Accounting Principles

Volume II

Accounting Principles

Volume II

Roger H. Hermanson, Ph.D., C.P.A.
Research Professor of Accounting
Ernst & Whinney Alumni Professor
Georgia State University

James Don Edwards, Ph.D., C.P.A.
J. M. Tull Professor of Accounting
The University of Georgia

R. F. Salmonson, Ph.D., C.P.A.
Professor Emeritus of Accounting
Michigan State University

AMERICAN INSTITUTE OF BANKING

 AMERICAN
BANKERS
ASSOCIATION
1120 Connecticut Avenue, N.W.
Washington, D.C. 20036

1986   Third edition

DOW JONES-IRWIN
Homewood, IL   60430

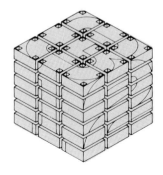

© BUSINESS PUBLICATIONS, INC., 1980, 1983, and 1986

ISBN 0-87094-776-1

Library of Congress Catalog Card No. 85–73267

Printed in the United States of America

1 2 3 4 5 6 7 8 9 0 K 3 2 1 0 9 8 7 6

Preface

This third edition of *Accounting Principles* is for use in introductory accounting courses, whether conducted in colleges and universities or in business settings. We recognize that people taking the first-year accounting course seek various careers. Some may choose accounting as a profession, while others will choose another area of business or possibly a nonbusiness career. All will find the ability to use and interpret accounting information valuable in both their work and their personal lives.

Accounting Principles covers both financial and managerial accounting topics, and serves as a foundation for subsequent courses in accounting and business. We assume that students using this text have a limited understanding of business concepts. Thus, when new terms and concepts are introduced they are defined, illustrated, and fully explained.

Two major reasons the previous edition of *Accounting Principles* had such "staying power" with adopters were that it was *readable* and *teachable*. These two attributes combined to make it easy for students to learn from the text. Early in the revision process we agreed to focus our work on improving readability and teachability even more. The result of our efforts is a text of which we are especially proud.

■ SPECIAL FEATURES THAT MAKE THIS EDITION MORE READABLE

☐ Introductions have been written for all chapters. We worked hard to make the introductions both interesting to read and helpful as a preview to the chapter. Students discover in the first paragraph of each chapter what the chapter contains and how the contents fit into the accounting process covered up to that point. The introductions give continuity to the text and show students how accounting concepts relate to each other.

☐ Summaries have been added to each chapter. The summary draws a complete picture of what the chapter covered. All topics presented are brought together in a logical review for the student. Every summary also gives the student a small "preview" of what the next chapter covers, giving continuity to the material.

☐ Organization of material has been improved based on feedback from adopters, suggestions by reviewers, and a serious study of the learning process itself by the authors and editors. New material is introduced only when the "proper stage has been set." These added transitional paragraphs between topic headings present students with the reasons for proceeding to the new material. The transitions alert students to the "building process" occurring within the chapter.

A lack of business experience among students sometimes prevents them from having a frame of reference for relating to accounting concepts and business transactions. In this edition we sought to involve the student more in real-life business applications as we introduced and explained the material.

☐ In Chapter 1 students become owners of their own business entities (a horse stable and a physical fitness center). References to "their" businesses in certain later chapters makes learning about accounting principles more personal and meaningful and also helps students learn and remember new material.

☐ A "Business Situation for Discussion" is located at the end of each chapter. These situations are taken from articles in current business periodicals (e.g., *The Wall Street Journal, Business Week, Management Accounting*) that relate to material covered in that chapter. These real-world examples demonstrate the business relevance of accounting.

☐ We have kept and revised our popular "Business Decision Problems" at the end of each chapter. These problems provide students with an opportunity to apply their newly learned accounting concepts to management situations in the business world.

☐ Numerous illustrations adapted from *Accounting Trends and Techniques* have been added in this edition to show the frequency of use in business of various accounting techniques. Scattered throughout the text, these illustrations give students real-world data to consider while learning about different accounting techniques.

Special attention was paid to improving the book's pedagogy in this edition. Specifically,

☐ Key terms are set in a second color for emphasis.

☐ End-of-chapter glossaries now contain the page number where the new term was first introduced and defined. Students can easily flip back to the original discussion and study the term's significance in context with the chapter material.

☐ A description of each exercise and problem is located beside each one in the left-hand margin. These descriptions let students know what they are expected to do in the problem.

Learning Aids for the Student—Supplementary Material

Study Guides.   Two comprehensive study guides are available, one for each half of the book. The study guides were developed in cooperation with Professor Gayle Rayburn, Memphis State University. The purpose of the study guides is to review and reinforce the concepts the student has learned in studying each chapter. Included for each chapter are learning objectives, reference outline, chapter review, a different demonstration problem and solution than is shown in the text, matching and true-false questions, completion questions and exercises, multiple-choice questions, and solutions to all exercises and questions.

Working Papers.   Two sets of working papers (one for each half of the text) are available for completing assigned exercises, problems, and business decision problems. In many instances, the working papers are partially filled in to reduce the "pencil pushing" required to solve the problems. The format and spacing used in the working papers are identical to the Instructor's Solutions Manual and to the transparencies. This feature makes it easier for the grader to compare the students' solutions to the authors' solutions.

Check Figures.   A list of check figures gives key amounts for the A and B series problems and Business Decision Problems in the text. Check figures are available in bulk free to adopters. Students can determine whether they are "on the right track" when working a problem by comparing their solution with the key amount given for a particular problem.

Practice Sets.   Four practice sets are available. Practice Set I, developed by Professor Margaret Mills, Tidewater Community College, Virginia, illustrates special journals and includes a work sheet for a retailing company. Practice Set II illustrates the accounting system used by a manufacturing company and was developed by Herbert A. O'Keefe, Georgia Southern College. Practice Set III illustrates the use of business papers for a retailing company. Practice Set IV is a microcomputer practice set that can be used with the Apple and IBM personal microcomputers. Practice Sets I, III, and IV may be used any time after Chapter 8 has been covered. Practice Set II may be used any time after Chapter 21 has been covered.

■ SPECIAL FEATURES THAT MAKE THIS EDITION MORE TEACHABLE

☐ We have included a vast amount of resource material *within* the text from which the instructor may draw: one of the largest selections of end-of-chapter exercises and problems available; two comprehensive review problems (after Chapters 4 and 6) that allow students to review all major concepts covered to that point; 28 Business Situations for Discussion to stimulate classroom discussion of accounting concepts; and financial statements of General Motors that can be used throughout the course to illustrate financial reporting.

☐ All end-of-chapter problem material (exercises, problems, and business decision problems) has been thoroughly revised.

☐ All end-of-chapter problem material has been traced back to the chapters to ensure that nothing is asked of a student that does not appear in the book. **This was a strength of the second edition,** ensuring that instructors could confidently assign problems without having to check for applicability.

☐ Demonstration problems and solutions are included for each chapter. Because of the positive response to this feature in the previous edition, we have added more of these problems. The problems help students to assess their own progress by showing them how problems that focus on the topic(s) covered in the chapter are worked before students do assigned homework problems.

☐ In Chapter 5 we now present two variations of the closing process: merchandise-related expense accounts are treated first as closing entries and then as adjusting entries. Instructors can choose which method(s) to teach.

☐ Chapter 17 has been reorganized so that it now covers only bond issuances and bond investments. (In the previous edition both bond and stock investments were covered in this chapter.) All investments in capital stock of other companies are now covered in Chapter 18. This change makes Chapter 17 more teachable and gives Chapter 18 more substance. This reorganization was suggested by users, and we agree that the result is a more logical organization of material.

☐ In Chapter 19, the statement of changes in financial position material covers both the working capital and cash concepts of funds. While both of these concepts are used in business, many texts cover only the working capital concept. We have included both concepts because a 1983 survey of 600 companies revealed that the cash concept was used by more than half of the companies.

☐ An important topic in accounting today, international accounting, is covered in an appendix at the back of the text. We believe that this coverage is the most complete of any introductory text. This appendix will assist in meeting the accreditation standard of the American Assembly of Collegiate Schools of Business regarding internationalizing the curriculum.

Teaching Aids for the Instructor—Supplementary Material

A complete package of supplemental teaching aids contains all you need to efficiently and effectively teach the course. For universities where graduate students or part-time instructors teach accounting principles, we have an excellent instructor's resource guide and test bank that will assist them in preparing both lectures and examinations. The test bank has been substantially increased, providing more multiple-choice questions as well as three more problems per chapter.

Instructor's Resource Guide.   This supplement was developed for the previous edition, and we found it to be extremely helpful to both new instructors of accounting and new adopters of our text. Revised for this edition, each chapter contains (1) a summary of major concepts that can serve as a handy lecture organizer; (2) a basic outline of the chapter headings; (3) learning objectives from the text repeated for the instructor's convenience; and (4) detailed lecture notes that also refer to specific end-of-chapter problem materials illustrating the concepts. Any of these formats can serve as effective lecture notes depending on the instructor's personal preference. Also included are (5) teaching transparency masters for each chapter that may be used to emphasize important points. Each chapter concludes with (6) a summary of the estimated time, level of difficulty, and content of each exercise and problem that is useful in deciding which items to cover in class or to assign as homework.

Solutions Manual.   The instructor's solutions manual contains sample syllabi for both quarter- and semester-basis courses. Detailed answers to the exercises, questions (Series A and B), comprehensive review problems, and business decision problems are given for each chapter. Teaching notes are included at the bottom of many problems to explain questions commonly asked by students. The use of large type and paper identically lined to the students' Working Papers facilitates grading.

Transparencies. Acetate transparencies of solutions to all exercises and problems are available free to adopters. These transparencies, while useful in many situations, are especially helpful when covering problems involving work sheets and in large classroom situations. The transparency solutions are formatted on the same lined working paper the students have in their supplemental Working Papers. The new large and bold type used facilitates projection, and the use of lines aids students' viewing.

Examination Material. In this edition we have provided adopters with *four* different formats of examination material. Instructors need only to select the exam(s) that best fits their personal needs and resources, and then request a copy from their local BPI sales representative. Any and all are available free upon adoption and by request.

1. Pre-Printed Achievement Tests. Three series of achievement tests—A, B, and C—have been prepared and printed, and are available in bulk to adopters. Each series consists of six one-hour exams and two two-hour final exams. In each series, three of the one-hour exams and a final exam cover Chapters 1–14, and the other three one-hour exams and a final exam cover Chapters 15–28. All questions are multiple choice for ease in grading.

2. Examination Book. This test bank, **expanded in this edition,** contains over 1,500 questions and problems to choose from in preparing examinations. It contains true-false and multiple-choice questions and short problems for each chapter. The multiple-choice questions may also be used to freshen up the Achievement Tests, while the short problems may be used to supplement or replace them for those instructors who object to the sole use of multiple-choice questions.

3. COMPUTEST. For instructors who have microcomputers, this form of exam preparation is convenient and effective. COMPUTEST is a microcomputer version of the Examination Book. It is available for use on the IBM PC, Apple II+, and Apple IIe. COMPUTEST can be used to prepare examinations by selecting questions and problems in a variety of ways. Instructors may even add their own exam material to the test bank. COMPUTEST is menu-driven and has a well-documented instruction manual.

4. TELETEST. TELETEST is an in-house testing service that will prepare your exams. TELETEST has its own bank of examination questions and problems (taken from the Examination Book). To use TELETEST, all the instructor needs to do is call our 800 number, ask for TELETEST, and give the required information to BPI's TELETEST service representative. Or the instructor can mail in the required information. Either way, within 72 working hours of receiving the required information, the instructor will be mailed a copy of the exam and an answer key.

■ SPECIAL FEATURES OF THIS EDITION THAT HELP STUDENTS LEARN ACCOUNTING

Students often come into accounting principles courses feeling anxious about learning the material. Recognizing that apprehension, we studied ways to make learning easier and came up with some helpful ideas on how to make this edition work even better for students. Our "study of learning" resulted in the following improvements in *Accounting Principles,* third edition. Specifically, we:

☐ Organized ideas for improved flow of material. The newly written introductions preview the chapter material, letting students know exactly where they are and where they are going. Transitional paragraphs are used to improve the flow and continuity of material. Carefully worded and designed headings are strategically placed in the chapters as signposts. The summaries review the material covered and show its relationship to the overall accounting process. Every summary ends with a reference to what the next chapter covers and how it relates to the chapter just covered.

☐ Included examples to associate concepts with experiences. Throughout the text we used examples taken from everyday life to relate an accounting concept being introduced or discussed to students' experiences. For example, to help the student differentiate between the accounting process and an accounting system we ask them to think of the difference between going on a trip (the process) by the back roads (system) or by the highway (an alternative system). In the chapter on inventory, we have them recall the "pre-inventory sales" they all have seen advertisements for and possibly attended. It is much easier to learn a subject if you can associate it with something familiar.

☐ Used an informal style and the active voice. Our research showed that for an accounting principles text today, an informal writing style and the active voice are more effective for learning than the formal style and passive voice. In this edition we use the pronoun *you* more to involve students with the text material.

☐ Added several new graphics. Learning is enhanced when a picture reinforces a verbal understanding of new material. Wherever possible, we have added graphic illustrations to help explain accounting concepts to students. For example, in Chapter 7 we have illustrated cash flows in a business. In Chapter 19 we have a diagram showing the typical types of transactions that affect working capital. Graphics have been added to reinforce accounting concepts.

We are indebted to many individuals for reviewing the manuscript of the third edition. In addition to those listed on the acknowledgments page, we are especially indebted to colleagues and students at our respective universities for their helpful suggestions.

Note to the Student

Professor Gayle Rayburn of Memphis State University has participated with the authors in revising the very comprehensive two-volume student Study Guide to assist you in understanding the material in this text. Students who used the study guide in the previous edition found it to be extremely helpful in maximizing their understanding and class performance. Each chapter of the Study Guide is keyed to a chapter of the text and provides learning objectives, a reference outline, a detailed chapter review, a demonstration problem and answer, matching questions concerning important new terms and concepts, completion questions and exercises, and true-false and multiple-choice questions. Answers to all exercises and questions are included in the Study Guide to provide you with immediate feedback on your responses. Explanations are also given for the answers to many of the true-false and multiple-choice questions. This student Study Guide, published by Business Publications, Inc., is available through your college bookstore. If it is not in stock, please ask your bookstore manager to order a copy for you.

■ ACKNOWLEDGMENTS

We are grateful to many individuals who have contributed to the development of this text. Special appreciation is due: Lane K. Anderson, Texas Tech University; Lloyd Badgett, University of Central Arkansas; Charles D. Bailey, Florida State University; Martin Batross, Franklin University; Atha Beard, Auburn University; Edgar T. Bitting, Elizabethtown College; Sallie Branscom, Virginia Western Community College; Robert M. Brown, Virginia Polytechnic Institute and State University; Bruce Caster, Valdosta State College; Trudy Chiaravalli, Lansing Community College; Charles Coleman, Bellvue Community College; G. Michael Crooch, Arthur Andersen & Co.; Lawrence Curbo, Memphis State University; Michael A. Dalton, Loyola University–New Orleans; Nita Dodson, University of Texas at Arlington; Linda Dykes, College of Charleston; George A. Fiebelkorn, Valdosta State College; Farrell G. Gean, Pepperdine University; Russell T. Gingras, Saginaw Valley State College; Daryl Gosse, Michigan State University; Raymond Green, Texas Tech University; Peter R. Grierson, University of Central Florida; Jean Gutman, University of Southern Maine; James O. Hicks, Jr., Virginia Polytechnic Institute and State University; George Holdren, University of Nebraska; James T. Hood, Northeast Louisiana University; the late Rita Huff, Sam Houston State University; Marty Jagers, University of South Carolina; Robert Kelley, Corning Community College; Dennis Knutson, Marquette University; Anthony T. Krzystofik, University of Massachusetts, Amherst; Tom Largay, Hudson College; Donald E. MacGilvera, Shoreline Community College; Alan P. Mayer-Sommer, Georgetown University; Thomas E. McLeod, University of Alabama, Birmingham; Katherine M. Means, University of Miami; Patricia H. Michel, Loyola College; Mary Middleton, Mercer University; Margaret Mills, Tidewater Community College; George S. Minmier, Memphis State University; John L. Nabholtz, Southern Methodist University; Herbert A. O'Keefe, Georgia Southern College; Philip R. Olds, Virginia Commonwealth University; Douglas Pfister, Lansing Community College; Thomas Phillips, Louisiana State University, Shreveport; Martin Premo, St. Bonaventure University; Cecily Raiborn, Loyola University–New Orleans; L. Gayle Rayburn, Memphis State University; Ruthie Reynolds, Tennessee State University; Arthur T. Roberts, University of Baltimore; David E. Rogers, Mesa College; Bonnie Stivers, Kennesaw College; Virgil E. Stone, Texas A & I University; James

Specht, North Dakota State University; G. A. Swanson, Tennessee Technological University; Mary J. Swanson, Mankato State University; Jean Tillery, Emory University; Deborah Turner, Georgia Institute of Technology; Joyce Valentine, Ernst & Whinney; James J. Wallace, Rochester Institute of Technology; Penny Wardlaw, University of Maryland; and Jackson A. White, University of Arkansas, Little Rock.

Roger H. Hermanson
James Don Edwards
R. F. Salmonson

Contents

PART

5

Corporations

Corporations: Formation, Administration, and Classes of Capital Stock

LEARNING OBJECTIVES

After studying this chapter, you should be able to:

1. State the advantages and disadvantages of the corporate form of business.
2. List the various kinds of stock and describe the differences between them.
3. Record transactions involving stock with par value, with stated value, or without par or stated value, issued for cash, property, or services.
4. Present in proper form the stockholders' equity section of a balance sheet.
5. List values commonly associated with capital stock and give their definitions.
6. Determine book values of both preferred and common stock.
7. Define and use correctly the new terms in the glossary.

In this chapter you begin your study of the corporate form of business organization. Although corporations are fewer in number than single proprietorships and partnerships, corporations possess the bulk of our business capital and currently supply us with most of our goods and services.

This chapter discusses the advantages and disadvantages of the corporation, how to form and direct a corporation, and some of the unique situations encountered in accounting for and reporting on the different classes of corporation stock.

■ THE CORPORATION

A **corporation** is an entity recognized by law as possessing an existence separate and distinct from its owners; that is, it is a separate legal entity. Endowed with many of the rights and obligations possessed by a person, a corporation can, for example, enter into contracts in its own name; buy, sell, or hold property; borrow money; hire and fire employees; and sue and be sued.

Corporations have proved to be remarkably well-suited vehicles for obtaining the huge amounts of capital necessary for large-scale business operations. Corporations acquire their capital by issuing shares of stock, which are the units into which the ownership of a corporation is divided. Investors buy shares of stock in a corporation for two basic reasons. First, investors expect the value of their shares to increase over time so that the stock may be sold in the future at a profit. Also, while investors hold stock, they expect the corporation to pay them dividends (usually in cash) in return for using their money. The various kinds of dividends and their accounting treatment are discussed in Chapter 16.

Advantages of the Corporation Form of Organization

Corporations have many advantages compared to single proprietorships and partnerships. The major advantages of a corporation over a single proprietorship are the same advantages a partnership has over a single proprietorship. Although corporations usually have more owners than partnerships, both have a broader base for investment, risk, responsibilities, and talent than do single proprietorships. Since corporations are more comparable to partnerships than single proprietorships, the discussion of advantages that follows relates to the partnership and corporation.

1. **Easy transfer of ownership.** In a partnership, a partner cannot transfer ownership in the business to another person if the other partners do not want the new person involved in the partnership. In a corporation, shares of stock are often traded on a stock exchange between unknown parties; one owner usually cannot dictate to whom shares can or cannot be sold by another owner.
2. **Limited liability.** Each partner in a partnership is personally responsible for all the debts of the business. In a corporation, the stockholders are not personally responsible for the corporation's debts; the maximum amount a stockholder can lose is the amount of his or her investment. However, for small corporations, banks and other lending institutions often require an officer of the corporation to sign the loan agreement, so the officer will have to pay if the corporation does not.
3. **Continuous existence of the entity.** In a partnership, many circumstances can cause the termination of the business entity. These same circumstances have no effect on a corporation because it is a legal entity separate and distinct from its owners.
4. **Professional management.** Generally, the partners in a partnership are also the managers of that business, but they may or may not have the necessary expertise to manage a business. In a corporation, most of the owners (stockholders) do not participate in the day-to-day operations and

management of the entity. Usually, professionals are hired to run the business on a daily basis.

5. **Separation of owners and entity.** Since the corporation is considered a separate legal entity, the owners do not have the power to bind the corporation to business contracts. This eliminates the potential problem of mutual agency that exists between partners in a partnership. In a corporation, one stockholder cannot jeopardize other stockholders through poor decision making.

Disadvantages of the Corporation

The corporate form of organization is not without its disadvantages. These include the following:

1. **Double taxation.** Because a corporation is a separate legal entity, its net income is subject to taxation twice. The corporation pays a tax on its income, and stockholders pay a tax on corporate income received as dividends.
2. **Government regulation.** Because corporations are created by law, they are subject to greater regulation and control than are single proprietorships and partnerships.
3. **Entrenched inefficient management.** A corporation may be burdened with an inefficient management that remains in control because it can use corporate funds to solicit the needed stockholder votes to back its positions. Stockholders scattered across the country, who individually own only small portions of a corporation's stock, usually find it difficult to organize and oppose existing management.
4. **Limited ability to raise creditor capital.** The limited liability of stockholders makes a corporation an attractive means for accumulating stockholder capital. At the same time, this limited liability feature limits the amount of creditor capital a corporation can amass because **creditors cannot look to the personal assets of stockholders for satisfaction of the debts of a corporation if the corporation cannot pay.** Thus, beyond a certain point, creditors will not lend some corporations money without the personal guarantee of a shareholder or officer of the corporation to repay the loan if the corporation does not.

Incorporating

Corporations are chartered by the state. Each state has a corporation act that permits the formation of corporations by qualified persons. Incorporators are persons seeking to bring a corporation into existence. Most state corporation laws require a minimum of three incorporators, each of whom must be of legal age and a majority of whom must be citizens of the United States.

The laws of each state view a corporation organized in that state as a domestic corporation and a corporation organized in any other state as a foreign corporation. If a corporation intends to conduct business solely within one state, it normally seeks incorporation in that state because most state laws are not as severe for domestic corporations as for foreign corporations. Corporations conducting interstate business usually incorporate in the state that has laws most advantageous to the corporation being formed. Important considerations in choosing a state are the powers granted to the corporation, the taxes levied, and the reports required.

Articles of Incorporation

Once incorporators agree on the state in which to incorporate, they apply for a corporate charter. A corporate charter is a contract between the state and the incorporators of a corporation, and their successors, granting the corporation its legal existence. The application for the corporation's charter is called the articles of incorporation.

After the information requested in the incorporation application form is supplied, the articles of the incorporation are filed with the proper office in the state of incorporation. Each state requires different information in the articles of incorporation, but, in general, most ask for the following information:

1. Name of corporation.
2. Location of principal offices.
3. Purposes of business.
4. Number of shares of stock authorized, class or classes of shares, and voting and dividend rights of each class of shares.
5. Value of assets paid in by the original subscribers (persons who contract to acquire shares).
6. Limitations on authority of the management and owners of the corporation.

Upon approval by the state office (which is frequently the secretary of state's office), the charter is granted, and the corporation is created.

Bylaws

As soon as the charter is obtained, the corporation is authorized to operate its business. The incorporators call the first meeting of the stockholders. Two of the purposes of this meeting are to elect a board of directors and to adopt the bylaws of the corporation.

The bylaws are a set of rules or regulations adopted by the board of directors of a corporation to govern the conduct of corporate affairs. The bylaws must be in agreement with the laws of the state and the policies and purposes in the corporate charter. The bylaws contain, along with other information, provisions for the following: (1) the place, date, and manner of calling the annual stockholders' meeting; (2) the number of directors and the method for electing them; (3) the duties and powers of the directors; and (4) the method for selecting officers of the corporation.

Organization Costs

Organization costs are costs of organizing a corporation, such as state incorporation fees and legal fees applicable to incorporation. These costs should be debited to an account called Organization Costs. Organization Costs are carried as an asset since they yield benefits over the life of the corporation; if the fees had not been paid, there would be no corporate entity. The account is classified on the balance sheet as an intangible asset and amortized over a period not to exceed 40 years. Most organization costs are written off fairly rapidly because they are small in amount, and a rapid amortization is allowed for tax purposes.

Directing the Corporation

The corporation is managed through the delegation of authority in a line from the stockholders to the directors to the officers, as shown in the organization chart in Illustration 15.1. The stockholders elect the board of directors. The board of directors formulates the broad policies of the company and selects the principal officers, who execute the policies.

Illustration 15.1

Typical Corporation's Organization Chart

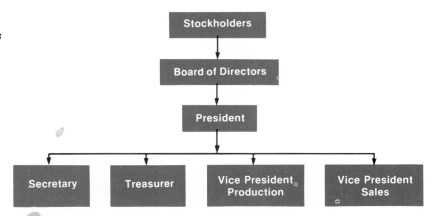

Stockholders. Stockholders do not have the right to participate actively in the management of the business unless they serve as directors and/or officers. But stockholders do have certain basic rights; these include the right to (1) dispose of their shares, (2) buy additional newly issued shares in a proportion equal to the percentage of shares already owned (called the **preemptive right**), (3) share in dividends when declared, (4) share in assets in liquidation, and (5) participate in management indirectly by voting at the stockholders' meeting.

The preemptive right is important to stockholders because it allows them to maintain their percentage of ownership in a corporation when additional shares are issued. For example, assume Joe Thornton owns 10% of the outstanding shares of Corporation X. When Corporation X decides to issue 1,000 additional shares of stock, Joe Thornton has the right to buy 100 (10%) of the new shares. Should he decide to do so, he will maintain his 10% interest in the corporation. If he does not wish to exercise his preemptive right, the shares may be sold to others.[1]

Normally, stockholders' meetings are held annually. At the annual stockholders' meeting, stockholders indirectly share in management by voting on such questions as changing the charter, increasing the number of authorized shares of stock to be issued, approving pension plans, selecting the independent auditor, and other related matters.

At stockholders' meetings, each stockholder is entitled to one vote for each share of voting stock held. Stockholders who do not personally attend the stockholders' meeting may vote by proxy. A **proxy** is a legal document signed

---

[1] The preemptive right has been eliminated by some corporations because its existence makes it difficult to issue large blocks of stock to the stockholders of another corporation to acquire that corporation.

by a stockholder, giving another designated person the authority to vote the stockholder's shares at a stockholders' meeting.

Board of Directors.   The **board of directors** is elected by the stockholders and is primarily responsible for formulating broad policies for the corporation. The board appoints administrative officers and delegates to them the execution of the policies established by the board. The board also has more specific duties including (1) authorizing contracts, (2) declaring dividends, (3) establishing executive salaries, and (4) granting authorization to borrow money. The decisions of the board are recorded in the minutes of its meetings. These minutes are an important source of information to the independent auditor, since they may serve as notice to record transactions (such as a dividend declaration) or to recognize that certain transactions may be taking place in the near future (such as a large loan).

Corporate Officers.   Officers of a corporation usually are specified in the corporation's bylaws. The number of officers and their exact titles vary from corporation to corporation, but most have a president, several vice presidents, a secretary, and a treasurer.

The president is the chief executive officer of the corporation. He is empowered by the bylaws to hire all necessary employees except those appointed by the board of directors.

Most corporations have more than one vice president. Each vice president is usually responsible for one particular corporate operation, such as sales, engineering, or production. The corporate secretary is responsible for maintaining the official records of the company and records the proceedings of meetings of stockholders and directors. The treasurer is accountable for corporate funds and may be charged with the general supervision of the accounting function within the company. A controller is usually directly charged with carrying out the accounting function. The controller usually reports to the treasurer of the corporation.

■ DOCUMENTS, BOOKS, AND RECORDS RELATING TO CAPITAL STOCK

Capital stock consists of transferable units of ownership in a corporation. Each unit of ownership is called a share of stock. Millions of shares of corporate capital stock are traded every business day on organized stock exchanges such as the New York Stock Exchange, the American Stock Exchange, and on the over-the-counter market. These sales (or "trades") seldom involve the corporation issuing the stock as a party to the exchange, but rather are made by existing stockholders to other individual or institutional investors. These trades are followed by the physical transfer of the stock certificates.

A **stock certificate** is a printed or engraved document serving as evidence that the holder owns a certain number of shares of capital stock. When a stockholder sells shares of stock, the stockholder signs over the stock certificate to the new owner who presents it to the issuing corporation. When the old certificate arrives at the issuing corporation, the certificate is canceled and attached to its corresponding stub in the stock certificate book. A new certificate is prepared for the new owner. The number of shares of stock outstanding at any time can be determined by summing the shares shown on the open stubs (stubs without certificates attached) in the stock certificate book.

Stockholders' Ledger

Among the more important records maintained by a corporation is the stockholders' ledger. The stockholders' ledger contains a group of subsidiary accounts showing the number of shares of stock currently held by each stockholder. Because it contains an account for **each** stockholder, in a large corporation this ledger may have more than a million individual accounts. Each stockholder's account shows the number of shares owned, their certificate numbers, and the dates on which shares were acquired or sold. Entries are made in terms of the number of shares rather than in dollars.

The stockholders' ledger contains the same information as the stock certificate book but summarizes it alphabetically by stockholder since a stockholder may own a dozen or more certificates, each representing a number of shares. This summary enables a corporation to determine the number of shares a stockholder is entitled to vote at a stockholders' meeting and to prepare one dividend check per stockholder rather than one per stock certificate.

Many large corporations with actively traded shares turn the task of maintaining reliable stock records over to an outside stock-transfer agent and a stock registrar. The stock-transfer agent, usually a bank or trust company, is employed by a corporation to transfer stock between buyers and sellers. The stock-transfer agent cancels the certificates covering shares sold, issues new stock certificates, and makes appropriate entries in the stockholder's ledger. New certificates are then sent to the stock registrar, typically another bank, that maintains separate records of the shares outstanding. This control system makes it difficult for a corporate employee to issue stock certificates fraudulently and steal the proceeds.

The Minutes Book

The minutes book, kept by the secretary of the corporation, is a record book in which actions taken at stockholders' and board of directors' meetings are recorded. The minutes book is the written authorization for many actions taken by corporate officers. All actions taken by the board of directors and the stockholders must be in accordance with the provisions contained in the charter and in the bylaws. The minutes book contains a variety of data, including the following:

1. A copy of the corporate charter.
2. A copy of the bylaws.
3. Dividends declared by the board of directors.
4. Authorization for the acquisition of major assets.
5. Authorization for borrowing.
6. Authorization for increases or decreases in capital stock.

■ CAPITAL STOCK AUTHORIZED AND OUTSTANDING

The corporate charter states the number of shares and the par value, if any, per share of each class of stock that the corporation is permitted to issue.

Capital stock authorized is the number of shares of stock that a corporation is entitled to issue as designated in its charter. <u>Par value</u> is an arbitrary amount printed on each stock certificate that may be assigned to each share of a given class of stock, usually at the time of incorporation.

A corporation might not issue all of its authorized stock immediately; some stock might be held for future issuance when additional funds are needed. If all authorized stock has been issued and more funds are needed, the consent of the state of incorporation will be required to increase the number of authorized shares.

The authorization to issue stock is not a transaction that results in a journal entry with a debit and credit. Instead, the authorization is noted in the capital stock account in the ledger (and often in the general journal) as a reminder of the number of shares authorized.

Capital stock outstanding is the number of authorized shares of stock that have been issued and that are currently held by stockholders. The total ownership of a corporation rests with the holders of the capital stock outstanding. If, for example, a corporation is authorized to issue 10,000 shares of capital stock but has issued only 8,000 shares, the holders of the 8,000 shares own 100% of the corporation.

Each outstanding share of stock of a given class is identical to any other outstanding share of that class with respect to the rights and privileges possessed. Shares authorized but not yet issued are referred to as unissued shares (there are 2,000 unissued shares in the above example). No rights or privileges attach to these shares until they are issued; they are not, for example, entitled to dividends, nor can they be voted at stockholders' meetings.

There is a difference between outstanding stock and issued stock. Issued stock includes shares that have been issued at some point in time, while outstanding shares are those shares that are currently held by stockholders. All outstanding stock is issued stock, but the reverse is not necessarily true. The difference is due to shares, called treasury stock, that have been returned to the corporation by stockholders. Treasury stock will be discussed in Chapter 16.

■ PAR VALUE AND NO-PAR CAPITAL STOCK

Par Value Stock

Many times par value stock is issued. As noted earlier, **par value** is an arbitrary amount assigned to each share of a given class of stock and printed on the stock certificate. Par value per share is no indication of the amount for which the stock will sell; it is simply the amount per share that is credited to the capital stock account for each share issued. Also, the total par value of all issued stock constitutes the legal capital of the corporation. The concept of legal capital exists to help protect creditors from losses. **Legal capital,** or <u>stated capital,</u> is an amount prescribed by law below which a corporation may not reduce stockholders' equity through declaration of dividends or other payments to stockholders. Legal capital does not guarantee that a company will be able to pay its debts, but it does serve to keep a company from compensating owners to the detriment of creditors.

No-Par Stock

Laws permitting the issuance of **no-par stock** (stock without par value) were first enacted in New York in 1912. Similar, but not uniform, legislation has since been passed in many states.

A corporation might issue no-par stock for two reasons. One reason is to avoid confusion. The use of a par value may confuse some investors because the par value usually does not conform to market value. When there is no par value, this source of confusion is avoided.

A second reason is related to state laws regarding the original issue price per share. A **discount on capital stock** is the amount by which the par value of shares issued exceeds their issue price. Thus, if stock with a par value of $100 is issued at $80, the discount is $20. Most states will not permit the original issuance of stock at a discount. Only a few states (e.g., Maryland and California) allow its issuance. The original purchasers of the shares are contingently liable for the discount unless they have transferred (by contract) the discount liability to subsequent holders. If the contingent liability has been transferred, the present stockholders are contingently liable to creditors for the difference between par value and issue price. Although this liability is seldom paid, the issuance of no-par stock avoids such a possibility.

No-Par Stock with a Stated Value

The board of directors of a corporation issuing no-par stock may assign a stated value to each share of capital stock. **Stated value** is an arbitrary amount assigned by the board of directors to each share of a given class of no-par stock. This stated value, like par value, may be set at any amount by the board, although some state statutes specify a minimum amount such as $5 per share. Stated value may be established either before or after the shares are issued, if not specified by applicable state law.

■ OTHER VALUES COMMONLY ASSOCIATED WITH CAPITAL STOCK

Market Value

Market value is the price at which shares of capital stock are bought and sold by investors in the market; it is generally the value of greatest interest to investors. Market price is directly affected by (1) all the factors that influence general economic conditions, (2) investors' expectations concerning the corporation, and (3) the corporation's earnings.

Book Value

Book value per share is the amount per share that each stockholder would receive if the corporation were liquidated without incurring any further expenses and if assets were sold and liabilities liquidated at their recorded amounts. A later section discusses book value per share in greater detail.

Liquidation Value

Liquidation value is the amount a stockholder will receive if a corporation discontinues operations and liquidates by selling its assets, paying its liabilities, and distributing the remaining cash among the stockholders. Since the assets might be sold for more or less than the amounts at which they are recorded in the corporation's accounts, liquidation value may be more or less than book value. If only one class of capital stock is outstanding, each stockholder will receive, per share, the amount obtained by dividing the remaining cash by the number of shares of stock outstanding. If two or more classes of stock are outstanding, liquidation values depend on the rights of the various classes.

Redemption Value

Certain capital stock may be issued with the stipulation that the corporation has the right to redeem it. Redemption value is the price per share at which a corporation may call in (or redeem) its capital stock for retirement.

■ CLASSES OF CAPITAL STOCK

Two classes of capital stock—common and preferred—may be issued by a corporation. These classes are discussed in the following sections.

Common Stock

If only one class of stock is issued, it is known as common stock. The rights of the stockholder are enjoyed equally by all the holders of shares. Common stock is usually referred to as the **residual equity** in the corporation. This means that all other claims against the corporation rank ahead of the claims of the common stockholder.

Preferred Stock

A corporation may also issue preferred stock. Preferred stock is capital stock that carries certain features not carried by common stock. Different classes of preferred stock may exist, each with slightly different characteristics.

Preferred stock is issued by a company for the following reasons: (1) to avoid the use of bonds that have fixed interest charges that must be paid regardless of the amount of net income; (2) to avoid issuing so many additional shares of common stock that earnings per share will be less in the current year than in prior years; and (3) to avoid diluting the common stockholders' control of the corporation, since preferred stockholders generally have no voting rights.

Unlike common stock, which has no set maximum or minimum dividend, the dividend return on preferred stock is usually stated at an amount per share or as a percentage of par value. Therefore, the amount of the dividend per share is usually fixed.

Illustration 15.2 shows the various classes and combinations of capital stock outstanding for a sample of 600 companies.

Illustration 15.2

Capital Structures

	1983	1982	1981	1980
Common stock with:				
No preferred stock	381	378	386	387
One class of preferred stock	157	150	140	133
Two classes of preferred stock	47	55	54	57
Three or more classes of preferred stock	15	17	20	23
Total companies	600	600	600	600

Source: American Institute of Certified Public Accountants, *Accounting Trends & Techniques* (New York: AICPA, 1984), p. 213.

■ TYPES OF PREFERRED STOCK

When a corporation issues both preferred and common stock, the preferred stock may be:

1. Preferred as to dividends. If it is, it may be:
   a. Cumulative or noncumulative.
   b. Participating or nonparticipating.
2. Preferred as to assets in the event of liquidation.
3. Convertible or nonconvertible.
4. Callable.

Stock Preferred as to Dividends

A **dividend** is a distribution of assets (usually cash) that represents a withdrawal of earnings by the owners. Dividends are similar in nature to withdrawals by single proprietors and partners.

Stock preferred as to dividends means that the preferred stockholders are entitled to a specified dividend per share before any dividend on common stock is paid. A **dividend on preferred stock** is the amount paid to preferred stockholders as a return for the use of their money. For no-par preferred stock, the dividend is stated as a specific dollar amount per share per year, such as $4.40. For par value preferred stock, the dividend is usually stated as a percentage of the par value, such as 8% of par value, although the dividend can be stated as a specific dollar amount per share. Most preferred stock has a par value.

Dividends on preferred stock usually are paid quarterly. A dividend—in full or in part—can be paid on preferred stock only if it is declared by the board of directors. In some states, preferred stock dividends can be declared only if the corporation has retained earnings (income that has been retained in the business) at least equal in dollar amount to the dividend declared.

Noncumulative Preferred Stock. **Noncumulative preferred stock** is preferred stock on which the right to receive a dividend expires if the dividend is not declared. When noncumulative preferred stock is outstanding, a dividend omitted or not paid in any one year need not be paid in any future year. Because omitted dividends are usually lost forever, noncumulative preferred stocks hold little attraction for investors and rarely are issued.

Cumulative Preferred Stock. **Cumulative preferred stock** is preferred stock for which the right to receive a basic dividend, usually each quarter, accumulates if the dividend is not paid. Unpaid cumulative preferred dividends must be paid before any dividends can be paid on the common stock. For example, assume a company has cumulative, $10 par value, 10% preferred stock outstanding of $100,000, common stock outstanding of $100,000, and retained earnings of $30,000. No dividends have been paid for two years. The preferred stockholders are entitled to dividends of $20,000 ($10,000 per year times two years) before any dividends can be paid to the common stockholders.

Dividends in arrears are cumulative unpaid dividends, including the passed quarterly dividends for the current year. Dividends in arrears are never shown as a liability of the corporation since they are not a legal liability until declared by the board of directors. But, since the amount of dividends in arrears may influence the decisions of users of a corporation's financial statements, such dividends should be, and usually are, disclosed in a footnote. An appropriate footnote might read: "Dividends in the amount of $20,000, representing two years' dividends on the company's 10%, cumulative preferred stock, were in arrears as of December 31, 1987."

Participating Preferred Stock. **Participating preferred stock** allows the preferred stockholders to receive dividends above the stated preference rate under certain conditions that are specified in the preferred stock contract. As an example of one of the many possible ways that a participation feature might work, assume that the preferred stock contract states that when the total dividend distributed to stockholders in a given year exceeds $8 per share to preferred shareholders and $8 per share to common shareholders, the remaining amount will be distributed in an equal amount per share to all stockholders. If there are 2,000 shares of preferred stock and 4,000 shares of common stock outstanding, a distribution of $108,000 would be shared as follows:

			Preferred	Common
1.	Preferred stockholders are paid their dividend (2,000 shares × $8)		$16,000	
2.	Common stockholders are paid an amount equal to the preferred dividend per share (4,000 × $8)			$32,000
3.	The remainder of the dividend is divided so as to pay the same amount per share:			
		Shares **Ratio**		
	Preferred	2,000 (2/6 × $60,000)	20,000	
	Common	4,000 (4/6 × $60,000)		40,000
	Total	6,000		
Total dividend			$36,000	$72,000

The preferred stockholders receive the first $16,000 of the current year's dividends. The common stockholders receive the next $32,000 of dividends. Any dividends over $48,000 per year are paid in an equal amount per share. In years when dividends are not sufficient to pay at least $48,000 of dividends, the distribution would be as follows:

Amount of dividends to be paid	Split between	
	Preferred	Common
$ 8,000 ..	$ 8,000	$ –0–
16,000 ..	16,000	–0–
24,000 ..	16,000	8,000
32,000 ..	16,000	16,000
40,000 ..	16,000	24,000

Participating preferred stock was popular in the early 1900s but has seldom been issued since that time. Most preferred stock is nonparticipating. **Nonparticipating preferred stock** is preferred stock that is entitled to its cumulative stated dividend only, regardless of the size of the dividend on common stock.

Stock Preferred as to Assets

Most preferred stocks are preferred as to assets in the event of dissolution and liquidation of the corporation. **Stock preferred as to assets** is preferred stock that receives special treatment in case of liquidation. Preferred stockholders are entitled to receive the par value (or a larger stipulated liquidation value) per share before any assets may be distributed to common stockholders. If there are cumulative preferred dividends in arrears at liquidation, they usually are payable even if there are not enough accumulated earnings to cover the dividends. Also, the cumulative dividend for the current year is payable. Stock may be preferred as to assets, dividends, or both.

Convertible Preferred Stock

Convertible preferred stock is preferred stock that is convertible into common stock of the issuing corporation. Many preferred stocks do not carry this special feature; they are nonconvertible. Holders of convertible preferred stock may exchange it, at their option, for a certain number of shares of common stock of the same corporation.

Investors find convertible preferred stock attractive because of the greater probability that the dividends on the preferred stock will be paid (as compared to dividends on common shares) and because the conversion privilege may be the source of substantial price appreciation. To illustrate this latter attraction, assume that the Olsen Company issued 1,000 shares of 6%, $100 par value convertible preferred stock at $100 per share. The stock is convertible at any time into four shares of Olsen $10 par value common stock, which has a current market value of $20 per share. In the next several years, the company reported sharply increased net income and increased the dividend on the common stock from $1 to $2 per share. Assume that the common stock now sells at $40 per share. The preferred stockholders can: (1) convert each share of preferred stock into four shares of common stock and increase the annual dividend they receive from $6 to $8; (2) sell their preferred stock at a substantial gain, since it will sell in the market at approximately $160 per share, the market value of the four shares of common stock into which it is convertible; or (3) continue to hold their preferred shares in the expectation of realizing an even larger gain at a later date.

Callable Preferred Stock

Most preferred stocks, nonconvertible or convertible, are **callable** at the option of the issuing corporation. Callable preferred stock means that at the option of the corporation, holders of nonconvertible preferred stock must surrender their stock to the company and holders of convertible preferred stock must either surrender their stock or convert it into common shares.

Preferred shares are usually callable at par value plus a small premium (the call premium) of 3% or 4% of the par value of the stock. A call premium is the difference between the amount at which a corporation calls its preferred stock for redemption and the par value of the stock. An issuing corporation may force conversion of **convertible** preferred stock by calling in the preferred stock for redemption. Holders of convertible preferred stock that is called may either surrender it or convert it into common shares. When preferred stockholders surrender their stock, the former holder receives par value plus the call premium, any dividends in arrears, and a prorated portion of the current period's dividend. If the market value of the common shares is higher than the amount that would be received in redemption, the holder of convertible preferred stock would be foolish not to convert the preferred shares into common shares. For instance, assume that a stockholder owns 1,000 shares of convertible preferred stock. Each share is callable at $104 per share, convertible into two common shares (currently selling at $62 per share), and entitled to $10 of unpaid dividends. If the issuing corporation calls in its preferred stock, the holder would receive either (1) $114,000 [($104 + $10) × 1,000] if the shares are surrendered, or (2) common shares worth $124,000 ($62 × 2,000) if the shares are converted. The holder should convert the shares.

A corporation might call in its preferred stock for many reasons: (1) the outstanding preferred stock may require, for example, a 12% annual dividend at a time when capital to retire the stock can be secured by issuing a new 8% preferred stock; (2) the issuing company may have been sufficiently profitable to enable it to retire the preferred stock out of earnings; or (3) the company may wish to force conversion of its convertible preferred stock because the cash dividend on the equivalent common shares will be less than the dividend on the preferred shares.

■ BALANCE SHEET PRESENTATION OF STOCK

At this point it may be helpful to see how capital stock is reported in the balance sheet. The stockholders' equity section of a corporation's balance sheet contains two main elements: paid-in capital and retained earnings. Paid-in capital is the part of stockholders' equity that normally results from cash or other assets invested by owners. Paid-in capital may also result from services performed for the corporation in exchange for capital stock and from certain other transactions to be discussed in Chapter 16. As stated earlier, retained earnings is the part of stockholders' equity resulting from net income. The Retained Earnings account is increased **periodically** by net income earned and decreased by net losses. In addition, Retained Earnings is **decreased** by **dividends** declared to stockholders. Since Retained Earnings is a capital account and represents accumulated net income, it normally has a **credit** balance. Retained earnings is discussed in more detail in Chapter 16.

The illustration below shows the proper financial reporting for preferred and common stock. Assume that a corporation is authorized to issue 10,000 shares of $100 par value, 6%, cumulative, convertible preferred stock, all of which have been issued and are outstanding; and 200,000 shares of $10 par value common stock, of which 80,000 shares are issued and outstanding. The stockholders' equity section of the balance sheet (assuming $450,000 of retained earnings) is:

Stockholders' equity:			
Paid-in capital:			
Preferred stock, $100 par value, 6%, cumulative, convertible; authorized, issued, and outstanding, 10,000 shares		$1,000,000	
Common stock, $10 par value; authorized, 200,000 shares; issued and outstanding, 80,000 shares		800,000	
Total paid-in capital			$1,800,000
Retained earnings			450,000
Total stockholders' equity			$2,250,000

A footnote to the balance sheet may be used to state the rate at which the preferred stock is convertible into common stock. Alternatively, the information could be disclosed in a parenthetical note within the description of preferred stock.

■ STOCK ISSUANCES FOR CASH

Issuance of Par Value Stock for Cash

Each share of capital stock (common or perferred) is either with par value or without par value, depending on the terms of the corporation's charter. The par value, if any, is stated in the charter and printed on the stock certificates issued. Par value may be any amount—1 cent, 10 cents, 16⅔ cents, $1, $5, or $100. Low par values of $10 or less are common in our economy.

As previously mentioned, par value gives no clue as to the stock's market value. Shares with a par value of $5 have sold in the market for well over $600, and many $100 par value preferred stocks have sold for considerably less than par. Par value is not even a reliable indicator of the price at which shares can be issued. Even in new corporations, shares are often issued at prices well in excess of par value and may even be issued for less than par value if state laws permit. However, par value does give the accountant a constant amount at which to record capital stock issuances in the capital stock accounts. Also, as stated earlier, the total par value of all outstanding shares is generally the legal capital of the corporation.

To illustrate the issuance of stock for cash, assume that 10,000 authorized shares of $20 par value common stock are issued at $22 per share. The following entry is made:

Cash		220,000	
Common Stock			200,000
Paid-in Capital in Excess of Par Value—Common			20,000
To record the issuance of 10,000 shares of stock for cash.			

Notice that the credit to the Common Stock account is the par value ($20) times the number of shares issued. The excess over par value ($20,000) is credited to Paid-In Capital in Excess of Par Value and is part of the paid-in capital contributed by the stockholders. Thus, **paid-in capital in excess of par (or stated) value** represents capital contributed to a corporation in addition to that assigned to the shares issued and recorded in capital stock accounts.

The paid-in capital section of the balance sheet appears as follows:

Paid-in capital:
Common stock, par value, $20; 10,000 shares
    authorized, issued, and outstanding $200,000
Paid-in capital in excess of par value—common . . .   20,000
    Total paid-in capital $220,000

Issuance of No-Par, Stated Value Stock for Cash

When no-par stock with stated value is issued, the shares are carried in the capital stock account at the stated value. Any amounts received in excess of the stated value per share represent a part of the capital of the corporation and should be credited to Paid-in Capital in Excess of Stated Value. The legal capital of a corporation issuing no-par shares with a stated value is generally equal to the total stated value of the shares issued.

As an illustration, assume that the DeWitt Corporation, which is authorized to issue 10,000 shares of capital stock without par value, assigns a stated value of $20 per share to its stock. The 10,000 authorized shares are issued for cash at $22 per share. The entry to record this transaction is:

Cash 220,000
    Common Stock   200,000
    Paid-in Capital in Excess of Stated Value—Common . . .   20,000
  To record issuance of 10,000 shares for cash.

The paid-in capital section of the balance sheet appears as follows:

Paid-in capital:
Common stock without par value, stated value, $20;
    10,000 shares authorized, issued, and outstanding $200,000
Paid-in capital in excess of stated value—common   20,000
    Total paid-in capital $220,000

The $20,000 received over and above the stated value of $200,000 is carried permanently as paid-in capital because it is a part of the capital originally contributed by the stockholders. But the legal capital of the DeWitt Corporation is $200,000.

Issuance of No-Par Stock without a Stated Value for Cash

If a corporation issues no-par stock without a stated value, the entire amount received is credited to the capital stock account. For instance, consider the above illustration of the DeWitt Corporation involving the issuance of no-par stock. If no stated value had been assigned, the entry would have been as follows:

Cash	220,000	
Common Stock		220,000
To record the issuance of 10,000 shares for cash.		

Because shares may be issued at different times and at differing amounts, the credit to the capital stock account in this situation is not at a uniform amount per share, in contrast to when par value shares or shares with a stated value are issued.

To continue our example, the paid-in capital section of the company's balance sheet would be as follows:

Paid-in capital:
  Common stock without par or stated value; 10,000
      shares authorized, issued, and outstanding $220,000
           Total paid-in capital $220,000

The actual capital contributed by stockholders is $220,000. In some states, the entire amount received for shares without par or stated value is the amount of legal capital. The legal capital in this example would then be equal to $220,000.

■ RECORDING CAPITAL STOCK ISSUED BY SUBSCRIPTION

Stock is often issued through subscriptions. A subscription is a contract to acquire a certain number of shares of stock at a specified price, with payment to be made at a specified date or dates. A **subscriber** is a person contracting to acquire the shares. Recording the issuance of capital stock by subscription involves three steps:

1. Receipt of subscriptions for the issuance of the capital stock.
2. Collection of the subscriptions.
3. Issuance of the stock certificates when subscriptions have been collected in full.

The subscriptions may be accompanied by a partial payment of the subscription. In other instances, no cash is paid until later.

The Stock Subscribed Account

Because stock certificates are not issued until a subscriber has paid in full, a separate account, Common (or Preferred) Stock Subscribed, is used to show the amount of stock subscribed but not yet outstanding. Subscribed stock is stock for which subscriptions have been received, but for which stock certificates have not yet been issued.

Issuance by Subscription of Par Value Stock

The following examples illustrate the conventional method for recording the issuance of par value stock by subscription. Shares are issued when subscriptions are fully paid. The data are for the Lake Company, organized as a corporation with 100,000 authorized shares of stock, of which 20,000 shares are already outstanding. The number of shares authorized is noted in memorandum form in both the general journal and the Common Stock account.

Issuance at Par Value.   If the stock has a par value of $100 and subscriptions at par value are received for 5,000 shares of stock on June 20, 1987, the entry is:

```
1987
June 20   Subscriptions Receivable—Common (5,000 × $100) .   500,000
                 Common Stock Subscribed . . . . . . . .                500,000
              To record subscriptions to 5,000 shares at par.
```

On June 30, 1987, 80% of the subscription price is collected from each of the subscribers. The journal entry to record this collection is:

```
1987
June 30   Cash . . . . . . . . . . . . . . . . . . .   400,000
                 Subscriptions Receivable—Common . . . . . .            400,000
              To record partial collection of the subscriptions.
```

If the subscription had originally been accompanied by an 80% partial payment, the two entries shown above would be combined as follows:

```
1987
June 20   Cash . . . . . . . . . . . . . . . . . .   400,000
          Subscriptions Receivable—Common . . . . . .   100,000
                 Common Stock Subscribed . . . . . . . .                500,000
              To record subscriptions to 5,000 shares at par and
              an 80% partial payment.
```

When subscriptions are collected in full on July 15, 1987, certificates are issued, and the following entries are prepared:

```
1987
July 15   Cash . . . . . . . . . . . . . . . . . .   100,000
                 Subscriptions Receivable—Common . . . . .             100,000
              To record collection of the remaining subscriptions.

     15   Common Stock Subscribed . . . . . . . .   500,000
                 Common Stock . . . . . . . . . . . .                  500,000
              Certificates issued for 5,000 shares paid in full.
```

Issuance at an Amount in Excess of Par Value.   If the $100 par value stock had been subscribed at $600,000 (an amount $100,000 in excess of par value), the entry would be:

```
1987
June 20   Subscriptions Receivable—Common (5,000 × $120) .   600,000
                 Common Stock Subscribed (5,000 × $100) . .             500,000
                 Paid-In Capital in Excess of Par Value—
                 Common . . . . . . . . . . . . . . .                  100,000
              To record subscriptions to 5,000 shares of $100
              par value common stock at $120 per share.
```

The collection of 80% of each subscription on June 30, 1987, would be recorded as follows:

```
1987
June 30  Cash  . . . . . . . . . . . . . . . . . . . . . .  480,000
               Subscriptions Receivable  . . . . . . . . .          480,000
               Received 80% on each of the subscriptions of
               June 20, 1987.
```

The entries to record the collection of the remaining 20% and issuance of the shares on July 15, 1987, would be:

```
1987
July 15  Cash  . . . . . . . . . . . . . . . . . . .  120,000
               Subscriptions Receivable—Common  . . . . .          120,000
               To record collection of the remaining subscriptions.

     15  Common Stock Subscribed  . . . . . . . . .  500,000
               Common Stock  . . . . . . . . . . . . .          500,000
               Certificates were issued for 5,000 shares paid in
               full.
```

When par value preferred stock instead of common stock is involved, the entries are the same except that the corresponding preferred stock account titles would be used.

Issuance by Subscription of No-Par Stock with a Stated Value

Assume the Lake Company shares above were no-par stock with a stated value of $100 per share. Assume that on June 20, 1987, subscriptions were received by the Lake Company for 5,000 shares at $120 per share; 80% of each of the subscriptions was collected on June 30, 1987. Certificates for these shares are to be issued on July 15 when the subscriptions are collected in full.

The journal entry needed to record the subscription on June 20 would be:

```
1987
June 20  Subscriptions Receivable—Common (5,000 × $120) .  600,000
               Common Stock Subscribed (5,000 × $100)  . .          500,000
               Paid-In Capital in Excess of Stated Value—
               Common  . . . . . . . . . . . . . . . . .          100,000
               Subscriptions received for 5,000 shares of no-par
               stock at $120 per share. The stated value is $100
               per share.
```

The entries for June 30 and July 15 would be identical to those shown above for par value stock issued in excess of par value.

Issuance by Subscription of No-Par Stock without a Stated Value

Now the subscription of no-par stock that has no stated value will be considered. Assume the Lake Company no-par common stock had no stated value and was subscribed for at $120 per share. The journal entry on June 20 would be:

```
1987
June 20  Subscriptions Receivable—Common  . . . . . . .  600,000
               Common Stock Subscribed .  . . . . . . . .          600,000
               To record subscriptions to 5,000 shares of no-par
               common stock without a stated value at
               $120 per share.
```

The entry for June 30 and the first entry on July 15 for the collection of the subscription would be the same as those shown for par value stock issued in excess of par value. The entry for the issuance of the shares on July 15 would be:

```
1987
July 15   Common Stock Subscribed  . . . . . . . . . .   600,000
              Common Stock  . . . . . . . . . . . . .              600,000
              Certificates were issued for 5,000 shares paid in
              full.
```

Balance Sheet Presentation of Subscriptions Receivable and Stock Subscribed

Illustration 15.3 presents the June 30, 1987, partial balance sheet for the Lake Company, assuming 5,000 shares of $100 par value stock were subscribed at $120 per share and that subscriptions receivable of $120,000 were still due as of June 30, 1987. Two accounts, Subscriptions Receivable—Common and Common Stock Subscribed, are included because the subscriptions of June 20 have not been collected in full.

Illustration 15.3

Partial Balance Sheet

THE LAKE COMPANY
Partial Balance Sheet
June 30, 1987

Assets

Current assets:
   Subscriptions receivable—common $120,000

Stockholders' Equity

Paid-in capital:
   Common stock, $100 par value per share;
     100,000 shares authorized:
      Issued and outstanding, 20,000 shares $2,000,000
     Subscribed but not issued, 5,000 shares (see
      subscriptions receivable) 500,000 $2,500,000
   Paid-in capital in excess of par value—common   100,000
       Total paid-in capital $2,600,000

The Common Stock Subscribed account is regarded as a temporary capital stock account. The $500,000 balance of this account represents the par value of shares subscribed but not yet issued. The balance of the Common Stock Subscribed account is presented immediately below the Common Stock account. The reference in Illustration 15.3 to subscriptions receivable (following the caption "Subscribed but not issued, 5,000 shares") informs the reader that $120,000 remains to be paid in before the 5,000 subscribed shares will be issued.

Subscriptions receivable normally will be collected within a matter of days or weeks. Subscriptions receivable are, therefore, properly classified as a current asset in the balance sheet. The account should be displayed separately and not included in the total of trade accounts receivable. In some instances, the subscriptions will not be collected within the coming operating cycle. The account, Subscriptions Receivable, is then properly classified as a noncurrent asset and preferably shown under the caption "Other assets" near the bottom of the assets section of the balance sheet.

Defaulted Subscriptions

A defaulted subscription occurs when a subscriber to a stock subscription contract fails to make a required installment payment. Since these contracts often call for an immediate initial cash payment, with the balance payable in periodic installments, the defaulting subscriber may have paid part of the total subscription price. State incorporation laws generally govern the disposition of the amount paid in and the balance of the contract. Three usual courses of action are: (1) the subscriber may receive as many shares as have been paid for in full, with the balance of the contract being canceled; (2) the amount paid in may be refunded (often after deducting any expenses and losses incurred in selling the shares to another party); or (3) the amount paid in may be declared forfeited to the corporation. In the third case, the amount retained should be credited to a Paid-In Capital from Defaulted Subscriptions account to indicate the source of the capital.

■ CAPITAL STOCK ISSUED FOR PROPERTY OR SERVICES

When capital stock is issued for property or services, the dollar amount of the exchange must be determined. Accountants generally record the transaction at the fair value of (1) the property or services received or (2) the stock issued, whichever is more clearly evident.

To illustrate, assume the owners of a tract of land deeded the land to a corporation in exchange for 1,000 shares of $12 par value common stock. The fair market value of the land can only be estimated. At the time of the exchange the stock has an established market value of $14,000. The required entry is:

Land	14,000	
Common Stock		12,000
Paid-in Capital in Excess of Par Value—Common		2,000
To record the receipt of land for capital stock.		

As another example, assume 100 shares of common stock with a par value of $40 per share are issued in exchange for legal services received in organizing a corporation. No shares had been recently traded, so they do not have an established market value. The attorney previously agreed to a price of $5,000 for these legal services but decided to accept stock in lieu of cash. In this example, the correct entry is:

Organization Costs	5,000	
Common Stock		4,000
Paid-In Capital in Excess of Par Value—Common		1,000
To record the receipt of legal services for capital stock.		

The services should be valued at the price previously agreed on since that value is more clearly evident than the market value of the shares. An asset account should be debited because these services will benefit the corporation indefinitely. The amount by which the value of the services received exceeds the par value of the shares issued is properly credited to a Paid-In Capital in Excess of Par Value—Common account.

■ BALANCE SHEET PRESENTATION OF PAID-IN CAPITAL IN EXCESS OF PAR (OR STATED) VALUE—COMMON OR PREFERRED

As already noted, amounts received in excess of the par or stated value of shares issued should be credited to an account called Paid-In Capital in Excess of Par (or Stated) Value—Common (or Preferred). The amounts received in excess of par or stated value should be carried in separate accounts for each class of stock issued. Using the following assumed data, the stockholders' equity section of the balance sheet of a company with both preferred and common stock outstanding would appear as follows:

Stockholders' equity:			
Paid-in capital:			
Preferred stock—$100 par value, 6% cumulative; 1,000 shares authorized, issued, and outstanding		$100,000	
Common stock—without par value, stated value $5; 100,000 shares authorized, 80,000 shares issued and outstanding		400,000	$500,000
Paid-in capital in excess of par or stated value:			
From preferred stock issuances		$ 5,000	
From common stock issuances		20,000	25,000
Total paid-in capital			$525,000
Retained earnings			200,000
Total stockholders' equity			$725,000

■ BOOK VALUE

The total book value of a corporation's outstanding shares is equal to the recorded net asset value of the corporation—that is, assets minus liabilities. Quite simply, **the amount of net assets is equal to stockholders' equity.** When **only** common stock is outstanding, **book value per share** is computed by dividing total stockholders' equity by the number of common shares outstanding plus common shares subscribed but not yet issued. In calculating book value, an assumption is made that (1) the corporation could be liquidated without incurring any further expenses, (2) the assets could be sold at their recorded amounts, and (3) the liabilities could be satisfied at their recorded amounts.

Assume the stockholders' equity of a corporation is as follows:

Stockholders' equity:		
Paid-in capital:		
Common stock without par value, stated value $10; authorized, 20,000 shares; issued and outstanding, 15,000 shares	$150,000	
Paid-in capital in excess of stated value	10,000	
Total paid-in capital		$160,000
Retained earnings		50,000
Total stockholders' equity		$210,000

The book value per share of the stock is determined as follows:

Total stockholders' equity	$210,000
Total shares outstanding	÷ 15,000
Book value per share	$ 14

When two or more classes of capital stock are outstanding, the computation of book value per share is more complex. The book value for each share of stock depends upon the rights of the preferred stockholders. Preferred stockholders typically are entitled to a specified liquidation value per share, plus cumulative dividends in arrears, if any, since most preferred stocks are preferred as to assets and are cumulative. In each case, the specific provisions in the preferred stock contract will govern.

To illustrate, the Celoron Corporation's stockholders' equity is as follows:

Stockholders' equity:
  Paid-in capital:
    Preferred stock, $100 par value, 5,000 shares . . $ 500,000
    Common stock, $10 par value, 200,000 shares . .   2,000,000
    Paid-in capital in excess of par value—preferred . .   200,000
    Retained earnings   400,000
          Total stockholders' equity $3,100,000

The preferred stock is 6%, cumulative, and nonparticipating. It is preferred as to dividends and as to assets in liquidation to the extent of the liquidation value of $100 per share, plus any cumulative dividends on the preferred stock Dividends for four years are unpaid. Book values of each class of stock ar· calculated as follows:

	Total	Per share
Total stockholders' equity	$3,100,000	
Book value of preferred stock (5,000 shares):		
Liquidation value (5,000 × $100) $500,000		
Dividends (four years at $30,000) 120,000	620,000	$124.00
Book value of common stock (200,000 shares) . .	$2,480,000	12.40

Notice that the paid-in capital in excess of par value—preferred did not get assigned to the preferred stock in determining the book values. Only the liquidation value and cumulative dividends on the preferred stock are assigned to the preferred stock.

Assume now that the features attached to the preferred stock in the above example are the same except that the preferred stockholders have the right to receive $103 per share in liquidation. The book values of each class of stock would be:

	Total	Per share
Total stockholders' equity	$3,100,000	
Book value of preferred stock (5,000 shares):		
Liquidation value (5,000 × $103) $515,000		
Dividends (four years at $30,000) 120,000	635,000	$127.00
Book value of common stock (200,000 shares) . .	$2,465,000	12.33

Book value rarely equals market value of a stock because many of the assets have increased in value due to inflation. Thus, the shares of many corporations are traded regularly at market prices different from their book values. The next chapter continues the discussion of stockholders' equity.

■ *SUMMARY*

A corporation is an association of individuals recognized by law as a separate legal entity. A corporation is granted legal existence when a proper application for incorporation is submitted to and approved by the appropriate state agency and a charter is granted. The board of directors selects officers to guide the corporation and carry out policies.

The corporate charter establishes a maximum number of shares that may be issued by the corporation; this is referred to as the total authorized stock. Stock that has been sold and is in the hands of stockholders is issued and outstanding.

Par value is an arbitrary dollar amount assigned to capital stock. No-par stock may be assigned a stated value by the board of directors. The legal capital of a corporation is generally computed as the number of issued shares times the par or stated value. If no-par stock has no stated value, the legal capital normally is equal to the amount received from stockholders for all issued shares.

The two classes of stock a corporation may issue are common and preferred stock. Common stock represents the residual equity in the corporation, and common stockholders are generally the only owners who are allowed to vote. Preferred stock has certain preference rights greater than common stock, such as preference in receiving dividends and/or in receiving assets in the event of liquidation of the corporation. Regarding dividends, preferred stock may be cumulative or noncumulative; it may also be participating or nonparticipating. As a special incentive to purchase preferred stock, such stock may be convertible into common shares of stock.

When a stock subscription is received, a subscriptions receivable account and a stock subscribed account will always be needed unless payment in full is received immediately and the stock is issued. Depending on the price agreed upon, an excess over par or stated value account may also be involved.

Capital stock issued for property or services is recorded at the fair market value of either the property or services received or the shares issued, whichever is more clearly evident. When shares are issued for an amount greater than their par or stated value, this excess should be credited to an account called Paid-In Capital in Excess of Par (or Stated) Value, with separate accounts established for each class of stock.

Since the stock market is frequently referred to as an economic indicator, the knowledge you now have on corporation stock issuances should help you relate to stocks traded in the market. Chapter 16 continues the discussion of paid-in capital and also discusses retained earnings, dividends, and treasury stock.

NEW TERMS INTRODUCED IN CHAPTER 15

Articles of incorporation

The application for the corporation's charter (575).

Board of directors

Elected by the stockholders and is primarily responsible for formulating broad policies for the corporation. The

board also authorizes contracts, declares dividends, establishes executive salaries, and grants authorization to borrow money (577).

Book value per share

Stockholders' equity per share; computed as the amount per share each stockholder would receive if the corporation were liquidated without incurring any further expenses and if assets were sold and liabilities liquidated at their recorded amounts (580).

Bylaws

A set of rules or regulations adopted by the board of directors of a corporation to govern the conduct of corporate affairs. The bylaws must be in agreement with the laws of the state and the policies and purposes in the corporate charter (575).

Call premium (on preferred stock)

The difference between the amount at which a corporation may call its preferred stock for redemption and the par value of the stock (585).

Callable preferred stock

If the stock is nonconvertible, it must be surrendered to the company when the holder is requested to do so. If the stock is convertible, it may be either surrendered or converted into common shares when called (585).

Capital stock

Transferable units of ownership in a corporation (577).

Capital stock authorized

The number of shares of stock that a corporation is entitled to issue as designated in its charter (579).

Capital stock outstanding

The number of shares of authorized stock that have been issued and that are currently held by stockholders (579).

Common stock

Shares of stock representing the residual equity in the corporation. If only one class of stock is issued, it is known as common stock. All other claims rank ahead of common stockholders' claims (581).

Convertible preferred stock

Preferred stock that is convertible into common stock of the issuing corporation (584).

Corporate charter

The contract between the state and the incorporators of a corporation, and their successors, granting the corporation its legal existence (575).

Corporation

An entity recognized by law as possessing an existence separate and distinct from its owners; that is, it is a separate legal entity. A corporation is granted many of the rights and placed under many of the obligations of a natural person. In any given state, all corporations organized under the laws of that state are **domestic corporations;** all others are **foreign corporations** (573–74).

Cumulative preferred stock

Preferred stock for which the right to receive a basic dividend accumulates if not paid; dividends in arrears must be paid before any dividends can be paid on the common stock (583).

Defaulted subscription

Occurs when a subscriber to a stock subscription contract fails to make a required installment payment (592).

Discount on capital stock

The amount by which the par value of shares issued exceeds their issue price. The original issuance of shares at a discount is illegal in most states (580).

Dividend

A distribution of assets (usually cash) that represents a withdrawal of earnings by the owners. Dividends are similar in nature to withdrawals by sole proprietors and partners (582).

Dividend on preferred stock

The amount paid to preferred stockholders as a return for the use of their money; usually a fixed or stated amount expressed in dollars per share or as a percentage of par value per share (582).

Dividends in arrears

Cumulative unpaid dividends, including passed quarterly dividends for the current year (583).

Domestic corporation

See Corporation.

Foreign corporation

See Corporation.

Incorporators

Persons seeking to bring a corporation into existence (574).

Legal capital (stated capital)

An amount prescribed by law (often par value or stated value of shares outstanding) below which a corporation may not reduce stockholders' equity through the declaration of dividends or other payments to stockholders (579).

Liquidation value

The amount a stockholder will receive if a corporation discontinues operations and liquidates by selling its assets, paying its liabilities, and distributing the remaining cash among the stockholders (581).

Market value

The price at which shares of stock are bought and sold in the open market (580).

Minutes book

The record book in which actions taken at stockholders' and board of directors' meetings are recorded (578).

Noncumulative preferred stock

Preferred stock on which the right to receive a dividend expires if the dividend is not declared (582).

Nonparticipating preferred stock

Preferred stock that is entitled to its stated cumulative dividend only, regardless of the size of the dividend paid on common stock (584).

No-par stock

Capital stock without par value, to which a stated value may or may not be assigned (580).

Organization costs

Costs of organizing a corporation, such as incorporation fees and legal fees applicable to incorporation (575).

Paid-in capital

Amount of stockholders' equity that normally results from the cash or other assets invested by owners; it may also result from services provided for shares of stock and certain other transactions (585).

Paid-in capital in excess of par (or stated) value—common or preferred

Capital contributed to a corporation in addition to that assigned to the shares issued and recorded in capital stock accounts (587).

Participating preferred stock

Preferred stock that is entitled to receive dividends above the stated preference rate under certain conditions specified in the preferred stock contract (583).

Par value

An arbitrary amount printed on each stock certificate that may be assigned to each share of a given class of stock, usually at the time of incorporation (579).

Preemptive right

The right of stockholders to buy additional shares in a proportion equal to the percentage of shares already owned (576).

Preferred stock

Capital stock that carries certain features or rights not carried by common stock. Preferred stock may be pre-ferred as to dividends, preferred as to assets, or preferred as to both dividends and assets. Preferred stock may be cumulative or noncumulative and participating or nonparticipating (581).

Proxy

A legal document signed by a stockholder, giving another person the authority to vote the stockholder's shares at a stockholders' meeting (576).

Redemption value

The price per share at which a corporation may call in (or redeem) its capital stock for retirement (581).

Retained earnings

The part of stockholders' equity resulting from net income; the account in which the results of corporate activity are reflected and to which dividends are charged (585).

Shares of stock

Units of ownership in a corporation (573).

Stated value

An arbitrary amount assigned by the board of directors to each share of a given class of no-par stock (580).

Stock certificate

A printed or engraved document serving as evidence that the holder owns a certain number of shares of capital stock (577).

Stock preferred as to assets

Means that in liquidation the preferred stockholders are entitled to receive the par value (or a larger stipulated liquidation value) per share before any assets may be distributed to common stockholders (584).

Stock preferred as to dividends

Means that the preferred stockholders are entitled to receive a specified dividend per share before any dividend on common stock is paid (582).

Stock registrar

Typically a bank that maintains records of the shares outstanding for a company (578).

Stock-transfer agent

Typically a bank or trust company employed by a corporation to transfer stock between buyers and sellers (578).

Stock without par value

See No-par stock.

Stockholders' ledger

Contains a group of subsidiary accounts showing the number of shares of stock currently held by each stockholder (578).

Subscribed stock

Stock for which subscriptions have been received but for which stock certificates have not been issued (588).

Subscribers

Persons who contract to acquire shares, usually in an original issuance of stock by a corporation (575).

Subscription

A contract to acquire a certain number of shares of stock, at a specified price, with payment to be made at a specified date or dates (588).

DEMONSTRATION PROBLEM 15–1

The Dey Company has paid all required preferred dividends through December 31, 1982. Its outstanding stock consists of 10,000 shares of $100 par value common stock and 4,000 shares of 6%, $100 par value preferred stock. During five successive years, the company's dividend declarations were as follows:

1983	$140,000
1984	84,000
1985	12,000
1986	24,000
1987	108,000

Required: Compute the amount of dividends that would have been paid to each class of stock in each of the last five years assuming the preferred stock is:

a. Cumulative and nonparticipating.
b. Noncumulative and nonparticipating.

Solution to demonstration problem 15–1

DEY COMPANY

		Assumptions	
Year	Dividends to	(a)	(b)
1983	Preferred . .	$ 24,000*	$ 24,000
	Common . .	116,000	116,000
1984	Preferred . .	24,000	24,000
	Common . .	60,000	60,000
1985	Preferred . .	12,000	12,000
	Common . .	–0–	–0–
1986	Preferred . .	24,000	24,000
	Common . .	–0–	–0–
1987	Preferred . .	36,000†	24,000‡
	Common . .	72,000	84,000

* (4,000 shares × $100 × 0.06).
† $24,000 + $12,000 preferred dividend missed in 1985.
‡ Only the basic $24,000 dividend is paid because the stock is noncumulative.

DEMONSTRATION PROBLEM 15–2

The Pinto Company has been authorized to issue 100,000 shares of $10 par value common stock and 1,000 shares of 14%, cumulative, nonparticipating preferred stock with a par value of $20.

Required: a.   Prepare the entries for the following transactions which all took place in June 1987:

1. 50,000 shares of common stock are subscribed at $40 per share, with a down payment of 25% of the issue price.
2. 750 shares of preferred stock are issued for cash at $30 per share.
3. 1,000 shares of common stock are issued in exchange for legal services received in the incorporation process. The fair market value of the legal services is $15,000.
4. The balance of the stock subscriptions is paid, and the stock is issued.

b.   Prepare the paid-in capital section of Pinto's balance sheet as of June 30, 1987.

Solution to demonstration problem 15–2

a.

1. Cash 500,000
   Subscriptions Receivable—Common 1,500,000
       Common Stock Subscribed 500,000
       Paid-In Capital in Excess of Par Value—Common . 1,500,000
   To record subscriptions to 50,000 shares at $40 per share, with 25% down payment.

2. Cash 22,500
       Preferred Stock 15,000
       Paid-In Capital in Excess of Par Value—Preferred . 7,500
   To record the issuance of 750 shares for cash, at $30 per share.

3. Organization Costs 15,000
       Common Stock 10,000
       Paid-In Capital in Excess of Par Value—Common . 5,000
   To record issuance of 1,000 shares in exchange for legal services.

4. Cash 1,500,000
       Subscriptions Receivable—Common 1,500,000
   To record collection of balance due on subscriptions.

   Common Stock Subscribed 500,000
       Common Stock 500,000
   To record issuance of certificates for 50,000 shares, fully paid.

b.

THE PINTO COMPANY
Partial Balance Sheet
June 30, 1987

Paid-in capital:
  Preferred stock, $20 par value per share; 1,000 shares
    authorized; issued and outstanding, 750 shares . . . . . $ 15,000
  Common stock, $10 par value per share; 100,000 shares
    authorized; issued and outstanding, 51,000 shares . . . . 510,000 $ 525,000
  Paid-in capital in excess of par value:
    From preferred stock issuances . . . . $ 7,500
    From common stock issuances 1,505,000   1,512,500
      Total paid-in capital $2,037,500

QUESTIONS

1. Cite the major advantages of the corporation form of business organization and indicate why each is considered an advantage.

2. What is meant by the statement that corporate income is subject to double taxation? Cite several other disadvantages of the corporation form of organization.

3. Why is Organization Expense not a good title for the account that records the costs of organizing a corporation? Could you justify leaving the balance of an Organization Costs account intact throughout the life of a corporation?

4. What are the basic rights associated with a share of capital stock if there is only one class of stock outstanding?

5. Explain the purpose or function of *(a)* the stockholders' ledger, *(b)* the minutes book, *(c)* the stock-transfer agent, and *(d)* the stock registrar.

6. What are the differences between par value stock and stock with no-par value?

7. Corporate capital stock is seldom issued for less than par value. Give two reasons why this is true.

8. Explain the terms *liquidation value* and *redemption value.*

9. What is the meaning of the terms *stock preferred as to dividends* and *stock preferred as to assets?*

10. What do the terms *(a) cumulative* and *noncumulative* and *(b) participating* and *nonparticipating* mean in regard to preferred stock?

11. A coporation has 1,000 shares of 8%, $100 par value, cumulative, preferred stock outstanding. Dividends on this stock have not been declared for three years. Is the corporation legally liable to its preferred stockholders for these dividends? How should this fact be shown in the balance sheet, if at all?

12. Explain why a corporation might issue a preferred stock that is both convertible into common stock and callable.

13. Explain the nature of the account entitled Paid-In Capital in Excess of Par Value. Under what circumstances is this account credited?

14. Explain the nature of the Subscriptions Receivable account. How should it be classified in the balance sheet? On what occasions is it debited or credited?

15. What is the general approach of the accountant in determining the dollar amount at which to record the issuance of capital stock for services or property other than cash?

16. Assuming there is no preferred stock outstanding, how can the book value per share of common stock be determined? Of what significance is it? What is its relationship to market value per share?

EXERCISES

E–1

Determine dividends for common and preferred stock

Welch Corporation has outstanding 1,000 shares of noncumulative, nonparticipating preferred stock and 2,000 shares of common stock. The preferred stock is entitled to an annual dividend of $10 per share before dividends are declared on common stock. What are the total dividends received by preferred stockholders and common stockholders if Welch Corporation distributes $28,000 in dividends in 1987?

E–2

Determine dividends for common and preferred stock

Burnett Corporation has 2,000 shares outstanding of cumulative, nonparticipating preferred stock and 6,000 shares of common stock. The preferred stock is entitled to an annual dividend of $6 per share before dividends are declared on common stock. No preferred dividends were paid for last year and the current year. What are the total dividends received by preferred stockholders if Burnett Corporation distributes $72,000 in dividends?

E–3

Determine dividends for common and preferred stock for five-year period

The preferred stock contract of Warwick Corporation specifies that the preferred shares will participate on an equal amount per share basis with the common shares after $2 has been distributed per share of preferred stock and common stock. There are 1,000 shares of preferred stock outstanding and 9,000 shares of common stock outstanding. Determine the dividends that will be paid to each class for the following years:

	Total dividend to be distributed
1987	$ 2,000
1988	10,000
1989	20,000
1990	25,000
1991	30,000

E–4

Journalize stock issuance

Doyle Company issued 10,000 shares of common stock for $105,000 cash. The common stock has a par value of $10 per share. Give the journal entry for the stock issuance.

E–5

Prepare entries for stock issuance

Green Company issued 20,000 shares of $20 par value common stock for $680,000. What is the journal entry for this transaction? What would the journal entry be if the common stock had no par or stated value?

E–6

Journalize stock subscriptions

Lewis Company has been authorized to issue 100,000 shares of $50 par value common stock, of which 20,000 shares are outstanding. On February 20, 1987, the company received subscriptions for 15,000 shares at $80 per share. What would be the journal entry on February 20, 1987?

E–7

Journalize stock issuance for property

One hundred shares of $50 par value common stock were issued to the incorporators of a corporation in exchange for land (which cost the incorporators $6,500 one year ago) needed by the corporation for use as a plant site. Experienced appraisers recently estimated the value of the land to be $7,500. What journal entry would be appropriate to record the acquisition of the land?

E–8

Journalize stock issuance to satisfy liability

Strickland Corporation owes a trade creditor $24,000 on open account which it does not have sufficient cash to pay. The trade creditor suggests that Strickland Corporation issue to him 750 shares of the company's $20 par value common stock, which is currently selling on the market at $32. Present the entry or entries that should be made on Strickland Corporation's books.

E–9

Journalize stock issuance for legal services

Why would a law firm ever consider accepting stock of a new corporation having a total par value of $30,000 as payment in full of a $45,000 bill for legal services rendered? If such a transaction occurred, give the journal entry the issuing company would make on its books.

E–10

Compute the book value and average price of common stock

The stockholders' equity section of the Hubert Company's balance sheet is as follows:

Stockholders' equity:
  Paid-in capital:
   Common stock without par value, $10 stated
    value; authorized 100,000 shares; issued
    and outstanding, 70,000 shares . . . . . $ 700,000
   Paid-in capital in excess of stated value . . . 272,000
    Total paid-in capital . . . . $ 972,000
   Retained earnings 108,000
    Total stockholders' equity $1,080,000

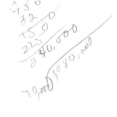

Compute the average price at which the 70,000 issued shares of common stock were sold. Compute the book value per share of common stock.

PROBLEMS, SERIES A

P15-1-A

Prepare partial balance sheet involving par value stock

Certain post-closing account balances for the Webb Company as of December 31, 1987, were as follows:

WEBB COMPANY Post-Closing Account Balances December 31, 1987	
Common Stock Subscribed, 4,000 shares	$100,000
Preferred Stock, 6%, $60 par; 2,000 shares authorized, issued, and outstanding	120,000
Common Stock, $25 par; 10,000 shares authorized, 6,000 shares issued and outstanding	150,000
Paid-In Capital in Excess of Par—Common	12,800
Subscriptions Receivable—Common	23,040
Paid-In Capital in Excess of Par—Preferred	6,000
Retained Earnings	18,840

Required: From the above list of accounts and balances, present in good form the stockholders' equity section of the December 31, 1987, balance sheet.

P15-2-A

Determine dividends for common stock and cumulative and noncumulative preferred stock

On January 1, 1983, the retained earnings of the Wilkins Company were $45,000. Net income for the succeeding five years was as follows:

1983	$30,000
1984	22,500
1985	500
1986	5,000
1987	27,500

The outstanding capital stock of the corporation consisted of 2,000 shares of preferred stock with a par value of $50 per share that pays a dividend of $2 per year and 8,000 shares of no-par common stock with a stated value of $25 per share. No dividends were in arrears as of January 1, 1983.

Required: Prepare schedules showing how the net income for the above five years was distributed to the two classes of stock if, in each of the years, the entire current net income was distributed as dividends and the preferred stock was:

a. Cumulative and nonparticipating.
b. Noncumulative and nonparticipating.

P15-3-A

Journalize stock subscriptions and issuances for cash and prepare resulting stockholders' equity section

The Blackmon Company had the following stockholders' equity and related accounts on January 1, 1987:

Subscriptions Receivable—Preferred Stock	$ 8,000
Preferred Stock, 8%, $10 par, 20,000 shares authorized, 10,000 shares issued	100,000
Preferred Stock Subscribed (2,500 shares)	25,000
Common Stock, $80 par, 10,000 shares authorized, 7,500 shares issued	600,000
Paid-In Capital in Excess of Par Value—Common	60,000
Retained Earnings	200,000

The following transactions occurred during 1987:

Transactions:

Jan. 10   Received the balance due on preferred stock subscribed; issued stock certificates.
Mar. 1   Received subscriptions for 5,000 shares of preferred stock at $14; 40% of the subscription price was paid in cash.
Aug. 3   Issued 2,000 shares of common stock for $92 cash per share.

Required:
a. Prepare journal entries for the transactions that occurred in 1987.
b. Prepare the stockholders' equity section of the balance sheet as of August, 3, 1987.

P15–4–A

Post transactions; prepare balance sheets for par value stock, stated value stock, and no-par or stated value stock

On July 3, 1987, the American Company was authorized to issue 15,000 shares of common stock; 3,000 shares were issued immediately to the incorporators of the company for cash at $40 per share. On July 5, an additional 300 shares were issued to the incorporators for services rendered in organizing the company.

On July 6, 1987, legal and printing costs of $1,500 were paid. These costs related to securing the corporate charter and the stock certificates.

On July 10, subscriptions were received from the general public for 4,500 shares at $36 per share, with 25% of the subscription price paid in cash immediately. The balance is due August 10, 1987.

Required:
a. Set up T-accounts, and post the above transactions. Then prepare the balance sheet of the American Company as of the close of July 10, 1987, assuming the authorized stock has a $20 par value.
b. Repeat *(a)* for the T-accounts involving stockholders' equity assuming the stock is no-par stock with a $30 stated value. Only prepare the stockholders' equity section of the balance sheet.
c. Repeat *(a)* for the T-accounts involving stockholders' equity assuming the stock is no-par stock with no stated value. Only prepare the stockholders' equity section of the balance sheet.

P15–5–A

Journalize stock subscriptions and issuance of stock for cash

On July 1, 1987, the York Company was authorized to issue 20,000 shares of $30 par value common stock. On July 7, subscriptions for 1,500 shares at $36 per share were received. The subscription contract requires a 10% immediate payment, with the remainder due on July 31. No stock certificates are to be issued until the subscriptions are paid in full.

Required:
a. Prepare the entries to record all transactions during July 1987, assuming the subscriptions are collected when due.
b. Prepare the July 1987 entries assuming the stock is no-par stock without a stated value.
c. Prepare the entry for July 7, 1987, assuming the subscriptions for the no-par stock are accompanied by cash payment in full and the stock is issued.

P15–6–A

Journalize stock transactions, including conversions; prepare stockholders' equity section

The Ballard Company received its charter on April 1, 1987, authorizing it to issue 5,000 shares of $100 par value, $8 cumulative, convertible preferred stock; 10,000 shares of $3 cumulative no-par preferred stock having a stated value of $5 per share and a liquidation value of $25 per share; and 100,000 shares of no-par common stock without a stated value.

On April 2, incorporators of the corporation acquired 50,000 shares of the common stock for cash at $20 per share, and 200 shares were issued to an attorney for services rendered in organizing the corporation. On April 3, the company issued all of its authorized shares of $8 convertible preferred stock for land valued at $400,000 and a building valued at $1,200,000. The property was subject to a mortgage of $600,000.

On April 4, subscriptions for 5,000 shares of the $3 preferred stock were received at $52 per share, with one half of the subscription price paid in cash. On April 8, the remaining 5,000 shares of $3 preferred stock were issued to an inventor for a patent. A subscription for 1,000 shares of common stock at $20 per share was also received, with a cash payment of $2,000 accompanying the subscription.

On April 25, the balance due on the April 4 subscriptions was collected, and the shares were issued. By April 30, the subscriber to 1,000 shares of common stock had failed to pay the balance of her subscription, which she had agreed to pay in 10 days. Shares were issued for her down payment, and the balance of the contract was canceled.

Required:
a. Prepare general journal entries for the above transactions.
b. Prepare the stockholders' equity section of the April 30, 1987, balance sheet. Assume retained earnings of $20,000.
c. Assume that each share of the $8 convertible preferred stock is convertible into six shares of common stock and that all of the preferred is converted on September 1, 1990. Give the required journal entry.

P15–7–A

Prepare stockholders' equity section; determine book values of stock; and determine dividends for each class of stock

The Heath Company issued all of its 2,500 shares of authorized preferred stock on January 1, 1986, at $206 per share. The preferred stock is no-par stock, has a stated value of $10 per share, is entitled to a cumulative basic preference dividend of $12 per share, is callable at $210 beginning in 1991, and is entitled to $200 per share in liquidation plus cumulative dividends. On this same date, Heath also issued its 5,000 authorized shares of no-par common stock with a $20 stated value at $100 per share.

On December 31, 1987, the end of its second year of operations, the company's retained earnings amounted to $160,000. No dividends have been declared or paid on either class of stock since the date of issue.

Required:
a. Prepare the stockholders' equity section of the Heath Company's December 31, 1987, balance sheet.
b. Compute the book value in total and per share of each class of stock as of December 31, 1987, assuming the preferred stock is nonparticipating.
c. If $110,000 of dividends are to be declared as of December 31, 1987, compute the amount payable to each class of stock assuming the preferred stock is nonparticipating.

P15–8–A

Determine book value for each class of stock

The stockholders' equity sections from three different corporations' balance sheets follow:

1. Stockholders' equity:
Paid-in capital:

Preferred stock, 7% cumulative and nonparticipating, $75 par value, 500 shares authorized and outstanding	$ 37,500
Common stock, $15 par value, 10,000 shares authorized and outstanding	150,000
Total paid-in capital	$ 187,500
Retained earnings	132,000
Total stockholders' equity	$ 319,500

2. Stockholders' equity:
Paid-in capital:

Preferred stock, 6% cumulative and nonparticipating, $25 par value, 10,000 shares authorized and outstanding	$ 250,000
Common stock, $75 par value, 30,000 shares authorized and outstanding	2,250,000
Total paid-in capital	$2,500,000
Retained earnings	27,500
Total stockholders' equity	$2,527,500

(The current year's dividends have not been paid.)

3. Stockholders' equity:
Paid-in capital:

Preferred stock, 7% cumulative and nonparticipating, $150 par value, 10,000 shares authorized and outstanding	$1,500,000
Common stock, $75 par value, 50,000 shares authorized and outstanding	3,750,000
Total paid-in capital	$5,250,000
Retained earnings (deficit)	(585,000)
Total stockholders' equity	$4,665,000

(Dividends have not been paid for 2 previous years or the current year.)

Required: Compute the book values per share of the preferred and common stock of each corporation assuming that in a liquidation the preferred stock receives par value plus dividends in arrears.

P15-9-A

Compute book values of a stockholder's preferred and common stock

Larson, Inc., is a corporation in which all of the outstanding preferred and common stock is held by the four Larson brothers. The brothers have an agreement stating that the remaining brothers will, upon the death of a brother, purchase from the estate his holdings of stock in the company at book value.

The stockholders' equity section of the balance sheet for the company on December 31, 1987, the date of the death of Edward Larson, shows:

Stockholders' equity:
Paid-in capital:

Preferred stock, 6%; $200 par value; $200 liquidation value; 4,000 shares authorized, issued, and outstanding	$ 800,000
Paid-in capital in excess of par—preferred	40,000
Common stock without par value, $10 stated value, 60,000 shares authorized, issued, and outstanding	600,000
Paid-in capital in excess of par—common	600,000
Retained earnings	80,000
Total stockholders' equity	$2,120,000

No dividends have been paid for the last year on the preferred stock, which is cumulative and nonparticipating. At the time of his death, Edward Larson held 2,000 shares of preferred stock and 10,000 shares of common stock of the company.

Required:

a. Compute the book value of the preferred stock.
b. Compute the book value of the common stock.
c. Compute the amount the remaining brothers must pay to the estate of Edward Larson for the preferred and common stock that he held at the time of his death.

PROBLEMS, SERIES B

P15-1-B

Prepare partial balance sheet involving par value stock

Certain post-closing account balances for Rigdon, Inc., as of December 31, 1987, were as follows:

RIGDON, INC.
Partial List of Post-Closing Account Balances
December 31, 1987

Paid-In Capital in Excess of Par Value—Preferred	$ 15,000
Common Stock Subscribed, 2,000 shares	100,000
Subscriptions Receivable—Common	120,000
Preferred Stock, 8%, $100 par value; 3,000 shares authorized, issued, and outstanding	300,000
Paid-In Capital in Excess of Par Value—Common	36,000
Common Stock, $50 par value; 30,000 shares authorized; 8,000 shares issued and outstanding	400,000
Retained Earnings	377,000

Required:

From the above list of account balances, prepare the stockholders' equity section of the December 31, 1987, balance sheet in good form.

P15-2-B

Determine dividends for common stock and cumulative and noncumulative preferred stock

The outstanding capital stock of the Precision Corporation consisted of 3,000 shares of 10% preferred stock, $100 par value, and 30,000 shares of no-par common stock with a stated value of $100. The preferred was issued at $164.80, the common at $192 per share. On January 1, 1983, the retained earnings of the company were $100,000. During the succeeding five years, net income was as follows:

1983	. . . . . .	$307,000
1984	. . . . . .	204,000
1985	. . . . .	19,200
1986	. . . . . .	64,000
1987	. . . . . .	265,000

No dividends were in arrears as of January 1, 1983, and during the five years 1983–87, the board of directors declared dividends in each year equal to net income of the year.

Required: Prepare a schedule showing the dividends declared each year on each class of stock assuming the preferred stock is:

a.   Cumulative and nonparticipating.
b.   Noncumulative and nonparticipating

P15–3–B

Journalize stock issuances for cash, services (organization costs), and property; prepare resulting balance sheet

On December 27, 1986, the Stoddard Company was authorized to issue 250,000 shares of $5 par value common stock. It then completed the following transactions:

Transactions:

1987
Jan. 14   Issued 45,000 shares of common stock at $6 per share for cash.
    29   Gave the promoters of the corporation 25,000 shares of common stock for their services in organizing the company. The board of directors valued these services at $155,000.
Feb. 19   Exchanged 50,000 shares of common stock for the following assets at fair market values:

Land	. . . . .	$ 45,000
Building	. . . .	110,000
Machinery	. . . .	150,000

Required: a.   Prepare general journal entries to record the transactions.
b.   Prepare the balance sheet of the company as of March 1, 1987.

P15–4–B

Prepare balance sheets for par value stock, stated value stock, and no-par or stated value stock

In the corporate charter that it received on May 1, 1987, the Woodard Company was authorized to issue 15,000 shares of common stock. The company issued 500 shares immediately to each of two of the promoters for $54 per share, cash.

On July 2, the company issued 100 shares of stock to a lawyer to satisfy a $5,600 bill for legal services rendered in organizing the corporation.

On July 3, subscriptions, accompanied by a 10% down payment, were received from the general public for 6,000 shares at $56 per share.

On July 5, the company issued 1,000 shares to the principal promoter of the corporation in exchange for a patent. Another 200 shares were issued to this same person for costs incurred and services rendered in bringing the corporation into existence.

Required: a.   Set up T-accounts, and post the above transactions. Then prepare a balance sheet for the Woodward Company as of July 5, 1987, assuming the authorized stock has a par value of $50 per share.
b.   Repeat part *(a)* for the stockholders' equity accounts, and prepare the stockholders' equity section of the July 5 balance sheet assuming the stock authorized has no par value but has a $20 per share stated value.
c.   Repeat part *(a)* for the stockholders' equity accounts assuming the stock authorized has neither par nor stated value. Only prepare the stockholders' equity section of the balance sheet.

P15–5–B

Journalize stock subscriptions and prepare resulting balance sheet

In the charter granted January 2, 1987, the Thomas Corporation was authorized to issue 2,000 shares of no-par common stock. The stock is to be issued under subscription agreements that call for immediate payment of one fourth of each subscription, with the remainder due on the first day of the following month.

On January 5, subscriptions for 600 shares at $25 per share were received, and on May 1 an additional 400 shares were subscribed at $30 per share. All subscriptions were collected in accordance with the agreements.

Required:
a. Prepare the entries to record all the transactions of January through May 1987, assuming no stock was issued until the subscriptions were paid in full.
b. Prepare the May 31, 1987, balance sheet assuming there were no transactions other than those described above.

P15-6-B

Journalize stock issuances for cash, property, and services; journalize stock subscriptions; and prepare resulting stockholders' equity section

On May 1, 1987, Conrad Company received a charter that authorized it to issue:

1. 4,000 shares of no-par preferred stock to which a stated value of $6 per share is assigned. The stock is entitled to a cumulative dividend of $4.80, convertible into two shares of common stock, callable at $104, and entitled to $100 per share in liquidation.
2. 1,500 shares of $200 par value, $10 cumulative preferred stock which is callable at $210 and entitled to $206 in liquidation.
3. 60,000 shares of no-par common stock to which a stated value of $20 is assigned.

Transactions:

May 1 All of the $4.80 cummulative convertible preferred was subscribed and issued at $102 per share, cash.
2 All of the $10 cumulative preferred was exchanged for inventory, land, and buildings valued at $64,000, $80,000, and $170,000, respectively.
2 Subscriptions were received for 50,000 shares of common at $40 per share, with 10% of the subscription price paid immediately in cash.
3 Cash of $6,000 was paid to reimburse promoters for costs incurred for accounting, legal, and printing services. In addition, 1,000 shares of common stock were issued to the promoters for their services.
31 All of the subscriptions to the common stock were collected and the shares issued.

Required:
a. Prepare journal entries for the above transactions.
b. Assume that retained earnings were $100,000. Prepare the stockholders' equity section of the May 31, 1987, balance sheet.

P15-7-B

Prepare stockholders' equity section; determine book values of stock; and determine dividends for each class of stock

On January 2, 1986, the date the Clark Company received its charter, it issued all of its authorized 3,000 shares of no-par preferred stock at $104 and all of its 12,000 authorized shares of no-par common stock at $40 per share. The preferred stock has a stated value of $50 per share, is entitled to a basic cumulative preference dividend of $6 per share, is callable at $106 beginning in 1988, and is entitled to $100 per share plus cumulative dividends in the event of liquidation. The common stock has a stated value of $10 per share.

On December 31, 1987, the end of the second year of operations, retained earnings were $90,000. No dividends have been declared or paid on either class of stock.

Required:
a. Prepare the stockholders' equity section of the Clark Company's December 31, 1987, balance sheet.
b. Compute the book value of each class of stock assuming the preferred stock is nonparticipating.
c. If $42,000 of dividends were declared as of December 31, 1987, compute the amount paid to each class of stock assuming the preferred stock is nonparticipating.

P15-8-B

Compute total market value for common stock; compute book value of common and preferred stock

The common stock of Mattox Corporation is selling on a stock exchange for $75 per share. The stockholders' equity of the corporation at December 31, 1987, consists of:

Stockholders' Equity:
Paid-in capital:
Preferred stock, 9% cumulative and nonparticipating, $100 par
value, 3,000 shares authorized and outstanding . . . . $ 300,000
Common stock, $60 par value, 30,000 shares
authorized and outstanding   1,800,000
Total paid-in capital $2,100,000
Retained earnings   295,500
Total stockholders' equity $2,395,500

Assume that in liquidation the preferred stock is entitled to par value plus cumulative unpaid dividends.

Required: a.   What is the total market value of all of the corporation's common stock?
  b.   If all dividends have been paid on the preferred stock as of December 31, 1987, what are the book values of the preferred stock and the common stock?
  c.   If two years' dividends were due on the preferred stock as of December 31, 1987, what are the book values of the preferred stock and common stock?

P15-9-B

Compute book values of a stockholder's preferred and common stock

Goode Corporation has an agreement with each of its 15 preferred and 30 common stockholders that in the event of the death of a stockholder, it will purchase at book value from the stockholder's estate or heirs the shares of Goode Corporation stock held by the deceased at the time of death. The book value is to be computed in accordance with generally accepted accounting principles.

Following is the stockholders' equity section of the Goode Corporation's December 31, 1987, balance sheet.

Stockholders' equity:
  Paid-in capital:
    $6 no-par preferred stock, $20 stated value;
      3,000 shares authorized, issued, and outstanding . . . . $ 60,000
    Common stock, $25 par value, 60,000 shares authorized,
      issued, and outstanding   1,500,000
    Paid-in capital in excess of stated value—preferred   336,000
    Paid-in capital in excess of par value—common   12,000
    Retained earnings   720,000
        Total stockholders' equity $2,628,000

The preferred stock is cumulative and entitled to $120 per share plus cumulative dividends in liquidation. No dividends have been paid for 1½ years.

A stockholder who owned 100 shares of preferred stock and 1,000 shares of common stock died on December 31, 1987. You have been employed by the stockholder's widow to compute the book value of each class of stock and to determine the price to be paid for the stock held by her late husband.

Required: Prepare a schedule showing the computation of the amount to be paid for the deceased stockholder's preferred and common stock.

BUSINESS DECISION PROBLEM 15-1

Compute dividends on preferred stock and common stock and determine their relationship to stock prices

Eastern Company and Western Company are two companies that have extremely stable net income amounts of $3,000,000 and $2,000,000, respectively. Both companies distribute all their net income as dividends each year. Eastern Company has 100,000 shares of $50 par value, 6% preferred stock and 500,000 shares of $5 par value common stock outstanding. Western Company has 50,000 shares of $25 par value, 8% preferred stock and 400,000 shares of $5 par value common stock outstanding. Both preferred stocks are cumulative and nonparticipating.

Required: a.   Compute the annual dividend per share of preferred stock and per share of common stock for each company.
  b.   Based solely on the above information, which common stock would you predict to have the higher market price per share? Why?

BUSINESS DECISION PROBLEM 15–2

Determine book values and their relationship to investment decisions

Frank Clayborn recently inherited $96,000 cash that he wishes to invest in one of the following securities: common stock of the Durden Corporation or common stock of the Simmons Corporation. Both corporations manufacture the same types of products and have been in existence for five years. The stockholders' equity sections of the two corporations' latest balance sheets are shown below:

DURDEN CORPORATION

Stockholders' equity:
Paid-in capital:
   Common stock, $25 par value, 30,000 shares authorized,
     issued, and outstanding . . . . $ 750,000
Retained earnings   690,000
     Total stockholders' equity $1,440,000

SIMMONS CORPORATION

Stockholders' equity:
Paid-in capital:
   Preferred stock, 8%, $100 par value, cumulative and
    nonparticipating, 4,000 shares authorized, issued,
    and outstanding   . . . . $ 400,000
   Common stock, $25 par value, 40,000 shares authorized,
     issued, and outstanding   1,000,000
Retained earnings   112,000
     Total stockholders' equity $1,512,000

The Durden Corporation has paid a cash dividend of $1.20 per share each year since its creation; its common stock is currently selling for $118 per share. The Simmons Corporation's common stock is currently selling for $96 per share. The current year's dividend and three prior years' dividends on the preferred stock are in arrears. The preferred stock has a liquidation value of $120 per share.

Required:

a. What is the book value per share of the Durden Corporation common stock and the Simmons Corporation common stock? Is book value the major determinant of market value of the stock?

b. Based solely upon the above information, which investment would you recommend? Why?

BUSINESS SITUATION FOR DISCUSSION

It Can Pay Off Big to Turn Common Into Preferred*

☐   When Teledyne Inc. bought back some 18% of its common shares in 1980, the company's executives got more or less what they had hoped for: a 28% higher price in a year's time. But when Advanced Systems Inc. swapped a new issue of preferred shares for 24% of its common in 1982, Chief Financial Officer Norman Walack got a lot more than he expected: a 100% jump in the common stock's price, from 11 a share to 22 a year later.

Shelling out cash to repurchase common shares has become an increasingly popular way for corporations to obtain, among other things, a more favorable balance between the market supply of their stock and the demand

* Reprinted from the March 5, 1984, issue of *Business Week,* (p. 76) by special permission. © 1984 by McGraw-Hill, Inc.

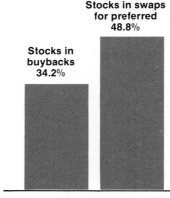

Swapping Preferred for Common: A Faster Track than Buybacks—Average Price Gain in 12 Months after Transactions in 1980–83 Period

Stocks in swaps for preferred 48.8%

Stocks in buybacks 34.2%

Data: Mitchell & Co.

for it. But, according to a study by Mitchell & Co., a Boston management-consulting firm, creating new preferred shares and swapping them for common stock is often more rewarding (see chart).

"Reacquiring common shares through an exchange of preferred stock generally does not hurt the company in any way, and avoids all the negatives that have thrown the entire stock-buyback idea into a deep well of controversy," says Carol Bruckner Coles, Mitchell's president and chief operating officer. While analysts increasingly criticize the costs of stock repurchases (BW—June 25), companies keep on doing them, for a variety of reasons: to reduce dividend payments, to gain an almost automatic assurance of higher earnings per share, to make feared takeover plots or proxy fights more difficult, and to reinvest excess cash in the companies' own "undervalued assets."

Thinking Big

The still relatively undiscovered method of swapping preferred serves the same purposes but skirts most of the pitfalls; about the only drawback to a company is that it may have to jack up its preferred dividend to compete with any rise in interest rates. The swappers, notes Coles, do not have to divert cash from more productive purposes, nor do they have to take on extra debt. "For a company that borrows funds to reacquire shares, interest charges may offset any earnings benefits and increase as well its debt-to-equity ratio," notes a Standard & Poor's Corp. analyst.

The stocks of companies that have resorted to straight buybacks, according to Mitchell analysts' calcu-

lations, increased, on average, over the past five years by about 30% above where the stock would have been without the repurchase. But the stocks of companies that have swapped preferred shares or, in some cases, even convertible debentures [unsecured bonds], for their common stock have, on the same basis, jumped an average of 199%. Thinking big helps, strategists contend: For maximum impact, the conversion should involve no fewer than 20% of outstanding shares.

Thus, not all stocks involved in swaps enjoy a surge in price. Manufacturers Hanover Trust Co., for example, pulled in only 11.8% of its common for new preferred shares in May, 1982. Result: Its common stock rose a meager 2% after a year. And Ashland Oil Inc. reacquired 14% of its common in January, 1980, with a $2.50-a-share dividend, in return for preferred shares that will pay a dividend almost twice that on its common stock. Dividends on preferred stock typically run up to 60% above the yield on common stocks. Even so, the Ashland common rose a disappointing 5%.

Snowball?

A large-scale preferred swap, however, may have preserved Development Corp. of America as a public company. Officers of the Hollywood (Fla.) real estate company had considered taking the company private, recalls Pedro Diaz, its chief financial officer. Then they had thought of economizing by cutting the dividend on the common stock. "But on second thought, we just decided to issue subordinated 12% debentures in exchange for about 27% of our common stock," he says. The stock, trading at about 5½ before the swap, rose to about 16 a year later.

That may, in part, explain why Advanced Systems' exchange of preferred shares was so well received. "Investors would do well to scout for companies that are in the process of, or about to offer, such a preferred-for-common stock swap," says Coles. Such offers have yet to snowball on Wall Street, "but we expect to see many more companies in the later half of the 1980s use this kind of a stock swap," says Coles.

Companies whose stocks are trading below their year-earlier prices, and which have authorized-but-unissued preferred stock, are likely to resort to such swaps. A number of steel companies, suggests Coles, could find the swaps rewarding. Among other logical candidates, she adds, are Johnson & Johnson, Gulf & Western Industries, Bristol-Meyers, and Revlon.

CHAPTER 16

Corporations: Paid-In Capital, Retained Earnings, Dividends, and Treasury Stock

LEARNING OBJECTIVES

After studying this chapter, you should be able to:

1. Identify the different sources of paid-in capital and describe how they would be presented in a balance sheet.

2. Give journal entries for a cash dividend, a large or small stock dividend, a stock split, a retained earnings appropriation, and an acquisition and reissuance of treasury stock.

3. Define extraordinary items and prior period adjustments and show their proper presentation in the financial statements.

4. Describe the proper accounting treatment of changes in accounting principle.

5. Define and use correctly the new terms in the glossary.

As owners of a corporation, stockholders provide much of the capital for the operation of the corporation. On the balance sheet, this ownership is shown as paid-in capital under stockholders' equity. Also included in stockholders' equity is the capital accumulated through the retention of earnings of the corporation (retained earnings). Paid-in capital is a relatively permanent portion of stockholders' equity; retained earnings are a relatively temporary portion of corporate capital and are the source of stockholders' dividends.

The preceding chapter discussed the paid-in capital obtained by issuing shares of stock for cash, other property, or services. In this chapter you will learn about additional sources of paid-in capital and other matters affecting stockholders' equity.

■ PAID-IN (OR CONTRIBUTED) CAPITAL

As you learned in the preceding chapter, paid-in capital, or contributed capital, refers to all of the contributed capital of a corporation, including that carried in the capital stock accounts. In the general ledger, no single account titled "Paid-in Capital" is maintained. Instead, a separate account is established for each source of paid-in capital.

Illustration 16.1 summarizes several sources of stockholders' equity and gives examples of general ledger account titles used to record increases and decreases in capital from each of these sources. Some of these general ledger accounts were discussed in Chapter 15; the others will be discussed in this chapter.

Illustration 16.1

Sources of Stockholders' Equity

Sources of stockholders' equity	Illustrative general ledger account titles
I. Capital paid in (or contributed).	
A. For, or assigned to, shares:	
1. Issued to the extent of par or stated value or the amount received for shares without par or stated value.	Common Stock 5% Preferred Stock
2. Subscribed but not issued to the extent of par or stated value or the amount subscribed for shares without par or stated value.	Common (Preferred) Stock Subscribed
3. To be distributed as a stock dividend.	Stock Dividend Distributable—Common (Preferred)
4. In addition to par or stated value:	
a. In excess of par.	Paid-In Capital in Excess of Par Value—Common (Preferred)
b. In excess of stated value.	Paid-In Capital in Excess of Stated Value—Common (Preferred)
c. Resulting from declaration of stock dividends.	Paid-In Capital—Stock Dividends
d. Resulting from reissue of treasury stock at a price above its acquisition price.	Paid-In Capital—Common (Preferred) Treasury Stock Transactions
B. Other than for shares, whether from shareholders or from others.	Paid-In Capital—Donations
II. Capital accumulated by retention of earnings (retained earnings).	
A. Appropriated retained earnings.	Appropriation per Loan Agreement
B. Free and unappropriated retained earnings.	Retained Earnings (Unappropriated)

The stockholders' equity section of the balance sheet should show the different sources of the corporation's paid-in capital since this is important information. For example, assume a corporation has issued both preferred and common stock at various times and amounts. The total paid-in capital in excess of par value currently is $25,000 for preferred stock and $15,000 for common stock. If only one Paid-In Capital in Excess of Par Value account were established for all classes of stock, it would be impossible to determine whether the capital came from preferred stock or from common stock issuances.

Paid-In Capital—Stock Dividends *Pay divides in Stock*

When a corporation declares a stock dividend, the corporation distributes additional shares of stock (instead of cash) to its present stockholders. In a later section, this chapter discusses and illustrates how the issuance of a stock dividend results in a credit to a Paid-In Capital—Stock Dividends account.

Paid-In Capital—Treasury Stock Transactions *(company buys back from the stockholder)*

Another source of capital is treasury stock transactions. **Treasury stock** is the corporation's own stock, either preferred or common, that has been issued and reacquired by the issuing corporation; it is legally available for reissuance. If a corporation reacquires shares of its own outstanding capital stock at one price and later reissues them at a higher price, corporate capital is increased by the difference between the two prices. If the reissue price is **less** than acquisition cost, corporate capital is decreased. Treasury stock transactions are treated at length later in this chapter.

Paid-In Capital—Donations

Occasionally, a corporation receives gifts of assets, such as a gift of a $500,000 building. These donated gifts increase stockholders' equity and are called **donated capital.** The entry to record the gift of a $500,000 building is a debit to Buildings and a credit to Paid-In Capital—Donations. The entry should be made in the amount of the $500,000 fair market value of the gift when received.

■ RETAINED EARNINGS

Retained earnings is that part of stockholders' equity resulting from earnings; it represents the source of certain assets received but not distributed to stockholders as dividends. Like paid-in capital, retained earnings is a source of assets received by a corporation. Paid-in capital is the actual investment by the stockholders; retained earnings is the investment by the stockholders through earnings not yet withdrawn.

The balance in the corporation's Retained Earnings account is the corporation's net income from the date the corporation began to the present, less the sum of dividends paid during this period. Net income increases Retained Earnings, while dividends decrease Retained Earnings in any given year. Thus, the balance in Retained Earnings represents the corporation's accumulated net income not distributed to stockholders.

When the Retained Earnings account has a debit balance, a **deficit** exists. A deficit is shown as retained earnings with a negative amount in the stockholders' equity section of the balance sheet. The title of the general ledger account need not be changed even though it contains a debit balance. The most common debits and credits made to Retained Earnings are for income (or losses) and dividends. Occasionally, other entries are made to the Retained Earnings account. Some of these entries are discussed later in the chapter.

■ PAID-IN CAPITAL AND RETAINED EARNINGS IN THE BALANCE SHEET

The following stockholders' equity section of a balance sheet presents the various sources of capital in proper form:

Stockholders' equity:

Paid-in capital:		
Preferred stock, 6% $100 par value; authorized, issued, and outstanding, 4,000 shares	$ 400,000	
Common stock, no par value, $5 stated value; authorized, issued, and outstanding, 400,000 shares	2,000,000	$2,400,000
Paid-in capital—		
From preferred stock issuances*	$ 40,000	
From donations	10,000	50,000
Total paid-in capital		$2,450,000
Retained earnings		500,000
Total stockholders' equity		$2,950,000

* This label is not the exact account title but is representative of the descriptions used on balance sheets. The exact account title could be used, but shorter descriptions are often shown.

In highly condensed, published balance sheets, the details regarding the sources of the paid-in capital in excess of par or stated value are often omitted and replaced by a single item, such as:

Paid-in capital in excess of par or stated value . . $50,000

will need to know this for test.

■ DIVIDENDS

Dividends are distributions of earnings by a corporation to its stockholders. Usually dividends are paid in cash, but additional shares of the corporation's own capital stock may also be distributed as dividends. Occasionally, dividends are paid in merchandise or other assets. Since dividends are the means whereby the owners of a corporation share in the earnings of the corporation, they usually are charged against retained earnings.

Before dividends can be paid, they must be declared by the board of directors and recorded in the minutes book. Three dividend dates are significant:

must be recorded

1. <u>Date of declaration.</u> This date indicates when the board of directors takes action in the form of a motion and declares that dividends should be paid. The board action creates the liability for dividends payable.
2. <u>Date of record.</u> This date is established by the board and means that the stockholders on the date of record will receive the dividends. The corporation's stockholders as of the date of record are determined from the corporation's records (the stockholders' ledger).
3. <u>Date of payment.</u> This date indicates when the dividend is actually paid to the stockholders.

entry

To illustrate how these three dates relate to an actual situation, assume the board of directors of the Allen Corporation declared a cash dividend on May 5, 1987 (date of declaration). The cash dividend declared is $1.25 per share to stockholders of record on July 1, 1987 (date of record), payable on

July 10 (date of payment). Since financial transactions occur on both the date of declaration (a liability is incurred) and on the date of payment (cash is paid), journal entries will be required on both of these dates. No journal entry is required on the date of record.

Illustration 16.2 shows the frequencies of dividend payments made by a sample of 600 companies for the years 1980–83. Cash dividends are far more numerous than stock dividends or dividends in kind (paid in merchandise or other assets).

Illustration 16.2

Types of Dividends

	Number of Companies			
	1983	*1982*	*1981*	*1980*
Cash dividends paid to common stock shareholders . . .	507	518	526	535
Cash dividends paid to preferred stock shareholders . . .	207	216	222	210
Stock dividends	14	17	21	27
Dividends in kind	6	3	6	—

Source: American Institute of Certified Public Accountants, *Accounting Trends & Techniques* (New York: AICPA, 1984), p. 313.

Cash Dividends

Cash dividends are cash distributions of net income by a corporation to its stockholders. To illustrate the entries for cash dividends, consider the following example. On January 21, 1987, a corporation's board of directors declares a 2% quarterly cash dividend on $100,000 (one fourth of the annual dividend on 1,000 shares of $100 par value, 8% preferred stock). The dividend will be paid on March 1, 1987, to stockholders of record on February 5, 1987. The entries at the declaration and payment dates are as follows (no entry is made on the date of record):

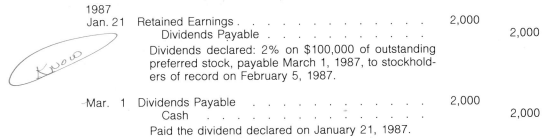

1987			
Jan. 21	Retained Earnings	2,000	
	Dividends Payable		2,000
	Dividends declared: 2% on $100,000 of outstanding preferred stock, payable March 1, 1987, to stockholders of record on February 5, 1987.		
Mar. 1	Dividends Payable	2,000	
	Cash		2,000
	Paid the dividend declared on January 21, 1987.		

Often a cash dividend is stated as so many dollars per share. For instance, the quarterly dividend could have been stated as $2 per share. When a cash dividend is declared, some companies debit a Dividends account instead of Retained Earnings. The Dividends account is then closed to Retained Earnings at the end of the fiscal year. Both methods are acceptable.

Once a cash dividend is declared and notice of the dividend is given to stockholders, generally it cannot be rescinded unless all stockholders agree to such action.[1] Thus, the credit balance in the Dividends Payable account appears as a current liability on the balance sheet.

---

[1] Stockholders might agree to rescind (cancel) a dividend that has already been declared if the company is in difficult financial circumstances and needs to retain the cash to pay bills or acquire assets that are needed to continue operations.

Stock Dividends

Stock dividends are payable in additional shares of the declaring corporation's capital stock. Stock dividend declarations usually call for the distribution of additional shares of the same class of stock as that held by the stockholders—for example, additional common stock to common stockholders. The usual accounting for a stock dividend distribution is to transfer a sum from retained earnings to permanent paid-in capital. The amount transferred for stock dividends is usually the fair market value of the distributed shares. Most states permit corporations to debit Retained Earnings or any paid-in capital accounts other than those representing legal capital for stock dividends. But in most circumstances Retained Earnings will be debited for the declaration of a stock dividend.

Stock dividends have no effect on the total amount of stockholders' equity. They merely decrease retained earnings and increase paid-in capital by an equal amount. Immediately after the distribution of a stock dividend, each share of similar stock has a lower book value per share. This decrease occurs because more shares are outstanding with no increase in total stockholders' equity.

Stock dividends do not affect the individual stockholder's percentage of ownership in the corporation. For example, if a stockholder owns 1,000 shares in a corporation having 100,000 shares of stock outstanding, that stockholder owns 1% of the outstanding shares. After a 10% stock dividend, the stockholder will still own 1% of the outstanding shares—1,100 of 110,000 outstanding.

There are several reasons why a corporation might declare a stock dividend:

1. Retained earnings may have become large relative to total stockholders' equity, or the corporation may simply desire a larger permanent capitalization. *Get money out of retained earnings*
2. The market price of the stock may have risen above a desirable trading range. A stock dividend will generally reduce the per share market value of the company's stock. *Dilutes the ownership*
3. The corporation may wish to have more stockholders (who might then buy their products) and expects to eventually increase their number by increasing the number of shares outstanding. Some of the stockholders receiving the stock dividend are likely to sell the shares to other persons.
4. Stock dividends may be used to silence stockholders' demands for dividends from a corporation that does not have sufficient cash to pay cash dividends.

Recording Stock Dividends

Does not have an effect on the company

Small Stock Dividends. A stock dividend of less than 20–25% of the previously outstanding shares is considered a "small stock dividend" and is assumed to have little effect on the market value of the shares. Thus, the dividend is accounted for at the present market value of the outstanding shares.

Assume a corporation is authorized to issue 20,000 shares of $100 par value common stock, of which 8,000 shares are outstanding. Its board of directors declares a 10% stock dividend (800 shares). The market price of the stock is $125 per share immediately before the stock dividend is announced. Since the distribution is less than 20–25% of the previously outstanding shares, the dividend is accounted for at market value. The entry for the declaration of the stock dividend on August 10, 1987, is:

```
1987
Aug. 10   Retained Earnings (800 shares × $125)  . . . . .   100,000
             Stock Dividend Distributable—Common
             (800 shares × $100)  . . . . . . . . .                    80,000
          Paid-In Capital—Stock Dividends
             (800 shares × $25)  . . . . . . . . . .                   20,000
          To record the declaration of a 10% stock dividend;
          shares to be distributed on September 20, 1987,
          to stockholders of record on August 31, 1987.
```

The entry to record the issuance of the shares is:

```
1987
Sept. 20  Stock Dividend Distributable—Common  . . . . .    80,000
             Common Stock  . . . . . . . . . . . .                     80,000
          To record the distribution of 800 shares of com-
          mon stock as authorized in stock dividend de-
          clared on August 10, 1987.
```

The **Stock Dividend Distributable—Common account** is a stockholders' equity (paid-in capital) account that is credited for the par or stated value of the shares distributable when recording the declaration of a stock dividend. Since a stock dividend distributable is not to be paid with assets, it is not a liability. If a balance sheet is prepared between the date the 10% dividend is declared and the date the shares are issued, the proper statement presentation of the effects of the stock dividend is:

```
Stockholders' equity:
  Paid-in capital:
    Common stock, $100 par value; authorized, 20,000 shares;
      issued and outstanding, 8,000 shares  . . . . . . . .   $800,000
    Stock dividend distributable on September 20, 1987,
      800 shares at par value  . . . . . . . . . . .             80,000
    Total par value of shares issued and to be issued  . . . .  $880,000
    Paid-in capital from stock dividends  . . . . . . . . . .     20,000
      Total paid-in capital  . . . . . . . . . . . .                       $ 900,000
  Retained earnings  . . . . . . . . . . . . . . . .                        150,000
      Total stockholders' equity  . . . . . . . . . .                      $1,050,000
```

Suppose, on the other hand, that the common stock in the above example is no-par stock and has a stated value of $50 per share. In this case, the entry to record the declaration of the stock dividend (when the market value is $125) is:

```
Retained Earnings (800 shares × $125) . . . . . . . . .   100,000
    Stock Dividend Distributable—Common
      (800 shares × $50)  . . . . . . . . . . .                      40,000
    Paid-In Capital—Stock Dividends (800 shares × $75)  . .          60,000
    To record the declaration of a stock dividend.
```

The entry to record the issuance of the stock dividend is:

```
Stock Dividend Distributable—Common . . . . . . . . .    40,000
    Common Stock  . . . . . . . . . . . . . .                       40,000
    To record the issuance of the stock dividend.
```

Large Stock Dividends.   Stock dividends of more than 20–25% of the previously outstanding shares are considered to be large stock dividends. Since one purpose of a large stock dividend is to reduce the market value of the stock so the shares can be traded more easily, the old market value of the stock should not be used in the entry. Such dividends are accounted for at their **par** or **stated** value rather than at their fair market value. Stocks without par or stated value are accounted for at the amounts established by the laws of the state of incorporation or by the board of directors.

To illustrate the treatment of a stock dividend of more than 20–25%, assume X Corporation has been authorized to issue 10,000 shares of $10 par value common stock, of which 5,000 shares are outstanding. X Corporation declares a 30% stock dividend (1,500 shares) on September 20, 1987, to be issued on October 15, 1987. The required entries are:

1987			
Sept. 20	Retained Earnings (1,500 shares × $10)	15,000	
	Stock Dividend Distributable		15,000
	To declare a 30% stock dividend.		
Oct. 15	Stock Dividend Distributable	15,000	
	Common Stock		15,000
	To issue the 30% stock dividend.		

No paid in capital [handwritten margin note]

Note that in contrast to the small stock dividend that was accounted for at market value, the 30% stock dividend is accounted for at par value (1,500 shares × $10 = $15,000). Because of the differences in accounting for large and small stock dividends, the relative size of the stock dividend must be determined before making any journal entries.

Stock Splits

A stock split is a distribution of additional shares of the issuing corporation's stock for which the corporation receives no assets. The purpose of a stock split is to cause a large reduction in the market price per share of the outstanding stock. In the usual stock split, the number of shares outstanding is increased, while the par value per share is decreased. A two-for-one split doubles the shares outstanding, a three-for-one split triples the shares, and so on. The par value per share is usually reduced at the same time so that the total dollar amount credited to common stock remains the same. For instance, in a two-for-one split, the par value per share is usually halved.[2]

The entry to record a stock split depends on the particular circumstances. Usually, only the number of shares outstanding and the par or stated value need to be changed in the records. Thus, a two-for-one stock split in which the par value of the shares is decreased from $20 to $10 would be recorded as follows:

Common stock—$20 par value	100,000	
Common Stock—$10 par value		100,000
To record a two-for-one stock split. 5,000 shares of $20 par value common stock were replaced by 10,000 shares of $10 par value common stock.		

---

[2] If a corporation *reduces* the par value of its stock without issuing more shares, say, from $100 to $60 per share, then $40 per share must be removed from the appropriate capital stock account and credited to Paid-In Capital—Recapitalization. Further discussion of this process, called recapitalization, is beyond the scope of this text.

Legality of Dividends

In the preceding chapter you learned that corporate laws differ as to their provisions on the legality of a dividend. The **legal** or **stated capital** of a corporation is established by state law as that portion of the stockholders' equity that must be maintained intact, unimpaired by dividend declarations or other distributions to stockholders. The legal capital is often established at an amount equal to the par or stated value of the shares issued or at an amount equal to a minimum price per share issued.

The objective of these state corporate laws is to protect the corporation's creditors whose claims are superior to the corporation's stockholders. To illustrate the significance of the legal capital concept, assume a corporation has severe financial difficulty and is about to go out of business. If there were no legal capital restriction on dividends, the stockholders of a corporation in financial difficulty might attempt to pay themselves a cash dividend leaving no funds available for the corporation's creditors.

The board of directors of a corporation possesses sole power to declare dividends. The legality of a dividend generally depends on the amount of retained earnings available for dividends—not on the net income of any one period or the size of the cash balance. Dividends may be paid in periods in which losses are incurred, provided retained earnings and the cash position justify the dividend. And in some states, dividends may be declared from current earnings even though there is an accumulated deficit. The financial advisability of declaring a dividend depends on the cash position of the corporation.

Liquidating Dividends

Normally, dividends are reductions of retained earnings since they are distributions of the corporation's net income. However, dividends may be distributions of contributed capital. These dividends are called liquidating dividends.

Liquidating dividends are debited to a paid-in capital account. Corporations should disclose to stockholders the source of any dividends that are not distributions of net income by indicating which paid-in capital account was debited as the result of the dividend. The legality of liquidating dividends depends on the precise source of the paid-in capital and the laws of the state of incorporation.

■ RETAINED EARNINGS APPROPRIATIONS

The amount of a corporation's retained earnings that may be paid as cash dividends may be less than total retained earnings for several reasons, contractual or voluntary. For example, a loan contract may state that part of a corporation's $100,000 of retained earnings is not available for cash dividends until the loan is paid, or a board of directors may decide that assets resulting from net income should be used for plant expansion rather than cash dividends. These contractual or voluntary restrictions or limitations on retained earnings are called retained earnings appropriations.

Retained earnings appropriations may be formally recorded by transferring amounts from Retained Earnings to accounts such as "Appropriation for Loan Agreement" or "Retained Earnings Appropriated for Plant Expansion." Retained earnings appropriations are sometimes referred to as retained earnings reserves.

Appropriations of retained earnings may also be made for pending litigation, for debt retirement, for contingencies in general, and for other purposes. Such appropriations do not reduce total retained earnings. Their purpose is merely to disclose to balance sheet readers that a portion of retained earnings is not available for cash dividends. Thus, the recording of these appropriations simply guarantees that the corporation will limit its outflow of cash dividends while repaying a loan, expanding a plant, or taking on some other costly endeavor. Recording retained earnings appropriations does not involve the setting aside of cash for the indicated purpose. The establishment of a separate fund would require a specific directive from the board of directors. Thus, the only entry required to record the appropriation of $25,000 of retained earnings to fulfill the provisions in a loan agreement is:

Retained Earnings	25,000	
Appropriation per Loan Agreement		25,000
New account To record restriction on retained earnings.		

When the retained earnings appropriation has served its purpose of restricting dividends and the loan has been repaid, the board of directors may decide to return the appropriation intact to Retained Earnings. The entry to do this is:

Appropriation per Loan Agreement	25,000	
Retained Earnings		25,000
To return balance in Appropriation per Loan Agreement account to Retained Earnings.		

Retained Earnings Appropriations in the Balance Sheet

In the balance sheet, retained earnings appropriations should be shown in the stockholders' equity section as follows:

Bal Sheet

Stockholders' equity:			
Paid-in capital:			
Preferred stock, $50 par value; 500 shares authorized, issued, and outstanding		$25,000	
Common stock, $5 par value; 10,000 shares authorized, issued, and outstanding		50,000	
Total paid-in capital			$ 75,000
Retained earnings:			
Appropriated:			
Per loan agreement		$25,000	
Unappropriated		20,000	
Total retained earnings			45,000
Total stockholders' equity			$120,000

Note that a retained earnings appropriation does not reduce stockholders' equity; it merely earmarks (restricts) a portion of that equity for a specific reason.

The formal practice of recording and reporting retained earnings appropriations is a practice that is decreasing and is being replaced by footnote explanations such as the following:

> Note 7. Retained earnings restrictions. According to provisions in the loan agreement, retained earnings available for dividends are limited to $20,000.

Such footnotes appear after the formal financial statements in a section called "Notes to Financial Statements." The Retained Earnings account in the balance sheet would be referenced as follows: "Retained Earnings (see note 7) . . . $45,000."

Changes in the composition of retained earnings reveal important information about a corporation to financial statement users. A separate formal financial statement is issued to disclose such changes. This statement is called the statement of retained earnings.

■ THE STATEMENT OF RETAINED EARNINGS

Most corporations include four financial statements in their annual reports to stockholders: a balance sheet, an income statement, a statement of retained earnings, and a statement of changes in financial position (to be discussed in Chapter 19). A statement of retained earnings is a formal statement showing the items causing changes in unappropriated and appropriated retained earnings during a stated period of time. Changes in unappropriated retained earnings usually consist of the addition of net income (or deduction of net loss) and the deduction of dividends and appropriations. Changes in appropriated retained earnings consist of increases or decreases in appropriations.

A typical statement of retained earnings is shown in Illustration 16.3. The only new appropriation during 1987 was an additional $35,000 for plant expansion. This new $35,000 is added to the $25,000 beginning balance in that account and subtracted from unappropriated retained earnings.

Illustration 16.3

Statement of Retained Earnings

WARD CORPORATION Statement of Retained Earnings For Year Ended December 31, 1987		
Unappropriated retained earnings:		
January 1, 1987, balance		$180,000
Add: Net income		80,000
		$260,000
Less: Dividends	$15,000	
Appropriation for plant expansion	35,000	50,000
Unappropriated retained earnings, December 31, 1987		$210,000
Appropriated retained earnings:		
Appropriation for plant expansion, January 1, 1987, balance	$25,000	
Add: Increase in 1987	35,000	$ 60,000
Appropriation for contract obligation, January 1, 1987, balance		20,000
Appropriated retained earnings, December 31, 1987		$ 80,000
Total retained earnings, December 31, 1987		$290,000

■ TREASURY STOCK

Treasury stock is the corporation's own capital stock that has been issued and then reacquired by the corporation; it has not been canceled and is legally available for later reissuance. Thus, treasury stock is not classified as **unissued stock** because unissued stock is stock that has never been issued.

As you may recall, if a corporation has additional **authorized** but **unissued** shares of stock that are to be issued after the date of original issue, the preemptive right requires that additional authorized and unissued shares must, in most states, be offered first to existing stockholders on a prorata basis. However, treasury stock may be reissued without violating the preemptive right provisions of state laws; that is, treasury stock does not have to be offered to current stockholders on a prorata basis.

A corporation may reacquire its own capital stock as treasury stock to (1) cancel and retire the stock, (2) reissue the stock later at a higher price, (3) reduce the number of shares outstanding and thereby increase earnings per share, or (4) use the stock for issuance to employees. If the intent of reacquisition is cancellation and retirement, the treasury shares exist only until they are retired and canceled by formal reduction of the authorized capital.

Most state corporate laws consider treasury stock as issued but not outstanding for dividend or voting purposes, since the shares are no longer in the possession of stockholders. But treasury shares usually are considered to be outstanding for purposes of determining legal capital. Thus, the legal capital would include outstanding shares plus those held in the corporation's treasury. In states that consider treasury stock part of legal capital, the cost of treasury stock may not exceed the amount of retained earnings at the date the shares are reacquired. The purpose of this regulation is to protect creditors by preventing the corporation from using funds to purchase stock instead of paying its debts when the corporation is in financial difficulty. Thus, if a corporation is subject to such a law (as is assumed in this text), the retained earnings available for dividends are limited to the amount in excess of the cost of the treasury shares on hand.

Acquisition and Reissuance of Treasury Stock

When treasury stock is acquired, the stock is recorded at cost in a debit-balanced stockholders' equity account called Treasury Stock.[3] Reissuances are credited to the Treasury Stock account at the cost of acquisition. Any excess of the reissue price over cost is credited to Paid-In Capital—Treasury Stock Transactions because it represents additional paid-in capital.

To illustrate, assume that on February 18, 1987, the Hillside Corporation reacquired 100 shares of its outstanding common stock for $55 each. (The company's stockholders' equity consisted solely of common stock and retained earnings.) On April 18, 1987, the company reissued 30 shares for $58 each. The entries are:

---

[3] Another acceptable method of accounting for treasury stock transactions is called the par value method. Further discussion of the par value method is left to intermediate accounting texts.

```
1987
Feb. 18   Treasury Stock—Common (100 shares × $55) . . .      5,500
              Cash . . . . . . . . . . . . . . . . . . . .                 5,500
          Acquired 100 shares of treasury stock at $55.


Apr. 18   Cash (30 shares × $58) . . . . . . . . . . . .      1,740
              Treasury Stock—Common (30 shares × $55) . .            1,650
              Paid-In Capital—Common Treasury Stock
                  Transactions . . . . . . . . . . . . . .             90
          Reissued 30 shares of treasury stock at $58; cost
          $55 per share.
```

When the reissue price of subsequent shares is **less** than the acquisition price, the difference between cost and reissue price is debited to Paid-In Capital—Common Treasury Stock Transactions. But this account is not permitted to develop a debit balance. By definition, no paid-in capital account can have a debit balance. If the Hillside Corporation reissued an additional 20 shares at $52 per share on June 12, 1987, the entry is:

```
1987
June 12   Cash (20 shares × $52) . . . . . . . . . . .       1,040
          Paid-In Capital—Common Treasury Stock
              Transactions . . . . . . . . . . . . . . .        60
              Treasury Stock—Common (20 shares × $55) . .            1,100
          Reissued 20 shares of treasury stock at $52; cost
          $55 per share.
```

At this point, the credit balance in the Paid-In Capital—Common Treasury Stock Transactions account is $30. If the remaining 50 shares are reissued on July 16, 1987, for $53 per share, the entry is:

```
1987
July 16   Cash (50 shares × $53) . . . . . . . . . . .       2,650
          Paid-In Capital—Common Treasury Stock
              Transactions . . . . . . . . . . . . . . .        30
          Retained Earnings . . . . . . . . . . . . . .         70
              Treasury Stock—Common (50 shares × $55) . .            2,750
          Reissued 50 shares of treasury stock at $53; cost
          $55 per share.
```

Note that the Paid-In Capital—Common Treasury Stock Transactions account credit balance has been exhausted. If more than $30 is debited to that account, it would develop a debit balance. Thus, the remaining $70 of the excess of cost over reissue price is regarded as a special distribution to the stockholders involved and is debited to the Retained Earnings account.

When stockholders **donate** stock to a corporation, the treatment is slightly different. Since donated treasury shares have no cost, only a memo entry is made when they are received.[4] The only formal entry required is to debit Cash and credit the Paid-In Capital—Donations account when the stock is reissued. For example, if donated treasury stock is sold for $5,000, the entry is:

```
Cash . . . . . . . . . . . . . . . . . . . . . .      5,000
    Paid-In Capital—Donations . . . . . . . . . . .          5,000
To record the sale of donated treasury stock.
```

---

[4] The method illustrated here is called the *memo* method. Other acceptable methods of accounting for donated stock are the *cost* method and *par value* method. These latter two methods are discussed in intermediate accounting texts.

Treasury Stock in the Balance Sheet

When treasury stock is held on a balance sheet date, it customarily is shown in that statement at cost, as a deduction from the sum of total paid-in capital and retained earnings, as follows:

Stockholders' equity:
Paid-in capital:
Common stock, authorized and issued, 20,000 shares, of which 2,000 shares
are in the treasury $200,000
Retained earnings (including $22,000 restricted by acquisition of treasury stock) . . 80,000
Total paid-in capital and retained earnings $280,000
Less: Treasury stock at cost, 2,000 shares 22,000
Total stockholders' equity $258,000

Stockholders' Equity in the Balance Sheet

Much of what has been discussed so far in Chapters 15 and 16 can be summarized through presentation of the stockholders' equity section of the balance sheet of a hypothetical corporation (Illustration 16.4). This partial balance sheet shows (1) the amount of capital assigned to shares outstanding; (2) the capital contributed for outstanding shares in addition to that assigned to the shares; (3) other forms of paid-in capital; and (4) retained earnings, appropriated and unappropriated.

Illustration 16.4

Stockholders' Equity Section of the Balance Sheet

HYPOTHETICAL CORPORATION
Partial Balance Sheet
December 31, 1987

Stockholders' Equity:
Paid-in capital:
Preferred stock, 8%, $100 par value; 2,000 shares authorized,
issued, and outstanding . . . . $ 200,000
Common stock, $10 par value; authorized, 100,000 shares,
issued, 80,000 shares of which 1,000 are held in the
treasury $800,000
Stock dividend distributable on common stock on January 15,
1988, 7,900 shares 79,000 879,000
Paid-in capital—
From common stock issuances . . . . $ 40,000
From stock dividends 60,000
From treasury stock transactions 30,000
From donations 50,000 180,000
Total paid-in capital $1,259,000
Retained earnings:
Appropriated:
Per loan agreement $250,000
Unappropriated (restricted to the extent of $20,000, the cost of
treasury shares held) 150,000
Total retained earnings 400,000
Total paid-in capital and retained earnings $1,659,000
Less: Treasury stock, common, 1,000 shares at cost 20,000
Total stockholders' equity $1,639,000

■ NET INCOME INCLUSIONS AND EXCLUSIONS

Accounting has long faced the problem of what to include in the net income reported for a period. Should net income include only the revenues and expenses related to normal operations? Or should it include unusual, nonrecurring gains and losses? And further, should the determination of net income for 1987, for example, include an item that can be clearly associated with a prior year, such as additional federal income taxes for 1986? Or should such items, including corrections of errors, be carried directly to retained earnings? How are the effects of making a change in accounting principle (like a change in depreciation methods) to be reported?

APB Opinion No. 9 (December 1966) sought to provide answers to some of these questions. The *Opinion* directed that unusual and nonrecurring items that have an earnings or loss effect be classified as extraordinary items (reported in the income statement) or as prior period adjustments (reported in the statement of retained earnings). Extraordinary items were to be reported separately after net income from regular continuing activities.

The reporting of extraordinary items, changes in accounting principle, and prior period adjustments is shown in Illustrations 16.5 (p. 626) and 16.7 (p. 629). For these illustrations, assume the following facts:

1. Anson Company had a taxable gain in 1987 of $40,000 from voluntary early retirement of debt (extraordinary item).
2. The company changed depreciation methods in 1987 (change in accounting principle), and the cumulative effect of the change was a $6,000 decrease in prior years' depreciation expense.
3. In 1987, it was discovered that the $200,000 cost of land acquired in 1986 had been expensed for both financial accounting and tax purposes. A prior period adjustment was made in 1987.
4. Anson Company has 1,000,000 shares of common stock outstanding.
5. The current tax rate is 40%. As a separate legal entity, corporations are required to pay federal income taxes.

Extraordinary Items

Prior to 1973, there was a tendency for companies to report a gain or loss as an extraordinary item if it was **either** unusual in nature or occurred infrequently. As a result, companies were inconsistent in the financial reporting of certain gains and losses. This inconsistency led to the issuance of *APB Opinion No. 30* (September 1973). *Opinion No. 30* redefined extraordinary items as those that are unusual in nature **and** that occur infrequently. Note that both conditions must be met—unusual nature and infrequent occurrence. Whether an item is unusual and infrequent is to be determined in light of the environment in which the company operates. Examples include gains or losses that are the direct result of a major casualty (a flood), a confiscation of property by a foreign government, or a prohibition under a newly enacted law. *FASB Statement No. 4* further directs that gains and losses from the voluntary early **extinguishment** (retirement) of debt are extraordinary items.

Extraordinary items are to be included in the determination of periodic

Illustration 16.5 *Income Statement*

ANSON COMPANY
Income Statement
For the Year Ended December 31, 1987

Net sales		$41,000,000
Other revenues		2,250,000
Total revenue		$43,250,000
Cost of goods sold	$22,000,000	
Administrative, selling, and general expenses	12,000,000	34,000,000
Net income before income taxes		$ 9,250,000
Federal income taxes (40%)		3,700,000
Net income before extraordinary item and the cumulative effect of a change in accounting principle (net income from regular operations)		$ 5,550,000
Extraordinary item:		
Gain on voluntary early retirement of debt	$ 40,000	
Less: Tax effect (40%)	16,000	24,000
Net income after extraordinary item		$ 5,574,000
Change in accounting principle:		
Cumulative positive effect on prior years' income of changing to a different depreciation method (net of 40% tax effect of $2,400)		3,600
Net income		$ 5,577,600
Earnings per share of common stock:		
Net income before extraordinary item and the cumulative effect of a change in accounting principle		$5.550
Extraordinary item		0.024
Cumulative effect on prior years' income of changing to a different depreciation method		0.004
Net income		$5.578

Extraordinary item

Change in accounting principle

Income before extraordinary item

Income after extraordinary item

Earnings per share

net income, but disclosed separately (net of their tax effects, if any) in the income statement. As shown in the income statement presented in Illustration 16.5, income before extraordinary items must be reported and then income after extraordinary items is reported. **Income before extraordinary items** is income from operations less applicable income taxes.

Gains or losses related to ordinary business activities are not extraordinary items regardless of their size. For example, material write-downs of uncollectible receivables, obsolete inventories, and intangible assets are not extraordinary items. But such items may be separately disclosed as part of net income from regular operations.

Illustration 16.6 shows that in a sample of 600 companies for the years 1980–83, the number reporting extraordinary items has increased each year. Also, the total number of extraordinary items reported has increased each year.

Illustration 16.6

Extraordinary Items

	1983	1982	1981	1980
Number of companies:				
Presenting extraordinary items . . .	84	69	53	47
Not presenting extraordinary items . .	516	531	547	553
Total companies	600	600	600	600
Total extraordinary items	95	79	57	48

Source: Based on American Institute of Certified Public Accountants, *Accounting Trends & Techniques* (New York: AICPA, 1984), p. 303.

Changes in Accounting Principle

A company's reported net income and financial position can be altered materially by changes in accounting principle. Changes in accounting principle are changes in accounting methods pertaining to such items as inventory and depreciation. Examples of changes in accounting principle are a change in inventory valuation method from Fifo to Lifo or a change in depreciation method from accelerated to straight line. According to *APB Opinion No. 20*, a company should consistently apply the same accounting methods from one period to another. But a change may be made if the newly adopted method is preferable and if the change is adequately disclosed in the financial statements. In the period in which a change in principle is made, the nature of the change, its justification, and its effect on net income must be disclosed in the financial statements. Also, the cumulative effect of the change on prior years' income (net of tax) must be shown in the income statement for the year of change (see Illustration 16.5).

As an example of a change in accounting principle, assume that Anson Company purchased a machine on January 2, 1985, for $30,000. The machine has a useful life of five years with no scrap value expected. Anson Company decided to depreciate the machine for financial reporting purposes using the sum-of-the-years'-digits method. At the beginning of 1987, the company decided to change to the straight-line method of depreciation. The cumulative effect of the change in accounting principle is computed as follows:

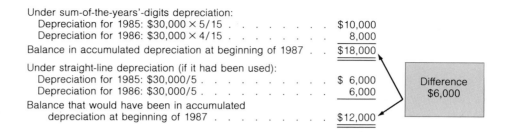

Under sum-of-the-years'-digits depreciation:
     Depreciation for 1985: $30,000 × 5/15 . . . . $10,000
     Depreciation for 1986: $30,000 × 4/15   8,000
Balance in accumulated depreciation at beginning of 1987 . . $18,000

Under straight-line depreciation (if it had been used):
     Depreciation for 1985: $30,000/5 . . . . $ 6,000
     Depreciation for 1986: $30,000/5   6,000
Balance that would have been in accumulated
     depreciation at beginning of 1987 . . . . $12,000

Difference
$6,000

The accumulated depreciation account balance would have been $6,000 less under the straight-line method. Also, depreciation expense over the two years would have been $6,000 less. Assume that federal income tax would have been $2,400 more ($6,000 × 0.4). The net effect of the change is $6,000 − $2,400 = $3,600. Therefore, Anson Company corrects the appropriate account balances by reducing (debiting) the accumulated depreciation account balance by $6,000, crediting an account entitled Cumulative Effect of Change in Accounting Principle for $3,600 (which will be closed to Retained Earnings during the normal closing process), and crediting Federal Income Taxes Payable for $2,400. The journal entry would be:

Accumulated Depreciation—Machinery   6,000
     Cumulative Effect of Change in Accounting Principle . . .   3,600
     Federal Income Taxes Payable   2,400
   To record the effect of changing from sum-of-the-years'-digits
   depreciation to straight-line depreciation on machinery.

The cumulative effect of changing to the straight-line depreciation method is reported in Illustration 16.5 at the after-tax amount of $3,600.

Prior Period Adjustments

According to *FASB Statement No 16,* prior period adjustments consist almost entirely of corrections of errors in previously published financial statements. Corrections of abnormal, nonrecurring errors that may have been caused by the improper use of an accounting principle or by mathematical mistakes are considered to be prior period adjustments. Normal, recurring corrections and adjustments, which follow inevitably from the use of estimates in accounting practice, are not treated as prior period adjustments. Also, mistakes corrected in the same year they occur are not prior period adjustments. To illustrate a prior period adjustment, suppose that land purchased in 1986 by the Anson Company at a total cost of $200,000 was recorded in an expense account instead of in the Land account. Discovery of the error on May 1, 1987, after publication of the 1986 financial statements, would require a prior period adjustment. The adjustment would be recorded directly in the Retained Earnings account. Assuming the error had resulted in an $80,000 underpayment of taxes in 1986, the entry to correct the error would be:

1987
May 1   Land   200,000
            Federal Income Taxes Payable   80,000
            Retained Earnings (or Prior Period Adjustment—
              Land)   120,000
     To correct an accounting error expensing land.

Prior period adjustments are not reported in the income statement but are shown in the financial statements as adjustments to the opening balance of retained earnings in the statement of retained earnings (Illustration 16.7).

Illustration 16.7   *Statement of Retained Earnings*

(handwritten annotation: net of the tax effect)

| Prior period adjustment | |

ANSON COMPANY
Statement of Retained Earnings
For the Year Ended December 31, 1987

Retained earnings, January 1, 1987	$ 5,000,000
Prior period adjustment:	
Correction of error of expensing land (net of tax effect of $80,000)	120,000
Adjusted retained earnings, January 1, 1987	$ 5,120,000
Add: Net income	5,577,600
	$10,697,600
Less: Dividends	500,000
Retained earnings, December 31, 1987	$10,197,600

Accounting for Tax Effects

Most extraordinary items, changes in accounting principle, and prior period adjustments will affect the amount of income taxes required to be paid by a corporation. A question arises as to how to report the income tax effect of these items. *APB Opinion No. 9* recommends that all of these items be reported **net of their tax effects,** as shown in Illustration 16.5 and 16.7. Net-of-tax effect means that items are shown at the dollar amounts remaining after deducting the income tax effects. Thus, the total effect of an extraordinary item, change in accounting principle, or prior period adjustment is shown in one place. Net income before extraordinary items represents the results of transactions (including income taxes) that are normal for the business and may be expected to recur. The tax effect of an item may be shown separately, as it is for the gain on voluntary early retirement of debt in Illustration 16.5. Alternatively, the tax effect may be mentioned parenthetically with only the net amount shown (see change in accounting principle in Illustration 16.5 and correction of error illustrated in 16.7).

■ EARNINGS PER SHARE

(handwritten annotation: EPS — net income divided by # of common shares)

A major item of interest to investors and potential investors is how much a company earned during the current year, both in total and for each share of stock outstanding. The earnings per share amount is calculated only for the common shares of ownership. Earnings per share (EPS) is computed as net income available to common stockholders divided by the number of common shares outstanding. Income available to common stockholders is net income less any dividends on preferred stock.

EPS is usually calculated and presented for each major category on the face of the income statement. In other words, an EPS calculation is made for ordinary income after taxes, extraordinary items, and changes in accounting principle. Note in Illustration 16.5 that the EPS amounts are reported at the bottom of the income statement.

Stockholders can compare the EPS of two companies more easily than total dollars of earnings. EPS is useful in making decisions about the price to pay for stock and the return on that investment. Also, EPS is related to market price per share of stock in that if EPS increases, generally market price per share also increases. EPS is covered in more detail in Chapter 20.

Summary of Illustrative Financial Statements

Note especially the following facts in Illustrations 16.5 and 16.7:

1. Net income of $5,550,000 before the extraordinary item and the cumulative effect of an accounting change is more representative of the continuing earning power of the company than is the final net income figure of $5,577,600.
2. The gain on retirement of debt is reported at its actual impact upon the company—that is, net of its tax effect.
3. EPS is reported both before ($5.550) and after ($5.578) the extraordinary item and the cumulative effect of a change in accounting principle.
4. The correction of the $200,000 error adds only $120,000 to retained earnings. This is because the mistake was included in the 1986 tax return and taxes were therefore underpaid by $80,000. In the 1987 return, the $80,000 of taxes would have to be paid.

■ POSSIBLE FUTURE CHANGE IN INCOME STATEMENT FORMAT

In December 1984, the FASB published *Concepts Statement No. 5, "Recognition and Measurement in Financial Statements of Business Enterprise."* [5] Rather than suggesting radical changes in present accounting practice, the Concepts Statement endorses present practice while allowing for gradual evolutionary changes. One such future change may be in the format of the income statement. The statement may become a statement of earnings and comprehensive income. "Earnings" would generally be computed like income after extraordinary items is presently calculated. Then cumulative account adjustments (such as changes in accounting principle) and other nonowner changes in equity would be added or deducted in arriving at "comprehensive income." The lower part of the statement would appear as follows:

Earnings	xx
+or— Cumulative account adjustments (e.g., cumulative effect of changes in accounting principle)	xx
+or— Other nonowner changes in equity (e.g., gains or losses on market changes in noncurrent marketable equity securities*) . .	xx
Comprehensive income	xx

* This item is discussed in Chapter 18.

---

[5] FASB, "Recognition and Measurement in Financial Statements of Business Enterprises," *Statement of Financial Accounting Concepts No. 5* (Stamford, Conn., 1984). Copyright © by the Financial Accounting Standards Board, High Ridge Park, Stamford, Connecticut 06905, U.S.A. Copies of the complete document are available from the FASB.

Concepts statements are part of the conceptual framework. This framework serves as a guide for the FASB in establishing accounting standards that resolve future accounting and reporting questions. Therefore, we are not certain that this change in format will be required in the future but wanted you to be aware of the possible change.

■ SUMMARY

The term *paid-in-capital* is applied to all of the contributed capital of a corporation, including that part carried in the capital stock accounts. The stockholders' equity section of the balance sheet should show the different sources of paid-in capital.

Retained earnings is that part of stockholders' equity resulting from net income. The balance in Retained Earnings consists of net income (or loss) of the corporation from the date business began to the present, less total dividends declared and certain other deductions during the same period.

The typical dividend is a cash distribution of corporate income to stockholders. A corporation may also distribute additional shares of its own capital stock (a stock dividend) as a dividend.

Stock dividends of less than 20% to 25% are recorded at current market value. Stock dividends greater than 20% to 25% are recorded at par or stated value. The amount transferred to the capital stock account is equal to the par or stated value of the shares issued. For stocks without par or stated value, the amount is established by law or by the board of directors.

A stock split is a distribution of additional shares of the issuing company's stock for which the corporation receives no assets. The par value per share is usually reduced (e.g., in a two-for-one split, the par value per share is usually halved) so that the total dollar amount credited to Common Stock remains the same. Retained earnings appropriations are restrictions on the declaration of cash dividends. Retained earnings appropriations are reported as a part of total retained earnings in the balance sheet.

Changes in retained earnings reveal important information about a company to interested parties. Thus, a statement of retained earnings is prepared, which shows the items that caused increases or decreases in retained earnings during a specified period of time.

Shares of capital stock that have been issued and are then reacquired by the issuing corporation are called treasury stock. Such stock is considered issued but not outstanding. The cost of treasury stock is reported as a deduction from total stockholders' equity. If treasury stock is reissued at more than cost, the difference between cost and reissue price is recorded in a Paid-In Capital— Common (Preferred) Treasury Stock Transactions account. If treasury stock is reissued at less than cost, the Paid-in Capital—Common (Preferred) Treasury Stock Transactions account is debited for the difference between cost and reissue price until its credit balance is exhausted. Any remaining debit needed to balance the journal entry is to Retained Earnings.

Donated treasury shares have no cost. The only formal entry made for them is to credit the entire amount received upon reissue to a Paid-In Capital— Donations account.

Extraordinary items are gains or losses that are both unusual in nature and infrequent in occurrence. They are reported on the income statement, net of their tax effects, separately from the results of ordinary operations. Changes in accounting principle also must be separately disclosed (net of their tax effect) in the income statement. Prior period adjustments are material adjustments primarily resulting from current corrections of accounting errors that occurred in prior years. They are treated as adjustments (net of their tax effect) to the opening balance of retained earnings in the statement of retained earnings.

This chapter completes the study of stockholders' equity. In Chapter 17, you will learn about bonds—another source of capital for companies and a vehicle for investment by investors. Perhaps someday you will buy bonds issued by a company.

NEW TERMS INTRODUCED IN CHAPTER 16

Cash dividends

Cash distributions of net income by a corporation to its stockholders (615).

Changes in accounting principle

Changes in accounting methods pertaining to such items as inventory and depreciation (627).

Contributed capital

All capital paid into a corporation, including that carried in capital stock accounts (612).

Date of declaration (of dividends)

The date the board of directors takes action in the form of a motion that dividends be paid (614).

Date of payment (of dividends)

The date of actual payment of a dividend, or issuance of additional shares in the case of a stock dividend (614).

Date of record (of dividends)

The date established by the board to determine who will receive a dividend (614).

Deficit

A debit balance in the Retained Earnings account (613).

Dividends

Distribution of earnings by a corporation to its stockholders (614).

Dividends (cash)

See Cash dividends.

Dividends (stock)

See Stock dividends.

Donated capital

Results from donation of assets to the corporation, which increases stockholders' equity (613).

Earnings per share (EPS)

Earnings to the common stockholders on a per share basis, computed as net income available to common stockholders divided by the number of common shares outstanding (629).

Extraordinary items

Items that are unusual in nature and that occur infrequently; reported in the income statement net of their tax effects, if any (625).

Income available to common stockholders

Net income less any dividends on preferred stock (629).

Income before extraordinary items

Income from operations less applicable income taxes, if any (627).

Liquidating dividends

Dividends that are a return of contributed capital, not a distribution chargeable to retained earnings (619).

Net-of-tax effect

Used for extraordinary items, prior period adjustments, and changes in accounting principle, whereby items are shown at the dollar amounts remaining after deducting the effects of such items on income taxes, if any, payable currently (629).

Paid-in capital

All of the contributed capital of a corporation, including that carried in capital stock accounts. When the words *paid-in capital* are included in the account title, the account contains capital contributed in addition to that assigned to the shares issued and recorded in the capital stock accounts (612).

Paid-In Capital—Treasury Stock Transactions

The account credited when treasury stock is reissued for more than its cost; this account is debited to the extent of its credit balance when such shares are reissued at less than cost (622).

Prior period adjustments

Consist almost entirely of corrections of errors in previously published financial statements. Prior period adjustments are reported in the statement of retained earnings net of their tax effects, if any (628).

Retained earnings

That part of stockholders' equity resulting from earnings; the account to which the results of corporate activity, including prior period adjustments, are carried and to which dividends and certain items resulting from capital transactions are charged (613).

Retained earnings appropriations

Contractual or voluntary restrictions or limitations on retained earnings that reduce the amount of dividends that may be declared (619).

Statement of retained earnings

A formal statement showing the items causing changes in unappropriated and appropriated retained earnings during a stated period of time (621).

Stock dividends

Dividends that are payable in additional shares of the declaring corporation's capital stock (616).

Stock Dividend Distributable—Common account

The stockholders' equity account that is credited for the par or stated value of the shares distributable when recording the declaration of a stock dividend (617).

Stock split

A distribution of additional shares of the issuing corporation's stock for which the corporation receives no assets. The purpose of a stock split is to cause a large reduction in the market price per share of the outstanding stock (618).

Treasury stock

Shares of capital stock issued and reacquired by the issuing corporation; they have not been formally canceled and are available for reissuance (613, 622).

DEMONSTRATION PROBLEM 16–1

The Benston Corporation has outstanding 10,000 shares of $100 par value common stock.

Required: Prepare the entries to record:

a. The declaration of a cash dividend of $1 per share.
b. The declaration of a stock dividend of 10% at a time when the market value per share is $125.
c. The declaration of a stock dividend of 40% at a time when the market value per share is $130.

Solution to demonstration problem 16–1

a. Retained earnings (or Dividends) 10,000
     Dividends Payable   10,000
To record declaration of a cash dividend.

b. Retained Earnings (or Stock Dividends) (1,000 × $125). . 125,000
     Stock Dividend Distributable—Common (1,000 × $100)   100,000
     Paid-In Capital—Stock Dividends   25,000
To record declaration of a small stock dividend (10%).

c. Retained Earnings (4,000 × $100) 400,000
     Stock Dividend Distributable—Common   400,000
To record declaration of a large stock dividend (40%).

DEMONSTRATION PROBLEM 16–2

Following are selected transactions of the Morgan Company:

Transactions:

1. The company acquired 200 shares of its own $100 par value common stock, previously issued at a premium of 5%, for $20,600 cash.
2. Fifty of the treasury shares were reissued at $110 per share, cash.
3. Seventy of the treasury shares were reissued at $95 per share, cash.
4. Stockholders of the corporation donated 100 shares of their common stock to the company.
5. The 100 shares of treasury stock received by donation were reissued for $9,000.

Required: Prepare the necessary journal entries to record the above transactions.

Solution to demonstration problem 16–2

1. Treasury Stock 20,600
       Cash 20,600
       Acquired 200 shares at $20,600 ($103 per share).

2. Cash (50 × $110 per share) 5,500
       Treasury Stock (50 × $103 per share) 5,150
       Paid-In Capital—Treasury Stock Transactions 350
       Reissued 50 shares at $110 per share; cost is $5,150.

3. Cash (70 × $95 per share) 6,650
   Paid-In Capital—Treasury Stock Transactions 350
   Retained Earnings 210
       Treasury Stock (70 × $103 per share) 7,210
       Reissued 70 shares at $95 per share; cost is $7,210.

4. Stockholders donated 100 shares of common stock to the company.

5. Cash 9,000
       Paid-In Capital—Donations (100 × $90 per share) . . . 9,000
       Reissued donated shares at $90 per share.

DEMONSTRATION PROBLEM 16–3

Selected account balances of the Clark Company at December 31, 1987, are:

Common stock—no par value; 100,000 shares authorized, issued, and outstanding; stated value of $20 per share	2,000,000
Retained earnings	570,000
Dividends payable (in cash, declared December 15 on preferred stock)	16,000
Preferred stock—8%, par value, $200; 1,000 shares authorized, issued, and outstanding	200,000
Paid-in capital from donation of plant site	100,000
Paid-in capital in excess of par value—preferred	8,000

Required: Present in good form the stockholders' equity section of the balance sheet.

Solution to demonstration problem 16–3

CLARK CORPORATION
Partial Balance Sheet
December 31, 1987

Stockholders' Equity:
  Paid-in capital:
    Preferred stock, 8%, par value, $200; 1,000 shares authorized,
      issued, and outstanding . . . . $ 200,000
    Common stock, no par value, stated value of $20 per share;
      100,000 shares authorized, issued, and outstanding   2,000,000
    Paid-in capital from donation of plant site   100,000
    Paid-in capital in excess of par value—preferred   8,000
        Total paid-in capital $2,308,000
  Retained earnings   570,000
        Total stockholders' equity $2,878,000

QUESTIONS

1. What are the two main elements of stockholders' equity in a corporation? Explain the difference between them.

2. Name several sources of paid-in capital. Would it suffice to maintain one account called Paid-In Capital for all sources of paid-in capital? Why or why not?

3. What is the effect of each of the following on the total stockholders' equity of a corporation: *(a)* declaration of a cash dividend, *(b)* payment of a cash dividend already declared, *(c)* declaration of a stock dividend, and *(d)* issuance of a stock dividend already declared?

4. The following dates are associated with a cash dividend of $50,000: July 15, July 31, and August 15. Identify each of the three dates, and give the journal entry required on each date, if any.

5. How should a declared but unpaid cash dividend be shown on the balance sheet? How should a declared but unissued stock dividend be shown?

6. On May 8, the board of directors of the Tanner Corporation declared a dividend, payable on June 5 to stockholders of record on May 17. On May 10, Power sold his capital stock in the Tanner Corporation directly to Bright for $10,000, endorsing his stock certificate and giving it to Bright. Bright placed the stock certificate in her safe. On May 30, Bright sent the certificate to the transfer agent of the Tanner Corporation for transfer. Who received the dividend? Why?

7. What are liquidating dividends?

8. What is the purpose of a retained earnings appropriation?

9. Does accounting for treasury stock resemble accounting for an asset? Is treasury stock an asset? If not, where is it properly shown in a balance sheet?

10. What are some possible reasons for a corporation to acquire its own capital stock as treasury stock?

11. What are extraordinary items? Where and how are they reported?

12. Give an example of a change in accounting principle. How are the effects of changes in accounting principle reported?

13. What are prior period adjustments? Where and how are they reported?

14. Why are stockholders and potential investors interested in the amount of a corporation's EPS? What does the EPS amount reveal that total earnings do not?

EXERCISES

E-1

Prepare stockholders' equity section of balance sheet

The trial balance of the Cane Corporation at December 31, 1987, had the following account balances:

Common Stock, no par value; 200,000 shares authorized,
  issued, and outstanding; stated value of $5 per share $1,000,000
Notes Payable, 12% due May 1, 1988   125,000
Retained Earnings, Unappropriated   625,000
Dividends Payable in Cash, declared December 15, on
  preferred stock   3,000
Appropriation per Loan Agreement   120,000
Preferred Stock, 6%, par value $50; 2,000 shares
  authorized, issued, and outstanding   100,000
Paid-In Capital in Excess of Stated Value—Common Stock . . .   75,000
Paid-In Capital in Excess of Par Value—Preferred Stock   10,000

Present in good form the stockholders' equity section of the balance sheet.

E-2

Prepare journal entries for cash dividends

Leonard Company has issued all of its authorized 5,000 shares of $50 par value common stock. On February 1, 1987, the board of directors declared a dividend of $1.50 per share payable on March 15, 1987, to stockholders of record on March 1, 1987. Give the necessary journal entries.

E-3

Prepare journal entries for stock split and small stock dividend

May Corporation's stockholders' equity consisted of 30,000 authorized shares of $20 par value common stock, of which 15,000 shares had been issued at par, and retained earnings of $750,000. The company then split its stock, two for one, by changing the par value of the old shares and issuing new $10 par shares.

a. Give the required journal entry to record the stock split.
b. Suppose instead that the company declared and later issued a 10% stock dividend. Give the required journal entries, assuming that the market value on the date of declaration is $25 per share.

E-4

Prepare journal entries for cash dividend when treasury stock is held

The stockholders' equity section of Howard Company's balance sheet on December 31, 1987, shows 100,000 shares of authorized and issued $20 stated value common stock, of which 9,000 shares are held in the treasury. On this date, the board of directors declared a cash dividend of $2 per share payable on January 21, 1988, to stockholders of record on January 10. Give dated journal entries for the above.

E-5

Prepare journal entry for small stock dividend and discuss large stock dividend

Swanson Company has outstanding 75,000 shares of common stock without par or stated value, which were issued at an average price of $18 per share, and retained earnings of $720,000. The current market price of the common stock is $27 per share. Total authorized stock consists of 500,000 shares.

a. Give the required entry to record the declaration of a 10% stock dividend.
b. If, alternatively, the company declared a 30% stock dividend, what additional information would you need before making a journal entry to record the dividend?

E-6

Prepare journal entry for appropriation of retained earnings and explain

The balance sheet of Echols Company contains the following:

Appropriation per loan agreement $750,000

a. Give the journal entry made to create this account.
b. Explain the reason for the appropriation's existence and its manner of presentation in the balance sheet.

E-7

Prepare journal entries for acquisition and reissuance of treasury stock

Trestle Company had outstanding 50,000 shares of $30 stated value common stock, all issued at $36 per share, and had retained earnings of $1,200,000. The company reacquired 2,000 shares of its stock for cash at book value from the widow of a deceased stockholder.

a. Give the entry to record the reacquisition of the stock.
b. Give the entry to record the subsequent reissuance of this stock at $75 per share.
c. Give the entry required if the stock is instead reissued at $45 per share and there have been no prior treasury stock transactions.

E-8

Prepare journal entry(ies) for reissuance of donated stock

Merlin Company received 200 shares of its $25 stated value common stock on December 1, 1987, as a donation from a stockholder. On December 15, 1987, it reissued the stock for $7,800 cash. Give the journal entry or entries necessary for these transactions.

E-9

Prepare income statement and statement of retained earnings

April Company has revenues of $20 million, expenses of $16 million, a tax-deductible earthquake loss (its first such loss) of $1 million, and a tax-deductible loss of $1.5 million resulting from the voluntary early extinguishment (retirement) of debt. The income tax rate is 40%. The company's beginning-of-the-year retained earnings were $7.5 million, and a dividend of $500,000 was declared.

a. Prepare an income statement for the year.
b. Prepare a statement of retained earnings for the year.

E-10

Prepare statement of retained earnings

The Sherwin Company had retained earnings of $21,000 as of January 1, 1987. In 1987, Sherwin Company had sales of $60,000, cost of goods sold of $36,000, and other operating expenses, excluding taxes, of $12,000. In 1987, Sherwin Company discovered that it had, in error, depreciated land over the last three years resulting in a balance in the accumulated depreciation account of $12,000. The tax rate for Sherwin Company is 40%. Present in proper form a statement of retained earnings for the year ended December 31, 1987.

E-11

Calculate EPS; present information in income statement format

The following information relates to the L. M. Stevens Corporation for the year ended December 31, 1987:

Average shares per year

Common stock outstanding	75,000 shares
Net income before extraordinary items . .	$952,000
Extraordinary gain	$ 90,000

Calculate EPS for the year ended December 31, 1987. Present the information in the same format as would be used in the corporation's income statement.

E-12

Calculate EPS; comment on resulting amount

The Metro Company had common stock outstanding of 200,000 and 215,000 shares at December 31, 1987 and 1988, respectively. Net income for these two years was as follows:

December 31, 1987	$1,840,000
December 31, 1988	1,920,000

a. Calculate EPS for the years ended December 31, 1987, and 1988.
b. What might the resulting figures tell a potential investor or stockholder?

PROBLEMS, SERIES A

P16–1–A

Present stockholders' equity section of balance sheet

The trial balance of the Nail Corporation as of December 31, 1987, contains the following selected balances:

Notes Payable, 17%, due May 1, 1989	$1,000,000
Allowance for Doubtful Accounts	15,000
Common Stock without par value, $5 stated value; 300,000 shares authorized, issued, and outstanding.	1,500,000
Retained Earnings, Unappropriated	125,000
Dividends Payable in cash declared December 15 on preferred stock . .	3,500
Appropriation for Pending Litigation	150,000
Preferred Stock, 6%, $50 par value; 3,000 shares authorized issued, and outstanding	150,000
Paid-In Capital—Donations	100,000
Paid-In Capital in Excess of Par Value—Preferred	2,500

Required: Present in good form the stockholders' equity section of the balance sheet.

P16–2–A

Prepare journal entries for cash dividend and small stock dividend

The stockholders' equity section of the Justin Company's December 31, 1986, balance sheet follows:

Stockholders' equity:
  Paid-In capital:
    Capital stock—common, $60 par value; authorized, 2,000 shares;

issued and outstanding, 1,000 shares	$60,000
Paid-in capital in excess of par value	3,000
Total paid-in capital	$63,000
Retained earnings	24,000
Total stockholders' equity	$87,000

On July 15, 1987, the board of directors declared a cash dividend of $6 per share, which was paid on August 1, 1987. On December 1, 1987, the board declared a stock dividend of 10%, and the shares were issued on December 15, 1987. Market value of the stock was $72 on December 1 and $84 on December 15.

Required: Prepare journal entries for the above dividend transactions.

P16–3–A

Prepare journal entries for appropriations of retained earnings

The ledger of the Mooreberry Company includes the following account balances on September 30, 1987:

Appropriation for Contingencies	$ 84,000
Appropriation for Plant Expansion	156,800
Retained Earnings, Unappropriated	280,000

During the month of October 1987, the company took action to:

1. Increase the appropriation for contingencies by $25,200.
2. Decrease the appropriation for plant expansion by $65,800.
3. Establish an appropriation per loan agreement, with an annual increase of $21,000.
4. Declare a cash dividend of $63,000.

Required: Prepare the general journal entries to record the transactions of the Mooreberry Company.

P16–4–A

Present statement of retained earnings

Using the information given in Problem 16–3–A, prepare a statement of retained earnings for the Mooreberry Company for the period ended October 31, 1987.

P16–5–A

Prepare journal entries for retained earnings appropriation and small stock dividend

Following are selected transactions of the Allana Corporation:

Transactions:

1982
Dec. 31   By action of the board of directors, $90,000 of retained earnings was appropriated to provide for future expansion of the company's main building. (On the last day of each of the four succeeding years, the same action was taken. You need not make entries for these years.)

1987
Jan. 3   Obtained, at a cost of $900, a building permit to construct a new wing on the main plant building.
July 30   Paid $360,000 to the Able Construction Company for completion of the new wing.
Aug. 4   The board of directors authorized the release of the sum appropriated for expansion of the plant building.
      4   The board of directors declared a 10% common stock dividend on the 25,000 shares of $100 par value common stock outstanding. The market price on this date was $132 per share.

Required: Prepare journal entries to record all of the above transactions.

P16–6–A

Present statement of retained earnings

The following information relates to the Summers Corporation for the year 1987:

Net income for the year	$ 700,000
Dividends declared on common stock	98,000
Dividends declared on preferred stock	56,000
Retained earnings, January 1, unappropriated	2,100,000
Appropriation for retirement of bonds	280,000
Balance in "Appropriation for possible loss of a lawsuit," no longer needed on December 31 because of favorable court decision, is (at directors' orders) returned to unappropriated retained earnings	350,000

Required: Prepare a statement of retained earnings for the year ended December 31, 1987.

Extra credit

P16–7–A

Prepare journal entries for treasury stock transactions and for cash dividends; present stockholders' equity section

The stockholders' equity of the Joyner Company as of December 31, 1986, consisted of 20,000 shares of authorized and outstanding $10 par value common stock, paid-in capital in excess of par of $48,000, and retained earnings of $80,000. Following are selected transactions for 1987:

Transactions:

May   1   Acquired 3,000 shares of its own common stock at $20 per share.
June 1   Reissued 500 shares at $24.
     30   Reissued 700 shares at $18.
Oct. 1   Declared a cash dividend of $1 per share.
     31   Paid the cash dividend declared on October 1.

Net income for the year was $16,000. No other transactions affecting retained earnings occurred during the year.

Required: a.   Prepare general journal entries for the above transactions.
b.   Prepare the stockholders' equity section of the December 31, 1987, balance sheet.

P16–8–A

Prepare journal entries for stock transactions, cash dividend, small stock dividend, and retained earnings appropriation; prepare statement of retained earnings and stockholders' equity section of balance sheet

The stockholders' equity section of Todd Company's December 31, 1986, balance sheet appears below:

Stockholders' equity:

Paid-in capital:

Preferred stock: $50 par value, 5%; authorized, 5,000 shares; issued and outstanding, 2,500 shares		$125,000
Common stock without par or stated value; authorized, 50,000 shares; issued, 25,000 shares of which 500 are held in treasury		187,500
Paid-in capital in excess of par—preferred		2,500
Total paid-in capital		$315,000

Retained earnings:

Appropriated:			
For plant expansion		$ 12,500	
Unappropriated (restricted as to dividends to the extent of $5,000, the cost of the treasury stock held)		105,000	
Total retained earnings			117,500
Total			$432,500
Less: Treasury stock, common at cost (500 shares)			5,000
Total stockholders' equity			$427,500

Following are selected transactions which occurred in 1987:

Transactions:

Jan. 13   Subscriptions were received for 550 shares of previously unissued common stock at $11.

Feb. 4   A plot of land was accepted as payment in full for 500 shares of common, and the stock was issued. Closing market price of the common stock on this date was $10 per share.

Mar. 24   All of the treasury stock was reissued at $12 per share.

June 22   All stock subscriptions were collected in full, and the shares were issued.

23   The regular semiannual dividend on the preferred stock was declared.

30   The preferred dividend was paid.

July 3   A 10% stock dividend was declared on the common stock. Market price on this date was $14.

18   The stock dividend shares were issued.

Oct. 4   The company reacquired 105 shares of its common stock at $12.

Dec. 18   The regular semiannual dividend on the preferred stock and a $0.20 per share dividend on the common stock were declared.

31   Both dividends were paid.

31   An additional appropriation of retained earnings of $2,500 for plant expansion was authorized.

Required:

a.   Prepare journal entries to record the 1987 transactions.

b.   Prepare a statement of retained earnings for the year 1987, assuming net income for the year was $21,562.

c.   Prepare the stockholders' equity section of the December 31, 1987, balance sheet.

P16–9–A

Present income statement and statement of retained earnings

Selected data of the Pate Company for the year ended December 31, 1987, are:

Sales, net	$800,000
Interest expense	72,000
Cash dividends on common stock	120,000
Selling and administrative expense	196,000
Cash dividends on preferred stock	56,000
Rent revenue	320,000
Cost of goods sold	520,000
Flood loss (has never occurred before)	160,000
Interest revenue	72,000
Other revenue	120,000
Depreciation and maintenance on rental equipment	216,000
Stock dividend on common stock	240,000
Litigation loss	320,000
Cumulative positive effect on prior years' income of changing to a different depreciation method	64,000

The applicable federal income tax rate is 40%. All above items of expense, revenue, and loss are included in the computation of taxable income. The litigation loss resulted from a court award of damages for patent infringement on a product that the company produced and sold in 1983 and 1984, but was discontinued in 1984. Retained earnings as of January 1, 1987, were $4,480,000. Assume there were 10,000 shares of common stock outstanding for the entire year.

Required: Prepare an income statement and a statement of retained earnings for 1987.

PROBLEMS, SERIES B

P16-1-B

Present stockholders' equity section of balance sheet

Following are selected data and accounts of Leather, Inc., as of May 31, 1987:

Paid-In Capital in Excess of Par Value—Preferred	$ 4,200
Retained Earnings, Unappropriated	72,000
Allowance for Doubtful Accounts	24,000
Common Stock without par value, stated value $30; 20,000 shares	
authorized, issued, and outstanding	600,000
Appropriation for Retirement of Bonds	90,000
Dividends Payable (cash)	3,600
Paid-In Capital in Excess of Stated Value—Common	24,000
Notes Payable, 17%, due April 1, 1993	360,000
Preferred Stock: 7%, par value $60; 2,000 shares authorized,	
issued, and outstanding	120,000
Paid-In Capital—Donations	18,000

Required: Present the stockholders' equity section of the company's balance sheet as of May 31, 1987.

P16-2-B

Prepare journal entries for cash dividend and small stock dividend

The only stockholders' equity items of the Health Company at June 30, 1987, are:

Stockholders' equity:		
Paid-in capital:		
Common stock, $100 par value, 5,000 shares authorized,		
3,000 shares issued and outstanding	$300,000	
Paid-in capital in excess of par value	120,000	
Retained earnings	120,000	
Total stockholders' equity	$540,000	

On August 4, a 4% cash dividend was declared, payable on September 3. On November 16, a 10% stock dividend was declared. The shares were issued on December 1. The market value of the common stock was $180 per share on November 16 and $177 per share on December 1.

Required: Prepare journal entries for the above transactions.

P16-3-B

Prepare stockholders' equity section of balance sheet

The bookkeeper of C. J. Simpson Company has prepared the following incorrect statement of stockholders' equity for the year ended December 31, 1987:

Stockholders' equity:	
Paid-in capital:	
Preferred stock, 6%, cumulative (8,000 shares) . .	$ 418,000
Common stock (50,000 shares)	1,190,000
Retained earnings	682,000
Total stockholders' equity	$2,290,000

The authorized stock consists of 12,000 shares of preferred stock with a $50 par value and 75,000 shares of common stock, $20 par value. The preferred stock was issued on two occasions; first, 5,000 shares at par; and second, 3,000 shares at $56 per share. The 50,000 shares of common stock were issued at $26 per share. Five thousand shares of treasury common stock were reacquired for $110,000; the bookkeeper deducted the cost of the treasury stock from the Common Stock account.

Required: Prepare the correct stockholders' equity section of the balance sheet at December 31, 1987.

P16-4-B

Prepare journal entries for stock dividend, treasury stock transactions, and retained earnings appropriation

The stockholders' equity of the Wayne A. Rutledge Company at January 1, 1987, is as follows:

Common stock, stated value of $5, 100,000 shares
  authorized, 60,000 shares issued $300,000
Paid-in capital in excess of stated value   50,000
Appropriation per loan agreement   18,800
Unappropriated retained earnings   106,000
Treasury stock (3,000 shares at cost) . . . . .   (18,000)

During 1987, the following transactions occurred in the order listed:

Transactions:

1. Issued 10,000 shares of stock for $92,000.
2. Declared a 4% stock dividend when the market price was $12 per share.
3. Sold 1,000 shares of treasury stock for $10,800.
4. Issued stock certificates for the stock dividend declared in transaction (2).
5. Bought 2,000 shares of treasury stock for $16,800.
6. Increased the appropriation by $10,800 per loan agreement.

Required: Prepare journal entries as necessary for the above transactions.

P16-5-B

Prepare journal entries for retained earnings appropriation, asset acquisition, and stock dividend

Following are selected transactions of the Salter Corporation:

Transactions:

1980
Dec. 31 The board of directors authorized the appropriation of $50,000 of retained earnings to provide for the future acquisition of a new plant site and the construction of a new building. (On the last day of the six succeeding years, the same action was taken. You need not make entries for these six years.)

1985
Jan. 2 Purchased a new plant site for cash, $100,000.
Mar. 29 Entered into a contract for construction of a new building, payment to be made within 30 days following completion.

1987
Feb. 10 Following final inspection and approval of the new building, the Dome Construction Company was paid in full, $500,000.
Mar. 10 The board of directors authorized release of the retained earnings appropriated for the plant site and building.
Apr. 2 A 5% stock dividend on the 100,000 shares of $50 par value common stock outstanding was declared. The market price on this date was $55 per share.

Required: Prepare journal entries for all of the above transactions.

P16–6–B

Present statement of retained earnings

Following are selected data of the Sailsbury Corporation at December 31, 1987:

Net income for the year	$384,000
Dividends declared on preferred stock	54,000
Retained earnings appropriated for future plant expansion during the year	180,000
Dividends declared on common stock	48,000
Retained earnings, January 1, unappropriated	540,000
Directors ordered that the balance in the "Appropriation per loan agreement," related to a loan repaid on March 31, 1987, be returned to unappropriated retained earnings	360,000

Required: Prepare a statement of retained earnings for the year ended December 31, 1987.

P16–7–B

Prepare journal entries for treasury stock transactions and for cash dividend; present stockholders' equity section of balance sheet

The stockholders' equity of the Ryerson Company on December 31, 1986, consisted of 1,000 authorized and outstanding shares of $9 cumulative preferred stock, stated value $30 per share, which were originally issued at $149 per share; 100,000 shares authorized and outstanding of $20 stated value common stock, which were originally issued at $20; and retained earnings of $140,000. Following are selected transactions and other data relating to 1987:

Transactions:

1.   The company reacquired 2,000 shares of its common stock at $42.
2.   One thousand of the treasury shares were reissued at $36.
3.   Stockholders donated 1,000 shares of common stock to the company. These shares were immediately reissued at $32 to provide working capital.
4.   The first quarter's dividend of $2.25 per share was declared and paid on the preferred stock. No other dividends were declared or paid during 1987.

The company suffered a net loss of $28,000 for the year 1987.

Required: a.   Prepare journal entries for the numbered transactions above.
b.   Prepare the stockholders' equity section of the December 31, 1987, balance sheet.

P16–8–B

Prepare journal entries to close retained earnings appropriation and for treasury stock transactions and cash dividends; present statement of retained earnings and stockholders' equity section of balance sheet

The stockholders' equity section of the Hodges Company's October 31, 1986, balance sheet appears below:

Stockholders' equity:

Paid-in capital:			
Preferred stock: $50 par value, 6%; 1,000 shares authorized, 350 shares issued and outstanding			$ 17,500
Common stock: $5 par value; 100,000 shares authorized, 40,000 shares issued and outstanding			200,000
Paid-in capital from donation of plant site			12,500
Total paid-in capital			$230,000
Retained earnings:			
Appropriated:			
Appropriation for contingencies		$10,000	
Unappropriated		27,750	
Total retained earnings			37,750
Total stockholders' equity			$267,750

During the ensuing fiscal year, the following transactions were entered into by the Hodges Company:

Transactions:

1.   The appropriation of $10,000 of retained earnings had been authorized in October 1986 because of the likelihood of an unfavorable court decision in a pending lawsuit. The suit was brought by a

customer seeking damages for the company's alleged breach of a contract to supply the customer with certain products at stated prices in 1985. The suit was concluded on March 6, 1987, with a court order directing the company to pay $8,750 in damages. These damages were not deductible in determining income tax liability. The board ordered the damages paid and the appropriation closed. The loss does not qualify as an extraordinary item.

2. The company acquired 1,000 shares of its own common stock at $7.50 in May 1987. On June 30, it reissued 500 of these shares at $6.

3. Dividends declared and paid during the year were 6% on preferred stock, and 15 cents per share on common stock. Both dividends were declared on September 1 and paid on September 30, 1987.

For the fiscal year, the company had net income after income taxes of $9,500, excluding the loss of the lawsuit.

Required:
a. Prepare general journal entries for the numbered transactions above.
b. Prepare a statement of retained earnings for the year ended October 31, 1987.
c. Prepare the stockholders' equity section of the October 31, 1987, balance sheet.

P16-9-B

Present income statement and statement of retained earnings

Selected data for the Shafer Company for 1987 are given below:

Common stock—$10 par value	$1,000,000
Sales, net	870,000
Selling and administrative expenses	160,000
Cash dividends declared and paid	60,000
Cost of goods sold	400,000
Depreciation expense	60,000
Interest revenue	10,000
Loss on write-down of obsolete inventory	20,000
Retained earnings (as of 12/31/86)	1,000,000
Earthquake loss	48,000
Cumulative negative effect on prior years' income of changing from straight-line to an accelerated method of computing depreciation	32,000

The applicable federal income tax rate is 40%. All of the items of expense, revenue, and loss are included in the computation of taxable income. The earthquake loss resulted from the first earthquake experienced at the company's location. In addition, the company discovered that in 1986 it had erroneously charged to expense the $80,000 cost of a tract of land purchased that year and had made the same error on its tax return for 1986.

Required:
a. Prepare an income statement for the year ended December 31, 1987.
b. Prepare a statement of retained earnings for the year ended December 31, 1987.

BUSINESS DECISION PROBLEM 16-1

Determine amount of dividends received and effects on stock prices

The stockholders' equity section of the Seeley Corporation's balance sheet for June 30, 1987, is shown below:

Stockholders' equity:
Paid-in capital:		
Common stock—$5 par value; authorized 200,000 shares, issued and outstanding 80,000 shares		$ 400,000
Paid-in capital in excess of par value		240,000
Total paid-in capital		$ 640,000
Retained earnings		380,000
Total stockholders' equity		$1,020,000

On July 1, 1987, the corporation's directors declared a 10% stock dividend distributable on August 2 to stockholders of record on July 16. On November 1, 1987, the directors voted a $0.60 per share annual cash dividend payable on December 2 to stockholders of record on November 16. For four years prior to 1987, the corporation had paid an annual cash dividend of $0.63.

Bill Hale owns 8,000 shares of Seeley Corporation's common stock, which he purchased five years ago. The market value of his stock was $12 per share on July 1, 1987, and $10.91 per share on July 16, 1987.

Required:

a. What amount of cash dividends will Hale receive in 1987? How does this amount differ from the amount of cash dividends Hale received in the previous four years?

b. For what logical reason did the price of the stock drop from $12 to $10.91 on July 16, 1987?

c. Is Hale better off as a result of the stock dividend and the $0.60 cash dividend than he would have been if he had just received the $0.63 dividend? Why?

BUSINESS DECISION PROBLEM 16–2

Analyze journal entries for impropriety and make subsequent corrections

Shown below are some journal entries made by the bookkeeper for the Royal Corporation:

1. Retained Earnings   3,000
        Reserve for Doubtful Accounts   3,000
      To record bad debts expense.

2. Retained Earnings   12,000
        Reserve for Depreciation   12,000
      To record depreciation expense.

3. Retained Earnings   30,000
        Reserve for Plant Expansion . . . . :   30,000
      To record retained earnings appropriation.

4. Retained Earnings   2,000
        Stock Dividend Distributable   2,000
      To record 10% stock dividend declaration (100 shares to be distributed—$20 par value, $30 market value).

5. Stock Dividend Distributable   2,000
        Common Stock   2,000
      To record distribution of stock dividend.

6. Treasury Stock   8,000
        Cash   8,000
      To record acquisition of 200 shares of $20 par value common stock at $40 per share.

7. Cash   4,400
        Treasury Stock   4,400
      To record sale of 100 treasury shares at $44 per share.

8. Cash   1,700
        Treasury Stock   1,700
      To record sale of 50 treasury shares at $34 per share.

9. Common Stock   4,000
        Dividends Payable   4,000
      To record declaration of cash dividend.

10.	Dividends Payable	4,000	
	Cash		4,000

To record payment of cash dividend.

Required: Analyze the above journal entries in connection with their explanations and decide whether each is correct or incorrect. The explanations are all correct. If a journal entry is incorrect, prepare the journal entry that should have been made.

BUSINESS SITUATION FOR DISCUSSION

The Troubles that Led to ITT's Dividend Shocker*

☐   Giant ITT [International Telephone and Telegraph] Corp., which has been scrabbling to gain a toehold in the newly competitive U.S. telecommunications market, stunned Wall Street by slashing its dividend nearly two-thirds, to $1 per share annually from $2.76. After the brief announcement of the cut came from Chairman Rand V. Araskog late July 10, trading in ITT's stock was delayed on the New York Stock Exchange for more than an hour on July 11, and by the end of the day ITT's stock had lost nearly a third of its value, closing at $21.

The dividend cut will save ITT about $262 million a year, but that amount is unlikely to solve the company's problems. Less than a third of its revenues come from telecommunications, but other key businesses—notably its Hartford Insurance Group and forest-products operations—have not been performing up to expectations. ITT declined to discuss the dividend cut beyond its brief announcement, but consultants and analysts who deal with the company say its main weakness is a lack of strategic planning.

Big-Ticket Sales

In telecommunications, ITT has concentrated in Europe, while competitors such as Northern Telecom, Rolm, and NEC have been selling big-ticket telecommunications equipment in the U.S. in competition with AT&T for nearly a decade. ITT's only major U.S. products are conventional telephones, a small private branch exchange (PBX) system for offices, and an aging switch for telephone company central offices. It is still adapting its state-of-the-art European central office switch, which cost $1 billion to develop, to the U.S. market. Doing so will cost as much as $250 million more by 1989, says William W. Ambrose, an industry analyst with Northern Business Information Inc.

_____
* Reprinted from the July 23, 1984, issue of *Business Week* (p. 77) by special permission. © 1984 by McGraw-Hill, Inc.

ITT has also shown scant ability to develop integrated office and communications products. For example, it recognized a need to market a personal computer, but the first ones it began to ship in June were stand-alone models that do not communicate with its PBX—or any other ITT product. And the company is only now establishing a task force to decide the direction it should take in communications services in the U.S.

One reason for the lack of focus, consultants say, is that there is little continuity in management. "It seems like every three weeks people change jobs," says one. More damaging, perhaps, is the sense that internal politics are occupying management. "It's devastating to see how far their eye has shifted from the external world to what's most important inside ITT," says Robin Williamson, a consultant with Logica Inc. in New York.

Success in the new telecommunications fields may be the key to ITT's future, but it will have to pay for it from its past. Yet its cash cow, Hartford insurance, has been having severe problems. Last year Hartford's commercial lines suffered an operating loss of $109 million, even after investment income. Although prices have firmed recently following a disastrous couple of years for the entire industry, an insurance executive notes that it takes "about 15 months for price increases to work their way through the income statement." That means ITT may yet have to contribute to Hartford instead of harvesting cash from it.

Takeover Target?

ITT's forest-products business has not provided much help. The company has had it on the block for several years, but, says an industry executive, nobody is interested in timberland these days.

Most of these problems have been kept secret. One analyst notes that as late as July 5, ITT was reassuring investors that the dividend was safe. Now Araskog seems to have damaged his credibility on Wall Street, and with its book value at $39 per share, the company seems vulnerable to takeover.

CHAPTER 17

Bonds Payable and Bond Investments

LEARNING OBJECTIVES

After studying this chapter, you should be able to:

1. Describe the features of bonds and tell how bonds differ from shares of stock.
2. List the advantages and disadvantages of financing with long-term debt and prepare examples showing how financial leverage is employed.
3. Explain how interest rates affect bond prices and what causes a bond to sell at a premium or discount.
4. Apply the concept of present value to compute the price of a bond.
5. Prepare journal entries to account for bonds payable.
6. Prepare journal entries to account for bond investments.
7. Define and use correctly the new terms in the glossary.

In previous chapters you learned that corporations obtain cash for recurring business operations from stock issuances, profitable operations, and short-term borrowing (current liabilities). However, when situations arise that require large amounts of cash, such as the purchase of a building, corporations also raise cash from long-term borrowing, that is, by issuing bonds. The issuing of bonds results in a Bonds Payable account. The first part of this chapter discusses the issuing of bonds and accounting for bonds payable.

Since corporations are legal entities, they, like individuals, can invest in stocks and bonds issued by other corporations that are regularly traded on national exchanges. These types of investments can offer a rate of return substantially greater than a savings account. The second part of this chapter discusses bond investments. Stock investments are discussed in Chapter 18.

■ BONDS PAYABLE

A bond is a long-term debt, or liability, owed by its issuer. Physical evidence of the debt lies in a negotiable bond certificate. Long-term notes usually mature in 10 years or less, while bond maturities often run for 20 years or more. A bond derives its value primarily from two promises made by the borrower to the lender, or bondholder. The borrower promises to pay (1) the face value or **principal amount** of the bond on a specific maturity date in the future, and (2) periodic interest at a specified rate on face value at stated dates, usually semiannually, until the maturity date.

A bond issue generally consists of a large number of $1,000 bonds, rather than one very large bond. For example, a company seeking to borrow $100,000 would issue one hundred $1,000 bonds, rather than one $100,000 bond. In this way, investors with less cash to invest are able to purchase some of the bonds.

Comparison with Stock

A bond differs from a share of stock in several ways:

1. A bond is a debt or liability of the issuer, while a share of stock is a unit of ownership.
2. A bond has a maturity date when it must be paid. A share of stock does not mature; stock remains outstanding indefinitely unless the company decides to retire it.
3. Most bonds require stated periodic interest payments by the company. In contrast, dividends to stockholders are payable only when declared; even preferred dividends may be passed in a particular period if the board of directors so decides.
4. Bond interest is deductible by the issuer in computing both net income and taxable income, while dividends are not deductible in either computation.

Selling (Issuing) Bonds

A company seeking to borrow millions of dollars generally will not be able to borrow from a single lender. In such an instance, the company will sell (issue) bonds to the public to secure the funds needed. Usually a bond issue is sold through an investment company or banker, called an underwriter. The underwriter performs many tasks for the issuer, such as advertising, selling, and delivering the bonds to the purchasers. The underwriter often guarantees the issuer a fixed price for the bonds, expecting to earn a profit by selling the bonds for more than the fixed price.

When bonds are sold to the public, many purchasers are involved. Rather than deal with each purchaser individually, the issuing corporation appoints a trustee to represent the bondholders. The trustee usually is a bank or trust company. The main duty of the trustee is to see that the borrower fulfills the provisions of the bond indenture. A bond indenture is the contract or loan agreement under which the bonds are issued. The indenture deals with matters such as the interest rate, maturity date and maturity amount, possible restrictions on dividends, repayment plans, and other provisions relating to the debt. If bond indenture provisions are not adhered to, the issuer is said to be in default. The trustee is expected to take action to force the issuer to comply with the indenture.

Characteristics of Bonds

All bonds have two common characteristics: (1) they promise to pay cash or other assets; and (2) they come due, or mature. In other respects, bonds may differ; they may be secured or unsecured bonds, registered or unregistered (bearer) bonds, and term or serial bonds. These differences and others are discussed below. Certain bond features are matters of legal necessity, such as the way interest is paid and ownership is transferred. Such differences usually do not affect the issue price of the bonds. Other features, such as convertibility into common stock, are designed to make the bonds more attractive to potential purchasers. These added features, called "sweeteners," may increase the issue price of a bond.

Secured Bonds.   A secured bond is a bond for which specific property has been pledged to ensure its payment. Mortgage bonds are the most common type of secured bonds. A mortgage is a legal claim (lien) on a specific property which gives the bondholder the right to sell the pledged property if the company fails to make required payments.

Unsecured Bonds.   An unsecured bond is called a debenture bond, or simply a debenture. A debenture is a bond backed only by the general creditworthiness of the issuer, not by a lien on any specific property. A financially sound company will be able to issue debentures more easily than a company experiencing financial difficulty.

Registered Bonds.   A registered bond is a bond in which the owner's name appears on both the bond certificate and in the record of bond owners kept by the bond issuer or its agent, the registrar. Bonds may be registered as to principal (or face value of the bond) or as to both principal and interest. If a bond is registered as to both, interest on the bond is paid by check. Most bonds in our economy are registered as to principal only. Ownership of registered bonds is transferred by endorsing the bond and registering it in the new owner's name. Registered bonds are easily replaced if lost or stolen.

Unregistered (Bearer) Bonds.   An unregistered (bearer) bond is assumed to be the property of its holder or bearer, since the owner's name does not appear on the bond certificate or in a separate record. Ownership is transferred by physical delivery of the bond.

Coupon Bonds.   A coupon bond is a bond not registered as to interest. A coupon bond carries detachable coupons for the interest it pays. At the end of each interest period, the coupon for the period is clipped and presented to a stated party, usually a bank, for collection.

Term Bonds and Serial Bonds.   A term bond is a bond that matures on the same date as all other bonds in a given bond issue. Serial bonds are bonds in a given bond issue with maturities spread over several dates. For instance, one fourth of the bonds may mature on December 31, 1988, another one fourth on December 31, 1989, and so on.

Callable Bonds. A callable bond contains a provision that gives the issuer the right to call (buy back) the bond before its maturity date. The provision is similar to the call provision in some preferred stocks. A company might exercise this call right if outstanding bonds bear interest at a much higher rate than the company would have to pay if it issued new but similar bonds now. The exercise of the call provision normally requires the company to pay the bondholder a call premium of about $30 to $70 per $1,000 bond. A call premium is the price paid in excess of face value that the issuer of bonds is required to pay to redeem (call) bonds before their maturity date.

Convertible Bonds. A convertible bond is a bond that may be exchanged, at the bondholder's option, for shares of stock of the issuing corporation. A convertible bond has a stipulated conversion rate of some number of shares for each $1,000 bond. Any type of bond may be convertible, but this feature usually is added to rather risky debenture bonds to make them more attractive to investors.

Bonds with Stock Warrants. A stock warrant allows the bondholder to purchase shares of common stock at a fixed price for a stated period of time. Warrants issued with long-term debt may be detachable or nondetachable. A bond with nondetachable warrants is virtually the same as a convertible bond; the holder must surrender the bond in order to acquire the common stock. Detachable warrants allow bondholders to keep their bonds and still purchase shares of stock through exercise of the warrants.

Advantages of Issuing Debt

Several advantages come from raising cash by issuing bonds rather than stock. First, the current stockholders of a corporation do not have to dilute or surrender their control of the company if needed funds can be obtained by borrowing rather than issuing more shares of stock. It may also be less expensive to issue debt rather than additional stock because the interest payments made to bondholders are tax deductible while dividends are not. But probably the most important reason is that the use of debt may increase the earnings of stockholders through favorable financial leverage.

Favorable Financial Leverage. A company has favorable financial leverage when borrowed funds are used to increase earnings per share (EPS) of common stock. Increased EPS usually result from earning a higher rate of return than the rate of interest paid for the borrowed money. For example, suppose a company borrowed money at 10% and earned a 15% rate of return. The 5% difference increases earnings.

A more complex example of favorable financial leverage is provided in Illustration 17.1. The two companies in the illustration are identical in every respect except in the way they are financed. Company A issued only capital stock, while Company B issued equal amounts of 10% bonds and capital stock. Both companies have $20,000,000 of assets, and both earned $4,000,000 of

Illustration 17.1

Favorable Financial Leverage

COMPANIES A AND B CONDENSED STATEMENTS
Balance Sheets
January 1, 1987

	Company A	Company B
Total assets	$20,000,000	$20,000,000
Bonds payable, 10%		$10,000,000
Stockholders' equity (capital stock)	$20,000,000	10,000,000
Total equities	$20,000,000	$20,000,000

Income Statements
For the Year Ended December 31, 1987

	Company A	Company B
Net income from operations	$ 4,000,000	$ 4,000,000
Interest expense		1,000,000
Net income before income taxes	$ 4,000,000	$ 3,000,000
Income taxes (40%)	1,600,000	1,200,000
Net income	$ 2,400,000	$ 1,800,000
Number of common shares outstanding	2,000,000	1,000,000
Earnings per share (EPS)	$1.20	$1.80
Rate of return on assets employed (both companies $4,000,000/$20,000,000)	20%	20%
Rate of return on stockholders' equity:		
Company A ($2,400,000/$20,000,000)	12%	
Company B ($1,800,000/$10,000,000)		18%

income from operations. If we divide income from operations by assets ($4,000,000 ÷ $20,000,000), we see that both companies earned 20% on assets employed. Yet B's stockholders fared far better than A's. The ratio of net income to stockholders' equity is 18% for B, while it is only 12% for A.

The 6% difference can be explained as follows:

Operating income earned on $10,000,000 debt (20%)	$2,000,000
Interest paid on the debt (10%)	1,000,000
Net increase in income before taxes due to debt	$1,000,000
Less income taxes (40%)	400,000
Net increase in income due to debt financing	$ 600,000

Net increase in income due to debt financing as a percentage of stockholders' equity, $600,000/$10,000,000 = 6%.

Assume that both companies issued their stock at the beginning of 1987 at $10 per share. B's $1.80 EPS are 50% greater than A's $1.20 EPS. This EPS difference probably would cause B's shares to sell at a substantially higher market price than A's shares. B's larger EPS would also allow a larger dividend on B's shares.

Company B, in the above illustration, is employing financial leverage, or is said to be trading on the equity. The company is using its stockholders' equity as a basis for securing funds on which a fixed return is paid. Company B expects to earn more from the use of such funds than their fixed after-tax cost, and as a result, Company B increases its rate of return on stockholders' equity and EPS.[1]

---

[1] Issuing bonds is only one method of using leverage. Other methods of using financial leverage include issuing preferred stock or long-term notes.

Disadvantages of Issuing Debt

Several disadvantages accompany the use of debt financing. First, the borrower has a fixed interest payment that must be met each period to avoid default. Use of debt also reduces a company's ability to sustain a major loss. For example, suppose that both Company A and Company B mentioned above sustain losses for 1987 of $11,000,000. At the end of 1987, Company A will still have $9,000,000 of stockholders' equity and can continue operations with a chance of recovery, as shown below. Company B, on the other hand, would have negative stockholders' equity of $1,000,000, and the bondholders could force the company to liquidate if B could not make interest payments as they came due.

	Partial Balance Sheets **December 31, 1987**	
	Company A	*Company B*
Stockholders' equity:		
Paid-in capital:		
Common stock	$ 20,000,000	$ 10,000,000
Retained earnings	(11,000,000)	(11,000,000)
Total stockholders' equity	$ 9,000,000	$ (1,000,000)

Debt financing also causes a company to experience unfavorable financial leverage when income from operations falls below a certain level. **Unfavorable financial leverage** results when the cost of borrowed funds exceeds the revenue they generate; it is the opposite of favorable financial leverage. In the above example, if income from operations fell to $1,000,000, the rates of return on stockholders' equity would be 3% for A and zero for B, as shown in the schedule below:

	Income Statements **For the Year End December 31, 1987**	
	Company A	*Company B*
Net income from operations	$1,000,000	$1,000,000
Interest expense		1,000,000
Net income before income taxes	$1,000,000	$ –0–
Income taxes (40%)	400,000	–0–
Net income	$ 600,000	$ –0–
Rate of return on stockholders' equity:		
Company A ($600,000/$20,000,000)	3%	
Company B ($0/$10,000,000)		0%

Another disadvantage of issuing debt is that loan agreements often require the maintenance of a certain amount of working capital (Current assets − Current liabilities) and place limitations on dividends and additional borrowings.

Accounting for Bonds

When a company issues bonds, it incurs a long-term liability on which periodic interest payments must be made, usually twice a year. If interest dates fall on other than balance sheet dates, interest will need to be accrued in the proper periods. The following example illustrates the accounting for bonds issued at face value on an interest date.

Bonds Issued at Face Value on an Interest Date.   Valley Company has an accounting year ending on December 31. On December 31, 1987, the company issued 10-year, 12% bonds with a $100,000 face value of cash for $100,000. The bonds are dated December 31, 1987, call for semiannual interest payments on June 30 and December 31, and mature on December 31, 1997. Valley Company made all required cash payments when due. The entries for the 10 years are summarized below.

On December 31, 1987, the date of issuance, the entry is:

```
1987
Dec. 31  Cash . . . . . . . . . . . . . . . .    100,000
             Bonds Payable . . . . . . . . . . . .           100,000
         To record bonds issued at face value.
```

On each June 30 and December 31 for 10 years, beginning June 30, 1988 (ending June 30, 1997), the entry would be:

```
Each year
June 30
and
Dec. 31  Bond Interest Expense ($100,000 × 0.12 × ½) . .    6,000
             Cash . . . . . . . . . . . . . . . .           6,000
         To record periodic interest payment.
```

On December 31, 1997, the maturity date, the entry would be:

```
1997
Dec. 31  Bond Interest Expense . . . . . . . . . . .    6,000
         Bonds Payable . . . . . . . . . . . . . .    100,000
             Cash . . . . . . . . . . . . . . . .           106,000
         To record bond redemption and final interest
         payment.
```

Note that no adjusting entries are needed when an interest payment date falls on the last day of the accounting period. The income statement for each of the 10 years 1988–97 would show Bond Interest Expense of $12,000 ($6,000 × 2); the balance sheet at the end of each of the years 1987–95 would report bonds payable of $100,000 in long-term liabilities. At the end of 1996, the bonds would be reclassified as a current liability because they will be paid within the next year.

But the real world is seldom so uncomplicated. For example, assume the Valley Company bonds were dated October 31, 1987, issued on that same date, and pay interest each April 30 and October 31. In this case, an adjusting entry is needed on December 31 to accrue interest for two months, November and December. That entry would read:

```
1987
Dec. 31  Bond Interest Expense ($100,000 × 0.12 × 2/12) . .    2,000
             Bond Interest Payable . . . . . . . . . . .           2,000
         To accrue two months' interest expense.
```

The April 30, 1988, entry would be:

```
1988
Apr. 30   Bond Interest Expense ($100,000 × 0.12 × 4/12)  . .     4,000
          Bond Interest Payable  . . . . . . . . . . .            2,000
              Cash . . . . . . . . . . . . . . . . . .                       6,000
              To record semiannual interest payment.
```

The October 31, 1988, entry would be:

```
1988
Oct. 31   Bond Interest Expense  . . . . . . . . . . .            6,000
              Cash . . . . . . . . . . . . . . . . . .                       6,000
              To record semiannual interest payment.
```

Each year similar entries would be made for the semiannual payments and the year-end accrual. The $2,000 Bond Interest Payable would be reported as a current liability on the December 31 balance sheet for each year.

Bonds Issued at Face Value between Interest Dates.   Bonds are not always issued on the date they start to bear interest. Regardless of when the bonds are physically issued, interest starts to accrue from the **most recent** interest date. Investors purchasing such bonds after they begin to accrue interest are required to pay for the interest accrued since the preceding interest date. The issuer of the bonds is required to pay holders of the bonds a full six months' interest at each interest date. Thus, the bondholders will be reimbursed for this accrued interest when they receive their first six-month interest check. The bonds are reported to be selling at a stated price "plus accrued interest."

Using the facts for the Valley Company bonds dated December 31, 1987, suppose Valley Company issued its bonds on May 31, 1988, instead of on December 31, 1987. The entry required is:

```
1988
May 31   Cash  . . . . . . . . . . . . . . . . . .       105,000
             Bonds Payable  . . . . . . . . . . . .                 100,000
             Bond Interest Payable ($100,000 × 0.12 × 5/12) .         5,000
             To record bonds issued at face value plus accrued
             interest.
```

This entry records the amount of cash received for the accrued interest as a liability.

The entry required on June 30, 1988, when the full six months' interest is paid, is:

```
1988
June 30   Bond Interest Expense ($100,000 × 0.12 × 1/12)  . .     1,000
          Bond Interest Payable  . . . . . . . . . . .            5,000
              Cash  . . . . . . . . . . . . . . . . .                       6,000
              To record bond interest payment.
```

This entry records $1,000 interest expense on the $100,000 of bonds that were outstanding for one month. The $5,000 is the amount previously collected from the bondholders on May 31 as accrued interest and is now being returned to them.

Bond Prices and Interest Rates

The price of a bond issue sold to investors often differs from its face value. A difference between face value and issue price will exist whenever the contract rate of interest on the bonds differs from the market rate of interest for similar bonds. The **contract rate of interest** (also called the **stated, coupon,** or **nominal rate**) is stated in the bond indenture and printed on the face of each bond. The contract rate is used to determine the actual amount of cash that will be paid each interest period. The **market interest rate,** also called the **effective interest** or **yield rate,** is the minimum rate of interest investors are willing to accept on bonds of a particular risk category. The market rate fluctuates from day to day, responding to the supply of, and demand for, money.

Contract and market rates of interest are likely to differ. The contract rate must be set before the bonds are actually sold to allow time for such activities as printing the bonds. By the time the bonds are sold and the market rate becomes known, the contract rate could be higher or lower than the market rate. **If the contract rate is higher than the market rate, the bonds will sell for more than face value.** Investors will be attracted to bonds offering a contract rate greater than the market rate for such bonds and will bid up their price. **If the contract rate is lower than the market rate, the bonds will sell for less than face value.** Investors will not be interested in bonds bearing a contract rate less than the market rate until their price falls. The amount a bond sells for above face value is called a **premium;** if bonds are sold for less than face value, the reduction is called a **discount.**

The effect of selling a bond at a premium or discount is to change the **contract** rate of interest on the bond to the **market** rate. To illustrate this concept, consider the following short-term note. Assume that you loaned the McNeil Company $9,800 on its $10,000, 10% note which matures in one year. The contract interest rate is 10%. But, if McNeil pays the note at maturity, the effective (actual) rate of interest is about 12.2%. At the end of the year, the McNeil Company must pay the principal of the note ($10,000) plus interest for one year at 10% ($10,000 × 0.10 = $1,000) or a total of $11,000. Your actual interest earned is $1,200—the difference between the amount collected, $11,000, and the amount loaned, $9,800. The effective rate of interest is 12.2% ($1,200/$9,800) per annum, simple interest. This is a simple example of how a discount on a loan can adjust the contract rate of interest to the market rate.

Computing Bond Prices

Computing long-term bond prices is a more complex process than finding the effective rate of interest on a one-year note at simple interest. The process involves finding **present values** using compound interest. The concepts of future value and present value are explained in the Appendix to this chapter. If you do not understand the present value concept, you should read the Appendix before continuing.

Buyers and sellers negotiate a price that will yield the going rate of interest for bonds of a particular risk class. The price investors will pay for a given bond issue is equal to the present value of the bonds. Present value is computed by discounting the promised cash flows from the bonds—principal and interest—using the market, or effective, rate. Market rate is used because the bonds must yield at least this rate or investors will be attracted to alternative investments. The life of the bonds is stated in terms of interest (compounding) periods. The interest rate used is the effective rate **per interest period,** which often is found by dividing the annual rate by the number of times interest is paid per year. For example, if the annual rate is 12%, the semiannual rate is 6%.

Bond prices usually are quoted as percentages of face value—100 means 100% of face value, 97 means 97% of face value, and 103 means 103% of face value. For example, a $100,000 face value bond issued at 103 has a price of $103,000.

Bonds Issued at Face Value. The specific steps involved in computing the price of a bond are illustrated by the following example. Assume 12% bonds with a $100,000 face value are issued by Carr Company to yield 12%. The bonds are dated and issued on June 30, 1987, call for semiannual interest payments on June 30 and December 31, and mature on June 30, 1990.[2] The bonds will sell at face value because they offer 12% and investors seek 12%. There is no reason for potential purchasers to offer a premium or demand a discount. One way to prove the bonds would be sold at face value is by showing that their present value is $100,000:

	Cash flow	×	Present value factor	=	Present value
Principal of $100,000 due in six interest periods multiplied by present value factor for 6% from Table 3, Appendix C (end of text)	$100,000	×	0.70496	=	$ 70,496
Interest of $6,000 due at end of each of six interest periods multiplied by present value factor for 6% from Table 4, Appendix C (end of text)	$6,000	×	4.91732	=	29,504
Total price (present value)					$100,000

This schedule shows that if investors seek an effective rate of 6% per six-month period, they should pay $100,000 for these bonds. **Notice that the same number of interest periods and semiannual interest rates are used in discounting both the principal and interest payments to their present values.** The entry to record the sale of these bonds on June 30, 1987, debits Cash and credits Bonds Payable for $100,000.

Bonds Issued at a Discount. Assume the $100,000, 12% Carr Company bonds are sold to yield a current market rate of 14% annual interest, or 7% per semiannual period. The present value (selling price) of the bonds is computed as follows:

	Cash flow	×	Present value factor	=	Present value
Principal of $100,000 due in six interest periods multiplied by present value factor for 7% from Table 3, Appendix C (end of text)	$100,000	×	0.66634	=	$66,634
Interest of $6,000 due at end of each of six interest periods multiplied by present value factor for 7% from Table 4, Appendix C (end of text)	$6,000	×	4.76654	=	28,599
Total price (present value)					$95,233

---

[2] Bonds do not normally mature in such a short time; we use a three-year life for illustrative purposes only.

Note that in computing the present value of the bonds, the actual $6,000 cash interest payment that will be made each period is still used. **The amount of cash paid by the company as interest does not change with changes in the market interest rate.** But the market rate per semiannual period—7%—does change, and this new rate is used to find interest factors in the tables.

The journal entry to record issuance of the bonds is:

```
1987
June 30  Cash . . . . . . . . . . . . . . . . . . . . .    95,233
         Discount on Bonds Payable . . . . . . . .        4,767
            Bonds Payable . . . . . . . . . . . .                  100,000
         To record bonds issued at a discount.
```

In recording the bond issue, Bonds Payable is credited for the face value of the debt. The difference between face value and price received is debited to Discount on Bonds Payable, a contra account to Bonds Payable. Bonds payable and the discount on bonds payable are reported in the balance sheet as follows:

```
Long-term liabilities:
   Bonds payable, 12%, due July 1, 1990 . . . . .   $100,000
      Less: Discount on bonds payable . . . . .        4,767   $95,233
```

The $95,233 is called the carrying value, or net liability, of the bonds. Carrying value is the face value of the bonds minus any unamortized discount or plus any unamortized premium. Unamortized premium on bonds payable is discussed in the next section.

Bonds Issued at a Premium.   Assume that Carr Company issued the $100,000 face value of 12% bonds to yield a current market rate of 10%. The bonds would sell at a premium calculated as follows:

	Cash flow	×	Present value factor	=	Present value
Principal of $100,000 due in six interest periods multiplied by present value factor for 5% from Table 3, Appendix C (end of text)	$100,000	×	0.74622	=	$ 74,622
Interest of $6,000 due at end of each of six interest periods multiplied by present value factor for 5% from Table 4, Appendix C (end of text)	$6,000	×	5.07569	=	30,454
Total price (present value)					$105,076

The journal entry to record the issuance of the bonds is:

```
1987
June 30  Cash . . . . . . . . . . . . . . . . . . . . .   105,076
            Bonds Payable . . . . . . . . . . . .                  100,000
            Premium on Bonds Payable . . . . . . .                   5,076
         To record bonds issued at a premium.
```

The carrying value of these bonds at issuance is $105,076, consisting of face value of $100,000 and premium of $5,076. The premium is shown on the balance sheet as an addition to bonds payable.

Discount/Premium Amortization

When bonds are issued at a premium or discount, bond interest expense recorded each period differs from bond interest actually paid in cash. A discount **increases** and a premium **decreases** the amount of interest expense. For example, if the Carr Company bonds with a face value of $100,000 were issued for $95,233, the total interest cost of borrowing would be $40,767: $36,000 (six payments of $6,000) plus the discount of $4,767. If the bonds had been issued at $105,076, the total interest cost of borrowing would be $30,924: $36,000 less the premium of $5,076. The $4,767 discount or $5,076 premium must be allocated or charged to the six periods that benefit from the use of borrowed money. Two methods are available for amortizing a discount or premium on bonds—the straight-line method and the effective interest rate method.

Interest expense is recorded at a **constant amount** under the straight-line method and at a **constant rate** under the interest method. *APB Opinion No. 21* states that the straight-line method may be used **only when it does not differ materially from the second method to be discussed, the effective interest rate method.** In many cases, the differences will not be material.

The Straight-Line Method. The straight-line method of amortization is a procedure that allocates an equal amount of discount or premium to each month the bonds are outstanding. The amount is calculated by dividing the discount or premium by the total number of months from the **date of issuance** to the maturity date. For example, if the Carr Company bonds with a face value of $100,000 were sold for $95,233, the $4,767 discount would be charged to interest expense at a rate of $132.42 ($4,767/36) per month. Total discount amortization for six months would be $794.52 ($132.42 × 6). Interest expense for each six-month period then would be $6,794.52 [$6,000 + ($132.42 × 6)]. The entry to record the expense on December 31, 1987, would be:

```
1987
Dec. 31  Bond Interest Expense  . . . . . . . . . . .  6,794.52
             Cash  . . . . . . . . . . . . . . . . .                6,000.00
             Discount on Bonds Payable (132.42 × 6)   . .             794.52
         To record interest payment and discount
         amortization.
```

To illustrate the straight-line method applied to a premium, recall that the $100,000 face value Carr Company bonds sold for $105,076. The $5,076 premium on these bonds would be amortized at a rate of $141 ($5,076/36) per month. The entry for the first period's semiannual interest expense on bonds sold at a premium is:

```
1987
Dec. 31  Bond Interest Expense . . . . . . . . . . .  5,154
         Premium on Bonds Payable ($141 × 6) . . . . . .    846
             Cash  . . . . . . . . . . . . . . . . .              6,000
         To record interest payment and premium
         amortization.
```

The Effective Interest Rate Method.   *APB Opinion No. 21* recommends an amortization procedure called the **effective interest rate method,** or simply the **interest method.** Under the interest method, **interest expense for any interest period is equal to the effective (market) rate of interest at the date of issuance times the carrying value of the bonds at the beginning of that interest period.** Using the Carr Company example of 12% bonds with a face value of $100,000 sold to yield 14%, the carrying value at the beginning of the first interest period is the selling price of $95,233. The interest expense for the first semiannual period would be recorded as follows:

```
1987
Dec. 31   Bond Interest Expense ($95,233 × 0.14 × ½) . . .    6,666
                 Cash ($100,000 × 0.12 × ½) . . . . . . . .            6,000
                 Discount on Bonds Payable . . . . . . . . .              666
             To record discount amortization and interest
             payment.
```

Note that interest expense is calculated using the **effective** interest rate. The cash payment is calculated using the **contract** rate. The discount amortized for the period is the difference between the two amounts.

After the above entry, the carrying value of the bonds is $95,899 ($95,233 + $666). The balance in the discount account was reduced by $666 to $4,101 ($4,767 − $666). Assuming the accounting year ends on December 31, the entry to record the payment of interest for the second semiannual period on June 30, 1988, is:

```
1988
June 30   Bond Interest Expense ($95,899 × 0.14 × ½) . . .    6,713
                 Cash ($100,000 × 0.12 × ½) . . . . . . . .            6,000
                 Discount on Bonds Payable . . . . . . . . .              713
             To record payment of six months' interest and to
             show discount amortization.
```

The effective interest rate method can also be applied to premium amortization. If the Carr Company bonds had been issued at $105,076 to yield 10%, the premium would be $5,076. Interest expense would be calculated in the same manner as for bonds sold at a discount. But the entry would differ somewhat, showing a debit to the premium account. The entry for the first interest period is:

```
1987
Dec. 31   Bond Interest Expense ($105,076 × 0.10 × ½)  . .    5,254
             Premium on Bonds Payable  . . . . . . . . .          746
                 Cash ($100,000 × 0.12 × ½) . . . . . . . .            6,000
             To record interest payment and premium
             amortization.
```

After the first entry, the carrying value of the bonds is $104,330 ($105,076 − $746). The premium account now carries a balance of $4,330 ($5,076 − $746). The entry for the second interest period is:

```
1988
June 30   Bond Interest Expense ($104,330 × 0.10 × ½)  . .    5,216
             Premium on Bonds Payable  . . . . . . . . .          784
                 Cash ($100,000 × 0.12 × ½) . . . . . . . .            6,000
             To record payment of six months' interest and to
             show premium amortization.
```

Discount and Premium Amortization Schedules. A discount amortization schedule (Illustration 17.2) and a premium amortization schedule (Illustration 17.3) can be used to aid in preparing entries for interest expense. Companies usually prepare such schedules when bonds are first issued, often using standard computer programs. The schedules are then referred to whenever journal entries for interest are to be made. Note that in each period the amount of interest expense changes; interest expense gets larger when a discount is involved and smaller when a premium is involved. This fluctuation occurs because the carrying value to which a constant interest rate is applied changes each interest payment date. With a discount, carrying value increases; with a premium, it decreases. But the actual cash paid as interest is always a constant amount determined by multiplying face value by the contract rate per interest period.

Illustration 17.2

Discount Amortization Schedule

(A) Interest payment date	(B) Interest Expense debit ($E \times 0.14 \times \frac{1}{2}$)	(C) Cash credit ($100,000 \times 0.12 \times \frac{1}{2}$)	(D) Discount on Bonds Payable credit (B − C)	(E) Carrying value of Bonds Payable (previous balance in E + D)
Issue price				$ 95,233
12/31/87	$ 6,666	$ 6,000	$ 666	95,899
6/30/88	6,713	6,000	713	96,612
12/31/88	6,763	6,000	763	97,375
6/30/89	6,816	6,000	816	98,191
12/31/89	6,873	6,000	873	99,064
6/30/90	6,936*	6,000	936	100,000
	$40,767	$36,000	$4,767	

* Includes rounding difference.

Note that total interest expense for the discount situation in Illustration 17.2 of $40,767 agrees with the earlier computation of total interest expense. In Illustration 17.3, total interest expense in the premium situation is shown as $30,924, which is equal to $36,000 (six $6,000 payments) **less** the $5,076 premium. In both illustrations, the carrying value of the bonds is equal to face value at the maturity date because the discount or premium has been fully amortized.

Adjusting Entry for Partial Period. Illustrations 17.2 and 17.3 can be

Illustration 17.3

Premium Amortization Schedule

(A) Interest payment date	(B) Interest Expense debit ($E \times 0.10 \times \frac{1}{2}$)	(C) Cash credit ($100,000 \times 0.12 \times \frac{1}{2}$)	(D) Premium on Bonds Payable debit (C − B)	(E) Carrying value of Bonds Payable (previous balance in E − D)
Issue price				$105,076
12/31/87	$ 5,254	$ 6,000	$ 746	104,330
6/30/88	5,216	6,000	784	103,546
12/31/88	5,177	6,000	823	102,723
6/30/89	5,136	6,000	864	101,859
12/31/89	5,093	6,000	907	100,952
6/30/90	5,048	6,000	952	100,000
	$30,924	$36,000	$5,076	

used to obtain amounts needed if interest must be accrued for a partial period. Instead of a calendar-year accounting period, assume the fiscal year of the bond issuer ends on August 31. Using the information provided in the premium amortization schedule (Illustration 17.3), the adjusting entry needed on August 31, 1987, is:

1987			
Aug. 31	Bond Interest Expense ($5,254 × 2/6)	1,751	
	Premium on Bonds Payable ($746 × 2/6)	249	
	Bond Interest Payable ($6,000 × 2/6)		2,000
	To record two months' accrued interest.		

This entry records interest for two months, July and August, of the six-month interest period ending on January 1, 1988. The first line of Illustration 17.3 shows the interest expense and premium amortization for the six months. The above entry thus records two sixths (or one third) of the amounts for this six-month period. The remaining four months' interest is recorded when the first payment is made on December 31, 1987. That entry reads:

1987			
Dec. 31	Bond Interest Payable	2,000	
	Bond Interest Expense ($5,254 × 4/6)	3,503	
	Premium on Bonds Payable ($746 × 4/6)	497	
	Cash		6,000
	To record interest expense and interest payment.		

Similar entries for August 31 and December 31 will be made in the remaining years in the life of the bonds. But the amounts will differ because the interest method of accounting for bond interest is being used. The entry for each June 30 would be as indicated in Illustration 17.3.

Redeeming Bonds Payable

Bonds may be (1) paid at maturity, (2) called, or (3) purchased in the market and retired. Each of these actions is referred to as redemption of bonds or the extinguishment of debt. If bonds are paid at maturity, any related discount or premium would have been amortized already. The only entry required at maturity would debit Bonds Payable and credit Cash for the face amount of the bonds.

An issuer may redeem some or all of its outstanding bonds before maturity date by calling them. Or bonds may be purchased in the market and retired. In either case, the accounting is the same. Assume that on January 1, 1989, bonds totaling $10,000 of the $100,000 face value bonds in Illustration 17.3 are called (or else purchased in the market) at 103, or $10,300. Accrued interest, if any, will be added to the price. But in this example, assume that the interest due on this date has been paid. A look at the last column on the line dated 12/31/88 in Illustration 17.3 reveals that the carrying value of the bonds is $102,723, which consists of Bonds Payable of $100,000 and Premium on Bonds Payable of $2,723. Since 10% of the bond issue is being redeemed, 10% must be removed from each of these two accounts. A loss is incurred for the excess of the price paid for the bonds, $10,300, over their carrying value, $10,272. The required entry reads:

```
1989
Jan. 1  Bonds Payable  . . . . . . . . . . . . . .       10,000
        Premium on Bonds Payable ($2,723 ÷ 10)  . . . .     272
        Loss on Bond Redemption ($10,272 − $10,300)  . .     28
            Cash  . . . . . . . . . . . . . . . . .                  10,300
        To record bonds redeemed.
```

According to *FASB Statement No. 4,* gains and losses from **voluntary early** retirement of bonds are extraordinary items, if material. Such gains and losses are reported in the income statement, net of their tax effects, as described in Chapter 16.

Serial Bonds

To avoid the burden of redeeming an entire bond issue at one time, **serial bonds** may be issued that mature over several dates. Assume that on June 30, 1982, Jasper Company issued $100,000 face value of 12% serial bonds at 100. Interest is payable each year on June 30 and December 31. A total of $20,000 of the bonds mature each year starting on June 30, 1987. Jasper Company has a calendar accounting year. Entries required for 1987 for interest expense and maturing debt are:

```
1987
June 30  Bond Interest Expense ($100,000 × 0.12 × ½)  . .    6,000
             Cash  . . . . . . . . . . . . . . . . . .               6,000
         To record interest payment.

     30  Serial Bonds Payable  . . . . . . . . . . .        20,000
             Cash  . . . . . . . . . . . . . . . . . .              20,000
         To record retirement of serial debt.

Dec. 31  Bond Interest Expense ($80,000 × 0.12 × ½)  . . .    4,800
             Cash  . . . . . . . . . . . . . . . . . .               4,800
         To record payment of semiannual interest expense.
```

Note that interest expense for the last six months of 1987 is calculated only on the remaining outstanding debt ($100,000 original issue less the $20,000 that matured on June 30, 1987). Each year after the amount of bonds maturing that year is retired, interest expense decreases proportionately. The $20,000 amount maturing the next year is reported as a current liability in each year-end balance sheet. The remaining debt is a long-term liability.

Bond Redemption or Sinking Funds

Investors in bonds typically are concerned about the safety of their investments. To reduce risk of default at maturity date, provisions in modern bond indentures often require that periodic payments be made to a bond redemption fund, often called a sinking fund. Such payments are to be used by the fund trustee (usually a bank) to redeem a stated amount of bonds annually and to pay accrued interest on those bonds. The trustee determines which bonds are to be called. The cash deposited with the trustee can be used **only** to redeem issuer's bonds and pay accrued interest on bonds redeemed.

To illustrate, assume Hand Company has 12% coupon bonds outstanding that pay interest on March 31 and September 30 and were issued at face value. The bond indenture required that the company pay a trustee the sum of $53,000 each September 30. The trustee is to use the funds to call $50,000 of Hand's bonds and to pay $3,000 accrued interest on bonds called. The entry for the payment to the trustee reads:

```
Sept. 30   Sinking Fund  . . . . . . . . . . . . . . .    53,000
              Cash  . . . . . . . . . . . . . . . .              53,000
           To record payment to trustee of required deposit.
```

The trustee calls $50,000 of bonds, pays for the bonds and accrued interest, and notifies the company. The trustee also bills the company for its fee and expenses incurred of $325. Assuming no interest has been recorded on these bonds for the period ended September 30, the entries are:

```
Sept. 30   Bonds Payable  . . . . . . . . . . . . .    50,000
           Bond Interest Expense . . . . . . . . . .    3,000
              Sinking Fund  . . . . . . . . . . . .              53,000
           To record bond redemption and interest paid by
           trustee.

      30   Sinking Fund Expenses  . . . . . . . . .      325
              Cash  . . . . . . . . . . . . . . . .                325
           To record trustee fee and expenses.
```

The $50,000 of bonds that must be retired during the coming year usually is described as "Current maturity of long-term debt" and reported as a current liability on the current year's balance sheet.

Convertible Bonds

A company may add to the attractiveness of its bonds by making them **convertible,** at each bondholder's option, into shares of the issuer's common stock. Bond conversions are accounted for by treating the carrying value of bonds surrendered as the capital contributed for shares issued.

Suppose a company has $10,000 face value of bonds outstanding. Each $1,000 bond is convertible into 50 shares of the issuer's $10 par value common stock. On May 1, when the carrying value of the bonds was $9,800, all of the bonds were presented for conversion. The entry required is:

```
May 1   Bonds Payable  . . . . . . . . . . . . . .    10,000
            Discount on Bonds Payable  . . . . . . . .            200
            Common Stock ($10,000 ÷ $1,000 = 10 bonds
              × 50 shares × $10 par) . . . . . . . . .          5,000
            Paid-In Capital in Excess of Par Value—Common .     4,800
        To record bonds converted into common stock.
```

The entry eliminates the $9,800 book value of the bonds from the accounts by debiting Bonds Payable for $10,000 and crediting Discount on Bonds Payable for $200. Common Stock is credited for the par value of the 500 shares issued (500 shares × $10 par). The excess amount ($4,800) is credited to Paid-In Capital in Excess of Par Value—Common.

■ BOND INVESTMENTS

Bonds may be purchased as either short-term or long-term investments. A company makes short-term investments in bonds to earn income on what might otherwise be idle cash. Such investments may yield a higher return than available alternatives. Long-term investments in bonds usually are made for reasons other than a return on idle cash. A company may invest on a long-term basis in another company to guarantee needed raw materials, or one company could be a dealer or distributor of the other company's products. In any event, the most common reason is to establish a long-term relationship between two companies. If short-term bond investments are marketable (readily salable) and are considered a temporary use of cash available for operations, they are reported as current assets. All other bond investments are long term and are reported in the Investments section of the balance sheet below current assets, whether marketable or not.

Short-Term Bond Investments

Short-term bond investments are recorded in a single account at cost, which includes the price paid for the bonds and often includes a broker's commission. If bonds are purchased between interest dates, investors pay for accrued interest and collect the amount paid later when the semiannual interest is received. **Premiums and discounts on short-term bond investments are not amortized because the length of time the bonds will be held is not known.**

To illustrate, assume that on May 31, 1987, Bay Company purchased as a short-term investment $10,000 face value, 12% bonds of Ace Company at 102, plus $100 of accrued interest from April 30. A $70 broker's commission was also paid. The entry required is:

```
1987
May 31  Temporary Investments (or Marketable Securities)
            ($10,200 + $70) . . . . . . . . . . . . . . .    10,270
        Bond Interest Receivable ($10,000 × 0.12 × 1/12) . .      100
            Cash . . . . . . . . . . . . . . . . . . . .              10,370
        To record bonds purchased.
```

On September 30, 1987, Bay sold the Ace bonds at 103.5, plus accrued interest of $500. A $70 broker's commission was charged on the sale. Before computing gain or loss on the sale, the broker's commission is deducted from selling price to compute net proceeds to the seller ($10,350 − $70 = $10,280). The gain or loss is the difference between net proceeds and cost. In this example, the gain is $10 ($10,280 − $10,270). Note that accrued interest does not affect the amount of gain or loss because it is paid for by the purchaser. The entry to record the sale is:

```
1987
Sept. 30  Cash ($10,350 + $500 − $70) . . . . . . . . . .    10,780
            Temporary Investments . . . . . . . . . . .              10,270
            Bond Interest Receivable (from above entry) . .             100
            Bond Interest Revenue ($10,000 × 0.12 × 4/12) .             400
            Gain on Sale of Temporary Investments  . . .                10
          To record sale of temporary investments.
```

The purchaser will receive the semiannual interest check from Ace Company to cover the $500 of accrued interest paid to Bay Company. Bay records only $400 of the $500 of interest received as interest revenue, since it held the bonds for only four months.

Long-Term Bond Investments

Long-term investments in bonds also are recorded in a single account at cost, which includes any premium or discount. A premium or discount on long-term bond investments is amortized, although it is not recorded in a separate account by the investing company as it is by the issuing company.

Bonds Purchased at a Discount.   Assume that on June 30, 1987, Mann Company purchased as a long-term investment $100,000 face value of Carr Company's 12% bonds for $95,233 (including broker's commission), a price that yields 14%. These bonds are the same Carr Company bonds that were described in Illustration 17.2. The entry to record the purchase is:

```
1987
June 30   Bond Investments . . . . . . . . . . . . . .        95,233
             Cash    . . . . . . . . . . . . . . . .                    95,233
          To record bonds purchased at a discount.
```

Note that the broker's commission paid to acquire the bonds was included in the debit to the Bond Investments account.

Since Mann intends to hold the bonds to maturity, the discount is amortized over the remaining life of the bonds. Either the straight-line method or interest method may be used to amortize the discount. We will use the interest method. Interest revenue on the bonds purchased by Mann is computed the same way the issuer's interest expense is computed: the bond price is multiplied by the effective rate per period. Discount amortization for Mann is also computed the same way it was for Carr Company; it is the difference between interest revenue (expense) and cash received (paid). The first period's interest revenue is $6,666 ($95,233 × 0.14 × ½). The discount amortized is $666 ($6,666 − $6,000). If Mann has a calendar accounting year, the required adjusting entry is:

```
1987
Dec. 31   Cash . . . . . . . . . . . . . . . . . .        6,000
          Bond Investments . . . . . . . . . . . . .        666
             Bond Interest Revenue   . . . . . . . . .                6,666
          To record accrued bond interest revenue.
```

Note that in the entry, the amount added to the Bond Investments account is equal to the discount amortized on the issuer's books. The discount is amortized even though it is not set up in a separate account on the investor's books. The original discount is $4,767, and this amount must be included in bond interest revenue on Mann's books during the life of the bonds. Illustration 17.4 shows how the $4,767 is added to periodic interest revenue and to Bond Investments. The debits gradually increase the Bond Investments account balance to face value at maturity date.

Mann's December 31, 1987, balance sheet would show Bond Investments of $95,899. If Mann's fiscal year ended on November 30, the adjusting entry on that date would be the same as the December 31 entry, except all amounts

Illustration 17.4

*Discount
Amortization
Schedule*

(A) Interest date	(B) Cash debit ($100,000 × 0.12 × ½)	(C) Bond Interest Revenue credit (E × 0.14 × ½)	(D) Bond Invest- ments debit (C − B)	(E) Carrying value of Bond Investments (previous balance in E + D)
Purchase price . .				$ 95,233
12/31/87	$ 6,000	$ 6,666	$ 666	95,899
6/30/88	6,000	6,713	713	96,612
12/31/88	6,000	6,763	763	97,375
6/30/89	6,000	6,816	816	98,191
12/31/89	6,000	6,873	873	99,064
6/30/90	6,000	6,936*	936	100,000
	$36,000	$40,767	$4,767	

* Includes rounding difference.

would be five sixths of the December 31 amounts and Bond Interest Receivable would be debited instead of Cash.

If the straight-line method were used, discount amortization would be $795 ($4,767/6) per period. Bond interest revenue would be $6,795 ($6,000 + $795).

Bonds Purchased at a Premium.   To illustrate accounting for bonds purchased at a premium, assume Ladd Company paid $105,076 for $100,000 face value of 12% bonds, a price that yields 10%. Ladd has a calendar-year accounting period. These bonds are the Carr Company bonds shown in Illustration 17.3. The entry to record the purchase would be:

```
1987
June 30   Bond Investments . . . . . . . . . . . . . .   105,076
              Cash   . . . . . . . . . . . . . . .                105,076
          To record bonds purchased at a premium.
```

Here again, interest revenue for the first interest period can be computed by multiplying the purchase price by the effective rate: $105,076 × 0.10 × ½ = $5,254. The entry to record the $5,254 is:

```
1987
Dec. 31   Cash . . . . . . . . . . . . . . . . . . .   6,000
              Bond Investments   . . . . . . . . . .                746
              Bond Interest Revenue   . . . . . . . .              5,254
          To record bond interest revenue collected.
```

The premium is amortized by crediting the Bond Investments account. If bonds are held to maturity, the balance in the Bond Investments account would be gradually decreased to the maturity value of $100,000, as shown in Illustration 17.5. Bond interest revenue for the second six months can be read from Illustration 17.5, or it can be computed: ($105,076 − $746) × 0.10 × ½ = $5,216.

If the straight-line method were used, the periodic amortization of the premium would be $846 ($5,076/6). Interest revenue would be a constant semiannual $5,154 ($6,000 − $846).

Illustration 17.5

*Premium
Amortization
Schedule*

(A) Interest date	(B) Cash debit ($100,000 × 0.12 × ½)	(C) Bond Interest Revenue credit (E × 0.10 × ½)	(D) Bond Invest- ments credit (B − C)	(E) Carrying value of Bond Investments (previous balance in E − D)
Purchase price . .				$105,076
12/31/87	$ 6,000	$ 5,254	$ 746	104,330
6/30/88	6,000	5,216	784	103,546
12/31/88	6,000	5,177	823	102,723
6/30/89	6,000	5,136	864	101,859
12/31/89	6,000	5,093	907	100,952
6/30/90	6,000	5,048	952	100,000
	$36,000	$30,924	$5,076	

Sale of Bond Investments

When bond investments are sold, a gain or loss usually must be recorded. Gain or loss is computed as the difference between the price received and the carrying value of the bonds on the date sold. Suppose that on June 30, 1989, when their carrying value was $101,859 (Illustration 17.5), the Ladd Company sold all of its bonds for $102,500, less a $500 broker's commission. The required entry is:

```
1989
June 30  Cash  .  .  .  .  .  .  .  .  .  .  .  .  .  .  .  .  102,000
              Bond Investments  .  .  .  .  .  .  .  .  .             101,859
              Gain on Sale of Bond Investments  .  .  .  .               141
         To record sale of bond investments.
```

There was no accrued interest because the sale occurred on an interest payment date, and the payment of interest had already been recorded. The gain (or loss) on the sale is reported in the income statement, but not as an extraordinary item.

Valuation of Bond Investments

Short-term bond investments are carried and reported at cost. Long-term bond investments are carried and reported at amortized cost. Amortized cost is equal to acquisition cost plus discount amortized or less premium amortized. An exception exists when a substantial, permanent decline in market value occurs. Bond investments are then written down by debiting an account called Loss on Market Decline of Bond Investments and crediting Bond Investments.

Once bond investments have been written down, traditional accounting conservatism dictates they may not be written up, not even to their original cost, if market price recovers. The written down amount serves as the basis for computing gain or loss when the bonds are sold.

■ SUMMARY

A bond is a long-term liability that derives its value from two promises made to the purchaser: (1) the issuing company will repay the principal at a specified later time, and (2) the issuing company will make periodic interest payments until that time.

Bonds may be secured or unsecured, registered or unregistered (bearer), term or serial, and callable or noncallable. Some bonds have detachable interest coupons. Two features that may be added to bonds to make them a more desirable investment are convertibility to capital stock or detachable stock warrants.

Companies may issue bonds in order to avoid diluting the control of the corporation by the current stockholders. It also may be less expensive to issue bonds than stock, since the interest payments made to bondholders are tax deductible while dividend payments are not. The issuance of bonds may create favorable financial leverage for the issuing company. The major disadvantage of issuing debt is that the company becomes obligated to make a fixed payment of interest each period to the bondholders in order to avoid default.

Interest is generally paid in semiannual amounts. If interest payment dates and balance sheet dates do not coincide, interest must be accrued in the proper periods. When bonds are issued between interest payment dates, investors will pay for the interest accrued since the preceding interest date. This accrued interest is refunded to these investors on the next interest date.

A bond may be issued at face value, at a discount, or at a premium. Discounts and premiums exist because of differences between the stated rate of interest on a bond and the market rate of interest. If the market rate is greater than the stated rate, the bond will be issued at a discount. If the market rate is less than the stated rate, the bond will be issued at a premium. The issue price of a bond is equal to the present value of the principal plus the present value of the interest payments. The market rate of interest is used to find the present value.

If a bond is issued at a discount or premium, total interest expense differs from the amount of interest paid in cash each period. The discount or premium is amortized over the life of the bond either under the straight-line method or the effective interest rate method. The latter method is the recommended procedure. Under this method, interest expense is computed as the market rate of interest times the carrying value of the bonds at the beginning of the interest period. Cash interest to be paid is the contract rate of interest times the face (principal) of the bonds. The difference between these two amounts is the discount or premium to be amortized for the interest period.

A company can redeem its outstanding bonds in three ways: (1) pay at maturity, (2) call, or (3) purchase in the market and retire. If bonds are retired early, any related discount or premium must also be removed from the accounts. Also, serial bonds may be issued to avoid paying off an entire bond issue at once.

If a bond is convertible, the bondholder may convert it into capital stock prior to maturity. Bond conversions are accounted for by treating the carrying value of the bonds converted as the capital contributed for the shares issued.

Bonds may be purchased as either short-term or long-term investments. Investments in bonds are recorded at cost, including any commission. For short-term bonds, any premium or discount is not amortized. For long-term bonds, any discount or premium is amortized using either the interest method or the straight-line method. When bond investments are sold, a gain or loss is recorded as the difference between the selling price and carrying value of the investment.

Chapter 18 discusses stock investments of corporations. Some of these investments are for a small percentage of the outstanding shares and some are for a "controlling interest" of more than 50% of the outstanding shares. You will learn new terms such as *parent company* and *subsidiary company*.

APPENDIX: FUTURE VALUE AND PRESENT VALUE

The concepts of interest, future value, and present value are widely applied in business decision making. Therefore, accountants need to understand these concepts in order to properly record certain business transactions.

■ THE TIME VALUE OF MONEY

The concept of the time value of money stems from the logical preference for a dollar today rather than a dollar at any future date. Most individuals would prefer having a dollar today rather than at some future date because (1) the risk exists that the future dollar will never be received; and (2) if the dollar is on hand now it can be invested, resulting in an increase in total dollars possessed at that future date.

Most business decisions involve a comparison of cash flows in and out of the company. To be useful in decision making, such comparisons must be in terms of dollars of the same point in time, or "vintage." That is, the dollars held now must be accumulated or rolled forward, or future dollars must be discounted or brought back to today before comparisons are valid. Such comparisons involve future value and present value concepts.

■ FUTURE VALUE

The **future value** or **worth** of any investment is the amount to which a sum of money invested today will grow in a stated time period at a specified interest rate. The interest involved may be simple interest or compound interest. **Simple interest** is interest on principal only. For example, $1,000 invested today for two years at 12% simple interest will grow to $1,240 since interest is $120 per year. The principal of $1,000, plus 2 × $120, is equal to $1,240. **Compound interest** is interest on principal **and** on interest of prior periods. For example, $1,000 invested for two years at 12% compounded annually will grow to $1,254.40. Interest for the first year is $120 ($1,000 × 0.12). For the second year, interest is earned on the principal plus the interest of the previous year, $120. Thus, the interest for the second year is $134.40 ($1,120 × 0.12). Future value at the end of year 2 is $1,254.40. The $1,254.40 is found by adding the second year's interest ($134.40) to the value at the beginning of the second year ($1,120). These computations of future worth may be portrayed graphically (see Illustration 17.6).

Illustration 17.6

*Compound Interest
and Future Value*

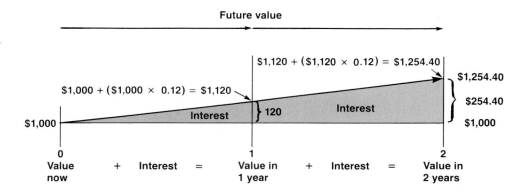

Illustration 17.6 shows the growth of $1,000 to $1,254.40 when the interest rate is 12% compounded annually. The effect of compounding is $14.40—the interest in the second year that was based on the interest computed for the first year, or $120 × 0.12 = $14.40.

The task of computing the future worth to which any invested amount will grow at a given rate for a stated period is aided by the use of interest tables. An example is Table 1 in Appendix C at the end of this text. To use the Appendix C tables, first determine the number of compounding periods involved. A compounding period may be any length of time, such as a day, a month, a quarter, a half-year, or a year, but normally not more than a year. The number of compounding periods is equal to the number of years in the life of the investment times the number of compoundings per year. Five years compounded annually is five periods, five years compounded quarterly is 20 periods, and so on.

Next, determine the interest rate per compounding period. Interest rates are usually quoted in annual terms; in fact, federal law requires statement of the interest rate in annual terms in certain situations. Divide the annual rate by the number of compounding periods per year to get the proper rate per period. Only with an annual compounding will the annual rate be the rate per period. All other cases involve a lower rate. For example, if the annual rate is 12% and interest is compounded monthly, the rate per period (one month) will be 1%.

To use the table in a given situation, find the number of periods involved in the Period column. Move across the table to the right, stopping in the column headed by the Interest Rate per Period, which yields a number called a **factor**. The **factor shows the amount to which an investment of $1 will grow for the periods and the rate involved.** To compute future worth of the investment, multiply the number of dollars in the given situation by this factor. For example, suppose your parents tell you that they will invest $8,000 at 12% for four years and give you the amount to which this investment grows if you graduate from college in four years. How much will you receive at the end of four years if the interest rate is 12% compounded annually? How much will you receive if the interest rate is 12% compounded quarterly?

To calculate these amounts, look at Appendix C, Table 1. In the intersection of the 4 period row and the 12% column, you find the factor 1.57352. Multiplying this factor by $8,000 yields $12,588.16, the answer to the first question. To answer the second question, look at the intersection of the 16 period row and the 3% column. The factor is 1.60471, and the value of your investment is

$12,837.68. The more frequent compounding would add $249.52 ($12,837.68 − $12,588.16) to the value of your investment. The reason for this difference in amounts is that 12% compounded quarterly is a higher rate than 12% compounded annually.

■ PRESENT VALUE

Present value is the current worth of a future cash receipt and is essentially the reverse of future value. In future value, a sum of money is possessed now, and its future value must be calculated. In present value, rights to future cash receipts are possessed now, and their current worth is to be calculated. Future cash receipts are discounted to find their present value. **To discount future receipts is to deduct interest from them.** If the proper interest rate is used, it should not matter to you whether you have cash in an amount equal to present value or have the rights to the larger amount of future receipts.

Assume that you have the right to receive $1,000 in one year. If the appropriate interest rate is 12% compounded annually, what is the present value of this $1,000 future cash receipt? You know that the present value is less than $1,000 because $1,000 due in one year is not worth $1,000 today. You also know that the $1,000 due in one year is equal to some amount, P, plus interest on P at 12% for one year. In other words, $P + 0.12P = $1,000$, or $1.12P = $1,000$. Dividing $1,000 by 1.12, you get $892.86; this amount is the present value of your future $1,000. If the $1,000 was due in two years, you would find its present value by dividing $892.86 by 1.12, which equals $797.20. Portrayed graphically, present value looks very much like future value, except for the direction of the arrows (see Illustration 17.7).

Illustration 17.7

Compound Interest and Present Value

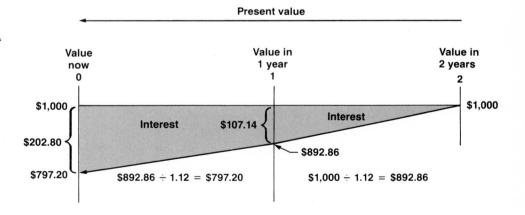

Appendix C, Table 3, contains present value factors for a number of periods and interest rates. Table 3 is used in the same manner as Table 1. For example, the present value of $1,000 due in four years at 16% compounded annually is $552.29, computed as $1,000 × 0.55229. The 0.55229 is the present value factor found in the intersection of the 4 period row and the 16% column.

As another example, suppose that you wish to have $4,000 in three years to pay for a vacation in Europe. If your investment will increase at a 20% rate compounded quarterly, how much should you invest now? To find the amount, you would use the present value factor found in Appendix C, Table 3, 12 period row, 5% column. This factor is 0.55684, which means that an investment of about 55½ cents today would grow to $1 in 12 periods at 5% per period. To have $4,000 at the end of three years, you must invest 4,000 times this factor (0.55684), or $2,227.36.

Present Value of an Annuity

An **annuity** is a series of equal cash flows (often called rents) spaced equally in time. The semiannual interest payments on a bond are a common example of an annuity. An illustration will be used to show how to calculate the present value of an annuity. Assume that $100 will be received at the end of each of the next three semiannual periods. The interest rate is 6% per semiannual period. It would be possible, by use of Appendix C, Table 3, to find the present value of each of the $100 payments as follows:

```
Present value of $100 due in:
   1 period   is 0.94340 × $100 = $ 94.34
   2 periods is 0.89000 × $100 =    89.00
   3 periods is 0.83962 × $100 =    83.96
Total present value   .   .   .   .   $267.30
```

Such a procedure could become quite tedious if the annuity consisted of 50 to 100 or more payments. Fortunately, tables are also available showing the present values of an annuity of $1 per period for varying interest rates and periods. See Appendix C, Table 4. For the annuity described above, a single factor can be obtained from the table to represent the present value of an annuity of $1 per period for three (semiannual) periods at 6% per (semiannual) period. This factor is 2.67301; it is equal to the sum of the present value factors for $1 due in one period, $1 in two periods, and $1 in three periods found in Appendix C, Table 3. When this factor is multiplied by $100, the number of dollars in each payment, it yields the present value of the annuity, $267.30. The present value of this annuity is presented graphically in Illustration 17.8.

Illustration 17.8

Present Value of an Annuity

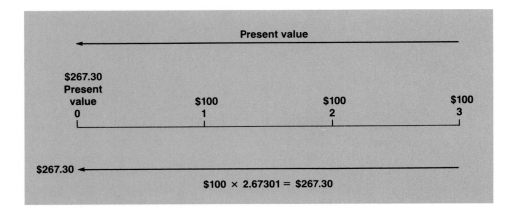

Illustration 17.8 shows that to find the present value of the three $100 cash flows, multiply the $100 by a present value of an annuity factor, 2.67301.

Suppose you won a prize in a lottery that awarded you your choice of $10,000 at the end of each of the next five years or $35,000 cash immediately. You believe you can earn interest on invested cash at 15% per year. Which option should you choose? To answer the question you should compute the present value of an annuity of $10,000 per period for five years at 15%. The present value is $33,521.60, ($10,000 × 3.35216). You should accept the immediate payment of $35,000 since it has the larger present value.

NEW TERMS INTRODUCED IN CHAPTER 17

Annuity

A series of equal cash flows spaced equally in time (672).

Bearer bond

See unregistered bond.

Bond

A long-term debt owed by its issuer. A **bond certificate** is a negotiable instrument and is the formal, physical evidence of the debt owed (648).

Bond indenture

The contract or loan agreement under which bonds are issued (648).

Bond redemption (or sinking) fund

A fund used to bring about gradual redemption of a bond issue (622).

Call premium

The price paid in excess of face value that the issuer of bonds may be required to pay to redeem (call) bonds before their maturity date (650).

Callable bond

A bond that gives the issuer the right to call (buy back) the bond before its maturity date (650).

Carrying value (of bonds)

The face value of bonds minus any unamortized discount or plus any unamortized premium. Sometimes referred to as **net liability** on the bonds when used for bonds payable (657).

Compound interest

Interest calculated on the principal and on interest of prior periods (669).

Contract rate of interest

The interest rate printed on the bond certificates and specified on the bond indenture; also called the **stated, coupon,** or **nominal rate** (655).

Convertible bond

A bond that may be exchanged, at the bondholder's option, for shares of stock of the issuing corporation (650).

Coupon bond

A bond not registered as to interest; it carries detachable coupons that are to be clipped and presented for payment of interest due (649).

Debenture bond

An unsecured bond backed only by the general credit worthiness of its issuer (649).

Discount (on bonds)

Excess of face value over issue or selling price (655).

Effective interest rate method (interest method)

A procedure for calculating periodic interest expense (or revenue) in which the first period's interest is computed by multiplying the carrying value of bonds payable (bond investments) by the market rate at the issue date. The difference between computed interest expense (revenue) and the interest paid (received), based on nominal rate times face value, is the discount or premium amortized for the period. Computations for subsequent periods are based on carrying value at the beginning of the period (659).

Face value

Principal amount, or maturity amount or value, of a bond (648).

Favorable financial leverage

An increase in EPS and rate of return on owners' equity resulting from earning a higher rate of return on borrowed funds than the fixed cost of such funds. **Unfavorable financial leverage** results when the cost of borrowed funds exceeds the income they generate, resulting in decreased income to owners (650).

Future value or worth

The amount to which a sum of money invested today will grow in a stated time period at a specified interest rate (669)

Interest method

See Effective interest rate method.

Market interest rate

The interest rate that an investor will earn on a bond investment by·paying a specified price for it and the rate of interest expense a borrower will incur by issuing bonds at that price. Also called **effective interest** or **yield rate** (655).

Mortgage

A legal claim (lien) on a specific property that gives the bondholder the right to sell the pledged property if the company fails to make required payments. A bond secured by a mortgage is called a **mortgage bond** (649).

Premium (on bonds)

Excess of selling or issue price over face value (655).

Present value

The current worth of a future cash receipt(s); computed by discounting future receipts at a stipulated interest rate (671).

Registered bond

A bond for which the owner's name appears on both the bond certificate and in the record of bond owners kept by the bond issuer or its agent, the registrar (649).

Secured bond

A bond for which specific property has been pledged to ensure its payment (649).

Serial bonds

Bonds in a given bond issue with maturities spread over several dates (649).

Simple interest

Interest on principal only (669).

Sinking fund

See Bond redemption fund.

Stock warrant

A right that allows the bondholder to purchase shares of common stock at a fixed price for a stated period of time. Warrants may be detachable or nondetachable (650).

Straight-line method of amortization

A procedure that, when applied to bond discount or premium, allocates an equal amount of discount or premium to each period in the life of a bond (658).

Term bond

A bond that matures on the same date as all other bonds in a given bond issue (649).

Trading on the equity

See Favorable financial leverage.

Trustee

Usually a bank or trust company appointed to represent the bondholders in a bond issue and to enforce the provisions of the bond indenture against the issuer (648).

Underwriter

An investment company that performs many tasks for the bond issuer in issuing bonds; may also guarantee the issuer a fixed price for the bonds (648).

Unfavorable financial leverage

Results when the cost of borrowed funds exceeds the revenue they generate; it is the reverse of **favorable financial leverage** (652).

Unregistered (bearer) bond

Ownership transfers by physical delivery (649).

Unsecured bond

A **debenture bond,** or simply a **debenture** (649).

DEMONSTRATION PROBLEM 17–1

Jackson Company issued $100,000 face value of 15%, 20-year bonds on April 30, 1987. The bonds are dated April 30, 1987, call for semiannual interest payments on April 30 and October 31, and are issued to yield 16% (8% per period).

Required: *a.* Compute the amount received for the bonds.

          b. Prepare an amortization schedule. Enter data in the schedule for only the first two interest periods. Use the interest method.

          c. Prepare journal entries to record issuance of the bonds, the first six months' interest expense on the bonds, the adjustment needed on December 31, 1987 (assuming Jackson's accounting year ends on that date), and the second six months' interest expense on April 30, 1988.

Solution to demonstration problem 17–1

a. Price received:

      Present value of principal: $100,000 × .04603 . . . $ 4,603

      Present value of interest: $7,500 × 11.92461 . . . <u>89,435</u>

      Total . . . . <u>$94,038</u>

b.

(A) Interest payment date	(B) Bond Interest Expense debit (E × 0.16 × ½)	(C) Cash credit ($100,000 × 0.15 × ½)	(D) Discount on Bonds Payable credit (B − C)	(E) Carrying Value of Bonds Payable (previous balance in E + D)
Issue price				$94,038
10/31/87	$7,523	$7,500	$23	94,061
4/30/88	7,525	7,500	25	94,086

c.

JACKSON COMPANY
GENERAL JOURNAL

1987

Apr. 30 Cash 94,038

          Discount on Bonds Payable 5,962

             Bonds Payable 100,000

          Issued $100,000 face value of 20-year, 15% bonds to

          yield 16%.

Oct. 31 Bond Interest Expense 7,523

          Discount on Bonds Payable 23

          Cash 7,500

          Paid semiannual bond interest expense.

Dec. 31 Bond Interest Expense ($7,525 × ⅓) 2,508

          Discount on Bonds Payable 8

          Bond Interest Payable ($7,500 × ⅓) 2,500

          To record accrual of two months' interest expense.

1988

Apr. 30 Bond Interest Payable 2,500

          Bond Interest Expense ($7,525 × ⅔) 5,017

          Discount on Bonds Payable 17

          Cash 7,500

          To record semiannual bond interest expense.

DEMONSTRATION PROBLEM 17–2

On May 31, 1987, Martin Company purchased $10,000 face value of 8%, 10-year bonds issued by Shane Company. The bonds mature on May 31, 1997, call for semiannual interest payments on May 31 and November 30, and were issued for cash of $8,754, a price that yields an effective rate of 10%. The bonds are considered a long-term investment by Martin Company, which has a December 31 accounting year-end.

Required Prepare journal entries to record the investment in the Shane bonds, to record the interest collected on November 30, 1987, and to adjust the accounts on December 31, 1987. Use the effective interest rate method.

Solution to demonstration problem 17–2

MARTIN COMPANY
GENERAL JOURNAL

1987
May 31 Bond Investments 8,754
     Cash 8,754
    To record purchase of $10,000 face value of bonds.

Nov. 30 Cash ($10,000 × 0.08 × ½) 400
    Bond Investments 38
     Bond Interest Revenue ($8,754 × 0.10 × ½) 438
    To record semiannual interest revenue.

Dec. 31 Bond Interest Receivable ($10,000 × 0.08 × $\frac{1}{12}$) 67
    Bond Investments 6
     Bond Interest Revenue [($8,754 + $38) × 0.10 × $\frac{1}{12}$] 73
    To accrue one month's interest revenue.

QUESTIONS

1. What are the advantages of obtaining long-term funds by the issuance of bonds rather than additional shares of capital stock? What are the disadvantages?

2. What is a bond indenture? What parties are usually associated with it? Explain why.

3. Explain what is meant by the terms *coupon, callable, convertible,* and *debenture.*

4. What is meant by the term *trading on the equity?*

5. When bonds are issued between interest dates, why is it appropriate that the issuing corporation should receive cash equal to the amount of accrued interest in addition to the issue price of the bonds?

6. Why might it be more accurate to describe a sinking fund as a bond redemption fund?

7. Indicate how each of the following items should be classified in a balance sheet on December 31, 1987.

 a. Cash balance in a sinking fund.
 b. Accrued interest on bonds payable.

 c. Debenture bonds payable due in 1997.
 d. Premium on bonds payable.
 e. First-mortgage bonds payable, due July 1, 1988.
 f. Discount on bonds payable.
 g. First National Bank—Interest account.
 h. Convertible bonds payable due in 1990.

8. Why is the effective interest rate method of computing periodic interest expense considered theoretically preferable to the straight-line method?

9. Why would an investor whose intent is to hold bonds to maturity pay more for the bonds than their face value?

10. Describe the amortization of a premium or discount on a short-term bond investment.

11. Describe the amortization of a premium or discount on a long-term bond investment.

12. Under what circumstances should bond investments be written down below their carrying value?

EXERCISES

E–1

Record issuance of bonds, adjusting entry, and payment of interest

On September 30, 1988, the Farrell Company issued $120,000 face value of 18%, 10-year bonds dated August 31, 1988, at 100, plus accrued interest. Interest is paid semiannually on February 28 and August 31. Farrell's accounting year ends on December 31. Prepare journal entries to record the issuance of these bonds, the accrual of interest at year-end, and the payment of the first interest coupon.

E–2

Record bond investments, adjusting entry, and collection of interest

Meal Company, with an accounting year ending on December 31, bought $5,000 face value of the bonds in Exercise E–1 on September 30. Prepare entries to record the purchase, the necessary year-end adjusting entry, and the receipt of the first six months' interest.

E–3

Compute bond interest expense; show how bond price determined

On December 31, 1986, Thomas Company issued $200,000 face value of 8%, 10-year bonds for cash of $164,149, a price to yield 11%. The bonds pay interest semiannually and mature December 31, 1996.

a. State which is higher, the effective rate of interest or the nominal rate.
b. Compute the bond interest expense for the first six months of 1987 using the interest method.
c. Show how the $164,149 price must have been determined.

E–4

Record bond investment and first period's interest

Booker Company purchased bonds with a face value of $40,000 issued by Thomas Company (Exercise E–3) as a long-term investment on December 31, 1987. Prepare the journal entry to record the investment. Also, prepare the entry to record the receipt of interest on the bonds for the first six months of 1987 using the interest method.

E–5

Calculate interest using straight-line amortization

Compute the annual interest expense on the bonds in Exercise E–3 and the interest revenue on the bonds in Exercise E–4, assuming the bond discount is amortized using the straight-line method.

E–6

Prepare entry to record interest payment

After recording the payment of the interest coupon due on June 30, 1988, the accounts of the Hallwood Company showed Bonds Payable of $100,000 and Premium on Bonds Payable of $3,524. Interest is payable semiannually on June 30 and December 31. The five-year, 12% bonds have a face value of $100,000 and were originally issued to yield 10%. Prepare the entry to record the payment of interest on December 31, 1988. Use the interest method.

E–7

Record call of bonds and payment of interest

On June 30, 1988 (a semiannual interest payment date), Flowers Company redeemed all of its $200,000 face value of 10% bonds outstanding by calling them at 106. The bonds were originally issued on June 30, 1984, at 100. Prepare the entry to record the payment of the interest and the redemption of the bonds on June 30, 1988.

E–8

Record conversion of bonds

After interest was paid on September 30, 1988, $16,000 face value of the LeClair Company's $160,000 face value of outstanding bonds were converted into 2,000 shares of the company's $5 par value common stock. Prepare the entry to record the conversion assuming the bonds were issued at 100.

E–9

Record accrued interest, and purchase and retirement of bonds

On August 31, 1987, the Caster Company, as part of the provisions of its bond indenture, acquired $60,000 of its outstanding bonds on the open market at 96 plus accrued interest. These bonds were originally issued at face value and carry a 12% interest rate, payable semiannually. The bonds are dated November 30, 1976, and pay semiannual interest on May 31 and November 30. Prepare the entries required to record the accrual of the interest to the acquisition date on the bonds acquired and the acquisition of the bonds.

E–10

Record interest received for six-month period given adjusting entry previously made

On December 31, 1988, the end of its accounting year, Sorg Company prepared an adjusting entry to record $6,667 of accrued interest revenue earned on 12% bonds with a $150,000 face value that were purchased on August 31, 1988, to yield 14%. The bonds are dated August 31, 1988, and call for semiannual interest payments on August 31 and February 28. Prepare the entry on February 28, 1989, to record the interest revenue, the discount amortization, and the collection of interest.

E–11

Record sinking fund transactions

The P Company is required to make a deposit of $72,000 plus semiannual interest expense of $2,160 on October 31, 1987, to the trustee of its sinking fund so that the trustee can redeem $72,000 of P's bonds on that date. The bonds were issued at 100. Prepare the entries required on October 31 to record the sinking fund deposit, the bond retirement, payment of interest (due on that date), and payment of trustee expenses, assuming the latter amount is $225.

E–12

Prepare journal entries related to temporary investment in bonds

On June 30, 1987, Cove Company purchased as a temporary investment $10,000 face value of Bay Company's 12% bonds at 101. In addition to the purchase price, Cove paid $200 of accrued interest from April 30 and a $70 broker's commission.

On September 30, 1987, Cove sold the Bay bonds at 102.5, plus accrued interest of $500, and less a $70 broker commission.

Prepare journal entries on Cove Company's books to record the purchase and sale of the Bay Company bonds.

E–13

Determine present value (based on Appendix)

(Based on the Appendix) What is the present value of a lump-sum payment of $22,000 due in five years if the market rate of interest is 10% per year (compounded annually) and the present value of $1 due in five periods at 10% is 0.62092?

E–14

Determine present value of a series of future payments (based on Appendix)

(Based on the Appendix) What is the present value of a series of semiannual payments of $2,000 due at the end of each six months for the next five years if the market rate of interest is 10% per year and the present value of an annuity of $1 for 10 periods at 5% is 7.72173?

PROBLEMS, SERIES A

P17–1–A

Compute two prices on bond issue and first period's interest

Rouse Company is seeking to issue $250,000 face value of 10%, 20-year bonds. The bonds are dated June 30, 1987, call for semiannual interest payments, and mature on June 30, 2007.

Required:

a. Compute the price investors should offer if they seek a yield of 8% on these bonds. Also, compute the first six months' interest assuming the bonds are issued at that price. Use the interest method.

b. Repeat part *(a)* assuming investors seek a yield of 12%.

P17–2–A

Record bond interest expense and accrual for partial period

On March 31, 1987, Maxwell Corporation issued $200,000 face value of 8%, 10-year bonds. The bonds call for semiannual interest payments on March 31 and September 30, and they mature on March 31, 1997. Maxwell received cash of $175,076, a price that yields 10%.

Required:

Assume that Maxwell's accounting year ends on December 31. Prepare entries to record the bond interest expense on September 30, 1987, the adjustment needed on December 31, 1987, and the bond interest expense on March 31, 1988, using the interest method.

P17–3–A

Record issuance of bonds, payment of interest, and partial period accrual; record purchase and receipt of interest on investor's books

On December 1, 1987, Stine Company issued $300,000 of 18%, 10-year bonds dated June 30, 1987, at 100. Interest on the bonds is payable semiannually on June 30 and December 31. The company's accounting period ends on December 31. Quarterly financial statements are prepared, so adjusting entries are prepared at the end of each quarter.

Required:

a. Prepare journal entries to record the issuance of the bonds; the December 31, 1987, interest payment; and the adjusting entry needed on March 31, 1988.

b. Assume that Vail Corporation bought $60,000 of the Stine Company bonds on December 1, 1987, as a long-term investment. Vail's year-end is December 31. Prepare all journal entries for Vail Corporation for these bonds through December 31, 1987.

P17–4–A

Compute issue price of bonds; prepare amortization schedule; journalize bond issuance and interest payment

Clover Company issued $50,000 face value of 16%, 20-year bonds on June 30, 1987. The bonds are dated June 30, 1987, call for semiannual interest payments on June 30 and December 31, and are issued to yield 12% (6% per period).

Required:

a. Compute the amount received for the bonds.

b. Prepare an amortization schedule similar to that shown in Illustration 17.3. Enter data in the schedule for the first two interest periods only. Use the interest method.

c. Prepare journal entries to record the issuance of the bonds and the first six months' interest expense on the bonds assuming Clover has a calendar-year accounting period.

17–5–A

Record bond investment, first two periods' interest, and sale of bonds

Haverty Company purchased $20,000 face value of the Clover Company bonds (Problem P17–4–A) when they were issued on June 30, 1987, as a long-term investment.

Required:

a. Prepare entries to record the purchase of the bonds and the receipt of the first two interest payments, assuming Haverty's accounting year ends on December 31. Use the interest method.

b. Assume that the Haverty Company sold all of these bonds on July 1, 1997, for cash of $24,000 after detaching the interest coupons due the preceding day. The bonds have a carrying value, properly adjusted to that date, of $24,588. Prepare the journal entry to record the sale.

P17–6–A

Compute price of bonds; prepare amortization schedule; journalize bond issuance and record two interest payments

Maddox Company issued $300,000 face value of 10%, 20-year bonds on June 30, 1987. The bonds are dated June 30, 1987, call for semiannual interest payments on June 30 and December 31, and are issued to yield 12% (6% per period).

Required:

a. Compute the amount received for the bonds.

b. Prepare an amortization schedule similar to that shown in Illustration 17.2. Enter data in the schedule for the first two interest periods only. Use the interest method.

c. Prepare entries to record the issuance of the bonds and the first two interest payments on the bonds, assuming Maddox has an accounting year that ends on December 31.

P17–7–A

Record bond investment, first two interest checks, and call of bonds

Sherwood Corporation, with a calendar-year accounting period, purchased as a long-term investment 60,000 face value of the Maddox bonds (Problem P17–6–A) when they were issued on June 30, 1987.

Required:

a. Prepare journal entries to record the purchase of the bonds and the receipt of the first two interest payments. Use the interest method.

b. Assume that on June 30, 1997, Maddox called all of the bonds at 105. The properly adjusted carrying value of the bonds on this date was $53,118. Sherwood received a check for $63,000. The collection of the semiannual interest due on this date had already been recorded. Prepare the entry to record the receipt of the $63,000.

c. If the investment had been a short-term investment, would the discount be amortized?

P17–8–A

Record serial bond transactions and show financial reporting

Porter Company issued $100,000 face value of 18% bonds on June 30, 1987, at face value. The bonds are dated June 30, 1987, call for semiannual interest payments on June 30 and December 31, and mature at the rate of $10,000 per year on June 30, beginning in 1992. The company's accounting year ends on December 31.

Required:

a. Prepare journal entries to record the interest payment for the six months ending June 30, 1992; the maturing of the bonds on June 30, 1992; and the interest payment on December 31, 1992.

b. Show how the bonds will be presented in the company's balance sheet for December 31, 1992.

PROBLEMS, SERIES B

P17–1–B

Compute two prices on bond issue and first period's interest

Harte Company is seeking to issue $200,000 face value of 10%, 15-year bonds. The bonds are dated June 30, 1987, call for semiannual interest payments, and mature on June 30, 2002.

Required:

a. Compute the price investors should offer if they seek a yield of 8% on these bonds. Also, compute the first six months' interest assuming the bonds are issued at this price. Use the interest method.

b. Repeat part *(a)* assuming investors seek a yield of 12%.

P17–2–B

Record bond interest expense payment and accrual for partial period

On March 31, 1987, Royston Corporation issued $160,000 face value of 10%, 10-year bonds. The bonds call for semiannual interest payments on March 31 and September 30 and mature on March 31, 1997. Royston received cash of $141,647, a price that yields 12%.

Required:

Assume that Royston's accounting year ends on December 31. Prepare entries to record the bond interest expense on September 30, 1987, the adjustment needed on December 31, 1987, and the bond interest expense on March 31, 1988, using the interest method.

P17–3–B

Record issuance of bonds and payment of interest; record purchase and accrual of interest on investor's books

On December 1, 1987, Kirby Corporation issued $450,000 of 16%, 10-year bonds dated September 30, 1987, at 100. Interest on the bonds is payable semiannually on March 31 and September 30 upon presentation of the appropriate coupon. All of the bonds are of $1,000 denomination. The company's accounting period ends on December 31.

All of the first interest period's coupons on the bonds are presented to the company's bank and paid on March 31, 1988. All of the second interest period's coupons on the bonds are received and paid on September 30, 1988.

Required:

a. Prepare all necessary journal entries for the above transactions through September 30, 1988, including the adjusting entry needed at December 31, 1987.

b. Novel Company purchased $150,000 of Kirby Corporation's bonds on December 1, 1987, as a long-term investment. Novel Company prepares financial statements on December 31. Prepare all journal entries for Novel Company relating to the bonds through December 31, 1987.

P17–4–B

Compute issue price of bonds; prepare amortization schedule; journalize bond issuance; accrue interest

Horn Company issued $80,000 face value of 15%, 20-year bonds on September 30, 1987. The bonds are dated September 30, 1987, call for semiannual interest payments on March 31 and September 30, and are issued to yield 16% (8% per period).

Required:

a. Compute the amount received for the bonds.

b. Prepare an amortization schedule similar to that shown in Illustration 17.2. Enter data in the schedule for the first two interest periods only. Use the interest method.

c. Prepare journal entries to record the issuance of the bonds, the adjustment needed on December 31, 1987; and payment of the first six months' interest expense on the bonds, assuming Horn Company has a calendar-year accounting period.

P17–5–B

Record bond investment, full and partial period's interest, and sale of bonds

Ferrell Company purchased, as a long-term investment, $32,000 face value of the Horn Company bonds (Problem 17–4–B) when they were issued on September 30, 1987.

Required:

a. Prepare entries to record the purchase of the bonds, the receipt of the first six months' interest, and the adjustment needed on June 30, 1988, assuming Ferrell's fiscal year ends on that date. Use the interest method.

b. Assume that the Ferrell Company sold all of these bonds on September 30, 1997, for cash of $31,840 after detaching the interest coupon due on this date. The bonds have a carrying value, properly adjusted to that date, of $30,443. Prepare the journal entry to record the sale.

P17–6–B

Compute price of bonds; prepare amortization schedule; journalize bond issuance, payment of first period's interest, and accrual of partial period's interest

Handley Company issued $200,000 face value of 18%, 20-year bonds on March 31, 1987. The bonds are dated March 31, 1987, call for semiannual interest payments on March 31 and September 30, and are issued to yield 16% (8% per period).

a. Compute the amount received for the bonds.

b. Prepare an amortization schedule similar to that shown in Illustration 17.3. Enter data in the schedule for the first two interest periods only. Use the interest method.

c. Prepare entries to record the issuance of the bonds, the first six months' interest on the bonds, and the adjustment needed on December 31, 1987, assuming Handley's year ends on that date.

P17–7–B

Record bond investment, collection of full period's interest, accrual of partial period's interest, and call of bonds

Collins Corporation, with a December 31 accounting year-end, purchased as a long-term investment $60,000 face value of the Handley's bonds, (Problem P17–6–B) when they were issued on March 31, 1987.

Required: a. Prepare journal entries to record the purchase of the bonds, the receipt of the first six months' interest, and the adjustment needed on December 31, 1987. Use the interest method.

b. Assume that on September 30, 1997, Handley called all of the bonds at 105. The properly adjusted carrying value of the bonds on this date was $65,918. Collins received a check for $63,000. The collection of the semiannual interest due on this date had already been recorded. Prepare the entry to record the receipt of the check from Handley Company for the redemption of the bonds.

c. If the investment had been a short-term investment, would the premium be amortized?

P17-8-B

Record serial bond transaction and show financial reporting

Tillman Company issued $280,000 face value of 16% serial bonds on June 30, 1987, at face value. The bonds are dated June 30, pay interest semiannually on June 30 and December 31, and mature at the rate of $56,000 per year. The first group of bonds matures on June 30, 1992. The company's accounting period ends on December 31.

Required: a. Prepare journal entries to record the interest payment of June 30, 1992; the maturing of $56,000 of bonds on June 30, 1992; and the entry to record the interest payment on December 31, 1992.

b. Show how the bonds will be presented in the company's balance sheet for December 31, 1992.

BUSINESS DECISION PROBLEM 17–1

Analyze two financing proposals; decide whether investment should be made

A company is trying to decide whether to invest $1,000,000 on plant expansion and $500,000 to finance a related increase in inventories and accounts receivable. The $1,500,000 expansion is expected to increase business volume substantially. Profit forecasts indicate that net income from operations will rise from $800,000 to $1,100,000. The income tax rate will be about 40%. Net income last year was $457,500. Interest expense on debt now outstanding is $35,000 per year. There are 200,000 shares of common stock currently outstanding.

The $1,500,000 needed can be obtained in two alternative ways:

1. Finance entirely by issuing additional shares of common stock at an expected issue price of $37.50 per share.
2. Finance two thirds with bonds, one third with additional stock. The bonds would have a 20-year life, bear interest at 10%, and would sell at face value. The issue price of the stock would be $40 per share.

Required: Should the investment be made? If so, which financing plan would you recommend? (Hint: Calculate EPS for last year and for future years under each of the alternatives.)

BUSINESS DECISION PROBLEM 17–2

Decide on which of two bond issues to purchase

You are an investor in stocks and bonds of various companies. An account executive of a brokerage firm has brought the following bonds to your attention:

1. C Company bonds—remaining life, 12 years; interest rate 6%, payable semiannually. Price: $650 per $1,000 bond.
2. R Company bonds—remaining life, 13 years; interest rate 15%, payable semiannually. Price: $1,150 per $1,000 bond.

From a study of available alternatives, you reach the conclusion that either of these bonds would be a suitable investment if the yield were 12% (6% per period).

Required: In which of the above bonds should you invest, if either? Explain.

BUSINESS SITUATION FOR DISCUSSION

Street Smart
Jeffrey M. Laderman

Managers Who Outguess the Bond Market*

The $100 million in fixed-income accounts at Century Capital Associates is now entirely in commercial paper and other cash equivalents—a situation that often gives rise to grumbling from clients who are paying for supervision of a portfolio of bonds. Managers James W. Harpel, 46, and Paul A. Zoschke, 44, find their position frustrating but defend it vigorously. "We expect higher interest rates, so we're in very short maturities," says Harpel. "Your judgment on whether to be short or long makes all the difference in this business."

Harpel's judgment has made the critical difference since he started managing fixed-income accounts in 1977. This year, a disaster for most bond managers, Harpel and Zoschke—who joined the firm in January—are up about 7.7% on a total-return basis, compared with 4.67% for the Shearson Lehman Government/Corporate Index. From 1977 through 1983, Century Capital's fixed-income portfolio was up 112.2%, compared with 66.9% for the Shearson Lehman index.

Turning Bearish

Furthermore, Harpel's firm—which is known for equity management—has provided above-average returns without resorting to the higher-yielding "junk" bonds (BW—June 4). While Harpel, a senior partner, focuses on macroeconomics and interest-rate forecasting, Zoschke, as director of fixed-income research, helps out with "sectoral" analysis, finding the mix of securities and maturities that will provide optimal returns.

With a bias toward the short maturities, Century Capital trailed the 1982–83 bull market in bonds. "I was late in buying bonds," admits Harpel. But he made a smart move by turning bearish in June of 1983—just a few weeks after the low in interest rates and the peak in bond prices—and shifting into cash. Expecting a period of gradually rising short-term rates in early 1984, Harpel and Zoschke bought floating-rate notes, which are typically issues of bank holding companies that pay interest in line with short-term rates.

But by the end of the first quarter of this year, the managers were becoming edgy about the exposure of money-center banks to shaky Third World debtors. So they sold off the floaters and fled to cash in time to avoid the disastrous sinking of the floater market in May (BW—July 9).

Right now, Harpel and Zoschke have the funds parked in top-rated commercial paper and short-term investment funds, what could be called bank-managed money market mutual funds for institutions. They are not impressed by the recent bond market rally. "It's too soon in the business cycle to be the real thing," says Harpel. "Credit demands are still likely to increase." Thus, the duo do not expect to buy long-term Treasury bonds again until the onset of a recession, which, because of the economy's strength, they think is 12 to 18 months away.

Faster Payback

When it appears that a recession will force interest rates downward, Zoschke says the best play is deep-discount, mortgage-backed securities such as the Government National Mortgage Assn. (GNMA) pass-through certificate with an 8% coupon. When interest rates are declining, says Zoschke, an investor gets additional price appreciation because the yield spread between mortgages and government bonds typically narrows. But there is another kicker: When mortgage rates decline, homes sales pick up, increasing the number of older, lower-rate mortgages that are paid off.

So, says Zoschke, an investor with a Ginnie Mae bought for 70¢ on the dollar finds an increasing number of mortgage prepayments paid back at par. In addition, when the rate of prepayments increases, the GNMA typically rises in price to anticipate the faster payback. Such extra dollars can kick in an additional 2% return—and in fixed-income investing, that is a lot of money.

Stock Investments— Cost, Equity, and Consolidations

LEARNING OBJECTIVES

After studying this chapter, you should be able to:

1. Prepare journal entries to account for stock investments.
2. Distinguish between the cost and equity methods of accounting for stock investments.
3. Describe the nature of parent and subsidiary corporations.
4. Prepare consolidated financial statements through the use of a consolidated statement work sheet.
5. Identify the differences between purchase accounting and pooling of interests accounting.
6. Describe the uses and limitations fo consolidated financial statements.
7. Define and use correctly the new terms in the glossary.

You may have read about a large company attempting to "take over" a smaller company by acquiring a controlling interest (more than 50% of the outstanding shares) in that "target" company. Some of these takeover attempts are "friendly" (not resisted by the target company) and some are "unfriendly" (resisted by the target company). If the attempt is successful, the two companies become one business entity for accounting purposes, and consolidated financial statements are prepared. The company that takes over another company is called the parent company; the company acquired is called the subsidiary company. This chapter discusses accounting for parent and subsidiary companies.

When a corporation purchases the stock of another corporation, the method of accounting for the stock investment depends on the corporation's **motivation** for making the investment and the **relative size** of the investment. A corporation's motivation for purchasing the stock of another company may be as (1) a temporary investment of excess cash; (2) a long-term investment in a substantial percentage of another company's stock to ensure a supply of a required raw material (for example, when large oil companies invest heavily in, or purchase outright, "wildcat" oil drilling companies); or (3) a long-term investment for expansion (when a company purchases another profitable company rather than starting a completely new business operation). On the balance sheet, the first type of investment is classified as a current asset, and the last two types are classified as long-term (noncurrent) investments. As explained in the chapter, the size of the investment determines whether the investment is accounted for by using the cost method or the equity method.

■ COST AND EQUITY METHODS

Two different methods can be used by an investor to account for investments in common stock: the cost and equity methods. The **cost method** is a method of accounting for stock investments in which the investor company records its investment at cost (price paid at acquisition) and does not adjust the investment account balance subsequently. Dividends received from the investee are credited to a Dividend Revenue account. The **equity method** is a method of accounting for stock investments where the investment is initially recorded at cost. The investment account is then adjusted periodically for the investor company's share of the investee's income, losses, and dividends as they are reported by the investee.

The Accounting Principles Board has identified the circumstances under which each method can be used. Each of those circumstances is illustrated in this chapter. The general rules for determining the appropriate method of accounting are summarized below:

Types of common stock investment	Method of accounting required by Accounting Principles Board* in most cases
All short-term investments	Cost
Long-term investments of:	
Less than 20%	Cost
20%–50%	Equity
More than 50%:	
Consolidated subsidiary	Cost or equity
Nonconsolidated subsidiary	Equity

* As is true in most instances in accounting, there are some exceptions to these requirements, but they are beyond the scope of this text.

■ ACCOUNTING FOR SHORT-TERM STOCK INVESTMENTS AND FOR LONG-TERM STOCK INVESTMENTS OF LESS THAN 50%

The cost method is used to account for all short-term stock investments. When a company owns less than 50% of the outstanding stock of another corporation as a long-term investment, one of two methods of accounting is used depending on the percentage of ownership. The cost method is used for long-term investments when the purchasing company owns 20% or less of the outstanding stock of the other company and does not exercise significant control over that company. The equity method is used when the purchasing company acquires from 20% to 50% of the outstanding stock, or when it holds less than 20% but still exercises significant control over the investee company. Thus, the cost method is used for all short-term investments as well as for almost all long-term stock investments of 20% or less.

Cost Method for Short-Term Investments and for Long-Term Investments of 20% or Less

Under the cost method, stock investments are recorded at cost—the cash paid in most instances. Most stocks are purchased from other investors (not the issuing company) through brokers who execute "trades" in an organized market, such as the New York Stock Exchange. Thus, cost will usually consist of the price paid for the shares, plus a broker's commission.

For example, assume that Brewer Corporation purchased as a temporary investment 1,000 shares of Cowen Company's $10 par value common stock at 14⅛, plus a $175 broker's commission. Stock prices are quoted in dollars and fractions of one dollar; thus, 14⅛ means $14.125 per share. The entry needed by Brewer to record its investment is:

```
Current Marketable Equity Securities (1,000 shares
   × $14.125 plus $175 commisssion) . . . . . . . . .    14,300
   Cash . . . . . . . . . . . . . . . . . . . . . .                14,300
Purchased 1,000 shares of Cowen common stock as a
short-term investment at 14⅛, plus commission.
```

If the stock had been purchased as a long-term investment, the account debited would have been **Noncurrent** Marketable Equity Securities. Note that the par value of Cowen's stock is not relevant to the investing corporation. Par value of shares owned is of little, if any, significance to the investing corporation.

Accounting for Cash Dividends Received.   Investments in stock provide dividend revenue. As a general rule, cash dividends are debited to Cash and credited to Dividend Revenue when received by the investor. The only exception to this general rule is when a dividend is declared in one accounting period that is payable in the next. This exception allows a company to record the revenue in the proper accounting period. Assume that Cowen Company declared a $1 per share cash dividend on December 1, 1987, to stockholders of record as of December 20, payable on January 15, 1988. The following entry should be made in 1987:

```
1987
Dec. 1  Dividends Receivable . . . . . . . . . . . . .    1,000
            Dividend Revenue  . . . . . . . . . . . .              1,000
        To record $1 per share cash dividend on Cowen
        common stock, payable January 15, 1988.
```

When the dividend is collected on January 15, Cash is debited and Dividends Receivable is credited:

```
1988
Jan. 15  Cash  .  .  .  .  .  .  .  .  .  .  .  .  .  .  .  .    1,000
              Dividends Receivable  .  .  .  .  .  .  .  .  .  .              1,000
         To record the receipt of a cash dividend.
```

Stock Dividends and Stock Splits.   As discussed in Chapter 16, a company might declare a stock dividend rather than a cash dividend. An investor does not recognize revenue upon receipt of the additional shares of stock from a stock dividend. The investor merely records the number of additional shares received and reduces the cost per share for each share held. For example, if Cowen Company distributed a 10% stock dividend in February 1988, Brewer Corporation, which held 1,000 shares at a cost of $14,300, would receive another 100 shares and would then hold 1,100 shares at a cost per share of $13 ($14,300/ 1,100 shares). Similarly, when a corporation declares a stock split, the investor would note the shares received and the reduction in the cost per share.

Sale of Stock Investments.   When shares are sold, the gain or loss on the sale is the difference between the net proceeds received and the carrying value of the shares sold. Assume, for example, that on May 1, 1988, Brewer sold 500 of the Cowen shares at $17 per share, less a $200 broker's commission. The entry needed to record the sale of shares at a gain is:

```
1988
May 1   Cash [(500 × $17) − $200]  .  .  .  .  .  .  .  .  .    8,300
             Current Marketable Equity Securities
                  (500 × $13)  .  .  .  .  .  .  .  .  .  .  .  .              6,500
             Gain on Sale of Stock Investments  .  .  .  .  .  .              1,800
        To record sale of 500 shares of Cowen common
        stock.
```

(Remember that the cost per share was reduced to $13 after the stock dividend was received in February 1988.)

The entries shown above are appropriate whenever less than 20% of the outstanding stock is held, regardless of whether the investment is temporary or long term. The only difference is in the use of the current or noncurrent distinction in the investment account title. Investments are classified as current or noncurrent, depending on the management's intention to hold the investment for a short period (one year or less) or a long period (more than one year).

Generally the cost of the above investments remains the carrying value until the investments are sold. The FASB has, however, required a year-end valuation procedure for such investments to provide better information to users of financial statements.

Subsequent Valuation of Stock Investments under the Cost Method

FASB Statement No. 12 (1975) governs the valuation of **marketable equity securities** that are being accounted for under the cost method. Marketable refers to the fact that the stocks are readily salable; equity securities are common and preferred stocks.

The FASB *Statement* requires companies to adjust the carrying value to the lower-of-cost-or-market (LCM) method at year-end for portfolios (groups) of these investment securities.[1] Current investments and noncurrent investments

---

[1] Lower-of-cost-or-market method was applied to inventories in Chapter 9.

in marketable equity securities are considered to be two separate investment portfolios, and LCM is applied independently to each of these portfolios.[2] Suppose the market value is lower than the cost. The write-down to market is journalized through the use of a **valuation account** called Allowance for Market Decline of Current (Noncurrent) Marketable Equity Securities. The valuation account is used rather than a direct credit to the investment account, because the LCM valuation is based on the **total** value of the securities held in each portfolio. Basing the valuation on the total value allows stock investments that have increased in value to offset other investments that have decreased in value.

Current Marketable Equity Securities. To illustrate the application of the LCM method to **current marketable equity securities,** assume that Hanson Company has the securities shown in Illustration 18.1 in its current investment stock portfolio.

Illustration 18.1

Stock Portfolio of Hanson Company

Company	No. of shares	Cost per share	Market price per share	Total cost	December 31, 1987, total market	Increase/ (decrease) in market value
A	200	$35	$40	7,000	$ 8,000	$ 1,000
B	400	10	15	4,000	6,000	2,000
C	100	90	50	9,000	5,000	(4,000)
				$20,000	$19,000	$(1,000)

Applying the LCM method reveals that the portfolio should be written down by $1,000—from $20,000 to $19,000. Note that the increases in the market values of Company A and Company B shares offset $3,000 of the $4,000 decrease in market value of the Company C shares, leaving only the net decrease of $1,000. The journal entry required at the end of 1987 is:

```
1987
Dec. 31  Net Unrealized Loss on Current Marketable
             Equity Securities  . . . . . . . . . . . .    1,000
                Allowance for Market Decline of Current
                    Marketable Equity Securities .  .  .  .  .  .  .         1,000
             To record unrealized loss from market decline of
             current marketable equity securities.
```

Note that the debit is to the account, Net Unrealized Loss on Current Marketable Equity Securities. This loss is called unrealized because the securities have not been sold. However, the loss is reported in the income statement. The credit in the above entry is to the valuation account, Allowance for Market Decline of Current Marketable Equity Securities, which is a contra account to the Current Marketable Equity Securities account. (This account is somewhat similar to the Allowance for Doubtful Accounts.) The securities and the contra account are reported in the balance sheet as follows:

> **December 31, 1987**
> **Partial Balance Sheet**
>
> Current assets:
>   Marketable equity securities (cost of $20,000 less
>   allowance for market decline of $1,000) $19,000

---

[2] A portfolio is simply a group of stock investments that a company holds at a given time.

If Hanson Company sold all its temporary investments on January 1, 1988, the company would receive $19,000 (assuming no change in market values from the previous day). The loss on the sale results from market changes in 1987 rather than in 1988; the LCM procedure placed that loss in the proper year.

Assume now that in 1988 Hanson sold the Company B shares for $6,000, a $2,000 gain over cost of the shares. The entry for the sale is:

Cash	6,000	
Current Marketable Equity Securities		4,000
Realized Gain on Sale of Securities		2,000
To record sale of securities.		

Note that the $2,000 gain on the sale of Company B stock is calculated without reference to the current balance in the allowance account. The $1,000 credit balance in the allowance account did not change the carrying value of any individual security. The securities are still being carried in the asset account at the actual cost paid for them. **Realized gains and losses are calculated by comparing the net proceeds from the sale with the actual cost of the securities sold.** No changes are made to the allowance account during the year when stock investments are bought or sold.

A subsequent recovery in the market value of the portfolio is recognized by reducing the allowance. This reduction in the allowance increases the carrying value of the portfolio, but the portfolio may never be carried at more than its original cost. Assume that at the end of 1988, Hanson Company again determined the cost and market value of its portfolio. Assume that total cost is $16,000 (the cost of the Company A [$7,000] and the Company C [$9,000] shares). Total market value is $15,600. Thus, an allowance of only $400 is needed to state the portfolio at LCM. Since the allowance has a $1,000 balance, the following entry is necessary to reduce the balance of the allowance to $400:

1988		
Dec. 31 Allowance for Market Decline of Current		
Marketable Equity Securities	600	
Recovery of Market Value of Current		
Marketable Equity Securities		600
To record gain from recovery of market value of		
current marketable equity securities.		

The account credited is an unrealized gain and is reported in the income statement. If the total market value had risen above $16,000, only $1,000 of the recovery could be recognized. This restriction prevents the stock from being carried at more than its original cost. The securities and the allowance are shown in the 1988 balance sheet as follows:

Partial Balance Sheet
December 31, 1988

Current assets:
  Marketable equity securities (cost of $16,000 less allowance
    for market decline of $400) $15,600

Noncurrent Marketable Equity Securities.   Assume a portfolio of noncurrent (or long-term) marketable equity securities has a cost of $32,000 and a current market value on December 31, 1987, of $31,000. The treatment of the loss depends on whether it results from a temporary decline in the market value of the **portfolio** or from a permanent decline in the value of an **individual security.** Assume first that the loss is related to a "temporary" decline in the portfolio. The required entry is:

```
1987
Dec. 31   Net Unrealized Loss on Noncurrent
                Marketable Equity Securities . . . . . . .      1,000
              Allowance for Market Decline of Noncurrent
                  Equity Securities . . . . . . . . . . .                  1,000
          To record unrealized loss from market decline of
          noncurrent equity securities.
```

Information from both of the above accounts would appear in the balance sheet as follows:

Partial Balance Sheet
December 31, 1987

Investments:	
Noncurrent marketable equity securities (cost of $32,000 less allowance for market decline of $1,000)	$ 31,000
Stockholders' equity:	
Capital stock	$xxx,xxx
Additional paid-in capital	x,xxx
Total paid-in capital	$xxx,xxx
Less: Unrealized loss on noncurrent marketable equity securities . .	1,000
	$xxx,xxx
Retained earnings	xx,xxx
Total stockholders' equity	$xxx,xxx

Note that the unrealized loss for noncurrent marketable equity securities appears in the balance sheet as a deduction from total paid-in capital rather than in the income statement (as it does for current marketable equity securities). Alternatively, the unrealized loss could be reported as a deduction from total stockholders' equity. The unrealized loss on noncurrent securities is **not** included in the determination of net income because it is not expected to be realized in the near future. These securities are being held on a long-term basis and will probably not be sold soon. Losses on current securities are included in net income because, being related to a current asset, they are more likely to be realized by the company in the next period.

Later recoveries of market value up to the original cost of $32,000 are debited to the allowance and credited to the unrealized loss account. Thus, if the market value of the noncurrent portfolio increases by $1,700 by December 31, 1988, the adjusting entry is:

```
1988
Dec. 31   Allowance for Market Decline of Noncurrent
                Marketable Equity Securities . . . . . . .      1,000
              Net Unrealized Loss on Noncurrent Marketable
                  Equity Securities . . . . . . . . . . .                  1,000
          To record recovery of market value of noncurrent
          marketable equity securities.
```

Only $1,000 of the $1,700 increase in market value may be recorded. Recording more than $1,000 of the increase in market value would result in valuing the securities at **more** than their original cost, and generally accepted accounting principles do not permit recording such an increase in value, and the associated gain, until the securities are actually sold. The $1,000 increase may be recorded, however, because it represents a recovery in the securities' market value up to their original cost.

If a loss on an individual noncurrent security is determined to be "permanent," it is recorded as a realized loss and deducted in determining net income. The entry to record a permanent loss of $1,400 reads:

Realized Loss on Noncurrent Marketable Equity Securities . .	1,400	
Noncurrent Marketable Equity Securities		1,400
To record loss in value of noncurrent marketable equity securities.		

No part of the $1,400 loss is subject to reversal if the market price of the stock recovers. **The stock's reduced value is now its "cost," and values in excess of cost are not recorded until a sale occurs.**

■ THE EQUITY METHOD FOR LONG-TERM INVESTMENTS OF BETWEEN 20% AND 50%

When one company purchases between 20% and 50% of the outstanding stock of another company as a long-term investment, the purchasing company is said to have significant control over that company. In certain cases a company may have significant control even when the investment is less than 20%. Under either of these circumstances, the investment must be accounted for under the **equity method.**

When the equity method is used in accounting for stock investments, the purchasing company must recognize its share of the **purchased** company's income, regardless of whether or not dividends are received. The logic behind this treatment is that the investing company may exercise control over the declaration of dividends and thereby manipulate its own income by influencing the investee's decision to declare (or not declare) dividends.

Thus, when the **investee** reports income or losses, the **investor** company must recognize its share of the investee's income or losses. For example, assume that the Tone Company owns 30% of the Butch Company and the Butch Company reports $50,000 net income in the current year. Under the equity method, the Tone Company will make the following entry as of the year-end:

Investment in Butch Company	15,000	
Income from Butch Company ($50,000 × 0.30)		15,000
To recognize 30% of Butch Company's net income.		

The $15,000 income from Butch Company would be reported on Tone Company's income statement in the current year. The investment account has also increased by $15,000.

Furthermore, because dividends are a distribution of income to the owners of the corporation, if Butch Company declares and pays $20,000 in dividends, the following entry would also be required for the Tone Company:

Cash	6,000	
Investment in Butch Company ($20,000 × 0.30)		6,000
To record receipt of 30% of dividends paid by Butch Company.		

Under the equity method illustrated in these two entries, the investment in Butch Company account will always reflect Tone's 30% interest in the net assets of Butch Company.

■ ACCOUNTING FOR STOCK INVESTMENTS OF MORE THAN 50%

Many companies have expanded in recent years by purchasing a major portion, or all, of another company's outstanding voting stock. The purpose of such acquisitions ranges from seeking to ensure a source of raw materials (such as oil), desiring to enter into a new industry, or simply to receive income on the investment. Both corporations still remain separate legal entities, regardless of the investment purpose. In this section you will study how to account for business combinations.

Parent and Subsidiary Corporations

A corporation that owns more than 50% of the outstanding voting common stock of another corporation is referred to as the **parent company.** The corporation acquired and controlled by the parent company is known as the **subsidiary company.**

A parent company and its subsidiaries maintain their own accounting records and prepare their own financial statements. But, since the parent and its subsidiaries are **controlled** by a central management and are related to each other, the parent company usually is **required** to prepare one set of financial statements as if the parent and its subsidiaries taken together were a single enterprise. **Consolidated statements** are the financial statements that result from combining the parent's financial statement amounts with those of its subsidiaries. Preparation of consolidated statements is discussed in this section. Consolidated statements **must be prepared** when (1) one company owns a majority (more than 50%) of the outstanding voting common stock of another company and (2) the two companies are not in markedly dissimilar businesses. A bank and a manufacturing company, for example, are in markedly dissimilar businesses; they would not be required to present consolidated financial statements even if one owned a majority of the other.

Illustration 18.2 shows the consolidation policies for a sample of 600 companies for the years 1980–83. Most of the companies consolidated all significant subsidiaries, but approximately 170 companies did not. The unconsolidated subsidiaries were too dissimilar to the parent company's operations.

Eliminations

Financial transactions involving a parent and one of its subsidiaries or between two of the subsidiaries are called **intercompany transactions.** In preparing con-

Illustration 18.2

Consolidation Policies

	1983	1982	1981	1980
Nature of subsidiaries not consolidated:				
Finance related:				
Credit	97	102	94	97
Insurance	60	60	53	49
Leasing	18	21	24	22
Banks	5	4	6	5
Real estate	31	33	29	27
Foreign	17	20	19	28
	228	240	225	228
Number of companies:				
Consolidating all significant subsidiaries	419	414	423	422
Consolidating certain significant subsidiaries	172	180	168	170
Not presenting consolidated financial statements	9	6	9	8
Total companies	600	600	600	600

Source: American Institute of Certified Public Accountants, *Accounting Trends & Techniques* (New York: AICPA, 1984), p. 42.

solidated financial statements, the effects of intercompany transactions must be eliminated by making **elimination entries.** Elimination entries allow the presentation of all account balances as if the parent and its subsidiaries were a single economic enterprise. **Elimination entries are made only on a consolidated statement work sheet, not in the accounting records of the parent or subsidiaries.** After elimination entries are prepared, the amounts remaining for each account on the work sheet are totaled and used to prepare the consolidated financial statements.

To illustrate the need for elimination entries, assume Y Company organized the Z Company, receiving all of Z Company's $100,000 par value common stock for $100,000 cash. The parent records the following entry on its books:

```
Investment in Z Company . . . . . . . . . . . . . .   100,000
    Cash  . . . . . . . . . . . . . . . . . . . .            100,000
    To record an investment in Z Company. Purchased 100% of
    Z Company stock.
```

Z Company, the subsidiary, records the following on its books:

```
Cash  . . . . . . . . . . . . . . . . . . . . . .   100,000
    Common Stock  . . . . . . . . . . . . . . . .            100,000
    To record issuance of all of the common stock to Y
    Company.
```

An elimination entry is needed to offset the parent company's subsidiary investment account against the stockholders' equity accounts of the subsidiary. When the consolidated balance sheet is prepared, the required elimination on the work sheet is:

```
Common Stock—Z Company  . . . . . . . . . . . .   100,000
    Investment in Z Company  . . . . . . . . . . .            100,000
```

This elimination is required because the parent company's investment in the stock of the subsidiary actually represents an equity in the net assets of the subsidiary. Unless the investment is eliminated, the same resources will appear twice on the consolidated balance sheet—first as the investment account of the parent and second as the assets of the subsidiary. The elimination of Z Company's common stock is necessary to avoid double counting stockholders' equity. Viewing the two companies as if they were one, the Z Company common stock is really not outstanding; it is held within the consolidated group.

Consolidated financial statements present financial data as though the companies were a single entity. Since no entity can owe an amount to itself or be due an amount from itself, intercompany receivables and payables (amounts owed to and due from companies within the consolidated group) are items that must be eliminated during the preparation of consolidated financial statements. For example, assume a subsidiary company owes its parent company $5,000, as evidenced by a $5,000 note receivable on the parent's books and a $5,000 note payable on the subsidiary's books. In this case, no debt is owed to or due from any entity outside the consolidated enterprise, so those balances would be eliminated by an entry like the following that offsets the note receivable against the note payable:

```
Note Payable (subsidiary company) . . . . . . . . . .    5,000
        Note Receivable (parent company) . . . . . . . . .           5,000
    To eliminate intercompany receivables and payables.
```

Other intercompany balances would be similarly eliminated when consolidated statements are prepared.

■ CONSOLIDATED BALANCE SHEET AT TIME OF ACQUISITION

Acquisition of Subsidiary at Book Value

To combine assets and liabilities of a parent company and its subsidiaries, a consolidated statement work sheet similar to the one shown in Illustration 18.3 is prepared. A **consolidated statement work sheet** is an informal record on which elimination entries are made for the purpose of showing account balances as if the parent and its subsidiaries were a single economic enterprise. The first two columns of the work sheet show assets, liabilities, and stockholders' equity of the parent and subsidiary as they appear on each corporation's individual balance sheet. The pair of columns labeled Eliminations allows intercompany items to be offset and consequently eliminated from the consolidated statement. The final column shows the amounts that will appear on the consolidated balance sheet.

The work sheet shown in Illustration 18.3 consolidates the accounts of P Company and its subsidiary, S Company, on January 1, 1987. P Company acquired S Company on January 1, 1987, by purchasing all of its outstanding voting common stock for $106,000 cash, which was the **book value** of the stock. Book value is equal to stockholders' equity, or net assets. Thus, common stock ($100,000) plus retained earnings ($6,000) equals $106,000. When P Company acquired the S Company stock, P Company made the following entry:

```
Investment in S Company  . . . . . . . . . . . . .   106,000
        Cash . . . . . . . . . . . . . . . . . . . . . . . .          106,000
    To record investment in S Company.
```

The investment appears as an asset on P Company's balance sheet. By buying the subsidiary's stock, the parent acquired a 100% equity, or ownership, interest in the subsidiary's net assets. Thus, if both the investment account

Illustration 18.3

*Consolidated
Balance Sheet
Work Sheet*

P COMPANY AND SUBSIDIARY S COMPANY
Work Sheet for Consolidated Balance Sheet
January 1, 1987 (date of acquisition)

	P Company	S Company	Eliminations Debit	Eliminations Credit	Consolidated Amounts
Assets					
Cash	26,000	12,000			38,000
Notes receivable	5,000			(2) 5,000	
Accounts receivable, net	24,000	15,000			39,000
Inventory	35,000	30,000			65,000
Investment in S Company	106,000			(1) 106,000	
Equipment, net	41,000	15,000			56,000
Buildings, net	65,000	35,000			100,000
Land	20,000	10,000			30,000
	322,000	117,000			328,000
Liabilities and Stockholders' Equity					
Accounts payable	18,000	6,000			24,000
Notes payable		5,000	(2) 5,000		
Common stock	250,000	100,000	(1) 100,000		250,000
Retained earnings	54,000	6,000	(1) 6,000		54,000
	322,000	117,000	111,000	111,000	328,000

and the subsidiary's assets appear on the consolidated balance sheet, the same
resources will be counted twice. The Common Stock and Retained Earnings
accounts of the subsidiary also represent an equity interest in the subsidiary's
assets. Therefore, P's investment in S Company must be offset against S Company's stockholders' equity accounts so that the subsidiary's assets and the ownership interest in these assets appear only once on the consolidated statement.
This elimination is accomplished by entry *(1)* under eliminations on the work
sheet. The entry debits S Company's Common Stock for $100,000 and Retained
Earnings for $6,000 and credits Investment in S Company for $106,000. In
journal entry form, the elimination entry is:

```
Common Stock . . . . . . . . . . . . . . . . .   100,000
Retained Earnings . . . . . . . . . . . . . . .     6,000
    Investment in S Company . . . . . . . . . .               106,000
    To eliminate investment account and subsidiary stockholders'
    equity.
```

Entry *(2)* is required to eliminate the effect of an intercompany transaction
(intercompany debt in this case). On the date it acquired S Company, P Company loaned S Company $5,000. The loan is recorded as a $5,000 note receivable
on P's books and a $5,000 note payable on S's books. If the elimination entry
is not made on the work sheet, the consolidated balance sheet will show $5,000
owed to the consolidated enterprise **by itself.** From the viewpoint of the consolidated entity, neither an asset nor a liability exists. Therefore, entry *(2)* is made
on the work sheet to eliminate both the asset and liability. The entry debits

Notes Payable and credits Notes Receivable for $5,000. In general journal form, entry *(2)* is:

```
Notes Payable . . . . . . . . . . . . . . . . . . .     5,000
     Notes Receivable . . . . . . . . . . . . . . . .              5,000
     To eliminate intercompany payable and receivable.
```

In making elimination entries, it is important to understand that **the entries are made only on the consolidated statement work sheet; no elimination entries are made in the accounting records of either P Company or S Company.**

Acquisition of Subsidiary at a Cost above or below Book Value

In the previous illustration, P Company acquired 100% of S Company at a cost **equal** to book value. In some cases, subsidiaries may be acquired at a cost **greater than** or **less than** book value. For example, assume P Company purchased 100% of S Company's outstanding voting common stock for $125,000 (instead of $106,000). The book value of this stock is $106,000. Cost exceeds book value by $19,000. P Company's management may have paid more than book value because (1) the subsidiary's earnings prospects justify paying a price greater than book value or (2) the total fair market value of the subsidiary's assets exceeds their total book value.

According to the Accounting Principles Board *(APB Opinion No. 16),* in cases where cost exceeds book value because of expected above-average earnings, the excess should be labeled goodwill on the consolidated balance sheet. **Goodwill** is an intangible value attached to a business primarily due to above-average earnings prospects. On the other hand, if the excess is attributable to the belief that assets of the subsidiary are undervalued, then the asset values on the consolidated balance sheet should be increased to the extent of the excess.[3] In Illustration 18.4, it is assumed that $4,000 is due to the undervaluation of land owned by the company and the remaining $15,000 of the excess of cost over book value is attributable to expected above-average earnings. As a result, $4,000 of the $19,000 excess is added to Land, and the other $15,000 is identified as "Goodwill" on the work sheet and on the balance sheet (see Illustration 18.5).

The goodwill is established as part of the first elimination entry. Elimination entry *(1)* in Illustration 18.4 involves debits to the subsidiary's Common Stock for $100,000 and Retained Earnings for $6,000 and a credit to the parent's investment account for $125,000. Land is debited for $4,000, and Goodwill is debited for $15,000. In journal form, entry *(1)* is:

```
Common Stock . . . . . . . . . . . . . . . . . .    100,000
Retained Earnings . . . . . . . . . . . . . . . .      6,000
Land . . . . . . . . . . . . . . . . . . . . . . .      4,000
Goodwill . . . . . . . . . . . . . . . . . . . . .     15,000
     Investment in S Company . . . . . . . . . . .              125,000
     To eliminate investment and subsidiary stockholders' equity and
     to establish increased value of land and goodwill.
```

Entry *(2)* is the same as elimination entry *(2)* in Illustration 18.3. Entry *(2)* eliminates the intercompany loan by debiting Notes Payable and crediting Notes Receivable for $5,000.

After these elimination entries are made, the remaining amounts are com-

---

[3] *APB Accounting Principles* (Chicago: Commerce Clearing House, Inc., 1973), vol. II, p. 6655.

Illustration 18.4

Consolidated Balance Sheet Work Sheet

P COMPANY AND SUBSIDIARY S COMPANY
Work Sheet for Consolidated Balance Sheet
January 1, 1987 (date of acquisition)

	P Company	S Company	Eliminations Debit	Eliminations Credit	Consolidated Amounts
Assets					
Cash	7,000	12,000			19,000
Notes receivable	5,000			(2) 5,000	
Accounts receivable, net	24,000	15,000			39,000
Inventory	35,000	30,000			65,000
Investment in S Company	125,000			(1) 125,000	
Equipment, net	41,000	15,000			56,000
Buildings, net	65,000	35,000			100,000
Land	20,000	10,000	(1) 4,000		34,000
Goodwill			(1) 15,000		15,000
	322,000	117,000			328,000
Liabilities and Stockholders' Equity					
Accounts payable	18,000	6,000			24,000
Notes payable		5,000	(2) 5,000		
Common stock	250,000	100,000	(1) 100,000		250,000
Retained earnings	54,000	6,000	(1) 6,000		54,000
	322,000	117,000	130,000	130,000	328,000

bined and extended to the column labeled "Consolidated Amounts." The amounts in this column are then used to prepare the consolidated balance sheet shown in Illustration 18.5. Notice that the $15,000 debit to Goodwill is carried to the Consolidated Amounts column and appears as an asset in the consolidated balance sheet.

Under some circumstances a parent company may pay less than book value of the subsidiary's net assets. In such cases it is highly unlikely that a "bargain" purchase has been made. The most logical explanation for the price paid is that some of the subsidiary's assets are overvalued. The Accounting Principles Board requires that the excess of book value over cost be used to reduce proportionately the value of the noncurrent assets acquired.[4]

Acquisition of Less than 100% of Subsidiary

Sometimes a parent company acquires less than 100% of the outstanding voting common stock of a subsidiary. For example, assume P Company acquired 80% (instead of 100%) of S Company's outstanding voting common stock. P Company is the majority stockholder, but another group of stockholders exists that owns the remaining 20% of the stock. Stockholders who own less than 50% of a subsidiary's outstanding voting common stock are called minority stockholders, and their claim, or interest in the subsidiary is called the **minority**

---

[4] Ibid., p. 6655.

Illustration 18.5

Consolidated Balance Sheet

P COMPANY AND SUBSIDIARY S COMPANY
Consolidated Balance Sheet
January 1, 1987

Assets

Current assets:

Cash	$ 19,000	
Accounts receivable, net	39,000	
Inventory	65,000	
Total current assets		$123,000

Property, plant, and equipment

Equipment, net	$ 56,000	
Buildings, net	100,000	
Land	34,000	
Total property, plant, and equipment		190,000
Goodwill		15,000
Total assets		$328,000

Liabilities and Stockholders' Equity

Current liabilities:

Accounts payable		$ 24,000

Stockholders' equity:

Common stock	$250,000	
Retained earnings	54,000	
Total stockholders' equity		304,000
Total liabilities and stockholders' equity		$328,000

---

interest. Minority stockholders have an interest in the subsidiary's net assets and share subsidiary income or loss with the parent company.

Illustration 18.6 shows the elimination entries that are required when P Company purchases 80% of S Company's stock for $90,000. The book value of the stock acquired by P Company is $84,800 (80% of $106,000). Assume no assets are undervalued. Therefore, the excess of cost ($90,000) over book value ($84,800) of $5,200 can be attributed to S Company's above-average earnings prospects (goodwill).

The first elimination entry *(1)* eliminates S Company's stockholders' equity by debiting Common Stock for $100,000 and Retained Earnings for $6,000. Minority interest is established by crediting a Minority Interest account for $21,200 (20% of $106,000). The investment account is eliminated by crediting Investment in S Company for $90,000. The debit required to make the debits equal the credits is $5,200. The $5,200 is debited to Goodwill. In journal form, the elimination entry *(1)* is:

Common Stock	100,000	
Retained Earnings	6,000	
Goodwill	5,200	
Investment in S Company		90,000
Minority Interest		21,200

To eliminate investment and subsidiary's stockholders' equity and to establish minority interest and goodwill.

The second elimination entry *(2)* is the same as in the preceding illustrations. The entry eliminates intercompany debt by debiting Notes Payable and crediting Notes Receivable for $5,000.

On the consolidated balance sheet (Illustration 18.7), minority interest appears between the liabilities and stockholders' equity sections.

Illustration 18.6

Consolidated Balance Sheet Work Sheet

P COMPANY AND SUBSIDIARY S COMPANY
Work Sheet for Consolidated Balance Sheet
January 1, 1987 (date of acquisition)

	P Company	S Company	Eliminations Debit	Eliminations Credit	Consolidated Amounts
Assets					
Cash	42,000	12,000			54,000
Notes receivable	5,000			(2) 5,000	
Accounts receivable, net	24,000	15,000			39,000
Inventory	35,000	30,000			65,000
Investment in S Company	90,000			(1) 90,000	
Equipment, net	41,000	15,000			56,000
Buildings, net	65,000	35,000			100,000
Land	20,000	10,000			30,000
Goodwill			(1) 5,200		5,200
	322,000	117,000			349,200
Liabilities and Stockholders' Equity					
Accounts payable	18,000	6,000			24,000
Notes payable		5,000	(2) 5,000		
Common stock	250,000	100,000	(1) 100,000		250,000
Retained earnings	54,000	6,000	(1) 6,000		54,000
Minority interest				(1) 21,200	21,200
	322,000	117,000	116,200	116,200	349,200

Illustration 18.7

Consolidated Balance Sheet

P COMPANY AND SUBSIDIARY S COMPANY
Consolidated Balance Sheet
January 1, 1987

Assets

Current assets:
Cash . . . . $ 54,000
Accounts receivable, net 39,000
Inventory 65,000
   Total current assets $158,000

Property, plant, and equipment:
Equipment, net . . . . $ 56,000
Buildings, net 100,000
Land 30,000
   Total property, plant, and equipment . .   186,000
Goodwill   5,200
Total assets $349,200

Liabilities and Stockholders' Equity

Liabilities:
Accounts payable . . . . $ 24,000
Minority interest   21,200
Stockholders' equity:
Common stock $250,000
Retained earnings 54,000
   Total stockholders' equity   304,000
Total liabilities and stockholders' equity . . $349,200

■ ACCOUNTING FOR INCOME, LOSSES, AND DIVIDENDS OF A SUBSIDIARY

If a subsidiary is operating profitably, its net assets and retained earnings increase. When the subsidiary pays dividends, both the parent company and minority stockholders share in the distribution. All transactions of the subsidiary are recorded in the accounting records of the subsidiary in a normal manner.

As noted earlier, two different methods used by an investor to account for investments in common stock are the **cost** and **equity methods.** The general rules for determining the appropriate method of accounting are again summarized below.

Percent of outstanding voting common stock of investee owned by investor	Method of accounting required by Accounting Principles Board in most cases
Less than 20%	Cost
20%–50%	Equity
More than 50%:	
Consolidated subsidiary	Cost or equity
Nonconsolidated subsidiary . . .	Equity

According to the table, a parent company can use either the cost or equity method of accounting for its investment in a consolidated subsidiary. This choice is allowed because the investment account is eliminated during the consolidation process; therefore, the results are identical after consolidation.

Cost Method for Investments in Subsidiaries

Under the cost method, the parent (investor) company records its investment in a subsidiary at cost (price paid at acquisition) and does not adjust the investment account balance subsequently. Dividends received from the subsidiary (investee) are recorded by debiting Cash and crediting Dividend Revenue. Thus, the investment account balance normally does not change under the cost method.

Equity Method for Investments in Subsidiaries

The equity method for investments in subsidiaries works just as we described earlier when applied to investments of 20% to 50% in nonconsolidated subsidiaries.

Under the equity method, as with the cost method, the parent company initially records its investment at cost. The major difference between the two methods is that the equity method calls for the investment account to be adjusted periodically for the parent company's share of the subsidiary's income, losses, and dividends as they are reported by the subsidiary. The parent company's share of the subsidiary's income is debited to the investment account and credited to an account labeled Income of S (subsidiary) Company.

For example, assume the subsidiary S Company, mentioned in the preceding illustrations, earned $20,000 during 1987. P Company owns 80% of S Company. P Company would record its share of S Company's income in the following manner:

```
Investment in S Company  . . . . . . . . . . .  . . . . .     16,000
     Income of S Company ($20,000 × 0.80) . . . . . . . .                16,000
     To record 80% of subsidiary's income.
```

The $16,000 debit to the investment account **increases the parent's equity in the subsidiary company.** The Income of S Company account will be closed at the end of the period to Income Summary, which then is closed to P Company's Retained Earnings.

If a subsidiary incurs a loss, the parent company debits a loss account and credits the investment account for the parent's share of the loss. For example, assume S Company incurs a loss of $10,000 in 1988. Since P Company still owns 80% of S Company, P Company records its share of the loss as follows:

```
Loss of S Company ($10,000 × 0.80)  . . . . . . . . .  . .     8,000
     Investment in S Company .  . . . . . . . . . . . .                  8,000
     To record 80% of subsidiary's loss.
```

The $8,000 debit is closed first to Income Summary, which then is closed to Retained Earnings; the $8,000 **credit reduces P Company's equity in the subsidiary.**

When a subsidiary declares and pays a dividend, the assets and retained earnings of the subsidiary are reduced by the dividend payment amount. When the parent company receives its share of the dividends, it debits the asset received (Cash, in this case) and credits the investment account. For instance, assume S Company declares a cash dividend of $8,000 in 1987. P Company's share of the dividend amounts to $6,400 ($8,000 × 0.80) and is recorded as follows:

```
Cash   . . . . . . . . . . . . . . . . . . . . .  . . . .     6,400
     Investment in S Company .  . . . . . . . . . . . . .                6,400
     To record dividend received from subsidiary.
```

The receipt of the dividend **reduces the parent's equity in the subsidiary** as shown by the credit to the investment account.

As noted earlier, a company may purchase all or part of another firm at more than book value and create goodwill on the consolidated balance sheet. The Accounting Principles Board in *APB Opinion No. 17* requires that all goodwill be amortized over a period not to exceed 40 years. This amortization is necessary under the equity method, but will be left to a more advanced text.

■ CONSOLIDATED FINANCIAL STATEMENTS AT A DATE AFTER ACQUISITION

As you have just seen, under the equity method the investment account on the parent company's books increases and decreases as the parent records its share of the income, losses, and dividends reported by the subsidiary. Thus, the balance in the investment account differs after acquisition from its balance on the date of acquisition. Consequently, the amounts eliminated on the consolidated statement work sheet will differ from year to year. As an illustration, assume the following facts:

1. P Company acquired 100% of the outstanding voting common stock of S Company on January 1, 1987. P Company paid $121,000 for stockholders' equity totaling $106,000. The excess of cost over book value is attributable to (a) an undervaluation of land amounting to $4,000 and (b) the remainder to S Company's above-average earnings prospects.
2. During 1987, S Company earned $20,000 from operations.
3. On December 31, 1987, S Company paid a cash dividend of $8,000.
4. S Company owes P Company $5,000 on a note at December 31.
5. Including its share (100%) of S Company's income, P Company earned $31,000 during 1987.
6. P Company paid a cash dividend of $10,000 during December 1987.
7. P Company uses the equity method of accounting for its investment in S Company.

The financial statements for the two companies as of December 31, 1987, are given in the first two columns of Illustration 18.8.

The type of work sheet shown in Illustration 18.8 will be used to prepare a consolidated income statement, statement of retained earnings, and balance sheet. Notice that in Illustration 18.8, P Company has a balance of $20,000 in its Income of S Company account and a balance of $133,000 in its Investment in S Company account. These balances are the result of the following journal entries actually made by P Company in 1987:

```
1987
Jan.  1  Investment in S Company  .  .  .  .  .   .  .  .  .  .   121,000
              Cash    .  .  .  .  .  .  .  .  .  .  .  .  .  .  .  .  .         121,000
         To record 100% investment in subsidiary.

Dec. 31  Investment in S Company  .  .  .  .  .  .  .  .  .  .    20,000
              Income of S Company    .  .  .  .  .  .  .  .  .          20,000
         To record income of subsidiary.

Dec. 31  Cash  .  .  .  .  .  .  .  .  .  .  .  .  .  .  .  .  .  .  .     8,000
              Investment in S Company   .  .  .  .  .  .  .  .          8,000
         To record dividends received from subsidiary.
```

The elimination entries on the work sheet in Illustration 18.8 are explained below.

Entry (1): During the year, S Company earned $20,000. P Company increased its investment account balance by $20,000. The first entry (1) on the work sheet eliminates the subsidiary's income from the investment account and Income of S Company ($20,000). This entry reverses the entries made on the books of P Company to recognize the parent's share of the subsidiary's income (December 31 entry above).

Entry (2): When S Company paid its cash dividend, P Company debited Cash and credited the investment account for $8,000 (December

Illustration 18.8

Consolidated Work
Sheet One Year after
Acquisition

P COMPANY AND SUBSIDIARY S COMPANY
Work Sheet for Consolidated Financial Statements
December 31, 1987

	P Company	S Company	Eliminations Debit	Eliminations Credit	Consolidated Amounts
Income Statement					
Revenue from sales	397,000	303,000			700,000
Income of S Company	20,000		(1) 20,000		
Cost of goods sold	(250,000)	(180,000)			(430,000)
Expenses (excluding de-					
preciation and taxes)	(100,000)	(80,000)			(180,000)
Depreciation expense	(7,400)	(5,000)			(12,400)
Income tax expense	(28,600)	(18,000)			(46,600)
Net income—carried forward	31,000	20,000			31,000
Statement of Retained Earnings					
Retained earnings— January 1:					
P Company	54,000				54,000
S Company		6,000	(3) 6,000		
Net income— brought forward	31,000	20,000			31,000
	85,000	26,000			85,000
Dividends:					
P Company	(10,000)				(10,000)
S Company		(8,000)		(2) 8,000	
Retained earnings— December 31— carried forward	75,000	18,000			75,000
Balance Sheet Assets					
Cash	38,000	16,000			54,000
Notes receivable	5,000			(4) 5,000	
Accounts receivable, net	25,000	18,000			43,000
Inventory	40,000	36,000			76,000
Investment in S Company	133,000		(2) 8,000	(3) 121,000	
				(1) 20,000	
Equipment, net	36,900	12,000			48,900
Buildings, net	61,700	33,000			94,700
Land	20,000	10,000	(3) 4,000		34,000
Goodwill			(3) 11,000		11,000
	359,600	125,000			361,600
Liabilities and Stockholders' Equity					
Accounts payable	19,600	2,000			21,600
Notes payable	15,000	5,000	(4) 5,000		15,000
Common stock	250,000	100,000	(3) 100,000		250,000
Retained earnings— brought forward	75,000	18,000			75,000
	359,600	125,000	154,000	154,000	361,600

31 entry above). The second entry *(2)* restores the investment account to its balance before the dividends from S Company were deducted. That is, P Company's investment account is debited and S Company's dividends account is credited for $8,000. On a consolidated basis, a company cannot pay a dividend to itself.

Entry *(3):* This entry eliminates the original investment account balance ($121,000) and the subsidiary's stockholders' equity accounts as of the date of acquisition (retained earnings of $6,000 and common stock of $100,000). The entry also establishes goodwill of $11,000 and increases land by $4,000 to account for the excess of acquisition cost over book value.

After the first three entries have been made, the investment account contains a zero balance from the viewpoint of the consolidated entity.

Entry *(4):* This entry eliminates the intercompany debt of $5,000.

After the eliminations have been made, the corresponding amounts are added together and placed in the Consolidated Amounts column. The net income row in the Income Statement section is carried forward to the net income row in the Statement of Retained Earnings section. Likewise, the ending retained earnings row in the Statement of Retained Earnings section is carried forward to the retained earnings row in the Balance Sheet section. The final work sheet column is then used to prepare the consolidated income statement (Illustration 18.9), consolidated statement of retained earnings (Illustration 18.10), and consolidated balance sheet (Illustration 18.11).[5] As stated earlier, amortization of goodwill is ignored in the illustration.

■ PURCHASE VERSUS POOLING OF INTERESTS

In the illustrations in this chapter, it has been assumed that the parent company acquired the subsidiary's common stock in exchange for cash. The acquiring company could also have used assets other than cash in the exchange. This kind of transaction—the exchange of cash or other assets for the common stock of another company—is called a purchase. When assets other than cash are used, the cost of the acquired company's stock is the fair market value of the assets given up or of the stock received, whichever can be more clearly and objectively determined.

Another way a company can acquire the common stock of another company is to issue common stock of its own in exchange for the other company's common stock. In such cases, the stockholders of both companies maintain a joint ownership interest in the combined company. Such a business combination involving the issuance of common stock in exchange for common stock is

---

[5] Appendix A at the back of the text shows consolidated financial statements for an actual corporation.

Illustration 18.9

Consolidated Income Statement

P COMPANY AND SUBSIDIARY S COMPANY
Consolidated Income Statement
For the Year Ended December 31, 1987

Revenue from sales		$700,000
Cost of goods sold		430,000
Gross margin		$270,000
Expenses (excluding depreciation and taxes)	$180,000	
Depreciation expense	12,400	
Income tax expense	46,600	239,000
Net income		$ 31,000

Illustration 18.10

Consolidated Statement of Retained Earnings

P COMPANY AND SUBSIDIARY S COMPANY
Consolidated Statement of Retained Earnings
For the Year Ended December 31, 1987

Retained earnings, January 1, 1987	$54,000
Net income	31,000
	$85,000
Dividends	10,000
Retained earnings, December 31, 1987	$75,000

Illustration 18.11

Consolidated Balance Sheet

P COMPANY AND SUBSIDIARY S COMPANY
Consolidated Balance Sheet
December 31, 1987

Assets

Current assets:		
Cash	$ 54,000	
Accounts receivable, net	43,000	
Inventory	76,000	
Total current assets		$173,000
Property, plant, and equipment:		
Equipment, net	$ 48,900	
Buildings, net	94,700	
Land	34,000	
Total property, plant, and equipment		177,600
Goodwill		11,000
Total assets		$361,600

Liabilities and Stockholders' Equity

Current liabilities:		
Accounts payable	$ 21,600	
Notes payable	15,000	
Total liabilities		$36,600
Stockholders' equity:		
Common stock	$250,000	
Retained earnings	75,000	
Total stockholders' equity		325,000
Total liabilities and stockholders' equity		$361,600

classified as a pooling of interests if it meets all the criteria cited in *APB Opinion No. 16.* If a combination resulting from an exchange of stock does not qualify as a pooling of interests, it must be recorded as a purchase.

The purchase and pooling of interests methods are **not** alternatives that can be applied to the same situation. Given the circumstances surrounding a particular business combination, only one of the two methods—purchase or pooling of interests—is appropriate. *APB Opinion No. 16* specifies 12 conditions that must be met before a business combination can be classified as a pooling of interests. Two of these conditions are: (1) the combination must be effected in one transaction or be completed within one year in accordance with a specific plan, and (2) one corporation must issue only its common stock in exchange for 90% or more of the voting common stock of another company. **If all 12 conditions specified by the APB are met, the resulting business combination must be accounted for as a pooling of interests. Otherwise, the purchase method must be used to account for the combination.**

When the pooling of interests method is used, the parent company's investment is recorded at the **book value of the subsidiary's net assets** (assets minus liabilities). Since the investment is recorded at the book value of the subsidiary's net assets, there can be no goodwill or changes in asset valuations from consolidation. The subsidiary's retained earnings at date of acquisition become a part of the consolidated retained earnings, whereas under the purchase method they do not. Also, under the pooling of interests method, all subsidiary income for the year of acquisition is included in the consolidated net income in the year of acquisition. Under the purchase method only that portion of the subsidiary's income that arises after the date of acquisition is included in consolidated net income.

From the above discussion, it should be apparent that these two methods will lead to significant differences in financial statement amounts. For instance, under the purchase method, any excess of investment cost over the book value of the ownership interest acquired must be used to increase the value of any assets that are undervalued or must be recognized as goodwill from consolidation. Under the pooling of interests method, on the other hand, book value—rather than cost—is the amount of the investment. Thus, whenever cost exceeds book value, either more depreciation or more amortization will be recorded under the purchase method than under the pooling of interests method, and consolidated net income will be smaller under the purchase method than under the pooling of interests method.

Illustration 18.12 shows the number of business combinations involving the two methods that occurred in a sample of 600 companies for the years 1980–83. The purchase method was used much more extensively than the pooling of interests method.

Illustration 18.12

Business Combinations

	1983	1982	1981	1980
Pooling of interests . .	26	24	30	34
Purchase method . .	154	145	156	159

Source: Based on American Institute of Certified Public Accountants, *Accounting Trends & Techniques* (New York: AICPA, 1984), p. 47.

■ USES AND LIMITATIONS OF CONSOLIDATED STATEMENTS

Consolidated statements are of primary importance to stockholders, managers, and directors of the parent company. The parent company benefits from the income and other financial strengths of the subsidiary. Likewise, the parent company suffers from a subsidiary's losses.

On the other hand, consolidated statements are of very limited use to the creditors and minority stockholders of the subsidiary. The subsidiary's creditors have a claim against the subsidiary alone; they cannot look to the parent company for payment. Minority stockholders in the subsidiary do not benefit or suffer from the parent company's operations. They benefit only from the subsidiary's income and financial strengths; they suffer only from the subsidiary's losses and financial weaknesses. Therefore, the subsidiary's creditors and minority stockholders are more interested in the subsidiary's individual financial statements than in the consolidated statements.

■ *SUMMARY*

When one corporation purchases the stock of another corporation, the method of accounting for the investment depends on the investor company's motivation for making the investment and the relative size of the investment. Investors account for investments in common stock by using the cost method or the equity method.

All short-term investments in stock and all long-term investments of less than 20% are accounted for by the cost method. Under the cost method, the investor company generally records cash dividends as revenue when they are received. Stock dividends received on investments and stock splits are not revenue; they merely reduce the cost per share of stock owned. When stock investments are sold, the gain or loss is equal to the difference between the selling price and the carrying value of the stock owned.

Under the cost method, when marketable equity securities are carried at cost, the lower-of-cost-or-market (LCM) method is applied to the current and noncurrent investment portfolios at the end of the accounting period. Total cost is compared to total market value of the stocks held in each portfolio. If market value is less than cost, a net unrealized loss exists that will be shown in a contra asset account, Allowance for Market Decline of Current (Noncurrent) Marketable Equity Securities. Net unrealized losses on current marketable equity securities are closed each period and reported in the income statement. By contrast, net unrealized losses on noncurrent marketable equity securities are not closed at the end of the period. Such losses on long-term stock investments are shown in the balance sheet as a debit-balanced stockholders' equity account.

The value of a corporation's investment portfolios may be increased to reflect a subsequent recovery in market value, but the portfolios may never be written up above their original cost. The net unrealized gains associated with the recovery in market value are handled in the same manner as the unrealized losses on market decline. If a loss associated with an individual noncurrent security is considered permanent, that loss is considered to be a realized loss and is reported as such in the income statement. The cost of that investment is reduced by the amount of the realized loss.

Long-term investments in stock must be accounted for under the equity method when (1) the investor purchases between 20% and 50% of the investee company's outstanding stock, (2) the investor purchases less than 20% of the investee company's outstanding stock but still exercises significant control over the investee, or (3) the investor owns more than 50% of the investee company but does not include the investee in the investor's consolidated financial statements. Under the equity method, the investment account balance is adjusted to reflect the investor's proportional ownership of the net assets of the investee. Investee income increases the investment account balance, while investee losses and dividends paid by the investee to the investor decrease that balance.

A corporation that owns a majority of the outstanding voting common stock of another corporation is called a parent company; the corporation controlled by the parent company is known as a subsidiary. The combined financial statements of the parent company and subsidiary company are called consolidated financial statements.

In preparing consolidated financial statements, work sheets are useful in making the necessary elimination entries. Such entries are required to eliminate certain intercompany items to show the assets, liabilities, stockholders' equity, revenues, expenses, and dividend accounts as if the parent and subsidiary were a single economic entity. Included in the items to be eliminated are the parent's investment account; subsidiary's stockholders' equity accounts; and intercompany receivables, payables, revenues, expenses, and dividends.

In certain instances, a parent company may acquire a subsidiary at a cost above or below the book value of the subsidiary's stock. Any excess of cost over book value increases the value of undervalued assets or is recognized as goodwill from consolidation. Any excess of book value over cost reduces the values of noncurrent assets acquired.

When a parent company owns less than 100% but more than 50% of the outstanding voting common stock of a subsidiary, the interest not owned by the parent company is called the minority interest and is held by minority stockholders. The minority stockholders have an interest in the subsidiary's net assets and share in the subsidiary's income with the parent company.

A business combination may be classified as either a purchase or a pooling of interests. A purchase results when the acquiring company exchanges cash, other assets, and debt securities (and, sometimes, preferred and common stock) for the net assets or the common stock of another company. A pooling of interests results when the acquiring company issues common stock in exchange for common stock and certain other conditions have been satisfied. Only one of the two methods is appropriate, given the circumstances surrounding a particular business combination.

Consolidated financial statements are of primary importance to the stockholders, managers, and directors of parent companies. On the other hand, the minority stockholders and creditors of the subsidiary companies are more interested in the individual subsidiary's financial statements.

Since it is fairly common to read that a large corporation has purchased a controlling interest in a smaller corporation, this chapter will help you understand what actually happens to the accounting records of the two companies when this occurs. In Chapter 19, we discuss a new financial statement—the statement of changes in financial position.

NEW TERMS INTRODUCED IN CHAPTER 18

Consolidated statement work sheet

An informal record on which elimination entries are made for the purpose of showing account balances as if the parent and its subsidiaries were a single economic enterprise (694).

Consolidated statements

The financial statements that result from combining the parent's financial statement amounts with those of its subsidiaries (after certain eliminations have been made). The consolidated statements reflect the financial position and results of operations of a single economic enterprise (692).

Cost method

A method of accounting for stock investments in which the investor company records its investment at cost (price paid at acquisition) and does not adjust the investment account balance subsequently. Dividends received from the investee are credited to a Dividend Revenue account (685).

Elimination entries

Entries made on a consolidated statement work sheet to remove certain intercompany items and transactions. Elimination entries allow the presentation of all account balances as if the parent and its subsidiaries were a single economic enterprise (693).

Equity method

A method of accounting for stock investments where the investment is initially recorded at cost. The investment account is then adjusted periodically for the investor company's share of the investee's income, losses, and dividends as they are reported by the investee (685).

Goodwill

An intangible value attached to a business primarily due to above-average earnings prospects (696).

Intercompany transactions

Financial transactions involving a parent and one of its subsidiaries or between two of the subsidiaries (692).

Minority interest

The claim, or interest, of the stockholders who own less than 50% of a subsidiary's outstanding voting common stock. The minority stockholders have an interest in the subsidiary's net assets and share the subsidiary's earnings with the parent company (697).

Parent company

A corporation that owns more than 50% of the outstanding voting common stock of another corporation (692).

Pooling of interests

A business combination that meets certain criteria specified in *APB Opinion No. 16,* including the issuance of common stock in exchange for common stock (706).

Purchase

A transaction in which one company issues cash or other assets to acquire common stock of another company (704).

Subsidiary company

A corporation acquired and controlled by a parent corporation; control is established by ownership of more than 50% of the subsidiary's outstanding voting common stock (692).

DEMONSTRATION PROBLEM 18–1

Following are selected transactions and other data for the Shane Company for 1987:

Transactions:

Mar. 21   Purchased 600 shares of Tay Company common stock at $32.50 per share, plus a $300 broker's commission. Also purchased 100 shares of Raynor Company common stock at $150 per share, plus a $250 broker's commission. Both investments are expected to be temporary.

June 2   Received cash dividends of $1 per share on the Tay common shares and $2 per share on the Raynor common shares.

Aug. 12 Received shares representing a 100% stock dividend on the Raynor shares.

    30 Sold 100 shares of Raynor common stock at $80 per share, less a $240 broker's commission.

Sept. 15 Received shares representing a 10% stock dividend on the Tay common stock. Market price today was $35 per share.

Dec. 31 Per share market values for the two investments in common stock are: Tay, $30.50; and Raynor, $71. Both investments are considered temporary.

Required: Prepare journal entries to record the above transactions and the necessary adjustments for a December 31 closing.

Solution to demonstration problem 18–1

SHANE COMPANY
GENERAL JOURNAL

1987
Mar. 21 Current Marketable Equity Securities 35,050
    Cash 35,050
    To record purchase of 600 shares of Tay common stock for $19,800 and 100 shares of Raynor common stock for $15,250.

June 2 Cash 800
    Dividend Revenue 800
    To record cash dividends: $600 Tay, and $200 Raynor.

Aug. 12 Received 100 shares of Raynor common stock as a 100% stock dividend. The new cost per share is $15,250 ÷ 200 shares = $76.25.

    30 Cash 7,760
    Current Marketable Equity Securities 7,625
    Gain on Sale of Current Marketable Equity Securities . . . 135
    To record sale of current marketable equity securities.
    Proceeds = $8,000 − $240; cost = $76.25 × 100 shares.

Sept. 15 Received 60 shares of Tay common stock as a 10% stock dividend. New cost per share is $19,800 ÷ 660 shares = $30.00.

Dec. 31 Net Unrealized Loss on Current Marketable Equity Securities . . 195
    Allowance for Market Decline of Current Marketable Equity
    Securities 195
    To write current marketable equity securities down to market value:

	Cost	*Market*	*Inc. (Dec.) in Market Value*
Tay common stock . . .	$19,800	$20,130*	$ 330
Raynor common stock . .	7,625	7,100†	(525)
Total	$27,425	$27,230	$(195)

* $30.50 × 660 shares = $20,130.
† $71.00 × 100 shares = $ 7,100.

DEMONSTRATION PROBLEM 18–2

The Stiller Company acquired all of the outstanding voting common stock of Meara Company on January 2, 1987, for $200,000 cash. On the date of acquisition, the balance sheets for the two companies were as follows:

	Stiller Company	Meara Company
Assets		
Cash	$ 50,000	$ 20,000
Accounts receivable	60,000	25,000
Notes receivable	10,000	5,000
Inventory	75,000	50,000
Investment in Meara Company	200,000	–0–
Plant and equipment, net	202,000	130,000
Total assets	$597,000	$230,000
Liabilities and Stockholders' Equity		
Accounts payable	$ 50,000	$ 30,000
Notes payable	15,000	10,000
Common stock—$5 par value	350,000	100,000
Retained earnings	182,000	90,000
Total liabilities and stockholders' equity . .	$597,000	$230,000

Also on January 2, 1987, Meara Company borrowed $10,000 from Stiller Company by giving a note. The excess of cost over book value is attributable to Meara Company's above-average earnings prospects.

Required: Prepare a work sheet for a consolidated balance sheet on the date of acquisition.

Solution to demonstration problem 18–2

STILLER COMPANY AND SUBSIDIARY MEARA COMPANY
Work Sheet for Consolidated Balance Sheet
January 2, 1987 (date of acquisition)

	Stiller Company	Meara Company	Eliminations Debit	Eliminations Credit	Consolidated Amounts
Assets					
Cash	50,000	20,000			70,000
Accounts receivable	60,000	25,000			85,000
Notes receivable	10,000	5,000		(2) 10,000	5,000
Inventory	75,000	50,000			125,000
Investment in Meara Co.	200,000			(1) 200,000	
Plant and equipment, net	202,000	130,000			332,000
Goodwill			(1) 10,000		10,000
	597,000	230,000			627,000
Liabilities and Stockholders' Equity					
Accounts payable	50,000	30,000			80,000
Notes payable	15,000	10,000	(2) 10,000		15,000
Common stock—$5 par	350,000	100,000	(1) 100,000		350,000
Retained earnings	182,000	90,000	(1) 90,000		182,000
	597,000	230,000	210,000	210,000	627,000

QUESTIONS

1. Explain the main problem encountered in classifying marketable securities in the balance sheet.

2. Describe the valuation bases used for marketable equity securities.

3. Explain briefly the accounting for stock dividends and stock splits from the investor's point of view.

4. What is the purpose of preparing consolidated financial statements?

5. Under what circumstances must consolidated financial statements be prepared?

6. Why is it necessary to make elimination entries on the consolidated statement work sheet? Are these elimination entries also posted to the accounts of the parent and subsidiary? Why or why not?

7. Why might a corporation pay an amount in excess of the book value for a subsidiary's stock? Why might it pay an amount less than the book value of the subsidiary's stock?

8. The item "Minority interest" often appears as one amount in the consolidated balance sheet. What does this item represent?

9. How do a subsidiary's earnings, losses, and dividends affect the investment account of the parent when the equity method of accounting is used?

10. When must each of the following methods be used to account for a business combination?

    a. Purchase
    b. Pooling of interests

11. List three differences that exist between the purchase and pooling of interests methods of accounting for business combinations.

12. Why are consolidated financial statements of limited usefulness to the creditors and minority stockholders of a subsidiary?

EXERCISES

E-1

Prepare entries for temporary investment in marketable equity securities

Flint Company purchased 100 shares of Perry Company stock at a total cost of $1,260 on July 1, 1987. At the end of the accounting year (December 31, 1987), the market value for these shares was $1,140. By December 31, 1988, the market value had risen to $1,320. This is the only marketable equity security that Flint Company owns. The company classifies the securities as current assets. Give the entries necessary at the date of purchase and at December 31, 1987, and 1988.

E-2

Prepare entries for temporary investment in marketable equity securities

On July 1, 1987, Tuber Company purchased 100 shares of Sun Company capital stock as a temporary investment at $56.40 per share plus a commission of $60. On July 15, a 10% stock dividend was received. Tuber received a cash dividend of 60 cents per share on August 12, 1987. On November 1, Tuber sold all of the above shares for $69.60 per share, less a commision of $66. Prepare entries to record all of the above transactions in Tuber Company's accounts if this investment is classified under current assets.

E-3

Apply LCM rule to marketable equity securities

The Newport Company has marketable equity securities that have a market value at year-end that is $1,120 below their cost. Give the required entry if:

a. The securities are current assets.
b. The securities are noncurrent assets and the loss is considered to be temporary.
c. The securities are noncurrent assets and the loss is considered to be permanent.

State where each of the accounts debited in *(a), (b),* and *(c)* would be reported.

E-4

Prepare elimination entry as of the date of acquisition

On February 1, 1987, the Benz Company acquired 100% of the outstanding voting common stock of the BFW Company for $700,000 cash. The stockholders' equity of the BFW Company consisted of common stock, $560,000, and retained earnings, $140,000. Prepare (a) the entry to record the investment in BFW Company and (b) the elimination entry that would be made on the work sheet used to prepare a consolidated balance sheet as of the date of acquisition.

E-5

Prepare entries to record and eliminate an investment in subsidiary

The Douglas Corporation acquired, for cash, 80% of the outstanding voting common stock of Table Company. On the date of its acquisition, the Table Company's stockholders' equity consisted of common stock, $490,000, and retained earnings, $182,000. The cost of the investment exceeded the book value by $25,200 and was attributable to above-average earnings prospects. Prepare (a) the entry to record the investment in Table Company and (b) the elimination entry that would be made on the work sheet used to prepare consolidated financial statements as of the date of acquisition.

E-6

Compute difference between cost and book value of common stock investments

On January 1, 1987, Company A acquired 85% of the outstanding voting common stock of Company C. On that date, Company C's stockholders' equity consisted of:

Stockholders' equity:
Common stock, $30 par; 15,000 shares authorized, issued, and outstanding	$450,000
Retained earnings	112,500
Total stockholders' equity	$562,500

Compute the difference between cost and book value in each of the following cases:

a.   Company A pays $478,125 cash for its interest in Company C.
b.   Company A pays $562,500 cash for its interest in Company C.
c.   Company A pays $435,000 cash for its interest in Company C.

E-7

Compute balance in investment account and minority interest at year-end

Company X purchased 90% of Company Y's outstanding voting common stock on January 2, 1987. Company X paid $465,000 for an equity of $405,000 representing—$270,000 common stock, and $135,000 of retained earnings. The difference was due to undervalued land owned by Company Y. Company Y earned $54,000 during 1987 and paid cash dividends of $18,000.

a.   Compute the balance in the investment account on December 31, 1987.
b.   Compute the amount of the minority interest on (1) January 2, 1987, and (2) December 31, 1987.

E-8

Prepare equity method entries for an investment

Neal Company owns 75% of Black Company's outstanding common stock and uses the equity method of accounting. Black Company reported net income of $117,000 for 1987. On December 31, 1987, Black Company paid a cash dividend of $31,500. In 1988, Black Company incurred a net loss of $22,500. Prepare entries to reflect these events on Neal Company's books.

E-9

Compute book value, difference between cost and book value, and minority interest of an investment

The January 1, 1987, stockholders' equity section of Brown Company's balance sheet appears below:

Stockholders' equity:
Paid-in capital:		
Common stock—$24 par value: authorized, 100,000 shares; issued and outstanding, 75,000 shares		$1,800,000
Paid-in capital in excess of par value		300,000
Total paid-in capital		$2,100,000
Retained earnings		180,000
Total stockholders' equity		$2,280,000

Ninety percent of Brown Company's outstanding voting common stock was acquired by Red Company on January 1, 1988, for $2,004,000. Compute (a) the book value of the investment, (b) the difference between cost and book value, and (c) the minority interest.

PROBLEMS, SERIES A

P18–1–A

Prepare entries for noncurrent investments in marketable equity securities

On September 1, 1987, Oakdale Company purchased the following long-term investments:

1. One thousand shares of Nail Company capital stock at $73.20 plus broker's commission of $480.
2. Five hundred shares of Hammer Company capital stock at $117.60 plus broker's commission of $420.

Cash dividends of $1.50 per share on the Nail capital stock and $1.20 per share on the Hammer capital stock were received on December 7 and December 10, respectively.

On December 31, 1987, per share market values are: Nail, $76.80; and Hammer, $109.20.

Required:

a. Prepare journal entries to record the above transactions.
b. Prepare the necessary adjusting entry(ies) at December 31, 1987, to adjust the carrying values assuming that market price changes are believed to be permanent.
c. Repeat part (b), assuming the changes in market prices are expected to be temporary.

P18–2–A

Prepare entries for temporary investments in marketable equity securities

Da-Lite, Inc. purchased on July 2, 1986, 100 shares of Light Company $60 par value common stock as a temporary investment at $96 per share, plus a commission of $72. A 20% stock dividend was received on December 15, 1987.

On July 15, 1988, a cash dividend of $1.20 per share was received. On September 15, 1988, the Light Company split its $60 par value common shares two for one.

On November 2, 1988, Da-Lite sold 100 shares of Light common stock at $60, less commissions and taxes of $48.

Required:

a. Prepare journal entries to record all of the above 1988 transactions.
b. How would you recommend that the remaining shares be classified in the December 31, 1988, balance sheet if still held at that date?
c. Assume the shares were considered current assets at the end of 1986, at which time their market value was $93.60 per share. At the end of 1987, the shares had a market value of $78.90. Prepare any necessary adjusting entries for the end of 1986 and 1987.

P18–3–A

Prepare equity method entries for an investment and eliminating entries for consolidated work sheet

Lion Company acquired 90% of the outstanding voting common stock of Seagull Company on January 1, 1987, for $630,000 cash. Lion Company uses the equity method. During 1987, Seagull reported $126,000 of net income and paid $42,000 in cash dividends. The stockholders' equity section of the December 31, 1986, balance sheet for Seagull follows:

Stockholders' equity:

Common stock—$7 par	$560,000
Retained earnings	140,000
Total stockholders' equity . .	$700,000

Required:

a. Prepare general journal entries to record the investment and the effect of Seagull earnings and dividends on Lion Company's accounts.
b. Prepare the elimination entry that would be made on the work sheet for a consolidated balance sheet as of the date of acquisition.

P18–4–A

Prepare equity method entries for an investment

Hadley Company acquired 68% of the outstanding voting common stock of Summer Company for $1,428,000 on January 1, 1986. The investment is accounted for under the equity method. During the years 1986–88, Summer Company reported the following:

	Net income (loss)	Dividends paid
1986 . .	$242,480	$145,320
1987 . .	62,160	37,240
1988 . .	(3,920)	9,310

Required: a.   Prepare general journal entries to record the investment and the effect of the subsidiary's income, losses, and dividends on Hadley Company's accounts.

b.   Compute the investment account balance on December 31, 1988.

P18–5–A

Prepare work sheet for consolidated balance sheet at acquisition

Ivory Company acquired all of the outstanding voting common stock of Jade Company on January 3, 1987, for $201,600. On the date of acquisition, the balance sheets for the two companies were as follows:

	Ivory Company	Jade Company
Assets		
Cash	$ 33,600	$ 28,800
Accounts receivable	64,800	60,000
Notes receivable	36,000	9,600
Inventory	93,600	43,200
Investment in Jade Company	201,600	
Equipment, net	172,800	79,200
Total assets	$602,400	$220,800
Liabilities and Stockholders' Equity		
Accounts payable	$ 62,400	$ 19,200
Common stock—$15 par value	288,000	139,200
Retained earnings	252,000	62,400
Total liabilities and stockholders' equity	$602,400	$220,800

Required: Prepare a work sheet for a consolidated balance sheet on the date of acquisition.

P18–6–A

Prepare work sheet and consolidated balance sheet at acquisition

Dark Company acquired all of the outstanding voting common stock of Dawn Company on January 2, 1987, for $360,000. On the date of acquisition, the balance sheets for the two companies were as follows:

	Dark Company	Dawn Company
Assets		
Cash	$ 75,000	$ 22,500
Accounts receivable	36,000	30,000
Notes receivable	15,000	9,000
Inventory	114,000	72,000
Investment in Dawn Company	360,000	
Equipment, net	102,000	61,500
Buildings, net	277,500	138,000
Land	117,000	37,500
Total assets	$1,096,500	$370,500
Liabilities and Stockholders' Equity		
Accounts payable	$ 66,000	$ 30,000
Notes payable	18,000	21,000
Common stock—$30 par value	795,000	297,000
Retained earnings	217,500	22,500
Total liabilities and stockholders' equity	$1,096,500	$370,500

The management of Dark Company thinks that the Dawn Company's land is undervalued by $13,500. The remainder of the excess of cost over book value is due to superior earnings potential.

On the date of acquisition, Dawn Company borrowed $15,000 from Dark Company by giving a note.

Required: a.   Prepare a work sheet for a consolidated balance sheet on the date of acquisition.

b.   Prepare a consolidated balance sheet for January 2, 1987.

P18-7-A

Prepare work sheet for consolidated financial statements

Refer back to Problem 18–6–A. Dark Company uses the equity method. Assume the following are taken from the adjusted trial balances of Dark Company and Dawn Company on December 31, 1987:

	Dark Company	Dawn Company
Cash	$ 72,000	$ 30,358
Accounts receivable	46,128	34,500
Notes receivable	28,500	7,500
Inventory, December 31	127,500	84,000
Investment in Dawn Company	376,613	
Equipment, net	95,625	57,655
Buildings, net	263,625	131,100
Land	117,000	37,500
Cost of goods sold	672,000	180,000
Expenses (excluding depreciation and taxes) . .	180,000	67,500
Depreciation expense	20,250	10,745
Income tax expense	47,472	10,292
Dividends	39,750	14,850
Total of the accounts with debit balances . . .	$2,086,463	$666,000
Accounts payable	$ 60,000	$ 31,500
Notes payable	22,500	15,000
Common stock—$30 par value	795,000	297,000
Retained earnings	217,500	22,500
Revenue from sales	960,000	300,000
Income of Dawn Company	31,463	
Total of the accounts with credit balances . . .	$2,086,463	$666,000

There is no intercompany debt at the end of the year.

Required: Prepare a work sheet for consolidated financial statements on December 31, 1987. Ignore the amortization of goodwill.

P18-8-A

Prepare consolidated income statement, statement of retained earnings, and balance sheet

Using the work sheet from Problem 18–7–A, prepare the following items:

a.   Consolidated income statement for the year ended December 31, 1987.
b.   Consolidated statement of retained earnings for the year ended December 31, 1987.
c.   Consolidated balance sheet for December 31, 1987.

PROBLEMS, SERIES B

P18-1-B

Prepare entries for temporary investments in marketable equity securities

The Evans Company acquired on July 15, 1987, 200 shares of Tom Company $120 par value capital stock at $116.40 per share plus a broker's commission of $144. On August 1, 1987, Evans Company received a cash dividend of 72 cents per share. On November 3, 1987, it sold 100 of these shares at $126 per share less a broker's commission of $96. On December 1, 1987, the Tom Company issued shares comprising a 100% stock dividend declared on its capital stock on November 18.

On December 31, 1987, the end of the calendar-year accounting period, the market quotation for Tom's common stock was $55.20 per share. The decline was considered to be temporary.

Required: a. Prepare journal entries to record all of the above data assuming the securities are considered temporary investments and are to be valued at LCM.

   b. Assume Tom Company has become a major customer. If the shares are held for affiliation purposes, indicate how they should be shown in the balance sheet.

P18–2–B

Prepare entries for temporary investments in marketable equity securities; compare entries to those for long-term investments

On October 17, 1986, Pitcher Company purchased the following common stocks at the indicated per share prices that included commissions:

300 shares of Cee Company common stock @ $72 . .	$21,600
500 shares of Dee Company common stock @ $48 . .	$24,000
800 shares of Fey Company common stock @ $24 . .	$19,200
	$64,800

On December 31, 1986, the market prices per share of the above common stocks were Cee, $74.40, Dee, $45.60, and Fey, $18.

Summarized, the cash dividends per share received in 1987 were Cee, $2.40; Dee, $1.20; and Fey, $0.90. Also, a 100% stock dividend (300 shares) was received on the Cee Company common stock after the cash dividend was paid.

On December 31, 1987, the per share market prices were Cee, $40.80; Dee, $38.40; and Fey, $24.

All of the changes in market prices given above are considered temporary.

Required: a. Prepare journal entries for all of the above, including calendar year-end adjusting entries, assuming the shares of common stock acquired are considered short-term investments.

   b. If the securities acquired are considered long-term investments, how would the entries made in (a) differ?

   c. For both parts (a) and (b), give the descriptions (titles) and the dollar amounts of the items that would appear in the income statements for 1986 and 1987.

P18–3–B

Prepare equity method entries for an investment and eliminating entries for consolidated work sheet

On January 1, 1987, Raven Company acquired 80% of the outstanding voting common stock of the Dalton Company for $336,000 cash. Raven Company uses the equity method. During 1987, Dalton reported $56,000 of net income and paid $24,000 in dividends. The stockholders' equity section of the December 31, 1986, balance sheet for Dalton follows:

Stockholders' equity:	
Common stock—$7 par . . .	$350,000
Retained earnings	70,000
Total stockholders' equity . .	$420,000

Required: a. Prepare the general journal entry to record the investment and the effect on Dalton's income and dividends on Raven Company's accounts.

   b. Prepare the elimination entry that would be made on the work sheet for a consolidated balance sheet as of the date of acquisition.

P18–4–B

Prepare entries for investment, compute year-end balance in investment account

Technix Company acquired 75% of the outstanding voting common stock of Harmon Company for $481,600 cash on January 1, 1986. The investment is accounted for under the equity method. During 1986, 1987, and 1988, Harmon Company reported the following:

	Net income (loss)	Dividends paid
1986 . .	$119,280	$96,880
1987 . .	(15,120)	–0–
1988 . .	36,120	24,080

Required: a. Prepare general journal entries to record the investment and the effect of the subsidiary's income, losses, and dividends on Technix company's accounts.

   b. Compute the balance in the investment account on December 31, 1988.

P18–5–B

Prepare a work sheet for consolidated balance sheet at acquisition

Tide Company acquired 100% of the outstanding voting common stock of Houston Company on January 2, 1987, for $121,600 cash. On the date of acquisition, the balance sheets for the two companies were as follows:

	Tide Company	Houston Company
Assets		
Cash	$ 9,600	$ 22,400
Accounts receivable	22,400	28,800
Notes receivable	16,000	9,600
Inventory	40,000	24,000
Investment in Houston Company	121,600	
Equipment, net	35,200	44,800
Total assets	$244,800	$129,600
Liabilities and Stockholders' Equity		
Accounts payable	$ 25,600	$ 8,000
Notes payable	19,200	
Common stock—$32 par value	160,000	96,000
Retained earnings	40,000	25,600
Total liabilities and stockholders' equity	$244,800	$129,600

Also on January 2, 1987, Tide Company borrowed $9,600 from Houston Company by giving a note.

Required: Prepare a work sheet for a consolidated balance sheet as of the date of acquisition.

P18–6–B

Prepare work sheet and consolidated balance sheet; prepare consolidated balance sheet

Outland Company acquired 100% of the outstanding voting common stock of Paul Company on January 2, 1987, for $450,000. On the date of acquisition, the balance sheets for the two companies were as follows:

	Outland Company	Paul Company
Assets		
Cash	$ 52,500	$ 30,000
Accounts receivable	39,000	24,000
Notes receivable	60,000	15,000
Inventory	82,500	39,000
Investment in Paul Company	450,000	
Equipment, net	108,000	75,000
Buildings, net	315,000	165,000
Land	127,500	67,500
Total assets	$1,234,500	$415,500
Liabilities and Stockholders Equity		
Accounts payable	$ 19,500	$ 22,500
Notes payable	15,000	18,000
Common stock—$15 par value	900,000	300,000
Retained earnings	300,000	75,000
Total liabilities and stockholders' equity	$1,234,500	$415,500

The excess of cost over book value is attributable to the above-average earnings prospects of Paul Company. On the date of acquisition, Paul Company borrowed $12,000 from Outland Company by giving a note.

Required:
a. Prepare a work sheet for a consolidated balance sheet as of the date of acquisition.
b. Prepare a consolidated balance sheet for January 2, 1987.

P18-7-B

Prepare work sheet for consolidated financial statements

Refer back to Problem 18–6–B. Outland Company uses the equity method. Assume the following are taken from the adjusted trial balances of Outland Company and Paul Company on December 31, 1987:

	Outland Company	Paul Company
Cash	$ 58,500	$ 52,500
Accounts receivable	63,000	30,000
Notes receivable	52,500	7,500
Inventory, December 31	82,500	47,850
Investment in Paul Company	465,000	
Equipment, net	102,600	71,250
Buildings, net	302,400	158,400
Land	127,500	67,500
Cost of goods sold	300,000	105,000
Expenses (excluding depreciation and taxes)	120,000	45,150
Depreciation expense	18,000	10,350
Income tax expense	97,500	31,500
Dividends	90,000	18,000
Total of the accounts with debit balances	$1,879,500	$645,000
Accounts payable	$ 22,500	$ 30,000
Notes payable	24,000	15,000
Common stock—$15 par value	900,000	300,000
Retained earnings—January 1	300,000	75,000
Revenue from sales	600,000	225,000
Income of Paul Company	33,000	
Total of the accounts with credit balances	$1,879,500	$645,000

There is no intercompany debt at the end of the year.

Required: Prepare a work sheet for consolidated financial statements on December 31, 1987. Ignore the amortization of goodwill.

P18-8-B

Prepare consolidated income statement, statement of retained earnings, and balance sheet

Using the work sheet from Problem P18–7–B, prepare the following items:

a. Consolidated income statement for the year ended December 31, 1987.
b. Consolidated statement of retained earnings for the year ended December 31, 1987.
c. Consolidated balance sheet for December 31, 1987.

BUSINESS DECISION PROBLEM 18-1

Classify a portfolio of marketable equity securities as current or noncurrent investments

You are the CPA engaged to audit the records of Antoy Company. You find that your client has a portfolio of marketable equity securities that has a market value (in total) that is $100,000 less than the total cost of the portfolio. You ask the vice president for finance if the client expects to sell these securities in the coming year. He answers that he doesn't know. The securities will be sold if additional cash is needed to finance operations. When you ask for a cash forecast, you are told that one has been prepared that covers the next year. It shows no need to sell the marketable securities.

Required: How would you recommend that the client's portfolio of marketable securities be classified in the balance sheet? Why? Does it really make any difference whether the secuities are classified as current or noncurrent? Explain.

BUSINESS DECISION PROBLEM 18–2

18–2

Prepare a consolidated balance sheet

On January 2, 1987, Max Company acquired 60% of the voting common stock of York Corporation for $240,000 cash. The excess of cost over book value was due to above-average earnings prospects. Max and York are engaged in similar lines of business. Max has hired you to help it prepare consolidated financial statements and has already collected the following information for both companies as of January 2, 1987:

	Max Company	York Corporation
Assets		
Cash	$ 24,000	$ 18,000
Accounts receivable	36,000	42,000
Inventories	96,000	72,000
Investment in York Corporation	240,000	
Plant and equipment, net	312,000	246,000
Total assets	$708,000	$378,000
Liabilities and Stockholders' Equity		
Accounts payable	$ 48,000	$ 18,000
Common stock—$24 par	480,000	240,000
Retained earnings	180,000	120,000
Total liabilities and stockholders' equity . .	$708,000	$378,000

Required:

a. Max believes that consolidated financial statements can be prepared simply by adding together the amounts in the two individual columns. Is Max correct? If not, why not?

b. Prepare a consolidated balance sheet for the date of acquisition.

BUSINESS SITUATION FOR DISCUSSION

An SEC crackdown on "cute accounting" is making lots of people nervous.
Edited by Richard Green

Indecent Disclosure*
Jill Andresky

Experienced investors are accustomed to searching for bogus earnings—everything from debt-for-equity swaps to income from partially held subsidiaries. All of this, at least, can be found somewhere in annual reports. But how can a shareholder scrutinize things he can't see?

That's why the Securities & Exchange Commission is launching an earnest attack on what Commissioner James Treadway calls "cute accounting." The focus here isn't so much on traditional ploys to hype reported profits as it is on several controversial methods of sweeping losses and mistakes under the rug. "When you have a

period of economic recession, there is a tendency for liberties to be taken," explains Treadway. "Some people become overly aggressive, others can become downright dishonest."

Just a few weeks ago, for example, the SEC launched proceedings against Digilog, the computer manufacturer, and its auditor. . . . The charge: failure to consolidate losses from another company that should have been shown as a subsidiary. According to the SEC, Digilog's 1982 pretax earnings were really $1.2 million. The company claimed a figure that was twice that high.

Digilog and its chairman quickly signed a consent decree to end the SEC probe. But . . . [the auditor] refuses to back down. "We're going to litigate," says . . . [the] general counsel for the Big Eight firm. The issue here involves what is called a "nonsubsidiary subsidiary" and confusion about whether its income should be consolidated.

Here's how a nonsubsidiary subsidiary works: A company funds a risky new venture, making sure its ownership in the venture never exceeds 50%. That way there

* *Forbes,* August 13, 1984, p. 92. Reprinted with permission.

is no requirement to consolidate earnings. But suppose that the funding company keeps notes convertible at will to a majority of the venture's outstanding shares. As soon as the fledgling project starts to show a profit, the parent converts its notes and consolidates the income. Can you find out if this hanky-panky is going on? Only if you are lucky and the firm discloses the deal in footnotes. Otherwise, the company can take losses without clueing in the investors.

The SEC's Treadway thinks these arrangements are a sham—and they surely look that way. But prominent accountants are less quick to judge. Says Arthur Wyatt, managing director of accounting principles at Arthur Andersen: "The SEC has always been adamant that you cannot consolidate unless you own over 50% of an entity's voting shares. Now all of a sudden they come along and require consolidation where there isn't any voting interest. No one knows what the guidelines are."

The use of nonsubsidiary subsidiaries, however, is only one loss-hiding technique that has caught the commission's eye. Allocation of contract expenses is a second trouble spot. Say an aircraft manufacturer with large startup expenses convinces auditors that, while it has firm orders to build only 100 fighters, it actually anticipates selling 200. This simple assumption can significantly cut annual writeoffs for companies. But these days such moves are risky. Last year the SEC censured . . . [the auditor] for permitting Litton Industries to defer, without adequate basis, $328 million in costs that related to a big Navy contract.

Another clever way to bury bad news involves portfolio valuation. The Financial Accounting Standards Board says that when a company owns stocks and bonds, it should use the lower of cost or market value when it comes time to put the securities on its books. But there are clever ways to interpret that rule.

The SEC, for example, began proceedings against Clabir Corp. for substantially overstating its portfolio value. The diversified manufacturer held a 10% equity position in U.S. Industries. But Clabir didn't rely on the NYSE current price to value its U.S. Industries shares. Instead, Clabir relied on an oral offer from U.S. Industries to buy back its stock at a price 58% higher than the then current NYSE trading price, thus avoiding a writedown. The SEC thought that wasn't proper.

The new search for hidden losses nearly always involves matters that accountants see as judgment calls. This puts the profession on edge. "In our own firm, if something is not a straightforward accounting issue, we now almost always insist that clients talk to the SEC before the fact," says one Big Eight auditor, who requests anonymity. "It's kind of like having the IRS audit your tax return before you file it."

From an intelligent shareholder's viewpoint, however, the issue seems clear: Getting a little bad news today is surely better than lots of bad news tomorrow.

PART

6

Analysis of Financial Statements

CHAPTER 19

Statement of Changes in Financial Position

LEARNING OBJECTIVES

After studying this chapter, you should be able to:

1. List the major sources and uses of funds.
2. Explain why net income for a period is not equal to working capital or cash provided by operations.
3. Prepare a statement of changes in financial position—working capital basis.
4. Prepare a statement of changes in financial position—cash basis.
5. Prepare a working paper for a statement of changes in financial position.
6. Define and use correctly the new terms in the glossary.

In your study of the statement of income and retained earnings (as separate statements or combined) and the balance sheet, you may have realized that these financial statements do not answer all the questions raised by users of financial statements. Such questions include: How much working capital or cash was generated by the company's operations? Why is such a profitable company only able to pay such small dividends? How much was spent for new plant and equipment, and where did the company get the funds for the expenditures? How was the company able to pay a dividend when it incurred a net loss for the year?

The statement that provides information to answer these types of questions is called the statement of changes in financial position. This statement, also called a funds statement, reports the flow of funds into and out of a business in an accounting period. A statement of changes in financial position is required for each period for which financial statements are presented.[1]

A statement of changes in financial position can be prepared using two

---
[1] APB, "Reporting Changes in Financial Position," *APB Opinion No. 19* (New York: AICPA, 1971), par. 7.

alternative concepts or formats—working capital basis and cash basis. In this chapter you learn about these two concepts of funds and the procedures used to prepare the statement of changes in financial position under each concept.

■ USES OF THE STATEMENT OF CHANGES IN FINANCIAL POSITION

The **statement of changes in financial position** summarizes the financing and investing activities of a company for a period; it reports on past management decisions on such matters as issuance of capital stock or sale of long-term bonds. The statement reports on the flow of working capital or cash in the business. This information is available only in bits and pieces from the other financial statements. Because working capital and cash flows are vital to a company's financial health, the statement of changes in financial position provides useful information to management and other interested parties, especially creditors and investors.

Management Uses

Since the statement of changes in financial position presents all significant financing and investing activities, management can see the effects of its past major policy decisions in quantitative form by reviewing the statement. The statement may show a flow of funds from operations large enough to finance all projected capital needs internally rather than having to issue long-term debt or additional stock. Or, if the company has been experiencing working capital or cash shortages, management can use the statement to determine why such shortages are ocurring. After reviewing the statement, management may decide to reduce dividends in order to conserve funds and reduce cash shortages.

Creditor and Investor Uses

Information on the statement of changes in financial position may provide creditors and investors with valuable clues to:

1. The extent to which internally generated funds cover projected capital needs.
2. The likelihood of the company's paying or increasing future dividends.
3. Management's preferences toward financing and investing.
4. The company's ability to make principal and interest payments on its debt.
5. The feasibility of a planned expansion in the light of available resources.

■ THE CONCEPT OF FUNDS

The term *funds,* in a broad sense, means all financial resources of a company. But the definition of funds in reference to the statement of changes in financial position has a much more precise meaning. **Funds** are often defined as **working capital** or as **cash.** Either definition is an acceptable basis on which to prepare a statement of changes in financial position.

Funds Defined as Working Capital

Funds have typically been defined as working capital for purposes of preparing the statement of changes in financial position. Working capital is equal to current assets minus current liabilities. **Using the working capital definition of funds, the effects of any transaction that increases or decreases working capital are included in the statement of changes in financial position.** The borrowing of cash by the use of long-term bonds would be included because the transaction increases total current assets, thus **increasing** working capital. The purchase of a plant asset on a short-term credit basis would be included because it **reduces** working capital by increasing total current liabilities. Defining funds as working capital also permits the exclusion of many routine transactions. Examples of transactions that may be excluded are collection of an account receivable or payment of an account payable. The first transaction merely substitutes one current asset (cash) for another (accounts receivable). The second transaction reduces a current asset (cash) and reduces a current liability (accounts payable). Both transactions change the **composition** of working capital, but not the **amount** of working capital.

Illustration 19.1 diagrams the transactions that affect working capital. Four basic transaction types are identified that affect sources and uses of working capital.

Illustration 19.1

Typical Transactions that Affect Working Capital

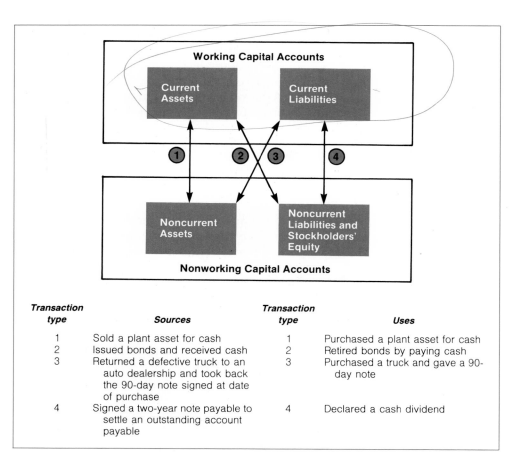

Transaction type	Sources	Transaction type	Uses
1	Sold a plant asset for cash	1	Purchased a plant asset for cash
2	Issued bonds and received cash	2	Retired bonds by paying cash
3	Returned a defective truck to an auto dealership and took back the 90-day note signed at date of purchase	3	Purchased a truck and gave a 90-day note
4	Signed a two-year note payable to settle an outstanding account payable	4	Declared a cash dividend

Funds Defined as Cash

When funds are defined as cash, the effects of any transaction that increases or decreases cash are included in the statement of changes in financial position. Many examples can be given, including transactions involving cash received from the collection of accounts receivable and the sale of plant assets, as well as cash payments to retire long-term or short-term debt. When the cash basis of funds is strictly applied, only the effects of transactions involving cash are reported.

Other Significant Financing and Investing Activities

Strict adherence to the cash or working capital concept of funds could lead to the omission of the effects of significant transactions from the statement of changes in financial position. For example, a company might double the total dollar amount of its assets by issuing common stock for land and buildings. Since this transaction does not change the amount of working capital (no current asset or current liability was affected) nor does it change the amount of cash, it would not appear on the statement of changes of financial position if either of the above concepts of funds was strictly applied. But, in developing the principles underlying the presentation of changes of financial position, *APB Opinion No. 19* requires a business to report **all significant** financing and investing activities, regardless of whether the cash or working capital definition of funds is used; this is known as the all financial resources concept. Because the above transaction is a significant investing and financing event, its effects would be reported on the company's statement of changes of financial position.

Major Sources and Uses of Funds

A source of funds is a transaction that brings funds (working capital or cash) into the business, while a use of funds is a transaction that removes funds from the business. Operations generally are the major source of funds, although unsuccessful operations can result in a use of funds. The major sources and uses of funds are presented in Illustration 19.2.

The organization of the statement of changes in financial position parallels the organization of Illustration 19.2. The **sources** from which the Company obtained funds during the period are reported in one section of the statement

Illustration 19.2

Sources and Uses of Funds

Sources of Funds

Operations (if positive inflow)

Borrowing

Disposal of assets

Investments by owners

Uses of Funds

Operations (if negative drain)

Repayment of borrowing

Purchase of assets

Distributions to owners

Pool of Funds

under a title such as "Financial resources provided." Another section, with a title such as "Financial resources applied," reports the various **uses** to which the funds were put during the period. The dollar amount of difference between the sources and the uses equals the **net change** (increase or decrease) in working capital or cash, depending on the funds concept being used.

■ FUNDS FROM OPERATIONS

Funds provided by operations can be measured in two ways. One way is to deduct from sales only those operating expenses that consumed funds. Alternatively, the indirect, or addback, method of determining funds provided by operations starts with net income and adjusts net income for items that affected reported net income but did not affect funds. Since the addback method is used almost exclusively in actual practice, this method will be used in this chapter.

The most common example of an operating expense that does not affect funds is depreciation expense. The journal entry to record depreciation requires a debit to an expense account and a credit to an accumulated depreciation account. This transaction has no effect on funds and therefore should not be included when measuring funds from operations. Because depreciation is deducted in arriving at net income, net income understates funds from operations. If net income is used as a starting point in measuring funds from operations, depreciation expense must be added back to net income.

Consider the following example. Company A had net income for the year of $20,000 after deducting depreciation of $10,000. Company B had a net loss for the year of $4,000 after deducting $10,000 of depreciation. Although Company B experienced a loss, the company has a positive funds flow from operations as shown below:

	Company A	Company B
Net income (loss)	$20,000	$ (4,000)
Add depreciation expense (which did not require use of funds)	10,000	10,000
Positive funds flow from operations	$30,000	$ 6,000

Company B's loss would have had to exceed $10,000 for there to be a negative flow of funds from operations for the company.

There are other expenses and losses that are added back to net income because they do not actually use funds of the company; these addbacks are often called nonworking capital (or nonfund) charges or expenses. The items added back include amounts of depletion that were expensed, amortization of intangible assets such as patents and goodwill, amortization of discount on bonds payable, and losses from disposals of noncurrent assets.

To illustrate the addback of the losses from disposals of noncurrent assets, assume that Quick Company sold a piece of equipment for $6,000. The equipment had cost $10,000 and had accumulated depreciation of $3,000. The journal entry to record the sale is:

```
Cash . . . . . . . . . . . . . . . . . . . . . . . . . . .      6,000
Accumulated Depreciation . . . . . . . . . . . . . . . . .      3,000
Loss on Sale of Equipment . . . . . . . . . . . . . . . . .     1,000
    Equipment . . . . . . . . . . . . . . . . . . . . .                10,000
    To record disposal of equipment at a loss.
```

The only "funds" account in the above journal entry is Cash. The $6,000 inflow from the sale of the equipment will be shown on the statement of changes in financial position as a source of funds. The loss amount ($1,000) was deducted in calculating net income but does not reduce working capital. Thus, the loss must be added back to net income in converting net income to funds from operations.

Certain revenues and gains included in arriving at net income do not provide working capital; these items are called **nonworking capital (or nonfund) credits or revenues.** These revenues and gains must be deducted from net income in order to compute funds provided by operations. Such items include gains from disposals of noncurrent assets and income from investments carried under the equity method.

To illustrate why the gain on the disposal of a noncurrent asset must be deducted from net income, assume that Quick Company sold the equipment mentioned above for $9,000. The journal entry to record the sale is:

```
Cash . . . . . . . . . . . . . . . . . . . . . . . . . . .      9,000
Accumulated Depreciation . . . . . . . . . . . . . . . . .      3,000
    Equipment . . . . . . . . . . . . . . . . . . . . .                10,000
    Gain on Sale of Equipment . . . . . . . . . . . . . .                2,000
    To record disposal of equipment at a gain.
```

The $9,000 inflow is shown as a source of funds. The gain does not affect working capital, yet it was added in calculating net income. Thus, the gain must be deducted in converting net income to funds from operations.

■ STATEMENT OF CHANGES IN FINANCIAL POSITION—WORKING CAPITAL BASIS

This section of the chapter covers the procedures followed to prepare a statement of changes in financial position on a working capital basis. This procedure is illustrated using the financial statements and additional data for the Welby Company given in Illustration 19.3. The first step is to determine the change in working capital. The second step is to analyze all of the noncurrent accounts for changes that affected working capital. The third step is to arrange the information gathered in steps 1 and 2 into the format required for the statement of changes in financial position.

Step 1: Determining the Change in Working Capital

APB Opinion No. 19 states that a separate statement of changes in working capital should accompany the statement of changes in financial position. Such a statement lists all current assets and current liabilities, their beginning and ending balances, and the changes in these balances summarized into a single amount—the net change in working capital.

A statement of changes in working capital is presented in Illustration 19.4.

Illustration 19.3

Financial Statements and Other Data

WELBY COMPANY
Balance Sheets
December 31, 1986, and 1987

	December 31	
	1987	1986
Assets		
Cash	$ 21,000	$ 10,000
Accounts receivable	30,000	20,000
Inventory	26,000	30,000
Plant assets	70,000	50,000
Accumulated depreciation	(10,000)	(5,000)
Total assets	$137,000	$105,000
Liabilities and Stockholders' Equity		
Accounts payable	$ 9,000	$ 15,000
Accrued liabilities	2,000	–0–
Common stock ($10 par value)	90,000	60,000
Retained earnings	36,000	30,000
Total liabilities and stockholder's equity	$137,000	$105,000

WELBY COMPANY
Income Statement
For the Year Ended December 31, 1987

Sales		$140,000
Cost of goods sold		100,000
Gross margin		$ 40,000
Operating expenses and taxes	$ 25,000	
Depreciation	5,000	30,000
Net income		$ 10,000

Additional data:
1. Plant assets purchased for cash during 1987 amounted to $20,000.
2. Common stock with a par value of $30,000 was issued at par for cash.
3. Cash dividends declared and paid in 1987 totaled $4,000.

Illustration 19.4

Statement of Changes in Working Capital

WELBY COMPANY
Statement of Changes in Working Capital
For the Year Ended December 31, 1987

	December 31		Working capital	
	1987	1986	Increase	Decrease
Current assets				
Cash	$21,000	$10,000	$11,000	
Accounts receivable	30,000	20,000	10,000	
Inventory	26,000	30,000		$ 4,000
Total current assets	$77,000	$60,000		
Current liabilities:				
Accounts payable	$9,000	$15,000	6,000	
Accrued liabilities	2,000	–0–		2,000
Total current liabilities	$11,000	$15,000		
Working capital	$66,000	$45,000		
Increase in working capital				21,000
			$27,000	$27,000

Alternatively, a **schedule of changes in working capital components** may be presented immediately under the statement of changes in financial position, as in Illustration 19.5. This schedule shows only the change in each working capital item summarized into a single amount.

In Illustration 19.4, note that changes in current assets of the Welby Company cause working capital to change in the same direction, while changes in current liabilities cause working capital to change in the opposite direction. Thus, the $11,000 increase in cash, the $10,000 increase in accounts receivable, and the $6,000 decrease in accounts payable increased working capital. The $4,000 decrease in inventory and the $2,000 increase in accrued liabilities decreased working capital.

Illustration 19.4 indicates that Welby's working capital increased $21,000 during the year. Once the change in working capital is determined—a $21,000 increase in this case—the change must be explained by analyzing the noncurrent accounts. The statement of changes in financial position reports the causes of the change in working capital.

Step 2: Analyzing the Noncurrent Accounts

At first, it may seem quite unusual to seek the causes of the change in working capital by looking at the noncurrent (nonworking capital) accounts. But bear in mind that a transaction recorded **solely** in two working capital accounts can never increase or decrease working capital. Consider the effects on working capital of collections of receivables, purchases of merchandise, and payment of accounts payable. These transactions change the **composition** of working capital, but not its **amount.** Thus, it is the noncurrent accounts that must be analyzed to find transactions affecting the amount of working capital. In the Welby Company example, there are four noncurrent accounts to analyze: Plant Assets, Accumulated Depreciation, Common Stock, and Retained Earnings.

1. Because of the importance of working capital from operations, the analysis of the noncurrent accounts begins by reviewing the Retained Earnings account. Retained Earnings is the account to which net income or loss for the period was closed. The $6,000 increase in this account consists of $10,000 of net income less $4,000 of dividends. The net income amount can be found in the income statement. Both net income and dividends must be entered on the statement of changes in financial position in Illustration 19.5. The $4,000 of dividends reduced working capital when they were declared and credited to a current liability account, Dividends Payable. The declaration of dividends is a **use of working capital** and is shown under "Financial resources applied." The $10,000 net income is used as the starting figure in determining working capital from operations. Net income of $10,000 is entered on the statement in the financial resources provided section under "Working capital from operations."
2. The Plant Assets account increased by $20,000 during the year. The additional data indicate that plant assets of $20,000 were purchased during the period. A purchase of plant assets is a use of funds and will be shown under "Financial resources applied."
3. The $5,000 increase in the accumulated depreciation account equals the amount of depreciation expense shown in the income statement for the period. Because depreciation does not affect or use up working capital,

under the addback method it must be added back to net income on the statement of changes in financial position to convert net income to working capital provided by operations.

4. The $30,000 increase in common stock resulted from the issuance of stock at par value, as disclosed in the additional data (item 2). An issuance of stock is a source of funds to a company and will be shown on the statement of changes in financial position under "Financial resources provided."

Step 3: Arranging Information into Statement of Changes in Financial Position Format

After all the noncurrent accounts have been analyzed, the statement of changes in financial position can be prepared from the information generated in the last step. Illustration 19.5 presents the statement of changes in financial position for Welby Company. Note that in Illustration 19.5, a schedule of changes in working capital components is shown at the bottom of the statement of changes in financial position.

The completed statement of changes in financial position has two major sections: financial resources provided and financial resources applied. The headings "Sources of working capital" and "Uses of working capital" could have been used instead of the all-inclusive headings shown. However, the "Financial resources" headings seem appropriate because of the requirement of reporting all significant financial and investing activities.

Note that the first item appearing in the "Financial resources provided" section is working capital from operations; this is due to the major significance of this item on the funds of a company. Also note the use of the addback

Illustration 19.5

Statement of Changes in Financial Position—Working Capital Basis

WELBY COMPANY
Statement of Changes in Financial Position—Working Capital Basis
For the Year Ended December 31, 1987

Financial resources provided:		
Working capital from operations:		
Net income		$10,000
Add nonworking capital expenses:		
Depreciation		5,000
Working capital from operations		$15,000
Issuance of common stock		30,000
Total financial resources provided		$45,000
Financial resources applied:		
Purchase of plant assets	$20,000	
Dividends declared	4,000	
Total financial resources applied		24,000
Increase in working capital		$21,000
Schedule of changes in working capital components:		
Increase (decrease) in current assets:		
Cash	$11,000	
Accounts receivable	10,000	
Inventory	(4,000)	
		$17,000
Increase (decrease) in current liabilities:		
Accounts payable	$(6,000)	
Accrued liabilities	2,000	(4,000)
Increase in working capital		$21,000

method, starting with net income and adjusting it for nonworking capital items. The other item shown in the "Provided" section is the funds generated from the issuance of the common stock.

In the "Financial resources applied" section, both the purchase of plant assets and the dividends declared are shown. These items both are uses of funds of the company.

The last line in the statement of changes in financial position is the amount of working capital provided or used during the year. This amount should equal the amount shown on the schedule of changes in working capital.

■ STATEMENT OF CHANGES IN FINANCIAL POSITION—CASH BASIS

As noted earlier, the statement of changes in financial position can be prepared on a cash basis instead of a working capital basis. Such a statement deals primarily with reporting the sources and uses of cash and is often referred to simply as a cash flow statement.

A cash basis statement of changes in financial position differs from one focusing on working capital primarily in the funds from operations section. A cash basis statement reports both cash and working capital from operations. Cash flow from operations is the net amount of cash received or disbursed on items that normally appear on the income statement. It is obtained by converting accural basis net income to a cash basis amount.

Cash Provided by Operations

There are two steps in converting net income to cash basis income. First, convert net income to working capital from operations by adding back or deducting from net income those items that did not use up or provide working capital. Second, convert working capital from operations to cash from operations by including the changes that occurred in current accounts other than cash. Applying these two steps to the Welby Company financial statements and other data in Illustration 19.3 yields the following schedule:

Net income		$10,000
Add expenses not reducing working capital—depreciation		5,000
Working capital from operations		$15,000
Effects of changes in components of operating working capital on cash:		
Increase in accounts receivable	$(10,000)	
Decrease in inventory	4,000	
Decrease in accounts payable	(6,000)	
Increase in accrued liabilities	2,000	(10,000)
Cash provided by operations		$ 5,000

The $10,000 increase in accounts receivable represents the difference between accrual basis sales revenue and cash collected from customers (sales revenue on a cash basis). An increase in accounts receivable indicates that accrual basis sales revenue was greater than cash basis sales revenue, and a decrease in accounts receivable indicates the opposite. Therefore, the $10,000 increase in accounts receivable must be deducted from accrual basis net income to convert it to cash basis income.

The changes in the balances of inventory and of accounts payable represent the difference between accrual basis cost of goods sold and cash paid for inventory purchases (cash basis cost of goods sold). We will first examine the effect of the change in inventory. If all the purchases had been for cash, then cost of goods sold on the cash basis would equal total purchases for the period. Total purchases were $96,000, computed as follows:

Ending inventory	$ 26,000
+Cost of goods sold	100,000
Cost of goods available for sale	$126,000
−Beginning inventory	30,000
Purchases	$ 96,000

Notice that the $4,000 decrease in inventory causes accrual basis cost of goods sold to be $4,000 greater than purchases. If we continue to assume that the total amount of purchases equals the amount of cash paid for purchases, then the higher cost of goods sold means that accrual basis income will be less than cash basis net income. Consequently, the $4,000 decrease in inventory must be added back to accrual basis net income to convert it to cash basis income.

However, not all purchases were made for cash. The $6,000 decrease in accounts payable represents the difference between purchases made on account and cash paid to suppliers during the period. A decrease in accounts payable means that more cash was paid than there were purchases, so cash basis cost of goods sold is greater than the amount of purchases. Thus, the $6,000 decrease in accounts payable must be deducted from accrual basis net income to convert it to cash basis income.

The correctness of the preceding analysis is demonstrated by the following computation:

Accounts payable, January 1	$ 15,000
Purchases (from prior schedule)	96,000
Total	$111,000
Accounts payable, December 31	9,000
Cash paid to suppliers during the year	102,000

Cash basis cost of goods sold is $102,000, or $2,000 more than the accrual basis amount. Net income on a cash basis is $2,000 less than the accrual basis amount. The $2,000 deduction agrees with the net amount of the individual analyses: $6,000 deducted for the decrease in accounts payable, and $4,000 added for the decrease in inventory nets out to a $2,000 deduction.

Accrued liabilities would be handled in a manner similar to accounts payable. Prepaid expenses would be treated the same as accounts receivable or inventory. These conversion procedures can be summarized as follows:

For changes in these working capital items:	Make these adjustments to convert accrual basis net income to cash basis net income:	
	Add	**Deduct**
Accounts receivable	Decrease	Increase
Inventory	Decrease	Increase
Prepaid expenses	Decrease	Increase
Accounts payable	Increase	Decrease
Accrued liabilities	Increase	Decrease

Notice in the above summary that all changes in current asset accounts are handled in a similar manner. Also, all changes in current liability accounts are handled in a similar manner, but that manner is exactly the opposite from the handling of the current asset changes. A more condensed table to use in making these adjustments is:

For changes in:	Add the change to working capital from operations	Deduct the change from working capital from operations
Current assets	Decreases	Increases
Current liabilities	Increases	Decreases

In applying the rules given in the table, a decrease in a current asset is added to working capital from operations; an increase in a current asset is deducted from working capital from operations. For current liabilities, increases are added and decreases are deducted.

The complete adjustment or conversion procedure used in the following comprehensive example is summarized below:

Accrual basis net income
+ Expenses and losses not reducing working capital
− Revenues and gains not producing working capital
= Working capital from operations
+ or − Changes in working capital accounts related to operations[2]
= Cash from operations

Statement of Changes in Financial Position—Cash Basis Preparation

The complete statement of changes in financial position—cash basis for Welby Company is presented in Illustration 19.6. A comparison of this statement with the one in Illustration 19.5 shows that the two statements are virtually identical, except for the section "Effects of changes in components of operating working capital on cash" in the cash basis statement (Illustration 19.6). There are two reasons for this similarity:

1. Most sources and uses of funds involve cash receipts and disbursements and would be reported in the same way whether cash or working capital was the focus of attention.
2. The cash basis statement was prepared by focusing on working capital first and then making the adjustments necessary to convert working capital from operations to cash from operations.

---

[2] An example of a change in a working capital item that does not affect operations is a change in dividends payable. We have avoided such items in this text and problems to simplify the coverage. Such items are covered in intermediate accounting texts.

Illustration 19.6

Statement of Changes in Financial Position—Cash Basis

WELBY COMPANY
Statement of Changes in Financial Position—Cash Basis
For the Year Ended December 31, 1987

Financial resources provided:

Cash from operations:		
Net income		$10,000
Add nonworking capital expenses:		
Depreciation		5,000
Working capital from operations		$15,000
Effects of changes in components of operating working capital on cash:		
Increase in accounts receivable	$(10,000)	
Decrease in inventory	4,000	
Decrease in accounts payable	(6,000)	
Increase in accrued liabilities	$ 2,000	(10,000)
Cash provided by operations		$ 5,000
Issuance of common stock		30,000
Total financial resources provided		$35,000
Financial resources applied:		
Purchase plant assets	$20,000	
Dividends paid	4,000	
Total financial resources applied		24,000
Increase in cash		$11,000

■ COMPREHENSIVE ILLUSTRATION

Presented and discussed below is a more complete example of the procedures followed to prepare a statement of changes in financial position—cash basis. A working paper (shown later in Illustration 19.9) is used to aid in preparing the statement. The working paper in Illustration 19.9 could, with only minor revision, be adapted to a working capital focus.[3]

The basic data for the example are found in Illustrations 19.7 and 19.8, which present the statement of income and retained earnings (combined) and comparative balance sheets of the United States Corporation. Assume the following information about the noncurrent accounts is available:

1. There were no purchases of investments during the year. Investments with an $8,000 cost were sold for $9,700.
2. Land and buildings with a cost of $65,000 ($45,000 for the buildings and $20,000 for the land) were acquired, subject to a mortgage note of $35,000.
3. During the year, the corporation disposed of equipment that had an original cost of $20,000 and accumulated depreciation of $16,500. The equipment was sold for $2,600.
4. The common stock was sold for cash.

The working paper in Illustration 19.9 for the United States Corporation is used to analyze the transactions and prepare the statement of changes in

---

[3] The use of a working paper to prepare a statement of changes in financial position—working capital basis is shown in the solution to the demonstration problem at the end of the chapter.

Illustration 19.7

Statement of Income and Retained Earnings

UNITED STATES CORPORATION		
Statement of Income and Retained Earnings		
For the Year Ended December 31, 1987		
Net sales		$1,464,200
Cost of goods sold		871,150
Gross margin		$ 593,050
Operating expenses:		
Salaries	$215,000	
Depreciation ($3,250, buildings; $31,050, equipment)	34,300	
Supplies	7,320	
Advertising	90,000	
Taxes, payroll and other	26,000	
General administrative expenses	123,780	
Total operating expenses		496,400
Net income from operations		$ 96,650
Other revenue:		
Interest revenue	$ 1,950	
Gain on sale of long-term investments	1,700	3,650
		$ 100,300
Other expenses:		
Interest expense	$ 3,800	
Loss on sale of equipment	900	4,700
Net income before federal income taxes		$ 95,600
Deduct: Federal income taxes		45,250
Net income to retained earnings		$ 50,350
Retained earnings, January 1		84,100
		$ 134,450
Deduct: Dividends declared and paid		18,000
Retained earnings, December 31		$ 116,450

financial position. The discussion that follows will describe the items and trace their effects in the entries made on the working paper.

The steps in preparing the working paper are described below:

1. Enter the account balances of all balance sheet accounts at the beginning of the period in the first column and at the end of the period in the fourth column. Notice that the debit items are listed first, followed by the credit items.
2. Total the debits and the credits in the first and fourth columns to make sure that debits equal credits in each column.
3. Write "Financial resources provided" immediately below the total of the credit items. Skip sufficient lines on which to record all sources of funds; then write "Financial resources applied."
4. Entries for analyzing transactions are entered in the second and third columns. The entries, which may be made in any order, serve two functions: (a) they explain the change in each account, and (b) they record the sources and uses of funds. These entries will be discussed individually.
5. Total the debits and credits in the second and third columns; they should be equal. There will be one pair of totals for the balance sheet items and another pair for the sources and uses of funds. The bottom portion of the working paper is used to prepare the formal statement of changes in financial position.

Illustration 19.8

*Comparative
Balance Sheet*

UNITED STATES CORPORATION
Comparative Balance Sheet
December 31, 1986, and 1987

	1987	1986	Increase/ decrease*
Assets			
Current assets:			
Cash	$ 46,300	$ 40,900	$ 5,400
Accounts receivable net	112,160	101,000	11,160
Inventories	130,600	115,300	15,300
Prepaid expenses	3,100	4,700	1,600*
Total current assets	$292,160	$261,900	$30,260
Investments	$ 17,000	$ 25,000	$ 8,000*
Property, plant, and equipment			
Land	$100,000	$ 80,000	$20,000
Buildings	175,000	130,000	45,000
Accumulated depreciation—buildings	(29,750)	(26,500)	(3,250)
Equipment	198,000	175,000	23,000
Accumulated depreciation—equipment	(57,650)	(43,100)	(14,550)
Total property, plant, and equipment	$385,600	$315,400	$70,200
Total assets	$694,760	$602,300	$92,460
Liabilities and Stockholders' Equity			
Current liabilities:			
Accounts payable	$ 91,420	$ 86,870	$ 4,550
Accrued liabilities	9,890	12,230	2,340*
Estimated federal income tax liability	12,000	14,100	2,100*
Total current liabilities	$113,310	$113,200	$ 110
Long-term liabilities:			
Mortgage note payable, 10% (on land and buildings)	$ 35,000	$ –0–	$35,000
Bonds payable, 8%, due 1991	40,000	40,000	–0–
Total long-term liabilities	$ 75,000	$ 40,000	$35,000
Total liabilities	$188,310	$153,200	$35,110
Stockholders' equity			
Common stock, stated value, $50 per share	$390,000	$365,000	$25,000
Retained earnings	116,450	84,100	32,350
Total stockholders' equity	$506,450	$449,100	$57,350
Total liabilities and stockholders' equity	$694,760	$602,300	$92,460

Completing the Working Paper

The working paper in Illustration 19.9 is completed by analyzing the change in each noncash balance sheet account. Although this procedure may seem odd at first, remember that the focus of this working paper is on cash and that every change in cash is accompanied by a change in a noncash balance sheet account. After entries have been properly made to analyze all changes in noncash balance sheet accounts, the working paper will show all sources and uses of cash. The explanations below are keyed by numbers to the entries on the working paper.

Entry (1). The beginning and ending cash balances are compared to determine the change for the year, which is a $5,400 increase. An entry is made on the working paper debiting Cash for $5,400 and crediting Increase in Cash for the Year under "Financial resources applied." This entry indicates that of the cash flowing into the company during the year, $5,400 was used to increase the Cash balance. The entry also sets out the change in cash that the statement seeks to explain. No further attention need be paid to cash in completing the working paper.

Attention is now directed toward changes in other balance sheet accounts. These accounts can be dealt with in any order. But, in order to group certain items, the noncurrent accounts are analyzed first.

Entry (2). Investments is the first noncurrent account. The additional information discloses that investments were sold at a gain, which was recorded in the following manner:

Cash	9,700	
Investments		8,000
Gain on Sale of Investments		1,700

Illustration 19.9

Working Paper for Statement of Changes in Financial Position—Cash Basis

UNITED STATES CORPORATION
Working Paper for Statement of Changes in Financial Position—Cash Basis for the Year Ended, December 31, 1987

	Account Balances 12/31/86	Analysis of Transactions for 1987		Account Balances 12/31/87
		Debit	**Credit**	
Debits				
Cash	40,900	(1) 5,400		46,300
Accounts Receivable	101,000	(10) 11,160		112,160
Inventories	115,300	(11) 15,300		130,600
Prepaid Expenses	4,700		(12) 1,600	3,100
Investments	25,000		(2) 8,000	17,000
Land	80,000	(3) 20,000		100,000
Buildings	130,000	(3) 45,000		175,000
Equipment	175,000	(5) 43,000	(4) 20,000	198,000
Totals	671,900			782,160
Credits				
Accumulated Depreciation— Buildings	26,500		(6) 3,250	29,750
Accumulated Depreciation— Equipment	43,100	(4) 16,500	(6) 31,050	57,650
Accounts Payable	86,870		(13) 4,550	91,420
Accrued Liabilities	12,230	(14) 2,340		9,890
Federal Income Tax Liability	14,100	(15) 2,100		12,000
Mortgage Note Payable	–0–		(3) 35,000	35,000
Bonds Payable	40,000			40,000
Common Stock	365,000		(7) 25,000	390,000
Retained Earnings	84,100	(9) 18,000	(8) 50,350	116,450
Totals	671,900	178,800	178,800	782,160

Illustration 19.9

(concluded)

	Account Balances 12/31/86	Analysis of Transactions for 1987		Account Balances 12/31/87
		Debit	**Credit**	
Financial Resources Provided:				
By Operations:				
Net Income		(8) 50,350		
Depreciation—Buildings		(6) 3,250		
Depreciation—Equipment		(6) 31,050		
Loss on Sale of Equipment		(4) 900		
Gain on Sale of Investments			(2) 1,700	
Increase in Accounts Receivable			(10) 11,160	
Increase in Inventories			(11) 15,300	
Decrease in Prepaid Expenses		(12) 1,600		
Increase in Accounts Payable		(13) 4,550		
Decrease in Accrued Liabilities			(14) 2,340	
Decrease in Federal Income Tax				
Liability			(15) 2,100	
Other Sources:				
Sale of Investments		(2) 9,700		
Assumption of Mortgage Note		(3) 35,000		
Sale of Equipment		(4) 2,600		
Issuance of Common Stock		(7) 25,000		
Financial Resources Applied:				
Acquisition of Land and Buildings			(3) 65,000	
Acquisition of Equipment			(5) 43,000	
Payment of Cash Dividends			(9) 18,000	
Increase in Cash for Year			(1) 5,400	
Totals		164,000	164,000	

Since cash changes and their causes are the focus of the working paper, the following entry is made on the working paper to show the source of cash.

Sale of Investments	9,700	
Investments		8,000
Gain on sale of investments		1,700

The working paper now shows that $9,700 cash was provided by the sale of investments. The entry also removes the $1,700 gain on sale of investments from cash provided by operations because this amount is already included as part of the cash provided by sale of investments. If the $9,700 cash received from the sale is reported and the gain is not removed from cash provided by operations, the $1,700 gain is shown or counted twice. Note that the working paper entry is identical to the original journal entry for the sale, except for the $9,700 debit. Instead of debiting Cash, a properly described source of cash is debited. The sources and uses of cash are shown in the lower section of the working paper. The $8,000 credit accounts fully for the change (decrease) in the Investments account balance; if it had not fully accounted for the change, there would have to be other transactions involving the Investments account to analyze and report.

Entry (3). The changes in the Land and Buildings accounts resulted from the following entry:

Land	20,000	
Buildings	45,000	
Cash		30,000
Mortgage Note Payable		35,000

This transaction requires two entries on the working paper. First, Land and Buildings are debited for $20,000 and $45,000, respectively, and a cash applied item described as "Acquisition of Land and Buildings" is credited for $65,000. Second, a source of cash called "Assumption of Mortgage Note" is debited and Mortgage Note Payable is credited for $35,000. In other words, the transaction is treated as if the mortgage note was issued for cash, and then $65,000 cash had been spent to acquire land and buildings. This transaction is an example of a significant financing and investing activity that must be included on the statement even though part of it did not affect funds.

Entry (4). The Equipment account shows a net increase of $23,000 resulting from two transactions: a $43,000 purchase and a $20,000 retirement. The net change in the account must be analyzed to show both cash applied and cash provided.

Data relating to the $20,000 retirement were included in the additional information given. The computation of the loss on sale can be summarized as follows using data provided in the additional information:

Cost of equipment sold (given)	$20,000
Less: Accumulated depreciation (given)	16,500
Book value of equipment sold	$ 3,500
Less: Cash received (given)	2,600
Loss on sale (as shown in Income statement)	$ 900

The complete working paper entry for the sale of equipment is:

Sale of Equipment	2,600	
Accumulated Depreciation—Equipment	16,500	
Loss on Sale of Equipment	900	
Equipment		20,000

This entry records the cash provided by sale of equipment under the "Other sources" section on the working paper and explains part of the changes in the Equipment and the Accumulated Depreciation—Equipment accounts. The loss is added back to net income because it is a noncash item that was deducted in arriving at net income. The loss has exactly the same effect as depreciation expense.

Entry (5). This entry debits the Equipment account and credits Acquisition of Equipment for the $43,000 cash spent to acquire new equipment. The $43,000 debit to Equipment along with the $20,000 credit to Equipment in entry (4) fully accounts for the $23,000 increase in the account.

Entry (6). This entry adds $3,250 building depreciation and $31,050 equipment depreciation back to net income and credits the respective accumulated depreciation accounts. The $31,050 credit to the accumulated depreciation account for equipment less the $16,500 debit to this account in entry *(4)* explains fully the increase in this account from $43,100 to $57,650.

Entry *(7)*. This entry shows the $25,000 cash received from sale of common stock as an "Other source" of cash. The entry also explains completely the change in the Common Stock account. If stock had been sold for more than its stated value of $50 per share, the excess would be recorded in a separate Paid-In Capital in Excess of Stated Value account. But only the total amount of cash received from the issuance would have been reported on the statement of changes in financial position as a single figure because only the total amount received is significant.

Entry *(8)*. The statement of income and retained earnings reveals that net income for 1987 was $50,350. Entry *(8)* records the $50,350 as the starting point in measuring cash from operations and credits Retained Earnings as a partial explanation of the change in that account.

Entry *(9)*. This entry debits Retained Earnings and credits Payment of Cash Dividends for the $18,000 of dividends declared and paid. The entry also completes the explanation of the change in Retained Earnings ($84,100 + $50,350 − $18,000 = $116,450). Notice that on the cash basis statement the dividends must be **paid** to be included as funds applied. Under the working capital basis they only had to be declared because the declaration increases dividends payable (thereby reducing working capital).

If Retained Earnings had changed for reasons other than net income or cash dividends, the causes of the changes must be determined in order to decide whether they should be reported in the statement of changes in financial position. Transactions such as stock dividends and stock splits would **not** be reported on the statement of changes in financial position because they lack significance from an analytical viewpoint and because these items never affect cash or working capital. But an entry must be made on the working paper to explain the changes caused by a stock dividend or split, even if cash was not affected. All changes in all noncash accounts must be explained to show that a change affecting cash was not overlooked.

The next task is to analyze changes in current accounts other than Cash. All the current accounts of the United States Corporation are closely related to operations, and their changes are included in converting net income to cash from operations. The changes in the current accounts are analyzed in the manner previously discussed (see pages 733–35).

Entry *(10)*. The $11,160 increase in accounts receivable must be deducted from net income when converting it to cash from operations. If accounts receivable increased, sales to customers exceeded cash received from customers. Accrual basis on a cash basis. To convert net income to a cash basis, the $11,160 must be deducted.

The working paper technique used makes the recording of these effects almost mechanical. Accounts Receivable must be debited for $11,160 to increase it from $101,000 to $112,160. If Accounts Receivable is debited, a credit must be entered for an item that can be entitled "Increase in Accounts Receivable." The increase is deducted from net income in converting it to cash from operations.

Entry *(11)* is virtually a duplicate of entry *(10)*, except that it involves inventories rather than receivables.

Entry *(12)* is similar to the above two entries, except that it has the opposite effect because prepaid expenses decreased.

Entry *(13)* records the effect of an increase in accounts payable on net income in converting it to cash from operations.

Entries *(14)* and *(15)* record the effects of decreases in two other current liability accounts in converting net income to cash from operations.

The analysis of the noncash accounts is now complete. To be sure that a change has not been overlooked, the debits and credits in the middle two columns opposite the 1986 balances are added to or subtracted from those balances, line by line. If the working paper has been properly prepared, the results will be the 1987 balances listed in the fourth column. For example, the $43,000 debit is added to the beginning balance for Equipment, and the $20,000 credit deducted to get an ending balance of $198,000.

Next, the debits and credits for the balance sheet account entries and for the statement of changes in financial position items are added to make sure that they are equal in both sections. Note that entries made in the working paper are used only to derive cash flows into and out of the company. These entries are not entered in the company's accounting system because the transactions that caused the fund flows have already been recorded.

The Formal Statement

The data in the lower section of the working paper are now used to prepare the formal statement of changes in financial position—cash basis shown in Illustration 19.10. A standard format has not been prescribed for this statement. Both the APB and the FASB have recommended experimentation using alternative forms.

Two features of Illustration 19.10 should be noted. First, the two sections are headed "Financial resources provided" and "Financial resources applied" reflecting the reporting of all significant financing and investing activities as required by *Opinion No. 19*. The headings are appropriate since an exchange involving assumption of liability on a mortgage note for land and buildings is reported. Also note that the statement reports both working capital and cash provided by operations.

Working Paper for Statement of Changes in Financial Position—Working Capital Basis

Entries *(2)* through *(9)* shown above for a statement of changes of financial position prepared under the cash basis analyze noncurrent account changes that had a cash effect. Since cash is an element of working capital, the same entries would be made in preparing a statement of changes of financial position focusing on working capital.

The first line of a working paper for a statement of changes of financial position—working capital basis for the United States Corporation would show $148,700 of working capital at the end of 1986 and $178,850 at the end of 1987. Entry *(1)* would debit Working Capital for $30,150 and credit Increase in Working Capital on the last line of the working paper. This single working capital amount would be substituted for the six current asset and current liability accounts listed on the working paper for a statement of changes of financial position—cash basis.

Also, note in the United States Corporation illustration that entries for net income and nonworking capital charges and credits are grouped to make it easy to compute working capital from operations. This amount is $83,850,

Illustration 19.10

Statement of Changes in Financial Position—Cash Basis

UNITED STATES CORPORATION Statement of Changes in Financial Position—Cash Basis For the Year Ended December 31, 1987		
Financial resources provided:		
By operations:		
Net income		$ 50,350
Add: Charges not requiring outlay of funds:		
Depreciation—building	$ 3,250	
Depreciation—equipment	31,050	
Loss on sale of equipment	900	35,200
		$ 85,550
Deduct: Credits not providing funds:		
Gain on sale of investments		1,700
Working capital provided by operations		$ 83,850
Effect of change in components of operating working capital on cash:		
Increase in accounts receivable	$(11,160)	
Increase in inventories	(15,300)	
Decrease in prepaid expenses	1,600	
Increase in accounts payable	4,550	
Decrease in accrued liabilities	(2,340)	
Decrease in federal income tax liability	(2,100)	(24,750)
Cash provided from operations		$ 59,100
Other resources provided:		
Sale of investments	$ 9,700	
Assumption of mortgage note	35,000	
Sale of equipment	2,600	
Issuance of common stock	25,000	72,300
Total financial resources provided		$131,400
Financial resources applied:		
Acquisition of land and building	$ 65,000	
Acquisition of equipment	43,000	
Payment of cash dividends	18,000	
Total financial resources applied		126,000
Increase in cash for the year		$ 5,400

computed by adding the first four items shown in the lower section of the working paper in Illustration 19.9 and deducting the $1,700 gain (see page 740).

Losses on the Working Paper

If a company incurs a net loss for a period, the entry on the working paper debits Retained Earnings and credits Net Loss under Financial Resources Provided by Operations. Then the net loss is adjusted for the nonfund items. For instance, depreciation and other nonfund expenses are added back and may more than offset the net loss. If so, the company will have funds provided by operations even though it had a net loss. If these nonfund adjustments do not offset the entire loss, then the company will have funds applied to operations. If the adjustments for the nonfund items result in funds provided by operations, all data relative to the net loss and its adjustments are shown in the "Resources provided" section of the statement of changes in financial position. If funds were applied to operations, all data relative to the net loss and its adjustments will be shown in the "Resources applied" section.

■ WORKING CAPITAL OR CASH FLOWS

In the past, statements of changes in financial position have generally focused on working capital flows. Such statements were prepared for several reasons. Accurate information was needed about the flows of liquid assets (working capital) through a company because such flows are the lifeblood of a business. Yet constant changes in accounting principles yielded net income amounts that often were not good measures of such liquid assets flows from operations. In addition, attention focused on working capital rather than cash because little significance was attached to the composition of working capital. In general, working capital turned over in a business quickly enough so that if not now in cash form, it would be shortly.

The Shift toward Cash Flows

Recent events suggest that in the future, statements of changes in financial position will focus increasingly on cash flows. Many companies experience severe cash flow, not working capital, problems. The FASB noted the importance of cash flows in the Conceptual Framework Project, stating "that the reporting of meaningful components of cash flows is generally more useful than reporting changes in working capital."[4] Shortly after the publication of this statement, the Financial Executives Institute (FEI) recommended that its members adopt the cash basis in preparing a statement of changes in financial position.[5] The FEI represents approximately 95% of the companies with securities traded on the New York Stock Exchange and the American Stock Exchange.

Illustration 19.11 shows that for a sample of 600 companies the emphasis has shifted steadily from working capital to cash. In 1980, only 59 of the companies emphasized cash flows, while in 1983 more than half did so.

Illustration 19.11

Definitions of "Funds" in Statement of Changes in Financial Position

	1983	1982	1981	1980
Changes in working capital	286	346	466	541
Changes in cash	314	254	134	59
Total	600	600	600	600

Source: Based on American Institute of Certified Public Accountants, *Accounting Trends & Techniques* (New York: AICPA, 1984), p. 366.

The shifting of attention from working capital flows to cash flows also is supported by developments in modern finance. The investment decision is seen more clearly as one in which cash outlays are compared with expected cash returns, appropriately discounted for time and risk. Management, investors, and creditors are all alike in that each "invests" cash to get future cash returns. Thus, information is needed to enable users to make predictions of the amounts,

---

[4] FASB, "Reporting Income, Cash Flows, and Financial Position of Business Enterprises," *Proposed Statement of Financial Accounting Concepts,* Exposure Draft (Stamford, Conn., 1981), p. xi.

[5] Financial Executives Institute, *Alert,* December 14, 1981.

timing, and uncertainty surrounding expected cash receipts. Information also is needed to provide feedback on prior assessments of cash flow.

Information on prior **cash** flows provides a better basis for making predictions of cash flows than does information on prior **working capital** flows. Cash flows often differ sharply from working capital flows. For example, a rapidly expanding business that increases its working capital by expanding inventories and accounts receivable may not have enough cash to meet current bills. Cash flow analysis, rather than working capital analysis, is required to reveal such problems.

■ *SUMMARY*

The statement of changes in financial position is one of the four major financial statements prepared by companies. The purpose of the statement of changes in financial position is analytical in that it attempts to explain how financial resources were acquired during a period, how financial resources were used, and what the net effect was on a company's working capital or cash position. Being an analytical tool, the statement of changes in financial position is an excellent means for assessing the quality of an organization's management.

Financial resources or funds are commonly defined as either working capital or cash. In the past, statements of changes in financial position have generally focused on working capital flows. Recent events suggest, however, that the emphasis in coming years will increasingly be on cash flows. Whichever definition of funds is used, the statement must report the effects of **all significant financing** and **investing activities,** even those that do not directly affect funds. This is known as the all financial resources concept.

In preparing a statement of changes in financial position—working capital basis, the first step is to prepare a schedule of changes in working capital. Then each noncurrent balance sheet account is analyzed to see what effect changes in it had on working capital during the period. These changes in noncurrent account balances are organized in terms of representing either financial resources provided or financial resources applied during the period. Finally, the statement is prepared using the analyses of the noncurrent accounts.

The statement of changes in financial position—cash basis focuses on cash flows into and out of an organization. A key element in the preparation of the cash basis statement is the adjustment of the income statement from an accrual basis to a cash basis. Changes in noncurrent balance sheet accounts are analyzed for their effects on working capital just as is done when the working capital basis is used. Then, all current accounts other than Cash are analyzed for changes in order to adjust working capital from operations to cash from operations. Finally, the resulting cash inflows and cash outflows are organized into a formal statement of changes in financial position—cash basis.

This chapter illustrated the use of a working paper to help in preparing a statement of changes in financial position. The working paper may be used with either a working capital or cash basis statement of changes in financial position; it helps to analyze changes in accounts and helps to format the final presentation of the statement of changes in financial position.

Now that you have studied the statement of changes of financial statement, you should realize its importance in presenting a more complete picture of the business operations of a company. In Chapter 20, you will learn how to analyze and interpret a company's financial statements so that you can better judge its solvency and profitability.

NEW TERMS INTRODUCED IN CHAPTER 19

All financial resources concept

This concept requires that a business report all significant financing and investing activities, regardless of whether the cash or working capital definition of funds is used (727).

Cash flow from operations

The net amount of cash received or disbursed for a given period on items that normally appear on the income statement. Usually obtained by converting accrual basis net income to a cash basis amount (733).

Cash flow statement

Another title for a statement of changes in financial position prepared on a cash basis; sometimes used as a title for a statement or schedule showing cash flows into and out of a business together with beginning and ending cash balances (733).

Financial resources applied

An all-inclusive title used to describe the uses made of a company's resources in a period. In certain instances, the more restrictive titles of working capital applied or cash applied may be substituted (731).

Financial resources provided

The most all-inclusive title used to describe the sources of the resources flowing into a company in a period. In certain instances, the more restrictive titles such as "sources of working capital" or "sources of cash" may be appropriate (732).

Funds

Broadly speaking, the financial resources of a company; often defined as working capital or as cash (725).

Indirect method

A way of determining cash or working capital from operations that starts with net income and adjusts for expenses and revenues that do not affect cash or working capital. Also called the **addback** method (728).

Nonworking capital (or nonfund) charges or expenses

Expenses and losses that are added back to net income because they do not actually use funds of the company.

The items added back include amounts of depletion that were expensed, amortization of intangible assets such as patents and goodwill, amortization of discount on bonds payable, and losses from disposals of noncurrent assets (728).

Nonworking capital (or nonfund) credits or revenues

Revenues and gains included in arriving at net income that do not provide working capital; an example is a gain on the sale of a noncurrent asset (729).

Source of funds

A transaction that brings funds (working capital or cash) into the business (727).

Statement of changes in financial position

A statement that reports the flows of cash or working capital into and out of a business in a given time period; it also shows significant financing and investing activities that do not involve cash or working capital flows (725).

Statement of changes in working capital

A statement listing all current assets and current liabilities, their beginning and ending balances, and the changes in these balances summarized into a single amount—the net change in working capital. The **schedule of changes in working capital components** shows only the change in each working capital item summarized into a single amount (729).

Use of funds

A transaction that removes funds (working capital or cash) from the business (727).

Working capital

A possible definition of funds; equal to current assets minus current liabilities (726).

Working capital from operations

Working capital generated by the regular operations of a business; usually computed as net income plus nonworking capital expenses deducted in arriving at net income, minus nonworking capital revenues included, and less certain gains which are included in the total proceeds received from sale of a noncash or nonworking capital asset (731).

DEMONSTRATION PROBLEM

Given below are comparative balance sheets of the Dells Corporation as of June 30, 1986, and June 30, 1987. Also given are the income statement for the year ended June 30, 1987, and certain additional data.

DELLS CORPORATION
Comparative Balance Sheet
June 30, 1986, and 1987

	1987	1986	Increase decrease*
Assets			
Current assets:			
Cash	$ 30,000	$ 80,000	$ 50,000*
Accounts receivable	160,000	100,000	60,000
Inventory	100,000	70,000	30,000
Prepaid rent	20,000	10,000	10,000
Total current assets	$310,000	$260,000	$ 50,000
Property, plant, and equipment:			
Equipment	$400,000	$200,000	$200,000
Accumulated depreciation	(60,000)	(50,000)	(10,000)
Total property, plant, and equipment . . .	$340,000	$150,000	$190,000
Total assets	$650,000	$410,000	$240,000
Liabilities and Stockholders' Equity			
Current liabilities:			
Accounts payable	$ 50,000	$ 40,000	$ 10,000
Notes payable—bank	–0–	50,000	50,000*
Accrued salaries	10,000	20,000	10,000*
Federal income tax payable	30,000	20,000	10,000
Total current liabilities	$ 90,000	$130,000	$ 40,000*
Stockholders' equity:			
Common stock, $10 par	$300,000	$100,000	$200,000
Paid-in capital in excess of par	50,000	–0–	50,000
Retained earnings	210,000	180,000	30,000
Total stockholders' equity	$560,000	$280,000	$280,000
Total liabilities and stockholders' equity	$650,000	$410,000	$240,000

DELLS CORPORATION
Statement of Income and Retained Earnings
For the Year Ended June 30, 1987

Sales		$1,000,000
Cost of goods sold	$600,000	
Salaries and wages	200,000	
Rent	40,000	
Depreciation	20,000	
Interest	3,000	
Loss on sale of equipment	7,000	870,000
Net income before federal income taxes . .		$ 130,000
Federal income taxes		60,000
Net income		$ 70,000
Retained earnings, July 1, 1986		180,000
		$ 250,000
Dividends		40,000
Retained earnings, June 30, 1987		$ 210,000

Additional data

1. Equipment with a cost of $20,000, on which $10,000 of depreciation had been recorded, was sold for cash. Additional equipment was purchased.
2. Stock was issued for cash.

Required: Using the data given for the Dells Corporation, prepare a statement of changes in financial position—working capital basis. Prepare a working paper by examining Illustration 19.9 and reading the description given on page 743 for preparing a working paper on the working capital basis.

Solution to demonstration problem

	Account Balances 6/30/86	Analysis of Transactions for Fiscal Year Debit	Credit	Account Balances 6/30/87
DELLS CORPORATION Working Paper for Statement of Changes in Financial Position—Working Capital Basis For the Year Ended June 30, 1987				
Debits				
Working Capital	130,000	(1) 90,000		220,000
Equipment	200,000	(5) 220,000	(4) 20,000	400,000
Totals	330,000			620,000
Credits				
Accumulated Depreciation	50,000	(4) 10,000	(3) 20,000	60,000
Common Stock	100,000		(6) 200,000	300,000
Capital in Excess of Par	–0–		(6) 50,000	50,000
Retained Earnings	180,000	(7) 40,000	(2) 70,000	210,000
Totals	330,000	360,000	360,000	620,000
Financial resources provided:				
By operations:				
Net income		(2) 70,000		
Add: Depreciation		(3) 20,000		
Loss on sale of equipment		(4) 7,000		
Other sources:				
Sale of equipment		(4) 3,000		
Sale of common stock		(6) 250,000		
Financial resources applied:				
Purchase of equipment			(5) 220,000	
Declaration of cash dividends			(7) 40,000	
Increase in working capital				
during year			(1) 90,000	
Totals		350,000	350,000	

DELLS CORPORATION
Statement of Changes in Financial Position—Working Capital Basis
For the Year Ended June 30, 1987

Financial resources provided:

By operations.			
Net income		$ 70,000	
Add: Depreciation	$20,000		
Loss on sale of equipment	7,000	27,000	
Working capital provided by operations .			$ 97,000
Other sources of working capital:			
Sale of equipment			3,000
Sale of common stock			250,000
Total working capital provided			$350,000
Financial resources applied:			
Purchase of equipment		$220,000	
Declaration of cash dividends		40,000	
Total working capital applied			260,000
Increase in working capital			$ 90,000

Schedule of changes in working capital components:

Increases (decreases) in current assets:		
Cash	$(50,000)	
Accounts receivable	60,000	
Inventory	30,000	
Prepaid rent	10,000	$ 50,000
Increase (decrease) in liabilities:		
Accounts payable	$ 10,000	
Notes payable—bank	(50,000)	
Accrued salaries	(10,000)	
Federal income tax payable	10,000	(40,000)
Increase in working capital		$ 90,000

QUESTIONS

1. What are the concepts of funds used in a statement of changes in financial position?

2. When funds are defined as working capital, what are the major sources of funds in a business? What are the major uses of funds?

3. Explain the difference between the direct and indirect methods for computing working capital from operations.

4. What are nonfund (nonworking capital or noncash) expenses? How are they treated in computing working capital from operations?

5. Describe the treatment of a gain on the sale of equipment in preparing a statement of changes in financial position.

6. In the preparation of a statement of changes in financial position—working capital basis, why are the noncurrent accounts analyzed rather than the current accounts?

7. Does the declaration or payment of dividends affect working capital? Why?

8. Depreciation is often referred to as a source of funds. Is it a source of funds? Explain.

9. In what respects does cash flow analysis differ from working capital flow analysis?

10. Why is it unlikely that cash flow from operations will be equal to net income for the same period?

11. If the net income for a given period is $25,000, does this mean that there is an increase of cash of the same amount? Why or why not?

12. Why might a company have a positive inflow of cash from operations even though operating at a net loss?

13. Why might an analysis of working capital flows be unsuitable for short-run planning?

14. Give two reasons why analysts seem to prefer cash flow statements to statements that report working capital flows.

EXERCISES

E-1

Report specific items on statement of changes in financial position

Indicate how the following data should be reported in a statement of changes in financial position—working capital basis. A company purchased land valued at $24,000 and a building valued at $48,000 by payment of $12,000 by check, signing a $18,000 interest-bearing note due in six months, and assuming a $42,000 mortgage on the property.

E-2

Report specific items on statement of changes in financial position

A company sold equipment having an original cost of $8,400, on which $4,800 of depreciation had been recorded, for $6,000. The gain was included in net income. How should these data be shown in the statement of changes in financial position? Why?

E-3

Report specific items on statement of changes in financial position

The following data are from the Automobile and Accumulated Depreciation—Automobile accounts of a certain company:

Automobile

Date			Debit	Credit	Balance
1987					
Jan.	1	Balance brought forward			4,800
July	1	Traded for new auto		4,800	–0–
		New auto	5,280		5,280

Accumulated Depreciation—Automobile

			Debit	Credit	Balance
Jan.	1	Balance brought forward			3,600
July	1	One-half year's depreciation		600	4,200
		Auto traded	4,200		–0–
Dec. 31		One-half year's depreciation		660	660

The old auto was traded for a new one and cash was paid in the exchange. The income statement for the year shows a loss on the exchange of autos of $360.

For all amounts involved, indicate the descriptions of these amounts and their exact locations in a statement of changes in financial position—working capital basis.

E-4

Compute change in working capital

Following are balance sheet data for the Badger Corporation:

	December 31, 1987	December 31, 1986
Cash	$ 65,800	$ 36,400
Accounts receivable	197,400	187,600
Inventory	116,200	142,800
Prepaid expenses	12,600	15,400
Plant assets (net of accumulated depreciation)	329,000	322,000
Accounts payable	170,800	177,800
Accrued liabilities	56,000	57,400
Capital stock	420,000	420,000
Retained earnings	74,200	49,000

Calculate the change in working capital for the year 1987.

E-5

Compute cash used to purchase plant assets

Refer to the information in Exercise E-4. Assume that the depreciation recorded in 1987 was $21,000. Compute the cash used to purchase plant assets assuming no assets were sold or scrapped in 1987.

E-6

Prepare statement of changes in financial position—working capital basis

Use the data in Exercise E-4. Assume that net income for 1987 was $33,600, that depreciation was $21,000, and that dividends declared and paid were $8,400. Prepare a statement of changes in financial position—working capital basis.

E-7

Compute working capital provided by operations

Assume that a company's net income for the year was $28,000, patent amortization was $700, loss on sale of patents was $1,400, depreciation was $2,800, gain on sale of equipment was $840, and accumulated depreciation on equipment was $14,000. Compute working capital from operations.

E-8

Compute sales on a cash basis and its effect on cash provided by operations

A company's financial statements for a given year show sales of $800,000, net income of $80,000, and accounts receivable on January 1 of $70,400 and $75,200 on December 31. *(a)* Compute sales on a cash basis (cash collections). *(b)* Compute the effect of the above information on net income as a measure of cash from operations.

E-9

Compute cost of goods sold on a cash basis and its effect on cash provided by operations

The income statement of a company shows net income of $80,000. Inventory on January 1 was $81,600 and on December 31 was $100,800, and accounts payable for merchandise purchases were $60,800 on January 1 and $67,200 on December 31. Compute the effects of the above information on net income as a measure of cash from operations.

E-10

Compute cash provided by operations

The operating expenses (including $16,000 of depreciation) of a company for a given year were $160,000. Net income was $80,000. Prepaid Insurance decreased from $4,800 to $3,200 during the year, while Accrued Wages increased from $6,400 to $9,600 during the year. Compute the effects of the above on net income as a measure of cash from operations.

E-11

Prepare partial statement of changes in financial position

Assume that the data in Exercises E-8, E-9, and E-10 above are for the same company. Prepare the section of the statement of changes in financial position showing conversion of net income to cash from operations. Show both working capital and cash from operations.

E-12

Indicate treatment of dividend

Dividends payable increased by $4,800 during the year in which total dividends declared were $96,000. What amount of dividends would appear in the statement of changes in financial position—working capital basis? What amount would appear in the same statement prepared under the cash basis?

E-13

Prepare a statement of changes in financial position—cash basis

Refer to the data in Exercises E-4 and E-6. Prepare a statement of changes in financial position—cash basis.

PROBLEMS, SERIES A

P19–1–A

Prepare statement of changes in financial position—working capital basis

Following are comparative ledger balance data and a statement of retained earnings for the year ended May 31, 1987, for Scott Company (in thousands of dollars):

	May 31	
	1987	1986
Debits		
Cash	$ 126	$ 112
Accounts receivable, net	252	288
Inventories	300	248
Investment in subsidiary	190	160
Land	140	100
Buildings and equipment	866	760
Patents	22	32
Total	$1,896	$1,700
Credits		
Accumulated depreciation . . .	$ 156	$ 120
Accounts payable	180	128
Taxes payable	32	24
Bonds payable	400	400
Common stock, $100 par	800	800
Retained earnings	328	228
Total	$1,896	$1,700

Statement of Retained Earnings

Balance, May 31, 1986	$ 228
Net income	200
	$ 428
Dividends declared	100
Balance, May 31, 1987	$ 328

Additional data:

1. Additional shares of stock of the subsidiary company were acquired for cash as an investment.
2. A tract of land adjacent to land owned was purchased during the year.
3. Depreciation of $60,000 and patent amortization of $10,000 were charged to expense during the year.
4. New equipment with a cost of $130,000 was purchased during the year, while fully depreciated equipment with a cost of $24,000 was scrapped and discarded.

Required: Prepare a statement of changes in financial position—working capital basis and include a comparative schedule of changes in working capital components. Try to do so without preparing a working paper so that your conceptual understanding of the statement may be strengthened.

P19–2–A

Prepare statement of changes in financial position—cash basis

Use the data for Problem P19–1–A. Prepare a statement of changes in financial position—cash basis.

P19–3–A

*Prepare working
paper and statement
of changes in
financial position—
working capital basis*

The income statement for the Bartley Company for the year ended December 31, 1987, shows:

Net sales		$768,000
Cost of goods sold	$450,000	
Operating expenses	120,000	
Major repairs	60,000	
Interest expense	18,000	
Loss on sale of equipment . .	9,600	657,600
Net income before taxes . .		$110,400
Federal income taxes . . .		57,600
Net income		$ 52,800

Comparative balance sheets for the company follow:

BARTLEY COMPANY
Comparative Balance Sheets
December 31, 1986, and 1987

	December 31	
	1987	*1986*
Assets		
Current assets:		
Cash	$ 57,600	$ 48,000
Accounts receivable, net	116,400	91,200
Inventories	252,000	216,000
Prepaid expenses	19,200	7,200
Total current assets	$445,200	$362,400
Property, plant, and equipment:		
Buildings	$120,000	$120,000
Accumulated depreciation—buildings	(66,000)	(60,000)
Equipment	222,000	156,000
Accumulated depreciation—equipment . . .	(75,600)	(72,000)
Total property, plant, and equipment . . .	$200,400	$144,000
Total assets	$645,600	$506,400
Liabilities and Stockholders' Equity		
Current liabilities:		
Accounts payable	$ 56,400	$ 90,000
Accrued liabilities	19,800	17,400
Federal income taxes payable	57,600	54,000
Wages payable	11,400	9,000
Total current liabilities	$145,200	$170,400
Long-term liabilities:		
Bonds payable (15%)	120,000	120,000
Total liabilities	$265,200	$290,400
Stockholders' equity:		
Paid-in capital:		
Capital stock—par $140	$300,000	$180,000
Paid-in capital in excess of par value . . .	30,000	–0–
Retained earnings	50,400	36,000
Total stockholders' equity	$380,400	$216,000
Total liabilities and stockholders' equity	$645,600	$506,400

Additional data:

1. Capital stock was issued for cash.
2. Accrued liabilities relate solely to operating expenses.
3. The depreciation on equipment for the year amounted to $18,000. The equipment sold had an original cost of $36,000.

4. Dividends declared and paid during the year totaled $38,400.
5. Accounts payable arose solely from purchases of merchandise.

Required: a. Prepare a working paper for a statement of changes in financial position—working capital basis. (See the solution to the demonstration problem.)
b. Prepare a statement of changes in financial position—working capital basis.

P19–4–A

Prepare working paper and statement of changes in financial position— cash basis

Use the data for problem P19–3–A.

Required: a. Prepare a working paper for a statement of changes in financial position—cash basis.
b. Prepare a statement of changes in financial position—cash basis.

P19–5–A

Prepare working paper and statement of changes in financial position— working capital basis

Given below are comparative balance sheet account balances and other data of the West Corporation:

	June 30	
	1987	1986
Debit balances		
Cash	$173,600	$ 95,200
Accounts receivable	539,000	310,800
Inventories	588,000	610,400
Prepaid insurance	2,800	4,200
Land	224,000	252,000
Buildings	1,568,000	868,000
Machinery and tools	616,000	336,000
Patent	5,600	7,000
Total	$3,717,000	$2,483,600
Credit balances		
Accumulated depreciation	$ 581,000	$ 366,800
Accounts payable	91,000	126,000
Accrued liabilities	61,600	8,400
Bank loans (90-day)	40,600	47,600
Mortgage bonds payable	280,000	140,000
Common stock, $100 par	1,260,000	420,000
Paid-in capital in excess of par value . .	42,000	–0–
Retained earnings	1,360,800	1,374,800
Total	$3,717,000	$2,483,600

Additional data:

1. Net income for the year was $56,000.
2. Patent amortization expense was $1,400.
3. Depreciation for the year was $256,200.
4. Dividends declared and paid were $70,000.
5. Additional common stock was issued at $105 per share.
6. The mortgage bonds were issued at face value as partial payment for a building valued at $700,000. Machinery and tools were purchased for $322,000.
7. There was a gain of $5,600 on the sale of land.
8. Fully depreciated machinery with a cost of $42,000 was scrapped and written off.

Required: a. Prepare a working paper for a statement of changes in financial position—working capital basis. (See the solution to the demonstration problem.)
b. Prepare the formal statement of changes in financial position—working capital basis.

P19-6-A

Prepare working paper and statement of changes in financial position—cash basis

Use the data in Problem P19-5-A.

a. Prepare a working paper for a statement of changes in financial position—cash basis.
b. Prepare a statement of changes in financial position—cash basis.

PROBLEMS, SERIES B

P19-1-B

Prepare statement of changes in financial position—working capital basis including a schedule of changes in working capital components

CAIN CORPORATION
Comparative Balance Sheets
December 31, 1986, and 1987

	December 31	
	1987	1986
Assets		
Cash	$ 36,000	$ 48,000
Accounts receivable, net	134,400	96,000
Inventory	240,000	192,000
Equipment	660,000	504,000
Accumulated depreciation	(192,000)	(168,000)
Investments	120,000	24,000
Total assets	$998,400	$696,000
Liabilities and Stockholders' Equity		
Accounts payable	$ 34,800	$ 30,000
Accrued liabilites	3,600	6,000
Capital stock—common—$12 par value . . .	600,000	480,000
Paid-in capital in excess of par value	240,000	120,000
Retained earnings	120,000	60,000
Total liabilities and stockholders' equity	$998,400	$696,000

Additional data:

1. Net income was $108,000 for the year.
2. Fully depreciated equipment costing $24,000 was sold for $6,000, and equipment costing $180,000 was purchased for cash.
3. Depreciation expense for the year was $48,000.
4. Investments were purchased for $96,000.
5. An additional 10,000 shares of common stock were issued for cash at $24 per share.
6. Cash dividends of $48,000 were declared.

Required: Prepare a statement of changes in financial position—working capital basis including a schedule of changes in working capital components.

P19-2-B

Prepare statement of changes in financial position—cash basis

Refer to the information in Problem P19-1-B. Prepare another statement of changes in financial position, this time using the cash basis.

P19–3–B

Prepare statement of changes in financial position—cash basis

---

GATLIN CORPORATION
Comparative Balance Sheets
June 30, 1986, and 1987

	June 30	
	1987	**1986**
Assets		
Current assets	$ 427,000	$ 329,000
Investment in stock of affiliated company	252,000	210,000
Buildings	532,000	392,000
Accumulated depreciation—buildings	(84,000)	(70,000)
Equipment	686,000	560,000
Accumulated depreciation—equipment	(210,000)	(168,000)
Total assets	$1,603,000	$1,253,000
Liabilities and Stockholders' Equity		
Current liabilities	$ 224,000	$ 168,000
Five-year note payable	140,000	–0–
Capital stock, par $140	1,120,000	980,000
Retained earnings	119,000	105,000
Total liabilities and stockholders' equity	$1,603,000	$1,253,000

Additional data:

1. Net income for year ended June 30, 1987, was $70,000.
2. Dividends declared amounted to $56,000.
3. Stock was issued at par for cash.
4. No equipment or building retirements occurred during the year.
5. The five-year note was issued to pay for a building erected on land leased by the company.
6. Additional shares of stock of the affiliated company were acquired for cash.
7. Equipment was also purchased for cash.

Required: Prepare a statement of changes in financial position—working capital basis. Try to do so without preparing a working paper so that your conceptual understanding of the statement might be strengthened.

P19–4–B

Prepare statement of changes in financial position—cash basis

Assume that the current assets and current liabilities in Problem P19–3–B consisted of the following:

	June 30, 1987	June 30, 1986
Current assets:		
Cash	$ 70,000	$ 56,000
Accounts receivable	224,000	112,000
Inventory	112,000	126,000
Prepaid expenses	21,000	35,000
Total current assets	$427,000	$329,000
Current liabilities:		
Accounts payable	$196,000	$126,000
Accrued liabilities	28,000	42,000
Total current liabilities	$224,000	$168,000

Required:
a. Use the data in Problem P19–3–B along with the above data and prepare a working paper for a statement of changes in financial position—cash basis.
b. Prepare a statement of changes in financial position—cash basis for Gatlin Corporation for the year ended June 30, 1987.

P19-5-B

Prepare working paper and statement of changes in financial position— working capital basis

---

LARSON CORPORATION
Comparative Balance Sheets
December 31, 1986, and 1987

	December 31	
	1987	**1986**
Assets		
Current assets:		
Cash	$ 30,000	$ 40,000
Accounts receivable	254,000	196,000
Inventories	244,000	224,000
Prepaid insurance	6,000	8,000
Total current assets	$ 534,000	$468,000
Property, plant, and equipment:		
Land	$ 100,000	$ 60,000
Buildings	400,000	200,000
Accumulated depreciations—buildings	(50,000)	(40,000)
Equipment	460,000	430,000
Accumulated depreciation—equipment	(250,000)	(200,000)
Total property, plant, and equipment	$ 660,000	$450,000
Total assets	$1,194,000	$918,000
Liabilities and Stockholders' Equity		
Current liabilities:		
Accounts payable	$ 164,000	$160,000
Federal income taxes payable	72,000	60,000
Accrued salaries and wages payable	8,000	6,000
Accrued liabilities	36,000	28,000
Total current liabilities	$ 280,000	$254,000
Long-term liabilities:		
Bonds payable—9%	200,000	200,000
Total liabilities	$ 480,000	$454,000
Stockholders' equity:		
Paid-in capital:		
Capital stock—common	$ 600,000	$400,000
Paid-in capital in excess of par	30,000	–0–
Retained earnings	84,000	64,000
Total stockholders' equity	$ 714,000	$464,000
Total liabilities and stockholders' equity	$1,194,000	$918,000

LARSON CORPORATION
Statement of Income and Retained Earnings
For Year Ended December 31, 1987

Sales, net		$1,800,000
Cost of goods sold		1,200,000
Gross margin		$ 600,000
Salaries and wages	$300,000	
Depreciation	74,000	
Insurance	4,000	
Other expenses	100,000	
Loss on sale of equipment	2,000	480,000
Net income before federal income taxes		$ 120,000
Federal income taxes		52,000
Net income		$ 68,000
Retained earnings, January 1, 1987		64,000
		$ 132,000
Less: Dividends declared and paid		48,000
Retained earnings, December 31, 1987		$ 84,000

Additional data:

1. Equipment having an original cost of $20,000, on which $14,000 of depreciation was recorded, was sold at a loss of $2,000. Equipment additions were for cash.
2. All of the additional capital stock issued during the year, plus $10,000 of cash, was exchanged for land and a building.

Required: a. Prepare a working paper similar to the one used to solve the demonstration problem. Use the working capital basis.
b. Prepare a statement of changes in financial position—working capital basis.

P19–6–B

Prepare working paper and statement of changes in financial position— cash basis

Refer to the data in Problem P19–5–B.

Required: a. Prepare a working paper for a statement of changes in financial position—cash basis.
b. Prepare a statement of changes in financial position—cash basis.

BUSINESS DECISION PROBLEM 19–1

Prepare a schedule showing working capital and cash provided by operations

Following are comparative ledger balances for the Newton Company:

	December 31	
	1987	**1986**
Debit balances		
Cash	$ 48,000	$ 30,000
Accounts Receivable	48,000	36,000
Inventory	72,000	42,000
Land	54,000	48,000
Building	72,000	72,000
Equipment	228,000	180,000
Goodwill	96,000	120,000
Total	$618,000	$528,000
Credit balances		
Accumulated Depreciation—Building	$ 24,000	$ 21,600
Accumulated Depreciation—Equipment	42,000	38,400
Accounts Payable	60,000	36,000
Accrued Liabilities	24,000	18,000
Capital Stock	252,000	240,000
Paid-In Capital—Stock Dividends	60,000	54,000
Paid-In Capital—Land Donation	12,000	–0–
Retained Earnings	144,000	120,000
Total	$618,000	$528,000

An analysis of the Retained Earnings account for the year reveals the following:

Balance, January 1, 1987		$120,000
Add:		
Net income for the year		78,000
		$198,000
Less:		
Cash dividends	$36,000	
Stock dividends	18,000	54,000
Balance, December 31, 1987		$144,000

handwritten margin notes: 18000, 12,000, 30,000 / 24,000, 6,000 / 30,000, 60,000, 60,000

Additional data:

   Equipment with a cost of $24,000 on which $21,600 of depreciation had been accumulated was sold during the year at a loss of $1,200. Included in net income is a gain on the sale of land of $7,200.

   The president of the Newton Company has set two goals for 1988: (1) increase working capital by $48,000 and (2) increase cash dividends to $72,000. The company's activities in 1988 are expected to be quite similar to those of 1987.

Required: Prepare a schedule showing working capital and cash provided by operations for 1987. Does it appear that the company can meet its president's goals for 1988? Explain?

BUSINESS DECISION PROBLEM 19–2

Prepare a statement of changes in financial position— cash basis

Video-Joy Inc. is a video games and supplies center owned and operated by Stan Brown. During 1987, the company replaced $72,000 of the center's fully depreciated equipment with new equipment costing $92,000. After paying a midyear dividend of $20,000, Stan found it necessary to borrow $20,000 from his bank on a 180-day note. He feels further borrowing may be needed since the Cash account is dangerously low at year-end.

   Given below are the income statement and a funds statement as Stan's accountant calls it, for 1987.

VIDEO-JOY
Income Statement
For Year Ended December 31, 1987

Sales		$800,000
Cost of goods sold	$560,000	
Operating expenses and taxes	198,800	758,800
Net income		$ 41,200

VIDEO-JOY
Funds Statement
For Year Ended December 31, 1987

Funds provided:		
From operations		
Net income		$ 41,200
Depreciation		20,000
Total funds from operations . . .		$ 61,200
Mortgage note issued		64,000
Total funds provided		$125,200
Funds applied:		
New equipment	$ 92,000	
Dividends	20,000	112,000
Increase in funds		$ 13,200

   Stan is very concerned about what he sees in the above statements and how it relates to what he knows has actually happened. He turns to you for help. Specifically, he wants to know why the funds statement shows an increase in funds when he knows the cash balance decreased from $44,000 to $6,000 during the year. He also wants to know why depreciation is shown as providing funds while the bank loan is not reported in the funds statement.

You believe that you can answer Stan's questions. You ask for and receive the following condensed balance sheet data:

VIDEO-JOY, INC.
Comparative Balance Sheets
December 31, 1986, and 1987

	December 31	
	1987	1986
Assets		
Current assets:		
Cash	$ 6,000	$ 44,000
Accounts receivable	71,200	52,800
Merchandise inventory	114,000	70,000
Prepaid expenses	2,800	1,200
Total current assets	$194,000	$168,000
Property, plant, and equipment		
Equipment	$160,000	$140,000
Accumulated depreciation	(44,000)	(96,000)
Total property, plant, and equipment	$116,000	$ 44,000
Total assets	$310,000	$212,000
Liabilities and Stockholders' Equity		
Current liabilities		
Accounts payable	$ 34,800	$ 40,000
Notes payable	20,000	–0–
Accrued liabilities	2,400	4,400
Total current liabilities	$ 57,200	$ 44,400
Long-term liabilities:		
Mortgage note payable	64,000	–0–
Total liabilities	$121,200	$ 44,400
Stockholders' equity:		
Common stock	160,000	160,000
Retained earnings	28,800	7,600
Total stockholders' equity	$188,800	$167,600
Total liabilities and stockholders' equity	$310,000	$212,000

Required: Prepare a statement that will show more clearly why the Video-Joy, Inc. center is having such a difficult time keeping sufficient cash on hand. Also answer Stan's questions.

BUSINESS SITUATION FOR DISCUSSION

Cash Flow: Why it Should be Stressed in Financial Reporting*

Many companies have been encouraged to change the formats of their funds statements to focus on cash and the components of cash flow. This article discusses some alternatives for how such a funds statement can be developed and presented.

Steven J. Golub and Harry D. Huffman,
Deloitte Haskins & Sells

☐   The ability of an enterprise to turn receivables and inventories into cash becomes more critical during periods of high interest rates. In our current economic environment, managers, businessmen, accountants, and investors are all directing their attention to cash flow. The need for relevant cash flow information has never been greater. Preparers and users of financial reports must be more cognizant of an enterprise's cash flow, liquidity, and financial flexibility, and must give such infor-

* *Financial Executive,* February 1984, pp. 34–35. Reprinted with permission.

mation the same amount of attention, if not more, that is devoted to an enterprise's reporting of next quarter's earnings per share.

In our view, the traditional funds statement, which generally has focused on working capital, is not as useful as a statement of cash flow, given the current economic climate. The presentation of cash flow from operations, a focus on cash and cash equivalents, and the segregation of an enterprise's activities into the main sources and uses of funds, in a funds statement, could help to fill this void.

Whenever an enterprise presents a complete set of financial statements prepared in accordance with generally accepted accounting principles, a funds statement is required. That requirement has existed since 1971, when the Accounting Principles Board issued Opinion No. 19, *Reporting Changes in Financial Position.* This allows either a cash or a working capital format for the funds statement. Initially, a large majority of enterprises adopted a working capital format. The exceptions were principally those enterprises for whom working capital was not a relevant concept because the enterprises did not segregate their assets and liabilities into current and noncurrent classifications.

A working capital format has the principal advantage of making the funds statement easier to prepare. The principal disadvantage, however, is that flows of working capital may not be indicative of cash flow. The business community has experienced situations where working capital provided by operations has been positive while cash provided by operations has been negative. This limitation of the working capital format and the increased emphasis on cash flow have resulted in increased adoption of the cash format.

*　*　*　*　*

Analysis and Interpretation of Financial Statements

LEARNING OBJECTIVES

After studying this chapter, you should be able to:

1. Explain how comparative financial statements may be used to analyze and appraise the financial position of a company and the results of its operations.

2. Calculate the amount of change in financial statement items for successive periods in dollars and percentages (horizontal and trend analysis).

3. Prepare common-size financial statements (vertical analysis).

4. Perform ratio analysis using the widely applied financial ratios and explain what each ratio seeks to show or measure.

5. Define and use correctly the new terms in the glossary.

As you will recall, the two primary objectives of every business are solvency and profitability. Solvency is the ability of a company to pay debts as they become due; it is reflected in the company's balance sheet. Profitability is the ability of a company to generate income; it is reflected in the company's income statement. Generally, all those interested in the affairs of a company are especially interested in a company's solvency and profitability.

This chapter discusses several common methods used to analyze and relate to one another the data in financial statements and, as a result, gain a clear picture of the solvency and profitability of a company. A company's financial statements are analyzed internally by management and externally by investors and creditors.

Management's analysis of financial statements primarily relates to **parts** of the company. Management conducts its analysis to plan, evaluate, and control operations within the company. The analysis by investors and creditors generally focuses on the company as a **whole.** Investors and creditors analyze financial statements to decide whether to invest in or extend credit to the company. In this chapter we discuss financial statement analysis as conducted by outside parties, such as investors and creditors, who rely primarily on a company's financial statements for their information.

■ OBJECTIVES OF FINANCIAL STATEMENT ANALYSIS

Financial statement analysis consists of applying analytical tools and techniques to financial statements and other relevant data to obtain useful information. This information is shown as significant relationships between data and trends in those data assessing the company's **past performance** and **current financial position.** The information shows the results or consequences of prior management decisions. In addition, the information is used to **make predictions** that may have a direct effect on decisions made by many users of financial statements.

Present company investors and potential company investors are both interested in the future ability of a company to earn profits—its profitability. These investors wish to predict future dividends and changes in the market price of the company's common stock. Since both dividends and price changes are likely to be influenced by earnings, investors may seek to predict earnings. The company's past earnings record is the logical starting point in predicting future earnings.

Sometimes outside parties are interested in predicting a company's solvency rather than its profitability. Short-term solvency is affected by the liquidity of the company. Liquidity is the state of possessing liquid assets, such as cash and other assets that will soon be converted into cash. Short-term debts must be paid soon, so liquid assets must be available for their payment. A bank that is asked to extend a 90-day loan to a company would be interested in that company's projected short-term liquidity. The company's predicted ability to repay the loan is likely to be based, at least partially, on proven past ability to pay off debts.

Long-term creditors are interested in a company's long-term solvency. A company is generally considered to be solvent when its assets exceed its liabilities so that it has a positive stockholders' equity. The larger the assets are in relation to the liabilities, the greater the long-term solvency of the company. The company's assets could shrink significantly before its liabilities would exceed its assets.

■ FINANCIAL STATEMENT ANALYSIS

Several types of analysis can be performed on a company's financial statements. All these analyses rely on comparisons or relationships of data because comparisons enhance the utility, or practical value, of accounting information. For example, knowing that a company's net income last year was $100,000 is not, by itself, very useful information. Some usefulness is added when it is known that the prior year's net income was $25,000. And even more useful information is gained if the amounts of sales and assets of the company are known. Such comparisons or relationships may be expressed as:

1. Absolute increases and decreases for an item from one period to the next.
2. Percentage increases and decreases for an item from one period to the next.

3. Trend percentages.
4. Percentages of single items to an aggregate total.
5. Ratios.

Items 1 and 2 make use of comparative financial statements. Comparative financial statements present the same company's financial statements for two or more successive periods in side-by-side columns. The calculation of dollar changes (see column 3 of Illustration 20.1 and column 9 of Illustration 20.2) or percentage changes (see column 4 of Illustration 20.1 and column 10 of Illustration 20.2) in the statement items or totals is known as horizontal analysis.

Illustration 20.1 *Comparative Balance Sheets*

THE KNIGHT CORPORATION
Comparative Balance Sheets
December 31, 1987, and 1988   **Exhibit A**

	December 31		Increase or decrease* 1988 over 1987		Percent of total assets December 31	
	(1) **1988**	*(2)* **1987**	*(3)* **Dollars**	*(4)* **Percent**	*(5)* **1988**	*(6)* **1987**
Assets						
Current assets:						
Cash	$ 80,200	$ 55,000	$25,200	45.8	12.6	10.0
Accounts receivable, net	124,200	132,600	8,400*	6.3*	19.6	24.1
Notes receivable	55,000	50,000	5,000	10.0	8.7	9.1
Inventories	110,800	94,500	16,300	17.2	17.4	17.1
Prepaid expenses	3,600	4,700	1,100*	23.4*	0.6	0.9
Total current assets	$373,800	$336,800	$37,000	11.0	58.8R	61.1R
Property, plant, and equipment:						
Land	$ 21,000	$ 21,000	$ –0–	–0–	3.3	3.8
Building	205,000	160,000	45,000	28.1	32.3	29.0
Less: Accumulated depreciation	(27,000)	(22,400)	(4,600)	21.0	(4.3)	(4.1)
Furniture and fixtures	83,200	69,800	13,400	19.2	13.1	12.7
Less: Accumulated depreciation	(20,800)	(14,100)	(6,700)	47.5	(3.3)	(2.6)
Total property, plant, and equipment . . .	$261,400	$214,300	$47,100	22.0	41.2R	38.9R
Total assets	$635,200	$551,100	$84,100	15.3	100.0	100.0
Liabilities and Stockholders' Equity						
Current liabilities:						
Accounts payable	$ 70,300	$ 64,600	$ 5,700	8.8	11.1	11.7
Notes payable	20,000	15,100	4,900	32.5	3.1	2.7
Taxes accrued	36,800	30,200	6,600	21.9	5.8	5.5
Total current liabilities	$127,100	$109,900	$17,200	15.7	20.0	20.0R
Long-term liabilities:						
Mortgage notes payable, land and building, 12%, 1990	43,600	60,800	17,200*	28.3*	6.9	11.0
Total liabilities	$170,700	$170,700	$ –0–	0.0	26.9	31.0
Stockholders' equity:						
Common stock, par value $10 per share . . .	$240,000	$200,000	$40,000	20.0	37.8	36.3
Retained earnings	224,500	180,400	44,100	24.4	35.3	32.7
Total stockholders' equity	$464,500	$380,400	$84,100	22.1	73.1	69.0
Total liabilities and stockholders' equity	$635,200	$551,100	$84,100	15.3	100.0	100.0

R Rounding difference.

Illustration 20.2 *Comparative Statements of Income and Retained Earnings*

THE KNIGHT CORPORATION
Comparative Statements of Income and Retained Earnings
For the Years Ended December 31, 1987, and 1988   **Exhibit B**

	Year ended December 31		Increase or decrease* 1988 over 1987		Percent of net sales	
	(7) 1988	(8) 1987	(9) Dollars	(10) Percent	(11) 1988	(12) 1987
Net sales	$986,400	$765,500	$220,900	28.9	100.0	100.0
Cost of goods sold	623,200	500,900	122,300	24.4	63.2	65.4
Gross margin	$363,200	$264,600	$ 98,600	37.3	36.8	34.6
Operating expenses:						
Selling	$132,500	$ 84,900	$ 47,600	56.1	13.4	11.1
Administrative	120,300	98,600	21,700	22.0	12.2	12.9
Total operating expenses	$252,800	$183,500	$ 69,300	37.8	25.6	24.0
Net operating income	$110,400	$ 81,100	$ 29,300	36.0	11.2	10.6
Other expenses	3,000	2,800	200	7.1	0.3	0.4
Net income before federal income taxes	$107,400	$ 78,300	$ 29,100	37.2	10.9	10.2
Federal income taxes	48,300	31,700	16,600	52.4	4.9	4.1
Net income	$ 59,100	$ 46,600	$ 12,500	26.8	6.0	6.1
Retained earnings, January 1	180,400	146,300	34,100	23.3		
	$239,500	$192,900	$ 46,600	24.2		
Dividends declared	15,000	12,500	2,500	20.0		
Retained earnings, December 31	$224,500	$180,400	$ 44,100	24.4		

This type of analysis helps detect changes in a company's performance and highlights trends.

Trend percentages (item 3) are similar to horizontal analysis except that a base year is selected and comparisons are made to the base year. Trend percentages are useful for comparing financial statements over **several years** because they disclose changes and trends occurring through time.

Information about a company can also be gained by the vertical analysis of the composition of a single financial statement, such as an income statement. Vertical analysis (item 4) consists of the study of a single financial statement in which each item is expressed as a **percentage of a significant total.** The use of vertical analysis is especially helpful in analyzing income statement data such as the percentage of cost of goods sold to sales or the gross margin on sales. For example, columns 11 and 12 of Illustration 20.2 show that in 1987, cost of goods sold was 65.4% of sales and decreased to 63.2% of sales in 1988.

Financial statements that show only percentages and no absolute dollar amounts are called common-size statements. All percentage figures in a common-size balance sheet are expressed as percentages of total assets (see columns 5 and 6 of Illustration 20.1), while all the items in a common-size income statement are expressed as percentages of net sales (see columns 11 and 12 of Illustration 20.2). The use of common-size statements facilitates vertical analysis of a company's financial statements. For instance, looking at columns 11 and 12 of Illustration 20.2 gives you a better idea of the relationship of each item to sales than looking at columns 7 and 8.

Ratios (item 5) are expressions of logical relationships between certain items in the financial statements. The financial statements of a single period are generally used. Many ratios can be computed from the same set of financial statements. A ratio can show a relationship between two items on the same financial statement or between two items on different financial statements (e.g., balance sheet and income statement). The choice of ratios to be prepared is limited only by the requirement that the items used to construct a ratio have a logical relationship to one another.

■ HORIZONTAL AND VERTICAL ANALYSIS: AN ILLUSTRATION

Illustrations 20.1 and 20.2 show comparative financial statements of the Knight Corporation for the years ended December 31, 1987, and 1988. These statements will serve as a basis for a more complete illustration of horizontal and vertical analysis of a balance sheet and a statement of income and retained earnings.

Analysis of Balance Sheet

Imagine that you are a prospective investor of the Knight Corporation and have acquired the comparative balance sheets shown in Illustrations 20.1 and 20.2. Columns 1, 2, and 3 in Illustration 20.1 show the absolute dollar amounts for each item for December 31, 1987, and December 31, 1988, and the change for the year. If the change between the two dates is an increase from 1987 to 1988, the change is shown as a positive figure. If the change is a decrease, it is followed by an asterisk (*). A few of the observations you could make from your horizontal analysis of Illustration 20.1 are:

1. Total current assets have increased $37,000, consisting largely of a $25,200 increase in cash, while total current liabilities have increased only $17,200.
2. Total assets have increased $84,100, while total liabilities have remained unchanged.
3. The increase in total assets has been financed by the sale of common stock, $40,000, and by the retention of earnings, $44,100.

Next, you study column 4 in Illustration 20.1, which expresses as a percentage the dollar change in column 3. Frequently, these percentage increases and decreases are more informative than absolute amounts, as is illustrated by the current asset and current liability changes. Although the absolute amount of current assets has increased more than twice the amount of current liabilities, the percentages reveal that current assets increased 11%, while current liabilities increased 15.7%. Thus, current liabilities are increasing at a rate faster than the current assets that will be used to pay them. But, in view of the substantial amount of cash possessed, the company is not likely to fail to pay its debts as they come due.

The percentages in column 4 lead you, the analyst, to several other observations. For one thing, the 28.3% decrease in mortgage notes payable indicates that interest charges will be lower; thus, this will tend to increase net income in the future. The 24.4% increase in retained earnings and the 45.8% increase in cash may indicate that higher dividends can be paid in the future.

Your vertical analysis of the Knight Corporation's balance sheet discloses each account's significance relative to total assets or equities. This comparison aids in assessing the importance of changes in each account. Columns 5 and 6 in Illustration 20.1 express the dollar amounts of each item in columns 1 and 2 as a percentage of total assets or equities. For example, although prepaid expenses declined $1,100 in 1988, a decrease of 23.4%, the account represents less than 1% of total assets and, therefore, probably does not have great significance. The vertical analysis also shows that total debt financing decreased by 4.1 percentage points, from 31% of total equities to 26.9% in 1988. At the same time, the percentage of stockholder financing to total assets of the company increased from 69.0% to 73.1%.

Analysis of Statement of Income and Retained Earnings

Illustration 20.2 provides you with the information to analyze the comparative statements of income and retained earnings of the Knight Corporation. Such a statement merely combines the income statement and the statement of retained earnings. Columns 7 and 8 in Illustration 20.2 show the dollar amounts for the years 1988 and 1987, respectively. Columns 9 and 10 show the absolute and percentage increase and decrease in each item from 1987 to 1988. The amounts and percentages in columns 11 and 12 are computed by dividing each item by net sales. Examination of the comparative statements of net income and retained earnings shows the following:

1. Sales increased 28.9% in 1988.
2. Gross margin increased 37.3% in 1988.
3. Selling expenses increased 56.1% in 1988.
4. Federal income taxes rose by 52.4% in 1988.
5. Net income increased 26.8%, while dividends increased 20.0%.
6. Net income per dollar of sales remained virtually constant over the two years (6.1% in 1987 and 6.0% in 1988).

Considering both horizontal and vertical analysis information, the analyst would conclude that an increase in the gross margin rate from 34.6% to 36.8%, coupled with a 28.9% increase in sales, resulted in a 37.3% increase in gross margin in 1988. The increase in net income was held to 26.8% because selling expenses increased 56.1% and income taxes increased 52.4%. Predicting net income for 1989 would be aided if you, the analyst, knew whether this increase in selling expenses is expected to recur. Other expenses remained basically the same, on a percentage-of-sales basis, over the two-year period.

Having completed the horizontal and vertical analysis of the balance sheet and statement of income and retained earnings of the Knight Corporation, you are ready to study trend percentages and ratio analysis. The last section in this chapter discusses some final considerations in financial statement analysis. Professional financial statement analysts use several tools and techniques to determine the solvency and profitability of companies.

■ TREND PERCENTAGES

Trend percentages are also referred to as index numbers and are used for the comparison of financial information over time to a base year. Trend percentages are calculated by:

1. Selecting a base year.
2. Assigning a weight of 100% to the amounts appearing on the base year financial statements.
3. Expressing the corresponding amounts shown on the other years' financial statements as a percentage of base-year amounts. The percentages are computed by dividing nonbase amounts by the corresponding base-year amounts and then multiplying the result by 100.

The following information is given to illustrate the calculation of trend percentages:

	1987	1988	1989	1990
Sales	$350,000	$367,500	$441,000	$485,000
Cost of goods sold	200,000	196,000	230,000	285,000
Gross margin	$150,000	$171,500	$211,000	$200,000
Operating expenses	145,000	169,000	200,000	192,000
Net income before taxes	$ 5,000	$ 2,500	$ 11,000	$ 8,000

If 1987 is the base year, trend percentages are calculated for each year by dividing sales by $350,000; cost of goods sold by $200,000; gross margin by $150,000; operating expenses by $145,000; and net income before income taxes by $5,000. After all divisions have been made, each result is multiplied by 100, and the resulting percentages that reflect trends appear as follows:

	1987	1988	1989	1990
Sales	100%	105%	126%	139%
Cost of goods sold	100	98	115	143
Gross margin	100	114	141	133
Operating expenses	100	117	138	132
Net income before taxes	100	50	220	160

Such trend percentages indicate changes that are taking place in an organization and highlight the direction of these changes. Percentages can provide clues to a user as to which items need further investigation or analysis. In reviewing trend percentages, a financial statement user should pay close attention to the trends in related items, such as the cost of goods sold in relation to sales. Trend analysis that shows a constantly declining gross margin rate may be a signal that future net income will decrease.

As useful as trend percentages are, they have one drawback. Expressing changes as percentages is usually straightforward as long as the amount in the base year is positive—that is, not zero or negative. A $30,000 increase in notes receivable cannot be expressed in percentages if the increase is from zero last year to $30,000 this year. Also, an increase from a loss last year of $10,000 to income this year of $20,000 cannot be expressed in percentage terms.

Proper analysis does not stop with the calculation of increases and decreases in amounts or percentages over several years. Such changes generally indicate areas worthy of further investigation. They are merely clues that may lead to significant findings. Accurate predictions depend on many factors including economic and political conditions; management's plans regarding new products, plant expansion, and promotional outlays; and the expected activities of competitors. Consideration of these factors in conjunction with horizontal analysis, vertical analysis, and trend analysis should provide a reasonable basis for predicting future performance.

■ RATIO ANALYSIS

Logical relationships exist between certain accounts or items in a company's financial statements. These accounts may appear on the same statement or they may appear on two different statements. The dollar amounts of the related accounts or items are set up in fraction form and called ratios. These ratios can be broadly classified as (1) liquidity ratios, (2) equity, or long-term solvency, ratios, (3) profitability tests, and (4) market tests.

Liquidity Ratios

Liquidity ratios are used to indicate a company's short-term debt-paying ability. Thus, these ratios are designed to show interested parties the company's capacity to meet maturing current liabilities.

Current, or Working Capital, Ratio.   Working capital is the excess of current assets over current liabilities. The ratio that relates current assets to current liabilities is known as the **current,** or **working capital, ratio.** The current ratio indicates the ability of a company to pay its current liabilities from current assets and, in this way, shows the strength of the company's working capital position.

The current ratio is computed by dividing total current assets by total current liabilities:

$$\text{Current ratio} = \frac{\text{Current assets}}{\text{Current liabilities}}$$

The ratio usually is stated in terms of the number of dollars of current assets to one dollar of current liabilities (although the dollar signs usually are omitted). Thus, if current assets total $75,000 and current liabilities total $50,000, the ratio is expressed as 1.5:1, meaning the company has $1.50 of current assets for each $1 of current liabilities.

The current ratio provides a better index of a company's ability to pay current debts than does the absolute amount of working capital. To illustrate, assume that Company A and Company B have current assets and current liabilities on December 31, 1987, as follows:

	Company A	Company B
Current assets *(a)*	$11,000,000	$200,000
Current liabilities *(b)*	10,000,000	100,000
Working capital *(a − b)*	$ 1,000,000	$100,000
Current ratio *(a ÷ b)*	1.1:1	2:1

Company A has 10 times as much working capital as Company B. But Company B has a superior debt-paying ability since it has $2 of current assets for each $1 of current liabilities. Company A has only $1.10 of current assets for each $1 of current liabilities.

Short-term creditors are particularly interested in the current ratio since the conversion of inventories and accounts receivable into cash is the primary source from which the company obtains the cash to pay short-term creditors. Long-term creditors are also interested in the current ratio because a company that is unable to pay short-term debts may be forced into bankruptcy. For this reason, many bond indentures, or contracts, contain a provision requiring that the borrower maintain at least a certain minimum current ratio. Remember from the last chapter that changes in long-term accounts can affect the total amount of working capital. Therefore, a company can increase its current ratio by issuing long-term debt or capital stock or by selling noncurrent assets.

A company must also guard against a current ratio that is too high, especially if caused by idle cash, slow-paying customers, and slow-moving inventory. Decreased net income can result when too much capital that could be used profitably elsewhere is tied up in current assets.

Refer back to the Knight Corporation data in column 4 of Illustration 20.1, which indicated that current liabilities are increasing more rapidly than current assets. This sort of observation can be made directly using changes in the current ratio. The Knight Corporation's current ratios for the two years follow:

| | December 31 | | Amount of increase |
	1988	1987	
Current assets *(a)*	$373,800	$336,800	$37,000
Current liabilities *(b)*	127,100	109,900	17,200
Working capital *(a − b)* . . .	$246,700	$226,900	$19,800
Current ratio *(a ÷ b)*	2.94:1	3.06:1	

Although Knight's working capital increased by $19,800, or 8.7%, its current ratio fell from 3.06 to 2.94, reflecting the fact that its current liabilities increased faster than its current assets.

Acid-Test (or Quick) Ratio.   The current ratio is not the only measure of a company's short-term debt-paying ability. Another measure, called the **acid-test** (or **quick**) **ratio,** is the ratio of quick assets (cash, marketable securities, and net receivables) to current liabilities. The formula for the acid-test ratio is:

$$\text{Acid-test ratio} = \frac{\text{Quick assets}}{\text{Current liabilities}}$$

Inventories and prepaid expenses are excluded from this computation because they might not be readily convertible into cash. Short-term creditors are interested particularly in this ratio since it relates the "pool" of cash and immediate cash inflows to immediate cash outflows.

The acid-test ratios for 1987 and 1988 for the Knight Corporation are:

	December 31		Amount of increase
	1988	1987	
Quick assets *(a)*	$259,400	$237,600	$21,800
Current liabilites *(b)*	127,100	109,900	17,200
Net quick assets *(a − b)* . . .	$132,300	$127,700	$ 4,600
Acid-test ratio *(a ÷ b)*	2.04:1	2.16:1	

In deciding whether the acid-test ratio is satisfactory, it is necessary to consider the **quality** of the marketable securities and receivables. An accumulation of poor quality marketable securities or receivables, or both, could cause an acid-test ratio to appear deceptively favorable. Poor quality when referring to marketable securities means securities that are likely to generate losses upon sale; poor quality receivables are those that may be uncollectible or not collectible until long past due. The quality of receivables depends primarily on their age, which can be assessed by preparing an aging schedule or by calculating the accounts receivable turnover. (Refer to Chapter 8 for a discussion of an accounts receivable aging schedule.)

Accounts Receivable Turnover.   Turnover is the relationship between the amount of an asset and some measure of its use. **Accounts receivable turnover** is the number of times per year that the average amount of receivables is collected. The ratio is calculated by dividing net credit sales by average net accounts receivable, that is, accounts receivable after deducting the allowance for doubtful accounts:

$$\text{Accounts receivable turnover} = \frac{\text{Net credit sales (or net sales)}}{\text{Average net accounts receivable}}$$

When a ratio compares an income statement item (like net credit sales) with a balance sheet item (like accounts receivable) the balance sheet item should be an average. Ideally, average net accounts receivable should be computed by averaging the end-of-month balances or end-of-week balances of net accounts receivable outstanding during the period. The greater the number of observations used, the more accurate the resulting average. Often though, only the beginning-of-year and end-of-year balances are averaged because this information is easily obtainable from comparative financial statements. Sometimes a formula calls for the use of an average balance, but only the year-end amount is available. Then the analyst must use the year-end amount.[1]

In theory, only net credit sales should be used in the numerator of the accounts receivable turnover ratio because those are the only sales that generate accounts receivable. But, if cash sales are relatively small or their proportion to total sales remains fairly constant, reliable results can be obtained by using total net sales. In most cases, the analyst may have to use total net sales because

---

[1] These general comments about the use of averages in a ratio apply to the other ratios involving averages discussed in this chapter.

the separate amounts of cash sales and credit sales are not reported on the income statement.

Accounts receivable turnover for the Knight Corporation is shown below. Since beginning-of-year data for 1987 are not provided in Illustration 20.1, assume net accounts receivable on January 1, 1987, totaled $121,200.

	1988	1987	Amount of increase or decrease*
Net sales (a)	$986,400	$765,500	$220,900
Accounts receivable:			
January 1	$132,600	$121,200	$ 11,400
December 31	124,200	132,600	8,400*
Total (b)	$256,800	$253,800	$ 3,000
Average accounts receivable (c) (b ÷ 2 = c) . .	$128,400	$126,900	
Turnover of accounts receivable (a ÷ c) . . .	7.68	6.03	

The turnover ratio provides an indication of how quickly the receivables are being collected. For the Knight Corporation in 1988, the turnover ratio indicates that accounts receivable are collected, or "turned over," slightly more than seven times per year. This ratio may be better understood and more easily compared with a company's credit terms if it is converted into a number of days, as is illustrated the next ratio.

Number of Days' Sales in Accounts Receivable. The **number of days' sales in accounts receivable** ratio, which also is called the **average collection period for accounts receivable,** is calculated as follows:

$$\text{Number of days' sales in accounts receivable (average collection period of accounts receivable)} = \frac{\text{Number of days in year (365)}}{\text{Accounts receivable turnover}}$$

The turnover ratios for the Knight Corporation given above can be used to show that the number of days' sales in accounts receivable decreased from about 61 days (365/6.03) in 1987 to 48 days (365/7.68) in 1988. The change means that the average collection period of the corporation's accounts receivable decreased from 61 to 48 days. Thus, the ratio measures the average liquidity of accounts receivable and gives an indication of their quality. Generally, the more rapid the collection period, the higher the quality of receivables. However, the average collection period will vary by industry; for example, they will be very rapid in utility companies and much slower in some retailing companies. A comparison of the average collection period with the credit terms extended customers by the company will provide further insight into the quality of the accounts receivable. For example, receivables arising under terms of 2/10, n/ 30 that have an average collection period of 75 days need to be investigated further. It is important to determine why customers are paying their accounts much later than expected.

Inventory Turnover. A company's inventory turnover ratio shows the number of times its average inventory is sold during a period. **Inventory turnover** is calculated as follows:

$$\text{Inventory turnover} = \frac{\text{Cost of goods sold}}{\text{Average inventory}}$$

Inventory turnover relates a measure of sales volume to the average amount of goods on hand to produce this sales volume.

Assume the inventory on January 1, 1987, for the Knight Corporation was $85,100. The following schedule shows that the inventory turnover increased slightly from 5.58 times per year in 1987 to 6.07 times per year in 1988. These turnover ratios can be converted to the number of days it takes a company to sell its entire stock of inventory; this is done by dividing 365 by the inventory turnover. For the Knight Corporation, the average inventory was sold in about 60 days (365/6.07) in 1988 as contrasted to about 65 days (365/5.58) in 1987.

	1988	1987	Amount of increase
Cost of goods sold (a)	$623,200	$500,900	$122,300
Inventories:			
January 1	$ 94,500	$ 85,100	$ 9,400
December 31	110,800	94,500	16,300
Total (b)	$205,300	$179,600	$ 25,700
Average inventory (c) (b ÷ 2 = c) . .	$102,650	$ 89,800	
Turnover of inventory (a ÷ c) . . .	6.07	5.58	

Other things being equal, the management that is able to maintain the highest inventory turnover ratio is considered most efficient. Yet, other things are not always equal. For example, a company that achieves a high inventory ratio by keeping extremely small inventories on hand may incur larger ordering costs, lose quantity discounts, and lose sales due to lack of adequate inventory. In attempting to earn satisfactory income, management must balance the costs of inventory storage and obsolescence and the cost of tying up funds in inventory against possible losses of sales and other costs associated with keeping too little inventory on hand.

Total Assets Turnover. **Total assets turnover** shows the relationship between dollar volume of sales and average total assets used in the business and is calculated as follows:

$$\text{Total assets turnover} = \frac{\text{Net sales}}{\text{Average total assets}}$$

This ratio measures the efficiency with which a company uses its assets to generate sales. The larger the total assets turnover, the larger will be the income on each dollar invested in the assets of the business.

For the Knight Corporation, the total assets turnover ratios for 1988 and 1987 are shown below. Assume total assets as of January 1, 1987, were $510,200.

	1988	1987	Amount of increase
Net sales (a)	$ 986,400	$ 765,500	$220,900
Total assets:			
January 1	$ 551,100	$ 510,200	$ 40,900
December 31	635,200	551,100	84,100
Total (b)	$1,186,300	$1,061,300	$125,000
Average total assets (c) (b ÷ 2 = c) . .	$ 593,150	$ 530,650	
Turnover of total assets (a ÷ c) . . .	1.66:1	1.44:1	

In 1987, each dollar of total assets produced $1.44 of sales; and in 1988, each dollar of assets produced $1.66 of sales. In other words, between 1987 and 1988, the Knight Corporation had an increase of $0.22 of sales per dollar of investment in assets.

Equity, or Long-Term Solvency, Ratios

Equity, or long-term solvency ratios show the relationship of debt and equity financing in a company.

Equity (or Stockholders Equity) Ratio.   The two basic sources of assets in a business are owners (stockholders) and creditors, and the interests of both groups are referred to as total equities. But in ratio analysis, the term *equity* generally refers only to stockholders' equity. Thus, the equity ratio indicates the proportion of total assets (or total equities) that is provided by stockholders (owners) on any given date. The formula for the equity ratio is:

$$\text{Equity ratio} = \frac{\text{Stockholders' equity}}{\text{Total assets (or total equities)}}$$

The Knight Corporation's liabilities and stockholders' equity, taken from Illustration 20.1, are given below. The Knight Corporation's equity ratio increased from 69.0% in 1987 to 73.1% in 1988. The schedule below shows that the company's stockholders increased their proportionate equity in the company's assets by additional investment in the company's common stock and by retention of income earned during the year.

	December 31, 1988		December 31, 1987	
	Amount	Percent	Amount	Percent
Current liabilities	$127,100	20.0	$109,900	20.0
Long-term liabilities	43,600	6.9	60,800	11.0
Total liabilities	$170,700	26.9	$170,700	31.0
Common stock	$240,000	37.8	$200,000	36.3
Retained earnings	224,500	35.3	180,400	32.7
Total stockholders' equity	$464,500	73.1	$380,400	69.0
Total equity (equal to total assets) . .	$635,200	100.0	$551,100	100.0

The equity ratio must be interpreted carefully. From a creditor's point of view, a high proportion of stockholders' equity is desirable. A high equity ratio indicates the existence of a large protective buffer for creditors in the event a company suffers a loss. But from an owner's point of view, a high proportion of stockholders' equity may or may not be desirable. If borrowed funds can be used by the business to generate income in excess of the net after-tax cost of the interest on such borrowed funds, a lower percentage of stockholders' equity may be desirable.

To illustrate the effect of higher leveraging (i.e., a larger proportion of debt), assume that Knight Corporation could have financed its present operations with $40,000 of 12% bonds instead of 4,000 shares of common stock. The effect on income for 1988 would be as follows, assuming a federal income tax rate of 50%:

Net income as presently stated (Illustration 20.2)	$59,100
Deduct additional interest on debt (0.12 × $40,000)	4,800
	$54,300
Add reduced tax due to interest deduction (0.5 × $4,800) . .	2,400
Adjusted net income	$56,700

As shown, net income is reduced when leverage is increased by issuing bonds instead of common stock. But there are also fewer shares outstanding, so earnings per share (EPS) increase from $2.46 ($59,100/24,000 shares) to $2.84 ($56,700/20,000 shares). Since investors place heavy emphasis on EPS amounts, many companies in recent years have introduced large portions of debt into their capital structures in order to increase EPS.

It should be pointed out, though, that too low a percentage of owners' equity (too much debt) has its dangers. Financial leverage magnifies losses per share as well as EPS since there are fewer shares of stock over which to spread the losses. A period of business recession may result in operating losses and shrinkage in the value of assets, such as receivables and inventory, which in turn may lead to an inability to meet fixed payments for interest and principal on the debt. The result could be that the company may be forced into liquidation and the stockholders would lose their investments.

Stockholders' Equity to Debt Ratio. The relative equities of owners and creditors may be expressed in several ways. To say that creditors hold a 26.9% interest in the assets of the Knight Corporation on December 31, 1988, is equivalent to saying stockholders hold a 73.1% interest. In many cases, this relationship is expressed as a ratio—**stockholders' equity to debt ratio.**

$$\frac{\text{Stockholders' equity}}{\text{to debt ratio}} = \frac{\text{Stockholders' equity}}{\text{Total debt}}$$

Such a ratio for the Knight Corporation would be 2.23 : 1 ($380,400/$170,700) on December 31, 1987, and 2.72 : 1 ($464,500/$170,700) on December 31, 1988. This ratio is sometimes inverted and called the **debt to equity ratio.** Some analysts use only long-term debt rather than total debt in calculating these ratios. These analysts do not consider short-term debt to be part of the capital structure since it will be paid within one year.

Profitability Tests

Profitability is a very important measure of a company's operating success. Generally, there are two areas of concern when judging profitability: (1) relationships on the income statement that indicate a company's ability to recover costs and expenses, and (2) relationships of income to various balance sheet measures that indicate the company's relative ability to earn income on assets employed.

Rate of Return on Operating Assets.   The best measure of earnings performance without regard to the sources of assets is the relationship of net operating income to operating assets, which is known as the **rate of return on operating assets.** This ratio is designed to show the earning power of the company as a bundle of assets. By disregarding both nonoperating assets and nonoperating income elements, the rate of return on operating assets measures the profitability of the company in carrying out its primary business functions. The ratio can be broken down into two elements—the operating margin and the turnover of operating assets.

Operating margin reflects the percentage of each dollar of net sales that becomes net operating income. Net operating income excludes **nonoperating income elements.** These elements include extraordinary items; nonoperating revenues, such as interest revenue; and nonoperating expenses, such as interest expense and income taxes. The formula for operating margin is:

$$\text{Operating margin} = \frac{\text{Net operating income}}{\text{Net sales}}$$

Turnover of operating assets shows the amount of sales dollars generated for each dollar invested in operating assets. Year-end operating assets typically are used, even though in theory an average would be better. **Operating assets** are all assets actively used in producing operating revenues. **Nonoperating assets** are assets owned but not used in producing operating revenues; they include items such as land held for future use, a factory building rented to another company, and long-term bond investments. Total assets should not be used in evaluating earnings performance because they include nonoperating assets that do not contribute to the generation of sales. The formula for the turnover of operating assets is:

$$\text{Turnover of operating assets} = \frac{\text{Net sales}}{\text{Operating assets}}$$

The rate of return on operating assets of a company is equal to operating margin multiplied by turnover of operating assets. The more a company earns per dollar of sales and the more sales it makes per dollar invested in operating assets, the higher will be the return per dollar invested. Rate of return on operating assets is expressed by the following formulas:

$$\frac{\text{Rate of return}}{\text{on operating assets}} = \text{Operating margin} \times \text{Turnover of operating assets}$$

or

$$\frac{\text{Rate of return}}{\text{on operating assets}} = \frac{\text{Net operating income}}{\text{Net sales}} \times \frac{\text{Net sales}}{\text{Operating assets}}$$

Since net sales appears in both ratios (once as a numerator and once as a denominator), it can be canceled out, and the formula for rate of return on operating assets becomes:

$$\text{Rate of return on operating assets} = \frac{\text{Net operating income}}{\text{Operating assets}}$$

It is, however, more useful for analytical purposes to leave the formula in the form that shows margin and turnover separately since it provides more information to analysts.

The rates of return on operating assets for the Knight Corporation for 1988 and 1987 are calculated below.

	1988	1987	Amount of increase
Net operating income *(a)*	$110,400	$ 81,100	$ 29,300
Net sales *(b)*	$986,400	$765,500	$220,900
Operating assets* *(c)*	$635,200	$551,100	$ 84,100
Operating margin *(a ÷ b)*	11.19%	10.59%	
Turnover of operating assets *(b ÷ c)*	1.55:1	1.39:1	
Rate of return on operating assets *(a ÷ c)* . . .	17.34%	14.72%	

* For the Knight Corporation there were no nonoperating assets, so total assets are used in the calculation.

Securing Desired Rate of Return on Operating Assets.   Companies that are to survive in the economy must attain some minimum rate of return on operating assets. But this minimum can be attained in many different ways. To illustrate, consider a grocery store and a jewelry store, each with a rate of return of 8% on operating assets. The grocery store normally would attain this rate of return with a low margin and a high turnover, while the jewelry store would have a high margin and a low turnover as shown below:

	Margin	×	Turnover	=	Rate of return on operating assets
Grocery store . .	1%	×	8.0 times		8%
Jewelry store . .	20%	×	0.4 times		8%

Net Income to Net Sales.   Another measure of a company's profitability is the net income to net sales ratio, calculated as follows:

$$\text{Net income to net sales} = \frac{\text{Net income}}{\text{Net sales}}$$

This ratio measures the proportion of the sales dollar that remains after the deduction of all expenses. The computations for the Knight Company are:

	1988	1987	Amount of increase
Net income *(a)*	$ 59,100	$ 46,600	$ 12,500
Net sales *(b)*	$986,400	$765,500	$220,900
Ratio of net income to net sales *(a ÷ b)* . .	5.99%	6.09%	

Although the ratio of net income to net sales indicates the net amount of profit on each sales dollar, a great deal of care must be exercised in the use and interpretation of this ratio. The amount of net income includes all types of nonoperating items that may occur in a particular period; therefore, net income includes the effects of such things as extraordinary items and interest charges. Thus, a period that contains the effects of an extraordinary item will not be comparable to a period that contains no extraordinary items. Also, since interest expense is deductible in the determination of net income while dividends are not, net income is affected by the methods used to finance the firm's assets.

Net Income to Average Stockholders' Equity.   From the stockholders' point of view, an important measure of the income-producing ability of a company is the relationship of **net income to average stockholders' equity,** also called the **rate of return on average stockholders' equity,** or simply the **return on equity (ROE).** Stockholders are interested in the ratio of operating income to operating assets as a measure of the efficient use of assets by management. But stockholders are even more interested in knowing what return is earned by the company on each dollar of stockholders' equity invested. The formula for net income to average stockholders' equity is:

$$\frac{\text{Net income to average}}{\text{stockholders' equity}} = \frac{\text{Net income}}{\text{Average stockholders' equity}}$$

The ratios for the Knight Company are shown below. Assume that total stockholders' equity on January 1, 1987, was $321,500.

	1988	1987	Amount of increase
Net income *(a)*	$ 59,100	$ 46,600	$ 12,500
Total stockholders' equity:			
January 1	$380,400	$321,500	$ 58,900
December 31	464,500	380,400	84,100
Total *(b)*	$844,900	$701,900	$143,000
Average stockholders' equity *(c) (b ÷ 2 = c)*	$422,450	$350,950	
Ratio of net income to stockholders' equity *(a ÷ c)* . .	13.99%	13.28%	

The increase in the ratio from 13.28% to 13.99% would be regarded favorably by stockholders. This ratio indicates that for each average dollar of capital invested by a stockholder, the company earned nearly 14 cents in 1988.

Earnings per Share. Probably the measure used most widely to appraise a company's operations is **earnings per share (EPS)** of common stock. EPS is equal to earnings available to common stockholders divided by the weighted-average number of shares of common stock outstanding. The financial press regularly publishes actual and forecasted EPS amounts for many corporations, together with period-to-period comparisons. The Accounting Principles Board noted the significance attached to EPS by requiring that such amounts be reported on the face of the income statement.[2]

The calculation of EPS may be fairly simple or highly complex, depending on the corporation's capital structure. A company has a simple capital structure if it has no outstanding securities (e.g., convertible bonds, convertible preferred stocks, warrants, or options) that can be exchanged for common stock. If a company has such securities outstanding, it has a complex capital structure.

A company with a simple capital structure reports a single EPS amount calculated as follows:

$$\text{EPS of common stock} = \frac{\text{Net income available to common stockholders}}{\text{Weighted-average number of common shares outstanding}}$$

Earnings available to common stockholders is equal to net income minus the current year's preferred dividends, whether such dividends have been declared or not.

Determining the Weighted-Average Number of Shares. The denominator in the EPS fraction is the weighted-average number of common shares outstanding for the period. If the number of shares outstanding did not change during the period, the weighted-average number of shares outstanding would, of course, be the number of shares outstanding at the end of the period. The balance in the common stock account of Knight Corporation (Illustration 20.1) was $200,000 on December 31, 1987, and the common stock has a $10 par value. Assuming that no shares were issued or redeemed during 1987, the weighted-average number of shares outstanding was 20,000 ($200,000/$10 per share).

If the number of shares changed during the period, such a change increases or decreases the capital invested in the company and should affect earnings available to shareholders. To compute the weighted-average number of shares outstanding, the change in the number of shares is weighted by the fractional portion of the year that those shares were outstanding. Shares are only considered outstanding during those periods that the related capital investment is available to produce income.

To illustrate, note that Knight Corporation's common stock balance increased by $40,000 (4,000 shares) during 1988. Assume that 3,000 of these shares were issued on April 1 and the other 1,000 shares were issued October 1. The computation of weighted-average shares outstanding would be as follows:

20,000 shares × 1 year	20,000
3,000 shares × ¾ year (April–December)	2,250
1,000 shares × ¼ year (October–December)	250
Weighted-average number of shares outstanding	22,500

---

[2] Accounting Principles Board, "Reporting Earnings per Share," *Opinion No. 15* (New York: AICPA, 1969), par. 12.

An alternate method looks at the total number of shares outstanding, weighted by the fractional portion of the year that the number of shares was outstanding, as follows:

20,000 shares × ¼ year (January–March)	5,000
23,000 shares × ½ year (April–September)	11,500
24,000 shares × ¼ year (October–December)	6,000
Weighted-average number of shares outstanding	22,500

Note that both methods give the same result.

Since the Knight Corporation had no preferred stock outstanding in either 1987 or 1988, EPS of common stock is computed as follows:

	1988	1987	Amount of increase
Net income *(a)*	$59,100	$46,600	$12,500
Average number of shares of common stock outstanding *(b)*	22,500	20,000	2,500
EPS of common stock *(a ÷ b)*	$2.63	$2.33	

The better than 13% increase in EPS from $2.33 to $2.63 would probably be viewed quite favorably by the Knight Corporation's stockholders.

EPS and Stock Dividends or Splits.   Increases in shares outstanding as a result of a stock dividend or split do not require weighting for fractional periods. Such shares do not increase the capital invested in the business and therefore do not affect income. All that is required is to restate all prior calculations of EPS using the increased number of shares. For example, assume a company reported EPS for 1987 of $1 ($100,000/100,000 shares) and earned $150,000 in 1988. The only change in common stock over the two years was a two-for-one stock split on December 1, 1988, which doubled the shares outstanding to 200,000. EPS for 1987 would be restated at $0.50 ($100,000/200,000 shares) and would be $0.75 ($150,000/200,000 shares) for 1988.

Primary EPS and Fully Diluted EPS.   In the merger wave of the 1960s, corporations often issued securities to finance their acquisitions of other companies. Many of the securities issued were "calls on common" or possessed "equity kickers." These terms mean that the securities were convertible into, or exchangeable for, shares of their issuers' common stock. As a result, many complex problems arose in computing EPS. *APB Opinion No. 15* provided guidelines for solving these problems. A company with a complex capital structure must present at least two EPS calculations, primary EPS and fully diluted EPS. Because of the complexities faced in the calculations, further discussion of these two EPS amounts must be reserved for an intermediate accounting text.

Times Interest Earned Ratio.   Creditors, especially long-term creditors, want to know whether a borrower can meet its required interest payments when they become due. A ratio that provides some indication of this ability is the times interest earned ratio, or **interest coverage ratio.** It is computed as follows:

$$\text{Times interest earned ratio} = \frac{\text{Income before interest and taxes}}{\text{Interest expense}}$$

The ratio is a rough comparison of cash inflow from operations with cash outflow for interest on debt. **Income before interest and taxes (IBIT)** is used in the numerator since there would be no income taxes if interest expense is equal to or greater than IBIT. Analysts disagree on whether the denominator should be only interest on long-term debt or all interest expense. We prefer the latter since failure to make any required interest payment is a serious matter.

Assume that a company has IBIT of $100,000 and that the interest expense for the same period is $10,000. The times interest earned ratio is 10:1. The company earned enough during the period to pay its interest expense 10 times over. Very low or negative interest coverage ratios suggest that the borrower could default on required interest payments. A company is not likely to be able to continue interest payments over many periods if it fails to earn enough income to cover them. On the other hand, interest coverage of 10 to 20 times suggests the company is not likely to default on interest payments.

Times Preferred Dividends Earned Ratio.   Preferred stockholders, like bondholders, must usually be satisifed with a fixed-dollar return on their investments. They are interested in the company's ability to make preferred dividend payments each year. This can be measured by computing the times preferred dividends earned ratio. It can be computed as follows:

$$\text{Times preferred dividends earned ratio} = \frac{\text{Net income}}{\text{Annual preferred dividends}}$$

Suppose a company has net income of $48,000 and has $100,000 ($100 par value) of 8% preferred stock outstanding. The number of times the annual preferred dividends are earned would be:

$$\frac{\$48,000}{\$8,000} = 6:1, \text{ or 6 times}$$

The higher this rate, the higher is the probability that the preferred stockholders will receive their dividends each year.

Market Tests

Certain ratios are computed using information from the financial statements and information about market price for the company's stock. These tests help investors and potential investors assess the relative merits of the various stocks in the marketplace.

The yield on a stock investment refers to either an earnings yield or a dividends yield.

Earnings Yield on Common Stock.   Thus, a company's earnings yield per share of common stock is calculated as follows:

$$\text{Earnings yield on common stock} = \frac{\text{EPS}}{\text{Current market price per share}}$$

Suppose, for example, that a company had common stock with an EPS of $2 and that the quoted market price of the stock on the New York Stock Exchange was $30. The earnings yield on common stock would be:

$$\frac{\$2}{\$30} = 6\tfrac{2}{3}\%$$

Price-Earnings Ratio.   When inverted, the earnings yield on common stock is called the price-earnings ratio. In the case cited above, the price-earnings ratio is:

$$\text{Price-earnings ratio} = \frac{\text{Current market price per share}}{\text{EPS}} = \frac{\$30}{\$2} = 15:1$$

Investors would say that this stock is selling at 15 times earnings, or at a multiple of 15. These investors might have a specific multiple in mind as being the one that should be used to judge whether the stock is underpriced or overpriced. Different investors will have different estimates of the proper price-earnings ratio for a given stock and also different estimates of the future earnings prospects of the company. These different estimates are two of the factors that cause one investor to sell stock at a particular price and another investor to buy at that price.

Dividend Yield on Common Stock.   The dividend paid per share of common stock is also of much interest to common stockholders. When the current annual dividend per share is divided by the current market price per share, the result is called the dividend yield on common stock. If the company referred to immediately above paid a $1.50 per share dividend, the dividend yield would be:

$$\frac{\text{Dividend yield on}}{\text{common stock}} = \frac{\text{Dividend per share}}{\text{Current market price per share}} = \frac{\$1.50}{\$30.00} = 5\%$$

Payout Ratio.   Using dividend yield, investors can compute the payout ratio on a stock. **Payout ratio** is computed as the dividend per share divided by EPS. The payout ratio for the above stock is:

$$\text{Payout ratio} = \frac{\text{Dividend per share}}{\text{EPS}} = \frac{\$1.50}{\$2.00} = 75\%$$

A payout ratio of 75% means that the company paid out 75% of the EPS in the form of dividends. Some investors are attracted by the stock of companies that pay out a large percentage of their earnings. Other investors are attracted by the stock of companies that retain and reinvest a large percentage of their earnings. The tax status of the investor has a great deal to do with this preference. Investors in very high tax brackets often prefer to have the company reinvest the earnings with the expectation that this will result in share price appreciation, which is taxed at capital gains rates when the shares are sold. Dividends are taxed at ordinary income rates, which have been much higher than capital gains rates.

Dividend Yield on Preferred Stock.   Preferred stockholders, as well as common stockholders, are interested in dividend yields. The computation of the dividend yield on preferred stock is similar to the common stock dividend yield computation. Suppose a company has 2,000 shares of $100 par value, 8% preferred stock outstanding that has a current market price of $110 per share. The dividend yield is computed as follows:

$$\text{Dividend yield on} \atop \text{preferred stock} = \frac{\text{Dividend per share}}{\text{Current market price per share}} = \frac{\$8}{\$110} = 7.27\%$$

Through the use of dividend yield rates, different preferred stocks having different annual dividends and different market prices can be compared.

■ FINAL CONSIDERATIONS IN FINANCIAL STATEMENT ANALYSIS

Standing alone, a single financial ratio may not be very informative. Greater insight can be obtained by computing and analyzing several related ratios for a company. The ratios presented in this chapter are summarized in Illustration 20.3.

Financial analysis relies heavily upon informed judgment. Percentages and ratios are guides to aid comparison and are useful in uncovering potential strengths and weaknesses. But the financial analyst should seek the basic causes behind changes and established trends.

Need for Comparable Data

Analysts must be sure that their comparisons are valid—especially when the comparison is of items for different periods or different companies. Consistent accounting practices must be followed if valid interperiod comparisons are to be made. Comparable intercompany comparisons are more difficult to secure. Accountants cannot do much more than disclose the fact that one company is using Fifo and another is using Lifo for inventory and cost of goods sold computations. Such a disclosure alerts analysts that intercompany comparisons of inventory turnover ratios, for example, may not be strictly comparable.

Also, when comparing a company's ratios to industry averages provided by an external source such as Dun & Bradstreet, the analyst must calculate the company's ratio in the same manner as the reporting service. Thus, if Dun & Bradstreet uses net sales (rather than cost of goods sold) to compute inventory turnover, so should the analyst. Net sales is used because cost of goods sold amounts are not computed and reported in the same manner by all companies. Ratios based on net sales may lead to different conclusions from those obtained using cost of goods sold because gross margin rates may differ. For example, two companies, Company A and Company B, may both have $100 sales and $10 average inventory for an identical inventory turnover based on sales of 10 ($100/$10). But, if Company A's gross margin rate is 40%, its inventory turnover based on cost of goods sold is 6 [($100 − $40)/$10]. If Company B's gross margin rate is 30%, its cost of goods sold is $70, and its inventory turnover is 7.

Influence of External Factors

Facts and conditions not disclosed by the financial statements may, however, affect their interpretation. A single important event may have been largely responsible for a given relationship. For example, a new product may have been unexpectedly put on the market by competitors, making it necessary for the company under study to sacrifice its inventory of a product suddenly ren-

Illustration 20.3   *Summary of Ratios*

Ratio	Formula	Significance
Current ratio	Current assets ÷ Current liabilities	Test of debt-paying ability
Acid-test (quick) ratio	Quick assets (Cash + Marketable securities + Net receivables) ÷ Current liabilities	Test of immediate debt-paying ability
Accounts receivable turnover	Net credit sales (or net sales)÷ Average net accounts receivable	Test of quality of accounts receivable
Number of days' sales in accounts receivable (average collection period of accounts receivable)	Number of days in year ÷ Accounts receivable turnover	Test of quality of accounts receivable
Inventory turnover	Cost of goods sold ÷ Average inventory	Test of whether or not a sufficient volume of business is being generated relative to inventory
Total assets turnover	Net sales ÷ Average total assets	Test of whether or not the volume of business generated is adequate relative to amount of capital invested in business
Equity ratio	Stockholders' equity ÷ Total assets (equities)	Index of long-run solvency and safety
Stockholders' equity to debt ratio	Stockholders' equity ÷ Total debt	Measure of the relative proportion of stockholders' and of creditors' equities
Rate of return on operating assets	Net operating income ÷ Operating assets or Operating margin × Turnover of operating assets	Measure of managerial effectiveness
Net income to net sales	Net income ÷ Net sales	Indicator of the net amount of net profit on each dollar of sales
Net income to average stockholders' equity	Net income ÷ Average stockholders' equity	Measure of what a given company earned for its stockholders from all sources as a percentage of the stockholders' investment
EPS of common stock	Net income available to common stockholders ÷ Weighted-average number of common shares outstanding	Tends to have an effect on the market price per share
Times interest earned ratio	Income before interest and taxes ÷ Interest expense	Indicates likelihood that creditors will continue to receive their interest payments
Times preferred dividends earned ratio	Net income ÷ Annual preferred dividends	Indicates likelihood that preferred stockholders will receive their dividend each year
Earnings yield on common stock	EPS ÷ Current market price per share	Useful for comparison with other stocks
Price-earnings ratio	Current market price per share ÷ EPS	Index of whether a stock is relatively cheap or expensive based on ratio
Dividend yield on common stock	Dividend per share ÷ Current market price per share	Useful for comparison with other stocks
Payout ratio on common stock	Dividend per share ÷ EPS	Index of whether company pays out a large percentage of earnings as dividends or reinvests most of its earnings
Dividend yield on preferred stock	Dividend per share ÷ Current market price per share	Useful for comparison with other preferred stocks

dered obsolete. Such an event would affect the percentage of gross margin to net sales severely. Yet there may be little or no chance that such an event will happen again.

General business conditions within the business or industry of the company under study must be considered. A corporation's downward trend in earnings, for example, is less alarming if the industry trend or the general economic trend is also downward.

Consideration should be given to the possible seasonal nature of the businesses under study. If the balance sheet date represents the seasonal peak in the volume of business, for example, the ratio of current assets to current liabilities may acceptably be much lower than if the balance sheet date is in a season of low activity.

The potential investor should realize that acquiring the ability to make informed judgments is a long process and does not occur overnight. Using ratios and percentages without thinking of underlying causes may lead to incorrect conclusions.

Impact of Inflation

The usefulness of conventional financial statements has been questioned in recent years more than ever before. There is one primary reason for this: financial statements fail to reveal the impact of inflation on the reporting entity. One of the primary rules to be followed in making comparisons is to be sure that the items being compared are comparable. The old adage is that one should not add apples and oranges and call the total either apples or oranges. Yet, the accountant does exactly this when dollars of different real worth are added or subtracted as if they were the same. The worth of a dollar declines during periods of inflation.

Considerable debate has existed over the proper response by accounting to inflation. Some argue that we should change our units of measure from the nominal, unadjusted dollar to a dollar of a constant purchasing power. Others maintain that only by adopting current cost as the attribute measured will the real effect of inflation on an entity be revealed. How each of these alternative approaches could be implemented and what they are likely to reveal were discussed in Chapter 13.

Need for Comparative Standards

Relationships between financial statement items become more meaningful when standards are available for comparison. Comparison with standards provides a starting point for all the analyst's thinking and leads to further investigation and, ultimately, to conclusions and business decisions. Such standards consist of (1) those that the analyst has in his or her own mind as a result of experience and observations, (2) those provided by the records of past performance and position of the business under study, and (3) those provided about other enterprises. Examples of this last type of standard are data available through trade associations, universities, research organizations (such as Dun & Bradstreet and Robert Morris Associates), and govermental units (such as the Federal Trade Commission).

It is important in financial statement analysis to remember that standards for comparison vary by industry and financial analysis must be carried out with knowledge of specific industry characteristics. For example, a wholesale grocery company would have large inventories to be shipped to retailers and a relatively small investment in plant, property, and equipment, while an electric utility company would have no inventory (except for repair parts) and a large investment in plant, property, and equipment.

Even within an industry, specific variations may exist. Acceptable current ratios, gross margin percentages, debt-to-equity ratios, and so forth vary widely depending on unique conditions within an industry. Therefore, it is important to know the industry in order to make comparisons that have real meaning.

■ SUMMARY

The data contained in financial statements represent a quantitative summary of a company's operations and activities. If managers, investors, and creditors are skillful in using these financial statements, they can learn much about a company's strengths, weaknesses, problems, operating efficiency, solvency, and profitability.

Many analytical techniques are available to assist managers and others in using financial statements and in assessing the direction and importance of trends and changes that are taking place in a company. Three such techniques have been discussed—dollar and percentage changes in statements (horizontal and vertical analysis), trend analysis, and ratio analysis. In regard to ratio analysis, we have discussed (1) liquidity ratios, (2) equity, or long-term solvency, ratios, (3) profitability tests, and (4) market tests.

Ratios and other analytical techniques are not ends in themselves but rather represent a starting point in evaluating an organization. Once ratios are computed, the analyst should look for the **basic causes** behind the changes and trends that are observed. In interpreting the findings of ratio analysis and the other analytical techniques discussed in the chapter, the analyst may rely on various standards for comparison. The analyst must also be concerned about the comparability of data between companies or over periods of time, about the influence of external factors such as competitive conditions in the industry and general business conditions, and about the impact of inflation on financial statements.

Playing the role of an analyst, as you did in this chapter, should make you aware of some of the techniques used and decisions made by professional financial statement analysts. This chapter should improve your understanding of the uses of financial statements.

So far in the text we have discussed only service companies and merchandising companies. In Chapter 21, we begin a discussion of the third type of business—manufacturing companies.

NEW TERMS INTRODUCED IN CHAPTER 20

Accounts receivable turnover

Net sales divided by average net accounts receivable (772).

Acid-test (quick) ratio

Ratio of quick assets (cash, marketable securities, net receivables) to current liabilities (771).

Common-size statements

Show only percentages and no absolute dollar amounts (766).

Comparative financial statements

Present the same company's financial statements for two or more successive periods in side-by-side columns (765).

Current ratio

The ratio that relates current assets to current liabilities (770).

Debt to equity ratio

Total debt divided by owners' equity (776).

Dividend yield on common stock

Dividend per share divided by current market price per share (783).

Dividend yield on preferred stock

Dividend per share divided by current market price per share (783).

Earnings per share (EPS)

Usually computed for common stock; earnings available to common stockholders (which equals net income less preferred dividends) divided by weighted-average number of shares of common stock outstanding (780).

Earnings yield on common stock

Ratio of current EPS to current market price per share (782).

Equity ratio

The ratio of stockholders' equity to total assets (or total equities) (775).

Horizontal analysis

Analysis of a company's financial statements for two or more successive periods showing percentage and/ or absolute changes from prior year. This type of analysis helps detect changes in a company's performance and highlights trends (765).

Inventory turnover

Cost of goods sold divided by average inventory (774).

Liquidity

State of possessing liquid assets, such as cash and other assets that will soon be converted into cash (764).

Net income to average stockholders' equity

Net income divided by average stockholders' equity; often called **rate of return on stockholders' equity,** or simply **return on equity (ROE)** (779).

Net income to net sales

Net income divided by net sales (778).

Nonoperating assets

Assets owned but not used in producing operating revenues (777).

Nonoperating income elements

Elements that are excluded from net operating income because they are not directly related to operations; includes such elements as extraordinary items, interest revenue, interest expense, and income taxes (777).

Number of days' sales in accounts receivable

The number of days in a year (365) divided by the accounts receivable turnover. Also called the **average collection period for accounts receivable** (773).

Operating assets

All assets actively used in producing operating revenues (777).

Operating margin

Net operating income divided by net sales (777).

Payout ratio (on common stock)

The ratio of dividends per share divided by EPS (783).

Price-earnings ratio

The ratio of current market price per share divided by the EPS of the stock (783).

Quick ratio

Same as acid-test ratio.

Rate of return on operating assets

(Net operating income ÷ Net sales) × (Net sales ÷ Operating assets). Result is equal to net operating income divided by operating assets (777).

Return on equity (ROE)

Net income divided by average stockholders' equity (779).

Stockholders' equity to debt ratio

Stockholders' equity divided by total debt; often used in inverted form and called the **debt to equity ratio** (776).

Times interest earned ratio

A ratio computed by dividing income before interest expense and income taxes by interest expense (also called **interest coverage ratio**) (781).

Times preferred dividends earned ratio

Net income divided by annual preferred dividends (782).

Total assets turnover

Net sales divided by average total assets (774).

Trend percentages

Similar to horizontal analysis except that a base year is selected and comparisons are made to the base year (766).

Turnover

The relationship between the amount of an asset and some measure of its use. See accounts receivable turnover, inventory turnover, and total assets turnover (772).

Turnover of operating assets

Net sales divided by operating assets (777).

Vertical analysis

The study of a single financial statement in which each item is expressed as a percentage of a significant total; for example, percentages of sales calculations (766).

Working capital ratio

Same as current ratio.

Yield (on stock)

The yield on a stock investment refers to either an earnings yield or a dividend yield (782). Also see Earnings yield on common stock and Dividend yield on common stock and preferred stock.

DEMONSTRATION PROBLEM 20–1

Comparative financial statements of the Roscoe Company for 1987 and 1988 follow:

ROSCOE COMPANY
Comparative Income Statements
For the Years Ended December 31, 1987, and 1988
(in thousands)

	1988	1987
Net sales	$800	$700
Cost of goods sold	497	427
Gross margin	$303	$273
Operating expenses	220	198
Net income before income taxes	$ 83	$ 75
Income taxes	33	30
Net income	$ 50	45

ROSCOE COMPANY
Comparative Balance Sheets
December 31, 1987, and 1988
(in thousands)

	1988	1987
Assets		
Cash	$ 23	$ 24
Accounts receivable	51	58
Inventory	85	63
Plant assets, net	177	178
Total assets	$336	$323
Liabilities and Stockholders' Equity		
Current liabilities	$ 60	$ 52
Long-term liabilities	70	70
Common stock	180	180
Retained earnings	26	21
Total liabilities and stockholders' equity	$336	$323

Required: a. Prepare comparative common-size income statements for 1987 and 1988.
              b. Perform a horizontal analysis of the comparative balance sheets.
              c. Comment on the results of *(a)* and *(b)*.

Solution to demonstration problem 20–1

a.

ROSCOE COMPANY
Common-Size Comparative Income Statements
For the Years Ended December 31, 1987, and 1988

	1988	1987
Net sales	100.00	100.00
Cost of goods sold	62.13	61.00
Gross margin	37.87	39.00
Operating expenses	27.50	28.29
Net income before income taxes . .	10.37	10.71
Income taxes	4.12	4.28
Net income	6.25	6.43

b.

ROSCOE COMPANY
Comparative Balance Sheets
December 31, 1987, and 1988
(in thousands)

	1988	1987	Increase or decrease* 1988 over 1987 Amount	Percent
Assets				
Cash	$ 23	$ 24	$ 1*	4.17*
Accounts receivable	51	58	7*	12.07*
Inventory	85	63	22	34.92
Plant assets, net	177	178	1*	0.56*
Total assets	$336	$323	$13	4.02
Liabilities and Stockholders' Equity				
Current liabilities	$ 60	$ 52	$ 8	15.38
Long-term liabilities	70	70	–0–	–0–
Common stock	180	180	–0–	–0–
Retained earnings	26	21	5	23.81
Total liabilities and stockholders' equity . .	$336	$323	$13	4.02

c.   The $100,000 increase in sales yielded only a $30,000 increase in gross margin because the gross margin rate decreased from 39% to 37.87%. Although operating expenses increased from $198,000 to $220,000, they declined relatively from 28.29% to 27.50% of sales. This change together with the change in gross margin combined to hold net income to an increase of $5,000, which represents a decline of 0.18% in the rate of net income to sales. The significant change in the balance sheet was the 35% increase in inventory that was financed by decreases in cash and accounts receivable and by increases in current liabilities and in retained earnings. The company is in a less liquid position at the end of 1988 than at the end of 1987.

DEMONSTRATION PROBLEM 20–2

The balance sheet and supplementary data for the Turner Corporation are shown below:

TURNER CORPORATION
Balance Sheet
December 31, 1987

Assets

Cash		$ 50,000
Marketable securities		30,000
Accounts receivable, net		70,000
Inventory		150,000
Building	$400,000	
Less: Accumulated depreciation	100,000	300,000
Total assets		$600,000

Liabilities and Stockholders' Equity

Accounts payable	$ 30,000
Bank loans payable	10,000
Mortgage notes payable, due in 1990	40,000
Bonds payable, 10%, due December 31, 1992 . .	100,000
Common stock, $100 par value	300,000
Retained earnings	120,000
Total liabilities and stockholders' equity	$600,000

Supplementary data:

1. 1987 net income: $60,000.
2. 1987 cost of goods sold: $540,000.
3. 1987 sales: $900,000.
4. Inventory, January 1, 1987: $100,000.
5. Interest expense: $15,000.
6. 1987 net income before interest and taxes: $130,000.
7. Net accounts receivable on January 1, 1987: $50,000.
8. Total assets on January 1, 1987: $540,000.

Required: Compute the following ratios:

a. Current ratio.
b. Acid-test ratio.
c. Accounts receivable turnover.
d. Inventory turnover.
e. Total assets turnover.
f. Equity ratio.
g. EPS of common stock.
h. Times interest earned ratio.

Solution to demonstration problem 20–2

a. Current ratio:

$$\frac{\text{Current assets}}{\text{Current liabilities}} = \frac{\$300,000}{\$40,000} = 7.5:1$$

b. Acid-test ratio:

$$\frac{\text{Quick assets}}{\text{Current liabilities}} = \frac{\$150,000}{\$40,000} = 3.75:1$$

c. Accounts receivable turnover:

$$\frac{\text{Net sales}}{\text{Average net accounts receivable}} = \frac{\$900,000}{\$60,000} = 15 \text{ times}$$

d. Inventory turnover:

$$\frac{\text{Cost of goods sold}}{\text{Average inventory}} = \frac{\$540,000}{\$125,000} = 4.32 \text{ times}$$

e. Total assets turnover:

$$\frac{\text{Net sales}}{\text{Average total assets}} = \frac{\$900,000}{\$570,000} = 1.58 \text{ times}$$

f. Equity ratio:

$$\frac{\text{Stockholders' equity}}{\text{Total assets}} = \frac{\$420,000}{\$600,000} = 70\%$$

g. EPS of common stock:

$$\frac{\begin{array}{c}\text{Net income available}\\ \text{to common stockholders}\end{array}}{\begin{array}{c}\text{Weighted-average number of}\\ \text{common shares outstanding}\end{array}} = \frac{\$60,000}{3,000} = \$20$$

h. Times interest earned ratio:

$$\frac{\text{Income before interest and taxes}}{\text{Interest expense}} = \frac{\$130,000}{\$15,000} = 8.67 \text{ to } 1, \text{ or } 8.67 \text{ times}$$

QUESTIONS

1. Distinguish between horizontal and vertical analysis of financial statements.

2. What are common-size financial statements? What item is assigned a value of 100% in the common-size income statement, and what item is assigned a value of 100% in the common-size balance sheet?

3. How do trend percentages differ from comparative financial statements?

4. What are the changes, absolute and percentage, if net income of $40,000 earned in 1988 is compared to a net loss sustained in 1987 of $10,000? What are the changes if the net loss was sustained in 1988 after earning net income in 1987?

5. Explain the meaning of this statement: "With 1979 equal to 100, net sales increased from 225 in 1987 to 260 in 1988."

6. Think of a situation where the current ratio is misleading as an indicator of short-term debt-paying ability. Does the acid-test ratio offer a remedy to the situation you have described? Describe a situation where the acid-test ratio will not suffice either.

7. A provision in a bond indenture requires the borrower to maintain positive working capital. Explain what this means and why such a provision is included in an indenture.

8. The higher the accounts receivable turnover rate, the better off is the company. Do you agree? Why?

9. Through the use of turnover ratios, explain why a company might seek to increase the volume of its sales even though such an increase can be secured only at reduced prices.

10. Of what significance is the equity ratio? What are the alternative ways of conveying the same information?

11. Before the John Company issued $10,000 of long-term notes (due more than a year from the date of issue) in exchange for a like amount of accounts payable, its acid-test ratio was 2:1. Will this transaction increase, decrease, or have no effect on *(a)* the current ratio and *(b)* the equity ratio?

12. How is rate of return on operating assets determined? Is it possible for two companies with "operating margins'' of 5% and 1%, respectively, both to have rates of return of 20% on operating assets? How?

13. Indicate which of the relationships illustrated in this chapter would be used to judge:
   a. The short-term debt-paying ability of the company.
   b. The overall efficiency of the company without regard to the sources of assets.
   c. The return to owners of a corporation.
   d. The safety of bondholders' interest.
   e. The safety of preferred stockholders' dividends.

14. Indicate how each of the following ratios or measures is calculated:
   a. Payout ratio.

   b. EPS of common stock.
   c. Price-earnings ratio.
   d. Earnings yield on common stock.
   e. Dividend yield on preferred stock.
   f. Times interest earned ratio.
   g. Times preferred dividends earned ratio.
   h. Return on stockholders' equity.

15. Explain why the EPS for 1986 must be adjusted in a three-year summary of earnings data (presented in 1988) for a 20% stock dividend distributed in June 1988.

16. Cite some deficiencies in accounting information that would limit its usefulness for analyzing a particular company over a 10-year period.

EXERCISES

E-1

Perform horizontal and vertical analysis

Income statement data for Black Company for 1987 and 1988 are given below:

	1988	1987
Net sales	$870,000	$645,600
Cost of goods sold . . .	609,600	418,800
Selling expenses	132,000	116,400
Administrative expenses . .	78,000	66,000
Income taxes	19,200	18,000

Prepare a horizontal and vertical analysis of the above income data in a form similar to that in Illustration 20.2. Comment on the results of this analysis.

E-2

Determine effects of various transactions on current ratio

A company engaged in the following three independent transactions:

1. Merchandise purchased on account, $200,000.
2. Machinery purchased for cash, $200,000.
3. Issued capital stock for cash, $200,000.

a. Compute the current ratio after each of these transactions assuming current assets were $400,000 and the current ratio was 1:1 before the transactions occurred.
b. Repeat part (a) assuming current assets were $400,000 and the current ratio was 2:1.
c. Repeat part (a) assuming current assets were $400,000 and the current ratio was 1:2.

E-3

Compute average number of days receivables are outstanding; determine effect of increase in turnover

A company has sales of $360,000 per year. Its average net accounts receivable balance is $120,000.

a. What is the average number of days accounts receivable are outstanding?
b. By how much would the capital invested in accounts receivable be reduced if the turnover could be increased to 6 without a loss of sales?

E-4

Compute inventory turnover

From the following partial income statement, calculate the inventory turnover for the period.

Net sales		$845,000
Cost of goods sold:		
Beginning inventory	$ 97,500	
Purchases	552,500	
Cost of goods available for sale . .	$650,000	
Less: Ending inventory	110,500	
Cost of goods sold		539,500
Gross margin		$305,500
Operating expenses		136,500
Net operating income		$169,000

E–5

Compute rate of return on operating assets

Picken, Inc. had net sales of $330,000, gross margin of $140,000, and operating expenses of $85,000. Total assets (all operating) were $275,000. Compute Picken's rate of return on operating assets.

E–6

Compute rate of return on stockholders' equity

Omega Company started 1987 with total stockholders' equity of $225,000. Its net income for 1987 was $60,000, and $10,000 of dividends were declared. Compute the rate of return on average stockholders' equity for 1987.

E–7

Compute EPS

The Cone Company had 60,000 shares of common stock outstanding on January 1, 1987. On April 1, 1987, it issued 20,000 additional shares for cash. The earnings available for common stockholders for 1987 were $200,000. What amount of EPS should the company report?

E–8

Compute weighted-average number of shares outstanding

Sapp Company started 1988 with 100,000 shares of common stock outstanding. On March 31 it issued 16,000 shares for cash, and on September 30 it purchased 8,000 shares for cash. Compute the weighted-average number of common shares outstanding for the year.

E–9

Compute EPS for current and prior year

A company reported EPS of $2 ($200,000/100,000 shares) for 1986, ending the year with 100,000 shares outstanding. In 1987, the company earned net income of $660,000, issued 40,000 shares of common stock for cash on September 30, and distributed a 100% stock dividend on December 31, 1987. Compute EPS for 1987, and compute the adjusted EPS for 1986 that would be shown in the 1987 annual report.

E–10

Compute times interest earned

A company paid interest of $12,000, incurred federal income taxes of $34,000, and had net income (after taxes) of $50,000. How many times was interest earned?

E–11

Compute times dividends earned and dividend yield

The Nash Company had 8,000 shares of $75 par value, 6%, preferred stock outstanding. Net income after taxes was $504,000. The market price per share was $90.

a. How many times were the preferred dividends earned?
b. What was the yield on the preferred stock assuming the regular preferred dividends were declared and paid?

E–12

Compute price-earnings ratio

A company had 9,000 shares of $100 par value common stock outstanding. Net income was $90,000. Current market price per share is $150. Compute the price-earnings ratio.

PROBLEMS, SERIES A

P20–1–A

Perform horizontal and vertical analysis

Neal Company's comparative statements of income and retained earnings for the years ended December 31, 1987, and 1988, and its comparative balance sheets as of the end of each of these years follow:

NEAL COMPANY
Comparative Statements of Income
and Retained Earnings
For the Years Ended December 31, 1987, and 1988
(in thousands)

	1988	1987
Net sales	$906,950	$864,270
Cost of goods sold	575,410	551,210
Gross margin	$331,540	$313,060
Operating expenses:		
Selling	$133,210	$141,350
Administrative	123,420	114,290
Total operating expenses	$256,630	$255,640
Net operating income	$ 74,910	$ 57,420
Interest expense	20,240	13,200
Income before income taxes	$ 54,670	$ 44,220
Income taxes	22,000	17,600
Net income	$ 32,670	$ 26,620
Retained earnings, January 1	82,500	66,880
	$115,170	$ 93,500
Dividends	11,770	11,000
Retained earnings, December 31	$103,400	$ 82,500

NEAL COMPANY
Comparative Balance Sheets
December 31, 1987, and 1988
(in thousands)

	1988	1987
Assets		
Current assets:		
Cash	$ 26,520	$ 14,430
Accounts receivable, net	75,530	73,450
Inventory	187,850	195,130
Total current assets	$289,900	$283,010
Plant asssets, net	244,400	232,700
Total assets	$534,300	$515,710
Liabilities and Stockholders' Equity		
Current liabilities:		
Accounts payable and accrued liabilities	$ 74,100	$158,210
Notes payable	52,000	130,000
Total current liabilities	$126,100	$288,210
Long-term liabilities:		
Bonds payable (due 1995)	156,000	–0–
Total liabilities	$282,100	$288,210
Stockholders' equity:		
Common stock	$130,000	$130,000
Retained earnings	122,200	97,500
Total stockholders' equity	$252,200	$227,500
Total liabilities and stockholders' equity	$534,300	$515,710

Required: a. Perform a horizontal and vertical analysis of the above financial statements in a manner similar to that shown in Illustrations 20.1 and 20.2.
b. Comment on the results obtained.

P20-2-A

Perform trend analysis

You are given the following data for Myra Corporation:

	1987	1988	1989	1990
Sales	$225,000	$257,500	$300,000	$425,000
Cost of goods sold . .	150,000	162,500	225,000	325,000
Gross margin	$ 75,000	$ 95,000	$ 75,000	$100,000
Operating expenses . .	60,000	64,000	73,500	88,000
Net operating income . .	$ 15,000	$ 31,000	$ 1,500	$ 12,000

Required:

a. Prepare a statement showing the trend percentages for each of the above items, using 1987 as the base year.

b. Comment on the trends noted.

P20-3-A

Compute working capital, current ratio, and acid-test ratio

The following data are for the Stoke Company:

	December 31, 1988	December 31, 1987
Notes payable (due in 90 days) . .	$ 47,000	$ 37,500
Merchandise inventory	150,000	130,000
Cash	62,500	80,000
Marketable securities	31,000	18,750
Accrued liabilities	12,000	13,750
Accounts receivable	117,500	115,000
Accounts payable	70,000	45,000
Allowance for doubtful accounts . .	15,000	9,500
Bonds payable, due 1992	97,500	100,000
Prepaid expenses	4,000	4,600

Required:

a. Compute the amount of working capital at both year-end dates.

b. Compute the current ratio at both year-end dates.

c. Compute the acid-test ratio at both year-end dates.

e. Comment briefly on the company's short-term financial position.

P20-4-A

Determine effects of various transactions on working capital and current ratio

Stevens Products, Inc. has a current ratio on December 31, 1987, of 2:1 before the following transactions were completed.

Transactions:

1. Sold a building for cash.
2. Exchanged old equipment for new equipment. (No cash was involved.)
3. Declared a cash dividend on preferred stock.
4. Sold merchandise on account (at a profit).
5. Retired mortgage notes that would have matured in 1995.
6. Issued a stock dividend to common stockholders.
7. Paid cash for a patent.
8. Temporarily invested cash in government bonds.
9. Purchased inventory for cash.
10. Wrote off an account receivable as uncollectible. Uncollectible amount is less than balance of the Allowance for Doubtful Accounts.
11. Paid the cash dividend on preferred stock that was declared earlier.
12. Purchased a computer and gave a two-year promissory note.
13. Collected accounts receivable.
14. Borrowed from the bank on a 120-day promissory note.
15. Discounted a customer's note. Interest expense was involved.

Required:

a. Indicate whether the amount of working capital will increase, decrease, or be unaffected by each of the transactions.

b. Indicate whether the current ratio will increase, decrease, or be unaffected by each of the transactions.

Consider each transaction independently of all the others.

P20–5–A

Prepare comparative financial statements in percentages; compute current, acid-test, and equity ratios for two years

The following are comparative balance sheets and other data of the Happer Corporation on December 31, 1987, and 1988:

HAPPER CORPORATION
Comparative Balance Sheets

	December 31, 1988	December 31, 1987
Assets		
Cash	$ 75,000	$ 85,000
Accounts receivable, net	65,000	75,000
Merchandise inventory	45,000	55,000
Plant assets, net	100,000	45,000
Total assets	$285,000	$260,000
Liabilities and Stockholders' Equity		
Accounts payable	$ 40,000	$ 25,000
Notes payable	35,000	43,000
Common stock	110,000	110,000
Retained earnings	100,000	82,000
Total liabilities and stockholders' equity	$285,000	$260,000
Other data:		
Sales	$460,000	$400,000
Gross margin	190,000	170,000
Selling and administrative expense	120,000	110,000
Interest expense	4,000	2,000
Cash dividends	38,000	15,000

During 1988, a note in the amount of $25,000 was given for equipment purchased at that price. Unlike the company's other notes, which are short term, the $25,000 note matures in 1992.

Required:

a. Prepare comparative income statements that show each item as a percentage of net sales. Ignore income taxes.
b. Prepare comparative balance sheets that show each item as a percentage of total assets.
c. Prepare a schedule that shows the percentage of each current asset to total current assets as of both year-end dates.
d. Compute the current ratios as of both dates.
e. Compute the acid-test ratios as of both dates.
f. Compute the equity ratio as of both dates.

P20–6–A

Compute rate of return on operating assets and demonstrate effects of various transactions on it

Selected data for three companies appear below:

	Operating assets	Net operating income	Net sales
Company 1	$ 585,000	$ 78,000	$ 858,000
Company 2	3,510,000	253,500	7,800,000
Company 3	15,600,000	2,047,500	14,625,000

Required:

a. Determine the operating margin, turnover of operating assets, and rate of return on operating assets for each company.
b. In the subsequent year the following changes took place (no other changes occurred):

Company 1 bought some new machinery at a cost of $65,000. Net operating income increased by $5,200 as a result of an increase in sales of $104,000.
Company 2 sold some equipment it was using which was relatively unproductive. The book value of the equipment sold was $260,000. As a result of the sale of the equipment, sales declined by $130,000 and operating income declined by $2,600.
Company 3 purchased some new retail outlets at a cost of $2,600,000. As a result, sales increased by $3,900,000 and operating income increased by $208,000.

1. Which company has the largest absolute change in—
    a. Operating margin ratio?
    b. Turnover of operating assets?
    c. Rate of return on operating assets?

2. Which one realized the largest dollar change in operating income? Explain this in relation to the changes in the rate of return on operating assets.

P20–7–A

Compute EPS, rate of return on sales and on stockholders' equity, and number of times interest earned for two years

You are given the following data for Michel Company:

	1988	1987
Net sales	$375,000	$262,500
Net income before interest and taxes	60,000	20,000
Net income	30,000	10,000
Interest expense	12,000	5,000
Stockholders' equity, January 1	375,000	250,000
Stockholders' equity, December 31	400,000	375,000
Common stock, par value $50, December 31 . .	200,000	120,000

Additional shares of common stock were issued on January 1, 1988.

Required: Compute the following for both 1987 and 1988. Then compare and comment.

a. EPS of common stock.
b. Net income to net sales.
c. Net income to average stockholders' equity.
d. Times interest earned ratio.

P20–8–A

Compute numerous standard ratios

The following condensed balance sheet and supplementary data are for the Moore Company for 1988:

MOORE COMPANY
Balance Sheet
December 31, 1988

Assets

Current assets:		
Cash	$ 300,000	
Marketable securities	175,000	
Accounts receivable, net	375,000	
Inventory	310,000	$1,160,000
Property, plant, and equipment:		
Plant assets, cost	$2,000,000	
Less: Accumulated depreciation	375,000	1,625,000
Total assets		$2,785,000

Liabilities and Stockholders' Equity

Current liabilities:		
Accounts payable	$ 200,000	
Bank loans payable (due in six months)	60,000	$ 260,000
Long-term liabilities:		
Mortgage notes payable, due in 1994	$ 237,500	
Bonds payable, 8%, due December 31, 2002 . .	450,000	687,500
Total liabilities		$ 947,500
Stockholders' equity:		
Common stock, par value $25 per share . . .	$1,350,000	
Paid-in capital in excess of par	87,500	
Retained earnings	400,000	1,837,500
Total liabilities and stockholders' equity		$2,785,000

Supplementary data:

1. 1988 interest expense, $40,000.
2. 1988 net sales, $2,000,000.
3. 1988 cost of goods sold, $1,350,000.
4. 1988 net income, $150,000.
5. 1988 income before interest and taxes, $350,000.
6. Inventory, December 31, 1987, $410,000.

Required: Calculate the following ratios. Where you would normally use the average amount for an item in a ratio, but the information is not available to do so, use the year-end balance. (Analysts sometimes have to do this.) Show computations.

a.   Current ratio.
b.   Net income to average stockholders' equity.
c.   Inventory turnover.
d.   Number of days' sales in accounts receivable (assume 365 days in 1988).
e.   EPS of common stock.
f.   Times interest earned ratio.
g.   Equity ratio.
h.   Net income to net sales.
i.   Total assets turnover.
j.   Acid-test ratio.

P20-9-A

***Determine effects on
ratios of change in
accounting method
(Fifo to Lifo)***

The Hulsey Company is considering switching from the Fifo method to the Lifo method of accounting for its inventory before it closes its books for the year. The January 1 inventory was $360,000. Following are data compiled from the adjusted trial balance at the end of the year:

Inventory, December 31 (Fifo) . .	$ 420,000	Current assets	$ 787,500
Current liabilities	300,000	Total assets (operating) . .	1,200,000
Net sales	1,050,000	Cost of goods sold . . .	607,500
Operating expenses	322,500		

If the switch to Lifo takes place, the December 31 inventory would be $375,000.

Required: a.   Compute the current ratio, inventory turnover ratio, and rate of return on operating assets assuming the company continues its use of Fifo.
b.   Repeat part *(a)* assuming the company adjusts its accounts to the Lifo inventory method.

PROBLEMS, SERIES B

P20–1–B

Perform horizontal and vertical analysis

Comparative statements of income and retained earnings for the years ending December 31, 1987, and 1988, and comparative balance sheets for the Lasky Company follow:

LASKY COMPANY
Comparative Statements of Income
and Retained Earnings
For the Years Ended December 31, 1987, and 1988
(in thousands)

	1988	1987
Net sales	$861,250	$745,000
Cost of goods sold	521,250	462,000
Gross margin	$340,000	$283,000
Operating expenses:		
Selling	$162,500	$133,500
Administrative	120,000	114,000
Total operating expenses	$282,500	$247,500
Net operating income	$ 57,500	$ 35,500
Interest expense	45,000	30,000
Income before income taxes	$ 12,500	$ 5,500
Income taxes	5,000	2,000
Net income	$ 7,500	$ 3,500
Retained earnings, January 1	5,500	2,500
	$ 13,000	$ 6,000
Dividends	750	500
Retained earnings, December 31	$ 12,250	$ 5,500

LASKY COMPANY
Comparative Balance Sheets
December 31, 1987, and 1988
(in thousands)

	1988	1987
Assets		
Current assets:		
Cash	$ 25,000	$ 38,000
Accounts receivable, net	60,000	56,000
Inventory	144,500	145,000
Total current assets	$229,500	$239,000
Plant assets, net	207,750	179,000
Total assets	$437,250	$418,000
Liabilities and Stockholders' Equity		
Current liabilities:		
Accounts payable and accrued liabilities	$100,000	$107,500
Notes payable	–0–	55,000
Total current liabilities	$100,000	$162,500
Long-term liabilities:		
Bonds payable (due 1994)	75,000	–0–
Total liabilities	$175,000	$162,500
Stockholders' equity:		
Common stock	$250,000	$250,000
Retained earnings	12,250	5,500
Total stockholders' equity	$262,250	$255,500
Total liabilities and stockholders' equity	$437,250	$418,000

Required:
   a. Perform a horizontal and vertical analysis of the above financial statements in a manner similar to that shown in Illustrations 20.1 and 20.2.
   b. Comment on the results of the analysis in part *(a)*.

P20-2-B

Perform trend analysis

You are given the following data for the Gulls Corporation:

	1987	1988	1989	1990
Sales	$350,000	$387,500	$455,000	$575,000
Cost of goods sold . .	225,000	237,500	265,000	375,000
Gross margin	$125,000	$150,000	$190,000	$200,000
Operating expenses . .	112,500	130,000	150,000	172,500
Net operating income . .	$ 12,500	$ 20,000	$ 40,000	$ 27,500

Required:
   a. Prepare a statement showing the trend percentages for each item above, using 1987 as the base year.
   b. Comment on the trends noted.

P20-3-B

Compute working capital, current ratio, and acid-test ratio

The following data are taken from the ledger of the Ryan Company:

	December 31, 1988	December 31, 1987
Allowance for doubtful accounts	$ 24,000	$ 19,000
Prepaid expenses	11,500	15,000
Accrued liabilities	70,000	62,000
Cash in Bank A	365,000	325,000
Wages payable	-0-	12,500
Accounts payable	238,000	195,000
Merchandise inventory	447,500	479,000
Bonds payable, due in 1992	205,000	198,000
Marketable securities	72,500	49,000
Notes payable (due in six months)	100,000	65,000
Accounts receivable	302,500	290,000

Required:
   a. Compute the amount of working capital at both year-end dates.
   b. Compute the current ratio at both year-end dates.
   c. Compute the acid-test ratio at both year-end dates.
   d. Comment briefly on the company's short-term financial position.

P20-4-B

Determine effects of various transactions on working capital and current ratio

On December 31, 1988, the Sledge Company's current ratio was 3:1 before the following transactions were completed.

Transactions:
  1. Purchased merchandise on account.
  2. Paid a cash dividend declared on November 15, 1988.
  3. Sold equipment for cash.
  4. Temporarily invested cash in marketable securities.
  5. Sold obsolete merchandise for cash (at a loss).
  6. Issued 10-year bonds for cash.
  7. Wrote off goodwill to retained earnings.
  8. Paid cash for inventory.
  9. Purchased land for cash.
 10. Returned merchandise which had not been paid for.
 11. Wrote off an account receivable as uncollectible. Uncollectible amount is less than balance in the Allowance for Doubtful Accounts.
 12. Accepted a 90-day note from a customer in settlement of customer's account receivable.
 13. Declared a stock dividend on common stock.

Required:
   a. Indicate whether the amount of working capital will increase, decrease, or be unaffected by each of the transactions.
   b. Indicate whether the current ratio will increase, decrease, or be unaffected by each of the transactions.

Consider each transaction independently of all the others.

P20-5-B

Prepare comparative financial statements in percentages; compute current, acid-test, and equity ratios for two years

The following information is for the Prader Company:

THE PRADER COMPANY
Comparative Balance Sheets

	December 31, 1988	December 31, 1987
Assets		
Cash	$ 25,000	$ 16,000
Accounts receivable, net	45,000	23,000
Merchandise inventory	35,000	28,000
Plant assets, net	36,000	27,000
Total assets	$141,000	$ 94,000
Liabilities and Stockholders' Equity		
Accounts payable	$ 19,000	$ 13,000
Notes payable	25,000	14,000
Common stock	65,000	46,000
Retained earnings	32,000	21,000
Total liabilities and stockholders' equity . .	$141,000	$ 94,000
Other data:		
Sales	$190,000	$145,000
Gross margin	115,000	95,000
Selling and administrative expense . . .	60,000	53,000
Interest expense	2,000	700

Cash dividends of $42,000 were paid in 1988. In 1988, plant assets were increased by giving a note of $4,500 for machinery of the same cost. The note matures October 1, 1991. All other notes are short term.

Required:

a. Prepare comparative income statements that show each item as a percentage of net sales. Ignore income taxes.

b. Prepare comparative balance sheets that show each item as a percentage of total assets.

c. Prepare a schedule that shows the percentage of each current asset to total current assets as of both year-end dates.

d. Compute the current ratios as of both dates.

e. Compute the acid-test ratios as of both dates.

f. Compute the equity ratio as of both dates.

P20-6-B

Compute rate of return on operating assets and demonstrate effects of various transactions on it

The Noble Company has net operating income of $312,500 and operating assets of $1,250,000. Its net sales are $2,500,000.

The accountant for the company computes the rate of return on operating assets after first computing the operating margin and the turnover of operating assets.

Required:

a. Show the computations the accountant made.

b. Indicate whether the operating margin and turnover will increase or decrease after each of the following changes. Then determine what the actual rate of return on operating assets would be. The events are not interrelated; consider each separately, starting from the original earning power position. No other changes occurred.

1. Sales were increased by $100,000. There was no change in the amount of operating income and no change in operating assets.

2. Management found some cost savings in the manufacturing process. The amount of reduction in operating expenses was $25,000. The savings resulted from the use of less materials to manufacture the same quantity of goods. As a result, average inventory was $10,000 lower than it otherwise would have been. Operating income was not affected by the reduction in inventory.

3. The company invested $50,000 of cash (received on accounts receivable) in a plot of land it plans to use in the future (a nonoperating asset); income was not affected.
4. The federal income tax rate increased and caused income tax expense to increase by $12,500. The taxes have not yet been paid.
5. The company issued bonds and used the proceeds to buy $250,000 of machinery to be used in the business. Interest payments are $12,500 per year. Operating income increased by $62,500 (net sales did not change).

P20–7–B

Compute EPS, rate of return on sales and stockholders' equity, and number of times interest earned for two years

You are given the following comparative data for the Carlyle Company:

	1988	1987
Net sales	$420,000	$260,000
Income before interest and taxes . . .	110,000	85,000
Net income	55,500	63,000
Interest expense	9,000	8,000
Stockholders' equity, December 31 (on December 31, 1986, $200,000) . .	305,000	235,000
Common stock, par value $50, December 31	260,000	230,000

Additional shares of common stock were issued on January 1, 1988.

Required: Compute the following for both 1987 and 1988. Then compare and comment.

a. EPS of common stock.
b. Net income to net sales.
c. Net income to average stockholders' equity.
d. Times interest earned ratio.

P20–8–B

Compute numerous standard ratios

The following balance sheet and supplementary data are for the Lynch Corporation for 1988:

LYNCH CORPORATION
Balance Sheet
December 31, 1988

Assets

Current assets:		
Cash	$ 112,500	
Marketable securities	60,000	
Accounts receivable, net	97,500	
Inventory	82,500	$ 352,500
Property, plant, and equipment:		
Plant assets, cost	$1,700,000	
Less: Accumulated depreciation	125,000	1,575,000
Total assets		$1,927,500

Liabilities and Stockholders' Equity

Current liabilities:		
Accounts payable	$ 85,000	
Bank loans payable	35,000	$ 120,000
Long-term liabilities:		
Mortgage notes payable, due in 1991	$ 45,000	
Bonds payable, 6% due December 31, 1990 . .	215,000	260,000
Total liabilities		$ 380,000
Stockholders' equity:		
Common stock, par value $50 per share . . .	$1,100,000	
Paid-in capital in excess of par value	40,000	
Retained earnings	407,500	1,547,500
Total liabilities and stockholders' equity		$1,927,500

Supplementary data:

1. 1988 net income, $150,000.
2. 1988 income before interest and taxes, $300,000.
3. 1988 cost of goods sold, $400,000.
4. 1988 net sales, $750,000.
5. Inventory on December 31, 1987, $72,500.
6. Total interest expense for the year, $12,900.

Required: Calculate the following ratios. Where you would normally use the average amount for an item in a ratio, but the information is not available to do so, use the year-end balance. (Analysts sometimes have to do this.) Show computations.

a. Current ratio.
b. Net income to average stockholders' equity.
c. Inventory turnover.
d. Number of days' sales in accounts receivable (assume 365 days in 1988).
e. EPS of common stock.
f. Times interest earned ratio.
g. Equity ratio.
h. Net income to net sales.
i. Total assets turnover.
j. Acid-test ratio.

P20–9–B

Determine effects on ratios of change in accounting method (Fifo to Lifo)

The Carter Company currently uses the Fifo method to account for its inventory but is considering a switch to Lifo before the books are closed for the year. Selected data for the year are:

Inventory, January 1	$137,500	Inventory, December 31 (Fifo)	$181,500
Current assets	346,500	Current liabilities	110,000
Total assets (operating)	550,000	Net sales	368,500
Cost of goods sold (Fifo)	214,500	Operating expenses	88,000
Inventory, December 31, (Lifo)	148,500		

Required:
a. Compute the current ratio, inventory turnover ratio, and rate of return on operating assets assuming the company continues using Fifo.
b. Repeat part *(a)* assuming the company adjusts its accounts to the Lifo method for ending inventory.

BUSINESS DECISION PROBLEM 20–1

Compute net income, identify reason for cash increase, state main sources of financing, and indicate further analyses needed

Shown below are the comparative balance sheets of the Dell Corporation for December 31, 1988 and 1987.

DELL CORPORATION
Comparative Balance Sheets
December 31, 1987, and 1988

	December 31, 1988	December 31, 1987
Assets		
Cash	$200,000	$ 40,000
Accounts receivable, net	36,000	48,000
Inventory	160,000	168,000
Plant and equipment	112,000	120,000
Total assets	$508,000	$376,000
Liabilities and Stockholders' Equity		
Accounts payable	$ 40,000	$ 40,000
Common stock	280,000	280,000
Retained earnings	188,000	56,000
Total liabilities and stockholders' equity . .	$508,000	$376,000

Required:
a. What was the net income for 1988 assuming there were no dividend payments?
b. What was the primary source of the large increase in the cash balance from 1987 to 1988?
c. What are the two main sources of assets for the Dell Corporation?
d. What other comparisons and procedures would you use to complete the analysis of the balance sheet begun above?

BUSINESS DECISION PROBLEM 20–2

Compute turnover ratios for four years and number of days sales in accounts receivable; evaluate effectiveness of company's credit policy

The information below was obtained from the annual reports of the Lyle Manufacturing Company:

	1985	1986	1987	1988
Net accounts receivable . .	$ 150,000	$ 300,000	$ 375,000	$ 500,000
Net sales	1,500,000	1,937,500	2,375,000	2,750,000

Required:
a. If cash sales account for 30% of all sales and credit terms are always 1/10, n/60, determine all turnover ratios possible and the number of days' sales in accounts receivable at all possible dates. (The number of days' sales in accounts receivable should be based on year-end accounts receivable and net credit sales.)
b. How effective is the company's credit policy?

BUSINESS DECISION PROBLEM 20–3

Analyze investment alternatives

Brenda Freeman is interested in investing in one of three companies (A, B, or C) by buying its common stock. The companies' shares are selling at about the same price. The long-term capital structures of the companies are as follows:

	Company A	Company B	Company C
Bonds with a 10% interest rate			$ 500,000
Preferred stock with an 8% dividend rate		$ 500,000	
Common stock, $10 par value	$1,000,000	500,000	500,000
Retained earnings	80,000	80,000	80,000
Total long-term equity	$1,080,000	$1,080,000	$1,080,000
Number of common shares outstanding . .	100,000	50,000	50,000

Ms. Freeman has consulted two investment advisers. One adviser believes that each of the companies will earn $62,500 per year before interest and taxes. The other adviser believes that each company will earn about $200,000 per year before interest and taxes.

Required: a.   Compute each of the following, using the estimate made by the first adviser and then the one made by the second adviser:

1. Earnings available for common stockholders assuming a 40% tax rate.
2. EPS of common stock.
3. Rate of return on total stockholders' equity.

b.   Which stock should Ms. Freeman select if she believes the first adviser?

c.   Are the stockholders as a group (common and preferred) better off with or without the use of long-term debt in the above companies?

BUSINESS SITUATION FOR DISCUSSION

Financial Statement Analysis—A Two-Minute Drill*

William L. Stone

* * * * *

Commercial loan officers often face the situation where they would like to make a quick appraisal of a financial statement. Some loan requests, for example, can be declined in short order because the financial statements reflect a weak condition. However, loan officers must have the skill to focus on those factors that would reveal that further discussion is fruitless. More important, they should be able to develop several pertinent questions regarding the problem areas of a company's operation as revealed by a brief analysis of the financial statements.

It is not uncommon for a loan applicant to present a loan officer with two or three years of financial statements in support of an application being presented orally. The loan officer does not have the luxury of analyzing the statements thoroughly while the applicant patiently sits in silence.

* * * * *

Within that two-minute period, the loan officer should be able to make an analysis that is thorough enough to reveal the company's problem areas on which the

subsequent questioning should focus. This article will explain how those two minutes can be spent most efficiently so that the loan officer will have a clear picture of the company's financial strengths and weaknesses.

* * * * *

Three ratios—current, debt to worth, and net profit margin—and three turnovers—receivables, inventory, and payables—form the basis of the two minute drill. These six relationships (turnovers are often referred to as ratios, but in the strictest sense, they are not ratios) were selected for several reasons. First, they are important indicators of a specific aspect of a company's financial condition. Second, taken together, they are indicative of the three important areas for credit purposes: liquidity, leverage, and profitability. Third, we can establish a standard that is easy to compute and understand against which a company's performance can be measured.

* * * * *

The writer suggests that loan officers have a simple worksheet available that looks like . . . [the table below].

Sample Worksheet

	1980	1981	1982
CR			2.1
D/W			0.9
NPM			5%
AR T/O			70
INV T/O			40
AP T/O			45

A quick glance . . . reveals that the company's financial condition for 1982 is pretty much in line except for the accounts receivable. The trap into which many loan officers fall is to stop once a chart . . . or a spread sheet is completed. On the contrary, no analysis has been accomplished yet. The numbers do not have any meaning until the loan officer understands what the numbers mean. What, for instance, do the numbers . . . indicate about the company's liquidity, leverage, and profitability? What problems—and therefore what areas of further inquiry—are indicated by the figures in . . . [the table]?

It should occur to readers that unless they go through an exercise such as the two-minute drill, they will have difficulty knowing what line of inquiry to pursue. The two-minute drill gives the loan officer the opportunity to focus on those areas of apparent weakness. An important side benefit is that the applicant realizes right away that the loan officer "understands" the applicant's business because he can ask direct, pertinent questions after only a brief review of the statements, for example, "What is your difficulty in collecting the money owed to you?" "Do you have a lot of obsolete inventory?" Are you being pressured by your trade creditors to bring your payables current?"

It is worth emphasizing again the cautions that appear near the beginning of this article. Briefly, the two-minute drill is not intended to be a substitute for a thorough analysis of a credit. Rather, it provides quick estimates of several important financial relationships that can serve as a basis for inquiries in the early stages of the application process.

*   *   *   *   *

PART 7

Accounting in Manufacturing Companies

CHAPTER 21

Income Measurement in Manufacturing Companies

LEARNING OBJECTIVES

After studying this chapter, you should be able to:

1. Name the three basic components of manufacturing costs incurred to produce a product.

2. Describe the difference between product costs and period costs and explain why proper classification is essential.

3. Describe the general pattern of the flow of costs through the accounting system of a manufacturing company under periodic inventory procedure and under perpetual inventory procedure.

4. Describe the differences in financial reporting by a merchandiser and a manufacturer and prepare a statement of cost of goods manufactured, an income statement, and a balance sheet for a manufacturer.

5. Prepare journal entries to account for the production activities of a manufacturer under both periodic and perpetual procedure.

6. Define and use correctly the new terms in the glossary.

So far in this text, you have studied accounting as it pertains to service businesses and merchandising businesses (retailers and wholesalers). This chapter focuses on accounting for manufacturing businesses.

If you owned a retail appliance store, you would purchase appliances, such as refrigerators and ranges, and sell them to customers. To determine your profitability, the cost of purchasing the appliances would be accounted for and subtracted from your gross sales as cost of goods sold. However, if instead you owned the manufacturing company that made the appliances, your cost of goods sold would be based on manufacturing costs.

Accounting for manufacturing costs is more complex than accounting for costs of merchandise purchased that is ready for sale. This chapter explains and illustrates the procedures to account for manufacturing costs. Terms such as raw materials, work in process, finished goods, direct labor, indirect labor, and manufacturing overhead are part of manufacturing accounting. The basic accounting process discussed throughout the text also applies to manufacturing companies.

■ MERCHANDISER AND MANUFACTURER ACCOUNTING DIFFERENCES

Perhaps the most important accounting difference between merchandisers and manufacturers relates to the difference in the nature of their activities. A merchandiser purchases goods that are already in their finished state and ready to be sold. On the other hand, a manufacturer must purchase raw materials and use production equipment and employee labor to transform the raw materials into finished products. Thus, while a merchandiser has only one type of inventory—merchandise available for sale—a manufacturer has three types—unprocessed materials, partially complete work in process, and ready-for-sale finished goods. Three different inventory accounts (instead of one) are necessary to show the cost of inventory in various stages of production.

A comparison of a manufacturer's cost of goods sold section of the income statement with that of a merchandiser is shown in Illustration 21.1. There are two major differences in the cost of goods sold sections: (1) goods ready to be sold are referred to as **merchandise inventory** by a merchandiser and as **finished goods inventory** by a manufacturer, and (2) **cost of purchases** for a merchandiser is equivalent to **cost of goods manufactured** by a manufacturer.

Illustration 21.1

Cost of Goods Sold Comparison

Merchandiser		Manufacturer	
Cost of goods sold:		Cost of goods sold:	
Merchandise inventory, January 1	$ 25,000	Finished goods inventory, January 1	$ 40,000
Cost of purchases	165,000	Cost of goods manufactured (from statement of cost of goods manufactured)	250,000
Cost of goods available for sale	$190,000	Cost of goods available for sale	$290,000
Merchandise inventory, December 31	30,000	Finished goods inventory, December 31	50,000
Cost of goods sold	$160,000	Cost of goods sold	$240,000

■ COST CLASSIFICATIONS

Cost is a financial measure of the resources used or given up to achieve a stated purpose. In manufacturing companies, costs can be classified as (1) manufacturing or nonmanufacturing costs, (2) product costs or period costs, and (3) fixed or variable costs. Each of these classifications of costs will be discussed.

Manufacturing Costs

The total cost of manufacturing a product is referred to as **manufacturing cost, factory cost,** or **product cost.** Manufacturing cost includes three cost elements: (1) direct materials costs, (2) direct labor costs, and (3) manufacturing overhead costs.

Direct Materials.   **Direct materials** have three characteristics: (1) they are included in the finished product, (2) they are used only in the manufacture of the product, and (3) they are clearly and easily traceable to the product. For example, iron ore is a direct material to a steel company because the iron ore is clearly traceable to the finished product, steel. In turn, steel becomes a direct material to an automobile manufacturer.

The cost of direct materials includes the net invoice price of the actual quantity used plus delivery charges. Some companies also include storage and handling costs. Direct materials inventory may be accounted for using any of the inventory cost methods discussed in Chapter 9, including specific identification, Fifo, Lifo, or average cost.

Some materials (such as glue and thread used in manufacturing furniture) may become part of the finished product, but tracing those materials to the product would require great cost and effort. For this reason, these materials are referred to as indirect materials or supplies and are included in manufacturing overhead. **Indirect materials** are materials that are used in the manufacture of a product but cannot or will not, for practical reasons, be traced directly to the products being manufactured.

Direct Labor.   **Direct labor** costs include labor costs of all employees actually working on materials to convert them into finished goods. As with direct materials costs, direct labor costs of a product include only those labor costs that are clearly traceable to, or readily identifiable with, the finished product. Direct labor costs can be identified by showing that these costs vary in direct proportion to the number of units produced. Thus, the labor of machinists, assemblers, cutters, and painters can be classified as direct labor.

Direct labor cost is usually measured by multiplying the number of hours of direct labor by the hourly wage rate. Many employees receive fringe benefits—employer's payroll taxes, pension costs, paid vacations, etc. These fringe benefit costs can significantly increase the direct labor hourly wage rate. Although fringe benefit costs are occasionally accounted for as direct labor, they are normally included in manufacturing overhead because they can be traced to the product only at great cost and effort.

Some labor costs (for example, wages of materials handlers, custodial workers, and supervisors) tend to vary directly with the number of product units produced but are not accounted for as direct labor because the expense to trace these costs to product units would be too great. These labor costs are called indirect labor and are accounted for as manufacturing overhead. **Indirect labor** consists of the cost of services that cannot or will not, for practical reasons, be traced to the product being manufactured.

Manufacturing Overhead.   There are many alternative names for manufacturing overhead, including factory indirect costs, factory burden, and manufacturing expense. **Manufacturing overhead** is a "catchall" classification, since it includes all manufacturing costs except for those costs accounted for as direct materials and direct labor. Manufacturing overhead costs are manufacturing costs that must be incurred but that cannot or will not be traced directly to specific units produced. As noted earlier, manufacturing overhead may include certain materials and labor costs that could theoretically be accounted for as direct materials or direct labor.

Manufacturing overhead contains a number of other costs that are related to the manufacturing process, such as depreciation and maintenance on machines, supervisors' salaries, and factory utility costs. Illustration 21.2 summarizes most manufacturing overhead costs and details some examples of indirect materials and indirect labor.

Illustration 21.2

Manufacturing Overhead Costs

Repairs and maintenance on factory buildings and equipment	Payroll taxes and fringe benefits for manufacturing employees
Depreciation on factory buildings and equipment	Overtime wage premiums on direct labor
Insurance and taxes on factory property and inventories	Indirect labor:
Indirect materials:	Janitors
Lubricants	Supervisors
Adhesives	Engineers
Cleaners, etc.	Timekeepers
Write-off of hand tools	Toolroom personnel
Utilities for factory buildings	Materials storeroom personnel, etc.
	Cost accountant

Note from the illustration that overtime wage premiums on direct labor are commonly included in manufacturing overhead rather than in direct labor cost. The logic behind this practice is that the need for employees to work overtime normally results from an overall production backlog, not from the need to manufacture a given product line. For example, in a company that manufactures three products, employees may work overtime on any one of the three products, depending on the **arbitrary scheduling by the production manager.** In such situations, the need for overtime is due to the combined time requirements of all three products and should not be directly charged to any one product unless that product was clearly the sole cause of the overtime.

Manufacturing Cost Terminology.   It is often useful for decision-making purposes to classify costs according to their relation to the finished product or the manufacturing process. For this reason, there are special terms to identify these classifications. The sum of direct materials costs and direct labor costs incurred to manufacture a product is called prime cost. The sum of direct labor cost and manufacturing overhead cost is called conversion cost because these costs are incurred in the conversion of the direct materials into finished goods. The relationship of these cost terms is shown in Illustration 21.3.

Nonmanufacturing Costs

Nonmanufacturing costs differ from manufacturing costs in that they relate to selling and administrative functions rather than to manufacturing. Nonmanufacturing costs are generally classified as either selling costs or administrative costs.

Selling Costs.   Selling costs are costs incurred to obtain customer orders and get the finished product into the customers' possession. Advertising, market

Illustration 21.3

Cost Relationships

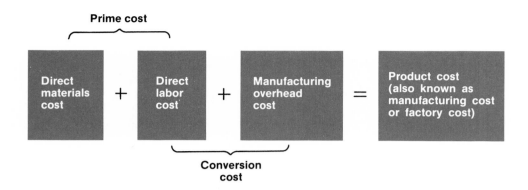

research, sales salaries and commissions, and delivery and storage of finished goods are examples of selling costs. The costs of delivery and storage of finished goods are considered to be selling costs since they are incurred **after** production has been completed. Therefore, the costs of storing **materials** are included in manufacturing overhead, whereas the costs of storing **finished goods** are a part of selling costs. Keep in mind that retailers, wholesalers, manufacturers, and service organizations all have selling costs.

Administrative Costs.   Administrative costs are nonmanufacturing costs that include the costs of top administrative functions and various staff departments such as accounting, data processing, and personnel. Examples of administrative costs are executive salaries, clerical salaries, office expenses, office rent, donations, research and development costs, and legal costs. As with selling costs, all organizations have administrative costs.

Product and Period Costs

Costs in manufacturing companies can also be classified as product costs and period costs. This distinction is important for income determination purposes.

Product costs are costs incurred in the manufacture of products and are assigned to units of the product produced by a manufacturing company. These costs include costs of direct materials, direct labor, and manufacturing overhead.

Period costs are not assigned to units of a product; they are related more closely to periods of time rather than to products produced. These costs cannot be traced directly to the manufacture of a specific product. For this reason, period costs are expensed (deducted from revenues) in the period in which they are incurred. To illustrate, assume a company pays its sales manager a fixed salary. Even though the manager may be working on projects that will benefit the company in future accounting periods, the sales manager's salary is expensed in the period in which it is incurred because the expense cannot be traced to the production of a product. Thus, **all selling and nonfactory administrative costs are treated as period costs.**

Illustration 21.4 shows how product costs and period costs are reported in the financial statements of a manufacturing company. Note that product costs are not expensed when incurred but are expensed in the **period the goods are sold.** If product costs are incurred toward the end of period 1 and the goods are sold in period 2, the costs involved are expensed against revenues of period 2. In Illustration 21.4, finished products of $900,000 were sold to

Illustration 21.4

Statement Analysis of Period and Product Costs

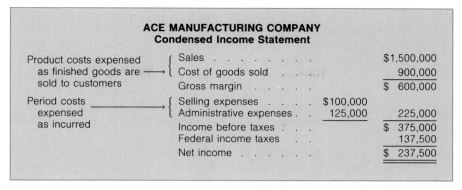

ACE MANUFACTURING COMPANY
Condensed Income Statement

Product costs expensed as finished goods are sold to customers →	Sales	$1,500,000
	Cost of goods sold	900,000
	Gross margin	$ 600,000
Period costs expensed as incurred →	Selling expenses $100,000	
	Administrative expenses 125,000	225,000
	Income before taxes	$ 375,000
	Federal income taxes	137,500
	Net income	$ 237,500

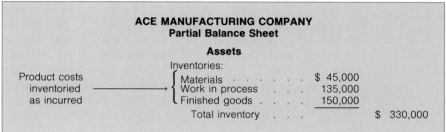

ACE MANUFACTURING COMPANY
Partial Balance Sheet

Assets

	Inventories:	
Product costs inventoried as incurred →	Materials	$ 45,000
	Work in process	135,000
	Finished goods	150,000
	Total inventory	$ 330,000

customers and expensed as cost of goods sold. The period costs, selling and administration expenses ($225,000), were expensed as incurred and deducted from gross margin on sales to compute income before taxes.

The ending inventories of a manufacturing company represent (1) materials, (2) work in process, and (3) finished goods. These three items are shown under "Inventories" in the balance sheet (see Illustration 21.4). These inventories are assets, and the product costs they contain are expensed in the period the goods are sold to customers. When items of finished goods inventory are sold, their costs are reported as an expense (cost of goods sold) on the income statement for the period of sale.

Fixed and Variable Costs

In addition to classifying costs by their relationships to the manufacturing process or to time periods, costs can be classified by how they respond to changes in the volume of manufacturing activity. Costs that are not affected in total amount by the volume of production activity are called fixed costs; costs that vary in total amount directly with changes in the volume of production activity are called variable costs.

Fixed Costs.   Fixed costs remain constant in total amount over wide variations in the level of manufacturing activity. For example, the annual license for an automobile may cost $50 whether the auto is driven 1,000 or 100,000 miles during the year. The same may hold true for the annual premium on an insurance policy for the auto. Property taxes, depreciation, rent, and executives' salaries are further examples of fixed costs. Fixed costs are basically time related, such as a one-year salary for the president, while variable costs are volume related, such as the total cost of motors necessary for some output of washing machines.

Fixed costs present a special problem in determining the unit cost of a product. Since total fixed costs do not change with the volume of production activity, cost **per unit** may vary widely if output varies. For example, assume that a company rents a factory building for $100,000 per year. The rental cost per ton of output is $1 if 100,000 tons are produced, $0.50 if 200,000 tons are produced, and only $0.10 if 1 million tons are produced. From this example you can see that **fixed cost per unit will decrease as the number of units produced increases and will increase as the number of units decreases.**

Variable Costs.   Variable costs are costs that vary directly in total amount with changes in the volume of production activity or output. Direct materials are a good example of a variable cost. For example, every washing machine produced by a manufacturer has one motor. If the motors cost $50 each, then the motor cost for one machine is $50; for two machines is $100; for three machines is $150; and so on. If profit plans call for the production of 10,000 washing machines, then the planned cost of the motors is $500,000. Similarly, the labor cost to install the motors is a variable cost.

Because fixed costs are basically time related, **total** fixed cost remains constant with volume changes, but fixed cost **per unit** varies inversely with the change in activity. Variable costs, on the other hand, remain constant on a **per unit** basis, but change **in total** in direct relation to the change in level of activity.

■ PERIODIC INVENTORY PROCEDURE

A manufacturer may use either periodic or perpetual inventory procedure. Recall from Chapter 5 that under periodic inventory procedure, accounts are brought to their proper balances only at the end of the accounting period by taking a physical inventory. Under perpetual inventory procedure, covered in Chapter 9, the inventory accounts are maintained at their proper balances throughout the period. This section discusses periodic inventory procedure applied in a manufacturing company. Perpetual inventory procedure is discussed in a later section in the chapter.

Accounts Used for Materials and Other Inventories

When a manufacturer uses periodic inventory procedure, the Materials Purchases, Transportation-In, Materials Purchase Returns and Allowances, and Materials Inventory accounts are used in the same manner as they are used by a retailer. Purchases during the period are debited to the Materials Purchases account. Transportation charges incurred on purchases are debited to Transportation-In. Returns of purchased materials and allowances granted on purchases are credited to Materials Purchase Returns and Allowances. Each of these accounts is closed through Manufacturing Summary to Income Summary at the end of the accounting period. The Materials Inventory account contains the beginning inventory amount until year-end, when the ending inventory is entered in the account during the closing process.

Since a manufacturer must account for unfinished goods still in various stages of production and completed goods that are yet to be sold, Work in Process Inventory and Finished Goods Inventory accounts are used. As with Materials Inventory, when a periodic inventory system is in use these inventory accounts will contain the beginning inventory amount until year-end, when a physical inventory is taken and the amount of ending inventory is entered in the accounts.

The following T-accounts show how the accounts are used by a manufacturer using a periodic inventory system:

Materials Purchases		**Transportation-In**	
Purchases of materials entered here	Closed through Manufacturing Summary to Income Summary at end of period	Freight charges incurred on purchases entered here	Closed through Manufacturing Summary to Income Summary at end of period

Materials Purchase Returns and Allowances		**Materials Inventory**	
Closed through Manufacturing Summary to Income Summary at end of period	Cost of materials returned to suppliers and amount of any allowances granted on purchases entered here	Beginning balance xx Ending balance xx Ending balance is entered at end of period based on a physical inventory	Beginning balance is closed through Manufacturing Summary to Income Summary at end of period

Work in Process Inventory		**Finished Goods Inventory**	
Beginning balance xx Ending balance xx Ending balance is entered at end of period based on a physical inventory	Beginning balance is closed through Manufacturing Summary to Income Summary at end of period	Beginning balance xx Ending balance xx Ending balance is entered at end of period based on a physical inventory	Beginning balance is closed to Income Summary at end of period

Estimation of Inventory Costs

When a manufacturer is using a periodic inventory system, inventory quantities are determined at year-end by making a physical count of the materials, work in process, and finished goods on hand. Once the **quantity** of these inventories has been established, their **cost** must be estimated.

Cost of the materials inventory on hand can be determined quite accurately by looking at purchase invoices to obtain purchase prices. Materials inventory cost is then calculated by multiplying the unit purchase price by the quantity of each type of item.

Estimating the cost of work in process or finished goods inventory is more complicated. For the average unit in work in process inventory and then for each unit in finished goods inventory, a manufacturer must estimate the:

1. Direct materials cost contained in each unit.
2. Direct labor cost incurred for each unit.
3. Manufacturing overhead applicable to each unit.

The amounts of materials *may* differ, while the amounts of labor and overhead *will* differ, for units in work in process inventory and units in finished goods inventory. Materials may be added at the beginning of the process, uniformly throughout the process, or near the end of the process. Direct labor is incurred throughout the manufacturing process. The sum of the three cost elements represents the product cost per unit contained in each of the inventories. The relevant product costs are then multiplied by the number of units in the work in process inventory and the number of units in the finished goods inventory to obtain the total costs of these inventories.

Direct Materials Cost. Direct materials cost in each unit of work in process and in each unit in finished goods can be established by referring to a materials specification list to determine the quantity of materials contained in each product. A materials specification list indicates what types and quantities of materials are used in manufacturing a product. Also, one must know when the materials are added in the production process in order to estimate what proportion of the materials is in the average unit in work in process inventory. Of course, all of the materials are in each unit in finished goods inventory. The relevant quantities are multiplied by the purchase invoice unit price to obtain the direct materials cost per unit.

Direct Labor Cost. The direct labor cost in each unit of a product is typically based on observations made by management to determine the **normal** amount of time it takes workers to complete the product. This amount of time multiplied by the hourly wage rate gives the direct labor cost per unit. In the case of products still in production, management estimates the percentage of completion of the good and determines the amount of direct labor cost applicable to work in process based on this percentage. Direct materials and direct labor costs may be estimated in this manner because these costs are clearly traceable to the product.

Manufacturing Overhead Cost. Since manufacturing overhead costs are not clearly traceable, they must be allocated to the product based on a manufacturing overhead rate. The **manufacturing overhead rate** expresses manufacturing overhead costs in relation to some measure of manufacturing activity. Manufacturing overhead costs often vary almost proportionately with the amount of direct labor used. More direct labor usually requires more supervisors, more utilities to operate the plant, and more maintenance and repairs on machinery used in production. Recall that the costs of such items are classified as manufacturing overhead costs. Consequently, manufacturing overhead rates are frequently expressed as either (1) a percentage of direct labor cost or (2) a certain dollar amount per direct labor-hour.

To illustrate the computation of a manufacturing overhead rate and the cost of ending inventories of work in process and finished goods, assume the following information is available for a company:

Direct materials used (100,000 units)	$600,000
Direct labor (50,000 hours)	500,000
Manufacturing overhead	400,000
Ending inventories (determined by physical count):	
Work in process	8,000 units
Finished goods	2,000 units

The company manufactures only one product—product P. All direct materials are issued to production at the start of the manufacturing process. Each unit of product contains one unit of direct materials. Therefore, the direct material cost per unit is $600,000 ÷ 100,000 units = $6. The direct labor cost per hour is $500,000 ÷ 50,000 hours = $10. Management estimates that each completed unit of product contains two hours of direct labor, while each unit still in production contains an average of one hour of direct labor. Thus, the direct labor cost per unit is $20 for finished goods and $10 for work in process.

The manufacturing overhead rate expressed as a percentage of direct labor cost is computed as follows:

$$\frac{\text{Total manufacturing overhead cost}}{\text{Total direct labor cost}} = \text{Manufacturing overhead rate}$$

$$\frac{\$400,000}{\$500,000} = 0.80 = 80\%$$

This overhead rate can be interpreted as saying that for every $1 spent on direct labor, we expect to spend $0.80 on manufacturing overhead.

The cost of the ending inventories of work in process and finished goods can now be determined as shown in Illustration 21.5.

Illustration 21.5

Computation of Work in Process and Finished Goods Inventories of Product P

Inventory	Estimated cost per unit				Estimated total inventory cost		
	Direct materials +	Direct labor +	Manufacturing overhead (80% of direct labor cost)	= Total	Total ×	Units in inventory =	Total ending inventory cost
Work in process . .	$6	$10	$ 8	$24	$24	8,000	$192,000
Finished goods . .	6	20	16	42	42	2,000	84,000

■ THE WORK SHEET FOR A MANUFACTURING COMPANY USING PERIODIC PROCEDURE

Remember that the major accounting difference between merchandisers and manufacturers is that merchandisers have only one type of inventory (merchandise) while manufacturers have three types (materials, work in process, and finished goods). This difference is further complicated by the fact that Work in Process and Finished Goods inventories are each composed of direct materials, direct labor, and manufacturing overhead costs allocated to production. These factors contribute to the complexity of determining the periodic cost of goods sold for a manufacturer. For this reason, manufacturers prepare a **statement of cost of goods manufactured** to support the cost of goods sold figure on the income statement. To aid in preparing the statement of cost of goods manufactured (as well as adjusting and closing entries), a work sheet can be used. The work sheet for a manufacturing company has a pair of columns for the statement of cost of goods manufactured, as shown in Illustration 21.6. The example in Illustration 21.6 focuses on the production-related accounts.

Illustration 21.6 *Manufacturing Work Sheet*

JERNIGAN MANUFACTURING COMPANY
Work Sheet for the Year Ended December 31, 1987

Account Titles	Trial Balance		Adjustments		Manufacturing Statement		Income Statement		Balance Sheet	
	Debit	Credit	Debit	Credit	Debit	Credit	Debit	Credit	Debit	Credit
Cash	62,000								62,000	
Accounts Receivable	160,000								160,000	
Allowance for Doubtful Accounts		500		(1) 1,500						2,000
Prepaid Insurance	7,500			(4) 6,500					1,000	
Inventories:										
Materials	40,000				40,000	38,000			38,000	
Work in Process	84,000				84,000	80,000			80,000	
Finished Goods	56,000						56,000	60,000	60,000	
Factory Building	400,000								400,000	
Accumulated Depreciation— Factory Building		40,000		(2) 20,000						60,000
Factory Equipment	460,000								460,000	
Accumulated Depreciation— Factory Equipment		92,000		(3) 46,000						138,000
Land	32,000								32,000	
Accounts Payable		60,000								60,000
Mortgage Payable, 10%		200,000								200,000
Common Stock—$5 Par Value		600,000								600,000
Retained Earnings, January 1		103,500								103,500
Sales		1,800,000						1,800,000		
Materials Purchases	480,000				480,000					
Transportation-In	6,000				6,000					

Account	Trial Balance Dr	Adjustments	Manufacturing Summary Dr	Manufacturing Summary Cr	Income Statement Dr	Income Statement Cr
Direct Labor	371,000	(5) 9,000	380,000			
Indirect Labor	62,500	(5) 2,500	65,000			
Supervisors' Salaries	127,000	(5) 3,000	130,000			
Maintenance and Repairs	17,000		17,000			
Utilities Expense	5,000		5,000			
Selling Expenses	199,500	(5) 500			200,000	
Administrative Expenses	184,500	(4) 500			185,000	
Interest Expense	20,000				20,000	
Factory Taxes	15,000		15,000			
Income Tax Expense	107,000				107,000	
	2,896,000	2,896,000				
Bad Debts Expense		(1) 1,500			1,500	
Depreciation Expense— Factory Building		(2) 20,000	20,000			
Depreciation Expense— Factory Equipment		(3) 46,000	46,000			
Insurance Expense—Factory		(4) 6,000	6,000			
Accrued Payroll Payable		(5) 15,000				15,000
		89,000	89,000			
		1,294,000	1,294,000	118,000	1,176,000	1,860,000
Manufacturing Summary (Cost of Goods Manufactured)			1,176,000	1,294,000	1,745,500	1,860,000
Net Income				114,500	114,500	
			1,293,000	1,293,000	1,860,000	1,860,000

(1) To record bad debts expense for the year.
(2) To record depreciation expense on factory building.
(3) To record depreciation expense on factory equipment.
(4) To record and distribute cost of expired insurance.
(5) To record and distribute cost of accrued payroll.

The Jernigan Manufacturing Company trial balance is taken from its ledger accounts at year-end. The administrative and selling expenses have been summarized in order to emphasize the company's production activities. The beginning-of-year inventory account balances for materials, work in process, and finished goods are $40,000, $84,000, and $56,000, respectively. The year-end inventory account balances are $38,000, $80,000, and $60,000, respectively.

Adjustments Columns

The required adjustments for the Jernigan Manufacturing Company appear in the **Adjustments columns** on the work sheet. The following information was used to prepare the adjustments:

1. The bad debts expense was estimated to be $1,500 for the year.
2. Depreciation on the factory building was $20,000.
3. Depreciation on the factory equipment was $46,000.
4. Insurance expiring during the year was $6,500. Of this amount, $6,000 applied to the factory building and equipment, and $500 applied to administrative offices (administrative expense).
5. Factory payroll accrued since the last payday was distributed as follows: direct labor, $9,000; supervisors' salary, $3,000; janitorial and maintenance, $1,800; materials storeroom personnel, $700; and finished goods storeroom personnel (selling expense), $500. Nonfactory employees were paid on December 31.

Based on the above information, the following adjusting entries need to be recorded on the work sheet of the Jernigan Manufacturing Company (see Illustration 21.6):

(1)	Bad Debts Expense	1,500	
	Allowance for Doubtful Accounts		1,500
	To record bad debt expense for the year.		
(2)	Depreciation Expense—Factory Building	20,000	
	Accumulated Depreciation—Factory Building		20,000
	To record depreciation on factory building.		
(3)	Depreciation Expense—Factory Equipment	46,000	
	Accumulated Depreciation—Factory Equipment		46,000
	To record depreciation on factory equipment.		
(4)	Insurance Expense—Factory	6,000	
	Insurance Expense—Administrative	500	
	Prepaid Insurance		6,500
	To record and distribute cost of expired insurance.		
(5)	Direct Labor	9,000	
	Supervisors' Salaries	3,000	
	Indirect Labor	2,500	
	Selling Expenses	500	
	Accrued Payroll Payable		15,000
	To record and distribute cost of accrued payroll.		

Manufacturing Statement Columns

The **Manufacturing Statement** columns show the total of all manufacturing costs **incurred** during the period. This total is referred to as cost to manufacture for the period. The first element of total manufacturing cost is materials used in production. The beginning materials inventory plus materials purchases and related transportation costs represent the total cost of materials available for production. Therefore, Materials Inventory, Materials Purchases, and Transportation-In are included in the Manufacturing Statement debit column of the work sheet. Materials remaining in inventory at the end of the period were not used, so the ending balance in materials inventory is included in the Manufacturing Statement credit column in order to remove that amount from the cost of materials issued to production.

Direct labor incurred in production and all manufacturing overhead costs incurred during the period are included in the Manufacturing Statement debit column because these items increase the cost of goods produced during the period.

Cost to manufacture, the total of all manufacturing costs for the period, represents the costs added to production. Cost of goods manufactured represents the total cost of all goods completed during the period and removed from production.

To determine the cost of goods manufactured, add the beginning work in process inventory to total manufacturing costs for the period and subtract the ending work in process inventory. Thus, the beginning balance of Work in Process Inventory is included in the Manufacturing Statement debit column and the ending balance of Work in Process Inventory is included in the credit column. Note that **the excess of total debits over total credits represents the cost of goods manufactured and is the total cost of all goods completed during the period.**

■ THE CLOSING ENTRIES

Closing entries for a manufacturing company using periodic inventory procedure are slightly different from closing entries prepared for a merchandiser. This difference is due to the use of a Manufacturing Summary account, which records the cost of goods produced during the period. As shown below, all of the items in the Manufacturing Statement columns are closed to the Manufacturing Summary account first (this balance is the cost of goods manufactured); then all items in the Income Statement columns are closed to Income Summary. Finally, the Income Summary account is closed to Retained Earnings.

Closing the Accounts in the Manufacturing Statement Columns

The first closing entry closes all of the accounts appearing in the Manufacturing Statement debit column (Illustration 21.6) by crediting those accounts. The debit is to Manufacturing Summary for the subtotal of the Manufacturing Statement debit column ($1,294,000):

```
1987
Dec. 31  Manufacturing Summary  . . . . . . . . . .  1,294,000
                 Materials Inventory (beginning)  . . . . .            40,000
                 Work in Process Inventory (beginning) . . .           84,000
                 Materials Purchases . . . . . . . . . .              480,000
                 Transportation-In  . . . . . . . . . . .               6,000
                 Direct Labor .  . . . . . . . . . . . .              380,000
                 Indirect Labor  . . . . . . . . . . . .               65,000
                 Supervisors' Salaries . . . . . . . . .              130,000
                 Maintenance and Repairs  . . . . . . .                17,000
                 Utilities Expense  . . . . . . . . . . .                5,000
                 Factory Taxes  . . . . . . . . . . . .                15,000
                 Depreciation Expense—Factory Building  . .            20,000
                 Depreciation Expense—Factory
                    Equipment  . . . . . . . . . . . .                 46,000
                 Insurance Expense—Factory  . . . . . .                 6,000
                 To close all accounts in the Manufacturing
                 Statement debit column to Manufacturing
                 Summary.
```

The second closing entry sets up the inventories that appear in the Manufacturing Statement credit column by debiting those accounts. The credit is to Manufacturing Summary for the subtotal of the Manufacturing Statement credit column ($118,000):

```
1987
Dec. 31  Materials Inventory (ending) . . . . . . . .    38,000
         Work in Process Inventory (ending)  . . . . .    80,000
                 Manufacturing Summary  . . . . . . .             118,000
                 To set up the ending inventories of materials
                 and work in process.
```

At this point in the closing process, the Manufacturing Summary account has a debit balance of $1,176,000. This amount represents the cost of goods manufactured during the period.

Closing the Accounts in the Income Statement Columns

The third closing entry closes all of the accounts in the Income Statement debit column by crediting those accounts. The debit is to the Income Summary account for the subtotal of the Income Statement debit column, $1,745,500.

```
1987
Dec. 31  Income Summary  . . . . . . . . . . . . .   1,745,500
                 Finished Goods Inventory (beginning)  . . .           56,000
                 Selling Expenses  . . . . . . . . . . .              200,000
                 Administrative Expenses  . . . . . . .               185,000
                 Interest Expense  . . . . . . . . . . .               20,000
                 Income Tax Expense . . . . . . . . . .               107,000
                 Bad Debts Expense  . . . . . . . . . .                 1,500
                 Manufacturing Summary  . . . . . . . .             1,176,000
                 To close all accounts in the Income Statement
                 debit column to Income Summary.
```

The fourth closing entry establishes the ending Finished Goods Inventory balance and closes the Sales account by debiting those accounts. The credit is to the Income Summary account for the subtotal of the Income Statement credit column, $1,860,000.

1987
Dec. 31   Finished Goods Inventory (ending)   60,000
           Sales   1,800,000
               Income Summary   1,860,000
           To set up the ending Finished Goods Inventory
           and close Sales to the Income Summary account.

At this point in the closing process the Income Summary account has a credit balance of $114,500, which is the amount of net income on the work sheet. The fifth (and last) closing entry closes the Income Summary account by debiting Income Summary and crediting Retained Earnings:

1987
Dec. 31   Income Summary   114,500
               Retained Earnings   114,500
           To close the Income Summary account to
           Retained Earnings.

■ FINANCIAL REPORTING BY MANUFACTURING COMPANIES

The major difference between a merchandiser and a manufacturer is in the types of inventories carried. Because inventories are reported on the balance sheet and also affect income (through cost of goods sold) on the income statement, the balance sheet and income statement of a merchandiser will differ from the balance sheet and income statement of a manufacturer.

The Statement of Cost of Goods Manufactured

The statement of cost of goods manufactured is used to support the cost of goods sold figure on the income statement. The two most important calculations on this statement are (1) the cost to manufacture and (2) the cost of goods manufactured. Careful attention should be given so that the terms **cost to manufacture** and **cost of goods manufactured** are not confused with one another or with cost of goods sold. The relationship between these terms is shown in Illustration 21.7. Cost to manufacture includes the costs of all **resources** put into production during the period. Cost of goods manufactured consists of the cost of all **goods completed** during the period; it includes "cost to manufacture" plus the beginning work in process inventory minus the ending work in process inventory. Cost of goods sold includes the cost of goods manufactured plus the beginning finished goods inventory minus the ending finished goods inventory.

Illustration 21.8 is the statement of cost of goods manufactured for the Jernigan Manufacturing Company for 1987. Note how the statement shows the costs incurred for materials, direct labor, and manufacturing overhead; it describes the total of these three costs as **cost to manufacture** during the period. When beginning work in process inventory is added and ending work in process is deducted, we obtain cost of goods manufactured (completed). Cost of goods sold does not appear on the cost of goods manufactured statement but is shown on the income statement.

In this illustration, all materials (both direct and indirect) are included in

Illustration 21.7

Relationship of Cost to Manufacture, Cost of Goods Manufactured, and Cost of Goods Sold

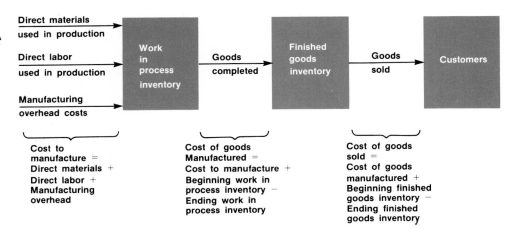

Cost to manufacture = Direct materials + Direct labor + Manufacturing overhead

Cost of goods Manufactured = Cost to manufacture + Beginning work in process inventory − Ending work in process inventory

Cost of goods sold = Cost of goods manufactured + Beginning finished goods inventory − Ending finished goods inventory

Illustration 21.8

Statement of Cost of Goods Manufactured

JERNIGAN MANUFACTURING COMPANY
Statement of Cost of Goods Manufactured
For the Year Ended December 31, 1987

Materials:

Materials inventory, January 1	$ 40,000	
Materials purchases	480,000	
Transportation-in	6,000	
Materials available for use	$526,000	
Less: Materials inventory, December 31	38,000	
Materials used		$ 488,000
Direct labor		380,000

Manufacturing overhead:

Indirect labor	$ 65,000	
Supervisors' salaries	130,000	
Maintenance and repairs	17,000	
Utilities expense	5,000	
Factory taxes	15,000	
Depreciation expense—factory building	20,000	
Depreciation expense—factory equipment	46,000	
Insurance expense—factory	6,000	
Total manufacturing overhead		304,000
Cost to manufacture		$1,172,000
Add: Work in process inventory, January 1		84,000
		$1,256,000
Less: Work in process inventory, December 31		80,000
Cost of goods manufactured		$1,176,000

the Materials Inventory account. Therefore, materials used consists of both direct materials and indirect materials. These amounts could have been separated and the amount of indirect materials could have been shown as a line item included under manufacturing overhead.

The Income Statement

Income statement preparation for a manufacturer may be considerably more complex than for a merchandiser. This is because a manufacturer incurs more types of costs than a merchandiser who buys goods that are ready for sale. In order to make the income statement more understandable to the readers of the financial statements, only the cost of goods manufactured is shown on the income statement. A statement of cost of goods manufactured has already been prepared to support this amount. The income statement for the Jernigan Manufacturing Company is shown in Illustration 21.9. The data are taken directly from the work sheet in Illustration 21.6. Notice in Illustration 21.9 the relationship of the statement of cost of goods manufactured to the income statement. The cost of goods manufactured appears in the cost of goods sold section as an addition to the beginning inventory of finished goods to derive the cost of goods available for sale. Cost of goods manufactured is shown in the same place that purchases would be presented on a merchandiser's income statement. When financial statements are released to the public, it is common practice to include previous years' income statements alongside the current year's for comparison.

Illustration 21.9

Income Statement of a Manufacturer

JERNIGAN MANUFACTURING COMPANY Income Statement For the Year Ended December 31, 1987		
Operating revenues:		
Sales		$1,800,000
Cost of goods sold:		
Finished goods inventory, January 1	$ 56,000	
Cost of goods manufactured (see statement of cost of goods manufactured)	1,176,000	
Cost of goods available for sale	$1,232,000	
Less: Finished goods inventory, December 31, 1987	60,000	
Cost of goods sold		1,172,000
Gross margin		$ 628,000
Operating expenses:		
Selling	$ 200,000	
Administrative	185,000	
Other operating expenses	1,500	
Total operating expenses		386,500
Net income from operations		$ 241,500
Nonoperating revenues and expenses:		
Interest expense		20,000
Net income before income taxes		$ 221,500
Less: Income tax expense		107,000
Net income		$ 114,500

The Balance Sheet

Unlike the balance sheet for a merchandiser, which reports a single inventory amount, the balance sheet for a manufacturer typically shows materials, work in process, and finished goods inventories separately. Illustration 21.10 shows the balance sheet for the Jernigan Manufacturing Company, using data taken from the work sheet in Illustration 21.6. A manufacturer's balance sheet may also show greater detail in the property, plant, and equipment section because of the significant investment in plant assets.

Illustration 21.10

Balance Sheet of a Manufacturer

JERNIGAN MANUFACTURING COMPANY
Balance Sheet
December 31, 1987

Assets

Current assets:

Cash		$ 62,000
Accounts receivable	$160,000	
Less: Allowance for doubtful accounts	2,000	158,000
Prepaid insurance		1,000
Inventories:		
Materials	$ 38,000	
Work in process	80,000	
Finished goods	60,000	178,000
Total current assets		$ 399,000

Property, plant, and equipment:

Land		$ 32,000
Factory building	$400,000	
Less: Accumulated depreciation	60,000	340,000
Factory equipment	$460,000	
Less: Accumulated depreciation	138,000	322,000
Total property, plant, and equipment		$ 694,000
Total assets		$1,093,000

Liabilities and Stockholders' Equity

Current liabilities:

Accrued payroll payable	$ 15,000	
Accounts payable	60,000	$ 75,000

Long-term liabilities

Mortgage payable		200,000
Total liabilities		$ 275,000

Stockholders' equity:

Common stock—$5 par value, 120,000 shares authorized, issued, and outstanding		$ 600,000
Retained earnings		218,000
Total stockholders' equity		$ 818,000
Total liabilities and stockholders' equity		$1,093,000

PERPETUAL INVENTORY PROCEDURE—THE GENERAL COST ACCUMULATION MODEL

Periodic inventory systems are designed to determine the **total** cost of goods manufactured and the **total** cost of goods sold at the end of the accounting period so that financial statements can be prepared. But in many manufacturing companies, a primary accounting objective is to measure the cost of manufacturing a product line on a **per unit** basis **during** the period so that timely cost control and product pricing decisions can be made. Under perpetual procedure, unit product costs are determined during the period, rather than estimated at the end of the period, by transferring the cost of direct materials, direct labor, and manufacturing overhead to work in process and then to finished goods inventory accounts as goods are processed. Unit costs are available throughout the period because they can be obtained quickly without having to take a physical inventory. Before proceeding with an illustration of perpetual inventory procedure, it is important to first understand the basic pattern of cost accumulation under perpetual inventory procedure in a manufacturing environment.

Product and Cost Flows

Under perpetual procedure, accounting records are usually set up so that the flow of costs through the records will match the physical flow of products through the production process, as shown in Illustration 21.11.

Illustration 21.11 *Product and Cost Flows*

The physical flow of the manufacturing process begins when materials are received from suppliers and placed in the materials storeroom. When needed for processing, the materials are moved from the materials storeroom to the production departments. During production, the materials are processed by laborers and machines and become partially manufactured products. At any time during production, these partially manufactured products are collectively known as **work in process.** Eventually the products are completed, at which time they are known as **finished goods.** The completed products are then moved to the finished goods storeroom for later sale and delivery to customers.

The accounting flow of costs under perpetual procedure follows the physical flow of the manufacturing process. The accounting records show the flow of direct material costs from Materials Inventory into Work in Process Inventory. Here, the costs of direct labor and other factory services are added. When the products are completed and transferred to the finished goods storeroom, their costs are removed from Work in Process Inventory and assigned to Finished Goods Inventory. As the goods are sold, the related costs are transferred from Finished Goods Inventory to Cost of Goods Sold.

Illustration 21.12 shows the manufacturing cost flows along with the selling, administrative, and financing costs of a company. These three expense categories plus the cost of goods sold are the total expenses of the company and are deducted from sales to arrive at net income.

Manufacturing Cost Flows under Perpetual Inventory Procedure Illustrated

Illustration 21.13 uses T-accounts to trace the flow of materials, labor, and overhead costs through the production process to finished goods inventory.

Illustration 21.12 *A Manufacturing Company's Total Operations*

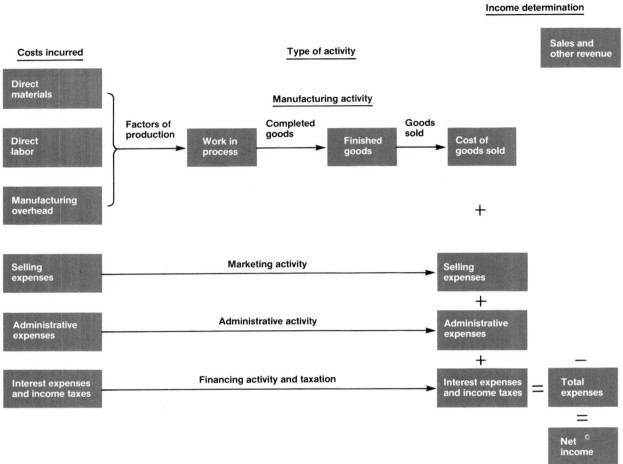

The sale of finished goods inventory to customers and the closing of the revenue and expense accounts for the year are then illustrated. Then the procedures followed in Illustration 21.13 are explained step by step, including examples of the journal entries necessary to record the transactions.

Flow of Direct and Indirect Materials Cost.   During July, $40,000 of materials and supplies were purchased on account; $28,000 of direct materials and $2,000 of indirect materials (supplies) were issued to production from the storeroom. The required entries (keyed numerically to the entries in the T-accounts in Illustration 21.13 are:

(1) Materials Inventory   40,000
      Accounts Payable   40,000
    To record purchases of materials and supplies on
    account.

(2) Work in Process Inventory   28,000
    Manufacturing Overhead   2,000
      Materials Inventory   30,000
    To record direct and indirect materials issued to
    production.

Note that purchases of both direct and indirect materials (supplies) are debited to Materials Inventory. But when materials are issued to production, direct materials are debited to Work in Process Inventory, while indirect materials are recorded in Manufacturing Overhead because they are not easily traceable to specific products.

Flow of Labor Costs.   Two kinds of labor costs must be accounted for in this procedure. **Payroll accounting** involves determining the total wages earned, the various deductions, and the net pay of each employee. **Labor cost accounting** involves determining which accounts are to be charged with what amount of labor costs. Under such a procedure, an account common to both groups is needed to tie together the separate accounting activities. This account is called Payroll Summary. The Payroll Summary account is a temporarily established (clearing) account that is debited when payrolls are prepared by the payroll department and credited when labor costs are distributed by the factory accounting department. Normally, the Payroll Summary account has a zero balance at the end of any accounting period. During the period, the account has a balance only because of the time lag between preparation of the payroll and classification of the payroll costs as direct or indirect labor.

The factory payrolls for July amounted to $75,000—direct labor of $60,000 and indirect labor of $15,000. Payroll withholdings amounted to $3,500 social security taxes, $8,000 federal income taxes, and $500 union dues. The entries required are:

(3)	Payroll Summary	75,000	
	FICA Taxes Payable		3,500
	Employees' Federal Income Taxes Payable . . .		8,000
	Employees' Union Dues Payable		500
	Accrued Payroll Payable		63,000
	To record factory payroll and various withholdings.		

(4)	Work in Process Inventory	60,000	
	Manufacturing Overhead	15,000	
	Payroll Summary		75,000
	To distribute labor costs for July.		

Accrued payroll shown in entry *(3)* will be paid in cash to the employees, while the amounts withheld will be paid at a later date on the employees' behalf to the federal government (social security taxes and federal income taxes) and the labor union (union dues). Entry *(4)* adds to Work in Process Inventory all labor cost traceable to the products being manufactured (direct labor), while nontraceable labor costs (indirect labor) are transferred to Manufacturing Overhead.[1]

Flow of Overhead Costs.   Indirect costs of operating the factory during the period included repairs of $1,000 paid in cash, property taxes of $1,500, expiration of prepaid equipment rent of $2,500, and insurance of $2,000, payroll

---

[1] Selling and administrative salaries are ignored since this chapter concentrates on aspects that are unique to a manufacturer.

Illustration 21.13   *Cost and Revenue Flowchart (Perpetual Inventory System)*

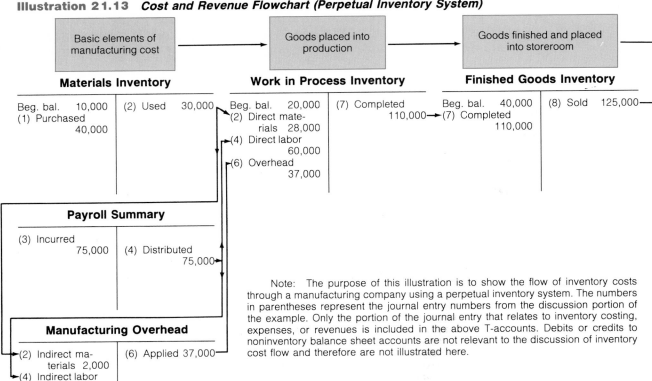

Note: The purpose of this illustration is to show the flow of inventory costs through a manufacturing company using a perpetual inventory system. The numbers in parentheses represent the journal entry numbers from the discussion portion of the example. Only the portion of the journal entry that relates to inventory costing, expenses, or revenues is included in the above T-accounts. Debits or credits to noninventory balance sheet accounts are not relevant to the discussion of inventory cost flow and therefore are not illustrated here.

taxes accrued of $3,500, utilities accrued of $4,000, and factory building depreciation of $5,500. Entry *(5)* below shows the recording of these indirect costs.

(5)	Manufacturing Overhead	20,000
	Cash	1,000
	Accrued Property Taxes Payable	1,500
	Prepaid Rent	2,500
	Prepaid Insurance	2,000
	Accrued Payroll Taxes Payable	3,500
	Accounts Payable	4,000
	Accumulated Depreciation—Factory Building . .	5,500
	To record factory indirect costs for July.	

Manufacturing overhead costs are as much a part of a period's production cost as are the costs of direct materials and direct labor. Manufacturing overhead costs must, therefore, be added to the Work in Process Inventory account; this is done in entry *(6)* below:

(6)	Work in Process Inventory	37,000
	Manufacturing Overhead	37,000
	To assign overhead to work in process.	

Manufacturing overhead costs are generally assigned to production using overhead rates. For purposes of this illustration however, it is assumed that **all** overhead incurred during July is assigned to production.

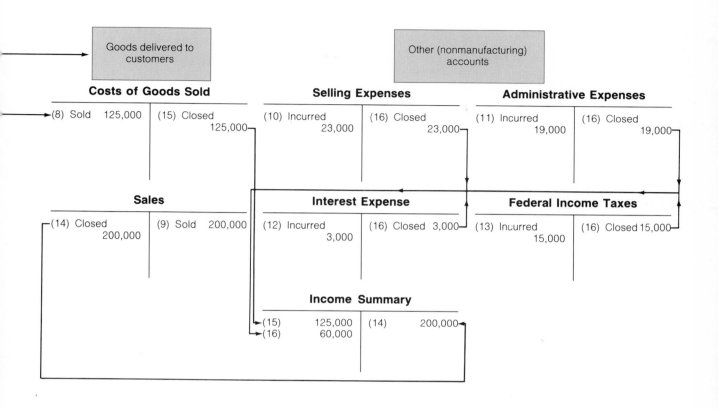

Flow of Finished Goods. As shown in Illustration 21.13, for product cost purposes Work in Process Inventory is charged with materials, labor, and overhead costs. When the goods are completed and transferred out of production, an entry is made to transfer their cost from Work in Process Inventory to Finished Goods Inventory. Assuming goods costing $110,000 were completed and transferred, the entry needed is:

(7)	Finished Goods Inventory	110,000	
	Work in Process Inventory		110,000
	To record transfer of completed goods.		

Now assume that goods costing $125,000 were sold on account for $200,000. Entries are required to transfer the cost of the inventory out of finished goods to cost of goods sold and to record the sale. The required entries are:

(8)	Costs of Goods Sold	125,000	
	Finished Goods Inventory		125,000
	To record cost of goods sold.		

(9)	Accounts Receivable	200,000	
	Sales		200,000
	To record sales on account.		

To complete the explanation of the entries in Illustration 21.13, assume that selling expenses of $23,000, administrative expenses of $19,000, interest expense of $3,000, and federal income taxes of $15,000 were incurred in July. The required entries are:

(10)	Selling Expenses	23,000	
	Various asset and liability accounts		23,000
	To record selling expenses incurred in July.		

(11)	Administrative Expenses	19,000	
	Various asset and liability accounts		19,000
	To record administrative expenses incurred in July.		

(12)	Interest Expense	3,000	
	Accrued Interest Payable		3,000
	To record interest expense incurred in July.		

(13)	Federal Income Taxes	15,000	
	Federal Income Taxes Payable		15,000
	To record estimated income taxes for July.		

Subsidiary records or accounts would be kept for the various types of selling and administrative expenses incurred. The credits in entries (10) and (11) would be to accounts such as Cash, Accounts Payable, Salaries Payable, and Accumulated Depreciation.

Although the accounts are usually closed only at the end of the accounting year, entry (14) records the closing of the Sales revenue account for the month of July as an illustration of the annual entry:

(14)	Sales	200,000	
	Income Summary		200,000
	To close Sales revenue account.		

Entries (15) and (16) are required to close the expense accounts:

(15)	Income Summary	125,000	
	Cost of Goods Sold		125,000
	To close Cost of Goods Sold account.		

(16)	Income Summary	60,000	
	Selling Expenses		23,000
	Administrative Expenses		19,000
	Interest Expense		3,000
	Federal Income Taxes		15,000
	To close other expense accounts.		

Entries (15) and (16) could be combined into one entry. Although it is not shown in Illustration 21.13, the closing process would be completed by transferring net income to the Retained Earnings account.

Income Summary	15,000	
Retained Earnings		15,000
To close Income Summary.		

Use of a Work Sheet under Perpetual Procedure

A manufacturing company using perpetual procedure can use the same work sheet as illustrated in Chapter 5. The work sheet has columns labeled Trial Balance, Adjustments, Adjusted Trial Balance, Income Statement, and Balance Sheet. The amounts shown in the trial balance for materials inventory, work in process inventory, and finished goods inventory will be the end of period balances. The amounts would be carried to the Balance Sheet debit column. The cost of goods sold amount will be included with the other expenses in the trial balance. All other steps in preparing the work sheet are as described in Chapter 5 and will not be illustrated here.

■ SUMMARY

This chapter focused on accounting for inventory and cost of goods sold for a manufacturer. Unlike a merchandiser (retailer or wholesaler), who purchases and resells goods that are already in their finished state, a manufacturer purchases raw materials and uses equipment and labor to process those materials into products for sale. While the merchandiser has only one inventory—merchandise available for sale—a manufacturer has three inventories—unprocessed materials, partially complete work in process, and ready-for-sale finished goods.

Manufacturing costs can be divided into direct materials, direct labor, and manufacturing overhead. Direct materials are materials that are (1) included in the finished product, (2) used only in the manufacture of the product, and (3) clearly and easily traceable to the product. Direct labor is the cost of labor by employees actually working on materials to convert them into finished goods. Manufacturing overhead includes all other manufacturing costs, except those that are accounted for as direct material or direct labor. Prime cost is a term used to refer to the sum of direct materials cost and direct labor cost, and conversion cost refers to the sum of direct labor cost and manufacturing overhead cost.

Product costs are costs incurred in the manufacture of products. They are associated with products rather than with periods of time. Product costs are considered to be the costs of manufacturing inventory, and they are expensed only when the related inventory is sold. Period costs, on the other hand, are more closely related to periods of time than to products produced. Period costs are expensed in the period in which they are incurred. All selling and nonmanufacturing administrative costs are treated as period costs.

Costs that remain constant in total amount over a wide range of variations in the level of manufacturing activity are considered to be fixed costs. Variable costs, on the other hand, vary in total amount directly with changes in the level of manufacturing activity.

Like merchandisers, manufacturers can use either periodic or perpetual inventory procedure to account for inventory costs. When a manufacturer uses periodic inventory procedure, the Materials Purchases, Transportation-In, Materials Purchase Returns and Allowances, and Materials Inventory accounts are used in the same manner as they are by a merchandiser. In addition, the manufacturer has to account for work in process and finished goods inventories. Use of a work sheet aids in the preparation of the necessary adjusting and closing entries to compute ending inventories and cost of goods sold.

When a periodic inventory system is in use, inventory quantities are determined at year-end by making a physical count of the materials, work in process, and finished goods on hand. After the quantity of these inventories has been established, their cost must be determined. Cost of the raw materials inventory may be determined by multiplying purchase cost per unit of material by the amount of material on hand. To obtain the cost of the work in process and finished goods inventories, the manufacturer must estimate the per unit cost of direct materials used, direct labor used, and manufacturing overhead incurred in producing each unit. The amounts of materials may differ, while the amounts of labor and overhead will differ, for units in work in process inventory and units in finished goods inventory. Direct materials cost per unit can be established by referring to a materials specification list for the product and knowing when materials are added in the production process. Direct labor cost per unit is normally based on observations made by management to determine the normal amount of time it takes workers to complete the product. Manufacturing overhead costs must be allocated to the product based on a manufacturing overhead rate, which expresses overhead costs in relation to some measure of manufacturing activity.

Under perpetual inventory procedure, accounting records are set up so that the flow of costs through the records matches the physical flow of products through the production process. All materials purchases are debited to the Materials Inventory account. Materials issued to production are credited to Materials Inventory; direct materials are debited to the Work in Process Inventory account, and indirect materials are debited to the Manufacturing Overhead account. All labor costs are recorded in a Payroll Summary account. Direct labor costs are credited to Payroll Summary and debited to Work in Process Inventory, while indirect labor costs are credited to Payroll Summary and debited to Manufacturing Overhead. Other factory overhead costs are also debited to Manufacturing Overhead. Overhead applied to production is credited to Manufacturing Overhead and debited to Work in Process Inventory. The cost of goods completed is transferred from the Work in Process Inventory account to the Finished Goods Inventory account, and the cost of goods sold is transferred from Finished Goods Inventory to Cost of Goods Sold.

Perpetual inventory systems are superior to periodic inventory systems in their ability to provide information about manufacturing costs during the accounting period so that timely cost control and pricing decisions can be made. Under a periodic inventory system, total cost of goods manufactured and total cost of goods sold are determined only at the end of the accounting period, and the per unit production costs can only be estimated. A perpetual inventory system, by contrast, provides per unit production cost information throughout the period. A perpetual inventory system involves considerably more detailed accounting records.

The balance sheet and income statement of a manufacturer differ from those of a merchandiser. The statement of cost of goods manufactured is a statement used by a manufacturer to show cost to manufacture and cost of goods manufactured for the period. Only cost of goods manufactured is shown in the income statement in order to make the income statement more understandable to readers of the financial statements. The balance sheet for a manufacturer typically shows materials, work in process, and finished goods inventories separately. A manufacturer's balance sheet may also show greater detail in property, plant, and equipment because of the significant investment in plant assets.

In Chapter 22, you continue your study of manufacturing costs. Without efficient cost systems for accumulating manufacturing costs, manufacturing companies cannot evaluate past performance and adequately plan for the future.

NEW TERMS INTRODUCED IN CHAPTER 21

Administrative costs

Nonmanufacturing costs that include the costs of top administrative functions and various staff departments such as accounting, data processing, and personnel (814).

Conversion cost

The sum of direct labor and manufacturing overhead costs (813).

Cost

A financial measure of the resources used or given up to achieve a stated purpose (811).

Cost of goods manufactured

Consists of the costs of all goods completed during the period; total manufacturing cost plus beginning work in process inventory minus ending work in process inventory (823, 825).

Cost to manufacture

Includes the costs of all resources put into production during the period (823, 825).

Direct labor

Labor costs of all employees actually working on materials to convert them into finished goods (812).

Direct materials

Materials that are (1) included in the finished product, (2) used only in the manufacture of the product, and (3) clearly and easily traceable to the product (812).

Factory cost

See Manufacturing cost.

Finished goods

Completed manufactured products ready to be sold; also, Finished Goods Inventory is the title of an inventory account maintained for such products (811).

Fixed costs

Costs that remain constant in total amount over wide variations in the level of manufacturing activity (815).

Indirect labor

The services of factory employees that cannot or will not, for practical reasons, be traced to the products being manufactured (812).

Indirect materials

Materials used in the manufacture of a product that cannot or will not, for practical reasons, be traced directly to the products being manufactured (812).

Manufacturing cost

The cost incurred to produce or create a product. It includes direct materials, direct labor, and manufacturing overhead costs (812).

Manufacturing overhead

All manufacturing costs except for those costs accounted for as direct materials and direct labor (812).

Manufacturing overhead rate

Expresses manufacturing overhead costs in relation to some measure of manufacturing activity (818).

Materials

Unprocessed items that will be used in the manufacturing process (811).

Period costs

Costs related more closely to periods of time than to products produced. Period costs cannot be traced directly to the manufacture of a specific product; they are expensed in the period in which they are incurred (814).

Prime cost

The sum of the direct materials costs and direct labor costs incurred to manufacture a product (813).

Product costs

(See also Manufacturing cost.) Costs incurred in the manufacture of products and assigned to units of the product produced by the manufacturing company. These costs include costs of direct materials, direct labor, and manufacturing overhead (814).

Selling costs

Costs incurred to obtain customer orders and get the finished product into the customer's possession (813).

Statement of cost of goods manufactured

An accounting report showing the cost to manufacture and the cost of goods manufactured (825).

Variable costs

Costs that directly vary in total amount with changes in the volume of production activity or output (816).

Work in process

Partially manufactured products; also, Work in Process Inventory is the title of an inventory account maintained for such products (811).

DEMONSTRATION PROBLEM

Data needed to prepare the work sheet of the Douglas Manufacturing Company are given below. The company uses a periodic inventory system.

1. The December 31, 1988, trial balance was taken from the general ledger of the company. (The inventories in the trial balance are those of January 1, 1988.)
2. The only entry in the Retained Earnings account during the year ended December 31, 1988, was a debit of $18,000 for the declaration of cash dividends.
3. The inventories at December 31, 1988, were as follows:

    a. Materials inventory $24,000
    b. Work in process inventory . . 44,000
    c. Finished goods inventory . . 34,000

Adjustments are as follows:

1. The allowance for doubtful accounts is to be adjusted to 5% of the accounts receivable.
2. Accrued wages and salaries are:

    Accrued direct labor $2,400
    Accrued sales salaries 4,000
    Accrued office and officers' salaries . . 6,000

3. Interest on the mortgage bonds was last paid on July 1.
4. Factory supplies used, $2,200.
5. Factory insurance expired during the period, $1,200.
6. Accrued factory taxes, $1,400.
7. Depreciation of factory building, $4,000.
8. Depreciation of machinery and equipment, $23,000.
9. Depreciation of office equipment, $1,000.

The Trial Balance columns of the work sheet and the proper totals of other columns on the work sheet have already been completed (see pages 840–41).

Required: Prepare the necessary adjusting entries for the work sheet, and extend the amounts in the work sheet Trial Balance columns (plus or minus any adjustments) to their proper columns.

Solution to demonstration problem

The adjusting entries for the Douglas Manufacturing Company for the year ended December 31, 1988, are shown below:

(1) Bad Debts Expense 3,800
      Allowance for Doubtful Accounts   3,800
    To increase allowance to 5% of outstanding accounts receivable:
      0.05 × $80,000 = $4,000; $4,000 − $200 = $3,800.

(2) Direct Labor 2,400
    Sales Salaries 4,000
    Office and Officers' Salaries 6,000
      Accrued Wages and Salaries Payable   12,400
    To record accrual of salaries and wages.

(3) Mortgage Bond Interest Expense 1,500
　　　　Bond Interest Payable . . . .　　　　　　　1,500
　　　To record accrual of 6 months' interest on bonds ($100,000
　　　$\times$ 0.03 $\times$ ½).

(4) Factory Supplies Expense 2,200
　　　　Factory Supplies on Hand . . . .　　　　　　　2,200
　　　To record factory supplies used.

(5) Factory Insurance Expense 1,200
　　　　Prepaid Factory Insurance . . . .　　　　　　　1,200
　　　To record expired factory insurance.

(6) Factory Taxes Expense 1,400
　　　　Accrued Taxes Payable . . . .　　　　　　　1,400
　　　To record the accrual of $1,400 of factory taxes.

(7) Depreciation Expense—Factory Building 4,000
　　　　Accumulated Depreciation—Factory Building . . . .　　　　　　　4,000
　　　To record depreciation on factory building.

(8) Depreciation Expense—Machinery and Equipment 23,000
　　　　Accumulated Depreciation—Machinery and Equipment .　　　　　　　23,000
　　　To record depreciation on machinery and equipment.

(9) Depreciation Expense—Office Equipment 1,000
　　　　Accumulated Depreciation—Office Equipment . . . .　　　　　　　1,000
　　　To record depreciation on office equipment.

The completed work sheet for the Douglas Manufacturing Company for the year ended December 31, 1988, is shown on pages 842–43.

THE DOUGLAS MANUFACTURING COMPANY
Work Sheet for the Year Ended December 31, 1988

Account Titles	Trial Balance		Adjustments		Manufacturing Statement		Income Statement		Balance Sheet	
	Debit	Credit	Debit	Credit	Debit	Credit	Debit	Credit	Debit	Credit
Cash	31,000									
Accounts Receivable	80,000									
Allowance for Doubtful Accounts		200								
Prepaid Factory Insurance	1,800									
Materials Inventory	20,000									
Work in Process Inventory	42,000									
Finished Goods Inventory	28,000									
Factory Supplies on Hand	2,800									
Land	16,000									
Factory Building	200,000									
Accumulated Depreciation— Factory Building		20,000								
Machinery and Equipment	230,000									
Accumulated Depreciation— Machinery and Equipment		46,000								
Small Tools	700									
Office Equipment	18,000									
Accumulated Depreciation— Office Equipment		2,600								
Accounts Payable		29,400								
Income and FICA Taxes Withheld		2,600								
Mortgage Bonds Payable, 3%		100,000								
Common Stock		300,000								
Retained Earnings		103,600								
Sales		800,000								
Sales Discounts	4,000									
Materials Purchases	240,000									
Purchase Returns		2,000								
Transportation-In	3,000									
Direct Labor	184,000									
Supervisors' Salaries	64,000									
Indirect Labor	16,000									

Account				Adjustments		Manufacturing		Income Statement	Balance Sheet
Building Maintenance and Repairs	2,200								
Maintenance of Machinery and Equipment	6,400								
Heat, Light, Power	2,400								
Factory Taxes Expense	9,800								
Small Tools Expense	3,100								
General Factory Expense	5,600								
Advertising and Sales Promotion	21,600								
Sales Salaries	60,000								
Sales Travel Expense	3,400								
Sales Office Expense	7,300								
Office and Officers' Salaries	90,000								
Stationery and Supplies Expense	2,200								
Office Taxes, Property and Payroll	4,800								
General Office Operating Expense	8,400								
Mortgage Bond Interest Expense	1,500								
Gain on Sale of Plant Assets		3,600							
	1,410,000	1,410,000							
Bad Debts Expense									
Factory Insurance Expense									
Accrued Wages and Salaries Payable									
Bond Interest Payable									
Factory Supplies Used									
Accrued Taxes Payable									
Depreciation Expense—Factory Building									
Depreciation Expense—Machinery and Equipment									
Depreciation Expense—Office Equipment									
				50,500	50,500				
Manufacturing Summary (Cost of Goods Manufactured)						632,700	632,700		
Net Income								837,600	678,900
								837,600	678,900

THE DOUGLAS MANUFACTURING COMPANY
Work Sheet for the Year Ended December 31, 1988

Account Titles	Trial Balance Debit	Trial Balance Credit	Adjustments Debit	Adjustments Credit	Manufacturing Statement Debit	Manufacturing Statement Credit	Income Statement Debit	Income Statement Credit	Balance Sheet Debit	Balance Sheet Credit
Cash	31,000								31,000	
Accounts Receivable	80,000								80,000	
Allowance for Doubtful Accounts		200		(1) 3,800						4,000
Prepaid Factory Insurance	1,800			(5) 1,200					600	
Materials Inventory	20,000				20,000	24,000			24,000	
Work in Process Inventory	42,000				42,000	44,000			44,000	
Finished Goods Inventory	28,000						28,000	34,000	34,000	
Factory Supplies on Hand	2,800			(4) 2,200					600	
Land	16,000								16,000	
Factory Building	200,000								200,000	
Accumulated Depreciation— Factory Building		20,000		(7) 4,000						24,000
Machinery and Equipment	230,000								230,000	
Accumulated Depreciation— Machinery and Equipment		46,000		(8) 23,000						69,000
Small Tools	700								700	
Office Equipment	18,000								18,000	
Accumulated Depreciation— Office Equipment		2,600		(9) 1,000						3,600
Accounts Payable		29,400								29,400
Income and FICA Taxes Withheld		2,600								2,600
Mortgage Bonds Payable, 3%		100,000								100,000
Common Stock		300,000								300,000
Retained Earnings		103,600								103,600
Sales		800,000						800,000		
Sales Discounts	4,000						4,000			
Materials Purchases	240,000				240,000					
Purchase Returns		2,000				2,000				
Transportation-In	3,000				3,000					
Direct Labor	184,000		(2) 2,400		186,400					
Supervisors' Salaries	64,000				64,000					
Indirect Labor	16,000				16,000					

Account	Trial Balance Dr	Trial Balance Cr	Adjustments Dr	Adjustments Cr	Manufacturing Dr	Manufacturing Cr	Income Statement Dr	Income Statement Cr	Balance Sheet Dr	Balance Sheet Cr
Building Maintenance and Repairs	2,200				2,200					
Maintenance of Machinery and Equipment	6,400				6,400					
Heat, Light, Power	2,400				2,400					
Factory Taxes Expense	9,800		(6) 1,400		11,200					
Small Tools Expense	3,100				3,100					
General Factory Expense	5,600				5,600					
Advertising and Sales Promotion	21,600						21,600			
Sales Salaries	60,000		(2) 4,000				64,000			
Sales Travel Expense	3,400						3,400			
Sales Office Expense	7,300						7,300			
Office and Officers' Salaries	90,000		(2) 6,000				96,000			
Stationery and Supplies Expense	2,200						2,200			
Office Taxes, Property, and Payroll	4,800						4,800			
General Office Operating Expense	8,400						8,400			
Mortgage Bond Interest Expense	1,500		(3) 1,500				3,000			
Gain on Sale of Plant Assets		3,600						3,600		
	1,410,000	1,410,000								
Bad Debts Expense			(1) 3,800				3,800			
Factory Insurance Expense			(5) 1,200		1,200					
Accrued Wages and Salaries Payable				(2) 12,400						12,400
Bond Interest Payable				(3) 1,500						1,500
Factory Supplies Used			(4) 2,200		2,200					
Accrued Taxes Payable				(6) 1,400						1,400
Depreciation Expense—Factory Building			(7) 4,000		4,000					
Depreciation Expense— Machinery and Equipment			(8) 23,000		23,000					
Depreciation Expense— Office Equipment			(9) 1,000				1,000			
			50,500	50,500						
Manufacturing Summary						70,000				
(Cost of Goods Manufactured)						562,700	562,700			
					632,700	632,700	810,200	837,600	678,900	
Net Income							27,400			27,400
							837,600	837,600	678,900	678,900

QUESTIONS

1. Identify the three elements of cost incurred in manufacturing a product, and indicate the distinguishing characteristics of each.

2. Why might a company claim that the total cost of employing a person is $10.30 per hour even though the employee's wage rate is $6.50 per hour? How should this difference be classified and why?

3. What is the typical accounting for the overtime wage premium paid to a direct laborer? Why?

4. Identify the two broad classifications of costs incurred by manufacturing companies and what is included in each. Indicate why it is important that costs be correctly classified.

5. Why are certain costs referred to as period costs? What are the major types of period costs incurred by a manufacturer?

6. Explain the differences between fixed costs and variable costs.

7. Explain how the income statement of a manufacturing company differs from the income statement of a merchandising company.

8. What is the general content of a statement of cost of goods manufactured? What is its relationship to the income statement?

9. Under perpetual inventory procedure what is the relationship between cost flows in the accounts and the flow of physical products through a factory?

EXERCISES

E-1

Classify various items according to types of costs

Given below are some costs incurred by an electrical appliance manufacturer. Classify these costs as direct materials, direct labor, manufacturing overhead, selling, or administrative.

a. President's salary.
b. Cost of electrical wire.
c. Cost of janitorial supplies.
d. Wages of assembly-line workers.
e. Cost of promotional displays.
f. Plant supervisor's salary.
g. Cost accountant's salary.
h. Research and development costs.
i. Cost of aluminum used for toasters.
j. Cost of market research survey.

E-2

Classify items as product or period costs

Classify the costs listed in Exercise E-1 as either product costs or period costs.

E-3

Identify variable cost items and prime cost items

Which of the items in Exercise E-1 would most likely vary directly with the number of appliances produced? Which would be considered prime costs?

E-4

Compute cost of goods manufactured

The following data pertain to the Thomas Company for the year ended December 31, 1987:

Materials inventory, January 1, 1987	$ 37,500
Materials inventory, December 31, 1987	50,000
Materials purchases	137,500
Direct labor	175,000
Work in process inventory, January 1, 1987	25,000

Work in process inventory, December 31, 1987 . .   37,500
Manufacturing overhead   100,000
Finished goods inventory, January 1, 1987   . . .   62,500
Finished goods inventory, December 31, 1987 . .   110,000

Compute the cost of goods manufactured and the cost of goods sold.

E–5

***Prepare journal
entries for labor
costs***

Bill Cash was paid $588 for 46 hours as an assembly-line worker at a manufacturing plant. This sum consisted of 40 hours regular time at $12 per hour and 6 hours overtime at time and a half.

a. Prepare the entry to distribute this labor cost to the accounts.
b. Prepare the entry to distribute the labor cost to the accounts assuming Bill is a salesman.
c. Prepare the entry assuming Bill is a factory supervisor.

E–6

***Compute
manufacturing
overhead rate***

Compute the manufacturing overhead rate for the Maddox Manufacturing Company based on direct labor costs, given the following information:

Estimated direct labor costs $750,000
Estimated manufacturing overhead costs . .   450,000

E–7

***Calculate estimated
ending inventory
costs***

The following data pertain to the TKR Company for the year ended December 31, 1987:

Estimated direct materials cost per unit included in work in
  process inventory for product D $22
Estimated direct materials cost per unit included in
  finished goods inventory for product D   22
Estimated direct labor cost per unit included in work in
  process inventory for product D   20
Estimated direct labor cost per unit included in
  finished goods inventory for product D   32
Manufacturing overhead rate . . . .   75% of direct labor cost
Units of product D included in work in process inventory   . .   300 units
Units of product D included in finished goods inventory . . .   150 units

Compute the ending work in process inventory and finished goods inventory for product D.

E–8

***Prepare cost and
revenue flowchart
under perpetual
inventory procedure***

The Flair Company uses perpetual inventory procedure. The following data are for the month of June:

1. Materials purchased on account, $78,000.
2. Direct materials issued, $90,000.
3. Repairs and maintenance on factory buildings, $9,000.
4. Factory depreciation, taxes, and utilities, $75,000.
5. Factory payroll for June, $54,000, including $4,800 of indirect labor. (Assume no withholdings.)
6. Manufacturing overhead is assigned in full to production.
7. Cost of goods completed and transferred, $247,500.
8. Cost of goods sold, $240.000.
9. Sales for the month on account, $450,000.

   The June 1 inventory account balances were:

Materials $24,000
Work in process   60,000
Finished goods   18,000

Prepare a cost and revenue flowchart similar to the one in Illustration 21.13, incorporating the above data.

E–9

***Prepare journal
entries under
perpetual inventory
procedure***

Prepare journal entries to record the transactions in Exercise E–8.

PROBLEMS—SERIES A

P21-1-A

Prepare statement of cost of goods manufactured and closing entries

The Manufacturing Statement columns of a work sheet prepared by Benton Manufacturing, Inc. at June 30, 1987, contain the following adjusted amounts:

Account Titles	Manufacturing Statement	
	Debit	Credit
Inventories:		
Materials	15,750	27,000
Work in Process	25,000	13,000
Materials Purchases	168,500	
Materials Purchase Returns		1,500
Transportation-In	17,500	
Direct Labor	112,500	
Indirect Labor	35,000	
Supervisors' Salaries	22,500	
Factory Building Rent	6,000	
Factory Utilities	18,000	
Factory Supplies Used	9,750	
Depreciation Expense—Machinery . .	25,000	
Other Factory Overhead	37,500	
	493,000	41,500
Manufacturing Summary		
(Cost of goods manufactured) . .		451,500
	493,000	493,000

Required:

a. Prepare a statement of cost of goods manufactured for Benton Manufacturing, Inc., for the year ended June 30, 1987.

b. Prepare all necessary closing entries, including the entry to establish the ending inventory balances and the entry to close the Manufacturing Summary account.

P21-2-A

Prepare statement of cost of goods manufactured and income statement

The information given below was taken from a work sheet prepared by the Davis Company on December 31, 1987:

Account Titles	Manufacturing Statement		Income Statement	
	Debit	Credit	Debit	Credit
Sales				925,000
Materials Purchases	118,750			
Materials Purchase Returns . . .		6,250		
Transportation-In	1,250			
Inventories:				
Materials	15,000	12,500		
Work in Process	32,500	27,000		
Finished Goods			45,000	37,500
Direct Labor	140,000			
Indirect Materials	4,000			
Overtime Wages	8,000			
Payroll Taxes—Factory . . .	42,500			
Utilities Expense	4,250			
Maintenance and Repairs . . .	1,500			
Selling Expenses			150,000	
Administrative Expenses . . .			225,000	
Property Taxes—Factory . . .	1,100			
Income Tax Expense			50,000	
Insurance Expense—Factory . .	1,500			
Depreciation Expense—Factory				
Building	7,500			
Depreciation Expense—Factory				
Equipment	10,000			
	387,850	45,750		
Manufacturing Summary				
(Cost of goods manufactured) . .		342,100	342,100	
	387,850	387,850	812,100	962,500
Net income			150,400	
			962,500	962,500

Required:

a. Prepare a statement of cost of goods manufactured for the Davis Company for the year ended December 31, 1987.

b. Prepare an income statement for the Davis Company for the year ended December 31, 1987.

P21-3-A

Prepare closing entries

Refer to the information given for the Davis Company in Problem 21-2-A. Prepare all necessary entries to set up the ending inventory balances and to close the books for 1987.

P21-4-A

Prepare statement of cost of goods manufactured, income statement, and closing entries

The following data were taken from the completed work sheet of Logo's Corner Manufacturing Company at December 31, 1987:

Direct labor	$300,000	Materials purchases	$	180,000
Indirect labor	37,500	Transportation-in		9,000
Factory supervision	66,000	Insurance expense (70%		
Selling and administrative		applicable to factory)		15,000
salaries	150,000	Repairs and maintenance		
Factory supplies used	9,000	expense		2,250
Inventories, January 1:		Utilities expense (70%		
Materials	12,000	applicable to factory)		4,500
Work in process	30,000	Payroll taxes (factory)		45,000
Finished goods	27,000	Depreciation expense (80%		
Inventories, December 31:		applicable to factory)		60,000
Materials	18,000	Delivery expense		24,000
Work in process	37,500	Sales		1,110,000
Finished goods	33,000	Other selling and		
		administrative expenses		30,000

Required: a. Prepare a statement of cost of goods manufactured for 1987.

b. Prepare an income statement for the year ended December 31, 1987 (ignore income taxes).

c. Prepare all necessary closing entries.

P21-5-A

Prepare work sheet, financial statements, and closing entries

Wand Products, Inc. prepared the following trial balance and supplementary information on December 31, 1987, the end of its first year of operations:

	Debits	*Credits*
Cash	$ 45,070	
Accounts Receivable	153,000	
Prepaid Factory Insurance . . .	9,492	
Factory Supplies on Hand . . .	14,916	
Office Supplies on Hand . . .	6,430	
Factory Machinery	362,000	
Factory Equipment	66,800	
Office Equipment	23,800	
Accounts Payable		$ 35,030
Mortgage Notes Payable . . .		80,000
Common Stock		500,000
Sales		644,470
Sales Returns	3,000	
Sales Discounts	6,170	
Materials Purchases	122,300	
Direct Labor	175,160	
Factory Supervision	32,500	
Indirect Labor	17,000	
Heat, Light, Power—Factory . .	33,564	
Machine Maintenance	9,200	
Rent of Factory	24,000	
Property Taxes—Factory . . .	3,200	
General Factory Expense . . .	11,520	
Sales Office Salaries	54,240	
Advertising Expense	8,400	
Rent of Sales Office	4,800	
Officers' Salaries	41,594	
Office Salaries	22,034	
Miscellaneous Office Expense . .	5,310	
Rent of Administrative Office . .	2,200	
Interest Expense	1,800	
	$1,259,500	$1,259,500

Supplementary information:

Inventories at December 31, 1987:

Materials	$17,800
Work in process	6,400
Finished goods	23,200

Information needed for adjustments:

1. Estimated bad debts expense for the year: 1% of net sales.
2. Factory insurance expired . . . . $ 2,292
3. Factory supplies used   13,066
4. Office supplies used   5,510

Depreciation rates:

5. Factory machinery 10%
6. Factory equipment 15%
7. Office equipment 7%
8. Accrued factory payroll at December 31, 1987:

Direct labor	$ 7,100
Factory supervision	950
	$ 8,050

9. Accrued salaries of December 31, 1987:

Sales office salaries	$ 2,000
Office salaries	1,140
	$ 3,140

10. Accrued rent of office (administrative) . . . . . $ 200
11. Accrued interest on mortgage note   600

Required: Using the information given, prepare the following for the year ended December 31, 1987:

a. Work sheet.
b. Statement of cost of goods manufactured.
c. Income statement (ignore income taxes).
d. Balance sheet.
e. Entries to set up the ending inventories and to close the accounts.

P21-6-A

Calculate manufacturing overhead rate, cost of ending work in process and finished goods inventories, cost of goods manufactured, and cost of goods sold

The Ideal Company incurred the following manufacturing costs for the first quarter of 1987:

Materials used	$384,600
Direct labor	620,000
Manufacturing overhead . .	496,000

The work in process and finished goods inventories were $64,800 and $268,000, respectively, on January 1, 1987. The production department provided the following information relating to the cost of the work in process and finished goods inventories on March 31, 1987:

		Estimated cost per unit	
	Units in inventory	Direct materials	Direct labor
Work in process:			
Product A	500	$ 8.00	$20.00
Product B	1,000	12.00	10.00
Finished goods:			
Product A	2,000	18.00	30.00
Product B	2,610	16.80	24.00

Required:

a. Compute the manufacturing overhead rate, based on direct labor cost.
b. Using the rate computed in (a), determine the cost of the inventories of work in process and finished goods at March 31, 1987.
c. Compute the cost of goods manufactured and the cost of goods sold during the first quarter of 1987.

P21-7-A

Prepare cost and revenue flowchart for perpetual inventory procedure

The McArthur Company uses perpetual inventory procedure. The following data are for the month of June:

1. Materials purchased on account, $67,200.
2. Direct materials issued, $78,400.
3. Repairs and maintenance on factory buildings, $8,400.
4. Factory depreciation, taxes, and utilities, $58,240.
5. Factory payroll for June, $50,400, including $4,480 of indirect labor.
6. Actual manufacturing overhead is assigned to production.
7. Cost of goods completed and transferred, $218,400.
8. Cost of goods sold, $224,000.
9. Sales for the month on account, $420,000.

The June 1 inventory account balances were:

Materials	$22,400
Work in process	56,000
Finished goods	16,800

Required: Using T-accounts, prepare a cost and revenue flowchart similar to the one shown in Illustration 21.13. Key your entries using the numbers given.

P21-8-A

Prepare journal entries and ending inventory balances under perpetual inventory procedure

The Penrod Company uses perpetual inventory procedure. Assume the inventories at August 1, 1987, were as follows:

Materials inventory	$30,800
Work in process inventory . . .	44,800
Finished goods inventory	63,000

Transactions:

1. During August, $112,000 of raw materials were purchased on account and $91,000 were issued to production.
2. The factory payrolls (gross) for August were $133,000. Direct labor was $98,000, and indirect labor was $35,000. Payroll withholdings included $8,400 of FICA taxes, $25,200 of federal income taxes, and $2,100 of union dues.
3. The indirect costs of production included machinery repairs of $2,100, equipment rental of $4,200, utilities of $14,000, payroll taxes of $8,400, amortization of prepaid insurance of $5,600, and factory building depreciation of $4,480.
4. Overhead was assigned in full to production.
5. Goods costing $196,000 were completed and transferred to finished goods inventory.
6. Goods costing $210,000 were sold on account for $308,000.

Required:
a. Give the journal entries for the above transactions.
b. Using T-accounts, compute the balance in each of the three inventory accounts at August 31, 1987.

P21–9–A

Prepare journal entries, income statement, and closing entries under perpetual inventory procedures

The Bailey Manufacturing Company, which uses perpetual inventory procedure, had the following transactions for the month of May 1987:

Transactions:

1. Materials and supplies purchased on account, $36,000.
2. Materials issued to production, $42,000; indirect materials issued, $3,000.
3. Repairs and maintenance on factory equipment, $2,250.
4. Recorded factory depreciation, $15,000; property taxes, $6,000; and utilities, $10,200.
5. Administrative salaries paid, $18,000.
6. Depreciation on administration building, $7,500.
7. Factory payroll (gross), $27,000; withholdings FICA taxes, $1,650; federal income taxes, $4,800.
8. Factory payroll distribution: direct labor, $24,600; indirect labor, $2,400.
9. Paid advertising expense, $750, and delivery expense, $525.
10. Sales salaries and commissions paid, $6,750.
11. Actual manufacturing overhead cost was assigned to production.
12. Cost of goods completed and transferred, $117,000.
13. Sales on account, $225,000; cost of goods sold, $120,000.
14. Other selling expenses, $420; other administrative expenses, $750; and interest expense, $60, were paid in cash.
15. Federal income taxes were accrued at 40% of net income from operations.

Required:
a. Prepare journal entries to record the May transactions.
b. Prepare an income statement for the Bailey Manufacturing Company for the month of May 1987.
c. Prepare closing entries at May 31, 1987.

PROBLEMS—SERIES B

P21–1–B

Prepare statement of cost of goods manufactured and closing entries

The following data are from a work sheet prepared by the Coleman Manufacturing Company at December 31, 1987:

Account Titles	Manufacturing Statement	
	Debit	Credit
Inventories:		
Materials	17,500	30,000
Work in Process	27,500	7,500
Materials Purchases (net)	187,500	
Transportation-In	25,000	
Direct Labor	125,000	
Indirect Labor	50,000	
Supervisors' Salaries	25,000	
Factory Utilities	20,000	
Factory Supplies Used	15,000	
Depreciation Expense—Factory Building . .	40,000	
Depreciation Expense—Equipment	30,000	
Other Manufacturing Overhead	75,000	
	637,500	37,500
Manufacturing Summary		
(Cost of goods manufactured)		600,000
	637,500	637,500

Required:

a. Using this information, prepare a statement of cost of goods manufactured for Coleman Manufacturing Company for the year ended December 31, 1987.

b. Prepare all necessary closing entries, including the entry to set up the new balances in the inventory accounts and the entry to close the Manufacturing Summary account.

P21-2-B

Prepare statement of cost of goods manufactured and income statement

The following account balances were taken from the December 31, 1987, work sheet for the Hollis Company:

Account Titles	Manufacturing Statement		Income Statement	
	Debit	Credit	Debit	Credit
Sales				450,000
Materials Purchases	120,000			
Transportation-In	1,000			
Inventories:				
Materials	10,000	9,500		
Work in Process	21,000	20,000		
Finished Goods			14,000	10,000
Direct Labor	95,000			
Utilities Expense	1,250			
Maintenance and Repairs	4,250			
Selling Expenses			50,000	
Administrative Expenses			46,250	
Income Tax Expense			25,000	
Insurance Expense—Factory . . .	3,000			
Depreciation Expense—Factory				
Building	5,000			
Depreciation Expense—Factory				
Equipment	11,500			
	272,000	29,500		
Manufacturing Summary				
(Cost of goods manufactured) . .		242,500	242,500	
	272,000	272,000	377,750	460,000
Net income			82,250	
			460,000	460,000

Required:
a. Prepare a statement of cost of goods manufactured for the Hollis Company for the year ended December 31, 1987.
b. Prepare an income statement for the Hollis Company for the year ended December 31, 1987.

P21-3-B

Prepare closing entries

Refer to the information given in Problem P21-2-B. Give all necessary entries to set up the ending inventory balances and to close the books of the Hollis Company on December 31, 1987.

P21-4-B

Prepare statement of cost of goods manufactured, income statement, and closing entries

The following account balances were taken in alphabetical order from the completed work sheet of Gerald Manufacturing, Inc. at December 31, 1987:

Administrative Salaries Expense* . .	$30,000	Inventories, December 31:	
Advertising and Promotion		Materials	$ 18,000
Expense	36,000	Work in Process	24,000
Depreciation Expense—Factory		Finished Goods	39,000
Equipment	21,000	Materials Purchases	90,000
Depreciation Expense—Office		Materials Purchase Returns	3,000
Equipment*	15,000	Rent—Factory	12,000
Depreciation Expense—Sales		Rent—Selling and	
Fixtures	12,000	Administrative*	45,000
Direct Labor	195,000	Repairs and Maintenance—	
Factory Supervision and		Factory	9,000
Inspection	18,000	Sales	660,000
Factory Supplies Used	18,000	Sales Salaries	30,000
Indirect Labor	15,000	Transportation-In	12,000
		Other Factory Overhead	27,000
Inventories, January 1:		Other Selling Expenses	15,000
Materials	6,000		
Work in Process	9,000		
Finished Goods	54,000		

* These amounts are to be allocated 40% to general (nonfactory) administration and 60% to the sales department.

Required: *a.* Prepare a statement of cost of goods manufactured for Gerald Manufacturing, Inc. for 1987.

    b. Prepare an income statement for the year ended December 31, 1987 (ignore taxes).

    c. Prepare all necessary closing entries.

P21-5-B

Prepare work sheet, all financial statements, and closing entries

The following trial balance and supplementary information pertain to the Allgood Manufacturing Company for the year ended June 30, 1987:

	Debits	Credits
Cash	$ 17,250	
Accounts Receivable	81,900	
Allowance for Doubtful Accounts		$ 300
Factory Supplies on Hand	17,550	
Office Supplies on Hand	1,275	
Materials Inventory	28,500	
Work in Process Inventory	6,300	
Finished Goods Inventory	18,000	
Prepaid Insurance—Factory	10,125	
Factory Machinery	67,500	
Accumulated Depreciation—Machinery		27,000
Factory Building	525,000	
Accumulated Depreciation—Building		31,500
Office Equipment	22,500	
Accumulated Depreciation—Office Equipment		6,750
Accounts Payable		60,800
Mortgage Note Payable (10%)		75,000
Common Stock ($10 par value)		435,000
Retained Earnings		18,600
Sales		745,900
Materials Purchases (net)	112,500	
Direct Labor	124,500	
Factory Supervision	21,300	
Indirect Labor	15,450	
Utilities—Factory	34,650	
Machine Maintenance	7,125	
Rent on Factory Equipment	3,000	
Property Taxes—Factory	4,200	
General Factory Costs	12,600	
Sales Office Salaries	60,750	
Selling Expenses	58,800	
Officers Salaries	75,000	
Administrative Expenses	40,500	
Interest Expense	3,750	
Income Taxes	30,825	
	$1,400,850	$1,400,850

Supplementary information:

Inventories, June 30, 1987:

    Materials $15,000

    Work in process 12,000

    Finished goods 22,500

Information needed for adjustments:

1. Estimated bad debts expense for the year: 1% of sales.

2. Factory insurance expired . . . . $ 8,325

3. Factory supplies used 16,762

4. Office supplies used 863

Depreciation rates per year are:

5.	Factory building	2%
6.	Factory machinery	20%
7.	Office equipment	15%
8.	Accrued factory payroll at June 30, 1987:	

Direct labor	$ 2,925
Factory supervision	900
Indirect labor	450
	$ 4,275

9. Accrued salaries at June 30, 1987:

Officers' salaries	$ 1,950
Sales office salaries	1,275
	$ 3,225

Required: Prepare the following for the year ended June 30, 1987:

a. Work sheet.
b. Statement of cost of goods manufactured.
c. Income statement.
d. Balance sheet.
e. Entries to set up the ending inventories and to close the accounts.

P21-6-B

Calculate manufacturing overhead rate and ending inventory amounts under periodic inventory procedure

The following information was taken from the December 31, 1987, statement of cost of goods manufactured of the Dean Corporation:

Direct materials used (100,000 units) . .	$150,000
Direct labor (100,000 hours)	450,000
Manufacturing overhead	396,000

All materials are issued to production at the beginning of the manufacturing process. Factory supervisors estimate that products still in production have received 1½ hours of direct labor per unit, while finished products have received 2 hours of direct labor per unit.

Required:

a. Compute the overhead rate for 1987 as a percentage of direct labor costs.
b. Estimate the per unit and total cost of the work in process and finished goods inventories. The year-end physical count showed 10,000 units still in production and 5,000 units In the finished goods storeroom.

P21-7-B

Prepare cost and revenue flowchart

The Gary Company uses perpetual inventory procedure. The operations for the quarter ended March 31, 1986, are summarized as follows:

1.	Materials purchased on account	$ 67,500
2.	Direct materials issued to production	82,500
3.	Indirect materials used (from materials inventory)	2,250
4.	Gross payroll costs incurred	102,000
5.	Payroll costs distributed:	
	Direct labor	75,000
	Indirect labor	27,000
6.	Other overhead costs incurred:	
	Depreciation of equipment	72,000
	Repairs and maintenance	11,250
	Utilities	18,750
	Other	9,750
7.	Selling expenses	52,500
8.	Administrative expenses	60,000
9.	Overhead costs actually incurred are assigned to production (determine from above data).	
10.	Cost of goods completed and transferred to finished goods inventory . .	300,000
11.	Cost of goods sold	270,000
12.	Sales on account	405,000

Inventory balances on January 1 were as follows:

Materials	$23,250
Work in process	28,500
Finished goods	67,500

Required: Using T-accounts, prepare a cost and revenue flowchart similar to Illustration 21.13. Key your entries using the numbers given.

P21-8-B

Prepare journal entries under perpetual inventory procedure

Assume each of the companies in this problem uses perpetual inventory procedure.

a. In June, Company L purchased on account $225,000 of direct materials and $60,000 of supplies. Also in June, $150,000 of direct materials and $30,000 of indirect materials (supplies) were issued by the storeroom to the production department.

Required: Prepare the necessary journal entries.

b. Company M's payroll department records indicate that the week's payroll amounted to $75,000 (gross pay) with the following amounts withheld:

FICA taxes	$ 2,700
Union dues	1,125
Federal income taxes	13,500

Further analysis reveals that of the $75,000, $52,500 was for direct labor. The indirect labor consists of the following wages and salaries:

Inspectors	$5,250
Supervisors	6,750
Janitors	1,500
Timekeepers	3,000
Toolroom personnel	4,500
Storeroom personnel	1,500

Required: Record the incurrence of the above labor costs and their distribution to the proper accounts.

c. In August, Company N incurred the following factory related costs: prepaid insurance expired, $1,500; depreciation of factory building, $3,750; prepaid rent expired, $2,250; payroll taxes, $5,700; utilities, $1,350; repairs, $675 (cash). The company assigns actual overhead costs to production at the end of each month.

Required: Prepare journal entries to record and assign overhead costs.

d. In September, Company O completed the production of goods costing $285,000 and transferred them to the finished goods storeroom. Also in September, Company O sold goods costing $262,500 to customers for $380,625, on account.

Required: Prepare journal entries to record these transactions.

P21-9-B

Prepare journal entries under perpetual inventory procedure; compute inventory balances; prepare income statement and closing entries

The following data relate to the Howell Company for the month of October 1987. The company uses perpetual inventory procedure.

1. Purchased materials on account, $105,000.
2. Materials issued to production, $120,000 (including $3,000 of indirect materials):
3. Factory payroll (gross) for the month, $138,000. Withholdings were $8,250 for FICA taxes and $24,000 for federal income taxes.
4. Payroll costs distributed: direct labor, $120,000; indirect labor, $18,000.
5. Other overhead costs incurred: factory depreciation, $105,000; property taxes, $24,000; repairs, $15,000; utilities, $12,000; and other, $9,000.
6. Selling expenses incurred, $90,000; administrative expenses incurred, $82,500.
7. Actual overhead costs were assigned to production.
8. Costs of goods completed and transferred, $390,000.
9. Sales on account, $600,000; cost of goods sold, $375,000.
10. Interest expense incurred, $450; federal income taxes payable, $26,250.

October 1 inventory balances were:

Materials	$27,000
Work in process	33,000
Finished goods	63,000

Required: a. Prepare journal entries to record the above transactions.

            b. Using T-accounts, compute the balance in each of the inventory accounts at the end of October.

            c. Prepare an income statement for the Howell Company for the month of October, 1987.

            d. Prepare the closing entries for October 31, 1987.

BUSINESS DECISION PROBLEM

Classify costs by behavior and type of production cost

A number of costs that would affect business decisions in manufacturing companies are listed below. These costs may be fixed or variable with respect to some measure of volume or output and may be classified as direct materials (DM), direct labor (DL), or manufacturing overhead (MO).

1. Glue used to attach labels to bottles containing a patented medicine.
2. Compressed air used in operating machines turning out products.
3. Insurance on factory building and equipment.
4. A production department supervisor's salary.
5. Rent on factory machinery.
6. Iron ore in a steel mill.
7. Oil, gasoline, and grease for forklift trucks.
8. Services of painters in building construction.
9. Cutting oils used in machining operations.
10. Cost of food in a factory employees' cafeteria.
11. Payroll taxes and fringe benefits related to direct labor.
12. The plant electricians' salaries.
13. Sand in a glass manufacturer.
14. Copy editor's salary in a book publisher.

Required: a. List the numbers 1 through 14 down the left side of a sheet of paper. After each number write the letters V (for variable) or F (for fixed) and either DM (for direct materials), DL (for direct labor), or MO (for manufacturing overhead) to show how you would classify the similarly numbered cost item given above.

            b. Which of your own answers given for part *(a)* could you challenge? Discuss.

BUSINESS SITUATION FOR DISCUSSION

Why We Should Account for the 4th Cost of Manufacturing*

Henry R. Schwarzbach and Richard G. Vangermeersch

Cost accounting may be 200 years behind the times. It continues to stress the same three types of product costs—raw materials, direct labor, and overhead, but ignores "machine labor."

Recent cost accounting texts note the growing mechanization of production but do not propose adding this fourth cost component, machine labor. The major reason for this neglect is that cost accounting practice has not been updated to reflect current manufacturing technol-

ogy. Texts tend to follow practice. For example, one major text states "in practice, however, machine time is rarely used (for allocating overhead) because of the added clerical cost and the difficulty of computing machine time on individual jobs." . . . Low-cost micro processors, digital clocks, and counters, however, now make it much less costly and difficult to track machine time.

We suggest here a revised approach to this old problem. The revised approach with the fourth class of product costs provides management with an improved picture of product costs and cost flows. Our concept is similar to the ideas espoused by accountant/engineer A. Hamilton Church in the early 1900s; however, data collection techniques of the early 1900s made this system costly to maintain. . . .

---

* Reprinted from the July 1984 issue of *Management Accounting*, (pp. 24–25). Copyright by the National Association of Accountants.

Accounting for the Cost of Key Machines

The first step in developing a cost system for the machine-intensive firm is to design cost and information collection systems for certain key machines and types of overhead. An analysis of a firm's production process may show that the costs of many machines will be best monitored and allocated as overhead items and not be managed as key machines. The first facet of the planning and control system for key machines is that of acquisition.

The acquisition of a key machine usually is a much more important decision than the hiring of a direct labor employee, even though personnel terminations have become a more difficult and serious matter in recent years. In contrast with the hiring decision for an employee, errors on the acquisition of a key machine are much more costly to the firm. For instance, the shop floor layout may have to be adjusted to accommodate the machine, employees may have to be laid off or retrained, and a large commitment of funds may have to follow the acquisition. Should the machine not operate up to standard however, termination is not an option.

A plan for placing the machine in operation (installation, personnel to operate, maintenance schedule, back up, and so on) is a necessity and should be fully developed before the acquisition transaction is completed. Management's job does not end after a machine is placed in operation. It must still be managed so that it operates efficiently and effectively from both a technical and cost perspective. We suggest that machine cost cards be developed for each key machine to aid in evaluating its cost effectiveness and in charging its cost to the products it helps produce.

22 Job Order and Process Cost Systems

After studying this chapter, you should be able to:

1. Describe and distinguish between the two major types of cost accumulation systems employed by manufacturing companies under perpetual inventory procedure.

2. Describe the documents used to accumulate product costs in a job order system and a process cost system.

3. Show how a predetermined overhead rate is computed and how it is used to assign overhead to production.

4. Discuss the determination of unit costs in a process cost system.

5. Prepare a production cost report for a process cost system and discuss its relationship to the Work in Process Inventory account.

6. Define and use correctly the new terms in the glossary.

This chapter continues the discussion of perpetual inventory procedure begun in Chapter 21. Perpetual inventory procedure is used when a manufacturing company wants to determine the costs of its product units **before** taking a physical inventory at year-end.

A product unit cost figure depends on many factors, such as which inventory costing method (Fifo, Lifo, or weighted-average) is chosen and how indirect costs (manufacturing overhead) are allocated to products. For some decisions, information about future costs is more relevant than product unit cost information based on past costs. The determination of product unit cost is always dependent on the type of cost accumulation system used by a company.

This chapter discusses the two major types of cost accumulation systems under perpetual procedure, the job order cost system and the process cost system. In each system, the goal is to **determine before year-end the unit costs of the products being manufactured.** These unit costs provide important data for management; they are used throughout the period to compute (1) cost of goods sold, (2) cost of work in process and finished goods ending inventories, (3) payments to be received under contracts based on "full" costs,[1] and (4) selling prices.

■ JOB ORDER COST SYSTEMS

A job order cost system is a cost accounting system in which the costs incurred to produce a product are accumulated for each individual job. For example, a job may consist of 1,000 chairs, 5 miles of highway, a single machine, a dam, or a building. A job cost system is generally used when the products being manufactured can be separately identified or when goods are produced to meet a customer's particular needs. Job costing is commonly used in construction, motion pictures, printing, and other industries where many heterogeneous (dissimilar) products are produced.

Under job order costing, an up-to-date record of the costs incurred on a job is kept in order to provide management with timely cost data. Reports to management can be revised as often as desired, even daily, on such matters as materials used, labor costs incurred, manufacturing overhead assigned, goods completed, total production costs incurred, and budgeted and actual cost comparisons.

Up-to-date information for each job is made available by maintaining a job order cost sheet for each job. A job order cost sheet is a form used to summarize the costs of direct materials, direct labor, and manufacturing overhead incurred for a job. It is the **key document** in the system. The file of job order cost sheets for jobs not yet completed represents the subsidiary ledger for the Work in Process Inventory account.

Illustration 22.1 depicts the cost flows in a job order cost system.

Illustration 22.1   *Cost Flows in a Job Order Cost System*

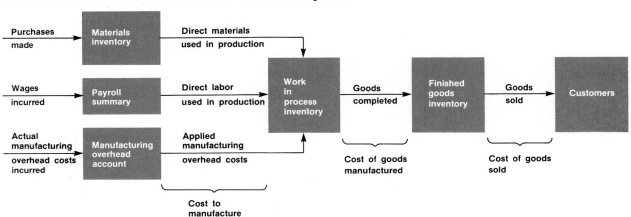

---

[1] A "full" cost contract basically guarantees the manufacturer total recovery of the costs incurred in producing the product and, usually, a specified profit margin.

Basic Records Used in Job Order Systems

Illustration 22.2 shows the basic records or source documents used in a job order cost system:

1. The job order cost sheet summarizes all costs—direct materials, direct labor, and applied manufacturing overhead—of producing a given job or batch of products. One sheet is maintained for each job order. When goods are completed and transferred, the job order cost sheets are transferred to a completed jobs file. The number of units and their unit costs are recorded on inventory cards supporting the Finished Goods Inventory account. An example of a job order cost sheet is shown in Illustration 22.2.

2. A stores (or materials) card is kept for each type of direct and indirect material maintained in inventory. The stores card shows the quantities (and costs) of each type of material received, issued, and on hand for which the storekeeper is responsible. When a job is started, direct materials are ordered from the storeroom on a materials requisition, which shows the types and quantities of the materials ordered.

3. The work ticket shows who worked on what job for how many hours and at what wage rate. All of each employee's daily hours must be accounted for on one or more work tickets.

Illustration 22.2 *Basic Records in a Job Order Cost System*

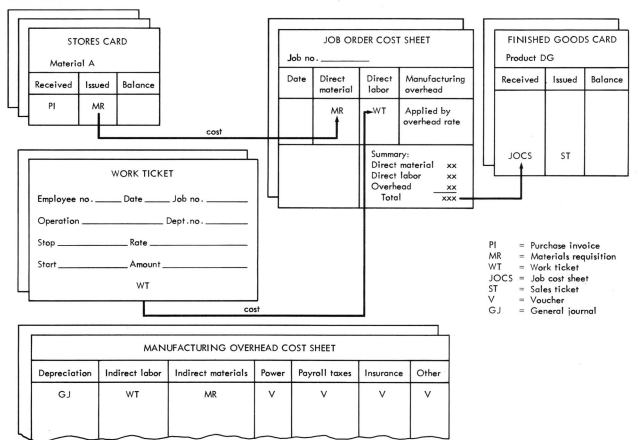

4. The manufacturing overhead cost sheet summarizes the various factory indirect costs incurred. One sheet is maintained for each production center.
5. A finished goods card is a running record of units and costs of products completed, sold, and on hand. A card is maintained for each type of product manufactured and sold.

The flow of manufacturing costs through the accounting system of a company using a job order cost system is shown in Illustration 22.3. To gain a full understanding of a job order cost system, this illustration should be studied carefully and related to the documents shown in Illustration 22.2 and to the journal entries in the following example.

Illustration 22.3   *Cost Flows in a Job Order Cost System*

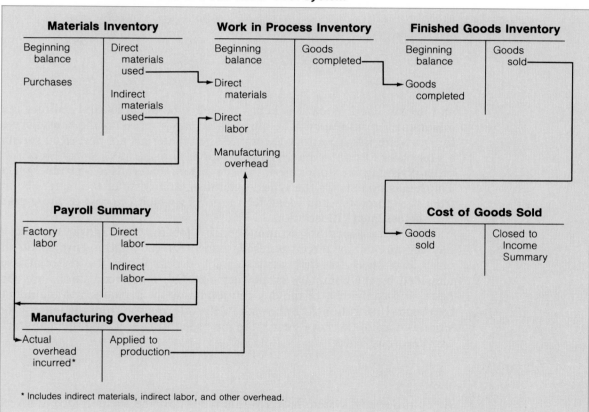

* Includes indirect materials, indirect labor, and other overhead.

The following section will explain the specific procedure followed in accounting for materials, labor, and manufacturing overhead costs in a job order cost system.

Accounting for Materials

As materials are received from vendors, they are placed in the materials storeroom. A stores (or materials) card is a perpetual inventory record that shows the quantities and costs of each type of material received, issued to a job,

Illustration 22.4

Materials Requisition

MATERIALS REQUISITION				
			Req. No.	R4
Storekeeper: Issue Following to Bearer			Date	6/4/87
			Dept. No.	1
Charge Job No. 201		Dept. Assembly		

Item	Quantity	Stock No.	Cost	Amount
DG	8,000	16	$3.00	$24,000

Entered on   Signed:
Job Order Cost Sheet

A TP
B N

and left on hand. A card is kept for each type of direct and indirect material maintained in inventory. The file of these cards serves as the subsidiary ledger for the Materials Inventory account. When materials are needed in production, a supervisor fills out a materials requisition. A **materials requisition** is a written order directing the store's clerk to issue certain materials to a production center. The requisition shows the types, quantities, and costs of the materials ordered from the storeroom and identifies the job to which the cost of those materials is to be assigned (Illustration 22.4).

The requisitions are accumulated by job number, and at the end of the day the amount of direct materials issued for each job is entered on the job order cost sheet for that particular job order. When the material issued is classified by the company as indirect material, those requisitions are accumulated, and at the end of the day the total amount is charged to manufacturing overhead. Illustration 22.2 shows how the information from the materials requisition is used in the store's card, the job order cost sheet, and the manufacturing overhead cost sheet.

Accounting for Labor

A job order cost system requires that labor costs be accumulated and recorded for each job. As each employee works on a particular job assignment, that employee fills out a **work (labor time) ticket,** which is a form used to record labor costs. Information recorded on the work ticket includes employee number, job number, number of hours worked, and any other important information. At the end of the day work tickets for each job are accumulated, and the total direct labor costs for each job are entered on the job order. A work ticket is shown in Illustration 22.2.

Work tickets are also used to accumulate and record indirect labor costs. When an employee is assigned work that is not directly related to any job (such as general maintenance work), this work is also recorded on a work ticket. Work not directly related to any job is indirect labor and is accounted for as part of manufacturing overhead. At the end of the day these tickets are accumulated, and the total indirect labor cost is recorded on the manufacturing overhead cost sheet.

The use of work tickets not only permits the accumulation and recording of direct labor costs for each job and indirect labor costs each day; it also provides control over the labor cost for each employee. Since each employee fills out a work ticket for each task performed, all of that employee's hours should be accounted for on one or more work tickets.

Accounting for Manufacturing Overhead

In order to exert some control over manufacturing overhead costs incurred, each production center or department must summarize its factory indirect costs. A manufacturing overhead cost sheet is the record used to summarize the various manufacturing overhead costs incurred. The file of manufacturing overhead cost sheets serves as the subsidiary ledger for the Manufacturing Overhead account. An example of a manufacturing overhead cost sheet was shown in Illustration 22.2.

Predetermined Overhead Rates.   In most manufacturing operations, unit costs are computed at the time a job is completed. The costs of direct materials and direct labor have already been entered on the job order cost sheet as a result of posting information from materials requisitions and work tickets. Each job must then be assigned its share of the manufacturing overhead costs.

In the last chapter, the manufacturing overhead rate was computed using actual overhead costs for the period. But most manufacturing companies prefer the use of a **predetermined** overhead rate rather than waiting to accumulate all overhead costs during a period and developing an actual manufacturing overhead rate. A predetermined overhead rate is calculated by dividing **estimated** total overhead costs for a period by an **expected level** of activity, such as total estimated direct labor-hours or direct labor cost for the period. Predetermined overhead rates are set at the **beginning** of the year in which they will be used.

Reasons for Using Predetermined Rates.   In addition to the need for current information on unit costs, other reasons for using a predetermined overhead rate in manufacturing operations include:

1. Overhead costs are seldom incurred uniformly throughout the year. For example, heating costs are larger during winter. No useful purpose is served by allocating less cost to a unit produced in the summer than to one produced in the winter. Use of a predetermined rate results in applying overhead based on direct labor cost, hours incurred, or some other measure of activity rather than on actual overhead incurred in a particular month.
2. Some overhead costs, like factory building depreciation, are fixed costs. Thus, if the volume of goods produced varies from month to month, there will be sharp fluctuations in average unit cost unless a predetermined rate is used.
3. Total unit costs of production are known sooner. Using a predetermined rate, overhead costs can be assigned to production when direct materials and direct labor costs are assigned. Without use of a predetermined rate,

unit costs would not be known until the end of the month or even later if bills for costs had not arrived by then. For example, the electric bill for the month of July will probably not arrive until August. If actual overhead were used to compute unit cost, products purchased in July could not be costed until August.

Computing Predetermined Overhead Rates.   Predetermined overhead rates are computed in the same basic manner as actual rates except that **estimated** rather than **actual** levels of activity and cost are used. As part of the budgeting process (discussed in Chapter 25), management estimates the level of manufacturing activity for the next year. This activity level is expressed in terms of some specified base, such as direct labor-hours or machine-hours. Next, expected overhead costs for the year are estimated, based on the expected level of activity. The overhead rate can then be calculated using the following formula:

$$\frac{\text{Estimated manufacturing overhead costs}}{\text{Expected level of activity (such as direct labor-hours)}} = \frac{\text{Predetermined}}{\text{overhead rate}}$$

This process of estimating the expected level of activity and the expected overhead costs and then calculating the predetermined overhead rate may be done for the company as a whole (if the company desires a single, company-wide overhead rate), or it may be done separately for each production center (department) within the company.[2] To illustrate the calculation of a predetermined overhead rate for a single production center, assume that the expected level of activity in a certain production center is 60,000 direct labor-hours. Assume also that, at that level of activity, the estimated overhead costs are $540,000.

The predetermined overhead rate would be:

$$\frac{\$540,000}{60,000 \text{ hours}} = \$9 \text{ per direct labor-hour}$$

Since Work in Process Inventory must contain amounts for direct materials, direct labor, and manufacturing overhead, the predetermined overhead rate is used to apply overhead to Work in Process Inventory. Actual amounts for direct materials and direct labor will already be posted to the Work in Process Inventory account from the materials requisitions and the work tickets. In the above situation, overhead would be applied to Work in Process Inventory at the rate of $9 of overhead for each **actual** direct labor-hour worked on a job. If 2,000 direct labor-hours have been worked, the journal entry to apply overhead is:

Work in Process Inventory	18,000	
Manufacturing Overhead		18,000
To apply overhead to Work in Process Inventory using a predetermined overhead rate of $9 per direct labor-hour.		

Note that the credit in the above entry is to the Manufacturing Overhead account. Actual manufacturing overhead is accumulated in the Manufacturing

---

[2] Sometimes separate rates are computed for variable overhead and fixed overhead. Later chapters illustrate how these separate rates may be useful.

Overhead account on the debit side. When overhead is applied to Work in Process Inventory, the Manufacturing Overhead account is credited. If the estimates used for overhead costs and expected level of activity are **exactly** the same as the actual amounts incurred for overhead and direct labor-hours worked, the Manufacturing Overhead account will have a zero balance at the end of the period.

Underapplied or Overapplied Overhead.   Because it is highly unlikely that the estimates used in computing the predetermined overhead rate will be exactly equal to the actual overhead cost or direct labor-hours worked, the Manufacturing Overhead account will normally have a debit or credit balance at the end of the period. A **debit** balance will remain if actual overhead exceeds the applied overhead for the period; in this case we say that the overhead is underapplied (underabsorbed). **Underapplied overhead** is the amount by which actual overhead costs incurred in a period exceed the overhead applied to production in that period. In contrast, a **credit** balance will remain if applied overhead exceeds actual overhead; in this case we say that overhead is overapplied or overabsorbed. **Overapplied overhead** is the amount by which the overhead applied to production exceeds the actual overhead costs incurred in that same period. Remember that overhead is applied to Work in Process Inventory (production) using the **predetermined** overhead rate times the **actual** level of activity (such as direct labor-hours) incurred during the period.

To illustrate the use of a predetermined overhead rate during a period, consider the following facts:

Estimated manufacturing overhead for year	$48,000
Estimated level of activity for year	80,000 direct labor-hours
Predetermined overhead rate ($48,000 ÷ 80,000 hours)	$0.60 per direct labor-hour
Actual overhead costs incurred during year	$45,000
Actual direct labor-hours worked	70,000 hours

The following journal entries are necessary to record the above information:

Manufacturing Overhead	45,000	
Various Accounts		45,000
To record actual manufacturing overhead costs incurred during period, machinery repair, indirect materials, etc.		
Work in Process Inventory	42,000	
Manufacturing Overhead		42,000
To apply manufacturing overhead to Work in Process Inventory at predetermined rate of $0.60 per direct labor-hour for 70,000 hours worked.		

It is essential to point out that in reality these entries are not made at a single point in time for these total amounts. The accountant will record actual manufacturing overhead (the first entry above) continuously during the period as indirect materials are issued to production, as work tickets are accumulated for indirect labor, and as other circumstances require entries (machinery repair, utility bills, etc.). The second entry above, to record applied manufacturing overhead, will be recorded each time a job is completed (in order to properly compute the total cost of the job) or at the end of each period (so that financial statements containing proper balances can be prepared).

Based on these two entries, the Manufacturing Overhead account will appear as follows:

Manufacturing Overhead

Actual costs	45,000	Applied to production	42,000
Balance	3,000		

The $3,000 debit balance is the amount of **underapplied** overhead during the period.

Reasons for Underapplied or Overapplied Manufacturing Overhead.

Two different factors determine whether overhead will be underapplied or overapplied for the period. The first factor has to do with the difference between the amount of indirect manufacturing cost actually incurred and the amount management estimated for the period. The second factor relates to the difference between the estimated level of manufacturing activity (expected activity) used to set the predetermined overhead rate and the actual level of activity on which overhead is applied.

A difference between actual and estimated overhead costs can arise because unanticipated events cause overhead costs to be more or less than the budgeted amount. High heating bills caused by a severe winter, excess repairs to factory machinery, and increases in prices of supplies are all examples of events that cause actual overhead costs to exceed expected costs and tend to result in underapplied overhead. Unanticipated cost savings, on the other hand, tend to cause overapplied overhead.

Unanticipated events can also cause the estimated and actual levels of activity to differ. For example, a company could find itself without essential raw materials and have to cut back production, or, alternatively, a company could produce a product that becomes a "fad" and have to increase production in order to meet demand. Recall that in every manufacturing business some overhead costs are fixed costs that do not change with the level of manufacturing activity. As a result, **total actual** overhead costs do not vary in direct proportion to the actual level of activity. However, applied overhead costs do vary in direct proportion to the actual level of activity because applied overhead is being applied to Work in Process Inventory at a constant amount per actual unit of activity (such as direct labor-hours). Therefore, if actual operations are at a higher level of activity than that used to set the predetermined overhead rate, more overhead will be applied to Work in Process Inventory than originally anticipated and will tend to cause overapplied overhead. Operating at a lower level than originally estimated will tend to cause underapplied overhead.

Disposition of Underapplied or Overapplied Manufacturing Overhead.

An underapplied or overapplied manufacturing overhead balance can be carried forward in monthly or quarterly (interim) financial statements if the probability exists that it will be reduced or offset by operations for the remainder of the year. If a balance in overhead remains at year-end, it can be allocated (or disposed of) to Work in Process Inventory, Finished Goods Inventory, and Cost of Goods Sold. This disposition is done by recomputing the cost of production for the year using actual overhead rates and adjusting the three account balances to their appropriate actual amounts. As an alternative, underapplied overhead can be charged off as a loss of the period, particularly if it resulted from idle production capacity or from unusual circumstances.

As a practical matter, however, **underapplied or overapplied overhead is usually transferred to Cost of Goods Sold.** Little distortion of net income or of assets results from this treatment if the amount transferred is small or if most of the goods produced during the year were sold. Thus, if the $3,000 of underapplied overhead in the previous example is a year-end balance, the journal entry to dispose of it will read:

Cost of Goods Sold	3,000	
Manufacturing Overhead		3,000
To dispose of underapplied overhead.		

Job Order Costing—an Example

To illustrate a job order costing system in use, the following example includes nine transactions of the Casting Company for the month of July. On July 1, the Casting Company had beginning inventories as follows:

Materials inventory (material A, $10,000; material B, $6,000; various indirect materials, $4,000)	$20,000
Work in process inventory (Job No. 106: direct materials, $4,200; direct labor, $5,000; and overhead, $4,000)	13,200
Finished goods inventory (500 units of product AB at a cost of $11 per unit)	5,500

Job No. 106, which was in process at the beginning of July, was completed in July. Of the two jobs started in July (Nos. 107 and 108), only Job No. 107 was completed by the end of July.

The transactions and the journal entries to record these transactions are given below. You may want to refer back to Illustration 22.3 to follow the cost flows in a job order cost system.

1. Purchased $10,000 of material A and $15,000 of material B on account.

Materials Inventory	25,000	
Accounts Payable		25,000
To record purchase of direct materials.		

2. Issued direct materials: material A to Job No. 106, $1,000; to Job No. 107, $8,000; to Job No. 108, $2,000; material B to Job No. 106, $2,000; to Job No. 107, $6,000; to Job No. 108, $4,000. Indirect materials issued to all jobs, $1,000.

Work in Process Inventory	23,000	
Manufacturing Overhead	1,000	
Materials Inventory		24,000
To record direct and indirect materials issued.		

3. Factory payroll for the month, $25,000; FICA and income taxes withheld, $4,000.

Payroll Summary	25,000	
Various liability accounts for taxes withheld		4,000
Accrued Wages Payable		21,000
To record factory payroll for July.		

4. **Factory payroll paid, $21,000.**

Accrued Wages Payable	21,000	
Cash		21,000
To record cash paid to factory employees in July.		

5. **Payroll costs distributed: direct labor, $20,000 (Job No. 106, $5,000; Job No. 107, $12,000; and Job No. 108, $3,000); and indirect labor, $5,000.**

Work in Process Inventory	20,000	
Manufacturing Overhead	5,000	
Payroll Summary		25,000
To distribute factory labor costs incurred.		

6. **Other indirect manufacturing costs incurred:**

Payroll taxes accrued	$ 3,000
Repairs (on account)	1,000
Property taxes accrued	4,000
Heat, light, and power (on account) . .	2,000
Depreciation	5,000
	$15,000

Manufacturing Overhead	15,000	
Accounts Payable		3,000
Accrued Payroll Taxes Payable		3,000
Accrued Property Taxes Payable		4,000
Accumulated Depreciation		5,000
To record manufacturing overhead costs incurred.		

7. **Manufacturing overhead applied to production (assume a predetermined rate of 80% of direct labor cost):**

Job No. 106, Product DG (0.80 × $5,000)	$ 4,000
Job No. 107, Product XY (0.80 × $12,000)	9,600
Job No. 108, Product OR (0.80 × $3,000)	2,400
	$16,000

Work in Process Inventory	16,000	
Manufacturing Overhead		16,000
To record application of overhead to production.		

8. **Jobs completed and transferred to finished goods storeroom (see Illustration 22.5 for details):**

Job No. 106 (4,000 units of product DG @ $6.30) . .	$25,200
Job No. 107 (10,000 units of product XY @ $3.56) . .	35,600
	$60,800

Finished Goods Inventory	60,800	
Work in Process Inventory		60,800
To record completed production for July.		

9. **Sales on account for the month: 500 units of product AB for $8,000, cost, $5,500; and 10,000 units of product XY for $62,000, cost, $35,600 (Job No. 107).**

```
Accounts Receivable . .  .  .  .  .  .  .  .  .  .  .  .  .  .  .  .  .    70,000
    Sales  .  .  .  .  .  .  .  .  .  .  .  .  .  .  .  .  .  .  .  .  .  .  .                      70,000
    To record sales on account for July.

Cost of Goods Sold  .  .  .  .  .  .  .  .  .  .  .  .  .  .  .  .  .  .    41,100
    Finished Goods Inventory   .  .  .  .  .  .  .  .  .  .  .  .  .  .                     41,100
    To record cost of goods sold in July.
```

After the above entries have been posted, the Work in Process Inventory and Finished Goods Inventory accounts appear (in T-account form) as follows:

Work in Process Inventory

July 1 balance	13,200	Completed	60,800
Direct materials used	23,000		
Direct labor cost incurred	20,000		
Overhead applied	16,000		
July 31 balance	11,400		

Finished Goods Inventory

July 1 balance	5,500	Sold	41,100
Completed	60,800		
July 31 balance	25,200		

On July 31, the Work in Process Inventory account has a balance of $11,400, which agrees with the total costs charged thus far to Job No. 108, as shown in Illustration 22.5. The balance consists of direct materials, $6,000; direct labor, $3,000; and manufacturing overhead, $2,400. Finished Goods Inventory has a balance on July 31 of $25,200, supported by the finished goods inventory card for Job No. 106 (Illustration 22.5), which shows that the 4,000 units of product DG on hand have a total cost of $25,200.

Ledger account entries like the ones given above, are often made from summaries of cost, and thus are recorded only at the end of the month. If, on the other hand, management wants to be informed more frequently as to costs incurred, details of the various costs can be recorded more often, even daily.

The main advantage of using a predetermined overhead rate is shown in this example. Three jobs were worked on during the month. Job No. 106 was started last month and completed in July. Job No. 107 was started and completed in July. And Job No. 108 was started but not finished in July. Each required different amounts of direct materials and direct labor. Under these conditions, there is simply no timely way to apply overhead to products without the use of a predetermined rate based on some common level of activity. Note that the use of a predetermined overhead rate permits the computation of unit costs to be made for Job Nos. 106 and 107 at the time of their completion rather than waiting until the end of the month. But this advantage is secured only at the expense of keeping more detailed records of the costs incurred. As discussed below, the other major cost accumulation system—process cost—requires far less record keeping, but the computation of unit costs is more complex.

Illustration 22.5 *Supporting Inventory Cards and Job Order Cost Sheets*

STORES CARD
Material A

Received	Issued	Balance
		$10,000
$10,000		20,000
	$1,000	19,000
	8,000	11,000
	2,000	9,000

STORES CARD
Material B

Received	Issued	Balance
		$ 6,000
$15,000		21,000
	$2,000	19,000
	6,000	13,000
	4,000	9,000

JOB ORDER COST SHEET (Product DG)   Job No. 106

Date	Direct Materials	Direct Labor	Manufacturing Overhead
July 1	$ 4,200	$ 5,000	$4,000
July	A: 1,000	5,000	4,000
	B: 2,000	$10,000	$8,000
	$7,200		

Job completed (4,000 units of product DG @ $6.30). Total cost, $25,200.

JOB ORDER COST SHEET (Product XY)   Job No. 107

Date	Direct Materials	Direct Labor	Manufacturing Overhead
July	A: $ 8,000	$12,000	$9,600
	B: 6,000		
	$14,000		

Job completed (10,000 units of product XY @ $3.56). Total cost, $35,600.

JOB ORDER COST SHEET (Product OR)   Job No. 108

Date	Direct Materials	Direct Labor	Manufacturing Overhead
July	A: $ 2,000	$3,000	$2,400
	B: 4,000		

Job incomplete (1,000 units of product OR). Cost to date, $11,400.

FINISHED GOODS CARD
Product AB

Received	Issued	Balance
		$5,500
	$5,500	–0–

FINISHED GOODS CARD
Product DG

Received	Issued	Balance
$25,200		$25,200

FINISHED GOODS CARD
Product XY

Received	Issued	Balance
$35,600		$35,600
	$35,600	–0–

■ PROCESS COST SYSTEMS

Many businesses manufacture huge quantities of a single product or similar products (paint, paper, chemicals, gasoline, rubber, and plastics) on a continuous basis over long periods of time. For these kinds of products, there is no separate job order; rather, production is ongoing over the year or even several years. In these types of operations, costs must be accumulated for **each process** that a product undergoes on its way to completion. The processes or departments serve as "cost centers" where costs are accumulated for the entire period (usually a month). These costs are divided by the number of units produced (tons, pounds, gallons, or feet) to get an average unit cost. The cost system used in these circumstances is called a process cost system. A process cost system (process costing) is a manufacturing cost system in which costs incurred to produce a product are accumulated according to the processes or departments a product goes through on its way to completion.

Basic System Design

As shown in Illustration 22.6, process cost systems have the same cost flows as found in a job order system. Costs of the factors of production are first recorded in separate accounts for materials inventory, labor, and overhead. Costs are then transferred to Work in Process Inventory. A process cost system usually has more than one Work in Process Inventory account. An account is kept for each processing center in order to determine the unit cost of each process.

The system depicted in Illustration 22.6 is one in which products are processed in a specified **sequential** order; that is, the products are started and processed in Department A, transferred to Department B and processed further, and then transferred to Finished Goods Inventory. For the purposes of illustration in this chapter, we will assume that all the process cost systems are sequential.

Process Costing Illustration

Assume that Ajax Company sells a chemical product that is processed in two departments. In Department A, basic materials are crushed, powdered, and blended. In Department B, the product is packaged and transferred to finished goods. This manufacturing process is shown in Illustration 22.7. Production and cost data for Ajax Company for the month of June are as follows:

	Department A	Department B
Units started, completed, and transferred	11,000	9,000
Units on hand at June 30, partially completed . .	–0–	2,000
Beginning inventory	$ –0–	$ –0–
Direct materials	16,500	1,100
Direct labor	5,500	5,880
Actual manufacturing overhead	4,500	5,600
Applied manufacturing overhead	4,400	5,880

Illustration 22.6 *Cost Flows in a Process Cost System*

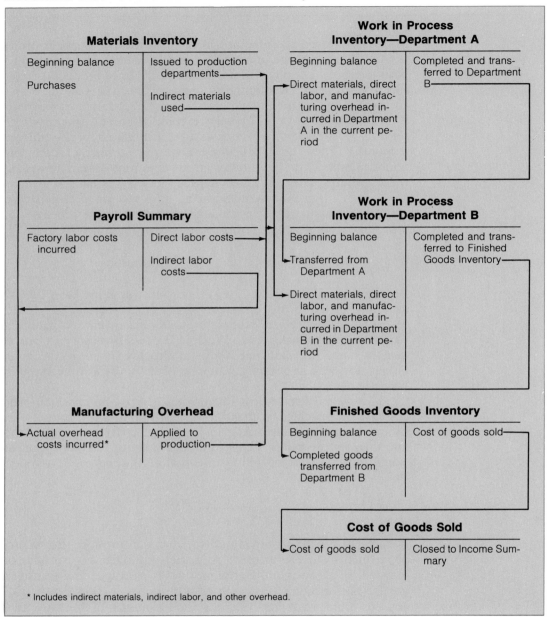

* Includes indirect materials, indirect labor, and other overhead.

In Department A, manufacturing overhead is applied on the basis of a predetermined rate of 80% of direct labor cost. In Department B, manufacturing overhead is applied at the rate of 100% of direct labor cost.

From these data, the Work in Process Inventory—Department A account can be constructed and summarized as follows:

Work in Process Inventory—Department A

Direct materials	16,500	Transferred to Department B—	
Direct labor	5,500	11,000 units @ $2.40	26,400
Applied overhead (80% of direct labor cost)	4,400		
Total	26,400		

Since all units started in June in Department A were completed and transferred to Department B, it follows that all costs assigned to those goods should also be transferred. The unit cost in Department A is computed by dividing $26,400 of total costs by the 11,000 units completed and transferred to get an average unit cost of $2.40.

Computations are seldom this simple. One complication is faced whenever partially completed inventories are present, as is true for Department B. Department B's Work in Process Inventory account for June is as follows before the cost of completed units is transferred out:

Work in Process Inventory—Department B

Transferred in from Department A	26,400	
Direct material	1,100	
Direct labor	5,880	
Overhead (100% of direct labor)	5,880	
Total	39,260	

Recall that direct materials, direct labor, and manufacturing overhead are product costs, that is, they "attach" to the product. Thus the "Transferred in from Department A" line in the T-accounts above represents the material, labor, and overhead costs assigned to products in Department A. These costs have "followed" the physical units to Department B.

The task now faced is to divide the $39,260 total costs charged to the department in June between the units transferred out and those remaining on hand in the department. The $39,260 cannot be divided by 11,000 to get an average unit cost because the 11,000 units are not alike; 9,000 are finished, and 2,000 are only partially finished. The problem is solved by using the concept of equivalent units of production.

Illustration 22.7

Product Flows in a Process Cost System (Ajax Company example)

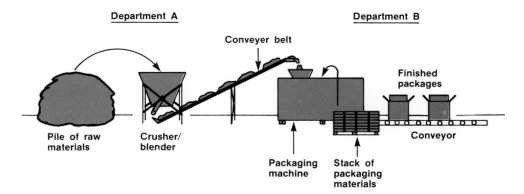

Equivalent Units.   Essentially, the concept of equivalent units involves expressing a given number of partially completed units as a smaller number of fully completed units. For example, 1,000 units brought to a 40% state of completion are equivalent to 400 units that are 100% complete. This concept is based on the fact that approximately the same amount of costs must be incurred to bring 1,000 units to a 40% level of completion as would be required to complete 400 units.

The first step in computing equivalent units produced in Department B for the example above is to determine the stage of completion of the unfinished units. These units are 100% complete as to transferred-in costs or they would not have been transferred out of Department A. But the units may have different stages of completion as to materials, labor, and overhead costs added in Department B. Assume that all materials are added at the beginning of the production process in Department B. Thus, both ending inventory and units transferred out are 100% complete as to materials, and equivalent production for materials is 11,000 units. Units are usually assumed to be at the same stage of completion regarding labor and overhead. This assumption is made because overhead is often applied to work in process on a direct labor basis (recall that direct labor and overhead together are termed *conversion costs*). Next, assume that the 2,000 units in ending inventory are, on the average, 40% complete as to conversion. Equivalent production for labor and overhead is 9,800 units—9,000 units transferred out fully complete and 2,000 brought to a 40% completion state, which is the equivalent of 800 fully completed units.

Once the equivalent units of production are known, unit costs of processing in Department B can be computed as follows:

	Transferred in	Materials	Conversion	Total
Costs to be accounted for:				
Charged to Department B . .	$26,400	$ 1,100	$11,760*	$39,260
Equivalent units	11,000	11,000	9,800†	
Unit costs	$2.40	$0.10	$1.20	$3.70

* Conversion costs consist of direct labor + overhead ($5,880 + $5,880).
† Units transferred out (9,000) + equivalent units in ending inventory (800).

Using the computed unit costs, the $39,260 of costs charged to Department B in June is divided between costs associated with units completed and transferred out and costs of units remaining in the department's ending inventory:

	Transferred in (@ $2.40)	Materials (@ $0.10)	Conversion (@ $1.20)	Total
Costs accounted for:				
Units completed and transferred out (9,000 units)	$21,600	$ 900	$10,800	$33,300
Units remaining in ending inventory (2,000 units)	4,800	200	960*	5,960
Costs accounted for	$26,400	$1,100	$11,760	$39,260

* Equivalent units = 800 units.

The $33,300 total costs transferred out consists of $21,600 of Department A's cost (9,000 × $2.40), $900 of materials costs (9,000 × $0.10), and $10,800 of conversion costs (9,000 × $1.20) or $3.70 per unit. The 2,000 units of ending inventory in Department B are fully complete as to materials and 40% complete as to conversion. Ending inventory cost, then, consists of the following:

Costs from Department A (2,000 × $2.40) . . .		$4,800
Costs added by Department B:		
Materials (2,000 × $0.10)	$200	
Conversion (800 equivalent units × $1.20) . .	960	1,160
Total cost of ending inventory		$5,960

The units transferred out of Department B will be carried in finished goods inventory at a cost of $3.70 each until they are sold, at which time the costs will be charged to Cost of Goods Sold.

The June journal entries for the above activities follow:

(1)	Work in Process Inventory—Department A	16,500	
	Work in Process Inventory—Department B	1,100	
	Materials Inventory		17,600
	To record materials placed in production in June.		
(2)	Payroll Summary	11,380	
	Various withholding accounts and accrued wages payable		11,380
	To record factory payroll for June.		
(3)	Work in Process Inventory—Department A	5,500	
	Work in Process Inventory—Department B	5,880	
	Payroll Summary		11,380
	To distribute factory labor costs (assuming that all such costs are chargeable directly to production departments).		
(4)	Manufacturing Overhead	10,100	
	Various accounts—cash, accounts payable, accruals, and accumulated depreciation		10,100
	To record actual overhead costs incurred in June.		
(5)	Work in Process Inventory—Department A	4,400	
	Work in Process Inventory—Department B	5,880	
	Manufacturing Overhead		10,280
	To apply overhead to production using predetermined rates based on direct labor cost: Department A, 80%; and Department B, 100%.		
(6)	Work in Process Inventory—Department B	26,400	
	Work in Process Inventory—Department A		26,400
	To record transfer of goods from Department A to Department B.		
(7)	Finished Goods Inventory	33,300	
	Work in Process Inventory—Department B		33,300
	To record transfer of completed goods from Department B to finished goods.		

Assuming that 6,000 completed units were sold in June at a price of $10 per unit on account, the following entries would be required:

(8)	Accounts Receivable	60,000	
	Sales		60,000
	To record sales on account.		

(9)	Cost of Goods Sold	22,200	
	Finished Goods Inventory		22,200
	To record cost of goods sold in June, 6,000 units @ $3.70.		

Production Cost Report. The key document in a process costing system is the production cost report. A **production cost report** shows both the flow of units and the flow of costs through a processing center. It also shows how these costs are divided between the cost of units completed and transferred out and the cost of units still in the processing center's ending inventory. This report is designed to make equivalent unit and unit cost computations easier.

To illustrate the preparation of a production cost report where there are partially completed beginning and ending inventories, assume the following data for Department 3 of the Storey Company, for the month of June 1987:

Units

Units in beginning inventory, complete as to materials, 60% complete as to conversion	6,000
Units transferred in from Department 2	18,000
Units completed and transferred out	16,000
Units in ending inventory, complete as to materials, 50% complete as to conversion	8,000

Costs

Cost of beginning inventory:		
Cost transferred in from preceding department in May	$12,000	
Materials added in May in Department 3	6,000	
Conversion costs (equal amounts of labor and overhead)	3,000	$21,000
Costs transferred in from preceding department in June		37,200
Costs added in Department 3 in June:		
Materials	$18,480	
Conversion (equal amounts of labor and overhead)	18,000	36,480
Total costs in beginning inventory and placed in production in Department 3 in June		$94,680

The production cost report for Department 3, shown in Illustration 22.8, is developed using the above data. There are four steps in the preparation of the production cost report:

1. Tracing the physical flow of the units through the production department.
2. Converting actual units to equivalent units.
3. Computing unit costs for each cost element.
4. Distributing the total cost between the units completed and transferred and the units remaining in the ending inventory.

These are the same four steps that were followed in the Ajax Company illustration of the process cost system.

The first step in the preparation of a production cost report is to trace the physical flow of actual units into and out of the department. The section entitled "UNITS" in Illustration 22.8 shows that 6,000 units were in the June beginning inventory and that 18,000 units were transferred in from the previous department, making a total of 24,000 units that must be accounted for. Of

Illustration 22.8 *Production Cost Report*

STOREY COMPANY
Production Cost Report—Department 3
For the Month of June 1987

	Actual units	Equivalent units		
		Transferred in	Materials	Conversion
UNITS:				
Units in beginning inventory	6,000			
Units transferred in from Department 2	18,000			
Units to be accounted for	24,000			
Units completed and transferred	16,000	16,000	16,000	16,000
Units in ending inventory*	8,000	8,000	8,000	4,000
Units accounted for	24,000	24,000	24,000	20,000

* Inventory is complete as to materials added, 50% complete as to conversion.

	Transferred in	Materials	Conversion	Total
COSTS:				
Costs to be accounted for:				
Costs in beginning inventory	$12,000	$ 6,000	$ 3,000	$21,000
Costs transferred in from Department 2	37,200			37,200
Costs added in Department 3		18,480	18,000	36,480
Costs to be accounted for	$49,200	$24,480	$21,000	$94,680
Equivalent units (as above)	24,000	24,000	20,000	
Unit costs (per equivalent unit)	$2.05	$1.02	$1.05	$4.12
Costs accounted for:				
Costs completed and transferred out	$32,800	$16,320	$16,800	$65,920
Costs remaining in ending inventory	16,400	8,160	4,200	28,760
Costs accounted for	$49,200	$24,480	$21,000	$94,680

these 24,000 units, 16,000 units were completed and transferred out (either to the next processing department or to finished goods), and 8,000 remained partially completed in Department 3 at the end of the month.

The next step is to convert actual units to equivalent units of production. The cost of production report illustrated uses an **average cost** procedure.[3] **Under an average cost procedure, the number of equivalent units for each cost element equals the number of units transferred out plus the number of equivalent units of that cost element in the ending inventory.** The number of units in beginning inventory and the degree of completion of the beginning inventory are not considered under the average cost method. In this example, since the units in the ending inventory are fully complete as to cost transferred in and as to materials, the number of equivalent units for each of these cost elements is 24,000 (16,000 units completed and transferred + 8,000 units in the ending inventory $\times$ 100% complete for transferred-in cost and for materials). But the units in ending inventory were only 50% complete as to conversion; therefore, equivalent units for conversion cost purposes are 20,000 (16,000 units completed and transferred + 8,000 units in the ending inventory $\times$ 50% complete for conversion).

---

[3] Discussion of Fifo and Lifo procedures in a process cost system is reserved for an advanced cost accounting text.

Now that equivalent units have been computed, the next step is to calculate unit costs. Costs are accumulated for each cost element of production—costs transferred in, materials, and conversion. Notice that the costs of beginning inventory and costs of the current month are totaled for each cost element. The summation of all costs charged to the department is referred to as "costs to be accounted for." These costs will either be transferred out or will appear in ending inventory of Department 3. Total cost assignable to each cost element is divided by the appropriate number of equivalent units of production related to that cost element to determine the cost per equivalent unit for that cost element. Since all costs for each cost element are totaled before the division, the unit costs computed are averages across the current and the prior period. As shown in Illustration 22.8, average per unit costs for June are as follows: transferred-in cost, $2.05; materials, $1.02; and conversion, $1.05. These costs are monitored closely by management for cost control purposes in the event that there are extreme fluctuations from one month to the next.

The last step is to distribute costs between the units completed and transferred out and those remaining in ending inventory. The units that were transferred out were fully complete as to all elements of production. Therefore, the 16,000 units can be multiplied by $4.12, the total cost per unit. The result is $65,920, the amount to be assigned to the next department as "cost transferred in" or to finished goods as the cost of current period production. The cost of ending inventory is computed as follows:

8,000 equivalent units transferred in @ $2.05	$16,400
8,000 equivalent units of materials costs @ $1.02 . .	8,160
4,000 equivalent units of conversion costs @ $1.05 . .	4,200
Total cost of ending inventory	$28,760

The sum of the ending inventory cost and the cost of the units transferred out must equal the total costs for which the department is accountable. Thus, a built-in check is provided to determine whether the procedures of cost allocation have been properly followed. Note that cost transferred out of $65,920 is added to ending inventory cost of $28,760, and the total equals costs accountable for of $94,680 as shown in the production cost report.

■ SUMMARY

Two major types of cost accumulation systems under perpetual inventory cost procedure are found in practice—the job order cost system and the process cost system. In each system, the goal is to determine before year-end the unit costs of the products being manufactured. Unit costs may be used throughout the period to compute (1) cost of goods sold, (2) cost of work in process and finished goods inventories, (3) payments to be received under contracts based on "full" cost, and (4) selling prices.

A job order cost system is a cost accounting system in which the costs incurred to produce a product are accumulated according to the individual job. A job order cost system is generally used when the products being manufactured can be grouped into separately identifiable jobs.

The key document in a job order cost system is the job order cost sheet, which summarizes the costs of direct materials, direct labor, and manufacturing overhead incurred for a job. The file of job order cost sheets for the incomplete jobs constitutes a subsidiary ledger for the Work in Process Inventory account. The actual costs of direct materials issued to a job and direct labor used on a job are recorded on the job order cost sheet. However, overhead cost is generally applied to the job through the use of a predetermined overhead rate.

A predetermined overhead rate is computed by dividing estimated overhead costs by the expected level of manufacturing activity. Overhead costs applied to production are debited to Work in Process Inventory and credited to the Manufacturing Overhead account. Actual overhead costs incurred are debited to Manufacturing Overhead and credited to Cash, various accounts payable, or similar accounts. Since overhead is applied via a predetermined, estimated overhead rate, it is unlikely that the actual costs debited to Manufacturing Overhead will equal the applied overhead that was credited to Manufacturing Overhead during the period. The debit balance (underapplied overhead) or credit balance (overapplied overhead) in the Manufacturing Overhead account can be allocated to Work in Process Inventory, Finished Goods Inventory, and Cost of Goods Sold, or it can simply be closed directly to Cost of Goods Sold.

A process cost system is a manufacturing cost system in which costs incurred to produce a product are accumulated according to the processes or departments a product goes through on its way to completion. A process cost system is generally used where huge quantities of a single product or similar products are manufactured on a continuous basis over long periods of time.

Computing per unit costs of products in a process cost system requires first computing the number of equivalent units completed during the period. Equivalent units must be determined for (1) units transferred-in (if this department receives products from a previous processing department), (2) materials, and (3) conversion. The costs of transferred-in units (if any), materials, and conversion are then divided by their respective numbers of equivalent units to obtain costs per equivalent unit. Finally, the numbers of equivalent units (for transferred-in units, materials, and conversion) in the units completed and transferred and in the ending work in process inventory are multiplied by their respective costs per equivalent unit to determine the total cost of the units completed and transferred and of the ending work in process inventory. This cost computation is performed on a production cost report, which is a key document in a process costing system.

The importance of accurate accounting for product unit costs should be evident to you. Without accurate cost accounting information, a manufacturing company cannot determine its selling prices, prepare accurate financial statements, or determine the cost of its ending inventory. Chapter 23 discusses how costs can be used to assess the efficiency of a manufacturing process.

NEW TERMS INTRODUCED IN CHAPTER 22

Equivalent units

A method of expressing a given number of partially completed units as a smaller number of fully completed units; for example, bringing 1,000 units to a 75% level of completion is the equivalent of bringing 750 units to a 100% level of completion (874).

Finished goods card

A running record of units and costs of products completed, sold, and on hand (861).

Job order cost sheet

A form used to summarize the costs of direct materials, direct labor, and manufacturing overhead incurred for a job. The job order cost sheets for all partially completed jobs form the subsidiary ledger for the Work in Process Inventory account (859).

Job order cost system (job costing)

A cost accounting system in which the costs incurred to produce a product are accumulated according to the individual job, such as a building, dam, 1,000 chairs, or 10 desks (859).

Manufacturing overhead cost sheet

A record that summarizes the various manufacturing overhead costs incurred (863).

Materials requisition

A written order directing the stores clerk to issue certain materials to a production center (862).

Overapplied (overabsorbed) overhead

The amount by which the overhead applied to production exceeds the actual overhead costs incurred in that same period (865).

Predetermined overhead rate

Calculated by dividing estimated total overhead costs for a period by the expected level of activity, such as direct labor-hours or direct labor costs for the period.

The use of a predetermined rate is a means of applying manufacturing overhead to production such that unit costs can be determined immediately after production has been completed (863).

Process cost system (process costing)

A manufacturing cost system in which costs incurred to produce a product are accumulated according to the processes or departments a product goes through on its way to completion (871).

Production cost report

A report that shows both the flow of units and the flow of costs through a processing center; it also shows how those costs are divided between the cost of units transferred out and the cost of units still in the processing center's ending inventory (876).

Stores (or materials) card

A record that shows the quantities and costs of each type of material received, issued to a job, and left on hand (861).

Underapplied (underabsorbed) overhead

The amount by which actual overhead costs incurred in a period exceeds the overhead applied to production in that period (865).

Work (labor time) ticket

A form used to record labor costs. Information recorded on the work ticket includes employee number, job number, number of hours worked, and any other important information; may be prepared for both direct and indirect labor (862).

DEMONSTRATION PROBLEM 22–1

Heille Company employs a job order cost system. As of January 1, 1987, its records showed:

Materials and supplies	$ 80,000
Work in process	172,000
Finished goods (50,000 units at $4)	200,000

The work in process inventory consisted of two jobs:

No.	Materials	Labor	Manufacturing overhead	Total
212	$30,000	$40,000	$20,000	$ 90,000
213	34,000	32,000	16,000	82,000
	$64,000	$72,000	$36,000	$172,000

Summarized below are manufacturing data for the company for 1987:

1. Materials and supplies purchased on account, $330,000.
2. Factory payrolls accrued, $680,000; FICA taxes withheld, $34,000; and federal income taxes withheld, $60,000.

3. Manufacturing overhead costs incurred: depreciation, $20,000; heat, light, and power, $8,000; and miscellaneous, $12,000.
4. Direct materials and supplies requisitioned: Job No. 212, $52,000; Job No. 213, $96,000; Job No. 214, $160,000; and indirect supplies requisitioned, $8,000.
5. Payrolls distributed: direct labor—Job No. 212, $80,000; Job No. 213, $160,000; Job No. 214, $240,000; factory supervision, $80,000; and other indirect labor, $120,000.
6. Overhead is assigned to work in process at 50% of direct labor costs.
7. Job Nos. 212 and 213 were completed.
8. Goods with a cost of $688,000 were sold for $900,000.

Required: Prepare general journal entries to record the above summarized data, as well as all closing entries for which you have sufficient information.

Solution to demonstration problem 22–1

HEILLE COMPANY
General Journal

(1) Materials Inventory 330,000
    Accounts Payable 330,000
    To record materials purchased on account.

(2) Payroll Summary 680,000
    FICA Taxes Withheld 34,000
    Federal Income Taxes Withheld 60,000
    Accrued Wages Payable 586,000
    To record accrued factory payrolls.

(3) Manufacturing Overhead 40,000
    Accumulated Depreciation 20,000
    Accounts Payable (Accrued Liabilities, Cash, etc.) 20,000
    To record various manufacturing overhead costs.

(4) Work in Process Inventory 308,000
    Manufacturing Overhead 8,000
    Materials inventory 316,000
    To record requisitions of materials and supplies:

        Job No. 212 . . . . $ 52,000
           213 96,000
           214 160,000
        Indirect supplies 8,000
                      $316,000

(5) Work in Process Inventory 480,000
    Manufacturing Overhead 200,000
    Payroll Summary 680,000
    To distribute labor costs:

    Direct labor to Work in Process Inventory:
      Job No. 212 . . . . $ 80,000
           213 160,000
           214 . . . . 240,000 $480,000

    Manufacturing overhead:
      Factory supervision . . . . $ 80,000
      Other indirect labor 120,000   200,000
                      $680,000

(6) Work in Process Inventory 240,000
    Manufacturing Overhead 240,000
    Overhead assigned: Job No. 212, $40,000; Job No. 213, $80,000; and Job No. 214, $120,000.

(7) Finished Goods Inventory   680,000
        Work in Process Inventory   680,000
   Completed and transferred jobs:
      No. 212 . . . . $262,000
      No. 213   418,000
                               $680,000

(8) Accounts Receivable   900,000
        Sales   900,000
   To record sales on account.

Cost of Goods Sold   688,000
    Finished Goods Inventory   688,000
   To record cost of goods sold.

Cost of Goods Sold   8,000
       Manufacturing Overhead   8,000
   To close underapplied manufacturing overhead.

Sales   900,000
       Income Summary   900,000
   To close Sales account.

Income Summary   696,000
       Cost of Goods Sold   696,000
   To close Cost of Goods Sold expense account.

DEMONSTRATION PROBLEM 22–2

AFA, Inc. uses a process cost system to accumulate the costs it incurs to produce aluminum awning stabilizers. The May 1 inventory consisted of 30,000 units, fully complete as to materials, 80% complete as to conversion. The beginning inventory cost of $240,000 consisted of $180,000 of costs transferred in from the molding department, $25,000 of finishing department material costs, and $35,000 of finishing department conversion costs. The costs incurred in the finishing department for the month of May appear below:

Costs from molding department (excluding costs in beginning
  inventory) $600,000
Costs added in finishing department in May (excluding costs in
  beginning inventory):
    Materials . . . . $ 53,000
    Conversion   109,480   162,480
                                     $762,480

The finishing department received 100,000 units from the molding department in May. During the month, 106,000 units were completed by the finishing department and transferred out. As of May 31, 24,000 units, complete as to materials and 60% complete as to conversion, were left in inventory of the finishing department.

Required: a. Prepare a production cost report for the finishing department for the month of May.
           b. Compute the average unit cost for conversion in the finishing department in April.

Solution to demonstration problem 22–2

a.

AFA, INC.
Finishing Department
Production Cost Report
For the Month Ending May 31

	Actual units	Transferred in	Materials	Conversion
		Equivalent units		
UNITS:				
Units in May 1 inventory	30,000			
Units transferred in	100,000			
Units to be accounted for	130,000			
Units completed and transferred	106,000	106,000	106,000	106,000
Units in May 31 inventory*	24,000	24,000	24,000	14,400†
Units accounted for	130,000	130,000	130,000	120,400

* Inventory is complete as to materials, 60% complete as to conversion.
† (24,000 × 60% = 14,400).

	Transferred in	Materials	Conversion	Total
COSTS:				
Costs to be accounted for:				
Costs in May 1 inventory	$180,000	$ 25,000	$ 35,000	$ 240,000
Costs transferred in	600,000			600,000
Costs added in department		53,000	109,480	162,480
Costs to be accounted for	$780,000	$ 78,000	$144,480	$1,002,480
Equivalent units (as above)	130,000	130,000	120,400	
Unit costs	$6.00	$0.60	$1.20	$7.80
Costs accounted for:				
Units completed and transferred out	$636,000	$ 63,600	$127,200	$ 826,800
Units remaining in May 31 inventory	144,000	14,400	17,280	175,680
Costs accounted for	$780,000	$ 78,000	$144,480	$1,002,480

b.   The unit cost of conversion in the finishing department in April was $1.46 [$35,000 ÷ (0.8 × 30,000)].

QUESTIONS

1. What is the basic purpose of any costing system?

2. What is a job order cost sheet? Explain how it is used.

3. How is a predetermined overhead rate calculated? Why is the use of a predetermined rate necessary in a perpetual inventory cost system?

4. Under what circumstances is the assignment of overhead to production by applying a predetermined rate definitely preferable to assigning actual overhead incurred?

5. What is a reason, other than errors in estimating costs, for overapplied overhead?

6. How does a process cost system differ from a job order cost system? What factors should be taken into consideration in determining which type of system should be employed?

7. What is meant by the term *equivalent units?* Of what use is the computation of the number of equivalent units of production?

8. Distinguish between the number of units completed and transferred during a period and the equivalent units for the same period.

9. Under what circumstances would the number of equivalent units of materials differ from the equivalent units of labor and overhead in the same department in the same period? Under what circumstances would they be the same?

10. What is the basic information reported in a production cost report?

11. Less effort is required to operate a job cost system than a process cost system. Do you agree or disagree? Explain.

EXERCISES

E–1

Compute job costs; prepare journal entries related to production activities

In September, Hays Company worked only on Job No. 714, completing it on September 30. During the month, the company purchased and used $5,000 of direct materials and incurred $7,500 of direct labor costs. Assuming manufacturing overhead is applied at the rate of 120% of direct labor costs, what is the total cost of Job No. 714? Prepare journal entries to assign the materials, labor, and manufacturing overhead costs to production and to record the transfer of Job No. 714 to finished goods inventory.

E–2

Compute job cost per unit; prepare journal entries to record transfer and sale

As of August 1, Job. No. 210 had already accumulated $7,500 in total costs. During August, Job No. 210 required $10,500 of direct materials and $21,000 of direct labor. Manufacturing overhead is applied to production at the rate of 80% of direct labor costs. Assuming completed Job No. 210 consisted of 800 units, what is the total cost per unit? Give the journal entries necessary to record the transfer of Job No. 210 to finished goods inventory and the ultimate sale of all 800 units at 150% of cost.

E–3

Prepare journal entries related to production; calculate unit cost (job order)

The Gable Company builds desks to fit customers' specifications. It engaged in the following transactions during June:

Transactions:

1. Purchased precut wood for desk tops, $15,000.
2. Wood and other direct materials were issued to production, $10,500.
3. Direct labor costs were $7,500.
4. Manufacturing overhead was assigned to production, $9,000.
5. Job No. 312 was completed and transferred.

Job No. 312 was the only order worked on in June, and it consisted of 5,000 desks. The total cost assigned to Job. No. 312 in May amounted to $6,750.

a. Journalize the transactions listed above.
b. Compute the cost per unit of Job No. 312.

E–4

Compute costs of three jobs

The Flower Company, which uses a job order cost system, engaged in the following activities during December:

1. Three jobs were started: Nos. 122, 123, and 124.
2. Direct materials issued:

   To Job 122 . . $2,500
   Job 123 . . 3,500
   Job 124 . . 2,000

3. Direct labor costs incurred:

   For Job 122 . . . 250 hours @ $7/hour
   Job 123 . . . 375 hours @ $6/hour
   Job 124 . . . 100 hours @ $8.50/hour

4. Assume manufacturing overhead is applied at the rate of $4 per direct labor-hour.

Compute the cost of each job, and give the necessary journal entry to record the transfer of Job No. 123 to Finished Goods Inventory.

E–5

Prepare journal entry for disposition of overhead

S Company estimated its manufacturing overhead for 1987 at $400,000. At the end of 1987, manufacturing overhead was overapplied by $1,500. Give the journal entry required to reflect a practical disposition of the manufacturing overhead balance.

E–6

Prepare journal entries for allocation of overhead

Using the data in Exercise E–5, assume the balance in Manufacturing Overhead is to be allocated to the following accounts in the amounts indicated: Work in Process Inventory, $200; Finished Goods Inventory, $300; and Cost of Goods Sold, $1,000. Give the journal entry to allocate the manufacturing overhead balance to these accounts.

E–7

Calculate equivalent units

In Department C, materials are added at the beginning of the process. The ending inventory in Department C in April, was 20% complete as to conversion costs. There were 600 units in beginning inventory, 7,200 units were started during the month, and 4,800 units were completed and transferred to finished goods inventory. Under the average method, what are the equivalent units of production for materials and conversion costs?

E–8

Calculate cost per equivalent unit; determine costs of units transferred and those reamining in ending inventory

The following cost data relate to Exercise E–7:

	Materials	Conversion	Total
Costs in beginning inventory . . .	$ 8,400	$ 4,200	$12,600
Costs incurred during month . . .	26,700	25,500	52,200
Total costs to be accounted for . .	$35,100	$29,700	$64,800

Compute the cost of goods completed and transferred to finished goods inventory and the cost of the ending work in process inventory.

PROBLEMS, SERIES A

P22–1–A

Compute predetermined overhead rate and total overhead cost of a job

a.   The Lawrence Company has established the following budget for 1987:

	Assembly	Packaging
Manufacturing overhead . .	$500,000	$ 700,000
Direct labor cost	$900,000	$1,100,000
Direct labor-hours	75,000	110,000
Machine-hours	37,500	100,000

Lawrence Company uses predetermined rates to apply manufacturing overhead. These rates are based on machine-hours in assembly and on direct labor costs in packaging.

Required: Compute the predetermined manufacturing overhead rate for each department.

b.   During June, the job cost sheet for Job No. 104 showed the following:

	Assembly	Packaging
Direct materials used . .	$12,000	$12,000
Direct labor cost . . .	$ 9,000	$ 3,750
Direct labor-hours . . .	750	375
Machine-hours	375	250

Required: Using the overhead rates computed in (a), compute the total manufacturing overhead cost of Job No. 104.

P22-2-A

Compute predetermined overhead rate and overhead cost of one job

Stockwell Company uses a job order cost system, applying manufacturing overhead at predetermined rates based on direct labor-hours in Department A and machine-hours in Department B. Budgeted estimates for 1987 are:

	Department A	Department B
Manufacturing overhead . .	$144,000	$192,000
Direct labor cost	$120,000	$132,000
Direct labor-hours	24,000	32,000
Machine-hours	16,000	48,000

Detailed cost records show the following for Job No. 105 which was completed in 1987:

	Department A	Department B
Materials used	$10,000	$500
Direct labor cost . . .	$ 8,000	$600
Direct labor-hours . .	200	100
Machine-hours	50	80

Required: a. Compute the predetermined overhead rates for 1987 for Departments A and B.

b. Compute the amount of manufacturing overhead applied to Job No. 105 in each department.

P22-3-A

Compute predetermined overhead rate and under- or overapplied overhead

Ballard Company applies overhead to production using a predetermined overhead rate based on machine-hours. Budgeted data for 1987 are:

Budgeted machine-hours	50,000
Budgeted manufacturing overhead . .	$290,000

Required: a. Compute the predetermined overhead rate.

b. Assume that in 1987, actual manufacturing overhead amounted to $332,500, and that 61,000 machine-hours were used. Compute the amount of underapplied or overapplied manufacturing overhead for 1987.

P22-4-A

Compute total and per unit costs of three jobs; calculate ending work in process inventory amount

Timothy Corporation employs a job order cost system. Its manufacturing activities in June 1987, its first month of operations, are summarized below:

	Job number		
	101	102	103
Direct materials cost	$18,000	$12,000	$27,000
Direct labor cost	$15,000	$13,500	$18,000
Direct labor-hours	1,500	1,600	2,000
Units produced	300	150	1,500

Manufacturing overhead is applied at a rate of $10.50 per direct labor-hour.
Job Nos. 101 and 102 were completed in June.

Required: a. Compute the amount of manufacturing overhead charged to each job.

b. Compute the total and unit cost of each completed job.

c. Prepare the entry, in general journal form, to record the transfer of completed jobs to finished goods inventory.

d. Compute the balance in the June 30, 1987, Work in Process Inventory account and provide a schedule of the costs charged to each incomplete job to support this balance.

P22–5–A

Compute cost of ending inventories of materials, work in process, and finished goods

The Apollo Company engaged in the following activities during 1987:

Materials purchased $195,000
Factory payroll incurred (all direct, all employees
  paid $5 per hour)   157,500

The following jobs were worked on during 1987:

	Job No. 1	Job No. 2	Job No. 3
Direct materials	$51,000	$39,000	$60,000
Direct labor	75,000	60,000	22,500
Manufacturing overhead (applied at $3.50 per direct labor-hour)	?	?	?

Job No. 1 was completed and sold (at 150% of cost), Job No. 2 was completed but not sold, and Job No. 3 was not completed.

Required: Compute the balance in each inventory account (Materials, Work in Process, and Finished Goods) at December 31, 1987.

P22–6–A

Prepare journal entries in job order system and T-accounts

Judson Company employs a job order cost system. As of January 1, 1987, its records showed the following inventory balances:

Materials $22,500
Work in process   43,000
Finished goods (25,000 units @ $2) . .   50,000

The work in process inventory consisted of two jobs:

Job No.	Materials	Direct labor	Manufacturing overhead	Total
212 . .	$ 7,500	$10,000	$5,000	$22,500
213 . .	8,500	8,000	4,000	20,500
	$16,000	$18,000	$9,000	$43,000

Summarized below are production and sales data for the company for 1987:

1. Materials purchased, $80,000.
2. Factory payroll costs incurred, $170,000.
3. Factory indirect costs incurred (other than indirect labor and indirect materials): depreciation, $5,000; heat, light, and power, $2,000; and miscellaneous, $3,000.
4. Materials requisitioned: direct materials for Job No. 212, $13,000; for Job No. 213, $24,000; and for Job No. 214, $40,000; supplies (indirect materials) requisitioned, $2,000.
5. Factory payroll distributed: direct labor to Job No. 212, $20,000; to Job No. 213, $40,000; and to Job No. 214, $60,000; indirect labor, $50,000.
6. Manufacturing overhead is assigned to work in process at the same rate per dollar of direct labor cost as in 1986.
7. Job Nos. 212 and 213 were completed.
8. Sales for the year amounted to $300,000; cost of goods sold, $172,000.

Required:
a. Prepare journal entries to record the above transactions.
b. Prepare all closing entries for which you have information.
c. Set up T-accounts for Materials Inventory, Payroll Summary, Manufacturing Overhead, Work in Process Inventory, Finished Goods Inventory, and Cost of Goods Sold. Post the parts of the entries made in *(a)* and *(b)* that affect these accounts.
d. Show that the total cost charged to incomplete jobs agrees with the balance in the Work in Process Inventory account.

P22-7-A

Prepare production cost report

The following information relates to the Cohn Company:

Units in beginning inventory	2,250
Cost of units in beginning inventory:	
Materials	$22,500
Conversion	$10,500
Units placed in production	60,000
Costs incurred during current period:	
Materials	$133,125
Conversion	$119,910
Units remaining in ending inventory (100% complete as to materials, 50% complete as to conversion) . .	3,750

Required: Prepare a production cost report using the average method.

P 22-8-A

Prepare production cost report

Health Company uses a process cost system to account for the costs incurred in making its single product, a health food called Vita-Myte. This product is processed first in Department A and then in Department B. Materials are added in both departments. Production for May was as follows:

	Department A	Department B
Units started or transferred in	150,000	112,500
Units completed and transferred out	112,500	90,000
Stage of completion of May 31 inventory:		
Materials	100%	80%
Conversion	50%	40%
Direct materials costs	$ 90,000	$ 16,200
Conversion costs	$262,500	$178,200

There was no May 1 inventory in either department.

Required: a.   Prepare a production cost report for Department A for May.
                b.   Prepare a production cost report for Department B for May.

PROBLEMS, SERIES B

P22-1-B

Compute predetermined overhead rate and total cost of a job

a. The John Company has established the following budget for 1987:

	Assembling	Welding
Manufacturing overhead . .	$350,000	$450,000
Direct labor cost	$600,000	$750,000
Direct labor-hours	50,000	75,000
Machine-hours	26,000	75,000

John Company uses predetermined rates to apply manufacturing overhead. These rates are based on machine-hours in assembling and on direct labor costs in welding.

Required: Compute the predetermined overhead rate for each department.

b. During May, the job cost sheet for Job No. 195 showed the following:

	Assembling	Welding
Direct materials used . .	$2,000	$8,000
Direct labor cost	$6,000	$2,500
Direct labor-hours . . .	500	250
Machine-hours	240	150

Required: Using the overhead rates computed in part *(a)*, compute the total cost of Job No. 195.

P22-2-B

Compute three different overhead rates and under- or overapplied manufacturing overhead using each rate; discuss disposition of over- or underapplied overhead

Manning Company intends to start a policy of using a predetermined rate to charge manufacturing overhead to production. Selected actual and budgeted production data and costs for 1987 follow:

	Budgeted	Actual
Manufacturing overhead . .	$300,000	$303,500
Direct labor-hours	37,500	38,000
Machine-hours	30,000	29,500
Units of production	100,000	97,500

Required:

a. Compute three possible rates by which the manufacturing overhead can be applied to production. Also compute the underapplied or overapplied manufacturing overhead for 1987 under each rate.

b. Theoretically, what disposition should be made for financial reporting of the underapplied or overapplied manufacturing overhead in part *(a)?*

P22-3-B

Compute total and per unit costs of four jobs; calculate ending work in process inventory

Carrington Corporation employs a job order cost system. Its manufacturing activities in July 1987, its first month of operation, are summarized below:

	Job number			
	201	202	203	204
Direct materials . .	$12,000	$8,700	$18,900	$9,000
Direct labor cost . .	$ 9,900	$9,000	$12,600	$3,600
Direct labor-hours . .	1,100	1,000	1,400	400
Units produced . .	200	100	1,000	300

Manufacturing overhead is applied at a rate of $3 per direct labor-hour for variable overhead and $4.50 per direct labor-hour for fixed overhead, for a total rate of $7.50 per direct labor-hour.

Job Nos. 201, 202, and 203 were completed in July.

Required:

a. Compute the amount of manufacturing overhead charged to each job.

b. Compute the total and unit cost of each completed job.

c. Prepare the entry, in general journal form, to record the transfer of completed jobs to finished goods inventory.

d. Compute the balance in the July 31, 1987, Work in Process Inventory account and provide a schedule of the costs charged to each incomplete job to support this balance.

P22-4-B

Prepare journal entries for a job order system; calculate cost of work in process inventory

The Newby Company's general ledger showed the following balances as of January 1, 1987:

Materials inventory	$ 75,000
Work in process inventory . .	33,750
Finished goods inventory . .	123,000

The work in process inventory consisted of the following:

Job No. 1858:

Material	$24,750
Labor	3,000
Manufacturing overhead . .	6,000
	$33,750

The following transactions took place in January:

Transactions:

1. Materials purchased on account, $210,000.

2. Materials issued during the month: direct, $150,000; indirect, $25,500. Of the direct materials issued,

$21,000 were assigned to Job No. 1858, with the balance going equally to Job Nos. 1859 and 1860.

3. Gross payroll for January was $112,500; FICA taxes withheld amounted to $6,000; federal income taxes withheld totaled $12,750.
4. The $112,500 payroll consisted of $90,000 of direct labor (one third charged to each job) and $22,500 of indirect labor.
5. Manufacturing overhead is applied at 200% of direct labor cost.
6. Job No. 1858 was completed.

Required: a. Prepare journal entries for the above transactions.
b. Compute the ending balance in Work in Process Inventory.

P22-5-B

Calculate equivalent units, costs per equivalent unit, cost of goods completed, and cost of ending inventory

The following data pertain to a production center of the Rockdale Company:

Work in process inventory, February 1, 5,000 units.

Direct materials	$ 5,250
Direct labor	2,500
Manufacturing overhead (150% of direct labor cost)	3,750
	$11,500

Units started in February	15,000

Costs incurred in February:

Direct materials	$15,150
Direct labor	23,000
Manufacturing overhead applied	?

The ending inventory consisted of 7,500 units (100% complete as to materials, 60% complete as to conversion).

Required: Compute the following:

a. Number of units completed and transferred to finished goods inventory.
b. The equivalent units of production for materials and conversion costs using the average method.
c. Cost per equivalent unit.
d. Cost of units completed and transferred.
e. Cost of ending inventory.

P22-6-B

Prepare production cost report

Vedder Company manufactures a product called Savem and determines product costs using a process cost system. Following are cost and production data for the handle department for the month of June:

	Units	Materials costs	Conversion costs
Inventory, June 1	30,000	$2,685	$ 3,300
Placed in production in June	90,000	8,115	14,340
Inventory, June 30	45,000	?	?

The June 30 inventory was 100% complete as to materials and 20% complete as to conversion.

Required: Prepare a production cost report using the average method.

P22–7–B

Prepare production cost report

Holcomb Company manufactures a product called DOG and determines product costs using a process cost system. Materials costing $11,000 were introduced at the start of processing, and $9,700 of conversion costs were incurred. During the period, 20,000 units of product were started, and 19,000 were completed. At the end of the period, 1,000 units were still in process and were 40% complete as to conversion.

Required: Prepare a production cost report using the average method.

P22–8–B

Prepare production cost report

Lee Drug Company manufactures an ointment for relieving sore muscles. The product is moved through two departments, mixing and bottling. Production and cost data for the bottling department in December follow:

Work in process, December 1 (30,000 pints):
Costs transferred in	$15,000
Materials costs	6,000
Conversion costs	4,000

Costs incurred in December:
Transferred in (90,000 pints) . .	$46,200
Materials costs	19,200
Conversion costs	18,365

All materials are added at the beginning of the bottling process. Ending inventory consists of 22,500 pints, 100% complete as to materials and 40% complete as to conversion.

Required: Prepare a production cost report for December using the average method.

BUSINESS DECISION PROBLEM

Determine how overhead should be applied; give advantages of predetermined rate; justify use of applied overhead

The Ball Manufacturing Company produces one product, an orange industrial dye. The demand for this dye is highly seasonal, and because of this, Ball adjusts its production schedule so that it is in line with demand (the dye is susceptible to spoilage). The president of Ball, Mona LeAnn, has received complaints from the sales department that it is having difficulty in setting a stable price for the dye. The sales department is under orders from Mrs. LeAnn to set prices on the basis of "cost plus 30% of cost." It complains that the cost figures it receives from the production manager vary widely from quarter to quarter, which in turn cause the selling price to fluctuate.

In an attempt to settle the dispute, Mrs. LeAnn calls the production manager, Charlie Serners, into her office for a conference. Mr. Serners reports that he has no choice but to change the cost every quarter, as to do otherwise would mean that a loss would result during periods of low demand. He tells Mrs. LeAnn that she has the numbers to back up this statement and reminds Mrs. LeAnn that figures don't lie. As proof, he offers the following information:

	First quarter	Second quarter	Third quarter	Fourth quarter
Direct materials	$ 90,000	$ 36,000	$ 18,000	$ 72,000
Direct labor	112,500	45,000	22,500	90,000
Variable manufacturing overhead . .	22,500	9,000	4,500	18,000
Fixed manufacturing overhead . . .	150,000	150,000	150,000	150,000
Total	$375,000	$240,000	$195,000	$330,000
Number of gallons to be produced . .	75,000	30,000	15,000	60,000
Cost per gallon	$5.00	$8.00	$13.00	$5.50

Mrs. LeAnn realizes that the root of the problem is manufacturing overhead. Manufacturing overhead costs cannot be reduced enough to make a difference during the periods of low demand. She asks Mr. Serners to find a better way to allocate the manufacturing overhead costs to each gallon of dye produced in order to arrive at a more uniform cost figure per gallon.

Required:
- a. How would you recommend to Mr. Serners that manufacturing overhead costs be assigned to production? How would this differ from his present method?
- b. What benefits would be gained by using your recommended solution?
- c. To justify your recommendation made in *(a)* above, recalculate the per gallon cost of the dye using your recommendation.

BUSINESS SITUATION FOR DISCUSSION

A Look at Accounting for Small Manufacturers*

George F. Hanks and Pamela L. Murphy

A company's profitability depends on its ability to control costs, as well as its ability to generate revenues, a fact that is overlooked by many small companies. Small manufacturing firms face many of the same accounting and control problems as large firms. The smaller the company, however, the less likely it is to possess the in-house expertise and other resources required to deal with those problems and the greater the probability is that the company is losing hard-earned dollars because of a lack of control.

We undertook a study in an effort to provide information that might be helpful to small manufacturing firms by identifying the most serious problem areas and by providing possible measures for correction. Efforts to improve accounting and related controls seem to be especially worthwhile in view of the country's existing economic situation and the resulting cash squeeze for firms of all sizes.

We studied 29 small manufacturing firms with the following specific objectives before us:

1. To evaluate the quality of four particular aspects of the accounting and control system;
2. To determine if any demographic factors, such as size or type of ownership, were related to the quality of the accounting and control systems; and
3. To make specific recommendations to correct areas that we observed to be particularly weak or common to many of the firms.

---

* Reprinted from the April 1984 issue of *Management Accounting* (pp. 40–44). Copyright by the National Association of Accountants.

Targets for Change

Over the past five years, information was gathered on the accounting systems of approximately 75 small manufacturing firms in eastern Indiana. These data were collected by graduate students who conducted on-site studies. From the total, 29 of the firms were selected for this study based on the completeness of the information received by the researchers.

We decided to center our investigation on four key aspects of control that we felt represented the essential features of an adequate manufacturing accounting system. The four were:

1. Cash control,
2. Materials control,
3. Cost accounting, and
4. Performance evaluation

* * * * *

The findings generally indicate that the accounting systems of the small manufacturers in this study are weak in each of the areas investigated. . . . Over half (51.7%) of the firms had very weak or somewhat weak material control systems. Fifty-five percent had weak cash control, while 69% had less than adequate cost accounting systems. Finally, a very large number of the firms (86%) made little or no attempt at measuring the performance of their operations beyond the use of the income statement. We found these overall findings surprisingly dismal.

* * * * *

Cost accounting was another general area in which the companies in the study were deficient. Almost 70% were judged to have inadequate cost accounting systems. A good cost accounting system serves two main purposes for a manufacturing firm: it allows the identification of cost which is necessary for control, and it allows the firm to compare actual costs incurred on work done to costs that were expected to be incurred. Cost accounting systems also are used for valuing work-in-process and finished-goods inventories and the computation of cost-of-goods sold for financial statements, but, from a management point of view, these benefits are secondary.

All of the companies studied were job shops but not all had job cost systems in use. In fact, several made no attempt to keep track of actually incurred cost at all. Undoubtedly, managers of small manufacturing firms often feel that their operations cannot justify the expense of a job cost system. However, an effective job cost system can be very simple using off-the-shelf time tickets and job cost sheets duplicated in-house. Even if only direct materials and direct labor are assigned to jobs, the effort will probably be worthwhile. With this information, management can determine where costs are being incurred, and make comparisons to original estimates (on the bid). This will determine how well the operation was performed and yield feedback information that may be useful in preparing future bids. While this comparison step seems so obvious, few firms actually took that step.

PART
8

Planning, Control, and Decision Making

CHAPTER 23 Control through Standard Costs

LEARNING OBJECTIVES

After studying this chapter, you should be able to:

1. Discuss the concept of a standard cost system, specifically addressing how standards are set and the advantages achieved through their use.
2. Calculate the six variances from standard and prepare journal entries based on that information.
3. Discuss possible reasons for the existence of variances and how the isolation of these variances can support a management by exception philosophy.
4. Discuss theoretical and practical methods for disposing of variances from standard.
5. Discuss standard costs in relation to job order or process cost systems (covered in Appendix).
6. Define and use correctly the new terms in the glossary.

You will recall that the job order and process cost systems discussed in Chapter 22 are based on actual historical cost data. Because these data say little about how efficiently operations were conducted, many companies find it helpful to introduce standard costs into their cost systems. Standard costs can be used in both job order and process cost systems as shown in the Appendix to this chapter.

Standard and actual cost systems differ in that an actual cost system collects **actual** costs for materials, labor, and manufacturing overhead, while a standard cost system gathers both actual costs and **standard** costs for these elements of production. The standard costs flow through the accounting system to determine a standard, or "normal," cost for finished goods inventory. Actual costs incurred during the period are then compared with standard costs to assist management in decision making and to determine whether proper control is being maintained over production costs.

This chapter discusses the nature of standard costs and how to compute the difference between an actual cost and a standard cost, which is called a variance. The variances discussed are: materials variances, labor variances, and overhead variances. As you work with variances you will become aware of how important variances are in controlling costs.

■ STANDARD COSTS

Possibly you have set goals in your own life that you have sought to achieve. These goals could well have been called standards. Periodically, you might measure your actual performance against these standards and analyze the differences. Similarly, management sets goals, such as standard costs, and compares actual costs with these goals to identify possible problems.

Nature of standard costs

A standard cost is a carefully predetermined measure of what a cost **should be** under stated conditions. A standard cost is not merely an estimate of what a cost will be; it represents a goal. If a standard is properly set, achieving it represents a reasonably efficient level of performance.

Standards are set in many ways, but to be of any real value they should be more than mere estimates found by extending historical trends into the future. Usually, engineering studies and time and motion studies are undertaken to determine the amounts of materials, labor, and other services required to produce a product. General economic conditions should also be considered in setting standards because economic conditions affect the cost of materials and other services that must be purchased by a manufacturing company. A standard cost is found for each manufactured unit of product by determining the standard costs of direct materials, direct labor, and manufacturing overhead needed to produce that unit.

Standard direct materials cost per unit is made up of the standard amount of material required to produce that unit multiplied by the standard price of the material. It is extremely important to distinguish between the terms *standard price* and *standard cost*. Standard price usually refers to the price per unit of inputs into the production process. For example, the price per pound of raw materials is a standard price. Standard cost, on the other hand, is the product of the standard quantity of an input required per unit of output times the standard price per unit of that input. For example, if the standard price of cloth is $3 per yard and the standard quantity of material required to produce a dress is 3 yards, then the standard direct materials cost of the dress is $9 (3 yards × $3 per yard). Similarly, the standard direct labor cost per unit for a product is computed as the standard number of hours needed to produce one unit multiplied times the standard labor or wage rate.

The standard manufacturing overhead cost of a unit is determined as follows. First, the expected level of output is determined for the year. This level of output is called the standard level of output. Next, the total budgeted manufacturing overhead cost at the standard level of output is determined. The total budgeted overhead cost includes both fixed and variable components. Total fixed cost is the same at every level of output. Variable overhead varies in direct proportion to the number of units produced. Finally, the standard manufacturing overhead cost per unit is computed by dividing the budgeted manufacturing overhead cost by the standard level of output. The result is an overhead cost (or rate) per unit of output. Sometimes accountants find the standard overhead cost (or rate) per direct labor-hour instead of per unit. To find the cost per unit, merely multiply the direct labor-hours per unit times the standard overhead cost per direct labor-hour. For instance, if the standard overhead cost per direct labor-hour is $5 and the standard number of direct labor-hours is two hours per unit, the standard overhead cost per unit is $10 ($5 × 2 hours).

■ COMPUTING VARIANCES

As stated earlier, standard costs represent **goals.** Standard cost is the amount that a cost should be under a given set of circumstances. The accounting records, however, contain information regarding **actual** costs. The amount by which actual cost differs from standard cost is called a **variance.** A variance is designated as favorable when actual costs are less than standard, and unfavorable when actual costs exceed standard. But it does not automatically follow that favorable and unfavorable variances should be equated with good and bad. As you will see, such an appraisal should only be made after the causes of the variance are known.

The following section explains how to compute the dollar amount of variances, a process called **isolating variances,** using data for the Beta Company. Beta Company manufactures and sells a single product, each unit of which has the following standard costs:

Materials—5 sheets at $6	$30
Direct labor—2 hours at $10	20
Manufacturing overhead—2 direct labor-hours at $5 . .	10
Total standard cost per unit	$60

Additional data regarding the production activities of the company will be presented as needed.

Materials Variances

The standard materials cost of any product is simply the standard **quantity** of materials that should be used multiplied by the **standard price** that should be paid for those materials. Actual costs may differ from standard costs for materials because the **price** paid for the materials and/or the **quantity** of materials used varied from the standard amounts management had set. These two factors are accounted for by isolating two variances for materials—a **price variance** and a **usage variance.**

There are several reasons for isolating two materials variances. First, different individuals may be responsible for each—a purchasing agent for the price variance and a production manager for the usage variance. Second, materials might not be purchased and used in the same period. The variance associated with the purchase should be isolated in the period of purchase, and the variance associated with usage should be isolated in the period of use. As a general rule, the sooner a variance can be isolated, the greater its value in cost control. Finally, it is unlikely that a single materials variance—the difference between the standard cost and the actual cost of the materials used—would be of any real value to management for effective cost control. A single variance would not show management what **caused** the difference, or one variance might simply offset another and make the total difference appear immaterial.

Materials Price Variance.   In a manufacturing company, the standard price for materials meeting certain engineering specifications is usually set by the purchasing and accounting departments. Consideration is given to factors such as market conditions, vendors' quoted prices, and the optimum size of a purchase order when setting a standard price. The materials price variance (MPV) is caused by paying a higher or lower price than the standard price set for materials. Materials price variance (MPV) is the difference between actual price paid (AP) and standard price allowed (SP) multiplied by the actual quantity of materials purchased (AQ). In equation form, the materials price variance is:

$$MPV = (AP - SP) \times AQ \text{ purchased}$$

To illustrate, assume that a new foreign supplier entered the market and the Beta Company was able to purchase 60,000 sheets of material from this supplier at a price of $5.90 each. Since the standard price set by management is $6 per sheet, the materials price variance is computed as:

$$MPV = (AP - SP) \times AQ \text{ purchased}$$
$$MPV = (\$5.90 - \$6.00) \times 60,000$$
$$MPV = \$-0.10 \times 60,000$$
$$MPV = \$-6,000 \text{ (favorable)}$$

The materials price variance of $6,000 is considered favorable since the materials were acquired for a price less than standard. (Why it is expressed as a negative amount will be explained later.) If the actual price had exceeded the standard price, the variance would be unfavorable because more costs would have been incurred than allowed by the standard.

In T-account form, the entry to record the purchase of the materials is:

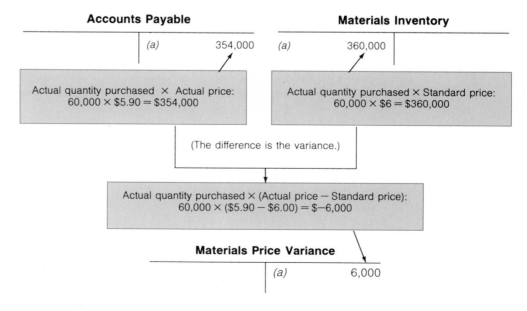

The general journal entry to record the purchase of materials is:

a.   Materials Inventory   360,000
      Materials Price Variance   6,000
      Accounts Payable   354,000
   To record the purchase of materials at less than
standard cost.

Note that the Accounts Payable account shows the actual debt owed to suppliers, while the Materials Inventory account shows the **standard** price of the actual quantity of materials **purchased.** The Materials Price Variance account shows the difference between actual price and standard price multiplied by the actual quantity purchased.

Materials Usage Variance.   Since the standard **quantity** of materials to be used in making a product is largely a matter of physical requirements or product specifications, it is usually set by the engineering department. But if the **quality** of materials used varies with price, the accounting and purchasing departments may take part in special studies to find the "right" quality.

The materials usage variance (MUV) is caused by using more or less than the standard amount of materials to produce a product or complete a process. **The variance shows only differences from standard caused by the quantity of materials used; it does not include any effect of variances in price.** Thus, the materials usage variance (MUV) is equal to actual quantity used (AQ) minus standard quantity allowed (SQ) multiplied by standard price (SP):

$$\text{MUV} = (\text{AQ used} - \text{SQ}) \times \text{SP}$$

To illustrate, assume that the Beta Company used 55,500 sheets of materials to produce 11,000 units of a product for which the standard quantity allowed is 55,000 sheets (5 × 11,000). Since the standard price of the material is $6 per sheet, the materials usage variance of $3,000 would be computed as follows:

$$\text{MUV} = (\text{AQ used} - \text{SQ}) \times \text{SP}$$
$$\text{MUV} = (55,500 - 55,000) \times \$6$$
$$\text{MUV} = 500 \times \$6$$
$$\text{MUV} = \$3,000 \text{ (unfavorable)}$$

The variance is unfavorable because more materials were used than the standard amount allowed to complete the job. If the standard quantity allowed had exceeded the quantity actually used, the materials usage variance would have been favorable.

The following T-accounts record the use of materials:

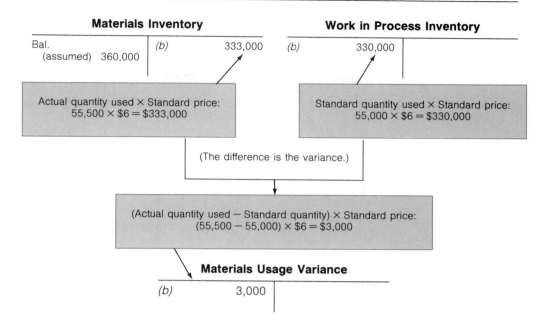

The general journal entry to record the use of materials is:

b. Work in Process Inventory 330,000
    Materials Usage Variance   3,000
      Materials Inventory   333,000
    To record the use of materials and to establish the
    materials usage variance.

The Materials Usage Variance shows the standard cost of the excess materials **used.** Note also that the Work in Process Inventory account contains both standard quantities and standard prices.

The equations for both of the above materials variances were expressed so that positive amounts were unfavorable variances and negative amounts were favorable variances. Unfavorable variances are debits in variance accounts because they add to the costs incurred, which are recorded as debits. Similarly, favorable variances are shown as negative amounts because they are reductions in costs. Thus, favorable variances are recorded in variance accounts as credits. This format will be used in this text, but a word of caution is in order. Far greater understanding is achieved if a variance is determined to be favorable or unfavorable by reliance upon reason or logic. If more materials were used than standard, or if a price greater than standard was paid, the variance is unfavorable. If the reverse is true, the variance is favorable.

Labor Variances

The standard labor cost of any product is equal to the standard quantity of labor time allowed multiplied by the wage rate that should be paid for this time. Here again it follows that the actual labor cost may differ from standard labor cost because of the **wages** paid for **labor,** the **quantity** of labor used, or both. Thus, there are two variances—a rate variance and an efficiency variance.

Labor Rate Variance. The **labor rate variance (LRV)** is caused by paying a higher or lower rate of pay than standard to produce a product or complete a process. The labor rate variance is similar to the materials price variance.

The labor rate variance (LRV) is computed by multiplying the difference between the actual direct labor-hour rate paid (AR) and the standard direct labor-hour rate allowed (SR) by the actual hours of direct labor services required (AH):

$$LRV = (AR - SR) \times AH$$

To continue the Beta Company example, assume that the direct labor payroll of the company consisted of 22,200 hours at a total cost of $233,100 (an average actual hourly rate of $10.50). Since management has set a standard direct labor-hour rate of $10 per hour, the labor rate variance is:

$$LRV = (AR - SR) \times AH$$
$$LRV = (\$10.50 - \$10.00) \times 22,200$$
$$LRV = \$0.50 \times 22,200$$
$$LRV = \$11,100 \text{ (unfavorable)}$$

The variance is positive and unfavorable because the actual rate paid exceeded the standard rate allowed. If the reverse were true, the variance would be favorable.

Labor Efficiency Variance. The standard amount of direct labor time (hours or minutes) needed to complete a product is usually set by the company's engineering department. The direct labor time standard may be based on time and motion studies, or it may be the subject of bargaining with the employees' union. The **labor efficiency variance (LEV)** is caused by using more or less than the standard amount of direct labor-hours to produce a product or complete a process. The labor efficiency variance is similar to the materials usage variance.

The labor efficiency variance (LEV) is computed by multiplying the difference between the actual direct labor-hours required (AH) and the standard direct labor-hours allowed (SH) by the standard direct labor-hour rate per hour (SR):

$$LEV = (AH - SH) \times SR$$

To illustrate, assume that the 22,200 hours of direct labor time worked by Beta Company employees resulted in 11,000 units of production. These 11,000 units have a standard direct labor time of 22,000 hours (11,000 units at 2 hours per unit). Since the standard direct labor rate is $10 per hour, the labor efficiency variance is $2,000, computed as follows:

$$LEV = (AH - SH) \times SR$$
$$LEV = (22,200 - 22,000) \times \$10$$
$$LEV = 200 \times \$10$$
$$LEV = \$2,000 \text{ (unfavorable)}$$

The variance is unfavorable since more hours than standard were required to complete the period's production. If the reverse were true, the variance would be favorable.

Illustration 23.1 shows the relationship between standard and actual direct labor cost and the computation of the labor variances; it is based on the following data relating to the Beta Company:

Standard direct labor time per unit	2 hours
Equivalent units produced in period	11,000 units
Standard labor rate per direct labor-hour	$10
Total direct labor wages paid (at average rate of $10.50 per hour) . .	$233,100
Actual direct labor hours worked	22,200 hours

The standard direct labor time allowed for the period's output is 22,000 hours (11,000 units at 2 hours per unit). The standard direct labor cost is $10 per hour; therefore, the standard direct labor cost for the output achieved is $220,000. The $220,000 is the amount of direct labor costs that will be assigned to inventory, regardless of the actual direct labor cost.

Illustration 23.1

Computation of Labor Variance

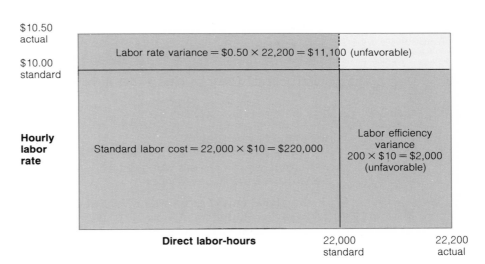

The unfavorable labor rate variance is the above-standard wages paid ($10.50 − $10.00 = $0.50 per hour) times the actual direct labor-hours worked (22,200), or $11,100. Note that the labor rate variance includes the above-standard wages paid on the 200 extra (above-standard) direct labor-hours used to secure the production—the lightly shaded area in the upper right-hand corner of Illustration 23.1. This variation from standard is actually caused by both extra hours and above-standard wages. But, as shown, it is included in the labor rate variance. The labor efficiency variance is the standard cost of the extra hours of direct labor required [(22,200 − 22,000) × $10 = $2,000]. This variance is unfavorable because more hours of direct labor were used than are allowed by the standard.

The charging of Work in Process Inventory with direct labor cost and the recording of the two labor variances for the Beta Company is shown in the T-accounts below.

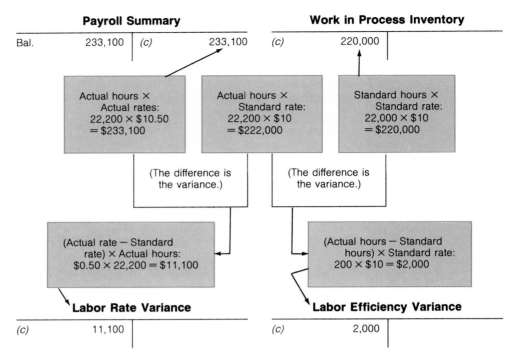

The general journal entry to charge the direct labor cost to work in process is:

c. Work in Process Inventory 220,000
    Labor Rate Variance 11,100
    Labor Efficiency Variance 2,000
        Payroll Summary   233,100
        To charge work in process with direct labor and to
        establish the two labor variances.

With the above entry, gross wages earned by direct-production employees ($233,100) are distributed as follows: $220,000 (the standard labor cost of production) to Work in Process Inventory and the balance to the two labor variance accounts. The unfavorable labor rate variance is not necessarily caused by paying employees more wages than they are entitled to receive. A more probable reason is either that more highly skilled employees (with higher wage rates) worked on production than originally anticipated, or that employee wage rates increased after the standard was developed and the standard was not revised. Favorable rate variances, on the other hand, could be caused by using less skilled (cheaper) labor in the production process. Typically, the hours of labor employed are more likely to be under management's control than the rates that are paid. For this reason, labor efficiency variances are generally watched more closely than labor rate variances.

Summary of Labor Variances.   The accuracy of the two labor variances can be checked by comparing their sum with the difference between actual and standard labor cost for a period. In the Beta Company illustration, this difference was:

Actual labor cost incurred (22,200 hours × $10.50) . $233,100
Standard labor cost allowed (22,000 hours × $10) . .   220,000
Total labor variance (unfavorable) . . . . $ 13,100

This $13,100 is made up of two labor variances, both unfavorable:

Labor efficiency variance (200 × $10) . . $ 2,000
Labor rate variance (22,200 × $0.50) . .   11,100
Total labor variance (unfavorable) . . . $ 13,100

Overhead Variances

In a standard cost system, manufacturing overhead is applied to the goods produced by means of a standard overhead rate. The rate is set prior to the start of the period by dividing the budgeted manufacturing overhead cost by a standard level of output or activity. Total budgeted manufacturing overhead will vary at different levels of standard output, but, since some overhead costs are fixed, total budgeted manufacturing overhead will not vary in direct proportion with output.

A flexible budget is used in isolating overhead variances and may be used in setting the standard overhead rate. A flexible budget shows the budgeted amount of manufacturing overhead for various levels of output.

The flexible budget for the Beta Company for the period is shown in Illustration 23.2. Note that it shows the variable and fixed manufacturing overhead costs expected to be incurred at three levels of activity: 90%, 100%, and 110% of capacity. For product costing purposes, the expected level of activity must be estimated in advance and a rate set based on that level. **The level chosen is called the standard volume of output.** This standard volume of output (or activity) may be expressed in terms of any of the activity bases that can be used in setting overhead rates. These activity bases include percent of capacity, units of output, and direct labor-hours, among others. In our example, standard volume is assumed to be 100% of capacity. At this level of operation, 10,000 units are expected to be produced and 20,000 direct labor-hours of services are expected to be used. Assume that Beta Company applies manufacturing overhead using a rate based on direct labor-hours. According to the flexible manufacturing overhead budget, the expected manufacturing overhead cost

Illustration 23.2

Flexible Manufacturing Overhead Budget

BETA COMPANY Flexible Manufacturing Overhead Budget			
Percent of capacity	90%	100%	110%
Direct labor-hours	18,000	20,000	22,000
Units of output	9,000	10,000	11,000
Variable overhead:			
Indirect materials	$ 7,200	$ 8,000	$ 8,800
Power	9,000	10,000	11,000
Royalties	1,800	2,000	2,200
Other	18,000	20,000	22,000
Total variable overhead	$36,000	$ 40,000	$ 44,000
Fixed overhead:			
Insurance	$ 4,000	$ 4,000	$ 4,000
Property taxes	6,000	6,000	6,000
Depreciation	20,000	20,000	20,000
Other	30,000	30,000	30,000
Total fixed overhead	$60,000	$ 60,000	$ 60,000
Total manufacturing overhead	$96,000	$100,000	$104,000
Standard overhead rate ($100,000 ÷ 20,000 hours) . .		$5	

at the standard volume (20,000 direct labor-hours) is $100,000, so the standard overhead rate is $5 per direct labor-hour ($100,000 ÷ 20,000 direct labor-hours).

Knowing the separate rates for variable and fixed overhead is sometimes useful. The variable overhead rate is $2 ($40,000 ÷ 20,000 hours) per hour, and the fixed overhead rate is $3 ($60,000 ÷ 20,000 hours) per hour. If the expected volume had been 18,000 direct labor-hours (90% of capacity), the standard overhead rate would have been $5.33 ($96,000 ÷ 18,000 hours). If the standard volume had been 22,000 direct labor-hours (110% of capacity), the standard overhead rate would have been $4.73 ($104,000 ÷ 22,000 hours). Note that the difference in rates is due solely to dividing fixed overhead by a different number of units. That is, the variable overhead cost per unit stays constant ($2 per direct labor-hour) regardless of the number of units expected to be produced, and only the fixed overhead cost per unit changes.

Continuing with the Beta Company illustration, assume that the company incurred $108,000 of actual manufacturing overhead costs in a period during which 11,000 units of product were produced. The actual costs would be debited to Manufacturing Overhead and credited to a variety of accounts such as Accounts Payable, Accumulated Depreciation, Prepaid Insurance, Accrued Property Taxes Payable, and so on. According to the flexible budget, the standard number of direct labor-hours allowed for 11,000 units of production is 22,000 hours. Therefore, $110,000 of manufacturing overhead is applied to production ($5 per direct labor-hour times 22,000 hours) by debiting Work in Process Inventory and crediting Manufacturing Overhead for $110,000.

The entry, in T-account form, to record the application of $110,000 of manufacturing overhead to production (22,000 hours at $5 per hour) would be:

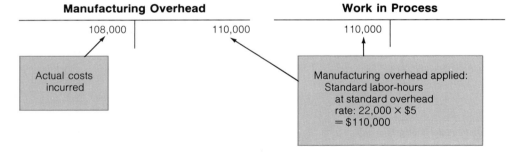

The general journal entry to apply manufacturing overhead to production would be:

Work in Process   110,000
        Manufacturing Overhead   110,000
    To apply manufacturing overhead to production (22,000
    hours at $5 per hour).

The above accounts show that manufacturing overhead has been overapplied to production by the $2,000 credit balance in the Manufacturing Overhead account. Manufacturing overhead will tend to be overapplied when actual production is greater than standard production.

The rate of $5 (which was based on output of 10,000 units) was used to apply manufacturing overhead when actual output was 11,000 units. The $5 is a **predetermined** rate set at the beginning of the year, when management **expected** to produce 10,000 units. Actual production achieved is not known until year-end.

Although various complex computations can be made for overhead variances, a simple approach will be used in this text. In this approach, known as the two-variance approach to overhead variances, only two variances are calculated—an overhead budget variance and an overhead volume variance.

The Overhead Budget Variance.   The overhead budget variance (OBV) (also called the spending or controllable variance) shows in one amount how economically overhead services were purchased and how efficiently they were used. This overhead variance is similar to a combined price and usage variance for materials or labor. The overhead budget variance (OBV) is equal to the difference between total actual overhead costs (Actual OH) and total budgeted overhead costs (BOH) for the **actual output attained.**

Total budgeted overhead costs are calculated as the variable overhead rate times the **standard direct labor-hours allowed for production achieved,** plus the constant amount of fixed overhead. For the Beta Company, this would be $2 variable overhead times 22,000 hours (11,000 units × 2 hours per unit), or $44,000 variable overhead plus $60,000 of fixed overhead—a total of $104,000. Since the total actual overhead was $108,000 and the total budgeted overhead was $104,000, then the overhead budget variance is computed as follows:

$$OBV = Actual\ OH - BOH$$
$$OBV = \$108,000 - \$104,000$$
$$OBV = \$4,000\ (unfavorable)$$

The variance is unfavorable because actual overhead costs were $108,000, while, according to the flexible budget, they should have been $104,000.

Overhead Volume Variance.   The overhead volume variance (OVV) is caused by producing at a level other than that used in setting the standard overhead application rate. The OVV shows whether plant assets produced more or fewer goods than expected. Because fixed overhead is not constant on a per unit basis, any deviation from planned production will cause the overhead application rate to be incorrect. The OVV is the difference between the budgeted amount of overhead for the **actual volume achieved** (BOH) and the applied overhead (Applied OH):

$$OVV = BOH - Applied\ OH$$

In the Beta Company illustration, the 11,000 units produced in the period have a standard labor allowance of 22,000 hours. Budgeted overhead was calculated when we computed the overhead budget variance. The flexible budget in Illustration 23.2 shows that the budgeted overhead for 22,000 direct labor-hours is $104,000. Overhead is applied to work in process on the basis of standard hours allowed for a particular amount of production, in this case 22,000 hours at $5 per hour. The overhead volume variance then is:

$$OVV = BOH - Applied\ OH$$
$$OVV = \$104,000 - \$110,000$$
$$OVV = \$-6,000\ (favorable)$$

Note that the amount of the overhead volume variance is related solely to fixed overhead. As Illustration 23.2 shows, fixed overhead at all levels of activity is $60,000. Since Beta Company used 100% of capacity, or 20,000 direct labor-hours, as its standard, the fixed overhead rate is $3 per direct labor-hour. Beta worked 2,000 (22,000 − 20,000) more standard hours than was expected. The overhead volume variance can also be calculated as follows:

$$\left(\begin{matrix} \text{Number of hours} \\ \text{used in setting} \\ \text{predetermined} \\ \text{overhead rates} \end{matrix} - \begin{matrix} \text{Number of standard} \\ \text{hours allowed} \\ \text{for production} \\ \text{level achieved} \end{matrix}\right) \times \begin{matrix} \text{Fixed over-} \\ \text{head rate} \\ \text{per hour} \end{matrix} = \begin{matrix} \text{Overhead} \\ \text{volume} \\ \text{variance} \end{matrix}$$

$$(20,000 \quad - \quad 22,000) \quad \times \quad \$3 \quad = \quad \$-6,000$$
(favorable)

The variance is favorable since the company achieved a higher level of production than was expected.

Recording Overhead Variances. Formal entries are made in the accounts showing the two parts of the $2,000 net overhead variance. The T-account entry for the Beta Company would be as follows (the debits and credits are keyed with the letter [*f*]):

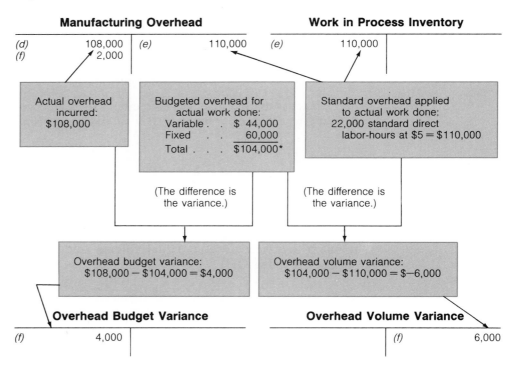

* From flexible budget. See Illustration 23.2.

The general journal entries related to overhead are as follows:

d. Manufacturing Overhead 108,000
      Various Accounts 108,000
    To record actual manufacturing overhead.

e. Work in Process   110,000
          Manufacturing Overhead   110,000
      To record the application of manufacturing overhead
      to work in process.

f. Manufacturing Overhead   2,000
    Overhead Budget Variance   4,000
          Overhead Volume Variance   6,000
      To record the variances related to overhead and close
      the Manufacturing Overhead account.

The first entry records the actual manufacturing overhead costs incurred during the period by Beta Company. The second entry applies manufacturing overhead to Work in Process at the rate of $5 per standard direct labor-hour (22,000). The final entry reduces the Manufacturing Overhead account balance to zero and recognizes the two variances calculated for overhead; these two variance accounts analyze the causes of the overapplied manufacturing overhead for the period.

Summary of Overhead Variances.   The accuracy of the two overhead variances can be easily determined by comparing the sum of the budget and volume variances with the difference between the costs of actual manufacturing overhead and applied manufacturing overhead (the amount of over- or underapplied overhead). For the Beta Company example, the difference between actual and applied manufacturing overhead was:

Actual manufacturing overhead incurred $108,000
Applied manufacturing overhead allowed (22,000 direct labor-hours
   × $5 per hour)   110,000
Total overhead variance (favorable) . . . . $ −2,000

This difference is made up of the two overhead variances:

Overhead budget variance—Unfavorable ($108,000 − $104,000) . . . . $ 4,000
Overhead volume variance—Favorable [$104,000 − (22,000 × $5)] . . .   −6,000
Total overhead variance (favorable) . . . . $−2,000

■ GOODS COMPLETED AND SOLD

To complete the standard cost system example using the Beta Company, assume that 11,000 units were completed and transferred to finished goods, 10,000 units were sold on account at a price equal to 160% of standard cost, there was no beginning or ending work in process inventory, and there was no finished goods beginning inventory. In the T-accounts below, entry *(g)* shows the transfer of the standard cost of the units completed, $660,000 (11,000 × $60), from Work in Process Inventory to Finished Goods Inventory. Entry *(h)* records the sales for the period, $960,000 (160% × $60 × 10,000). Entry *(i)* records the cost of goods sold, $600,000 (10,000 × $60).

Work in Process Inventory

(b) Materials	330,000	(g) Completed 660,000
(c) Labor	220,000	
(e) Manufacturing overhead	110,000	

Finished Goods Inventory

(g) Completed	660,000	(i) Sold 600,000

Accounts Receivable

(h)	960,000

Cost of Goods Sold

(i) Sold	600,000

Sales

	(h) 960,000

In journal entry form, entries *(g)*, *(h)*, and *(i)* are:

g. Finished Goods Inventory 660,000
   Work in Process Inventory 660,000
   To record the transfer of completed units to finished
   goods inventory.

h. Accounts Receivable 960,000
   Sales 960,000
   To record sales for the period.

i. Cost of Goods Sold 600,000
   Merchandise Inventory 600,000
   To record cost of goods sold for the period.

Work in Process Inventory has been debited with the standard cost of materials, labor, and manufacturing overhead for units put into production. Therefore, the entry recording the transfer of the standard cost of the completed units, $660,000 (11,000 × $60), reduces Work in Process Inventory to a zero balance. Note that Finished Goods Inventory is debited with the standard cost of goods completed and credited with the standard cost of goods sold. Thus, ending finished goods inventory consists of the units actually on hand (1,000) at their standard cost of $60 each, or $60,000. Sales for the period amount to 10,000 units at $96 each (160% of $60). It is fairly common practice to base selling prices at least partially on standard costs.

■ INVESTIGATING VARIANCES FROM STANDARD

Once all variances have been computed, management must decide which ones should be investigated further. Since numerous variances will occur, not all of them can be investigated. Management needs some selection guides. Possible guides include the (1) amount of the variance; (2) size of the variance relative to cost incurred; and (3) controllability of the cost associated with the variance—that is, whether it is considered controllable or noncontrollable. Statistical analysis may also be used in deciding which variances to investigate. For instance, the average value of actual costs could be determined for a period of time so that only those variances deviating from the average by more than a certain amount or percentage would be investigated. To decide which selection guides are most useful, management should seek the opinions of knowledgeable operating personnel.

Any analysis of variances is likely to disclose some variances that are controllable within the company and others that are not. For instance, quantities used are generally controllable internally. Prices paid for materials purchased may or may not be controllable. Management may discover that the purchasing agent is not getting competitive bids; therefore, the price paid for materials would have been controllable by seeking competitive bids. On the other hand, a raw materials shortage may exist which drives the price upward, and the price paid is beyond the buyer's control.

Another point to remember about the analysis of variances is that separate variances are not necessarily independent. For example, an unfavorable labor rate variance may result from using higher paid employees in a certain task. However, higher paid employees may be more productive, resulting in a favorable labor efficiency variance. These employees may also be more highly skilled and may waste less material, resulting in a favorable materials usage variance. Therefore, significant variances, both favorable and unfavorable, should be investigated.

■ DISPOSING OF VARIANCES FROM STANDARD

At the end of the year, variances from standard must be disposed of in the accounting records. The variances may be (1) viewed as losses due to inefficiency and closed to Income Summary; (2) allocated as adjustments to the recorded cost of Work in Process Inventory, Finished Goods Inventory, and Cost of Goods Sold; or (3) closed to Cost of Goods Sold. Theoretically, the alternative chosen should depend upon whether the standards set were reasonably attainable and whether the variances were controllable by company employees. For instance, an unfavorable materials usage or labor efficiency variance caused by carelessness or inefficiency may be considered a loss and closed to Income Summary because the standard was attainable and the variance was controllable. An unfavorable materials price variance caused by an unexpected price change may be considered an added cost and allocated to the inventory accounts and Cost of Goods Sold because the standard was unattainable and the variance was uncontrollable. As a practical matter, and especially if they are small, variances are usually closed to the Cost of Goods Sold account rather than allocated to the inventory accounts and to cost of goods sold.

Entry (j) in the T-accounts below reflects this practical disposition of the variances in the continuing example of the Beta Company:

Materials Price Variance				Materials Usage Variance				Labor Rate Variance			
(j)	6,000	(a)	6,000	(b)	3,000	(j)	3,000	(c)	11,100	(j)	11,100

Labor Efficiency Variance				Overhead Budget Variance				Overhead Volume Variance			
(c)	2,000	(j)	2,000	(f)	4,000	(j)	4,000	(j)	6,000	(f)	6,000

Cost of Goods Sold		
(i)	600,000	
(j)	8,100	

In general journal entry form, entry (j) is

j.	Materials Price Variance	. . . .	6,000	
	Overhead Volume Variance	. . . .	6,000	
	Cost of Goods Sold	. . . .	8,100	
	Materials Usage Variance	. . . .		3,000
	Labor Rate Variance	. . . .		11,100
	Labor Efficiency Variance	. . . .		2,000
	Overhead Budget Variance	. . . .		4,000

To close the variance accounts.

Variances are not reported separately in financial statements released to the public, but are simply included in the reported cost of goods sold amount. In reports prepared for internal use, the variances may be listed separately after cost of goods sold is shown at standard cost.

■ ADVANTAGES OF USING STANDARD COSTS

A number of benefits result from the use of a standard cost system. These include:

1. Improved cost control.
2. More useful information for managerial planning and decision making.
3. More reasonable inventory measurements.
4. Cost savings in record-keeping.
5. Possible reductions in production costs incurred.

Improved Cost Control. Cost control is gained mainly by setting standards for each type of cost incurred and then highlighting **exceptions,** or variances—instances where things are not going as planned. Variances provide a starting point for judging the effectiveness of managers in controlling the costs for which they are held responsible.

Assume, for example, that in a certain production center, actual direct materials cost was $52,015 and exceeded standard cost by $6,015. Knowing that actual direct materials cost exceeded standard cost by $6,015 is more useful than merely knowing actual direct materials cost amounted to $52,015. Now the cause of the excess of actual cost over standard cost can be investigated and action can be taken. Further investigation will show whether the exception was caused by factors under management's control. The exception (variance) may be caused by inefficient use of materials, or it may be the result of higher prices due to inflation. In either case, the standard cost system has served as an early warning system by highlighting a potential hazard for management.

More Useful Information for Managerial Planning and Decision Making. When management develops appropriate cost standards and succeeds in controlling production costs, then future actual costs should be fairly close to standard. As a result, standard costs can be used in preparing more accurate budgets and in estimating costs for bidding on jobs. A standard cost system can be valuable in top management planning and decision making.

More Reasonable Inventory Measurements. A standard cost system provides a more logical inventory valuation than an actual cost system. Unit costs for batches of identical products may differ widely under an actual cost system. This difference may be caused by a machine malfunction during the production of a given batch that resulted in more labor and overhead being charged to that batch. Under a standard cost system such costs would not be included in inventory. Rather, they would be charged to variance accounts after comparing actual costs to standard costs. Thus, in a standard cost system, all units of a given product are carried in inventory at the same unit cost. Logically, identical physical units produced in a given time period should be recorded at the same cost.

Cost Savings in Record-Keeping. Although a standard cost system may seem to require more detailed record-keeping than an actual cost system, the reverse is true. For example, in a job order system, detailed records must be kept of various types of materials used on each job as well as the various types and quantities of labor services received. In a standard cost system, standard cost sheets may be printed in advance showing quantities, unit costs, and total costs for the materials, labor, and overhead needed to produce a given amount of a certain product.

Possible Reductions in Production Costs Incurred. A standard cost system may lead to cost savings. The use of standard costs may cause employees to become more cost conscious and thus seek improved methods of completing their tasks. Only when employees become active in reducing costs can companies really become successful in cost control.

■ SUMMARY

A standard cost system gathers information about manufacturing costs incurred and the efficiency of manufacturing operations during the accounting period. A standard cost system can be used in both job order and process cost systems.

Standard costs are carefully predetermined measures of what costs should be under stated conditions. For each type of product manufactured, standard costs are established for **direct materials, direct labor,** and **manufacturing overhead.** The standard cost for each product unit produced is the sum of its standard direct materials cost, standard direct labor cost, and standard manufacturing overhead cost.

The amount by which the actual cost of a product unit differs from the standard cost of the unit is an exception or variance. A standard cost system highlights these variances. Six different types of variances are normally computed: materials price variance, materials usage variance, labor rate variance, labor efficiency variance, overhead budget variance, and overhead volume variance. Once variances are computed, management must decide which variances should be investigated further to determine the underlying causes of the variances.

Three inventory accounts—Materials Inventory, Work in Process Inventory, and Finished Goods Inventory—are carried at standard cost. Variances from standard are recorded separately in the respective variance accounts. At the end of the accounting period, variances must be disposed of in the accounting records. The variances may be (1) considered as losses due to inefficiency and closed to Income Summary; (2) allocated as adjustments to the recorded cost of Work in Process Inventory, Finished Goods Inventory, and Cost of Goods Sold; or (3) closed to Cost of Goods Sold. Theoretically, the alternative chosen by management to dispose of the variances should depend on whether the standards set were reasonably attainable and whether the variances were controllable by company employees. In actual practice, variances are usually closed to Cost of Goods Sold.

By using standard costs to control actual costs, management assumes responsibility for reducing the production costs of its products. In Chapter 24, you will learn about responsibility accounting in a broader sense. Many successful companies rely on responsibility accounting to make their business operations profitable.

APPENDIX: APPLYING STANDARD COSTS IN JOB ORDER AND PROCESS COST SYSTEMS

■ STANDARD COSTS IN A JOB ORDER COST SYSTEM

In a job order cost system, production quantities are known in advance. Thus, some variances can be isolated much earlier than in a process cost system (in which equivalent production is known only at the end of a period). This early isolation of variances is illustrated in the following example.

Assume that Company A accounts for the manufacture of its products in a job order cost system using standard costs. Its flexible budget shows that at the standard level of output, variable overhead is $24,000 and fixed overhead is $16,000 per month. At the standard activity level of 8,000 direct labor-hours, these figures yield a standard overhead rate of $5 per direct labor-hour. The variable portion of this rate is $3 ($24,000 ÷ 8,000 hours), and the fixed portion is $2 ($16,000 ÷ 8,000 hours).

Company A had no work in process inventory as of June 1. The standard specifications for the two jobs started during June are given below:

	Job 101	Job 102
Direct materials . . .	$20,000	$50,000
Direct labor:		
2,000 hours at $4 . .	8,000	
5,000 hours at $4 . .		20,000
Overhead:		
2,000 hours at $5 . .	10,000	
5,000 hours at $5 . .		25,000
Total standard cost . .	$38,000	$95,000

Company A's activities for June 1987 are summarized as follows:

a. Materials with a standard cost of $79,500 were purchased on account at an actual price of $80,150.

b. Standard direct materials were issued for both jobs. In addition, excess materials were requisitioned: Job No. 101, $400; and Job No. 102, $700.

c. Analysis of the factory payrolls debited to Payroll Summary shows they consisted of $10,000 of indirect labor ($4,000 variable and $6,000 fixed), and 6,000 hours of direct labor (Job No. 101, 1,980 hours and Job No. 102, 4,020 hours) at a cost of $24,600. Job No. 101 was completed.

d. Various overhead costs were incurred: variable, $14,500; and fixed, $10,200.

e. Standard overhead was assigned to production: Job No. 101, $10,000 (2,000 hours at $5 per hour), and Job No. 102, $20,100 (4,020 hours at $5 per hour). Even though Job No. 102 was incomplete at the end of the month, overhead needs to be assigned to it for proper valuation of Work in Process Inventory on the balance sheet.

f. Job No. 101 was completed and transferred to the finished goods storeroom.

g. Sales for the month—all units in Job No. 101 at a total price of $60,000.

The entries to record the above information and isolate the variances follow:

a. Materials Inventory 79,500
   Materials Price Variance 650
      Accounts Payable 80,150
   To record purchase of materials and to isolate materials price variance.

b. Work in Process Inventory 70,000
   Materials Usage Variance 1,100
      Materials Inventory 71,100
   To charge standard materials to production and to charge excess materials requisitioned to a variance account.

c. Work in Process Inventory 24,080
   Manufacturing Overhead 10,000
   Labor Rate Variance 600
      Labor Efficiency Variance 80
      Payroll Summary 34,600
   To distribute labor costs and to isolate labor variances:

   Job No. 101 (2,000 hours at $4) . . . . . . $ 8,000
   Job No. 102 (4,020 hours at $4) 16,080
   Total labor to Work in Process Inventory . . . $24,080

   Labor efficiency variance on Job No. 101: (1,980 actual hours − 2,000 standard hours) × $4 = $−80 (favorable).
   Labor rate variance: ($4.10 actual wage rate − $4.00 standard rate) × 6,000 hours = $600 (unfavorable).

d. Manufacturing Overhead 24,700
      Accounts Payable (and various other accounts) . . . 24,700
    To record incurrence of overhead costs.

e. Work in Process Inventory 30,100
      Manufacturing Overhead 30,100
    To apply standard overhead to production: Job No. 101—
    $10,000 (standard amount, job completed); Job No. 102—
    4,020 hours at $5 = $20,100 (based on standard labor,
    job incomplete).

f. Finished Goods Inventory 38,000
      Work in Process Inventory 38,000
    To record transfer of completed Job No. 101 at standard.

g. Accounts Receivable 60,000
      Sales 60,000
    To record sales for the month.

   Cost of Goods Sold 38,000
      Finished Goods Inventory 38,000
    To record cost of goods sold (Job No. 101, $38,000).

Note that in the above entries the materials and labor variances are isolated rather routinely in the recording process. But the overhead variances must be computed separately at the end of the period, unless standard production for the period is known earlier. For Company A, the overhead variances are computed as follows:

Overhead budget variance:
  Actual overhead (entries [c] and [d] above) $34,700
  Budgeted overhead (from flexible budget)
    (6,020* standard hours at $3 variable
    overhead + $16,000 fixed overhead) 34,060
      Unfavorable overhead budget variance . . . . . $ 640

Overhead volume variance:
  Budgeted overhead [(6,020* hours × $3) + $16,000] . . $34,060
  Standard overhead applied to production
    (6,020* hours at $5) 30,100
      Unfavorable overhead volume variance 3,960
Total unfavorable overhead variance $4,600

* 6,020 hours are used in the calculations because standard hours allowed for Job No. 101 are 2,000 and standard hours allowed this far on Job No. 202 are 4,020 for a total of 6,020 hours.

The following entry isolates the two overhead variances in the accounts:

Overhead Budget Variance 640
Overhead Volume Variance 3,960
    Manufacturing Overhead 4,600
  To set up separate overhead variance accounts.

Note that the credit to Manufacturing Overhead of $4,600 reduces that account to a zero balance (for previous entries to the account, see entries [c], [d], and [e] above), thus proving the accuracy of the computations.

Typically, the overhead variances and the materials and labor variances are summarized in a report prepared periodically for internal management. Such a report could be called a "Summary of Variances from Standard."

■ STANDARD COSTS IN A PROCESS COST SYSTEM

To provide a brief illustration of how standard costs might be incorporated into a process cost system, assume that Company P manufactures a product for which the standard specifications are:

Materials—2 pounds at $2 per pound . .	$4.00
Direct labor—0.5 hours at $4 per hour . .	2.00
Overhead—0.5 hours at $3 per hour . .	1.50
Total standard cost	$7.50

The fixed overhead included in the standard cost is based on a monthly flexible budget that shows budgeted variable overhead of $120,000 and budgeted fixed overhead of $60,000 at a standard activity level of 60,000 standard direct labor-hours. Thus, the variable overhead rate is $2 per direct labor-hour ($120,000 ÷ 60,000 hours), and the fixed overhead rate is $1 per direct labor-hour ($60,000 ÷ 60,000 hours). Since each unit only requires one-half hour to produce, total overhead assignable per unit is $1.50 ($3 per hour × ½ hour).

This example makes one change in the standard cost system illustrated earlier in the chapter: Work in Process will be charged with actual quantities and actual costs rather than standard quantities and standard costs, as shown previously. The variances will be calculated and placed in variance accounts at the end of the month. Alternatively, the materials price variance could be recorded when materials are purchased, and the labor rate variance could be recorded when direct labor is charged to Work in Process Inventory.

The entries to the Work in Process Inventory account for the month of May are summarized below:

Direct materials (180,500 pounds at $2.02)	$364,610
Direct labor (40,100 hours at $3.95)	158,395
Actual fixed overhead	58,700
Actual variable overhead	80,500
Total cost put into production	$662,205
Standard cost of units completed and transferred (70,000 at $7.50)	525,000
Balance, May 31, 1987	$137,205

Production records show that 70,000 units were completed and transferred and that 20,000 units of the product remain in process at the end of the month. These units are complete as to materials and 50% complete as to conversion. From this information, the equivalent production for the period in terms of standard units of product can be computed as follows:

	Materials	Labor and overhead (conversion)
Units started and finished	70,000	70,000
Equivalent units in ending inventory . .	20,000	10,000
Equivalent production	90,000	80,000

We now have enough information to calculate all of the variances presented in the "Summary of Variances from Standard" shown in Illustration 23.3.

Illustration 23.3

Summary of Variances from Standard

COMPANY P
Summary of Variances from Standard
Month Ended May 31, 1987

Materials:
    Price variance (180,500 pounds × $0.02) . . . . $ 3,610
    Usage variance (500 pounds × $2) 1,000

       Total unfavorable materials variance . . . . . . $ 4,610
Labor:
    Rate variance (40,100 hours × $−0.05) . . . . . . $−2,005
    Efficiency variance (100 hours × $4) 400
       Net favorable labor variance . . . .   −1,605
Overhead:
    Budget variance [fixed ($58,700 − $60,000) + variable
       ($80,500 − $80,000*)] . . . . $ −800
    Volume variance ($140,000 − $120,000) 20,000
       Net unfavorable overhead variance   19,200
Total variance from standard for the month $22,205

* (40,000 hours × $2).

Since the actual price paid for materials was $0.02 per pound above standard, the materials price variance is the actual usage of 180,500 pounds multiplied by $0.02. Since the standard materials allowed for 90,000 equivalent units is 180,000 pounds (90,000 × 2), the materials usage variance is $1,000 (500 pounds × $2). Both variances are unfavorable.

The average wage rate paid employees was $0.05 less than standard, resulting in a favorable rate variance of this amount multiplied by actual hours of 40,100. The standard labor-hours allowed for the production of the period (80,000 × 0.5 hours) is 100 hours less than the actual direct labor-hours used. Hence, an unfavorable labor efficiency variance was experienced.

Fixed overhead costs were $1,300 ($58,700 − $60,000) less than their budgeted amount, while variable overhead costs exceeded their **budgeted amount** for the actual production in May by $500 [$80,500 − (40,000 × $2)]. Together, these costs yield a net favorable variance of $800. Because the standard overhead applied to production of $120,000 (40,000 standard direct labor-hours × $3) is less than the budgeted overhead for the month of $140,000 [(40,000 standard direct-labor hours × $2) + $60,000], there is an unfavorable volume variance of $20,000. These variances amount to a net unfavorable overhead variance of $19,200. Added together, the materials, labor, and overhead variances amount to $22,205, the total variance (unfavorable) from standard for the month.

The variances shown in Illustration 23.3 can be formally recorded in the accounts by the following entry, thus removing the month's variances from Work in Process Inventory:

Materials Price Variance 3,610
Materials Usage Variance 1,000
Labor Efficiency Variance 400
Overhead Volume Variance 20,000
    Labor Rate Variance   2,005
    Overhead Budget Variance   800
    Work in Process Inventory   22,205
To set up variances from standard for the month.

Subtracting the $22,205 from the previously given balance of $137,205 in the Work in Process Inventory account leaves a balance of $115,000, which is equal to the standard cost of the ending inventory. The standard cost of the ending inventory can be separately computed as follows:

Direct materials (20,000 units, 100% complete, unit cost $4)	$ 80,000
Direct labor (20,000 units, 50% complete, unit cost $2) . .	20,000
Overhead (20,000 units, 50% complete, unit cost $1.50) . .	15,000
Total standard cost of ending inventory	$115,000

NEW TERMS INTRODUCED IN CHAPTER 23

Flexible budget

A budget that shows the expected amount of overhead for various levels of output; used in isolating overhead variances and setting standard overhead rates (905).

Labor efficiency variance (LEV)

A variance from standard caused by using more or less than the standard amount of direct labor-hours to produce a product or complete a process; computed as (Actual direct labor-hours − Standard direct labor-hours) × Standard rate per hour (902).

Labor rate variance (LRV)

A variance from standard caused by paying a higher or lower average rate of pay than standard to produce a product or complete a process; computed as (Actual rate per hour − Standard rate per direct labor-hour) × Actual direct labor-hours worked (902).

Materials price variance (MPV)

A variance from standard caused by paying a higher or lower price than standard for materials purchased; computed as (Actual price − Standard price) × Actual quantity purchased (899).

Materials usage variance (MUV)

A variance from standard caused by using more or less than the standard amount of materials to produce a product or complete a process; computed as (Actual quantity used − Standard quantity allowed) × Standard price (900).

Overhead budget variance (OBV)

A variance from standard caused by incurring more or less than the standard manufacturing overhead for the actual production volume achieved, as shown by a flexible budget; computed as Actual overhead − Budgeted overhead at actual production volume level (907).

Overhead volume variance (OVV)

A variance from standard caused by producing at a level other than that used in setting the standard overhead rates; computed as Budgeted overhead − Applied overhead (907).

Standard cost

A carefully predetermined measure of what a cost should be under stated conditions (897).

Standard level of output

A carefully predetermined measure of what the expected level of output should be for a specified period of time, usually one year (897).

Variance

A deviation of actual costs from standard costs; may be favorable or unfavorable. That is, actual costs may be less than or more than standard costs. Variances may relate to materials, labor, or manufacturing overhead (898).

DEMONSTRATION PROBLEM

The Baxter Company manufactures children's toys that are all identical. The standard cost of each toy is:

Direct materials:
  Three blocks of wood at $0.20 . . $0.60
  Direct labor (1 hour at $5) 5.00

Overhead:
  Fixed ($18,000 ÷ 60,000 units) . .   0.30
  Variable 0.40
                                    $6.30

The standard overhead rate is based on a volume of 60,000 units per month. In May, 50,000 units were manufactured. Detailed data relative to production are summarized below:

Materials purchased:
  160,000 blocks of wood at $0.22
Materials used:
  152,000 blocks of wood
Direct labor: 49,000 hours at $5.10
Fixed manufacturing overhead: $18,200
Variable manufacturing overhead: $20,350

From the above data, compute the six variances from standard for the month.

Solution to demonstration problem

Materials price variance:
  ($0.22 − $0.20) × 160,000 . . . . . $3,200 (unfavorable)

Materials usage variance:
  (152,000 − 150,000*) × $0.20 . . . .   400 (unfavorable)
      Net materials variance . . . . . . $3,600 (unfavorable)

Labor rate variance:
  ($5.10 − $5.00) × 49,000 . . . . . $4,900 (unfavorable)

Labor efficiency variance:
  (49,000 − 50,000) × $5.00 . . . . .   −5,000 (favorable)
      Total labor variance . . . . .   −100 (favorable)

Overhead budget variance:
  Actual ($18,200 + $20,350) $38,550
  Budgeted [$18,000 + (50,000 ×
    $0.40)]   38,000
      Overhead budget variance . . . . $ 550 (unfavorable)

Overhead volume variance:
  Budgeted − Applied [$38,000 −
    (50,000 × $0.70)] . . . .   3,000 (unfavorable)
      Total overhead variance . . . . .   3,550 (unfavorable)
  Total variance for month . . . . . . $7,050 (unfavorable)

* 50,000 units × 3 blocks per unit.

QUESTIONS

1. Is a standard cost an estimated cost? What is the primary objective of employing standard costs in a cost system? What are some of the other advantages of using standard costs?

2. Describe how the materials price and usage variances would be computed from the following data:

Standard—1 unit of material at $20 per unit.
Purchased—1,200 units of material at $20.25; used—995 units.
Production—1,000 units of finished goods.

3. When might a given company have a substantial favorable materials price variance and a substantial unfavorable materials usage variance?

4. What is the usual cause of a favorable or unfavorable labor rate variance? What other labor variance is isolated in a standard cost system? Of the two variances, which is more likely to be under the control of management? Explain.

5. Identify the type of variance indicated by each situation below and indicate whether it is favorable or unfavorable.

   a. The cutting department of a company during the week ending July 15 cut 12 size-S cogged wheels out of three sheets of 12-inch high-tempered steel. Usually three wheels of such size are cut out of each sheet.

   b. A company purchased and installed an expensive new cutting machine to handle expanding orders. This purchase and the related depreciation had not been anticipated when the overhead rate was set.

   c. Edwards, the band saw operator, was on vacation last week. Lands took his place for the normal 40-hour week. Edwards' wage rate is $5.40 per hour, while Lands's is $5.20 per hour. Production was at capacity last week and the week before.

6. Theoretically, how should an accountant dispose of variances from standard? How does an accountant typically dispose of variances?

7. Why are variances typically isolated as soon as possible?

8. Is it correct to consider favorable variances as always being desirable? Explain.

9. Why is it said that the use of standard costs permits the application of the principle of management by exception?

10. How do standards help in controlling production costs?

EXERCISES

E–1

Compute materials variances

During January, the cutting department completed 1,000 units of a product that had a standard materials cost of 2 square feet per unit at $1.20 per square foot. The actual material purchased consisted of 2,050 square feet at $1.10 per square foot, for a total cost of $2,255. The actual material used this period was 2,020 square feet. Compute the materials price and usage variances, indicating whether each is favorable or unfavorable

E–2

Compute materials variances; comment on possible causes

Hill Company produces a product which has the following standard costs:

Direct materials—4 pounds at $5 per pound . . .	$20
Direct labor—3 hours at $6 per hour	18
Manufacturing overhead—150% of direct labor . .	27
	$65

Hill's purchasing agent took advantage of a special offer from one of its suppliers to purchase 88,000 pounds of material at $4.10 per pound. Assume 11,000 units were produced and 68,200 pounds of material were used. Compute the variances for materials. Comment on the purchasing agent's decision to take the special offer.

E–3

Compute labor variances

Compute the labor variances in the following situation:

Actual direct labor payroll (21,500 hours at $4.50)	$96,750
Standard direct labor allowed per unit, 3.5 hours at $4.80 . .	$ 16.80
Production for month (in units)	5,500

E–4

Compute labor variances for two departments

During September, 150 units of a certain product were produced. This product has a standard direct labor cost of two hours per unit at $4.20 per hour in Department 1 and one hour per unit at $6 per hour in Department 2. Department 1 paid $1,140 for 295 direct labor-hours, and Department 2 incurred a cost of $1,008 for 160 direct labor-hours. Compute the labor variances for each department.

E–5

Compute labor variances; evaluate labor foreman

The Wheat Company manufactures a product which has a standard direct labor cost of two hours per unit at $5 per hour. In producing 6,500 units, the foreman used a different crew than usual, which resulted in a total labor cost of $59,800 for 10,400 hours. Compute the labor variances, and comment on the foreman's decision to use a different crew.

E-6

Compute overhead volume and budget variances

The following data relate to the manufacturing activities of the Warren Company for the first quarter of 1987:

Standard activity (units)	50,000
Actual production (units)	40,000
Budgeted fixed manufacturing overhead	$30,000
Variable overhead rate (per unit)	$4.00
Actual fixed manufacturing overhead	$31,000
Actual variable manufacturing overhead	$74,000

Compute the overhead budget variance and the overhead volume variance.

E-7

Compute overhead volume variance.

Assume that the actual production in Exercise E-4 was 44,000 units rather than 40,000. What was the overhead volume variance?

E-8

Close all variance accounts

The standard cost variance accounts of the Travis Company at the end of its fiscal year had the following balances:

Materials price variance (unfavorable)	$3,750
Materials usage variance (unfavorable) . . .	3,000
Labor rate variance (favorable)	2,250
Labor efficiency variance (unfavorable) . . .	8,250
Overhead budget variance (favorable) . . .	750
Overhead volume variance (unfavorable) . . .	4,500

Set up T-accounts for these variances, and enter the balances given above in the accounts. Then prepare one entry to record the closing of the variance accounts in the most practical manner.

PROBLEMS, SERIES A

P23-1-A

Compute materials variances

A certain product has a standard materials usage and cost of 2 pounds per unit at $7.00 per pound. During the month, 1,100 pounds of material were purchased at $7.30 per pound. Production for the month totaled 500 units requiring 980 pounds of materials.

Required: Compute the materials variances.

P23-2-A

Prepare entries in T-accounts for materials variances

During the month of March, a department completed 5,000 units of a product which has a standard materials usage and cost of 1.2 square feet per unit at $0.39 per square foot. The actual material used consisted of 6,100 square feet at an actual cost of $2,220.40. The actual purchase of this material amounted to 9,000 square feet at a total cost of $3,276.

Required: Using T-accounts, prepare entries *(a)* for the purchase of the materials and *(b)* for the issuance of materials to production.

P23-3-A

Compute labor variances

The C. T. Company makes plastic garbage bags. One box of bags requires 1.5 hours of direct labor at an hourly rate of $6. The company produced 100,000 boxes using 160,000 hours of direct labor at a total cost of $880,000.

Required: Compute the labor variances.

P23-4-A

Compute labor variances; prepare journal entries

The finishing department of the Case Company produced 20,000 units during the month of November. The standard number of direct labor-hours per unit is two hours. The standard rate per hour is $10.50. During the month, 41,000 direct labor-hours were worked at a cost of $461,250.

Required: a. Record the labor data in a journal entry, and post the entry to T-accounts.
b. Record the journal entry to dispose of any variances, and post the entry to the T-accounts.

P23-5-A

Compute overhead variances under two assumptions

The standard amount of output for the Buffalo plant of the XYZ Company is 50,000 units per month. Overhead is applied based on units produced. The flexible budget for the month for manufacturing overhead allows $37,500 for fixed overhead and $1 per unit of output for variable overhead. Actual overhead for the month consisted of $37,800 of fixed overhead with actual variable overhead given below.

Required: Compute the overhead budget variance and the overhead volume variance assuming actual production in units and actual variable overhead in dollars were:

a. 37,500 and $38,000.
b. 55,000 and $56,350.

P23-6-A

Compute overhead variances

The Lerner Company manufactures chalkboards for sale to various high schools and colleges. The expected volume of activity is 37,500 units. Standard direct labor is three hours per unit. At the 37,500 unit level of output, fixed manufacturing overhead is budgeted at $90,000, and variable manufacturing overhead is budgeted at $1.10 per hour. Overhead is applied based on standard direct labor-hours.

In July, 115,500 direct labor-hours were worked to achieve the standard level of output of 37,500 units. Actual manufacturing overhead for July consisted of $94,500 of fixed overhead and $135,000 of variable overhead.

Required: Compute the two overhead variances showing all computations.

P23-7-A

Compute materials, labor, and overhead variances

Based on a standard volume of output of 80,000 units per month, the standard cost of the product manufactured by the Woodward Company consists of:

Direct materials (0.25 pounds)	$1.00
Direct labor (0.5 hours)	3.80
Variable manufacturing overhead	2.50
Fixed manufacturing overhead ($120,000)	1.50
Total	$8.80

A total of 21,000 pounds of materials was purchased at $4.20 per pound. During the month of May, 82,000 units were produced with the following costs:

Direct materials used (20,650 pounds at $4.20) . .	$ 86,730
Direct labor (40,000 hours at $7.80)	312,000
Variable manufacturing overhead	208,000
Fixed manufacturing overhead	121,040

Required: Compute the materials price and usage variances, the labor rate and efficiency variances, and the overhead budget and volume variances (overhead is applied based on units produced).

**P23-8-A
(Based on the Appendix)**

Prepare journal entries under a job order standard cost accounting system; compute overhead variances

The Burch Manufacturing Company employs a job order standard cost accounting system. The standard cost of the material used is $0.80 per square foot, while the standard direct labor cost is $4 per hour. Manufacturing overhead is assigned to jobs at a rate of $3 per standard direct labor-hour. Based upon a standard volume of activity of 90,000 direct labor-hours, the flexible budget allows $90,000 of fixed overhead and $2 of variable overhead per standard direct labor-hour for the month of June 1987.

Work in process is charged with standard quantities and standard prices. On June 1, 1987, one job (No. 201) was in process, with the following standard costs already assigned:

Materials (2,500 square feet) $2,000
Labor (400 direct labor-hours) 1,600
Manufacturing overhead ($3 per standard direct
   labor-hour) 1,200
Total $4,800

When completed, the standard quantities for Job No. 201 are 6,000 square feet of material and 750 hours of direct labor.

During the month of June 1987, the following transactions and events occurred:

Transactions:

1. Purchased 900,000 square feet of material at $0.78 per square foot.
2. Materials issued:

Job No.	Actual quantity (square feet)	Standard quantity (square feet)
201	2,400	2,250
All others	630,000	631,800
	632,400	634,050

3. The direct labor costs and hours for the month were:

Incurred on—	Actual hours	Standard hours	Actual cost
Job No. 201	156	150	$ 651
All other jobs	76,644	76,500	310,449
	76,800	76,650	$311,100

4. The appropriate amount of overhead was assigned to the jobs.
5. Actual overhead incurred during the month was $232,500.
6. Job No. 201 was completed during the month. Other production also completed during the month had a standard cost of $780,000.

Required:
  a. Prepare general journal entries for each of the numbered transactions given above.
  b. Compute the overhead budget variance and the overhead volume variance for the month, and prepare the general journal entry(ies) to record them.

P23-9-A
(Based on the
Appendix)

Prepare journal
entries under a
process standard
cost system;
compute variances

The Swan Company employs a process cost system with standard costs to account for the product it manufactures in a two-step process through Departments I and II. The standard cost of this product in Department I consists of:

Direct materials (10 units at $8) . . . . $ 80
Direct labor (5 hours at $6) 30
Variable manufacturing overhead (5 hours at $4) . . 20
Fixed manufacturing overhead (5 hours at $2) . . 10
                         $ 140

The flexible overhead budget, based on 30,000 direct labor-hours as a standard volume of activity, allows $60,000 of fixed overhead plus $2 per direct labor-hour. Materials price variances are isolated at the time of purchase. Labor rate variances are isolated when direct labor is charged to Work in Process Inventory. Materials usage and labor efficiency variances are isolated at the end of the month when production is known. Standard overhead is assigned to production and overhead variances are isolated at the end of the month when production and actual costs are known.

There was no work in process inventory as of July 1, 1987, in Department I. Summarized data for the month are:

1. Purchased 60,500 units of material for $481,580.
2. Direct materials requisitioned by Department I, 55,290 units.
3. Of the payroll costs for the month, 24,950 direct labor-hours with a total cost of $149,880 are chargeable to Department I.
4. Total manufacturing overhead costs incurred by the department for the month consist of $60,450 of fixed overhead and $100,550 of variable overhead.

5. A total of 4,500 units was completed during the month; 1,000 units remain in process, 100% complete as to materials and 50% complete as to labor and overhead.
6. Manufacturing overhead is assigned to production on the basis of standard direct labor-hours.

Required:
a. Prepare journal entries to record the above summarized data. (In the illustration in the Appendix, all variances were isolated at the end of the period. Use logic to isolate them as required in this problem.)
b. Compute the materials usage variance and the labor efficiency variance, and prepare journal entries to remove them from work in process inventory.
c. Compute the overhead budget variance and the overhead volume variance, and prepare journal entries to record them.
d. Assuming that the variances isolated are for the year ending July 31, 1987, prepare an entry that represents a practical disposition of these variances.

PROBLEMS, SERIES B

P23–1–B

Compute materials labor variances; prepare journal entries

The following data apply to the Traylor Company for the month of April, when 1,320 finished units were produced:

Materials used: 4,320 pounds
Standard materials per finished unit: 3 pounds at $3 per pound
Materials purchased: 6,000 pounds at $3.25 per pound
Direct labor: 2,940 hours at a total cost of $23,520
Standard labor per finished unit: 2 hours at $7.60 per hour

Required
a. Compute the materials and labor variances.
b. Prepare journal entries to record the transactions involving these variances.

P23–2–B

Prepare entries in T-accounts for materials variances

During the month of December, the Glover Company produced 15,000 units of a product called Alpha. Alpha has a standard materials cost of two pieces per unit at $2 per piece. The actual material used consisted of 30,500 pieces at a cost of $57,950. Actual purchases of the materials amounted to 40,000 pieces at a cost of $76,000.

Required:
Using T-accounts, prepare entries for the purchase of materials and the issuance of materials to production.

P23–3–B

Calculate actual labor rate given standards and rate variance

Some of the records of Kirkland Company's repair and maintenance division have been lost in a fire. Salvaged records indicate that actual direct labor-hours for the period were 2,000. The *total* labor variance was $3,000, favorable (the difference between actual hours times actual rate and standard hours times standard rate). The standard labor rate was $7 per direct labor-hour and the labor rate variance was $600, unfavorable.

Required:
Compute the actual direct labor rate per hour.

P23–4–B

Compute labor variances; prepare journal entries

The Entertainment Division of the Stereo Company produced 5,000 stereos during the year ended December 31, 1987. The standard number of direct labor-hours per stereo is 2.5 at a standard rate of $6.75 per hour. During the year, 12,200 direct labor-hours were worked at a cost of $87,840.

Required:
a. Record the labor data in a journal entry, and post the entry to T-accounts.
b. Record the journal entry to dispose of any variances, and post the entry to the T-accounts.

P23–5–B

Compute overhead volume variances under different assumptions

The Felder Company computes its overhead rates based on a standard activity of 37,500 units. Fixed manufacturing overhead for 1987 is budgeted at $30,000. Actual fixed manufacturing overhead for 1987 was $29,000. Overhead is applied based on units produced.

Required: Compute the amount of the overhead volume variance for the year under each of the following assumptions regarding actual output:

a. 22,500 units.
b. 37,500 units.
c. 45,000 units.

P23-6-B

Compute overhead variances

The Video Company manufactures electronic games. The standard production volume is 25,000 direct labor-hours per month for 50,000 units. Fixed manufacturing overhead is budgeted at $250,000, while variable manufacturing overhead is budgeted at $4.40 per direct labor-hour. Overhead is applied based on standard direct labor-hours.

In April, 22,000 direct labor-hours were worked in producing 45,000 units. The actual manufacturing overhead for the month amounted to $238,000 fixed and $92,000 variable.

Required: Compute the two overhead variances showing all calculations.

P23-7-B
(Based on the Appendix)

Prepare journal entries under a process standard cost accounting system; compute variances

The Ceramics Company produces ceramic figurines which, although different in shape and color, are similar enough to be considered one product for standard costing purposes. The standard cost of each figurine consists of:

Direct materials:
   1 pound of clay at $0.60 per pound . . . . $ 0.60
   2 ounces of coloring pigment at $1.875 per ounce . .   3.75
Direct labor (½ hour at $15 per hour) 7.50

Manufacturing overhead:
   Fixed (total budgeted fixed overhead of $31,500
     divided by standard output of 35,000 units)   . . .   0.90 ($1.80 per direct
                                    labor-hour)
   Variable   . . . .   1.20 ($2.40 per direct
                                      labor-hour)

Total $13.95

In March, 25,000 units were manufactured, and 21,000 units were sold. Production data for March follow:

Materials purchased:
  51,000 pounds of clay at $0.585 per pound
  105,000 ounces of pigment at $1.95 per ounce

Materials used:
  23,500 pounds of clay and 48,000 ounces of pigment
Direct labor: 12,000 hours at $15.30
Fixed overhead: $25,200
Variable overhead: $31,875
The total overhead rate is $4.20 per standard direct labor-hour.

Required: Record the above data in journal entries, isolating variances as soon as possible. (In the illustration in the Appendix, all variances were isolated at the end of the period. Use logic to isolate them as required in this problem.)

P23-8-B
(Based on the Appendix)

Prepare journal entries under a job order standard cost accounting system; compute overhead variances

The Brooks Company maintains a job order standard cost accounting system. The standard cost of the plastic material it uses is $4 per pound, while the standard direct labor cost is $6 per hour. Manufacturing overhead is charged to the various jobs at a rate of $4 per standard direct labor-hour. This rate is based on a flexible budget. At a standard volume of activity of 240,000 direct labor-hours, the budget allows $480,000 of budgeted fixed overhead and $2 per standard direct labor-hour for variable overhead. Work in Process Inventory is charged with standard quantities and standard prices. There was no work in process inventory at May 1, 1987.

During May 1987, the following transactions and events occurred:

Transactions:

1. Purchased 240,000 pounds of plastic at $3.92.
2. Started the following jobs during the month:

Job No.	Standard units of material	Standard hours of labor
505	3,000	6,000
506	2,400	4,800
All others . . .	144,600	253,200
	150,000	264,000

3. Materials issued during the month:

Job No.	Pounds
505	3,060
506	2,370
All others	145,770
	151,200

4. Of the direct labor cost charged to Payroll Summary, the following amounts relate to the various jobs:

Job No.	Actual hours	Standard hours	Actual cost
505 . . .	6,120	6,000	$ 36,288
506 . . .	4,896	4,800	28,512
All others . .	220,800	217,200	1,321,680
	231,816	228,000	$1,386,480

5. Appropriate manufacturing overhead was charged to the various jobs.
6. Actual fixed manufacturing overhead incurred, $489,600; actual variable manufacturing overhead incurred, $451,200.
7. Job Nos. 505 and 506 were completed along with other production having a standard cost of $1,896,000

Required:

a. Prepare journal entries to record the above summarized data, isolating variances as soon as possible.
b. Compute the two overhead variances, and prepare the journal entries to record them.
c. Assuming that the variances isolated are for the year ending May 31, 1987, prepare an entry that represents a practical disposition of these variances.

P23–9–B
(Based on the Appendix)

Prepare journal entries under a process standard cost accounting system; compute variances

The Amigo Manufacturing Company manufactures a product by processing it through three successive departments, A, B, and C. A process cost system incorporating standard costs is used. The standard cost of the product in Department A consists of:

Materials (20 pounds at $2.25) . .	$ 45.00
Direct labor (3 hours at $9)	27.00
Fixed manufacturing overhead . . .	22.50
Variable manufacturing overhead . .	18.00
	$112.50

Materials price variances are recorded at the time of purchase with the result that materials are charged to production at actual quantity and standard price. Work in process is charged for actual costs incurred for labor and overhead, and variances are isolated at the end of the period, when production is known. Budgeted manufacturing overhead at the standard volume of output of 25,000 units per month is $562,500 plus $18 per unit completed.

There was no beginning work in process inventory on June 1, 1987, in Department A. Following are summarized data for the month of June for Department A:

1. Materials purchased, 450,000 pounds at $2.34.
2. Materials requisitioned, 440,310 pounds.
3. Of the charges to Payroll Summary, $539,910 represents the cost of 59,940 hours of direct labor received in Department A.
4. Actual overhead costs charged to Work in Process Inventory: fixed, $567,000; and variable, $363,892.50.
5. Units completed and transferred to Department B, 18,000; 4,000 units remain on hand in the department, 100% complete as to materials (which are added only at the beginning of the processing in the department) and 50% complete as to processing.

Required:
a. Prepare journal entries for the above summarized data. (In the illustration in the Appendix, all variances were isolated at the end of the period. Use logic to isolate the materials price variance as required in this problem.)
b. Compute the remaining five variances, and give one journal entry to remove the variances from the Work in Process Inventory—Department A account.
c. Can the overhead volume variance be logically related to the labor efficiency variance? Explain.

BUSINESS DECISION PROBLEM 23–1

Discuss possible causes for variances

Turn to Exercise E–8 in this chapter. For each of the variances listed, give a possible reason for its existence.

BUSINESS DECISION PROBLEM 23–2

Analyze situation where actual costs differ from standard costs; evaluate the two managers involved

Farris Johnson, the president of the Light Company, has a problem. It does not involve substantial dollar amounts but does involve the important question of responsibility for variances from standard costs. He has just received the following report:

Standard materials at standard price for the actual production in May . .	$18,000
Unfavorable materials price variance ($3.60 − $3.00) × 6,900 pounds	4,140
Unfavorable materials usage variance (6,900 pounds − 6,000 pounds) × $3	2,700
Total actual materials costs for the month of May (6,900 pounds at $3.60 per pound)	$24,840

Farris has discussed the unfavorable price variance with Linda Brewer, the purchasing officer. She agrees that under the circumstances she should be held responsible for most of the materials price variance. But she objects to the inclusion of $540 (900 pounds of excess materials used at $0.60 per pound). This, she argues, is the responsibility of the production department. If it had not been so inefficient in the use of materials, she would not have had to purchase the extra 900 pounds. On the other hand, Bob Hardin, the production manager, agrees that he is basically responsible for the excess quantity of materials used. But he does not agree that the above materials usage variance should be revised to include the $540 of unfavorable price variance on the excess materials used. "That's Linda's responsibility," he says.

Farris now turns to you for help. Specifically, he wants you to tell him:

a. Who is responsible for the $540 in dispute?
b. If responsibility cannot be clearly assigned, in which materials variance should the accounting department include the variance? Why?

c. Are there likely to be other circumstances where materials variances cannot be considered the responsibility of the manager most closely involved with them? Explain.

Required: Prepare written answers to the three questions asked by Farris.

BUSINESS SITUATION FOR DISCUSSION

Standard Costing Games that Managers Play*
Richard V. Calvasina and
Eugene J Calvasina

A standard cost system has three basic functions: collecting the actual costs of a manufacturing operation, determining the achievement of that manufacturing operation, and evaluating performance through the reporting of variances from standard. These variances provide managers with the information that directs them to areas that are not performing according to budget. Managers thus may be able, through the use of these data, to keep the cost centers under their control running efficiently and according to goals established during the planning stages.

Sometimes, however, the standards that are set do more to hinder the manager than to help. In the situations or "games" that we describe, the variance reporting, because of the standard set, at best has no value and, worse, actually may provide misinformation to the manager.

The Everlasting Standard Game

The first game we call the "Everlasting Standard." In this situation the company is either relatively small and has no industrial engineering department, or management may be under the mistaken belief that once a standard is set, it is set forever. The standard quantities for material and labor were set when the company first started making the product. Although it may be years later, the company may have revised just the costs for material and labor but not the quantities for material nor the time allotment for labor. Because these standards for material and labor are outdated, the efficiency variances for labor and material are no longer valid, so the managers receiving these reports have probably stopped even looking at them.

*   *   *   *   *

The Unbreakable Schedule Game

This standard costing game is an offshoot of "Everlasting Standard" but occurs over a shorter time span.

In the "Unbreakable Schedule" game, standard costs may be revised only on a set time schedule. It makes no difference what major changes in costs or production techniques may occur between the dates officially scheduled for revising standard cost cards; the cost card in force is the one used to prepare the variance reports for management. Again, as in the first game, the information (variances) presented is, in fact, misinformation. The basis used for calculating the variance, whether it be an efficiency or spending variance, is being compared to a "standard" that no longer reflects the real world.

*   *   *   *   *

The Methods Change Variance Game

In order to alleviate the problem of distorting labor efficiency variances, the "Methods Change Variance" is employed. This variance is calculated to determine the difference between the labor efficiency variance based on the old standard that is still in force and the labor efficiency variance that would have been calculated if the new standard, reflecting the current labor specifications, had been in effect. The need for presenting the second variance to management is apparent. The added cost of preparing two reports that must be combined at some point to reflect the true situation is less evident.

*   *   *   *   *

The Material Mix Game

The Material Mix variance is the materials version of the Methods Change Variance game. In this strategy, a combination of different ingredients is used in the manufacture of a product, and set quantities of each raw material item are specified. Without changing the specified ratio of ingredients in the cost card, management decides to change the amounts that are actually used. When this decision is made, someone usually states, "We are still creating the perfect product." The implication is that although we now have a different proportion of ingredients in our product there is no difference between our original recipe product and the new one. Invariably, the material mix variance resulting from this decision is favorable.

*   *   *   *   *

The All-Encompassing Product Standard

A slightly different version of the Material Mix game is one in which a company makes a multitude of products

* Reprinted from the March 1984 issue of *Management Accounting* (pp. 49–51, 77). Copyright by the National Association of Accountants.

that, based on outward appearances, seem to be identical, but because of different uses, different strengths of the product are needed. In order to obtain the different strengths, the ratio of the ingredients used is altered. In effect, the company makes many different products but employs only one standard product cost. This cost card represents the average of the strengths that are to be made. Based on this one average product cost card, mix and yield variances are calculated. The value of the yield variance is open to question, while a mix variance will result as long as the product strength does not match the strength on the cost card.

*   *   *   *   *

The Full Figure Standard Game

In this game the standard amounts for material, labor, and overhead costs may have been set realistically in the preliminary stages of the standard-setting process, but, somewhere along the line, a little extra is added here and there so that "achievable" standards are established. The sure sign that this game is being played to the hilt is that all variances reported for material, labor, and overhead are favorable. Also, if these "full figure standards" are used to establish selling prices, then the inventories of these overpriced goods increase rapidly.

*   *   *   *   *

The standard cost games we have described illustrate errors in methodology and uses that can creep into a standard cost system. If a standard cost system is to be a useful management tool, then standard costs, which are the foundation of this system, must be established on a current and positive basis and must be a realistic and a valid representation of actual management intentions. Because standards are usually set prior to an upcoming production period, they must reflect management's plans and goals for that future period. To do otherwise will result in mispriced inventories and performance reports and variances that are invalid. Instead of the standard cost system helping management, it will provide misinformation that will make it more difficult for management to control production systems.

CHAPTER 24

Responsibility Accounting; Segmental Analysis

LEARNING OBJECTIVES

After studying this chapter, you should be able to:

1. Discuss the concept of responsibility accounting.
2. Prepare responsibility accounting reports.
3. Prepare a segmental income statement showing the contribution to indirect expenses using the contribution margin format.
4. Determine return on investment, margin, and turnover for a segment.
5. Determine the residual income of a segment.
6. Define and use correctly the new terms in the glossary.

When a business is small, the owner usually oversees many different activities in the business. As a business grows, responsibility for some of these activities must be given to other persons. Obviously, the success of a business depends to a great extent on the persons responsible for these activities.

In this chapter you will learn about delegating authority to lower-level managers for managing various business activities and holding these lower-level managers responsible for the activities under their control. You will also learn how to assess the performance of these managers. The activities in a company are grouped into responsibility centers. The manager in charge of each center is responsible for controlling certain expenses. Sometimes the manager also has some control over revenues. The performance of each manager is measured in terms of the items of revenue and expense over which that manager has control. Various types of responsibility centers are discussed and illustrated. The chapter ends with a discussion of return on investment, which directly relates to the profitability of a company.

▌ RESPONSIBILITY ACCOUNTING

The term **responsibility accounting** refers to an accounting system that collects, summarizes, and reports accounting data relating to the responsibilities of individual managers. A responsibility accounting system provides information to evaluate each manager on revenue and expense items over which that manager has primary control (authority to influence). A responsibility accounting report contains only those items that are controllable by the responsible manager. If, however, both controllable **and uncontrollable** items are included in the report, the categories should be clearly separated. The identification of controllable items is a fundamental task in responsibility accounting and reporting.

To implement responsibility accounting in a company, the business entity must be organized so that responsibility is assignable to individual managers. The various company managers and their lines of authority (and the resulting levels of responsibility) should be fully defined. The organization chart in Illustration 24.1 demonstrates lines of authority and responsibility that could be used as a basis for responsibility reporting. If clear lines of authority and resulting levels of responsibility cannot be determined, it is very doubtful that responsibility accounting can be implemented effectively.

To identify the items over which each manager has control, the lines of authority should follow a specified path. For example, Illustration 24.1 shows that a plant supervisor may report to a plant manager, who reports to a vice president of manufacturing, who reports to the president. The president is ultimately responsible to stockholders or their elected representatives, the board of directors. In a sense, the president is responsible for all revenue and expense items of the company, since at the presidential level all items are controllable over some period of time. The president cannot delegate responsibility so as to avoid personal responsibility. But, the president will usually delegate authority

Illustration 24.1

A Corporate Functional Organization Chart Including Four Levels of Management (illustrates only manufacturing function from level three)

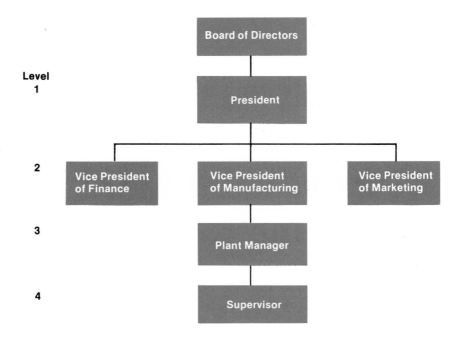

to lower-level managers since the president cannot keep fully informed of the day-to-day operating details of all areas of the business.

The manager's level in the organization also affects identification of the items over which that manager has control. The president is usually considered a first-level manager. Managers who report directly to the president are second-level managers. Notice on the organization chart in Illustration 24.1 that individuals at a specific management level are on a horizontal line across the chart. But not all managers at that level necessarily have equal authority and responsibility. The degree of a manager's authority will vary from company to company.

While the president may delegate much decision-making power, there are some revenue and expense items that will remain exclusively under the president's control. For example, in some companies, large capital (plant and equipment) expenditures may be approved only by the president. Depreciation, property taxes, and other related expenses should not, therefore, be designated as a plant manager's responsibility since these costs are not primarily under that manager's control.

The controllability criterion is crucial to the content of performance reports for each manager. For example, at the supervisor level, perhaps only direct materials and direct labor cost control are appropriate for measuring performance. A plant manager, however, has the authority to make decisions regarding many other costs that are not controllable at the supervisory level (such as salaries of supervisors); these other costs would be included in the performance evaluation of the plant manager, but not the supervisor.

■ THE CONCEPT OF CONTROL

Theoretically, a manager should have absolute control over an item to be held responsible for it. Unfortunately, absolute controllability is rare. Frequently, external or internal factors beyond a manager's control may affect revenues or expenses under that manager's responsibility. For example, the imposition of a 10% excise tax by a governmental agency may cause the price of the product to go up and thereby decrease sales of certain items in a specific segment. Although a particular manager may have the authority and responsibility for that segment of the company's sales, such a decline in revenues is beyond that manager's control. Another example would be the excessive use of raw materials in a production process under the control of a particular manager. Although the manager has the authority to control such expenses, that manager should not be held responsible for excess costs if the purchasing department bought low-quality materials that created an unusual amount of spoilage.

Therefore, the theoretical requirement that a manager should have absolute control over items for which that manager is held responsible often must be compromised, since most revenue and expense items have some degree of non-controllability in them. The manager is, thus, usually held responsible for items over which that manager has relative control. **Relative control** means that the manager has control over most of the factors that influence a given budget item. The use of relative control as a basis for evaluation may lead to some motivational problems in a company, since the manager is evaluated on results that may not reflect that manager's actual efforts. Nevertheless, most budget plans assign control on a relative basis in order to develop and use segmental budgets, which are discussed later in this chapter.

▌ RESPONSIBILITY REPORTS

A unique feature of a responsibility accounting system is the varying amount of detail included in the reports issued to different levels of management. Although the amount of detail varies, reports issued under a responsibility accounting system are interrelated. Totals from the report on one level of management are carried forward in the report to the management level immediately above. For example, a performance report to a supervisor would include actual and budgeted dollar amounts of all revenue and expense items under that supervisor's control. The responsibility report issued to a supervisor's plant manager would show only totals from all the supervisors' performance reports and any additional items under the plant manager's control, such as plant administrative expenses. The vice president of manufacturing's report would contain totals from all the plants plus any additional items under the vice president's control. Because a responsibility accounting system selectively condenses data, the report to the president includes summary totals of the subordinate levels plus any additional items under the president's control. In effect, the president's report should include **all** revenue and expense items in summary form since the president is responsible for controlling the profitability of the entire company.

The condensation of data as information flows upward to increasingly higher levels of management may seem to be a hindrance to performance analysis. Actually, this lack of detail results in "management by exception." **Management by exception** is the principle that upper-level management does not need to examine operating details at lower levels unless there appears to be a problem. Since businesses are becoming increasingly complex, it has become necessary to filter and condense accounting data so that these data may be analyzed quickly. Most executives do not have time to study detailed accounting reports and search for problem areas. Reporting only summary totals highlights those areas that need attention so that the executive can make more efficient use of available time.

The condensation of data that occurs in successive levels of management reports is justified on the basis that the appropriate manager will take the necessary corrective action. Thus, specific performance details need not be reported to superiors. For example, if direct labor cost has been excessively high in a particular department, that departmental supervisor should seek to find and correct the cause of the problem. When the plant manager questions the unfavorable budget variance of the department, the supervisor can inform the manager that corrective action was taken. Hence, it is not necessary to report to the vice president of manufacturing that a particular department within one of the plants is not operating satisfactorily, since the matter has already been resolved. Alternatively, if a manager's entire plant has been performing poorly, summary totals reported to the vice president of manufacturing will disclose this situation, and an investigation of the plant manager's problems may be indicated.

In preparing responsibility accounting reports, two basic methods are used to handle revenue or expense items. In the first approach, only those items over which a manager has direct control are included in the responsibility report for that management level. Any revenue and expense items that cannot be directly controlled are not included. The second approach is to include all revenue and expense items that can be traced directly **or** allocated indirectly to a particular manager, whether or not they are controllable. This second method represents a full-cost approach, which means **all** costs of a given area are disclosed in a single report. When this approach is used, care must be taken to separate controllable from noncontrollable items in order to differentiate those items for which a manager can and should be held responsible.

Features of Responsibility Reports

In order for accounting reports to be of maximum benefit, they must be **timely.** That is, reports should be prepared as soon as possible after the end of the performance measurement period. Timely reporting allows prompt corrective action to be taken. Reports that are delayed excessively lose their effectiveness as control devices. For example, a report on the previous month's operations that is not received until the end of the current month is virtually useless for analyzing poor performance areas and taking corrective action.

Reports should also be issued **regularly** so that trends can be spotted. Appropriate management action can be initiated before major problems occur. Regularity is also important so that managers will rely on the reports and become familiar with their contents.

The format of responsibility reports should be relatively simple and easy to read. Confusing terminology should be avoided. Results should be expressed in physical units where appropriate, since these may be more familiar and understandable to some managers. To assist management in quickly spotting budget variances, both budgeted (expected) and actual amounts should be reported. A budget variance is the difference between the budgeted and actual amounts of an item. Because variances highlight problem areas (exceptions), they are helpful in applying the management-by-exception principle. To help management evaluate performance to date, responsibility reports often include both a current period and a year-to-date analysis.

■ RESPONSIBILITY REPORTS—AN ILLUSTRATION

The following example shows how an organization's responsibility accounting reports are interrelated. The organization in this example has four management levels, as shown in Illustration 24.2. The managers we will focus on are the president, vice president of manufacturing, plant manager, and supervisor of the dye shop. A responsibility report would be prepared for each management level, as shown in Illustration 24.3.

Illustration 24.4 shows the detailed information included in the responsibility reports for each manager. These reports contain **only** the individual managers' controllable expenses. Notice that only **totals** from the dye shop supervisor's report are included in the plant manager's report. In turn, only totals from the plant manager's report are included in the report to the vice president,

Illustration 24.2

Organization Chart

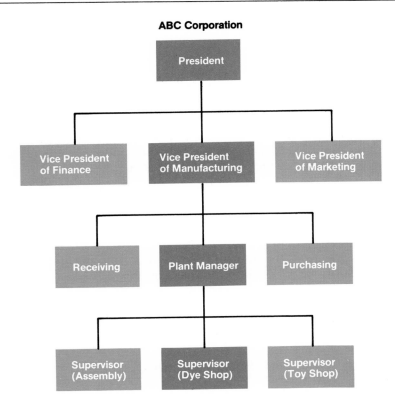

and so on. In this way, detailed data from the lower levels are summarized (condensed) and reported at the next higher level. You can see that at each level more and more costs become controllable. Also, controllable costs that were not included on lower-level reports are introduced into the reports for levels 3, 2, and 1. The only plant cost that is not included at the plant manager's level is the plant manager's salary, because it is noncontrollable by that plant

Illustration 24.3

Responsibility Reports

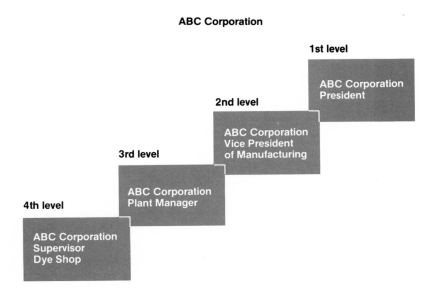

Illustration 24.4

Responsibility Reports for ABC Corporation

ABC CORPORATION
President

First level

Controllable expenses	Amount		Over or (under) budget	
	This month	Year to date	This month	Year to date
President's office expense	$ 1,000	$ 5,000	$ 100	$ 200
Manufacturing vice president's costs	18,800	93,000	600	800
Vice president, sales	8,700	19,000	400	800
Vice president, finance	4,000	15,000	800	900
Vice presidents' salaries	9,000	45,000	–0–	–0–
Total	$41,500	$177,000	$1,900	$2,700

ABC CORPORATION
Vice President of Manufacturing

Second level

Controllable expenses	Amount		Over or (under) budget	
	This month	Year to date	This month	Year to date
Vice president's office expense	$ 2,840	$ 9,500	$ (50)	$(800)
Plant manager's costs	7,880	43,000	250	500
Purchasing	380	2,500	100	200
Receiving	700	3,000	300	900
Salaries of plant manager and heads of purchasing and receiving	7,000	35,000	–0–	–0–
Total (include in report for next higher level)	$18,800	$93,000	$600	$ 800

ABC CORPORATION
Plant Manager

Third level

Controllable expenses	Amount		Over or (under) budget	
	This month	Year to date	This month	Year to date
Plant manager's office expense	$ 800	$ 9,100	$ (50)	$(100)
Dye shop costs	680	2,600	160	230
Toy shop costs	1,000	5,000	80	130
Assembly	400	1,300	60	240
Salaries of supervisors	5,000	25,000	–0–	–0–
Total (include in report for next higher level)	$7,880	$43,000	$250	$ 500

ABC CORPORATION
Supervisor, Dye Shop

Fourth level

Controllable expenses	Amount		Over or (under) budget	
	This month	Year to date	This month	Year to date
Repairs and maintenance	$200	$1,000	$ 10	$ 40
Supplies	180	850	80	95
Tools	100	300	(10)	81
Overtime	200	450	80	14
Total (include in report for next higher level)	$680	$2,600	$160	$230

manager. It is, however, controllable by the plant manager's supervisor, the vice president of manufacturing, and is included at that level of responsibility reporting.

Based on an analysis of these reports, the dye shop supervisor probably will take immediate action to see why supplies and overtime were significantly over budget this month. The plant manager may ask the supervisor what the problems were and whether they are now under control. The vice president may ask the same question of the plant manager. The president may ask each vice president why the budget was exceeded this month and what corrective action has been taken.

■ RESPONSIBILITY CENTERS

A segment is a fairly autonomous unit or division of a company defined according to function or product line. Traditionally, companies have been organized along functional lines. The segments or departments organized along functional lines perform a specified function (e.g., marketing, finance, purchasing, production, shipping). Recently, large companies have tended to organize segments according to product lines (e.g., electrical products division, shoe department, or food division).

A responsibility center is a segment of an organization for which a particular executive is responsible. There are three types of responsibility centers—expense (or cost) centers, profit centers, and investment centers. It is very important in designing a responsibility accounting system to examine the characteristics of each segment and the extent of the responsible manager's authority. Care must be taken to ensure that the basis for evaluating performance (i.e., expense center, profit center, or investment center) matches the characteristics of the segment and the authority of the segment's manager. The following sections of the chapter will discuss the characteristics of each of these types of centers and the appropriate bases for evaluating the performance of each type.

Expense Centers

An expense center is a responsibility center incurring only expense items and producing no direct revenue from the sale of goods or services. Examples of expense centers are service centers (e.g., the maintenance department or accounting department) or intermediate production facilities that produce parts for assembly into a finished product. **Managers of expense centers are held responsible only for specified expense items.**

The appropriate goal of an expense center is the **long-run** minimization of expenses. Short-run minimization of expenses may not be appropriate. For example, a production supervisor could eliminate maintenance costs for a short period of time, but in the long run, total costs might be higher due to more frequent machine breakdowns.

Profit Centers

A profit center is a responsibility center having both revenues and expenses. Since segmental earnings are usually defined as segmental revenues minus related expenses, the manager must be able to **control** both of these categories. The manager must have the authority to control selling price, sales volume, and all reported expense items. The manager's authority over all of these measured items is essential to proper performance evaluation. **Controllable profits of a segment** are shown when expenses under a manager's control are deducted from revenues under that manager's control.

Today, many companies are organizing segments as profit centers, including those that were normally considered expense centers. For example, consider the intermediate production facility mentioned in the last section which only produced output that becomes part of the final assembly in another segment. To enable the producing division to become a profit center rather than an expense center, a transfer price can be established.

Transfer Prices.   A **transfer price** is an artificial price used when goods or services are transferred from one segment to another segment within the same company. The transfer price is recorded as a revenue of the producing segment and as a cost, or expense, of the receiving segment. In using transfer prices, no cash actually changes hands between the segments. Instead, the transfer price is recorded as an internal accounting transaction.

Ideally, a transfer price should be the amount a part or service would cost if purchased from an outside party. Because such a "market" price might not be available, transfer prices often are determined on a cost-plus-profit-margin basis. In other cases, transfer prices are negotiated between the two segments, possibly with the help of an internal arbitration board.

No matter how the transfer price is determined, it is essential that the manufacturing segment manager have some degree of control over setting the price. If the manager does not have any control over the transfer price and output volume, the use of a profit center may not be a motivator.

Investment Centers

Closely related to the profit center concept is an investment center. An **investment center** is a responsibility center having revenues, expenses, and an appropriate investment base. When a segment is considered an investment center, it is evaluated according to the rate of return that it can earn on its investment base. **Return on investment (ROI),** also called rate of return, is computed by dividing segmental income by the appropriate investment base. For example, if a segment earns $100,000 on an investment base of $1,000,000, its ROI is 10%.

Determining the investment base to be used in the ROI calculation is a tricky matter. Normally, the assets available for use by the division make up the investment base of the division. But accountants disagree on whether depreciable assets should be included in the ROI calculation at original cost, original cost less accumulated depreciation, or current replacement cost. **Original cost** is the price paid to acquire an asset. **Original cost less accumulated depreciation** is the book value of the asset—the amount paid less total depreciation taken. **Current replacement cost** is the cost of replacing the present assets with similar assets in the same condition as those now in use. A different rate of return results from each of these measures. Therefore, management must select and agree upon an appropriate measure of investment base prior to making ROI calculations or interdivision comparisons.

Even after the investment base is defined, problems may still remain since many segment managers have limited control over some of the items included in the investment base of their segment. For instance, capital expenditure decisions for major plant assets are often made by top-level management rather than at the segment level. Therefore, the segment manager may have little control over the plant assets used by the segment. Another problem area may exist if the company has a centralized credit and collection department. In this case, the segment manager may have little or no control over the amount of accounts receivable included as segment assets since the manager cannot change the credit-granting or collection policies of the company.

Usually the above problems are overcome by realizing that if all segments are treated in the same manner, the inclusion of noncontrollable items in the investment base may have negligible effects. Comparisons of the ROI for all segments will then be based on a consistent treatment of items. It is important, though, that the segment managers agree to this treatment in order to avoid adverse reactions or decreased motivation.

Companies prefer to evaluate segments as investment centers because the ROI criterion facilitates performance comparisons between segments. Segments with more resources should produce more profits than segments with fewer resources, so it is difficult to compare the performance of segments of different sizes on the basis of profits alone. However, when ROI is used as a performance measure, performance comparisons take into account the differences in the sizes of the segments. The segment with the highest percentage ROI is presumably the most effective in using whatever resources it has.

Typical investment centers are large, autonomous segments of large companies. The centers are often separated from one another by location, types of products, functions, and/or necessary management skills. Segments such as these often seem to be separate companies to an outside observer. But the investment center concept can be applied even in relatively small companies in which the segment managers have control over the revenues, expenses, and assets of their segments.

■ SEGMENTAL ANALYSIS

So far, this chapter has described only the fundamentals of responsibility accounting. This section focuses specifically on segmental analysis.

Decentralization is the dispersion of decision-making authority among individuals at lower levels of the organization. In other words, the extent of decentralization refers to the degree of control that segment managers have over the revenues, expenses, and assets of their segments. When a segment manager has control over these three elements, the investment center concept can be applied to the segment. Thus, the more decentralized the decision making is in an organization, the more applicable is the investment center concept to the segments of the company. The more centralized the decision making is, the more likely one is to find responsibility centers established as expense centers.

Some of the advantages of decentralized decision making are:

1. Increased control over their segments trains managers for high-level positions in the company. The added authority and responsibility also represent "job enlargement" and often increase job satisfaction and motivation.

2. Top management can be more removed from day-to-day decision making at lower levels of the company and can manage by exception. When top management is not involved with routine problem solving, it can devote more time to long-range planning and to the company's most significant problem areas.

3. Decisions can be made at the point where problems arise. It is often difficult for members of top management to make appropriate decisions on a timely basis when they are not intimately involved with the problem they are trying to solve.

4. Since decentralization permits use of the investment center concept, performance evaluation criteria such as ROI and residual income can be used.

■ CONCEPTS USED IN SEGMENTAL ANALYSIS

The concepts of variable cost, fixed cost, direct cost, indirect cost, net income of a segment, and contribution to indirect expenses are used in segmental analysis. Each concept will be described, except for variable cost and fixed cost, which were discussed in Chapter 21.

Direct Cost and Indirect Cost

Costs may be either directly or indirectly related to a particular cost objective. A cost objective is a segment, product, or other item for which costs may be accumulated. In other words, a cost is not "direct" or "indirect" in and of itself. It is only "direct" or "indirect" in relation to a given cost objective.

A direct cost (expense) is specifically traceable to a given cost objective. An indirect cost (expense) is not traceable to a given cost objective but has been allocated to it. A particular cost (expense) can only be designated as direct or indirect by reference to a given cost objective, and a cost that is direct to one cost objective may be indirect to another. For instance, the salary of a segment manager may be a direct cost of a given manufacturing segment but an indirect cost of one of the products manufactured by that segment. In this example the segment and the product are two distinct cost objectives.

Since a direct cost is traceable to a cost objective, the cost is likely to be eliminated if the cost objective is eliminated. For instance, if the plastics segment of a business is closed down, the salary of the manager of that segment probably will be eliminated. Sometimes a direct cost would remain even if the cost objective were eliminated, but this is the exception rather than the rule.

An indirect cost is not traceable to a particular cost objective; therefore, it only becomes an expense of the cost objective through an allocation process. For example, consider the depreciation expense on the company headquarters building that is allocated to each of the segments of the company. The depreciation expense is a direct cost for the company headquarters, but it is an indirect cost to each segment. If a segment of the company is eliminated, the indirect cost for depreciation assigned to that segment will not disappear, the cost will simply be allocated among the remaining segments. In a given situation, it may be possible to identify an indirect cost that would be eliminated if the cost objective were eliminated, but this would be the exception to the general rule.

Since direct costs of a segment are clearly identified with that segment, these costs are often controllable by the segment manager. Since indirect costs become segment costs only through allocation, most indirect costs are noncontrollable by the segment manager. But care must be taken not to equate direct costs with controllable costs. For example, the salary of a segment supervisor may be direct to that segment and yet noncontrollable by that supervisor because supervisors cannot specify their own salaries.

■ NET INCOME OF A SEGMENT—EVALUATION CRITERIA FOR A PROFIT CENTER

When preparing internal reports on the performance of segments of a company, management often finds it important to classify expenses as fixed or variable and as direct or indirect to the segment. These classifications may be more useful to management than the traditional classifications of cost of goods sold, operating expenses, and nonoperating expenses that are used for external reporting in the company's financial statements. As a result, many companies prepare (for internal use) an income statement with the format shown in Illustration 24.5.

This format is called the contribution margin format for the income statement because it shows the contribution margin. Contribution margin is defined as sales revenue less variable expenses. Notice in Illustration 24.5 that all variable expenses are direct expenses of the segment. The second subtotal shown in the contribution margin format income statement (Illustration 24.5) is the segment's contribution to indirect expenses. Contribution to indirect expenses is defined as sales revenue less all direct expenses of the segment (both variable direct expenses and fixed direct expenses). The final total in the income statement is segmental net income, defined as segmental revenues less all expenses (direct expenses and allocated indirect expenses).

Earlier we stated that the performance of a profit center is evaluated on the basis of the segment's profits. It is tempting to use segmental net income to make this evaluation since total net income is used to evaluate the performance of the entire company. The problem with using segmental net income to evaluate performance is that segmental net income includes certain indirect expenses that have been allocated to the segment but are not directly related to it or its operations. Because segmental contribution to indirect expenses includes only revenues and expenses that are directly related to the segment, this amount is often more appropriate for evaluation purposes.

Illustration 24.5

Contribution Margin Format Income Statement—All Expenses Allocated

	Segment A	Segment B	Total
Sales	$1,000,000	$700,000	$1,700,000
Less: Variable expenses (all direct expenses)	500,000	410,000	910,000
Contribution margin	$ 500,000	$290,000	$ 790,000
Less: Direct fixed expenses	120,000	170,000	290,000
Contribution to indirect expenses	$ 380,000	$120,000	$ 500,000
Less: Indirect fixed expenses	90,000	160,000	250,000
Net income	$ 290,000	$ (40,000)	$ 250,000

Given the facts in Illustration 24.5, if management relied on segmental net income to judge segmental performance, management might conclude that Segment B should be eliminated since it shows a loss of $40,000. But this action would reduce overall company profits by $120,000, as shown below:

Reduction in corporate revenues		$700,000
Reduction in corporate expenses:		
Variable expenses	$410,000	
Direct fixed expenses	170,000	580,000
Reduction in corporate income		$120,000

Notice that the elimination of Segment B would not eliminate the $160,000 of allocated fixed costs. These costs would need to be allocated to Segment A if Segment B no longer existed.

To stress the importance of a segment's contribution to indirect expenses, many companies prefer the contribution margin income statement format presented in Illustration 24.6 rather than the format used in Illustration 24.5. The difference is that indirect fixed costs are not allocated to individual segments. Indirect fixed expenses are only shown in the total column for the computation of net income for the entire company. The computation for each segment stops with the segment's contribution to indirect expenses; this is the appropriate figure to use for evaluating the earnings performance of a segment. Only for the company as a whole is net income (revenues minus **all** expenses) computed; this is, of course, the appropriate figure to use for evaluating the company as a whole.

Arbitrary Allocations of Indirect Fixed Expenses. As stated above, indirect fixed expenses, such as depreciation on the corporate administration building or on the computer facility maintained at company headquarters, can only be allocated to segments on some arbitrary basis. There are two basic guidelines for allocating indirect fixed expenses—by the benefit received and by the responsibility for incurrence of the expense.

Allocation can be made on the basis of benefit received for certain indirect expenses. For instance, assume a corporate computer was used for a total of 10,000 hours by the entire company. If Segment K used 4,000 hours, it could be charged (allocated) with 40% of the computer's depreciation for the period, since Segment K received 40% of the total benefits for the period.

For certain other indirect expenses, allocation is based on responsibility for incurrence. For instance, assume that Segment M contracts with a magazine to run an advertisement that will benefit both Segment M and various other segments of the company. Many companies would allocate the entire cost of

Illustration 24.6

Contribution Margin Format Income Statement—Indirect Fixed Expenses Not Allocated

	Segment A	Segment B	Total
Sales	$1,000,000	$700,000	$1,700,000
Less: Variable expenses	500,000	410,000	910,000
Contribution margin	$ 500,000	$290,000	$ 790,000
Less: Direct fixed expenses	120,000	170,000	290,000
Contribution to indirect expenses	$ 380,000	$120,000	$ 500,000
Less: Indirect fixed expenses			250,000
Net income			$ 250,000

the advertisement to Segment **M** since it was responsible for incurring the advertising expense.

To further illustrate the allocation of indirect expenses based on a measure of benefit or responsibility for incurrence, assume that Daily Company operates two segments, **X** and **Y**. It allocates the following indirect expenses to its two segments using the designated allocation bases:

Expense	Allocation base
Home office building occupancy expense, $40,000	Net sales
Insurance expense, $25,000	Cost of segmental plant assets
General administrative expenses, $30,000 . .	Number of employees

The following additional data are provided:

	Segment X	Segment Y	Total
Sales (net)	$200,000	$300,000	$500,000
Segmental plant assets . .	$150,000	$200,000	$350,000
Number of Employees . .	40	60	100

The allocation of indirect expenses is as shown in the following expense allocation schedule:

	Segment X	Segment Y	Total
Home office building occupancy expense . .	$16,000[1]	$24,000[2]	$40,000
Insurance expense	10,714[3]	14,286[4]	25,000
General administrative expenses	12,000[5]	18,000[6]	30,000

1. $\dfrac{\$200,000}{\$500,000} \times \$40,000 = \$16,000.$

2. $\dfrac{\$300,000}{\$500,000} \times \$40,000 = \$24,000.$

3. $\dfrac{\$150,000}{\$350,000} \times \$25,000 = \$10,714.$

4. $\dfrac{\$200,000}{\$350,000} \times \$25,000 = \$14,286.$

5. $\dfrac{40}{100} \times \$30,000 = \$12,000.$

6. $\dfrac{60}{100} \times \$30,000 = \$18,000.$

When neither "benefit" nor "responsibility" can be used to allocate indirect fixed expenses, some other reasonable, but arbitrary, basis must be found. Often, for lack of a better approach, indirect expenses are allocated based on net sales. For instance, if segment X's net sales were 60% of total company sales, then 60% of the indirect expenses would be allocated to Segment X. Allocating expenses based on sales is not recommended because it reduces the incentive of a segment manager to increase sales, since this would result in more indirect expenses being allocated to that segment.

Having covered some basic concepts essential to segmental analysis, some specific procedures for performance evaluation will be presented.

■ INVESTMENT CENTER ANALYSIS

To this point, the segmental analysis discussion has concentrated on the contribution to indirect expenses and segmental net income approaches. Now we will introduce the investment base concept into the analysis. Two criteria that include the concept of investment base in the analysis are ROI (return on investment) and RI (residual income).

Return on Investment (ROI)

A segment that has a large amount of assets will usually earn more in an absolute sense than will a segment that has a small amount of assets. Therefore, absolute amounts of segmental income cannot be used to compare the performance of different segments. To measure the relative effectiveness of segments, a company must use ROI, which calculates the return (income) as a percentage of the assets employed (investment). The formula for return on investment is:

$$ROI = \frac{Income}{Investment}$$

To illustrate the difference between using absolute amounts and using percentages in evaluating a segment's performance, consider the data shown in Illustration 24.7 for a company with three segments. If absolute dollars of income are used to evaluate performance, Segment 2 appears to be doing twice as well as Segment 3. But the use of ROI as a criterion for evaluating the segments indicates that Segment 3 is really performing the best (25%), Segment 2 is next (20%), and Segment 1 is performing the worst (10%). ROI is therefore a more useful indicator of the relative performance of segments than absolute income.

Although ROI appears to be a quite simple and straightforward computation, there are several alternative methods for making the calculation. These alternatives focus on what is meant by "income" and "investment." Illustration 24.8 shows various definitions and applicable situations for each type of computation.

As discussed earlier in the chapter, alternative valuation bases include original cost, cost less accumulated depreciation, and current replacement cost. Each of the valuation bases has merits and drawbacks, as you will now see.

Cost less accumulated depreciation is probably the most widely used valuation base and is easily determined. But since there are many types of depreciation methods, comparisons between segments or companies may be difficult. Also,

Illustration 24.7

Computation of Return on Investment (ROI)

		Segment 1	Segment 2	Segment 3	Total
(a)	Income	$ 100,000	$ 500,000	$ 250,000	$ 850,000
(b)	Investment	1,000,000	2,500,000	1,000,000	4,500,000
	Return on investment (a) ÷ (b)	10%	20%	25%	18.89%

Illustration 24.8

Possible Definitions of "Income" and "Investment"

Situation	Definition of income	Definition of investment
1. Evaluation of the earning power of the company. Do not use for segments or segment managers due to inclusion of noncontrollable expenses.	Net income of the company.*	Total assets of the company.†
2. Evaluation of rate of income contribution of segment. Do not use for segment managers due to inclusion of noncontrollable expenses.	Contribution to indirect expenses.	Assets directly used by and identified with the segment.
3. Evaluation of income performance of segment manager.	"Controllable" income. This would begin with contribution to indirect expenses and would eliminate any revenues and direct expenses not under the control of the segment manager.	Assets under the control of the segment manager.

* Often *net operating income* is used; this is defined as income before interest and taxes.
† *Operating assets* are often used in the calculation. This definition excludes assets not used in normal operations.

as book value decreases, a constant income results in a steadily increasing ROI even though the segment's performance is unchanged. The use of original cost eliminates the problem of decreasing book value but has its own drawback. The investment in (cost of) old assets will be much less than an investment in new assets, so a segment with old assets can earn less than a segment with net assets and still realize the same ROI. Current replacement cost is difficult to use because replacement cost figures often are not available, but this base does eliminate some of the problems caused by the other two methods. Whichever valuation basis is adopted, all ROI calculations that are to be used for comparative purposes should be made consistently.

Expanded Form of ROI Computation.   The ROI formula can be broken into two component parts as follows:

$$\text{ROI} = \frac{\text{Income}}{\text{Sales}} \times \frac{\text{Sales}}{\text{Investment}}$$

The first part of the formula, Income/Sales, is called margin or return on sales. The margin refers to the percentage relationship of income or profits to sales. This percentage shows the number of cents of profit that are generated by each dollar of sales. The second part of the formula, Sales/Investment, is called turnover. Turnover shows the number of dollars of sales generated by each dollar of investment. Turnover measures how effectively each dollar of assets was used.

There are several ways to increase ROI:

1. A manager can concentrate on increasing profit margin while holding turnover constant. Pursuing this strategy means keeping selling prices constant and making every effort to increase efficiency and thereby reduce expenses.

2. A manager can concentrate on increasing turnover by reducing the investment in assets while holding income and sales constant. For example, working capital could be decreased, thereby reducing the investment in assets.
3. A manager can take actions that affect both margin and turnover. For example, disposing of nonproductive depreciable assets would decrease investment while also increasing income (through the reduction of depreciation expense). Thus, both margin and turnover would increase. An advertising campaign would probably increase sales and income. In this case, turnover would increase, and margin might increase or decrease depending on the relative amounts of the increases in income and sales.

Illustration 24.9 shows possible outcomes of some of these strategies to increase ROI.

Illustration 24.9

Strategies for Increasing ROI

Past year return on investment:

$$ROI = Margin \times Turnover$$
$$ROI = \frac{Income}{Sales} \times \frac{Sales}{Investment}$$
$$ROI = \frac{\$100,000}{\$2,000,000} \times \frac{\$2,000,000}{\$1,000,000}$$
$$ROI = 5\% \times 2 \text{ times}$$
$$ROI = 10\%$$

1. Increase margin through reducing expenses by $40,000; no effect on sales or investment.

$$ROI = \frac{\$140,000}{\$2,000,000} \times \frac{\$2,000,000}{\$1,000,000}$$
$$ROI = 7\% \times 2 \text{ times}$$
$$ROI = 14\%$$

2. Increase turnover through reducing investment in assets by $200,000; no effect on sales or income.

$$ROI = \frac{\$100,000}{\$2,000,000} \times \frac{\$2,000,000}{\$800,000}$$
$$ROI = 5\% \times 2.5 \text{ times}$$
$$ROI = 12.5\%$$

3(a). Increase margin and turnover by disposing of nonproductive depreciable assets; income increased by $10,000; investment decreased by $200,000.

$$ROI = \frac{\$110,000}{\$2,000,000} \times \frac{\$2,000,000}{\$800,000}$$
$$ROI = 5.5\% \times 2.5 \text{ times}$$
$$ROI = 13.75\%$$

3(b). Increase margin and turnover through increased advertising; sales increased by $500,000 and income by $50,000; no effect on investment.

$$ROI = \frac{\$150,000}{\$2,500,000} \times \frac{\$2,500,000}{\$1,000,000}$$
$$ROI = 6\% \times 2.5 \text{ times}$$
$$ROI = 15\%$$

3(c). Increase turnover through increased advertising; sales increased by $500,000 and income by $12,500; no effect on investment.

$$ROI = \frac{\$112,500}{\$2,500,000} \times \frac{\$2,500,000}{\$1,000,000}$$
$$ROI = 4.5\% \times 2.5 \text{ times}$$
$$ROI = 11.25\%$$

Residual Income

The use of ROI as the sole criterion for evaluating performance can result in what is termed suboptimization. Suboptimization occurs when a segment manager takes an action that is in the segment's best interest (i.e., raises that segment's ROI), but is not in the best interest of the company as a whole.

To prevent suboptimization, companies sometimes use the concept of residual income. Residual income (RI) is defined as the amount of income a segment has in excess of a desired minimum ROI. Each company sets its minimum ROI based on many factors, including expected growth rate, debt coverage, industry technology, and desired returns to stockholders. The formula for residual income is:

Residual income (RI) = Income − (Investment × Desired minimum ROI)

When RI is used to evaluate performance, the segment rated as the best is the segment with the greatest amount of RI rather than the one with the highest ROI.

To illustrate the value of using residual income to measure performance, assume the manager of Segment 3 in Illustration 24.10 has an opportunity to take on a project involving an investment of $100,000 that is estimated to return $22,000, or 22%, on the investment. Since the segment's ROI is currently 25%, the manager may decide to reject the project. However, from a company standpoint, ROI will increase from 18.89% to 18.96% if the project is accepted. The decision to reject the project is a valid decision from the manager's point

Illustration 24.10 *Computation of Residual Income (RI)*

Before acceptance of the project by Segment 3, the amounts are as follows:

		Segment 1	Segment 2	Segment 3	Total company
a.	Income	$ 100,000	$ 500,000	$ 250,000	$ 850,000
b.	Investment	1,000,000	2,500,000	1,000,000	4,500,000
c.	Rate of return on investment (ROI)	10%	20%	25%	18.89%
d.	Desired minimum ROI (10%)	$ 100,000	$ 250,000	$ 100,000	*
e.	Residual income	–0–	250,000	150,000	*

* The RI concept is generally not used for evaluating an entire company, since the problem of suboptimization, by definition, does not exist.

With acceptance of the project by Segment 3, the amounts would be as follows:

		Segment 1	Segment 2	Segment 3	Total company
a.	Income	$ 100,000	$ 500,000	$ 272,000*	$ 872,000
b.	Investment	1,000,000	2,500,000	1,100,000†	4,600,000
c.	Rate of return on investment (ROI)	10%	20%	24.7%	18.96%
d.	Desired minimum ROI (10%)	$ 100,000	$ 250,000	$ 110,000	
e.	Residual income	–0–	250,000	162,000	

* $250,000 + (22% of $100,000).
† $1,000,000 original investment + $100,000 new investment.

of view because to accept the project will cause the segment's ROI to decline. But from a company standpoint, ROI is 18.89%, and accepting the project would increase the overall company ROI.

The project opportunity for Segment 3 could earn in excess of the desired minimum ROI of 10%. In fact, it has residual income of $12,000 ($22,000 − 10% × $100,000). If residual income (RI) were applied as the basis for evaluating segmental performance, the manager of Segment 3 would accept the project because doing so would improve his or her segment's performance. That choice would also be beneficial to the entire company.

Critics of the residual income method complain that larger segments are likely to have the highest residual income. In a given situation it may be advisable to look at both ROI and RI in assessing performance.

Since it is always assumed that a manager will make choices that improve his or her segment's performance, the challenge is to select evaluation bases for segments that will result in managers making choices that benefit the entire company. When performance is evaluated on RI, choices that improve a segment's performance are more likely to be good for the entire company as well.

When calculating RI for a **segment,** the income and investment definitions are "contributions to indirect expenses" and "assets directly used by and identified with the segment." When calculating RI for a **manager** of a segment, the income and investment definitions should be "income controllable by the manager" and "assets under the control of the segment manager."

In evaluating the performance of a segment or a segment manager, comparisons should be made with (1) the current budget, (2) other segments or managers within the company, (3) past performance of that segment or manager, and (4) similar segments or managers in other companies. Consideration must be given to general economic conditions, market conditions for the product being produced, and so on. A superior segment in Company A may be considered superior because it is earning a return of 12%, which is above similar segments in other companies but below other segments in Company A. But segments in Company A may be more profitable because of market conditions and the nature of the company's products rather than because of the performance of the segment managers. Careful judgment must be used whenever performance is evaluated.

■ SEGMENTAL REPORTING IN EXTERNAL FINANCIAL STATEMENTS

Formerly, segmental information was reported only to management for internal decision-making purposes. In December 1976, the Financial Accounting Standards Board issued *Statement of Financial Accounting Standards No. 14,* "Financial Reporting for Segments of a Business Enterprise." This *Statement* requires publicly held companies to publish certain segmental information in their annual financial statements. Thus, external users of financial statements now have segmental information to aid them in their decisions regarding these companies. However, fewer details are presented in these external statements than in reports intended for management.

■ *SUMMARY*

A responsibility accounting system provides information to evaluate each manager on revenue and expense items over which that manager has primary control. Responsibility accounting reports contain only those items controlled by the responsible manager, or if noncontrollable items are included, the reports should clearly separate controllable from noncontrollable items. The identification of controllable items is a fundamental task in responsibility accounting and reporting.

Management by exception is the concept that upper-level management does not need to be concerned with operating details of subordinate levels unless there appears to be a problem. To accomplish management by exception, responsibility reports contain details only of activities immediately under the manager's control; only summary information of results from subordinate levels is presented. Also, responsibility reports should present both budgeted and actual results, as well as budget variances and year-to-date totals.

A responsibility center is a segment of an organization for which a particular executive is responsible. There are three types of responsibility centers—expense centers, profit centers, and investment centers.

A responsibility center having only expense items and producing no revenue from the sale of goods or services is properly accounted for as an expense center. Managers of expense centers are held responsible only for specified expense items.

A profit center has both revenues and expenses, so it is possible to calculate segmental income. A profit center manager is evaluated on controllable profits of the segment, the difference between revenue items under the manager's control and expense items under the manager's control. When a profit center sells its output only to other segments of the same company, controllable profits of the profit center are strongly influenced by the transfer price that is established for the "sale." It is essential that the manufacturing segment (profit center) manager have some control over setting the transfer price.

An investment center is a responsibility center that has revenues, expenses, and a specified investment base. Performance of an investment center and of an investment center's manager can be evaluated on the basis of return on investment (ROI). ROI is computed by dividing segmental income by the appropriate investment base.

A direct cost of a given cost objective can be traced directly to that cost objective. An indirect cost cannot be traced directly to a cost objective; it can be assigned to the cost objective only through a cost allocation process. A cost that is direct to one cost objective may be indirect with regard to another.

Segment contribution margin is the difference between net sales and variable expenses of a segment. Segment contribution to indirect expenses is the amount remaining after all direct expenses of the segment are deducted from the revenues generated by the segment. Segmental net income is the amount that remains after all of a segment's expenses (direct and indirect) are deducted from the segment's revenues. Since a segment's contribution to indirect expenses includes only items that are directly related to the segment, this amount indicates the effect on company profits if the segment were eliminated. Consequently, contribution to indirect expenses is often considered more appropriate than segmental net income for evaluation purposes.

Two different criteria exist for evaluating the performance of investment centers. Return on investment (ROI) directly compares segmental income to the segment's investment base. Both segmental income and the segment's investment base may be defined in a number of ways, any of which may be appropriate depending on the circumstances. The ROI computation can also be expanded to consider separately the effects of margin and turnover. The other criterion for evaluating investment center performance is residual income (RI), the amount by which segmental income exceeds a minimum desired ROI. Use of the RI criterion for segmental evaluation reduces the tendency toward suboptimization that can occur when managers are evaluated on ROI alone. Possibly both ROI and RI should be used in evaluating performance.

Chapter 25 discusses budgeting. Companies, like individuals, should plan for the future. A budget is one method of planning. Just as you may use a budget in managing your personal finances, budgets are an important tool of company management.

NEW TERMS INTRODUCED IN CHAPTER 24*

Budget variance

The difference between the budgeted and actual amounts of an item (935).

Contribution margin

Sales revenues less variable expenses (942).

Contribution margin format

An income statement format that shows the contribution margin (Sales — Variable expenses) for a segment (942).

Contribution to indirect expenses

The income of a segment remaining after direct expenses are deducted from segmental revenues (942).

Controllable profits of a segment

Profit of a segment when expenses under a manager's control are deducted from revenues under that manager's control (939).

Cost objective

A segment, product, or other item for which costs may be accumulated (941).

Current replacement cost

The cost of replacing the present assets with similar assets in the same condition as those now in use (939).

Decentralization

The dispersion of decision-making authority among individuals at lower levels of the organization (940).

Direct cost (expense)

A cost that is directly traceable to a given cost objective (941).

Expense center

A responsibility center producing only expense items and producing no direct revenue from the sale of goods or services. Examples include the accounting department and the maintenance department (938).

Indirect cost (expense)

A cost that is not traceable to a given cost objective but has been allocated to it (941).

Investment center

A responsibility center having revenues, expenses, and an appropriate investment base (939).

Management by exception

The principle that upper-level management does not need to examine operating details at lower levels unless there appears to be a problem (an exception) (934).

---

* Some terms listed in earlier chapters are repeated here for your convenience.

Margin (as used in ROI)

The percentage relationship of income (or profits) to sales.

$$\text{Margin} = \frac{\text{Income}}{\text{Sales}} \quad (946)$$

Original cost

The price paid to acquire an asset (939).

Original cost less accumulated depreciation

The book value of an asset—the amount paid less total depreciation taken (939).

Profit center

A responsibility center having both revenue and expense items (938).

Relative control

Means the manager has control over most of the factors that influence a given budget item (933).

Residual income (RI)

The amount of income a segment has in excess of a desired minimum ROI. Residual income is equal to Income − (Investment × Desired minimum ROI) (948).

Responsibility accounting

Refers to an accounting system that collects, summarizes, and reports accounting data according to the responsibilities of the individual managers. A responsibility accounting system provides information to evaluate each manager on revenue and expense items over which that manager has primary control (932).

Responsibility Center

A segment of an organization for which a particular executive is responsible (938).

Return on investment (ROI)

Calculates the return (income) as a percentage of the assets employed (investment).

$$\text{Return on investment} = \frac{\text{Income}}{\text{Investment}} \text{ or } \frac{\text{Income}}{\text{Sales}} \times \frac{\text{Sales}}{\text{Investment}}$$
$$(939, 945)$$

Segment

A fairly autonomous unit or division of a company (938).

Segmental net income

Final total in the income statement; segmental revenues less all expenses (direct expenses and allocated indirect expenses) (942).

Suboptimization

A situation that occurs when a segment manager takes an action that is in the segment's best interest but is not in the best interest of the company as a whole (948).

Transfer price

An artificial price used when goods or services are transferred from one segment to another segment within the same company (939).

Turnover (as used in ROI)

The number of dollars of sales generated by each dollar of investment.

$$\text{Turnover} = \frac{\text{Sales}}{\text{Investment}} \quad (946)$$

DEMONSTRATION PROBLEM

The Corey Company has two segments. Results of operations for 1987 follow:

	Segment 1	Segment 2	Total
Sales	$50,000	$75,000	$125,000
Variable expenses	35,000	45,000	80,000
Fixed expenses:			
Direct	5,000	14,000	19,000
Indirect			7,000

The company has total operating assets of $175,000; $160,000 of these assets are identified with particular segments as follows:

	Segment 1	Segment 2
Assets directly used by and identified with the segment	$60,000	$100,000

Required: a.   Prepare a statement showing the contribution margin, contribution to indirect expenses for each segment, and the total income for the Corey Company.

b.   Determine the return on investment for each segment and then for the entire company.

c.   Comment on the results of *(a)* and *(b)*.

Solution to demonstration problem

a.

COREY COMPANY
Income Statement Showing Segmental
Contributions to Indirect Expenses
For the Year Ended December 31, 1987

	Segment 1	Segment 2	Total
Sales	$50,000	$75,000	$125,000
Less: Variable expenses	35,000	45,000	80,000
Contribution margin	$15,000	$30,000	$ 45,000
Less: Direct fixed expenses	5,000	14,000	19,000
Contribution to indirect expenses	$10,000	$16,000	$ 26,000
Less: Indirect fixed expenses			7,000
Net income			$ 19,000

b.   1. $\text{ROI} = \dfrac{\text{Contribution to indirect expenses}}{\text{Assets directly used by and identified with the segment}}$

Segment 1   **Segment 2**

$\text{ROI} = \dfrac{\$10,000}{\$60,000} = 16.67\%$ $\text{ROI} = \dfrac{\$16,000}{\$100,000} = 16\%$

2. $\text{ROI} = \dfrac{\text{Net operating income}}{\text{Operating assets}} = \dfrac{\$19,000}{\$175,000} = 10.9\%$

c.   In Part *(a)*, Segment 2 showed a higher contribution to indirect expenses. But in *(b)*, Segment 1 showed a higher return on investment. The difference between these calculations shows that when a segment is evaluated as a profit center, the center with the highest investment base will usually show the best results. But when the segment is evaluated as an investment center, the segment with the highest investment base will not necessarily show the highest return. The computations in *(b)* also demonstrate that the return on investment for the company as a whole will be lower than the segments because of the increased investment base.

QUESTIONS

1. What is the fundamental principle of responsibility accounting?

2. Hope Company manufactures refrigerators. Below are listed several of the company's costs. Indicate whether or not the shop supervisor can control each of the costs.

a.   Depreciation.
b.   Repairs.
c.   Small tools.
d.   Supplies.
e.   Bond interest.

3. List five important factors that should be considered in designing reports for a responsibility accounting system.

4. How soon should accounting reports be prepared after the end of the performance measurement period? Explain.

5. Name and describe three types of responsibility centers.

6. Describe a segment of a business enterprise that is best treated as an expense center. List four indirect expenses that may be allocated to such an expense center.

7. Compare and contrast an expense center and an investment center.

8. What purpose is served by setting transfer prices?

9. What is the advantage of using investment centers as a basis for performance evaluation?

10. Which categories of items must a segment manager have control over for the investment center concept to be applicable?

11. What connection is there between the extent of decentralization and the investment center concept?

12. Give some of the advantages of decentralization.

13. Differentiate between a direct cost and an indirect cost of a segment. What happens to these categories if the segment to which they are related is eliminated?

14. Is it possible for a cost to be "direct" to one cost objective and "indirect" to another cost objective? Explain.

15. Describe some of the methods by which indirect expenses are allocated to a segment.

16. Give the general formula for return on investment (ROI). What are its two components?

17. Give the three sets of definitions for "income" and "investment" that can be used in ROI calculations, and explain when each set is applicable.

18. Give the various valuation bases that can be used for plant assets in investment center calculations. Discuss some of the advantages and disadvantages of these methods.

19. In what way is the use of the residual income (RI) concept superior to the use of ROI?

20. How is RI determined?

21. If the RI for segment manager A is $50,000 while the RI for segment manager B is $100,000, does this necessarily mean that B is a better manager than A? Explain.

EXERCISES

E-1

Prepare a responsibility report for a given management level

The following information refers to the toy shop of the Playtime Company for the month of May:

	Amount	Over or (under) budget
Supplies	$ 60,000	$(12,000)
Repairs and maintenance	300,000	24,000
Overtime	120,000	12,000
Salary of supervisor	36,000	(6,000)
Salary of plant manager	48,000	–0–
Allocation of company accounting costs	36,000	12,000
Allocation of depreciation	24,000	(6,000)

Using the above information, prepare a responsibility report for the *supervisor* of the toy shop for the month of May. (Ignore year-to-date expenses.)

E-2

Prepare an income statement for a segment in a contribution margin format

Present the following information for Segment D in the contribution margin format:

Sales	$1,000,000
Variable selling and administrative expenses . . .	75,000
Fixed direct manufacturing expenses	25,000
Variable manufacturing expenses	300,000
Fixed direct selling and administrative expenses . .	125,000

E-3

Prepare an income statement for a segment using the contribution margin format; determine effect of elimination of segment on company income

Given the following data, prepare a schedule that shows contribution margin, contribution to indirect expenses, and net income of the segment:

Direct fixed expenses . .	$ 90,000
Indirect fixed expenses . .	72,000
Sales	624,000
Variable expenses . . .	432,000

What would be the effect on company income if the segment were eliminated?

E-4

Allocate expenses to various segments using a specified allocation base

Three segments (X, Y, and Z) of the Rabb Company have net sales of $1,000,000, $600,000, and $200,000, respectively. A decision is made to allocate the pool of $80,000 of administrative overhead expenses of the home office to the segments, using net sales as the basis for allocation.

a. How much should be allocated to each segment?
b. If Segment Z is eliminated, how much will be allocated to X and Y?

E-5

Calculate ROI, margin, and turnover for a segment

Two segments (hardware and software) showed the following data for the most recent year:

	Hardware	Software
Contribution to indirect expenses . . .	$ 300,000	$ 360,000
Assets directly used by and identified		
with the segment	900,000	1,560,000
Sales	2,400,000	4,800,000

a. Calculate ROI for each segment in the most direct manner.
b. Calculate ROI using the margin and turnover components.

E-6

Determine the effect on margin, turnover, and ROI when the variables are altered

Determine the effect of each of the following on the margin, turnover, and ROI of the hardware segment in Exercise E-5. Consider each change independently of the others.

a. Direct variable expenses were reduced by $12,000, and indirect expenses were reduced by $24,000. Sales and assets were unaffected.
b. Assets used by the segment were reduced by $180,000, while income and sales were unaffected.
c. An advertising campaign increased sales by $240,000 and income by $60,000. Assets directly used by the segment were unaffected.

E-7

Calculate the ROI in evaluating the income performance of a segment manager and the rate of income contribution of a segment

For Segment C of the Cat Company, the following data are available:

Net income of the segment	$ 40,000
Contribution to indirect expenses	100,000
Controllable income	60,000
Total assets related to the segment	500,000
Assets directly used by the segment	300,000
Assets under the "control" of the segment manager . .	200,000

Determine the ROI for evaluating *(a)* the income performance of the manager of Segment C and *(b)* the rate of income contribution of the segment.

E-8

Determine RI in evaluating segments

The Rice Company has three segments: U, V, and W. Data concerning "income" and "investment" follow:

	Segment U	Segment V	Segment W
Contribution to indirect expenses . . .	$ 36,000	$ 72,000	$ 96,000
Assets directly used by and identified			
with the segment	240,000	480,000	1,080,000

Assuming that the minimum desired ROI is 10%, calculate the residual income (RI) of each of the segments. Do the results indicate that any of the segments should be eliminated?

E-9

Calculate ROI and RI in evaluating a manager

Assume that for Segment U in Exercise E–8, $12,000 of the direct expenses and $30,000 of the segmental assets are not under the control of the segment manager. Top management wishes to evaluate the segment manager's income performance. Calculate the manager's ROI and RI. (Because certain expenses and assets are not controllable by the segment manager, the minimum desired ROI is 15%.)

PROBLEMS, SERIES A

P24-1-A

Prepare responsibility reports for various levels of management

You are given the following information relevant to the Monroe Company for the year ended December 31, 1987. The company is organized according to functions.

Controllable expenses	Plant manager Budget	Plant manager Actual	Vice president of manufacturing Budget	Vice president of manufacturing Actual	President Budget	President Actual
Office expense	$3,000	$4,000	$ 5,000	$ 7,000	$10,000	$ 7,000
Printing shop	2,000	2,000				
Iron shop	1,000	900				
Toaster shop	8,000	7,000				
Purchasing			10,000	11,000		
Receiving			5,000	6,000		
Inspection			8,000	7,000		
Vice president of marketing					80,000	70,000
Controller					60,000	50,000
Treasurer					40,000	30,000
Vice president of personnel					20,000	30,000

Required: Prepare the responsibility accounting reports for the three levels of management—plant manager, vice president of manufacturing, and president.

P24-2-A

Evaluate responsibility centers as profit centers and investment centers

The Bay Corporation has three production plants (A, B, and C). These plants are treated as responsibility centers. Following is a summary of the results for the month of March 1987:

Plant	Revenues	Expenses	Investment base (gross assets)
A	$ 750,000	$375,000	$ 7,500,000
B	1,500,000	600,000	11,250,000
C	2,250,000	825,000	24,000,000

Required:

a. If the plants are treated as profit centers, which plant manager appears to have done the best job?

b. If the plants are treated as investment centers, which plant manager appears to have done the best job? (Assume that plant managers are evaluated in terms of ROI on gross assets.)

c. Do the results of profit center analysis and investment center analysis give different findings? If so, why?

P24-3-A

*Allocate indirect
expenses to
illustrate the
arbitrary nature of
expense allocation*

Denny Company allocates all of its home office expenses to its two segments, A and B. Given below are selected expense account balances and additional data upon which allocations are based:

Expenses (allocation bases)

Home office building expense (net sales)	$24,000
Buying expenses (net purchases)	21,000
Bad debts (net sales)	2,500
Depreciation of home office equipment (net sales) . .	6,600
Advertising expense (indirect, allocated on basis of relative amounts of direct advertising)	27,000
Insurance expense (relative amounts of equipment plus average inventory in department)	7,200

Additional data:

	Segment A	Segment B	Total
Purchases (net) . . .	$ 76,000	$24,000	$100,000
Sales (net)	160,000	40,000	200,000
Equipment (cost) . .	30,000	20,000	50,000
Advertising (direct) . .	8,000	4,000	12,000
Average inventory . .	50,000	20,000	70,000

Required:

a. Prepare a schedule showing the amounts of each type of expense allocable to Segments A and B using the above data and the bases of allocation.
b. Criticize some of these allocation bases.

P24-4-A

*Prepare schedule
showing
contribution margin
and contribution to
indirect expenses
using contribution
margin format;
prepare segmental
income statements*

Green, Inc. is a company with two segments, 1 and 2. Its revenues and expenses for 1987 follow:

	Segment 1	Segment 2	Total
Sales (net)	$320,000	$480,000	$800,000
Direct expenses:*			
Cost of goods sold	150,000	330,000	480,000
Selling	45,600	24,000	69,600
Administrative:			
Bad debts	10,000	6,000	16,000
Insurance	8,000	4,000	12,000
Interest	1,600	800	2,400
Indirect expenses (all fixed):			
Selling			60,000
Administrative			84,000

* All the direct expenses are variable except insurance and interest, which are fixed.

Required:

a. Prepare a schedule showing the contribution margin, the contribution to indirect expenses of each segment, and net income for the company as a whole. Do not allocate indirect expenses to the segments.
b. Assume that indirect selling expenses are to be allocated on the basis of net sales and that indirect administrative expenses are to be allocated on the basis of direct administrative expenses. Prepare a statement (starting with the contribution to indirect expenses) which shows the net income of each segment.
c. Comment on the appropriateness of the "income" amounts shown in parts *(a)* and *(b)* for determining the income contribution of the segments.

P24-5-A

Prepare an income statement for two segments using the contribution margin format; calculate the ROI for (1) the entire company, (2) each segment, and (3) each manager

The following data pertain to the operating revenues and expenses for the Vail Company for 1987:

	Segment C	Segment D	Total
Sales	$1,200,000	$600,000	$1,800,000
Variable expenses . . .	800,000	320,000	1,120,000
Direct fixed expenses . .	100,000	80,000	180,000
Indirect fixed expenses . .			240,000

Of the direct fixed expenses, $20,000 of those shown for Segment C and $18,000 of those shown for Segment D were not under the control of that segment's manager.

Regarding the company's total operating assets of $3,000,000 the following facts exist:

	Segment C	Segment D
Assets directly used by and identified with the segment	$1,200,000	$600,000
Assets under the "control" of the segment manager	1,000,000	500,000

Required:

a. Prepare a statement showing the contribution margin of each segment, the contribution to indirect expenses for each segment, and the total income of the Vail Company.
b. Determine the ROI for evaluating (1) the earning power of the entire company, (2) the rate of income contribution of each segment, and (3) the income performance of each segment manager.
c. Comment on the results of part *(b)*.

P24-6-A

Calculate ROI and RI for each segment and segment manager

The Albott Company operates with three segments, E, F, and G. Data regarding these segments follow:

	Segment E	Segment F	Segment G
Contribution to indirect expenses	$108,000	$ 60,000	$ 48,000
Income controllable by the manager	150,000	90,000	76,800
Assets directly used by and identified with the segment . .	600,000	480,000	240,000
Assets under the "control" of the segment manager . . .	528,000	426,000	216,000

Required:

a. Calculate the ROI for each segment and each segment manager. Rank them from highest to lowest.
b. Assume the minimum desired rates of return are 12% for a segment and 20% for a segment manager. Calculate the RI for each segment and each manager. Rank them from highest to lowest.
c. Repeat *(b)*, but assume the desired minimum rates of return are 17% for a segment and 25% for a segment manager. Rank them from highest to lowest.
d. Comment on the ranking achieved.

P24-7-A

Determine margin, turnover, and ROI for a segment and the effect on each when the variables are changed

The manager of the Tennis segment of the Sanford Corporation is faced with the following data for the year 1987:

Contribution to indirect expenses	$ 1,500,000
Assets directly used by and identified with the segment . .	18,750,000
Sales	30,000,000

Required:

a. Determine the margin, turnover, and ROI for the segment in 1987.
b. Determine the effect on margin, turnover, and ROI of the segment in 1988 if each of the following changes were to occur. Consider each one separately, and assume that any items not specifically mentioned remain the same as in 1987:

1. A campaign to control costs resulted in $300,000 of reduced expenses.
2. Certain nonproductive assets were eliminated. As a result "investment" decreased by $1,500,000 and expenses decreased by $120,000.

3. An advertising campaign resulted in increasing sales by $6,000,000, cost of goods sold by $4,500,000, and advertising expense by $900,000.

4. An investment was made in productive assets costing $1,500,000. As a result, sales increased by $600,000, and expenses increased by $90,000.

P24–8–A

Evaluate the desirability of adopting a new project using ROI, margin, and turnover

For the year ended December 31, 1987, the Adams Company reported the following information for the company as a whole and for one of its segments:

		Kitchen segment		
	Adams Company	Tile project	Floor project	Total
Sales	$9,600,000	$1,080,000	$480,000	$1,560,000
Income	1,800,000	480,000	60,000	540,000
Investment . .	7,200,000	1,440,000	168,000	1,608,000

The Adams Company anticipates that the above relationships (ROI, margin, turnover) will hold true for the upcoming year. The kitchen segment is faced with the possibility of adding a new project in 1988, with the following projected data:

	Appliance project
Sales	$360,000
Income	84,000
Investment	300,000

Required:

a. Determine the ROI for the Adams Company, the kitchen segment, and for the two projects (tile and floor) separately for the year ended December 31, 1987.

b. Using the above information, determine if the manager of the kitchen segment should add the appliance project if ROI is a deciding factor. What problem may be encountered?

P24–9–A

Evaluate the desirability of adopting a new project using RI

Using the data provided in P24–8–A, determine the residual income for all three projects and for the kitchen segment with and without the appliance project if the desired ROI is 25% (the ROI for the company as a whole). Should the appliance project be added if RI is a deciding factor?

PROBLEMS, SERIES B

P24–1–B

Prepare responsibility reports for various levels of management

You are given the following information relevant to Mitchell Company for the year ended December 31, 1987. The company is organized according to functions.

	Shop "A" supervisor		Plant manager		Vice president of manufacturing	
Controllable expenses	Budget	Actual	Budget	Actual	Budget	Actual
Office expense	$2,000	$1,000	$ 4,000	$ 5,000	$10,000	$ 9,000
Supervision	3,000	4,000				
Supplies (manufacturing) . .	4,000	5,000				
Tools	5,000	6,000				
Shop "B"			9,000	10,000		
Shop "C"			11,000	12,000		
Purchasing					14,000	17,000
Receiving					15,000	15,000
Inspection					16,000	8,000

Required:

Prepare the responsibility accounting reports for three levels of management—supervisor, plant manager, and vice president of manufacturing.

P24–2–B

Evaluate responsibility centers as profit centers and investment centers

The Norton Corporation has three production plants (K, L, and M). These plants are treated as responsibility centers. Following is a summary of the results for the month of April 1987:

Plant	Revenues	Expenses	Investment base (gross assets)
K	$ 150,000	$125,000	$ 600,000
L	200,000	75,000	800,000
M	1,050,000	800,000	5,500,000

Required:

a. If the plants are treated as profit centers, which plant manager appears to have done the best job?

b. If the plants are treated as investment centers, which plant manager appears to have done the best job? (Assume that plant managers are evaluated in terms of ROI).

c. Do the results of profit center analysis and investment center analysis give different findings? If so, why?

P24–3–B

Allocate indirect expenses to illustrate arbitrary nature of expense allocation

Surfrider, Inc. allocates expenses and revenues to the two segments that it operates. It extends credit to customers under a revolving charge plan whereby all account balances not paid within 30 days are charged interest at the rate of 1½% per month.

Given below are selected revenue and expense accounts and some additional data needed to complete the allocation of the one revenue amount and the expenses.

Revenue and expenses (allocation bases)

Revolving charge service revenue (net sales)	$ 40,000
Home office building occupancy expense (net sales)	30,000
Buying expenses (net purchases)	100,000
General administrative expenses (number of employees in department)	50,000
Insurance expense (relative average inventory plus cost of equipment and fixtures in each department)	12,000
Depreciation expense on home office equipment (net sales) . .	20,000

Additional data:

	Segment D	Segment E	Total
Number of employees	3	7	10
Sales (net)	$200,000	$400,000	$600,000
Purchases (net)	160,000	240,000	400,000
Average inventory	40,000	80,000	120,000
Cost of equipment and fixtures . .	60,000	120,000	180,000

Required:

a. Prepare a schedule showing allocation of the above items to Segments D and E.

b. Criticize some of these allocation bases.

P24–4–B

Prepare schedule showing contribution margin and contribution to indirect expenses using contribution margin format; prepare segmental income statements

Carey, Inc. is a diamond importer that operates two segments, A and B. The revenue and expense data for 1987 follow:

	Segment A	Segment B	Total
Net sales	$559,500	$923,000	$1,482,500
Direct expenses:*			
Cost of goods sold . . .	310,000	470,000	780,000
Selling	53,000	45,000	98,000
Administrative	15,000	10,000	25,000
Bad debts	4,000	11,000	15,000
Indirect expenses:			
Selling			210,000
Administrative			260,000

* All of the direct expenses are variable except administrative expense, which is fixed.

Required: a. Prepare a schedule showing the contribution margin, the contribution to indirect expenses of each segment, and net income for the company as a whole. Do not allocate indirect expenses to the segments.

b. Assume that indirect selling expenses are to be allocated to the segments on the basis of net sales (round to the nearest percent) and that indirect administrative expenses are to be allocated on the basis of direct administrative expenses. Prepare a statement (starting with the contribution to indirect expenses) that shows the net income of each segment.

c. Comment on the appropriateness of the "income" amounts shown in parts *(a)* and *(b)* for determining the income contribution of the segments.

P24–5–B

Determine the contribution margin using contribution margin format; calculate ROI for (1) the entire company, (2) each segment, and (3) each manager

The Davis Corporation has three segments. Following are the results of operations for 1987:

	Segment 1	Segment 2	Segment 3	Total
Sales	$30,000,000	$18,000,000	$12,000,000	$60,000,000
Variable expenses . .	21,600,000	10,200,000	8,100,000	39,900,000
Fixed expenses:				
Direct	4,200,000	1,500,000	600,000	6,300,000
Indirect				3,000,000

Of the direct fixed expenses, $300,000 of those shown for Segment 1, $210,000 of those shown for Segment 2, and $300,000 of those shown for Segment 3 were not under the control of that segment's manager.

For the company's total operating assets of $84,000,000, the following facts exist:

	Segment 1	Segment 2	Segment 3
Assets directly used by and identified with the segment	$42,000,000	$24,000,000	$12,000,000
Assets under the "control" of the segment manager	36,000,000	19,200,000	9,600,000

Required: a. Prepare a statement (in thousands of dollars) showing the contribution margin, the contribution to indirect expenses for each segment, and the total income of the Davis Corporation.

b. Determine the ROI for evaluating (1) the earning power of the entire company, (2) the rate of income contribution of each segment, and (3) the income performance of each segment manager.

c. Comment on the results of part *(b)*.

P24–6–B

Calculate ROI and RI for each segment and each segment manager

The Watson Company has three segments, R, S, and T. Data regarding these segments follow:

	Segment R	Segment S	Segment T
Contribution to indirect expenses	$ 720,000	$ 348,000	$120,000
Income controllable by the manager	792,000	378,000	144,000
Assets directly used by and identified with the segment . .	6,000,000	2,400,000	600,000
Assets under the "control" of the segment manager	5,760,000	2,280,000	540,000

Required: a. Calculate the ROI for each segment and each segment manager. Rank them from highest to lowest.

b. Assume the minimum desired rates of return are 10% for a segment and 12% for a segment manager. Calculate the RI for each segment and for each manager. Rank them from highest to lowest.

c. Repeat *(b)*, but assume that the desired minimum rates of return are 14% for a segment and 16% for a segment manager. Rank them from highest to lowest.

d. Comment on the rankings achieved.

P24-7-B

Determine margin, turnover, and ROI for a segment and the effect on each when the variables are changed

The Jacket segment of the Tweed Corporation reported the following data for 1987:

Contribution to indirect expenses	$ 525,000
Assets directly used by and identified with the segment . .	4,200,000
Sales	8,400,000

Required:

a.   Determine the margin, turnover, and ROI for the segment in 1987.

b.   Determine the effect on margin, turnover, and ROI of the segment in 1988 if each of the following changes were to occur. Consider each one separately, and assume that any items not specifically mentioned remain the same as in 1987:

1.   A new labor contract with the union increased expenses by $150,000 for 1988.
2.   A strike in early 1988 shut down operations for two months. Sales decreased by $2,250,000, cost of goods sold by $1,500,000, and other direct expenses by $450,000.
3.   Introduction of a new product caused sales to increase by $3,000,000, cost of goods sold by $2,100,000, and other direct expenses by $225,000. Operating assets increased by $450,000.
4.   An advertising campaign was launched. As a result, sales increased by $750,000, cost of goods sold by $525,000, and other direct expenses by $225,000.

P24-8-B

Evaluate the desirability of adopting a project using ROI, margin, and turnover

The following information is available for the Crenshaw Company as a whole and for the Golf segment for the year ending December 31, 1987.

	Crenshaw Company overall	Golf segment		
		Project A	Project B	Total
Sales	$8,000,000	$1,000,000	$1,500,000	$2,500,000
Income	900,000	200,000	180,000	380,000
Investment . . .	6,000,000	800,000	1,000,000	1,800,000

The Crenshaw Company anticipates that the above relationships (margin, turnover, and ROI) will hold true for the coming year. The Golf segment intends to add project C in 1988, with the following projected data:

Project C	
Sales . . .	$500,000
Income . . .	50,000
Investment . .	300,000

Required:

a.   Using the above information, determine the ROI for 1987 for the Crenshaw Company, the Golf segment, and for projects A and B separately.

b.   Using ROI information, should the manager of the Golf Segment undertake project C? What problems might be encountered in using ROI as a decision-making tool?

BUSINESS DECISION PROBLEM

Allocate unusual expenses to departments; determine controllable and noncontrollable expenses

Respond to each of the following situations:

a.   The Nelson Company manufactures water skis. The company's business is seasonal, and between August and December 10 skilled manufacturing employees are usually "laid off." In order to improve morale, the financial vice president suggested that these 10 employees not be laid off in the future. Instead it was suggested that they work in general labor from August to December but still be paid their manufacturing wages of $12 per hour. General labor personnel earn $6 per hour. What are the implications of this plan for the assignment of costs to the various segments of the business?

b. The Leed Company builds new homes. Ferris is in charge of the construction department. Among other responsibilities, Ferris hires and supervises the carpenters and other workers who build the homes. The Leed Company does not do its own foundation work. The construction of foundations is done by subcontractors hired by Kyte of the procurement department.

To start the development of a 500-home community, Kyte hired the Lye Company to build the foundations for the homes. On the day construction was to begin, the Lye Company went out of business. Consequently, construction was delayed six weeks while Kyte hired a new subcontractor. Which department should be charged with the cost of the delay in construction? Why?

c. Jack Blount is supervisor of Department 39 of the Sykes Company. The annual budget for the department is as follows:

	Annual budget for Department 39
Small tools	$ 10,800
Set up	12,000
Direct labor	13,200
Direct materials	24,000
Supplies	6,000
Supervision	36,000
Property taxes	6,000
Property insurance	1,200
Depreciation, machinery	2,400
Depreciation, building	2,400
Total	$114,000

Blount's salary of $24,000 is included in supervision. The remaining $12,000 in supervision is the salary of the assistant supervisor who is directly responsible to Blount.
Identify the budget items that are controllable by Blount.

BUSINESS SITUATION FOR DISCUSSION

Management*

Financial analysts group stresses need for segment reporting

☐   The need for good segment reporting, not only on an annual basis but on a quarterly basis as well, has increased in significance of late. It has become so important that the Financial Analysts Federation (FAF) is weighing the possibility of not presenting its annual Award for Excellence for financial reporting to a company if the company does not do an "outstanding job" of segment reporting in its quarterly reports.

The FAF is the professional organization of investment managers and securities analysts in North America with more than 15,000 members in 53 societies and chapters. Awards for excellence in corporate reporting are annually presented by the group.

According to Anthony T. Cope, CFA, of Wellington Management Company, Boston, Massachusetts, chairman of the FAF's corporate information committee, the suggestion made by a committee member that no award

be given a company that does not do a superior job of segment reporting "has merit; it will be carefully considered when criteria [for the 1984 awards] are established."

Cope said that the need for more segmented reporting is "another implication of the volatility and turmoil" of 1982, for which the most recent FAF awards were made.

What constitutes successful financial reporting? The FAF's corporate information committee suggests four elements:

☐   Clear presentation of information that goes beyond the minimum prescribed reporting requirements and helps to put company operations in perspective.

☐   Written commentary that is more than a recitation of historical facts but, rather, explains why important developments took place, that does not gloss over problems and adverse developments and that provides a judicious insight into the future.

☐   A timely, consistent and responsible investor relations program that genuinely seeks to inform the financial analyst in an unbiased way.

☐   An ability to articulate and communicate the business philosophy and principal strategies of management

* *Journal of Accountancy*, May 1984, p. 34. Copyright © 1984 by the American Institute of Certified Public Accountants, Inc. Reprinted with permission.

and the way in which management is organized to carry them out.

''Nothing more, and nothing less, will satisfy the demands of the increasingly turbulent investment and financial worlds,'' Cope said.

On segment disclosure in particular, analysts representing various industry specialties also suggest some guidelines:

☐ Be uniform in the way information is presented in each segment.
☐ Include segment sales and earnings graphs going back at least five years.
☐ Summarize the year's highlights and offer perspective on unusual events.
☐ Emphasize market size and growth rates or end users served by each segment and the backlog of key product lines.
☐ Break out foreign revenues, including export sales by segment.

Most analysts believe that, in order to grasp the prospects of a specific business, statements and breakdowns by product line and geographic market reported in the annual report, and on a regular and consistent basis thereafter, are essential.

CHAPTER 25 Budgeting

LEARNING OBJECTIVES

After studying this chapter, you should be able to:

1. Define a budget and name several kinds of budgets.
2. List several benefits of a budget.
3. List five general principles of budgeting.
4. Prepare a planned operating budget and its supporting budgets, such as the sales budget, production and purchases budgets, and other expense budgets.
5. Prepare flexible operating budgets.
6. Prepare a financial budget and its supporting budgets.
7. Define and use correctly the new terms in the glossary.

In planning the management of your personal finances, you may have only a general notion of the inflows and outflows of cash that will occur for a period. If the outflows exceed the inflows, you may have to borrow to cover the difference. If the inflows exceed the outflows, you may have excess cash to place in a bank or to invest.

At times, especially if you find that your cash position is tight, you may be tempted to prepare a written plan detailing your anticipated cash flows so that you may better control your finances. Such a written plan is a budget.

Companies usually prepare budgets so that they may plan for and then control their revenues (inflows) and expenses (outflows). Failure to prepare a budget could lead to significant cash flow problems or even financial disaster for a company. In fact, one of the leading causes of failure in small businesses is failing to plan and control operations through the use of budgets.

■ THE BUDGET—FOR PLANNING AND CONTROL

Time and wealth are scarce resources to all individuals and organizations, and use of these resources requires planning. But planning alone is insufficient. Control is also necessary to ensure that feasible plans are actually carried out. A tool widely used in planning and controlling the use of scarce resources is a **budget.**

There are many types of budgets. **Responsibility budgets,** which were examined in the preceding chapter, are designed to judge the performance of an individual segment or manager. **Capital budgets,** covered in Chapter 27, evaluate long-term capital projects such as the addition of equipment or the relocation of a plant. This chapter examines the **master budget,** which consists of a planned operating budget and a financial budget. The planned operating budget helps plan future earnings and results in a projected income statement. The financial budget helps management plan the financing of assets and results in a projected balance sheet.

Purposes of Budgets

A budget is a **plan** showing the company's objectives and how management intends to acquire and use resources to attain those objectives. A budget also shows how management intends to **control** the acquisition and use of resources in the coming period(s). A budget formalizes management's plans in quantitative terms. It also forces all levels of management to think ahead, anticipate results, and take action to remedy possible poor results.

Budgets may also be used to **motivate** individuals so that they strive to achieve stated goals. Budget-to-actual comparisons may be used to evaluate individual performance. For instance, the standard variable cost of producing a given part in a given cost center is a budget figure with which actual cost can be compared to help evaluate the performance of that cost center's manager. This type of comparison was illustrated in Chapter 23.

The preparation and use of budgets result in many other benefits. Business activities are better **coordinated;** managers **become aware of other managers' plans;** employees may become **cost conscious** and try to **conserve** resources; the organizational plan of the company may be **reviewed** more often and changed where necessary; and a breadth of **vision,** which might not otherwise be developed, is fostered. The planning process that results in a formal budget provides an opportunity for various levels of management to think through and commit future plans to writing. In addition, a properly prepared budget will allow management to follow the management-by-exception principle by devoting attention to activities that deviate significantly from planned levels. For all these reasons, the expected results, which are reflected in the budget, must be clearly stated.

Considerations in Preparing a Budget

Being uncertain about future developments is a poor excuse for failing to budget. In fact, the less stable the conditions, the more necessary and desirable is budgeting, although the process becomes more difficult. Obviously, stable operating conditions permit greater reliance on past experience as a basis for budgeting. But it must be emphasized that budgets are based on more than past results. Future plans must also be considered. The current year's expected activities as expressed in the budget are based on current conditions. As a result, budgeted performance is more useful than past performance as a basis for judging actual results.

A budget should describe management's assumptions relating to (1) the state of the economy over the planning horizon; (2) plans for adding, deleting, or changing product lines; (3) the nature of the industry's competition; and (4) the effects of existing or possible government regulations. If assumptions change during the budget period, the effects of the changes should be analyzed and included in the evaluation of performance.

Budgets are quantitative plans for the future. But they are based mainly on past experience adjusted for future expectations. Thus, accounting data related to the past play an important part in budget preparation. The accounting system and the budget are closely related. The details of the budget must agree with the company's ledger accounts. In turn, the accounts must be designed to assist in preparing the budget, financial statements, and interim financial reports to facilitate operational control.

Accounting data and budgeted projections should be compared often during the budget period, and any differences should be investigated. Yet budgeting is not a substitute for good management. Rather, the budget is an important tool of managerial control. Managers make decisions in budget preparation that serve as a plan of action.

Some General Principles of Budgeting

Budgeting involves the coordination of financial and nonfinancial planning to satisfy organizational goals and objectives. Although there is no foolproof method for preparing an effective budget, the following aspects should be carefully considered.

Top Management Support.   All management levels must be aware of the budget's importance to the company. Plans must be clearly stated. Overemphasis on the mechanics of the budget process should be avoided. Overall broad objectives for the corporation must be decided upon and communicated throughout the organization.

Participation in Goal Setting.   It is generally believed that employees are more likely to strive toward organizational goals if they participate in setting them. Employees may have significant information that would help the budget process. Also, the employees can be made aware of the interrelationships among budget items.

Responsibility Accounting.   Individuals should be informed of management's expectations. Only those costs over which an individual has predominant control should be used in evaluating that individual's performance. As noted in the previous chapter, responsibility reports often contain budget-to-actual comparisons.

Communication of Results.   People should be informed of their progress promptly and clearly. Effective communication implies (1) timeliness, (2) reasonable accuracy, and (3) understandability. Results should be communicated so that any necessary adjustments to performance can be made.

Flexibility.   If the basic assumptions underlying the budget change during the year, the budget should be restated. In this way, performance at the actual level of operations can be compared to expected performance at that level.

Behavioral Implications of Budgets

The term *budget* has negative connotations for many employees who feel they are **subjected** to a budget. Often in the past, management has **imposed** a budget without considering the opinions and feelings of the personnel affected. Such a dictatorial process may result in resistance to the budget. A number of reasons may underlie such resistance, including lack of understanding of the program, concern for status, and an expectation of increased pressure to perform. Employees may believe that the performance evaluation method is unfair or that the goals are unrealistic and unattainable. They may lack confidence in the way accounting figures are generated or may prefer a less formal communication and evaluation system. Often these fears are completely unfounded, but if an employee believes these problems exist, it will be very difficult to accomplish the objectives of budgeting.

Problems encountered with such **imposed** budgets have led accountants and management to participatory budgeting. Participatory budgeting means that all levels of management responsible for actual performance actively participate in setting operating goals for the coming period. Managers are more likely to understand, accept, and pursue goals if they are involved in formulating them.

Where do accountants fit into a participatory budgeting process? Accountants should be **compilers** or coordinators of the budget, not **preparers.** They should be on hand during the preparation process to present and explain significant financial data. Accountants must identify the relevant cost data that will enable management's objectives to be quantified in dollars, and they are responsible for meaningful budget reports. Accountants must continually strive to make the accounting system more responsive to managerial needs. That responsiveness, in turn, will increase confidence in the system.

Although budget participation has been used successfully in many companies, it does not always work. Studies have shown that in many organizations budget participation failed to make employees more motivated to achieve budgeted goals. Whether or not participation works depends on management's leadership style and on the organization's size and structure. Participation is not the answer to all the problems of budget preparation. It is one way to achieve better results in organizations that are receptive to that philosophy of participation.

▦ THE MASTER BUDGET

A master budget consists of a projected income statement (planned operating budget) and a projected balance sheet (financial budget) showing the organization's objectives and proposed ways of attaining them. The remainder of this chapter will concentrate on how to prepare a master budget. The master budget is emphasized because of its prime importance to financial planning and control in a business entity. Illustration 25.1 presents the major elements involved in preparing a master budget.

The budget preparation process flows from top to bottom in Illustration 25.1. The resulting projected income statement and balance sheet incorporate elements from all budgets and schedules prepared by individual segments or divisions.

The budgeting process starts with management's plans and objectives for the next period. These plans result in various policy decisions concerning selling price, distribution network, advertising expenditures, and environmental influences from which sales forecasts for the period (in units by product or product line) are made. Multiplying units by selling price gives the sales budget in

Illustration 25.1

A Flowchart of the Financial Planning Process (an overview)

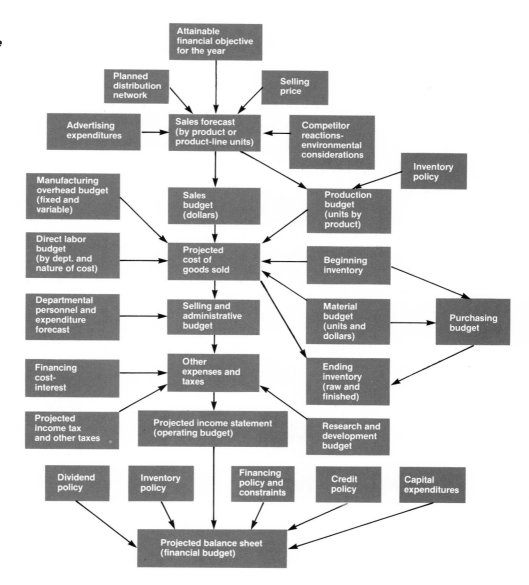

dollars. Projected cost of goods sold is based on expected production, sales volume, and inventory policy. Volume and inventory policies influence the preparation of the purchasing budget. Detailed budgets are made for each major type of manufacturing expense on both a cost center (responsibility) basis and in the aggregate.

The projected balance sheet is prepared using information contained in the planned operating budget; it is also influenced by policy decisions pertaining to dividends, inventory, credit, capital expenditures, and financial plans. The planning of capital expenditures will be described in Chapter 27. Financing by debt or stock issuances was discussed in earlier chapters.

This chapter cannot cover all areas of budgeting in detail; whole books are devoted to the subject. But the following presentation provides an overview of a budgeting procedure that has been used successfully by many business enterprises. Illustration 25.1 provides a frame of reference for the following discussion.

Preparing the Planned Operating Budget at the Expected Level of Operations

Since the projected balance sheet, or **financial budget,** depends on many items in the projected income statement, the logical starting point in preparing a master budget is the projected income statement, or **planned operating budget.** However, since the planned operating budget shows the net effect of many interrelated activities, several supporting budgets (sales, production, and purchases, to name a few) must be prepared before preparing the planned operating budget. The process begins with the sales budget.

The Sales Budget.   Preparing the sales budget is a critical step in the budgeting process. Most other budgets are derived from the sales budget. If the sales budget is not properly prepared, the entire operating budget will be inaccurate.

As you saw in Illustration 25.1, the sales budget is established by using the sales forecast. Generally, sales forecasts are based on a combination of past experiences and future expectations. The expected general level of economic activity and prospects for the industry as a whole must be considered. These prospects may be influenced by population growth, per capita income, new construction, population migration, and so on. The company's relative position in the industry must also be reviewed in light of any expected changes.

Allowances must be made for varying conditions that affect products, territories, or the strength of competitors. For example, the effect of any changes in the expected level of advertising expenditures must be estimated. Quotas may be developed for salespersons based on sales analyses by territory, by customer, by product, and so on.

The sales manager is usually responsible for the sales budget, which is prepared first in units and then in dollars. The remaining budgets that support the operating budget are based on the sales budget in units.

The Production Budget.   The **production budget** takes into account the units in the sales budget and the company's inventory policy. The production budget is first developed in units, but unit costs cannot be developed until production volume is known. Determining production volume is an important task. Careful scheduling is needed to maintain certain minimum quantities of inventory on hand while avoiding excessive inventory accumulation. The cost of carrying inventory on hand must be compared with the higher unit costs frequently encountered in producing relatively small batches of a product. **The principal objective of the production budget is to coordinate (in terms of time and quantity) the production and sale of goods.**

The production budget is often subdivided into budgets for materials, labor, and manufacturing overhead. Usually materials, labor, and some elements of manufacturing overhead will vary directly with production within a given relevant range of production. Fixed manufacturing overhead costs do not vary directly with production but are constant in total within a relevant range of production. For example, fixed manufacturing overhead costs may be $15,000 when production ranges from 60,000 to 80,000 units. However, when production is 80,001 to 95,000 units, the fixed manufacturing overhead costs might be $25,000. Management will need to determine which level of production will be the "relevant range" in order to accurately determine fixed manufacturing overhead costs.

Selling, Administrative, and Other Expense Budgets (Schedules).   Departmental personnel and expenditure forecasts are used to budget the amounts of selling and administrative expenses. Other expenses such as interest expense, income tax expense, and research and development expenses are also estimated.

Preparing the Financial Budget

Preparing a projected balance sheet, or financial budget, involves analyzing every balance sheet account. The beginning balance for each account is the amount shown on the balance sheet prepared at the end of the preceding period. Then, the effects of any planned activities on each account are considered. Many accounts will be affected by items appearing in the operating budget and by either cash inflows or outflows. Cash inflows and outflows are usually shown in a cash budget, which will be discussed later in the chapter.

The complexities encountered in preparing the financial budget often require the preparation of detailed schedules. These schedules analyze such things as planned accounts receivable collections and balances, planned material purchases, planned inventories, changes in all accounts affected by operating costs, and the amount of federal income taxes payable. Dividend policy, inventory policy, financing policy and constraints, credit policy, and planned capital expenditures also affect amounts shown in the financial budget.

■ THE MASTER BUDGET ILLUSTRATED

The first part of this chapter discussed some general concepts relating to the preparation of a master budget. This section illustrates step by step how to prepare a master budget for 1987 for the Leed Company.

Preparing the Planned Operating Budget in Units for the Leed Company

The planned operating budget is developed first in units rather than dollars. Because revenues and many expenses vary with volume, they can be forecasted more easily after sales and production quantities are established.

Illustration 25.2

Leed Company's Planned Production and Sales for First Two Quarters of 1987 (in units)

	Quarter ending	
	March 31, 1987	June 30, 1987
Beginning finished goods inventory . . .	10,000*	15,000
Add: Planned production	25,000	25,000
Units available for sale	35,000	40,000
Less: Sales forecast	20,000	35,000
Ending finished good inventory	15,000	5,000

* Actual on January 1.

To illustrate this step, assume that Leed's management forecasts sales for the year 1987 at 100,000 units. Quarterly sales are expected to be 20,000, 35,000, 20,000, and 25,000 units. We will assume that the company's policy is to stabilize production, so that 100,000 units will be produced uniformly throughout the year. Therefore, production will be at the rate of 25,000 units per quarter (100,000 units/four quarters). To simplify our example, assume there are no beginning or ending work in process inventories (although it would be equivalent and more realistic to assume that work in process inventories would remain at a constant amount throughout the year). Finished goods inventory on January 1, 1987, is 10,000 units. From these data, a schedule of budgeted sales and production in units is prepared, as shown in Illustration 25.2.

Notice that the above ending inventory must be allowed to fluctuate if sales vary and a stable production policy is maintained. Thus, the finished goods inventory is affected by the difference between production and sales. When establishing inventory policy, management has decided that it is less costly to deal with fluctuating inventories than with fluctuating production.

In Illustration 25.2 sales and production data were given for each period, and we had to solve for ending inventory. Sometimes we are given sales and ending inventory data (described as a certain percentage of the next period's sales), and we have to calculate the required level of production. Assume Leed Company wishes to have ending inventory equal to 50% of the next month's sales in units (30,000 units). In this latter instance, the following format may be used to calculate planned production:

Sales forecast (units)—current month	20,000
Add: Planned ending finished goods inventory . .	15,000*
Total units required for the period	35,000
Deduct: Beginning finished goods inventory . . .	10,000
Planned production (units)	25,000

* 50% × 30,000.

When management states that ending finished goods inventory must be a specified percentage of future sales, a constant production policy cannot be maintained unless sales each period are constant.

Preparing the Planned Operating Budget in Dollars

Next, dollars must be introduced into the analysis. A forecast of expected selling prices must be made and costs must be analyzed. The forecasted selling price and costs are shown in Illustration 25.3. Note that costs are classified

Illustration 25.3

*Budget Estimate of
Selling Price and
Costs*

LEED COMPANY
Budget Estimates of Selling Price and Costs
For the Quarters Ending March 31, and June 30, 1987

Forecasted selling price	$ 20
Manufacturing costs:	
Variable (per unit manufactured):	
Direct materials	2
Direct labor	6
Manufacturing overhead	1
Fixed overhead (total each quarter)	75,000
Selling and administrative expenses:	
Variable (per unit sold)	2
Fixed (total each quarter)	100,000

according to whether they are variable or fixed and are budgeted accordingly. As noted earlier, **variable costs** vary in total directly with production or sales. **Fixed costs** are unaffected in total by the relative level of production or sales. Thus, variable costs are budgeted as a constant dollar amount **per unit,** while fixed costs are budgeted only in total.

Management must now prepare a schedule to forecast cost of goods sold, the next major amount on the planned operating budget. This schedule is shown in Illustration 25.4. Notice that the beginning finished goods inventory amount for the quarter ending March 31 is the amount shown on the December 31, 1986, year-end balance sheet. Cost of goods manufactured is calculated using the variable costs of production from Illustration 25.3 plus an allocated amount of fixed manufacturing overhead ($75,000/25,000 units).

The amount of ending finished good inventory is the number of units determined to be in ending inventory (from Illustration 25.2) times the cost per unit manufactured during the period.

Illustration 25.4

*Schedule of Planned
Cost of Goods Sold*

LEED COMPANY
Planned Cost of Goods Sold

	Quarter ending	
	March 31, 1987	June 30, 1987
Beginning finished goods inventory	$130,000*	$180,000
Cost of goods manufactured:		
Direct materials (25,000 × $2)	$ 50,000	$ 50,000
Direct labor (25,000 × $6)	150,000	150,000
Variable manufacturing overhead (25,000 × $1)	25,000	25,000
Fixed manufacturing overhead (per Illustration 25.3)	75,000	75,000
Cost of goods manufactured (25,000 units at $12)	$300,000	$300,000
Goods available for sale	$430,000	$480,000
Ending finished goods inventory:		
(15,000 at $12)†	180,000	
(5,000 at $12)		60,000
Cost of goods sold	$250,000	$420,000

* Actual on January 1 (10,000 at $13); see balance sheet Illustration 25.9.
† First-in, first-out procedure assumed.

After cost of goods sold has been forecasted, a separate budget is prepared for all selling and administrative expenses. Several support schedules may be involved for items such as advertising expense, office expense, and payroll department expense. The schedules to support budgeted selling and administrative expenses are not illustrated here, but the total selling and administrative expenses for each of the first two quarters is entered into the planned operating budget in Illustration 25.5.

Illustration 25.5

Planned Operating Budgets

LEED COMPANY
Planned Operating Budgets
For Quarters Ending March 31 and June 30, 1987

	Quarter ending	
	March 31, 1987	June 30, 1987
Forecasted sales (20,000 and 35,000 at $20) (per Illustration 25.3)	$400,000	$700,000
Cost of goods sold (per Illustration 25.4)	250,000	420,000
Gross margin	$150,000	$280,000
Selling and administrative expenses:		
Variable (20,000 and 35,000 at $2) (per Illustration 25.3)	$ 40,000	$ 70,000
Fixed (per Illustration 25.3)	100,000	100,000
Total selling and administrative expenses	$140,000	$170,000
Net income before income taxes	$ 10,000	$110,000
Estimated federal income taxes (assumed to be 40%) . . .	4,000	44,000
Net income	$ 6,000	$ 66,000

The Planned Operating Budget Illustrated

Illustration 25.5 shows the resulting planned operating budget for the Leed Company. All of the items appearing in the planned operating budget except the income tax accrual have been discussed and explained. Income taxes are budgeted for Leed Company at an assumed rate of 40% of net income before taxes.

If the planned operating budget does not show the desired net income, new operating plans will have to be formulated, and a new budget will be developed. The purpose of preparing a planned operating budget is to gain some knowledge of the results of a period's activities before they actually occur.

Flexible Operating Budgets

Early in the chapter you learned that a budget should be adjusted for changes in assumptions or variations in the level of operations. A technique known as flexible budgeting, which was introduced in Chapter 23, is used to deal with budgetary adjustments. A **flexible operating budget** is a special kind of budget that provides detailed information about budgeted expenses (and revenues) at various levels of output.

Illustration 25.6 shows a flexible budget for Leed Company's manufacturing overhead costs at various levels of output. In this example, supplies are considered a strictly variable cost, increasing $200 each time production increases

Illustration 25.6

Flexible Budget for Manufacturing Overhead

Element of manufacturing overhead	Volume (percent of capacity)*			
	70%	*80%*	*90%*	*100%*
Supplies	$ 1,400	$ 1,600	$ 1,800	$ 2,000
Power	7,600	8,400	9,200	10,000
Insurance	4,500	4,500	5,000	5,000
Maintenance	5,800	6,200	7,200	8,000
Depreciation . . .	40,000	40,000	40,000	40,000
Supervision	35,000	35,000	35,000	35,000
	$94,300	$95,700	$98,200	$100,000

LEED COMPANY
Flexible Budget for Manufacturing Overhead

* Capacity is 100,000 units per period.

by 10% of capacity. In actuality, however, there are probably few costs that vary in an exact linear relationship with output. Power is a mixed (or semivariable) cost in this example. A **mixed cost** varies with volume, but not in direct proportion to the changes in volume. In the case of power cost, there is a fixed amount that Leed Company must pay, plus an additional $800 for each 10% increase in volume. Insurance and maintenance are considered **step variable** costs in this example since they increase in "steps" as volume increases. Depreciation and supervision, on the other hand, are completely fixed costs in this example since they are constant over the entire relevant range of activity.

A similar flexible budget could be prepared for selling and administrative expenses with supporting schedules for each expense item. Variable expenses are calculated for various levels of sales volume, while fixed costs remain constant within the relevant range.

Budget Variances.   When management uses a flexible budget to appraise a department's performance, the evaluation is based on the amounts budgeted for the level of activity actually experienced. The difference between actual costs incurred and the budgeted amount for that **same level of operations** is called a **budget variance.** Budget variances can indicate a department's or company's degree of efficiency, since they emerge from a comparison of "what was" with "what should have been."

To illustrate the computation of budget variances, assume that Leed Company prepared an overhead budget based on an expected volume of 100%. At this level of production, the budgeted amount for supplies is $2,000, or $0.02 per unit. By the end of the period $1,900 of supplies have been used. The first impression is that a favorable variance of $100 exists. But if actual production for the period was only 90,000 units (90% of capacity), there is actually an unfavorable variance of $100. This is because, according to the flexible operating budget, at 90% of capacity only $1,800 of supplies should have been used. Consequently, there appears to have been an inefficient use of supplies.

To give another example using the data in Illustration 25.6, maintenance may have been budgeted at $6,200 for a given period assuming the company planned to produce 80,000 units (80% of operating capacity). However, actual maintenance costs may have been $6,800 for the period. This result does not necessarily mean that an unfavorable variance of $600 was incurred. The variance depends on **actual production volume.** Assume once again that 90,000 units were produced during the period; maintenance costs are budgeted at $7,200 for that level of production. Therefore, there would actually be a favorable variance of $400 ($7,200 − $6,800).

Flexible budgets often show budgeted amounts for every 10% change in the level of operations, such as at the 70%, 80%, 90%, 100%, and 110% levels of capacity. But actual production may fall somewhere between levels, say, at 84%. When actual production falls between the levels shown in the flexible budget, the budgeted amounts at that level of operations must be calculated. The only kind of cost that does not have to be recalculated is a fixed cost since, by definition, it does not vary over the relevant range. For directly variable costs, the expected cost can be computed easily at any level since the cost is constant per unit of output. For mixed costs (partially fixed and partially variable), the budgeted amount for any operating level other than those presented can be computed using the following formula, assuming the relationship between costs and volume above a minimum level of costs is linear.

Budgeted amount = Fixed portion of costs
  + (Variable portion of cost per unit × Units of output)

Step variable costs may change only when a sufficiently large increase in production occurs, such as when one additional inspector must be added for every 20% increase in capacity used. Such step variable costs usually can be read directly from the flexible budget.

Flexible Operating Budget and Budget Variances Illustrated. As stated above, a flexible operating budget provides detailed information about budgeted expenses at various levels of activity. The main advantage of using a flexible operating budget along with a planned operating budget is that performance can be appraised on two levels. First, comparison of the actual results with the **planned** operating budget permits analysis of the deviation of actual output from expected output. Then, given the actual level of operations, actual costs can be compared with expected costs for **that** level of output, shown on the **flexible** operating budget. The use of flexible operating budgets gives a valid basis for comparison when actual production or sales volume differs from expectations.

A detailed planned operating budget and flexible operating budget for the Leed Company for the quarter ended March 31, 1987, are presented in Illustrations 25.7 and 25.8. The planned operating budget and flexible operating budget have been prepared using the data from Illustration 25.3. The planned operating budget was based on a sales forecast of 20,000 units and a production forecast of 25,000 units, while the actual results for the period, reported in Illustrations 25.7 and 25.8, show actual sales of 19,000 units and actual production of 25,000 units. The actual selling price was $20 per unit, the same price that had been forecast.

Illustration 25.7 shows the comparison of the actual results with the planned operating budget. Comparison of actual results with the planned operating budget yields some useful information, for it shows where actual performance deviated from planned performance. For example, sales were 1,000 units lower than expected, sales revenue was $20,000 less than expected, gross margin was $12,500 less than expected, and net income was $2,000 more than expected.

Illustration 25.7

Comparison of Planned Operating Budget and Actual Results

LEED COMPANY
Comparison of Planned Operating Budget and Actual Results
For Quarter Ended March 31, 1987

	Budget	Actual
Sales (budgeted 20,000 units, actual 19,000 units)	$400,000	$380,000
Cost of goods sold:		
Beginning finished goods inventory	$130,000	$130,000
Cost of goods manufactured (25,000 units):		
Direct materials	$ 50,000	$ 62,500
Direct labor	150,000	143,750
Variable manufacturing overhead	25,000	31,250
Fixed manufacturing overhead	75,000	75,000
Cost of goods manufactured	$300,000	$312,500
Goods available for sale	$430,000	$442,500
Ending finished goods inventory	180,000	200,000
Cost of goods sold	$250,000	$242,500
Gross margin	$150,000	$137,500
Selling and administrative expenses:		
Variable	$ 40,000	$ 28,500
Fixed	100,000	95,000
Total selling and administrative expenses	$140,000	$123,500
Net income before income taxes	$ 10,000	$ 14,000
Estimated federal income taxes (40%)	4,000	5,600
Net income	$ 6,000	$ 8,400

Illustration 25.8

Comparison of Flexible Operating Budget and Actual Results

LEED COMPANY
Comparison of Flexible Operating Budget and Actual Results
For Quarter Ended March 31, 1987

	Budget	Actual	Budget variance over/under*
Sales (19,000 units)	$380,000	$380,000	$ –0–
Cost of goods sold:			
Beginning finished goods inventory	$130,000	$130,000	$ –0–
Cost of goods manufactured (25,000 units):			
Direct materials	$ 50,000	$ 62,500	12,500
Direct labor	150,000	143,750	6,250*
Variable manufacturing overhead	25,000	31,250	6,250
Fixed manufacturing overhead	75,000	75,000	–0–
Cost of goods manufactured	$300,000	$312,500	$12,500
Goods available for sale	$430,000	$442,500	$12,500
Ending finished goods inventory	192,000	200,000	8,000
Cost of goods sold (19,000 units)	$238,000	$242,500	$ 4,500
Gross margin	$142,000	$137,500	$ 4,500*
Selling and administrative expenses:			
Variable	$ 38,000	$ 28,500	$ 9,500*
Fixed	100,000	95,000	5,000*
Total selling and administrative expenses	$138,000	$123,500	$14,500*
Net income before income taxes	$ 4,000	$ 14,000	$10,000
Estimated federal income taxes (40%)	1,600	5,600	4,000
Net income	$ 2,400	$ 8,400	$ 6,000

However, the comparison of actual results with the planned operating budget does not provide a basis for evaluating whether or not management performed efficiently at the actual level of operations. For example, Illustration 25.7 shows that cost of goods sold was $7,500 less than expected. But the meaning of this difference is not clear since the actual cost of goods sold relates to the 19,000 units actually sold, while the planned cost of goods sold relates to the 20,000 units that were expected. The planned operating budget projected sales revenue, cost of goods sold, and selling and administrative expenses based on a sales forecast of 20,000 units, but only 19,000 units were actually sold. The levels of activity are not the same, so the comparisons do not give valid information for expense control.

A valid analysis for expense control purposes can only be made by comparing actual results with a flexible operating budget that is based on the same levels of sales and production that actually occurred. That is the comparison shown in Illustration 25.8. The flexible budget shown in Illustration 25.8 is made up of several pieces. The flexible budget amounts for sales revenue and selling and administrative expenses come from a flexible sales budget (not illustrated) for 19,000 units of sales, and the flexible budget amounts for production costs come from a flexible production budget (also not illustrated) for 25,000 units of production. Since the actual level of production (25,000 units) in this case was the same as the planned level, the production costs shown in the planned operating budget and the flexible operating budget are the same.

In comparisons such as these, if the number of units produced is equal to the number sold, beginning and ending inventories often are not shown. Instead, the flexible operating budget may show the number of units actually sold multiplied by the budgeted unit cost of direct materials, direct labor, and manufacturing overhead. The actual costs for direct materials, direct labor, and manufacturing overhead are also shown for the number of units sold.

The comparison of the actual results with the flexible operating budget (Illustration 25.8) reveals some inefficiencies for items in the costs of goods manufactured section. For instance, direct materials cost was $2.50 per unit ($62,500/25,000) instead of the $2 expected. Direct labor cost was only $5.75 per unit ($143,750/25,000) instead of the $6 expected. Variable overhead was $1.25 per unit ($31,250/25,000) instead of the $1 expected.

Net income was $5,000 more than expected at a sales level of 19,000 units. The main reason for the increase in net income was the lower than expected amounts of selling and administrative expenses. Variable selling and administrative expenses were only $1.50 per unit ($28,500/19,000) instead of the $2 expected; fixed selling and administrative expenses were only $95,000 instead of the $100,000 expected.

After the planned operating budget has been prepared, management must then prepare a financial budget, or projected balance sheet. The steps in preparing the financial budget are described in the next section.

Preparing the Financial Budget for the Leed Company

To prepare a projected balance sheet, each balance sheet account must be analyzed. First, the beginning balance is taken from the balance sheet at the end of the preceding period. The Leed Company balance sheet as of December 31, 1986, is shown in Illustration 25.9. Management must consider the effects of planned activities on these balances. Many accounts will be affected by items shown in the planned operating budget, by cash inflows and outflows,

Illustration 25.9

Balance Sheet at Beginning of Period

LEED COMPANY
Balance Sheet
December 31, 1986

Assets

Current assets:
Cash		$ 130,000
Accounts receivable		200,000
Inventories:		
Materials	$ 40,000	
Finished goods	130,000	170,000
Prepaid expenses		20,000
Total current assets		$ 520,000

Property, plant, and equipment:
Land		$ 60,000
Buildings	$1,000,000	
Less: Accumulated depreciation	400,000	600,000
Equipment	$ 600,000	
Less: Accumulated depreciation	180,000	420,000
Total property, plant, and equipment		$1,080,000
Total assets		$1,600,000

Liabilities and Stockholders' Equity

Current liabilities:
Accounts payable	$ 80,000
Accrued liabilities	160,000
Federal income taxes payable	100,000
Total current liabilities	$ 340,000

Stockholders' equity:
Capital stock (100,000 shares of $10 par value)	$1,000,000
Retained earnings	260,000
Total stockholders' equity	$1,260,000
Total liabilities and stockholders' equity	$1,600,000

and by policy decisions of the company. The planned operating budget shown in Illustration 25.5 and the other illustrations previously given will be used to prepare Leed Company's financial budget for the first two quarters of 1987.

Accounts Receivable. To prepare a financial budget, several new schedules must be prepared. The first of these schedules is the accounts receivable schedule shown in Illustration 25.10. We will assume that 60% of the current quarter's sales for Leed Company will be collected in that quarter, and the remaining 40% will be collected in the following quarter. Thus, collections for the first quarter will be $440,000; that is, 60% of budgeted sales of $400,000 for the first quarter plus the uncollected sales of the previous quarter [0.6($400,000) + $200,000]. Second quarter collections will be $580,000 [0.6($700,000) + $160,000]. Several other assumptions have been made to simplify this schedule; for example, there are no sales returns or allowances, no discounts, and no uncollectible accounts. All sales are assumed to be on a credit basis.

Inventories. A schedule of planned materials purchases and inventories must also be prepared. Planned usage and cost per unit of materials are taken from the planned cost of goods sold schedule (Illustration 25.4). Assuming

Illustration 25.10

*Planned Accounts
Receivable
Collections and
Balances*

LEED COMPANY
Planned Accounts Receivable Collections and Balances

	Quarter ending	
	March 31, 1987	June 30, 1987
Planned balance at beginning of quarter	$200,000*	$160,000
Planned sales for period (per Illustration 25.5)	400,000	700,000
Total	$600,000	$860,000
Projected collections during quarter (per discussion in text) . .	440,000	580,000
Planned balance at end of quarter	$160,000	$280,000

* Actual on January 1.

Illustration 25.11

*Planned Materials
Purchases and
Inventories*

LEED COMPANY
Planned Materials Purchases and Inventories

	Quarter ending	
	March 31, 1987	June 30, 1987
Planned usage (25,000 × $2) (per Illustration 25.4) . .	$50,000	$50,000
Planned ending inventory (½ × 25,000 × $2) (per discussion in text)	25,000	25,000
Planned material available for use	$75,000	$75,000
Inventory at beginning of quarter	40,000*	25,000
Planned purchases for the quarter	$35,000	$50,000

* Actual on January 1.

no work in process inventories, there will be only materials and finished goods inventories.

Illustration 25.11 shows a schedule of planned purchases and inventories of materials for the Leed Company. Materials inventory is normally maintained at a level of one half of next quarter's planned usage. The $40,000 beginning inventory was greater than normal because of a strike threat in the supplier company. This threat has now passed, and the materials inventory will be reduced at the end of the first quarter to the normal planned level.

The calculation of planned ending finished goods inventories is included in Illustration 25.4.

Accounts Affected by Operating Costs. Individual schedules could be prepared for each of the accounts affected by operating costs. But for illustrative purposes a schedule will be prepared combining the analyses of all the accounts affected by materials purchases or operating costs.

The following assumptions are made:

1. All purchases of materials are made on account.
2. Direct labor incurred is credited to accrued liabilities.

3.   Manufacturing overhead incurred is credited to the following accounts:

	Quarter ending	
	March 31	June 30
Accounts Payable	$ 16,000	$ 13,000
Accrued Liabilities	60,000	64,000
Prepaid Expenses	6,000	5,000
Accumulated Depreciation—Building . .	5,000	5,000
Accumulated Depreciation—Equipment . .	13,000	13,000
Total	$100,000	$100,000

4.   Selling and administrative expenses incurred are credited to the following accounts:

	Quarter ending	
	March 31	June 30
Accounts Payable	$ 5,000	$ 10,000
Accrued Liabilities	130,000	154,000
Prepaid Expenses	2,000	3,000
Accumulated Depreciation—Building . .	1,000	1,000
Accumulated Depreciation—Equipment . .	2,000	2,000
Total	$140,000	$170,000

5.   Planned cash payments are as follows:

	Quarter ending	
	March 31	June 30
Accounts Payable . .	$ 80,000	$ 56,000
Accrued Liabilities . .	330,000	354,000
Prepaid Expenses . .	–0–	10,000
Total	$410,000	$420,000

Illustration 25.12 shows analyses of the accounts credited as a result of the above data. The illustration provides a considerable amount of information needed in constructing financial budgets for the quarters ended March 31, 1987, and June 30, 1987. The balances on both dates for Accounts Payable, Accrued Liabilities, Prepaid Expenses (the only debit balance account shown), Accumulated Depreciation—Building, and Accumulated Depreciation—Equipment are computed in the schedule.

Federal Income Taxes Payable.   A separate schedule could be prepared showing the changes in the Federal Income Taxes Payable account, but in this example, a brief discussion will suffice. Balances reported in the financial budgets assume that one half of the $100,000 liability shown in the December 31, 1986, balance sheet is paid in each of the first two quarters of 1987 (shown in Illustration 25.15 later in the chapter). The accrual for the current quarter is added (Illustration 25.5). Thus, the balance on March 31, 1987, is $54,000 ($100,000 − $50,000 + $4,000). The balance on June 30, 1987, is $48,000 ($54,000 − $50,000 + $44,000). On June 30, the balance equals the accrual for the current year, $4,000 for the first quarter and $44,000 for the second quarter.

Cash Budget.   After the above analyses have been prepared, sufficient information is available to prepare the cash budget and compute the balance

Illustration 25.12 *Analyses of Accounts Credited for Materials Purchases and Operating Costs*

LEED COMPANY
Analyses of Accounts Credited for Materials Purchases and Operating Costs

	Total debits	Accounts payable	Accrued liabilities	Prepaid expenses	Accumulated depreciation Building	Equipment
Purchases or operating costs, quarter ending March 31 (credits made to accounts shown at right):						
Direct materials (per Illustration 25.11)	$ 35,000	$ 35,000				
Direct labor (per Illustration 25.4)	150,000		$150,000			
Manufacturing overhead (per Illustration 25.4)	100,000	16,000	60,000	$ 6,000	$ 5,000	$ 13,000
Selling and administrative expenses (per Illustration 25.5)	140,000	5,000	130,000	2,000	1,000	2,000
Total	$425,000	$ 56,000	$340,000	$ 8,000	$ 6,000	$ 15,000
Beginning balances (per Illustration 25.9)		80,000	160,000	20,000*	400,000	180,000
Total		$136,000	$500,000	$12,000*	$406,000	$195,000
Planned cash payments (debits made to accounts shown)		80,000	330,000			
Planned balances, March 31		$ 56,000	$170,000	$12,000*	$406,000	$195,000
Purchases or operating costs, quarter ending June 30 (credits made to accounts shown at right):						
Direct materials (per Illustration 25.11)	$ 50,000	$ 50,000				
Direct labor (per Illustration 25.4)	150,000		$150,000			
Manufacturing overhead (per Illustration 25.4)	100,000	13,000	64,000	$ 5,000	$ 5,000	$ 13,000
Selling and administrative expenses (per Illustration 25.5)	170,000	10,000	154,000	3,000	1,000	2,000
Total	$470,000	$ 73,000	$368,000	$ 8,000	$ 6,000	$ 15,000
Total including March 31 balances		$129,000	$538,000	$ 4,000*	$412,000	$210,000
Planned cash payments (debits made to accounts shown)		56,000	354,000	10,000		
Planned balances, June 30		$ 73,000	$184,000	$14,000*	$412,000	$210,000

* Debit balance.

in the Cash account on March 31 and June 30, 1987. To prepare a cash budget, information about cash receipts and cash disbursements is required.

Cash Receipts.   The cash receipts schedule can be prepared from the information used to compute the accounts receivable schedule (Illustration 25.10). A schedule of planned cash receipts for the Leed Company is shown in Illustration 25.13.

Cash Disbursements.   Cash is needed to pay for purchases, wages, rent, interest, income taxes, cash dividends, and most other expenses. The amount of each cash disbursement may be obtained from other budgets or schedules. Illustration 25.14 shows the cash disbursements schedule for the Leed Company. The illustration shows where the information came from, except for the payment of federal income taxes and dividends. Income taxes, discussed earlier, are assumed to be 40% of net income before taxes. It is assumed that $20,000 of dividends will be paid in the first quarter and $40,000 in the second quarter.

Illustration 25.13   *Planned Cash Receipts*

LEED COMPANY
Planned Cash Receipts

	Quarter ending	
	March 31, 1987	*June 30, 1987*
Collections on accounts receivable:		
From preceding quarter's sales	$200,000	$160,000
From current quarter's sales	240,000 (0.6 × $400,000)	420,000 (0.6 × $700,000)
Total cash receipts (per Illustration 25.10) . .	$440,000	$580,000

Illustration 25.14

Planned Cash Disbursements

LEED COMPANY
Planned Cash Disbursements

	Quarter ending	
	March 31, 1987	*June 30, 1987*
Payment of accounts payable (per Illustration 25.12) . .	$ 80,000	$ 56,000
Payment of accrued liabilities (per Illustration 25.12) . .	330,000	354,000
Payment of federal income tax liability	50,000	50,000
Payment of dividends	20,000	40,000
Expenses prepaid (per Illustration 25.12)	–0–	10,000
Total cash disbursements	$480,000	$510,000

Once cash receipts and disbursements have been determined, a cash budget can be prepared for the Leed Company, as shown in Illustration 25.15. The **cash budget** is a plan indicating expected inflows and outflows of cash. This cash budget helps management to decide whether enough cash will be available for short-term needs. If the cash budget indicates a cash shortage at a certain

Illustration 25.15

Planned Cash Flows and Cash Balances

LEED COMPANY
Planned Cash Flows and Cash Balances

	Quarter ending	
	March 31, 1987	*June 30, 1987*
Planned balance at beginning of quarter	$130,000*	$ 90,000
Planned cash receipts:		
Collections of accounts receivable (per Illustration 25.13) . .	440,000	580,000
	$570,000	$670,000
Planned cash disbursements:		
Payment of accounts payable (per Illustration 25.12) . . .	$ 80,000	$ 56,000
Payment of accrued liabilities (per Illustration 25.12) . . .	330,000	354,000
Payment of federal income tax liability	50,000	50,000
Payment of dividends	20,000	40,000
Expenses prepaid (per Illustration 25.12)	–0–	10,000
Total cash disbursements	$480,000	$510,000
Planned balance at end of quarter	$ 90,000	$160,000

* Actual on January 1.

date, the company may need to borrow money on a short-term basis. If the expected cash balance appears to be higher than necessary, the company may wish to invest the extra funds for short periods to earn interest rather than leave the cash idle. Knowing of possible shortages or excess cash balances in advance will allow management sufficient time to plan for such occurrences.

The Financial Budget Illustrated

The preparation of the financial budget for the quarters ending March 31, 1987, and June 30, 1987, shown in Illustration 25.16 completes the master budget. Management now has information to help appraise the policies it has adopted before implementing them. If the results of these policies, as shown by the master budget, are unsatisfactory, the policies can be changed before serious problems arise. For example, the Leed Company management had a

Illustration 25.16 *Projected Balance Sheet*

LEED COMPANY
Projected Balance Sheet

	March 31, 1987	June 30, 1987
Assets		
Current assets:		
Cash (per Illustration 25.15)	$ 90,000	$ 160,000
Accounts receivable (per Illustration 25.10)	160,000	280,000
Inventories:		
Materials (per Illustration 25.11)	25,000	25,000
Finished goods (per Illustration 25.4)	180,000	60,000
Prepaid expenses (per Illustration 25.12)	12,000	14,000
Total current assets	$ 467,000	$ 539,000
Property, plant, and equipment:		
Land (per Illustration 25.9)	$ 60,000	$ 60,000
Buildings ($1,000,000 less accumulated depreciation of $406,000 and $412,000) (per Illustrations 25.9 and 25.12) . .	594,000	588,000
Equipment ($600,000 less accumulated depreciation of $195,000 and $210,000) (per Illustrations 25.9 and 25.12) . .	405,000	390,000
Total property, plant, and equipment	$1,059,000	$1,038,000
Total assets	$1,526,000	$1,577,000
Liabilities and Stockholders' Equity		
Current liabilities:		
Accounts payable (per Illustration 25.12)	$ 56,000	$ 73,000
Accrued liabilities (per Illustration 25.12)	170,000	184,000
Federal income taxes payable (per discussion on page 981)	54,000	48,000
Total current liabilities	$ 280,000	$ 305,000
Stockholders' equity:		
Capital stock (100,000 shares of $10 par value) (per Illustration 25.9)	$1,000,000	$1,000,000
Retained earnings (see below)	246,000*	272,000†
Total stockholders' equity	$1,246,000	$1,272,000
Total liabilities and stockholders' equity	$1,526,000	$1,577,000

* $260,000 (per Illustration 25.9) + Income of $6,000 − Dividends of $20,000.
† $246,000 + Income of $66,000 − Dividends of $40,000.

policy of stable production each period. The master budget shows that production can be stabilized even though sales fluctuate widely. But the planned ending inventory at June 30 may be considered somewhat low in view of the fluctuations in sales. Management now knows this in advance and can take corrective action if necessary.

Purchases Budget for a Merchandising Company

Throughout this chapter, discussion has centered on the preparation of operating and financial budgets for a **manufacturer.** Suppose a budget is being prepared for a **retail merchandising business,** such as a dress shop or a furniture store. In this case, a purchases budget will be prepared instead of a production budget. To compute the purchases for each quarter, the cost of the goods to be sold during the quarter and the inventory required at the end of the quarter must be estimated.

The purchases budget can be derived from the sales budget and the company's inventory policy. Using the Strobel Furniture Company as an example, suppose a sales budget was prepared as shown in Illustration 25.17. Assume that the company likes to maintain sufficient inventory to cover one half of the next quarter's sales. Cost of goods sold is 55% of sales. The ending inventory on December 31, 1986, was $8,250. The purchases budget can now be prepared, as shown in Illustration 25.18. For the first quarter of 1987, notice that the ending inventory is one half of the second quarter's cost of goods sold [0.5 × (55% of $80,000) = $22,000].

The Strobel Company would use the information in the purchases budget in preparing the cost of goods sold section of the planned operating budget,

Illustration 25.17

Sales Budget

STROBEL FURNITURE COMPANY Sales Budget Quarter Ending				
March 31, 1987	June 30, 1987	September 30, 1987	December 31, 1987	March 31, 1988
$30,000	$80,000	$50,000	$90,000	$40,000

Illustration 25.18

Purchases Budget

STROBEL FURNITURE COMPANY Purchases Budget Quarter Ending				
	March 31, 1987	June 30, 1987	September 30, 1987	December 31, 1987
Ending inventory desired*	$22,000	$13,750	$24,750	$11,000
Cost of goods sold (55% of sales)	16,500	44,000	27,500	49,500
Total	$38,500	$57,750	$52,250	$60,500
Less: Beginning inventory	8,250	22,000	13,750	24,750
Purchases required	$30,250	$35,750	$38,500	$35,750

* Next period's sales × 55% × 50%.

the cash disbursements schedules, and the inventory and accounts payable amounts on the financial budget.

■ *SUMMARY*

A budget is one of management's most useful tools for planning and controlling income, cash flow, and other aspects of a business. A well-prepared budget forces management to think ahead, anticipate results, and take action when actual results differ from expected results. Used effectively, a budget can motivate employees. Used ineffectively, a budget can cause employee disenchantment and possible disruption of operations.

Participation in the preparation of budgets generally improves the motivational aspects of budgeting. Participation gives the people who have responsibility for performance a voice in setting the goals for the forthcoming period.

The preparation of an effective budget requires top management support and timely communication of results. The accountant should strive to design the accounting system to reflect the operations of the business and at the same time to facilitate responsibility reporting.

There are several types of budgets. The two budgets discussed in this chapter are the planned operating budget and the financial budget. The planned operating budget (a projected income statement) helps management plan future earnings. The financial budget (a forecast balance sheet) helps management plan the financing of assets. Together, the planned operating budget and the financial budget are referred to as the master budget.

The preparation of the master budget begins with detail budgets that support the planned operating budget. First, a sales forecast is made to project the number of units to be sold in the upcoming year. Based on this sales forecast, the expected price, and the projected selling expenses, a sales budget can be proposed showing expected sales revenue and selling expenses. Next, management uses that sales forecast and the company's inventory policy to decide the number of units to produce in the next year. Once the level of operations is established, management can use production cost information to project the cost to manufacture, cost of goods manufactured, and cost of goods sold for the year. This information is presented in the production budget. Finally, budgets for administrative and other expenses are established, based on the levels of sales and of production established in the sales and production budgets. Collectively, these subsidiary budgets provide enough information for a projected income statement, which is the planned operating budget.

A budget variance is a deviation between actual performance and the expected performance for the actual level of operations. A flexible operating budget is a series of budgets, each of which corresponds to a different level of operations. A flexible operating budget amount shown for the actual level of operations serves as a standard for comparing a department's actual results with the expected results.

The use of a flexible operating budget along with a planned operating budget permits performance appraisal on two levels. First, comparison of the actual results with the planned operating budget permits the deviation from expected output to be analyzed. Then, given the actual level of operations, actual costs can be compared with expected costs for that level of output, shown on the flexible operating budget.

Preparing a projected balance sheet (or financial budget) involves analyzing every balance sheet account in light of the planned activities expressed in the income statement. A separate cash budget is usually prepared to show sources of, uses of, and net changes in cash for the period. The complexities involved in preparing the financial budget often require the preparation of supplemental schedules for various accounts on the balance sheet.

You must realize by now that the terms *management* and *decision making* go "hand in hand." Under normal economic conditions, poor decision making by management is usually the cause of business failures. In Chapter 26, short-term decision making is discussed.

NEW TERMS INTRODUCED IN CHAPTER 25*

Budget

A plan showing a company's objectives and proposed ways of attaining the objectives. Two major types of budgets are the (1) master budget and (2) control, or responsibility, budget (966).

Budgeting

The coordination of financial and nonfinancial planning to satisfy an organization's goals (967).

Budget variance

The difference between an actual cost incurred (or revenue earned) at a certain level of operations and the budgeted amount for that same level of operations (975).

Cash budget

A plan indicating expected inflows (receipts) and outflows (disbursements) of cash; it helps management decide whether enough cash will be available for short-term needs (983).

Financial budget

The projected balance sheet portion of a master budget (966, 970).

Fixed costs

Costs that are unaffected by the relative levels of production or sales (973).

Flexible operating budget

Provides detailed information about budgeted expenses and revenues at various levels of output (974).

Master budget

The projected income statement and projected balance sheet showing the organization's objectives and proposed ways of attaining them; includes supporting budgets for such areas as cash, sales, costs, and production; also called master profit plan. It is the overall plan of the enterprise and ideally consists of all of the various segmental budgets (968).

Mixed cost

A cost that varies with volume, but not in direct proportion to the changes in volume (975).

Participatory budgeting

A method of preparing the budget that includes the participation of all levels of management responsible for actual performance (968).

Planned operating budget

The projected income statement portion of a master budget (966, 970).

Production budget

Takes into account the units in the sales budget and the company's inventory policy (970).

Variable costs

Costs that vary directly with production or sales and are a constant dollar amount per unit of output over different levels of output or sales (973).

---

* Some terms defined in earlier chapters are repeated here for your convenience.

DEMONSTRATION PROBLEM

During January 1987, the Phoenix Company plans to sell 20,000 units of its product at a price of $20 per unit. Selling expenses are estimated to be $40,000 plus 2% of sales revenue. General and administrative expenses are estimated to be $30,000 plus 1% of sales revenue. Income tax expense is estimated to be 40% of net income before taxes.

Phoenix plans to produce 25,000 units during January with estimated variable costs per unit as follows: $2 for material, $5 for labor, and $3 for variable overhead. The fixed overhead cost is estimated at $20,000 per month. The finished goods inventory at January 1, 1987, is 4,000 units with a cost per unit of $10. The company uses Fifo inventory procedure.

Required: Prepare a projected income statement for January 1987.

Solution to demonstration problem

PHOENIX COMPANY
Projected Income Statement
For January 1987

Sales (20,000 × $20)		$400,000
Cost of goods sold (see Schedule 1)		212,800
Gross margin		$187,200
Selling expenses:		
Fixed	$ 40,000	
Variable (0.02 × $400,000)	8,000	
General and administrative expenses:		
Fixed	30,000	
Variable (0.01 × $400,000)	4,000	82,000
Net income before taxes		$105,200
Income taxes (40%)		42,080
Net income		$ 63,120

Schedule 1

PHOENIX COMPANY
Planned Cost of Goods Sold

Beginning finished goods inventory (4,000 × $10)		$ 40,000
Cost of goods manufactured:		
Direct materials (25,000 × $2)	$ 50,000	
Direct labor (25,000 × $5)	125,000	
Variable manufacturing overhead (25,000 × $3)	75,000	
Fixed manufacturing overhead	20,000	
Cost of goods manufactured (25,000 × $10.80)		270,000
Cost of goods available for sale		$310,000
Ending finished goods inventory (9,000 × $10.80)		97,200
Cost of goods sold		$212,800

QUESTIONS

1. What are three purposes of budgeting?

2. How does the management-by-exception concept relate to budgeting?

3. What are five basic principles which, if followed, should improve the possibility of preparing a meaningful budget? Why is each important?

4. What is the difference between an "imposed" budget and a "participatory" budget?

5. Define and explain a budget variance.

6. What are the two major budgets in the master budget? Which should be prepared first? Why?

7. Distinguish between a master budget and a responsibility budget.

8. The budget established at the beginning of a given period carried an item for supplies in the amount of $40,000. At the end of the period, the supplies used amounted to $44,000. Can it be concluded from these data that there was an inefficient use of supplies or that care was not exercised in purchasing the supplies?

9. Management must make certain assumptions about the business environment when preparing a budget. What areas should be considered?

10. Why is budgeted performance better than past performance as a basis for judging actual results?

EXERCISES

E-1

Prepare a schedule of planned sales and production

The Murphy Sock Company has decided to produce 30,000 pairs of socks at a uniform rate throughout 1987. The sales department of Murphy Sock Company has estimated sales for 1987 according to the following schedule:

	Sales in pairs
First quarter	8,000
Second quarter	6,500
Third quarter	7,500
Fourth quarter	10,500
Total for 1987	32,500

Assume the December 31, 1986, inventory is estimated to be 4,000 pairs of socks. Prepare a schedule of planned sales and production (in pairs) for the first two quarters of 1987.

E-2

Prepare a flexible production budget

Materials and labor of Nation Corporation are considered to be variable costs. Expected production for the year is 300,000 units. At that level of production, direct material cost is budgeted at $495,000, and direct labor cost is budgeted at $1,125,000. Prepare a flexible budget for materials and labor for possible production levels of 210,000, 240,000, and 270,000 units of product.

E-3

Compute budget variances

Assume that in Exercise E-2 actual production was 240,000 units, materials cost was $420,000, and labor cost was $800,000. What are the budget variances?

E–4

Prepare a schedule of planned collections and ending balance for accounts receivable

The following data apply to the collection of accounts receivable for the Wood Company:

Current balance—February 28—$100,000 (of which $40,000 relates to January sales and $60,000 relates to February sales)
Planned sales for March—$500,000

Assumptions: 70% of sales are collected in the month of sale, 20% in the following month, and the remaining 10% in the second month after the sale. Prepare a schedule of planned collections and ending balance for accounts receivable as of March 31, 1987.

E–5

Prepare an operating budget

The Oak Company expects to sell 60,000 units during the next quarter at a price of $24 per unit. Production costs (all variable) are $8 per unit. There are no fixed manufacturing costs. Variable selling and administrative expenses are $4 per unit and fixed costs are $200,000 in total. What is budgeted net income? (Do not consider taxes.)

E–6

Compute the budget variance for operations

Fixed production costs for the Bee Company are budgeted at $240,000 assuming 80,000 units of product. Actual sales for the period were 70,000 units, while actual production was 80,000 units. Actual fixed costs used in computing cost of goods sold amounted to $210,000. What is the budget variance?

E–7

Prepare a purchases budget

The shoe department of D & S Department Store has prepared a sales budget for the month of April calling for a sales volume of $40,000. The department expects to begin April with a $30,000 inventory and to end the month with a $32,000 inventory. Its cost of goods sold averages 70% of sales.

   Prepare a purchases budget for the department showing the amount of goods to be purchased during April.

E–8

Prepare an operating budget

The Reed Company projects sales of 100,000 units during May at $5 per unit. Variable production costs are $1.50 per unit. Variable selling and administrative expenses are $0.50 per unit; fixed costs are $190,000. Compute the budgeted net income before taxes.

PROBLEMS, SERIES A

P25–1–A

Determine budgeted cost of goods sold; prepare operating budgets

The Mitch Corporation prepares monthly operating and financial budgets. The operating budgets for June and July are based on the following data:

	Units produced	Units sold
June	100,000	90,000
July	90,000	100,000

All sales are at $20 per unit. Direct materials, direct labor, and variable manufacturing overhead are estimated at $2, $4, and $2 per unit, while total fixed manufacturing overhead is budgeted at $180,000 per month. Operating expenses are budgeted at $200,000 plus 10% of sales, while federal income taxes are budgeted at 40% of net income before taxes. The inventory at June 1 consists of 50,000 units with a cost of $11.40 each.

Required: *a.* Prepare monthly budget estimates of cost of goods sold assuming that Fifo inventory procedure is used.

b. Prepare planned operating budgets for June and July. (Use a single amount for cost of goods sold—as derived above.)

P25-2-A

Prepare a flexible operating budget

The computation of net operating income for the Ivey Company for 1986 follows:

Sales		$3,000,000
Cost of goods sold:		
Direct materials	$600,000	
Direct labor	400,000	
Variable manufacturing overhead . .	200,000	
Fixed manufacturing overhead . . .	400,000	1,600,000
Gross margin		$1,400,000
Selling expenses:		
Variable	$220,000	
Fixed	280,000	500,000
		$ 900,000
General and administrative expenses:		
Variable	$260,000	
Fixed	320,000	580,000
Net operating income		$ 320,000

An operating budget is prepared for 1987 with sales forecasted at a 25% increase in volume. Direct materials, direct labor, and all costs labeled above as variable are completely variable. Fixed costs are expected to continue as above except for a $40,000 increase in fixed general and administrative costs.

    Actual operating data for 1987 are given below:

Sales	$3,600,000
Direct materials	740,000
Direct labor	480,000
Variable manufacturing overhead	248,000
Fixed manufacturing overhead	410,000
Variable selling expenses	310,000
Fixed selling expenses	262,000
Variable general and administrative expenses . .	330,000
Fixed general and administrative expenses . . .	364,000

Required:

a. Prepare a budget report comparing the 1987 planned operating budget with actual 1987 data.

b. Prepare a budget report that would be useful in appraising the performance of the various persons charged with responsibility to provide satisfactory income. (Hint: Prepare budget data on a flexible basis.)

c. Comment on the differences revealed by the two reports.

P25-3-A

Prepare a planned operating budget and a flexible operating budget

a. The following data for the Prince Company are to be used in preparing its 1987 operating budget:

Plant capacity	100,000 units
Expected sales volume	90,000 units
Expected production	90,000 units
Actual production	90,000 units
Forecasted selling price	$10.00 per unit
Actual selling price	$11.25 per unit
Manufacturing costs:	
Variable (per unit):	
Direct materials	$3.00
Direct labor	$1.25
Manufacturing overhead	$1.875
Fixed manufacturing overhead . . .	$90,000
Selling and administrative expenses:	
Variable (per unit)	$1.00
Fixed	$50,000

Assume no beginning or ending inventory. Taxes are 40% of net income before taxes.

Required: Prepare a planned operating budget for the year ended December 31, 1987.

b. The actual operating data of the Prince Company for the year 1987 follow:

Sales		$900,000
Cost of goods sold:		
Direct materials	$281,250	
Direct labor	112,500	
Variable manufacturing overhead . .	168,750	
Fixed manufacturing overhead . . .	90,000	
Total	$652,500	
Less: Ending inventory		
($652,500 × 10/90)	72,500	$580,000
Gross margin		$320,000
Selling and administrative expenses:		
Variable	$ 85,000	
Fixed	60,000	$145,000
Net income before taxes		$175,000
Income taxes—at 40%		70,000
Net income		$105,000

Required: Using a flexible operating budget, analyze the efficiency of operations and comment on the company's sales policy.

Problem 25–4–A

Prepare a flexible budget for selling and administrative expenses

The Wilson Company wants you to prepare a flexible budget for selling and administrative expenses. The general manager and the sales manager have met with all the department heads, and they have provided you with the following information regarding selling and administrative expenses:

1. The company presently employs 30 full-time salespersons with a base salary of $300 each per month plus commissions and 10 full-time salespersons with a salary of $500 each per month plus commissions. In addition, the company employs nine regional sales managers with a salary of $1,800 per month, none of whom is entitled to any commissions.
2. If sales volume exceeds $7,500,000 per year, the company will need to hire four more salespersons, each at a salary of $300 per month plus commissions.
3. Sales commissions are either 10% or 5% of the selling price, depending on the product sold. Typically, a 10% commission applies on 60% of sales, and a 5% commission applies on the remaining 40% of sales.
4. Salespersons' travel allowances average $125 per month per salesperson (excluding managers).
5. Advertising expenses average $25,000 per month plus 5% of sales.
6. Selling supplies expense is estimated at 1% of sales.
7. Administrative salaries are $25,000 per month.
8. Other administrative expenses include the following:
    Rent—$4,000 per month
    Office supplies—2% of sales
    Other administrative expenses (telephone, etc.)—$1,000 per month

Required: Prepare a flexible budget for selling and administrative expenses for sales volumes of $6 million, $8 million, and $10 million per year.

P25–5–A

Prepare a schedule of planned cost of goods manufactured and sold

The King Company wants to prepare a schedule of planned cost of goods sold and ending inventory for the quarters ending September 30, 1987, and December 31, 1987. The following data relate to the expected activity for the two quarters:

1. Expected sales for the next three quarters are: $1,200,000 for the quarter ending September 30, 1987; $1,500,000 for the quarter ending December 31, 1987; and $816,000 for the quarter ending March 31, 1988.
2. The selling price is $30 per unit.
3. Due to demand, the company wishes to carry a beginning-of-the-period inventory equal to 25% of the following quarter's expected requirements.
4. Inventory of finished goods on June 30, 1987, is 10,000 units at $24 per unit.
5. Cost of production is estimated at:

Direct materials . . . . $4 per unit
Direct labor . . . . 8 per unit
Variable manufacturing overhead . . . . 2 per unit
Fixed manufacturing overhead . . . . 400,000 per quarter

6. There is no work in process inventory at the beginning or end of either period.
7. The company computes inventory on a Fifo basis.

Required: Prepare a schedule of planned cost of goods manufactured and sold for the quarters ending September 30, 1987, and December 31, 1987. (Hint: Prepare production schedules in units first.)

P25–6–A

Prepare a cash receipts schedule and a purchases budget

Park Company manufactures and sells bathroom fixtures. Estimated sales for the next three months are:

September 1987 . . . $300,000
October 1987 450,000
November 1987 350,000

Sales for August were $320,000. All sales are on account. Park Company estimates that 60% of the accounts receivable are collected in the month of sale with the remaining 40% collected the following month. The units sell for $25 each. The cash balance for September 1, 1987, is $68,000.

Generally, 60% of purchases are due and payable in the month of purchase with the remainder due the following month. Purchase cost per unit for materials is $15. The company maintains an end-of-the-month inventory of 1,000 units plus 10% of next month's unit sales.

Required: Prepare a cash receipts schedule for September and October and a purchases budget for August, September, and October.

P25–7–A

Prepare a cash budget

Refer to P25–6–A. In addition to the information given, selling and administrative expenses paid in cash are $100,000 per month.

Required: Prepare a monthly cash budget for September and October for the Park Company.

P25–8–A

Prepare a cash budget

The Hunt Company has gathered the following budget information for the quarter ending March 31:

Sales $540,000
Purchases 450,000
Salaries and wages . . 195,000
Rent 9,000
Supplies 6,000
Insurance 1,800
Other cash expenses . . 13,200

A cash balance of $36,000 is planned for January 1. Accounts receivable are expected to be $60,000 on January 1. All but one half of 1% of the January 1 balance will be collected in the quarter ending March 31. The company's sales collection pattern is 95% in the quarter of sale and 5% in the quarter after sale. Accounts payable will be $30,000 on January 1 and will be paid during the coming quarter. The company's purchases payment pattern is 75% in the quarter of purchase and 25% in the quarter after purchase. Expenses are paid in the quarter of incurrence.

Required: Prepare a cash budget for the quarter ending March 31.

P25–9–A

Prepare a master budget

May Corporation prepares annual budgets by quarters for its fiscal year ending June 30. Given below is its post-closing trial balance at December 31, 1986:

	Debits	Credits
Cash	$ 46,000	
Accounts Receivable	120,000	
Allowance for Doubtful Accounts . .		$ 4,000
Inventories	52,000	
Prepaid Expenses	4,000	
Furniture and Equipment	60,000	
Accumulated Depreciation		4,000
Accounts Payable		40,000
Accrued Liabilities		12,000
Notes Payable, 5% (due 1990) . .		160,000
Capital Stock		100,000
Retained Earnings (deficit)	38,000	
	$320,000	$320,000

All of the capital stock of May Corporation was recently acquired by Floyd White after the corporation had suffered losses for a number of years. After the purchase, White loaned substantial sums of money to the corporation, which still owes him $160,000 on a 5% note. Because of these past losses there are no accrued federal income taxes payable, but future earnings will be subject to taxation.

White is anxious to withdraw $40,000 from the corporation (as a payment on the note payable to him) but will not do so if it reduces the corporation's cash balance below $40,000. Thus, he is quite interested in the budgets for the quarter ending March 31, 1987.

Additional data:

1. Sales for the coming quarter are forecasted at $400,000; for the following quarter they are forecasted at $500,000. All sales are priced to yield a gross margin of 40%. Inventory is to be maintained on hand at the end of any quarter in an amount equal to 20% of the goods to be sold in the next quarter. All sales are on account, and 95% of the December 31, 1986, receivables plus 70% of the current quarter's sales will be collected during the quarter ending March 31, 1987.

2. Selling expenses are budgeted at $16,000 plus 6% of sales; $8,000 will be incurred on account, $22,000 accrued, $9,000 from expiration of prepaid rent and prepaid insurance, and $1,000 from allocated depreciation.

3. Purchasing expenses are budgeted at $11,600 plus 5% of purchases for the quarter; $3,000 will be incurred on account, $16,000 accrued, $4,600 from expired prepaid expenses, and $400 from allocated depreciation.

4. Administrative expenses are budgeted at $14,000 plus 2% of sales; $1,000 will be incurred on account, $12,000 accrued, $4,400 from expired prepayments, and $600 from allocated depreciation. Bad debts are estimated at 1% of sales.

5. Interest accrues at 5% on the notes payable and is credited to Accrued Liabilities.

6. All of the beginning balances in Accounts Payable and Accrued Liabilities, plus 80% of the current credits to Accounts Payable, and all but $10,000 of the current accrued liabilities will be paid during the quarter. A $6,000 insurance premium is to be paid prior to March 31, and a full year's rent of $48,000 is due on January 2.

7. Federal income taxes are budgeted at 40% of the net income before taxes. The taxes should be accrued separately, and no payments are due in the first quarter.

Required:
a. Prepare a planned operating budget for the quarter ending March 31, 1987, including supporting schedules for planned purchases and operating expenses.

b. Prepare a financial budget for March 31, 1987. Supporting schedules should be included that (1) analyze accounts credited for purchases and operating expenses, (2) show planned accounts receivable collections and balance, and (3) show planned cash flows and cash balance.

c. Will White be able to collect $40,000 on his note?

PROBLEMS, SERIES B

P25–1–B

Prepare a schedule showing budgeted production and a schedule showing the budgeted cost of goods sold

The Stafford Company prepares monthly operating and financial budgets. Estimates of sales in units are made for each month. Production is scheduled at a level high enough to take care of current needs and to carry into each month one half of that next month's unit sales. Direct materials, direct labor, and variable manufacturing overhead are estimated at $3, $5, and $2 per unit, and total fixed manufacturing overhead is budgeted at $100,000 per month. Sales for April, May, June, and July 1987 are estimated at 50,000, 60,000, 80,000, and 60,000 units. The inventory at April 1, 1987, consists of 25,000 units with a cost of $12 per unit.

Required:

a. Prepare a schedule showing the budgeted production in units for April, May, and June 1987.

b. Prepare a schedule showing the budgeted cost of goods sold for the same three months assuming that the Fifo method is used for inventories.

P25–2–B

Prepare a flexible operating budget

Following is a summary of operating data of the Sylvester Company for the year 1986:

Sales		$12,000,000
Cost of goods manufactured and sold:		
Direct materials	$2,100,000	
Direct labor	1,900,000	
Variable manufacturing overhead	600,000	
Fixed manufacturing overhead	1,300,000	5,900,000
		$ 6,100,000
Selling expenses:		
Variable	$ 600,000	
Fixed	500,000	1,100,000
		$ 5,000,000
General and administrative expenses:		
Variable	$ 300,000	
Fixed	1,900,000	2,200,000
Net operating income		$ 2,800,000

Sales volume for 1987 is budgeted at 90% of 1986 volume. Prices are not expected to change. The 1987 budget amounts for the various other costs and expenses differ from those reported in 1986 only for the expected volume change in the variable items.

The actual operating data for 1987 follow:

Sales	$9,600,000
Direct materials	2,140,000
Direct labor	1,920,000
Variable manufacturing overhead	630,000
Fixed manufacturing overhead	1,310,000
Variable selling expenses	780,000
Fixed selling expenses	490,000
Variable general and administrative expenses	335,000
Fixed general and administrative expenses	1,880,000

Required:

a. Prepare a report comparing the planned operating budget for 1987 with the actual results for that year.

b. Prepare a budget report that would be useful in pinpointing responsibility for the poor showing in 1987. (Hint: Prepare budget data on a flexible budget basis.)

P25–3–B

Prepare a planned operating budget and a flexible operating budget

a. The following data for the Jones Company are to be used in preparing its 1987 operating budget:

Plant capacity	1,000,000 units
Expected sales	900,000 units
Expected production	1,000,000 units
Forecasted sales price	$ 12.00

Manufacturing costs:
Variable (per unit):

Direct materials	4.50
Direct labor	1.50
Manufacturing overhead	1.00
Fixed manufacturing overhead	300,000

Selling and administrative expenses:

Variable (per unit)	0.50
Fixed	250,000

Assume no beginning inventory. Taxes are 40% of net income before taxes.

Required: Prepare a planned operating budget for the year ended December 31, 1987.

b. The actual results for the Jones Company for the year ended December 31, 1987, follow: (Note: The actual sales price was $13 per unit. Actual production [in units] was equal to actual sales [in units]).

Sales		$13,000,000
Cost of goods sold:		
Direct materials	$3,850,000	
Direct labor	1,575,000	
Variable manufacturing overhead . .	1,200,000	
Fixed manufacturing overhead . . .	300,000	6,925,000
		$ 6,075,000
Selling and administrative expense		
Variable	$ 500,000	
Fixed	250,000	750,000
Net income before taxes		$ 5,325,000
Income tax at 40%		2,130,000
Net income		$ 3,195,000

Required: Using a flexible operating budget, analyze the efficiency of operations. Comment on the results of 1987 and on the company's sales policy.

P25-4-B

Prepare a flexible budget for selling and administration expenses

The Clay Company wants you to prepare a flexible budget for selling and administrative expenses. The general manager and the sales manager have met with all the department heads, and they have provided you with the following information regarding selling and administrative expenses:

1. The company presently employs 40 full-time salespersons with a base salary of $200 each per month plus commissions. In addition, the company employs eight regional sales managers each with a salary of $18,000 per year and one general sales manager with a salary of $24,000 per year, none of whom is entitled to any commissions.
2. If sales volume exceeds $15 million per year, the company will need to hire five more salespersons and one more regional sales manager.
3. Sales commissions are either 5%, 3%, or 0% of the selling price, depending on the product sold. Typically, a 5% commission applies to 70% of sales, a 3% commission applies to 20% of sales, and no commission applies to the remaining 10% of sales.
4. Salespersons' travel allowances average $100 per month per salesperson (excluding managers).
5. Advertising expenses average $50,000 per month plus 2% of sales.
6. Selling supplies expense is estimated at 1% of sales.
7. Administrative salaries are $40,000 per month.
8. Other administrative expenses include the following:
   Rent—$5,000 per month
   Office supplies—1% of sales
   Other administrative expenses (telephone, etc.)—$1,200 per month

Required: Prepare a flexible budget for selling and administrative expenses for sales volumes of $12 million, $14 million, and $16 million per year.

P25-5-B

Prepare a schedule of planned cost of goods manufactured and sold

The Clock Manufacturing Company is in the process of preparing a schedule of planned cost of goods sold and ending inventory for the quarters ended March 31, 1987, and June 30, 1987. The following data relate to expected activity for the two quarters:

1. Sales are expected to be:

March quarter	$ 800,000
June quarter	600,000
September quarter	1,200,000

2. Selling price per unit is $40.
3. The company policy is to carry a beginning-of-the-period inventory equal to 20% of the next period's requirements. Beginning inventory at January 1, 1987, was 4,000 units at $25 per unit.
4. Cost of production is estimated at:

Direct materials	$ 6 per unit
Direct labor	14 per unit
Variable manufacturing overhead . . .	4 per unit
Fixed manufacturing overhead	76,000 per quarter

5. There is no work in process inventory at the beginning or end of either period.
6. Inventory is computed on a Fifo basis.

Required: Prepare a schedule of planned cost of goods sold for the quarters ended March 31 and June 30, 1987. (Hint: Prepare a production schedule in units first.)

P25-6-B

Prepare accounts receivable schedule and planned purchases schedule

Anderson Company has a cash balance of $44,000 on May 1, 1987. Anderson Company's product sells for $45 per unit. Actual and projected sales are:

March, actual	$640,000
April, actual	400,000
May, estimated	450,000
June, estimated	480,000
July, estimated	380,000

All sales are on account. Generally, 45% of the accounts receivable are collected in the month of sale, 40% in the second month, and 15% in the third month.

Generally, 65% of purchases are due and payable in the month of purchase and the remainder the following month. Purchase cost per unit for materials is $30. The company maintains an end-of-the-month inventory of 500 units plus 20% of the next month's unit sales.

Required: Prepare schedules for May and June showing:

a. Planned accounts receivable collections and balances.
b. Planned materials purchases and inventories. Round all units to the nearest whole number.

P25-7-B

Prepare a cash budget

Refer to P25-6-B. In addition to the information given, selling and administrative expenses are $840,000 per year, incurred and paid evenly throughout the year.

Required: Prepare a monthly cash budget for May and June for the Anderson Company.

P25-8-B

Prepare a cash budget

The Michaels Company has gathered the following budget information for the quarter ending September 30:

Sales	$360,000
Purchases	300,000
Salaries and wages	130,000
Rent	6,000
Supplies	4,000
Insurance	1,200
Other cash expenses	8,800

A cash balance of $24,000 is planned for July 1. Accounts receivable are expected to be $40,000 on July 1. All but one half of 1% of the July 1 balance will be collected in the quarter ending September 30. The company's sales collection pattern is 95% in the quarter of sale and 5% in the quarter after sale. Accounts payable will be $20,000 on July 1 and will be paid during the coming quarter. The company's purchases payment pattern is 75% in the quarter of purchase and 25% in the quarter after purchase. Expenses are paid in the quarter of incurrence.

Required: Prepare a cash budget for the quarter ending September 30.

P25-9-B

Prepare a master budget

WARREN CORPORATION Post-Closing Trial Balance December 31, 1986		
	Debits	*Credits*
Cash	$ 100,000	
Accounts Receivable	200,000	
Allowance for Doubtful Accounts		$ 15,000
Inventories	250,000	
Prepaid Expenses	30,000	
Land	250,000	
Buildings and Equipment	750,000	
Accumulated Depreciation		100,000
Accounts Payable		150,000
Accrued Liabilities (including income taxes) . .		100,000
Capital Stock		1,000,000
Retained Earnings		215,000
	$1,580,000	$1,580,000

The Warren Corporation, whose post-closing trial balance at December 31, 1986, appears above, is a rapidly expanding company. Sales in the last quarter of 1986 amounted to $1,000,000 and are projected at $1,250,000 and $2,000,000 for the first two quarters of 1987. This expansion has created a very tight cash position. Management is especially concerned about the probable cash balance at March 31, 1987, since a payment of $150,000 for some new equipment must be made upon delivery on April 2. The current cash balance of $100,000 is considered to be the minimum workable balance.

Additional data:

1. Purchases, all on account, are to be scheduled so that the inventory at the end of any quarter is equal to one third of the goods expected to be sold in the coming quarter. Cost of goods sold averages 60% of sales.
2. Selling expenses are budgeted at $50,000 plus 8% of sales; $10,000 is expected to be incurred on account, $120,000 accrued, $14,000 from expired prepayments, and $6,000 from allocated depreciation.
3. Purchasing expenses are budgeted at $35,000 plus 5% of purchases; $5,000 will be incurred on account, $65,000 accrued, $5,500 from expired prepayments, and $4,500 from allocated depreciation.
4. Administrative expenses are budgeted at $62,500 plus 3% of sales; $10,000 will be incurred on account, $55,000 accrued, $5,500 from expired prepayments, $4,500 from allocated depreciation. Bad debts are equal to 2% of current sales.
5. Federal income taxes are budgeted at 40% of net income before taxes and are recorded in accrued liabilities. Payments on these taxes are included in the payments on accrued liabilities discussed below.
6. All December 31, 1986, accounts payable plus 80% of current credits to this account will be paid in the first quarter. All of the December 31, 1986, accrued liabilities except for $30,000 will be paid in the first quarter. Of the current quarter's accrued liabilities, all but $120,000 will be paid during the quarter.

7   Cash outlays for various expenses normally prepaid will amount to $40,000 during the quarter.

8.   All sales are made on account; 80% of the sales are collected in the quarter in which made, and all of the remaining sales are collected in the following quarter, except for 2% which is never collected. The allowance for doubtful accounts shows the estimated amount of accounts receivable at December 31, 1986, arising from 1986 sales that will not be collected.

Required:

a.   Prepare an operating budget for the quarter ending March 31, 1987. Supporting schedules for planned purchases and operating expenses should be included.

b.   Prepare a financial budget for March 31, 1987. Include supporting schedules that (1) analyze accounts credited for purchases and expenses, (2) show planned cash flows and cash balance, and (3) show planned collections of accounts receivable and the accounts receivable balance.

c.   Will sufficient cash be on hand April 2 to pay for the new equipment?

BUSINESS DECISION PROBLEM

Prepare a cash budget

The Madden Company has applied at a local bank for a short-term loan of $125,000 starting on October 1. The loan will be repaid with interest at 10% on December 31. The bank's loan officer has requested a cash budget from the company for the quarter ending December 31. The following budget information is needed to prepare the cash budget:

Sales	$540,000
Purchases	300,000
Salaries and wages to be paid . .	105,000
Rent payments	6,000
Supplies (payments for)	4,000
Insurance payments	1,500
Other cash payments	18,500

A cash balance of $20,000 is planned for October 1. Accounts receivable are expected to be $40,000 on October 1. All of these accounts will be collected in the quarter ending December 31. In general, sales are collected as follows: 90% in the quarter of sale and 10% in the quarter after sale. Accounts payable will be $400,000 on October 1 and will be paid during the quarter ending December 31. All purchases are paid for in the quarter after purchase.

Required:

a.   Prepare a cash budget for the quarter ending December 31. Assume that the $125,000 loan will be made on October 1 and will be repaid with interest at 10% on December 31.

b.   Will the company be able to repay the loan on December 31? If the company desires a minimum cash balance of $15,000, will the company be able to repay the loan as planned?

BUSINESS SITUATION FOR DISCUSSION

Growing Concerns: Topics of particular interest to owners and managers of smaller businesses
(edited by David E. Gumpert)

Budget Choice: Planning vs. Control*
Neil C. Churchill

☐   The term "budget" tends to conjure up in the minds of many managers images of inaccurate estimates,

produced in tedious detail, which are never exactly achieved but whose shortfalls or overruns require explanations. And that is what budgets are like for many smaller businesses. This wasteful way of using budgets overlooks important managerial objectives that budgeting can help achieve.

*   *   *   *   *

. . . [The author] maintains that budgets should be considered from a broader perspective. He views them as having two primary functions: planning and control. Managers must decide which function is more important and then resolve a number of formulation issues. These include the initiation process, implementation, the period covered, whether the budget should be fixed or flexible, and how it should be used to evaluate performance. He concludes that large companies concerned about operational efficiency should focus on the coordination and control aspects of budgeting while small and innovative companies should be concerned with planning aspects. Whatever the focus, budget preparation and implementation are important in carrying out company strategy and in professionalizing the smaller company.

* * * * *

I [the author] start my classes on budgeting by displaying two situations on the blackboard:

Expenses

	Budgeted amount	Actual results
Budget 1 . .	$1000	$950
Budget 2 . .	750	850

Then I ask the class, "Which budget is better, assuming in both cases that the manager gets the job done in time, that the end result is the same quality of performance and customer satisfaction, and that the manager doesn't develop ulcers in the process of implementation?"

A heated argument usually follows. Most class participants eventually choose Budget 2 after being assured of equal results. A minority, however, hold out for Budget 1, which seems to them the "most reasonable."

These opposing views come together when I ask, "Which would be best for borrowing money on a one-loan-a-year basis?" In this case, the choice is almost always Budget 1. And when I then ask, "Which would

be best for motivating performance?" the majority of participants usually select Budget 2.

As this example shows, budgets can be used both for planning (Number 1) and for control (Number 2), although the same budget is not always optimal for both purposes.

Occasionally a company uses a budget with "stretch" in it for motivating performance—sales, for instance—and a more "realistic" budget for planning—expected sales, for example. More commonly, companies use the same document for both purposes. Large companies tend to use budgets mostly for control and smaller enterpreneurial companies use them primarily as planning tools.

But no matter whether it is used for planning or for control, a budget is more than a forecast. A forecast is a prediction of what may happen and sometimes contains prescriptions for dealing with future events. A budget, on the other hand, involves a commitment to a forecast to make an agreed-on outcome happen.

Budgets come in several variations. Cash budgets are especially important to new and growing businesses, whereas capital budgets are widely used if capital expenditures are important and recurring. Human-resource or "headcount" budgets (the capital budgets of service companies) serve as means of control in labor-intensive companies. But generally when the term *budget* is used, it refers to an operating budget containing an organization's detailed revenue and expense accounts grouped either by operating units, such as divisions or departments, or by products and product lines. Such a document is a central part of the management control system of many companies.

CHAPTER 26 Short-Term Decision Making

LEARNING OBJECTIVES

After studying this chapter, you should be able to:

1. Describe different cost behavior patterns.
2. Compute the break-even point for a company.
3. List the assumptions underlying cost-volume-profit analysis.
4. Apply cost-volume-profit analysis to practical situations.
5. Make short-term decisions involving relevant costs.
6. Differentiate between and compute net income under absorption and direct costing.
7. Define and use correctly the new terms in the glossary.

In making decisions, management must frequently distinguish between short-run decision making and long-run decision making. The term **short run** describes a time frame during which a company's management cannot change the effects of certain past decisions. The short-run time frame is often considered to be one year or less. In the short run, many costs, such as depreciation expense, are assumed to be fixed and unchangeable. Because of this assumption, short-run decision making uses different criteria than long-run decision making, under which all costs are subject to change.

In this chapter you will be introduced to some of the analytical tools that can be used to make short-run decisions. The chapter begins with a discussion of cost behavior patterns because the classification of costs as fixed or variable is the first step in using the analytical tools.

■ COST BEHAVIOR PATTERNS

Illustration 26.1 shows four basic cost behavior patterns: variable, fixed, mixed (semivariable), and step. As discussed in earlier chapters, **variable costs** vary directly with changes in volume of production or sales. Direct materials, direct labor, and sales commissions are examples of variable costs. In contrast, **fixed costs** remain constant over some relevant range of output, and are often described as time-related costs. Depreciation, insurance, property taxes, and administrative salaries are examples of fixed costs.

Illustration 26.1

Four Cost Patterns

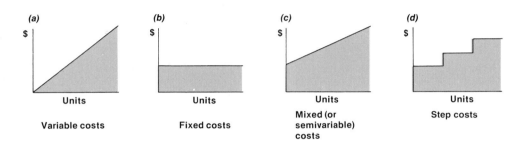

Mixed and step costs demonstrate both fixed and variable characteristics. A **mixed cost** contains a fixed portion of cost that will be incurred even when the plant is completely idle and a variable portion that will increase directly with production volume. An example of a mixed cost is electricity. A certain amount of cost is incurred in order for the company to have electrical service. As the plant operates, each additional kilowatt-hour of usage generates an additional amount of cost. A mixed cost may be separated into its fixed and variable components, as shown in Illustration 26.2.

A **step cost** remains constant in total over a range of output (or sales) but then increases in steps at certain points. A step cost may be either a step variable or a step fixed cost. The major difference between the two types is the size of the "steps." In both cases, there are fixed and variable components

Illustration 26.2

Separation of a Mixed Cost

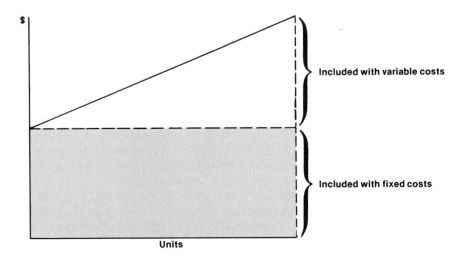

Illustration 26.3

Separation of a Step Variable Cost

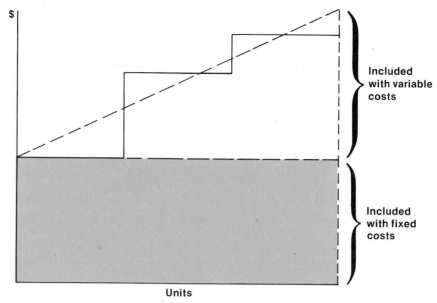

Even though step variable costs do not vary directly with changes in volume, they can be treated for planning purposes as though they are directly variable costs. The slanted dashed line represents the smoothing of the step variable cost into a directly variable cost.

of the cost. An example of a step variable cost is the cost of water. The utility company charges a flat fee for providing water (fixed component) and an additional amount depending on the quantity of water used (variable component). Unlike the variable charge for electricity, which is on an hour-by-hour basis, the charge for water may be stated in increments as follows: $10 for the first 1,000 gallons or less; $5 additional for use of 1,001 to 5,000 gallons; $8 additional for use of 5,001 to 10,000 gallons; and so on. This type of cost is shown in Illustration 26.3.

Supervisors' salaries are an example of a step fixed cost. At any level of production from 1 unit to 40,000 units, one supervisor is necessary at a salary of $20,000 per year. If the company produces at a level over 40,000 units but below 100,000 units, a second supervisor is needed at an additional cost of $20,000. A step fixed cost for supervisors' salaries is shown in Illustration 26.4.

For decision making, management must separate mixed and step costs into their fixed and variable components. A mixed cost can be easily broken down into these two components. The fixed portion of a mixed cost is included with other fixed costs, while the variable element is shown as directly changing with volume. A step variable cost is treated in the same manner as a mixed cost. The fixed portion of a step variable cost is treated as a fixed cost, and the remaining cost is treated as entirely variable.

Since a step fixed cost is fixed over a relatively wide range of activity, it is treated as entirely fixed for decision-making purposes. This is done by estimating the level of operations and then treating the step fixed cost expected at that level of operations as a fixed cost for decision making.

Although there are four basic cost behavior patterns, management must

Illustration 26.4

A Step Fixed Cost

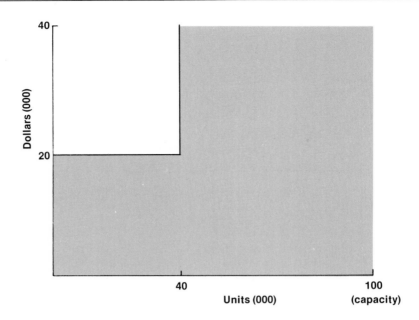

attempt to classify all types of costs into only two categories—variable and fixed. This simplification is necessary in order to visualize the ways in which costs will react to changes in production volume or sales.

Methods for Analyzing Costs

There are several methods available for breaking down a mixed or a step variable cost into its fixed and variable cost components. Two of these procedures are the scatter diagram and the high-low method.

The Scatter Diagram.   A scatter diagram shows plots of actual costs incurred for various levels of output or sales. The dots on the scatter diagram in Illustration 26.5 represent total actual maintenance costs for a company's

Illustration 26.5

Scatter Diagram

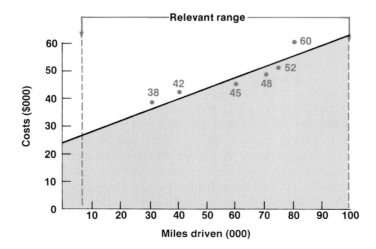

fleet of delivery trucks at various levels of past activity. A line is drawn through what appears visually to be the center of the pattern formed by the dots. In Illustration 26.5, the fixed element of the mixed cost is $23,000, since that is the amount of cost at zero volume of output. The line (called a regression line) rises from $23,000 to $63,000 over the range of 100,000 units. The variable cost portion can be computed as:

$$\frac{\$63,000 - \$23,000}{100,000 \text{ units}} = \$0.40 \text{ per unit}$$

The data in the chart suggest that the company's truck maintenance costs can be estimated at $23,000 plus 40 cents for every mile driven.

A more sophisticated technique, called the **least-squares method,** is often used to draw the regression line and divide mixed costs into their fixed and variable portions. The least-squares method is more precise, but since it involves statistical analysis, it will not be presented in this text.

The High-Low Method.   The high-low method is also widely used to identify the behavior of mixed costs. The **high-low method** uses only the highest and lowest points on a scatter diagram to draw a line representing a total mixed cost.

To illustrate, the lowest point in Illustration 26.5 is $38,000 of expense at 30,000 units of output, and the highest point is $60,000 at 80,000 units of output. The amount of variable cost per unit is found as follows:

$$\frac{\text{Change in cost}}{\text{Change in units}} = \frac{\$60,000 - \$38,000}{80,000 \text{ units} - 30,000 \text{ units}} = \frac{\$22,000}{50,000 \text{ units}} = \$0.44 \text{ per unit}$$

The fixed portion is then found as follows:

Total cost at 80,000 units of output	$60,000
Less: Variable cost at that level of output	
(80,000 × $0.44)	35,200
Fixed cost at all levels of output	
within the relevant range	$24,800

The high-low method is less precise than the scatter diagram since it uses only two data points in the computation. Either or both points may not be representative of the data as a whole.

■ COST–VOLUME–PROFIT (CVP) ANALYSIS

Cost-volume-profit (CVP) analysis (sometimes called **break-even analysis**) is used to determine what effects any changes in a company's selling prices, costs, and/or volume will have on income in the short run. The starting point of such an analysis is the company's break-even point. A company is said to "break even" for a given period if sales revenue and costs charged to that period are exactly equal. Thus, the **break-even point** is that level of operations at which a company realizes no net income or loss.

A careful and accurate cost-volume-profit (CVP) analysis requires knowledge of costs and their behavior (i.e., fixed or variable) as volume changes.

The types and quantities of cost data accumulated depend on the costs of obtaining the data compared to the benefits of having more refined information. Within this constraint, it is desirable to compute break-even points for each area of decision making within the company. Some important classifications of cost data for break-even analysis are by product, territory, salesperson, or class of customer.

A break-even point may be expressed in dollars of sales revenue or number of units produced or sold. No matter how the break-even point is expressed, it is still the point of zero income or loss.

To illustrate the calculation of a break-even point, assume the Muffet Manufacturing Company produces a single product that sells for $20. Fixed costs per period total $40,000, while variable cost is $12 per unit. The **variable cost rate,** which expresses variable cost as a percentage of sales, is 60% ($12 ÷ $20). That is, for each dollar of sales, the company incurs $0.60 of variable cost. The sales revenue needed to break even would be calculated as that point at which all costs are covered, but no income is generated. Therefore, the break-even point can be expressed as:

$$\text{Sales} = \text{Fixed costs} + \text{Variable costs}$$

or

$$S = FC + VC$$

Substituting the Muffet Company amounts of fixed costs and the variable cost rate in the formula gives the following:

$$
\begin{aligned}
S &= \$40,000 + 0.60S \\
S - 0.60S &= \$40,000 \\
0.40S &= \$40,000 \\
S &= \$40,000 \div 0.40 \\
S &= \$100,000
\end{aligned}
$$

Sales revenue at the break-even point is $100,000. To compute the break-even point in units, simply divide the $100,000 of sales by the $20 selling price per unit. This gives a break-even point of 5,000 units.

Alternatively, the break-even point in units could be calculated first. The break-even point in units involves a concept known as contribution margin. **Contribution margin** is the amount by which revenue exceeds variable costs of producing that revenue; it can be calculated on a per unit or total sales volume basis. On a per unit basis, the contribution margin for Muffet Company is $8, which equals the selling price of $20 less the variable cost per unit of $12. Contribution margin indicates the amount of money remaining after variable cost is covered. This remainder contributes to the coverage of fixed costs and to the generation of net income. The break-even point in units is computed by dividing total fixed costs by the contribution margin per unit.

$$\text{BEP}_{\text{units}} = \frac{\text{Fixed costs}}{\text{Contribution margin per unit}}$$

$$\text{BEP}_{\text{units}} = \frac{\$40,000}{\$8 \text{ per unit}}$$

$$= 5,000 \text{ units}$$

If the Muffet Company's production capacity is 20,000 units, then the break-even point is equal to 25% of capacity (5,000/20,000 = 25%).

An alternative method of finding the break-even point in sales dollars is to divide the total fixed costs by the contribution margin rate. The **contribution margin rate** expresses the contribution margin as a percentage of sales and is calculated by dividing the contribution margin per unit by the selling price per unit. The Muffet Company's contribution margin rate is:

$$\frac{\text{Contribution margin per unit}}{\text{Selling price per unit}} = \frac{\$20 - \$12}{\$20} = \frac{\$8}{\$20} = 0.40$$

Using this rate, the Muffet Company's break-even point in sales dollars is calculated as follows:

$$\text{BEP}_{\text{dollars}} = \frac{\text{Fixed costs}}{\text{Contribution margin rate}}$$

$$\text{BEP}_{\text{dollars}} = \frac{\$40,000}{0.40}$$

$$= \$100,000$$

Break-Even Chart

A **break-even chart** is a graph that shows the relationships between sales, costs, volume, and profit and also shows the break-even point. Illustration 26.6 presents the break-even chart for the Muffet Company. Each break-even chart or calculation is valid only for a specified relevant range of volume. The **relevant range** is the range of production or sales volume over which the basic cost behavior assumptions will hold true. For volumes outside these ranges, costs will behave

Illustration 26.6

The Break-Even Chart

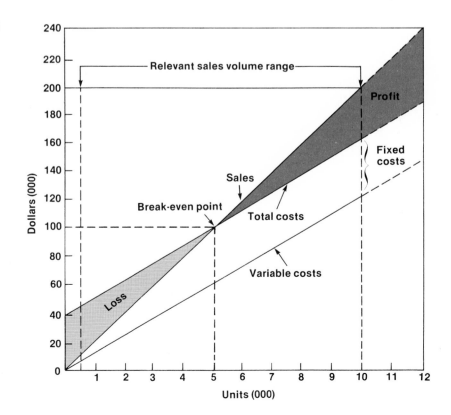

differently and will alter the assumed relationships. For example, if more than 10,000 units were produced by the Muffet Company, it might be necessary to increase plant capacity (thus incurring additional fixed costs) or to work extra shifts (thus incurring overtime charges and other inefficiencies). In either case, the cost relationships first assumed are no longer valid. Illustration 26.6 is based on cost data for Muffet Company in a relevant range of output from 500 to 10,000 units.

The chart in Illustration 26.6 shows that the break-even volume of sales is $100,000 (5,000 units at $20 per unit). At this level of sales, fixed costs and variable costs are exactly equal to sales revenue, as shown:

Revenues	$100,000
Less: Variable costs	60,000
Contribution margin	$ 40,000
Less: Fixed costs	40,000
Net income	$ –0–

The break-even chart could also be re-labeled to indicate contribution margin, as shown in Illustration 26.7.

The break-even charts show that a period of complete idleness will produce a loss of $40,000 (the amount of fixed costs), while output of 10,000 units will produce net income of $40,000. Other points on the graphs show that

Illustration 26.7

Break-Even Chart Showing that Fixed Costs Equal Contribution Margin at Break-Even Point

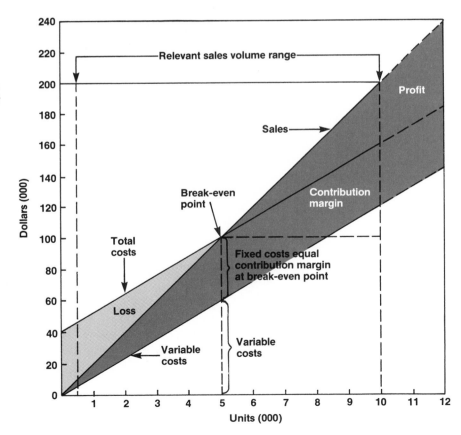

sales of 7,500 units will result in $150,000 of revenue. At that point, total costs amount to $130,000, leaving net income of $20,000. The charts also show that net income at any level of output can be found by multiplying the contribution margin per unit by the number of units sold and subtracting total fixed costs from the result.

Changing the Break-Even Point

A break-even point can be lowered or raised by changing selling price, variable cost per unit, or fixed costs. Lowering the break-even point means that the company can earn income at a lower volume of operations. If the selling price is increased or the variable cost per unit is decreased, the break-even point will be lower because the contribution margin per unit is larger. A larger contribution margin means that more of the selling price of each unit can be used to cover fixed costs. Similarly, if fixed costs are decreased, it takes fewer units sold to cover the smaller amount of fixed costs. These actions in reverse will create a higher break-even point. That is, lowering the selling price, increasing the variable cost per unit, or increasing fixed costs will raise the break-even point.

To illustrate the effects of changing the (1) selling price, (2) variable cost, or (3) fixed cost to lower the break-even point, assume that a company currently has a single product that sells for $60. Variable cost per unit is $15, or 25% of selling price, and fixed costs are $27,000. The break-even point is $36,000 of sales revenue, computed as follows:

$$S = FC + VC$$
$$S = \$27,000 + 0.25S$$
$$0.75S = \$27,000$$
$$S = \$36,000$$

As shown below, companies have a great deal of flexibility in the means of adjusting their break-even points. Companies attempt to operate at a level of operations **above** the break-even point in order to make a profit.

Increase Selling Price.   If the company can increase its selling price to $75 while keeping variable costs and fixed costs the same, the variable cost rate becomes 20%, ($15 ÷ $75). The break-even point will then decrease by $2,250:

$$S = FC + VC$$
$$S = \$27,000 + 0.20S$$
$$0.80S = \$27,000$$
$$S = \$33,750$$

Reduce Variable Cost.   If the company can reduce the variable cost per unit to $13.20 and thus reduce the variable cost rate to 22% of selling price, ($13.20 ÷ $60) the break-even point can be lowered:

$$S = FC + VC$$
$$S = \$27,000 + 0.22S$$
$$0.78S = \$27,000$$
$$S = \$34,615$$

Reduce Fixed Costs.   If the company can reduce its fixed costs by $3,000 to $24,000, the break-even point is again reduced:

$$S = FC + VC$$
$$S = \$24,000 + 0.25S$$
$$0.75S = \$24,000$$
$$S = \$32,000$$

Margin of Safety

If a company's current sales are above its break-even point, then the company is said to have a margin of safety equal to current sales less break-even sales. The margin of safety is the amount by which sales can decrease before a loss will be incurred. For example, assume a company currently has sales of $250,000 and its break-even sales are $200,000. The margin of safety is $50,000, computed as follows:

$$\text{Margin of safety} = \text{Current sales} - \text{Break-even sales}$$
$$= \$250,000 - \$200,000$$
$$= \$50,000$$

The margin of safety is sometimes expressed as a percentage, called the margin of safety rate. The margin of safety rate is equal to (Current sales − Break-even sales) ÷ Current sales. Using data from the company just discussed, the margin of safety rate would be computed as follows:

$$\text{Margin of safety rate} = \frac{\text{Current sales} - \text{Break-even sales}}{\text{Current sales}}$$
$$= \frac{\$250,000 - \$200,000}{\$250,000}$$
$$= 20\%$$

This means that sales volume could drop by 20% before a loss would be incurred.

Assumptions Made in Cost-Volume-Profit Analysis

Certain assumptions are made in CVP analysis:

1. Selling price, variable cost per unit, and total fixed costs remain constant through the relevant range. This means that more or fewer units could be sold at the same price and that there is no change in technical efficiency as volume changes.
2. The number of units produced equals the number of units sold.
3. In multiproduct situations, the product mix is known in advance. (Multiproduct situations are covered later in this chapter.)
4. Costs can be accurately classified into their fixed and variable portions.

Although these assumptions are sometimes criticized as being unrealistic in many situations, they are necessary in order to make the calculations.

Cost-Volume-Profit Analysis Illustrated

CVP analysis has many applications, several of which are illustrated below using data regarding an airline.

Calculating the Break-Even Point. A major airline wishes to know the number of seats that must be sold on a certain flight for the flight to break even. To solve this problem, costs must first be identified and separated into fixed and variable categories.

The fixed costs are the same regardless of the number of seats filled. Fixed costs include items such as the fuel required to fly the plane and crew (with no passengers) to its destination; depreciation on the plane used on the flight; and salaries of required crew members, gate attendants, and maintenance and refueling personnel. The variable costs will vary directly with the number of passengers. Variable costs include meals and beverages provided to passengers, baggage handling costs, and the cost of the additional fuel required to fly the plane with passengers to its destination. Each variable cost should be expressed on a per person basis.

Assume that after the various costs have been analyzed and classified as fixed or variable, the fixed costs for a given flight are $12,000. Variable costs are $25 per passenger, and tickets are sold at $125; thus the variable cost rate is 20% ($25 ÷ $125). This rate yields a contribution margin per ticket of $100 ($125 − $25). The contribution margin rate is 80% [($125 − $25) ÷ $125].

The break-even point can be expressed in sales revenue (dollars) or in number of passengers. The sales revenue needed to break even is computed as follows:

$$\text{Sales} = \text{Fixed costs} + \text{Variable costs}$$
$$S = FC + VC$$
$$S = \$12,000 + 0.20S$$
$$0.80S = \$12,000$$
$$S = \$15,000$$

The break-even point in dollars can also be computed as follows:

$$BEP_{\text{dollars}} = \frac{\text{Fixed costs}}{\text{Contribution margin rate}}$$
$$= \frac{\$12,000}{0.80}$$
$$= \$15,000$$

The break-even point in number of passengers (units) may be found by dividing fixed costs by the contribution margin per unit:

$$BEP_{\text{units}} = \frac{\text{Fixed costs}}{\text{Contribution margin per unit}}$$
$$= \frac{\$12,000}{\$125 - \$25}$$
$$= 120 \text{ passengers}$$

Calculating Sales Volume Needed for Desired Net Income. With a simple adjustment in the break-even formulas, CVP analysis can also show the sales volume needed to generate some desired level of net income. This adjustment is made by adding the desired income amount to the total costs that need to be covered. Management can then determine the necessary sales volume in dollars or units. For example, if the airline discussed above wishes to earn $8,000 of income on its flight, the company can calculate the amount of necessary sales revenue by the following formula:

$$Sales = Fixed\ costs + Variable\ costs + Desired\ net\ income$$

or

$$S = FC + VC + NI$$
$$S = \$12,000 + 0.20S + \$8,000$$
$$0.80S = \$20,000$$
$$S = \$25,000$$

If the airline wants to know how many passenger tickets must be sold in order to earn $8,000, a similar modification of another form of the break-even point formula will yield the desired calculation. Remembering that the contribution margin per ticket is $100, the number of tickets to be sold is computed as follows:

$$Number\ of\ units = \frac{Fixed\ costs + Desired\ net\ income}{Contribution\ margin\ per\ unit}$$
$$= \frac{\$12,000 + \$8,000}{\$100}$$
$$= \frac{\$20,000}{\$100}$$
$$= 200\ passengers$$

Calculating the Effect on Net Income of Changing Price. The break-even formula can also be used to determine the results if the price used in the formula is changed. To illustrate, assume that the flight normally carries 150 passengers (sales of $18,750 and net income of $3,000) and that a decision is made to increase ticket prices by 5%. If variable and fixed costs remain constant and passenger load does not change, net income will rise from $3,000 to $3,937.50 as shown:

$$S = FC + VC + NI$$
$$\$18,750\ (1.05) = \$12,000 + 0.20\ (\$18,750) + NI$$
$$\$19,687.50 = \$12,000 + \$3,750 + NI$$
$$\$19,687.50 = \$15,750 + NI$$
$$NI = \$3,937.50$$

We assume that variable costs would remain constant at 20% of original sales in the above illustration because a change in selling price has no effect on the variable costs associated with providing flight service. Income would rise by the entire amount of the price increase ($19,687.50 − $18,750 = $937.50) because all variable and fixed costs are already being covered by the original selling price.

Calculating Sales Needed to Maintain Net Income When Costs Change.
The break-even formula has yet another application; it can be used to calculate
the sales needed to maintain income when costs change. For example, if the
price of gasoline rises, both fixed and variable costs will increase for the airline.
Assume that fixed costs are increased by $4,000, and variable costs are increased
by $6.25 per passenger. Variable costs are now 25% ($31.25/$125) of sales
price. In order to maintain the current net income of $3,000 (on $18,750 of
sales), the airline will need to increase sales revenue to $25,333 as shown below.

$$S = FC + VC + NI$$
$$S = \$16,000 + 0.25S + \$3,000$$
$$0.75S = \$19,000$$
$$S = \$25,333 \text{ (or 203 passengers)}$$

Other Uses of CVP Analysis.   Management can also use its knowledge
of CVP relationships to determine whether to increase sales promotion costs
in an effort to increase sales volume or to accept an order at a lower-than-
usual price. In general, the careful study of break-even charts helps management
plan future courses of action. Indeed, it has been said that to be successful,
management must become "break-even minded."

Calculating Break-Even for a Multiproduct Company

When computing the break-even point for a multiproduct company, only dollars
of sales are used. In a multiproduct company, a given product mix is assumed
to be constant for CVP purposes. **Product mix** refers to the proportion of
the company's total sales attributable to each type of product sold. To illustrate
the computation of the break-even point for a multiproduct company, assume
the following historical data:

| | \multicolumn{8}{c}{Products} | | | | | | | |
| | 1 | | 2 | | 3 | | Total | |
	Amount	Per-cent	Amount	Per-cent	Amount	Per-cent	Amount	Per-cent
Sales	$60,000	100	$30,000	100	$10,000	100	$100,000	100
Less: Variable costs . . .	40,000	67	16,000	53	4,000	40	60,000	60
Contribution margin . .	$20,000	33	$14,000	47	$ 6,000	60	$ 40,000	40

The relationships shown in the Total column are used to compute the break-
even point. Variable costs are 60% ($60,000/$100,000) of total sales. If the
product mix is assumed to remain constant and fixed costs for the company
are $50,000, break-even sales are $125,000:

$$S = FC + VC$$
$$S = \$50,000 + 0.60S$$
$$0.40S = \$50,000$$
$$S = \$125,000$$

The $125,000 of sales can be specified by product by multiplying total sales dollars by the percent of product mix of each of the three products. The product mix for products 1, 2, and 3 is 60:30:10, respectively; that is, out of the $100,000 total sales, there were $60,000 sales of product 1, $30,000 sales of product 2, and $10,000 sales of product 3. Therefore, the company will have to sell $75,000 (0.6 × $125,000) of product 1, $37,500 (0.3 × $125,000) of product 2, and $12,500 (0.1 × $125,000) of product 3 in order to break even.

If there is any change in the mix of products sold, the break-even point will also change. The break-even point changes because each product has a different contribution margin. Also, if historical patterns of selling prices or variable costs are not expected to hold true in the future, projected sales and variable expenses should be used to determine expected percentages of variable expenses to total sales.

To illustrate the effects of such changes, assume that the product mix for products 1, 2, and 3 is expected to change to 20:30:50 in the upcoming period, as shown in the following chart. Also assume that total sales are $100,000 and that the variable costs for product 3 are expected to fall to 33% of the selling price. To compute the new break-even point, we again use the relationships shown in the Total column.

| | Products | | | | | | | |
| | 1 | | 2 | | 3 | | Total | |
	Amount	Per-cent	Amount	Per-cent	Amount	Per-cent	Amount	Per-cent
Sales . . .	$20,000	100	$30,000	100	$50,000	100	$100,000	100
Less: Variable costs . . .	13,333	67	16,000	53	16,667	33	46,000	46
Contribution margin . .	$ 6,667	33	$14,000	47	$33,333	67	$ 54,000	54

As shown in the Total column, variable costs are expected to fall to 46% of total sales in the upcoming period. The new break-even point will be $92,593 computed as follows:

$$S = FC + VC$$
$$S = \$50,000 + 0.46S$$
$$0.54S = \$50,000$$
$$S = \$92,593$$

Notice that the new break-even point is lower than the old one. Sales shifted from the lowest contribution margin product (product 1) to the highest contribution margin product (product 3), thereby increasing the contribution margin dollars available to cover fixed costs.

■ DIFFERENTIAL ANALYSIS

Another analytical tool of short-term decision making is differential analysis. Differential analysis involves analyzing the different costs and benefits that would arise from alternative solutions to a particular situation. **Relevant revenues or costs** in a given situation are future revenues or costs that differ depending on which alternative course of action is selected. **Differential revenue** is defined as the difference in revenues between two alternatives. **Differential cost or expense** is the difference between relevant costs for two alternatives.[1] Future costs that do not differ between alternatives are irrelevant and may be ignored since they will affect both alternatives similarly. Past costs, also known as **sunk costs,** are also not relevant in decision making because the costs have already been incurred and, therefore, cannot be changed no matter which alternative is selected.

For certain decisions, revenues do not differ between alternatives. Under those circumstances, management should select the alternative with the least cost. In other situations, costs do not differ between alternatives. Accordingly, the alternative that results in the greatest revenue should be selected. But many times both future costs and revenues differ between alternatives. In these situations, the alternative that results in the greatest positive difference between future revenues and expenses (costs) should be selected.

To illustrate relevant, differential, and sunk costs, assume that Jack Bennett had invested $400 in a tiller so that he could till gardens to earn $1,500 during the summer. He is now offered the opportunity of working at a horse stable feeding horses and cleaning stalls for a salary of $1,200 for the summer. The costs that he would incur in tilling are $100 for transportation and $150 for supplies. The costs he would incur at the horse stable are $100 for transportation and $50 for supplies. If Jack works at the stable, he would still have the tiller, and it would be used by his parents and loaned to friends at no charge. The tiller cost of $400 is not **relevant** to the decision because it is a **sunk** cost. The transportation cost of $100 is also not relevant because it is the same for both alternatives. The relevant costs and revenues are shown below:

	Performing tilling service	Working at horse stable	Differential
Revenues	$1,500	$1,200	$300
Costs	150	50	100
Net benefit in favor of tilling service			$200

Based on this differential analysis, Jack Bennett should perform his tilling service rather than work at the stable.

In many situations, total variable costs differ between alternatives while total fixed costs do not. But one cannot assume that variable costs are always differential costs and fixed costs are never differential costs. For example, the differential cost between operating at a production level of 40,000 units versus a production level of 60,000 units might include increases in both variable and fixed costs. This increase in fixed costs could be the result of a step fixed cost, such as that related to the number of supervisors necessary for a particular production level.

---

[1] Some authors equate relevant cost and differential cost. This text uses the term *relevant* to identify which costs should be considered in a situation and the term *differential* to identify the amount by which these costs differ.

The Nature of Fixed Costs

Up to this point in our discussion, fixed costs have been treated as if they were all alike. But two types of fixed costs should be identified. They are committed fixed costs and discretionary fixed costs.

Committed Fixed Costs.   Committed fixed costs relate to the basic facilities and organization structure that a company must have to continue operations. These costs are not changed in the short run without seriously disrupting operations. Examples of committed fixed costs are depreciation on buildings and equipment and salaries of key executives. In the short run, costs such as these are viewed as not being subject to the discretion or control of management. They result from past decisions that "committed" the company for a period of several years. For instance, once a company constructs a building to house production operations, it is committed to the use of the building for many years. Thus, the depreciation on that building is not as subject to control by management as are some other types of fixed costs.

Discretionary Fixed Costs.   In contrast to committed fixed costs, discretionary fixed costs are subject to management control from year to year. Each year management decides how much to spend on advertising, research and development, and employee training and development programs. Since these decisions are made each year, they are said to be under the "discretion" of management. Management is not locked in or committed to a certain level of expense for any more than one budget period. The next period it may change the level of expense or may eliminate it completely.

The philosophy of management can affect to some extent which fixed costs are committed and which discretionary. For instance, during the recession of the mid 1970s, some companies terminated persons in the upper levels of management, while other companies kept their "management team" intact. Thus, in some companies the salaries of top-level managers were discretionary while in others they were committed.

The discussion of committed fixed costs and discretionary fixed costs is relevant to CVP analysis. If a company's fixed costs are almost all committed fixed costs, it is going to have a more difficult time in reducing its break-even point for the next budget period than if most of its fixed costs are discretionary in nature. A company with a large proportion of discretionary fixed costs may be able to reduce fixed costs dramatically in a recessionary period. By doing this, it may be able to "run lean" and show some income even when economic conditions are difficult. Its chances of long-run survival may be enhanced.

Opportunity Cost

Another cost concept relevant to decision making is opportunity cost. An opportunity cost is the potential benefit that is forgone from **not** following the next best alternative course of action. For instance, assume that the two best uses of a plot of land are as a mobile home park (annual income of $100,000) and as a golf driving range (annual income of $60,000). The opportunity cost of utilizing the land as a mobile home park is $60,000, while the opportunity cost of utilizing the land as a driving range is $100,000. Opportunity costs are not recorded in the accounting records since they are the costs of **not** following a certain alternative. However, opportunity cost is a relevant cost in many decision problems because it represents a real sacrifice that comes about because one alternative is chosen instead of another.

Applications of Differential Analysis

To illustrate the application of differential analysis to specific decision problems, we will now consider five types of decisions: (1) setting prices of products; (2) accepting or rejecting special orders; (3) eliminating products, segments, or customers; (4) processing or selling joint products; and (5) deciding to make or buy. These five types of decisions are not the only applications of differential analysis, but they represent typical short-term business decisions to which differential analysis can properly be applied.

Setting Prices of Products.   When differential analysis is applied to pricing decisions, each possible price for a given product represents an alternative course of action. The sales revenues for each alternative and the costs that differ between alternatives are the relevant amounts in these decisions. Total fixed costs usually remain the same between pricing alternatives and, if so, may be ignored. In selecting a price for a product, the goal is to select the price at which total future revenues will exceed total future variable costs by the greatest amount or, in other words, the price that will result in the greatest **total** contribution margin.

A high price is not necessarily the price that will maximize income. There may be many substitutes for the product. If a high price is set, the number of units sold may decline substantially as customers switch to lower-priced competitive products. Thus, in the maximization of income, the expected volume of sales at each price is as important as the contribution margin per unit of product sold. In making any pricing decision, management should seek the combination of price and volume that will produce the largest **total** contribution margin. This combination is often difficult to identify in an actual situation since management may have to estimate the number of units that can be sold at each price.

For example, assume that a company has fixed costs of $10,000 and variable production costs of $5 per unit. Estimates of product demand are:

Choice	Demand
1 . . .	20,000 units at $4 per unit
2 . . .	15,000 units at $6 per unit
3 . . .	10,000 units at $8 per unit
4 . . .	5,000 units at $10 per unit

What price should be set for the product? Based on the calculations shown below, the company should select a price of $8 per unit (choice 3) since this will result in the greatest total contribution margin ($30,000).

Choice	Contribution margin per unit*	×	Number of units	=	Total contribution margin
1	$—1		20,000		$—20,000
2	1		15,000		15,000
3	3		10,000		30,000
4	5		5,000		25,000

* Sales price — Variable cost.

Accepting or Rejecting Special Orders. Sometimes management is faced with the opportunity to sell its product in two or more markets at two or more different prices. Price discrimination is unlawful under the Robinson-Patman Act unless it is justified by differences in costs of delivery or selling. Since such cost differences often exist, a single product may be marketed at more than one selling price. Differential analysis can be used to determine if special orders (orders at a price different from the norm) should be accepted.

The desirablility of keeping physical facilities and personnel working at capacity is obvious. Good business management requires keeping the cost of idleness at a minimum. When operations are at a level less than full capacity, additional business should be sought. Such additional business may be accepted at prices lower than average unit costs because the only relevant costs are the future **additional** costs that will be incurred. For the most part, the relevant costs will be variable costs, such as direct materials and direct labor.

To illustrate, assume that a given company produces and sells a single product that has a variable cost of $8 per unit. Annual capacity is 10,000 units, and annual fixed costs total $48,000. The selling price is $20 per unit, and production and sales are budgeted at 5,000 units. Thus, budgeted net income before taxes is $12,000, computed as follows:

Sales (5,000 units at $20) . . .		$100,000
Costs:		
Fixed	$48,000	
Variable (5,000 units at $8) . .	40,000	88,000
Net income before taxes . . .		$ 12,000

Assume an order for 3,000 units is received from a foreign distributor at a price of $10 per unit. This $10 price is only half of the regular selling price per unit and is also less than the average cost per unit of $17.60 ($88,000 ÷ 5,000 units). But the $10 price offered exceeds the variable cost per unit by $2. If the order is accepted, net income will be $18,000, computed as follows:

Sales (5,000 units at $20, 3,000 units at $10) . .		$130,000
Costs:		
Fixed	$48,000	
Variable (8,000 units at $8)	64,000	112,000
Net income before taxes		$ 18,000

To continue to operate at 50% capacity (producing 5,000 units) would produce net income of only $12,000. A contribution margin of $2 per unit on the new units will result from acceptance of the order; thus, net income will increase by $6,000. Because the regular market is unlikely to be affected by the export of the product at a sharply reduced price, the order should be accepted assuming it does not violate international trade agreements.

Differential analysis would provide the following calculations:

	(1) Accept order	(2) Reject order	Differential
Revenues	$130,000	$100,000	$30,000
Costs	64,000	40,000	24,000
Net benefit in favor of accepting order . .			$ 6,000

In summary, variable costs set a floor for the selling price in cost analyses. Even if the price exceeds variable costs only slightly, the additional business may make a contribution to income. But "contribution pricing" of marginal business often brings only short-term increases in income. Such pricing should be appraised in light of the long-range effects on company and industry price structures. In the long run, full costs must be covered.

Eliminating Products, Segments, or Customers.   Periodically, management has to decide whether to eliminate or retain certain products, segments, or customers. Differential analysis can be useful in this type of decision making. Since the income statement does not automatically associate costs with given products, segments, or customers, costs must be reclassified as those that **would be changed** by the elimination and those that **would not.** In effect, one must simply assume elimination and compare the reduction in revenues with the eliminated costs.

Usually costs such as direct materials, direct labor, and other variable costs would be eliminated and, therefore, become part of differential cost. The fixed costs will **normally** remain unaffected and, if so, are not relevant to the decision. If revenues lost from discontinuing the product, segment, or customer exceed the costs that would be eliminated, that item is making a positive contribution to profits and should, therefore, be retained unless a more profitable opportunity exists.

To illustrate, assume that the elimination of product R is being considered. Product R provides revenues of $100,000 annually and incurs costs of $110,000, $80,000 variable and $30,000 fixed. Therefore, product R creates an apparent annual loss of $10,000. But careful cost analysis reveals that if product R were dropped, the reduction in costs would be $80,000. The $30,000 fixed costs would continue to be incurred and would need to be covered by the remaining products of the company. The analysis is as follows:

	(1) Retain product R	(2) Drop product R	Differential
Revenues	$100,000	$–0–	$100,000
Costs	80,000	–0–	80,000
Net benefit of retaining product R . .			$ 20,000

This illustration shows that product R, even though it produces no net income itself, has been contributing $20,000 ($100,000 revenues − $80,000 variable costs) annually to covering the fixed costs of the business. In other words, product R has a contribution to indirect expenses of $20,000. Consequently, its elimination could be a costly mistake unless there is a more profitable use for the released facilities.

If there is a profitable alternative use for those facilities, the potential income from that alternative represents an opportunity cost of retaining product R. Assume, for example, that those facilities could be used to manufacture a product that would contribute $30,000 to the company's income. In this case, the relevant costs in the decision to retain product R are $110,000 ($80,000 of variable manufacturing costs and $30,000 of opportunity cost), while the relevant revenues are still $100,000. Therefore, the net advantage of keeping product R is $−10,000, meaning that product R should not be retained. Similarly, when analyzing the decision to replace product R with the alternative, the $20,000 contribution to indirect expenses that is foregone if product R is replaced becomes an opportunity cost of the alternative product.

Processing or Selling Joint Products.   In some manufacturing situations, several products result from a common raw material or manufacturing process; these products are called **joint products.** For instance, when crude oil is manufactured, a wide variety of fuels, solvents, lubricants, and residual petrochemicals are derived. Some of these products can be processed further or sold in their existing condition. Management can use differential analysis to decide whether to process a joint product further or to sell it in its present condition. **Joint costs** are those costs incurred up to the point where the joint products split off from each other. These costs are sunk costs in deciding whether to process a joint product further before selling it or to sell it in its condition at split off.

The following example will illustrate the issue of whether to process or sell joint products. Assume that Company Y manufactures two products, A and B, from a common manufacturing process. Each of the products could be sold in its present form or could be processed further and sold at a higher price. Data for both products are given below:

Product	Selling price per unit at split-off point	Cost per unit of further processing	Selling price per unit after further processing
A	$10	$6	$21
B	12	7	18

The differential revenues and costs of further processing of the two products are as follows:

Product	Differential revenue of further processing	Differential cost of further processing	Net advantage (disadvantage) of further processing
A	$11	$6	$ 5
B	6	7	(1)

Based on this analysis, product A should be processed further since it will increase income by $5 per unit sold. Product B should not be processed further, for doing so would decrease income by $1 per unit sold.

This same form of differential analysis should also be used in deciding whether **by-products,** the waste materials that result from the production of a product, should be discarded or processed further to be made salable. If the differential revenue of further processing exceeds the differential cost, then further processing should be done. If not, the waste material should be discarded.

Deciding to Make or Buy. Differential analysis can also be applied to make-or-buy decisions. A **make-or-buy decision** concerns whether to manufacture or purchase a part or material used in the manufacture of another product. The price that would be paid for the part if it were purchased is compared with the **additional costs** that would be incurred if the part were manufactured. If almost all of the manufacturing costs are fixed and would exist in any case, it is likely that manufacture rather than purchase of the part or material would be more economical.

To illustrate the application of differential analysis to a make-or-buy decision, assume that a company manufactures parts costing $6 for use in its final product. Cost components are materials, $3; labor, $1.50; fixed overhead costs, $1.05; and variable overhead costs, $0.45. The part could be purchased for $5.25. Since fixed overhead would presumably continue even if the part were purchased, manufacture of the part should be continued. The added costs of manufacturing amount to only $4.95 ($3.00 + $1.50 + $0.45). This amount is 30 cents per unit less than the purchase price of the part, as shown in the following analysis:

	(1) Make	(2) Buy	Differential
Costs	$4.95	$5.25	$0.30
Net advantage of making . .			$0.30

The opportunity cost of not utilizing the space for some other purpose should also be considered. If the opportunity cost of not using this space in its best alternative use is more than 30 cents per unit times the number of units produced, then the part should be purchased.

In some manufacturing situations, it is possible to avoid a portion of fixed costs by buying from an outside source. For example, if the part was no longer produced, a segment supervisor's salary (a fixed cost) could be eliminated, thereby reducing fixed costs by the amount of that salary. In such a situation, these fixed costs should be treated the same as variable costs in the analysis, since they would then be relevant costs.

It is also possible that the cost to manufacture may be only slightly less than the cost of purchasing the part or material. In this case, other factors should be considered, such as the competency of existing personnel to undertake manufacture of the part or material, the availability of working capital, and the cost of any loans than may be necessary.

■ ABSORPTION VERSUS DIRECT COSTING

As the final consideration in short-term decision making, a new form of income statement and product costing will be introduced. Currently, the most commonly accepted theory and method of product costing is called absorption or full costing. Under **absorption (or full) costing,** all production costs, including fixed manufacturing overhead, are accounted for as product costs and are allocated to the units of product produced during a period. Absorption costing is the theory on which the discussion of product costing in Chapters 21–25 was based. Another method, **direct (or variable) costing,** on the other hand, includes only variable manufacturing costs as product costs. All fixed manufacturing overhead costs are charged to expense in the period in which they are incurred. The difference between the income statements under the two methods is that absorption costing focuses on gross margin, while direct costing focuses on contribution margin.

The differences between absorption and direct costing can be seen by comparing the income statements that would result from applying each technique to the same data. Assume the Bradley Company had the following data related to manufacturing and sales activities for May 1987:

BRADLEY COMPANY
May, 1987

Beginning inventory (units) . .	–0–	Variable costs (per unit):	
Production (units)	10,000	Direct materials	$2.00
Sales (units)	9,000	Direct labor	1.00
Fixed costs:		Manufacturing overhead	0.30
Manufacturing overhead . .	$ 6,000	Total	$3.30
Selling expenses	15,000	Variable selling expenses (per unit) . .	$0.20
Administrative expenses . .	12,000	Selling price (per unit)	$8.00

Absorption Costing

Under absorption costing, fixed manufacturing overhead costs would be applied to the units of production at the rate of $0.60 per unit ($6,000/10,000 units). Therefore, the cost per unit of inventory is $3.90, the total of the direct materials, direct labor, and variable and fixed manufacturing overhead. All selling and administrative expenses are period costs. Illustration 26.8 contains the income statement for the Bradley Company prepared under absorption costing.

Generally, variable and fixed manufacturing costs do not appear as separate line items on the income statement; they are presented this way simply to illustrate that the fixed manufacturing costs are included as part of product cost and that some of these costs are included in ending inventory. Ending inventory is priced at "full cost" of $3.90 per unit ($39,000/10,000). Also, no distinction is made between fixed and variable selling expenses. These are totaled and shown under operating expenses of the period.

Absorption costing is required for external financial statement presentation and also for tax purposes. But, as shown throughout this chapter, a "full" cost approach is not necessarily the best approach for internal management decision making. Management often needs information on contribution margin

Illustration 26.8

Income Statement under Absorption Costing

BRADLEY COMPANY
Income Statement
For the Period Ending May 31, 1987

Sales (9,000 units at $8)		$72,000
Cost of goods sold:		
Variable costs of production (10,000 units at $3.30) . .	$33,000	
Fixed overhead costs	6,000	
Total costs of producing 10,000 units	$39,000	
Less: Ending inventory (1,000 units at $3.90)	3,900	35,100
Gross margin on sales		$36,900
Operating expenses:		
Selling ($15,000 fixed plus 9,000 at $0.20 each) . . .	$16,800	
Administrative	12,000	28,800
Net income before taxes		$8,100

rather than gross margin to calculate break-even points and make decisions regarding special-order pricing. Direct costing presents this information in a more obvious and prominent form.

Direct Costing

Under direct costing, all **variable** costs of production (direct materials, direct labor, and variable manufacturing overhead) are treated as product costs. Product costs attach to the product and only become an expense (cost of goods sold) when the products are sold. All **fixed** manufacturing overhead costs are considered period costs and are charged to expense in the period received. The logic behind this expensing of fixed manufacturing overhead is that such costs would be incurred whether there was production or whether the plant was idle; therefore, these fixed costs do not specifically relate to the manufacture of products. The direct costing income statement for Bradley Company for May 1987 is presented in Illustration 26.9.

Illustration 26.9

Income Statement under Direct Costing

BRADLEY COMPANY
Income Statement
For the Period Ending May 31, 1987

Sales (9,000 units at $8)		$72,000
Variable costs:		
Variable production costs incurred (10,000 units at $3.30) . .	$33,000	
Less: Ending inventory (1,000 units at $3.30)	3,300	29,700
Manufacturing margin		$42,300
Variable selling expenses (9,000 units at $0.20)		1,800
Contribution margin		$40,500
Fixed costs:		
Manufacturing overhead	$ 6,000	
Selling expenses	15,000	
Administrative expenses	12,000	33,000
Net income before taxes		$ 7,500

Notice in the direct cost income statement that the goods in inventory are carried at $3.30 per unit rather than at the $3.90 full cost. All variable costs are shown separately at the top of the statement as deductions from sales to disclose contribution margin for the month. All fixed costs are classified as period costs no matter what the source of the cost (manufacturing, selling, or administrative).

Comparing the Two Methods

Comparing the two income statements, there is a $600 difference in net income before taxes for the month and a $600 difference in ending inventory valuation. These differences are due to the treatment of fixed manufacturing overhead costs. Under absorption costing, each unit in ending inventory carries $0.60 of fixed overhead cost as part of product cost. There are 1,000 units in inventory at the end of the month; therefore, ending inventory under absorption costing includes $600 of fixed manufacturing overhead costs ($0.60 × 1,000 units) and is valued at $600 more than under direct costing. Under direct costing, **all** the fixed manufacturing overhead costs are charged off during the period rather than being deferred and carried forward to the next period as part of inventory cost. Therefore, $6,000 of fixed manufacturing overhead costs appear on the direct costing income statement as an expense, rather than $5,400 ($6,000 fixed manufacturing overhead costs $—600 fixed manufacturing overhead included in inventory) under absorption costing. Consequently, net income before taxes under direct costing is $600 less than under absorption costing because more expense is charged off during the period.

As a final point of emphasis, recognize that the difference between the two methods is **solely** in the treatment of fixed manufacturing overhead costs and income statement presentation. Selling and administrative expenses are treated as period costs under **both** methods. The only difference in regard to these costs is their placement on the income statement and the segregation of variable and fixed selling and administrative expenses. Variable selling and administrative expenses are **not** part of product cost under either method.

The analysis is slightly more complicated when both beginning and ending inventories are involved. The difference in net income before taxes is found by determining whether the amount of fixed manufacturing overhead costs included in inventory cost under absorption costing increased or decreased from the beginning to the end of the period. If that amount increased, net income before taxes under direct costing will be less than under absorption costing. If the amount of fixed manufacturing overhead costs included in inventory decreased during the period, net income before taxes under direct costing will be greater than under absorption costing. (Demonstration Problem 26–2 illustrates how to determine net income before taxes when both beginning and ending inventories are involved.)

As a general rule, the difference in net income before taxes under the two methods can be related to the **change** in inventories. Assuming a relatively constant level of production, if inventories increase during the year, then production exceeded sales, and reported net income before taxes will be less under direct costing than under absorption costing. Conversely, if inventories decreased, then sales exceeded production, and net income before taxes will be larger under direct costing than under absorption costing.

Direct costing is not currently considered acceptable for income measurement, inventory valuation, or tax purposes. Currently accepted practice requires that **all** costs of producing a product be attached to that product and treated as expenses only when the product is sold. But the type of information accumulated under direct costing, especially the classification of costs as fixed and variable, is very useful to management in understanding relationships between costs, volume, and profits. Since direct costing is such a valuable management tool, its use is likely to increase.

■ SUMMARY

The short term (or short run) is defined as that period of time in which the effects of certain past decisions cannot be changed. As a result, some costs are fixed in the short run, while others vary with changes in the level of activity. For purposes of short-term decision making, management must attempt to classify all costs as fixed or variable to understand how total costs will react to changes in the volume of production or sales.

There are four basic types of cost behavior patterns—variable costs, fixed costs, mixed (or semivariable) costs, and step costs. Various techniques exist for analyzing actual cost data to identify the underlying cost patterns. These techniques include the scatter diagram, the high-low method, and sophisticated statistical techniques like the least squares method.

The chapter discusses three topics related to short-term decision making— cost-volume-profit (CVP) analysis, differential analysis, and direct costing. CVP analysis is a technique used to estimate the relationship between selling prices, costs, the company's volume of operations, and net income in the short run. The starting point for CVP analysis is the company's break-even point, which means the level of operations at which revenues and costs are equal. Once that is determined, management can look at the changes in income that would result if selling prices, fixed costs, or variable costs were changed. In addition, management can compute the level of operations required to produce a certain amount of income.

Differential analysis is another tool of short-term analysis. In differential analysis, a particular set of alternatives is analyzed by looking at the revenues and costs or expenses that will differ in the future, depending on which alternative is chosen. Such revenues and costs are designated as relevant revenues and relevant costs for differential analysis. Differential revenue is the amount by which relevant revenues differ between alternatives. Differential cost or expense is the amount by which total expense differs between alternatives. In differential analysis, the preferred alternative is the one that provides the largest positive difference between differential revenue and differential expense. A number of specific types of decisions can be addressed through differential analysis including the following: setting prices of products; accepting or rejecting special orders; eliminating products, segments, or customers; processing or selling joint products; and deciding to make or buy.

Under absorption (or full) costing all manufacturing costs are treated as product costs. Under direct (or variable) costing only variable manufacturing costs are treated as product costs; fixed manufacturing overhead costs are considered to be period costs. Absorption costing is required for financial reporting purposes. Direct costing, however, provides cost information that is useful to management for many decision-making purposes, including CVP analysis and differential analysis. As a general rule, the difference in the net income before taxes computed under each of the methods is related to the change in inventories over the period. If there is no change in inventories, both methods give the same net income before taxes amount.

In this chapter you studied the importance of short-run planning. Chapter 27 discusses long-range planning regarding the acquisition of capital assets. All businesses must establish long-range goals and must plan for the future to be successful.

NEW TERMS INTRODUCED IN CHAPTER 26*

Absorption (or full) costing

A concept of costing under which all production costs, including fixed manufacturing overhead, are accounted for as product costs and allocated to the units produced during a period (1022).

Break-even analysis

See Cost-volume-profit analysis.

Break-even chart

A graph that shows the relationships between sales, costs, volume, and profit and also shows the break-even point (1007).

Break-even point

That level of operations at which revenues for a period are equal to the costs assigned to that period so that there is no net income or loss (1005).

By-products

The waste materials (which sometimes have a small market value compared to the main product) that result from the production of a product or products (1021).

Committed fixed costs

Costs relating to the basic facilities and organization structure that a company must have to continue operations. An example is depreciation on the factory building (1016).

Contribution margin

The amount by which revenue exceeds the variable costs of producing that revenue (1006).

Contribution margin rate

Contribution margin per unit divided by selling price per unit (1007).

Cost-volume-profit (CVP) analysis

An analysis of the effects that any changes in a company's selling prices, costs, and/or volume will have upon income (profits) in the short run. Also called break-even analysis (1005).

Differential analysis

An analysis of the different costs and benefits that would arise from alternative solutions to a particular problem (1014).

Differential cost or expense

The difference between the amounts of relevant costs for two alternatives (1015).

Differential revenue

The difference between the amounts of relevant revenues for two alternatives (1015).

Direct (or variable) costing

A concept of costing under which only variable manufacturing costs are accounted for as product costs and charged to the units produced during a period. All fixed manufacturing overhead is charged to expense in the period in which it is incurred (1022).

Discretionary fixed costs

Fixed costs that are subject to management control from year to year. An example is advertising expense (1016).

Fixed costs

Costs that remain constant (in total) over some relevant range of output (1002).

---

* Some terms listed in earlier chapters are repeated here for your convenience.

High-low method

A method used in dividing mixed costs into their fixed and variable portions. The high plot and low plot of actual costs are used to draw a line representing a total mixed cost (1005).

Joint costs

Those costs incurred up to the point where joint products split off from each other (1020).

Joint products

Two or more products resulting from a common raw material or manufacturing process (1020).

Least-squares method

A method used for dividing mixed costs into their fixed and variable portions; it uses statistical techniques to draw the regression line representing a total mixed cost (1005).

Make-or-buy decision

Concerns whether to manufacture or purchase a part or material used in the manufacture of another product (1021).

Margin of safety

Amount by which sales can decrease before a loss will be incurred (1010).

Margin of safety rate

Margin of safety expressed as a percentage; is equal to (Current sales − Break-even sales) ÷ Current sales (1010).

Mixed cost

Contains a fixed portion of cost that will be incurred even when the plant is completely idle and a variable portion that will increase directly with production volume (1002).

Opportunity cost

The potential benefit that is foregone from not following the next best alternative course of action (1016).

Product mix

The proportion of the company's total sales attributable to each type of product sold. Product mix may be defined either in terms of sales dollars or in terms of the number of units sold (1013).

Relevant revenues or costs

Revenues or costs that will differ in the future depending on which alternative course of action is selected (1015).

Relevant range

The range of production or sales volume over which the basic cost behavior assumptions will hold true (1007).

Scatter diagram

A diagram that shows plots of actual costs incurred for various levels of output or sales; it is used in dividing mixed costs into their fixed and variable portions (1004).

Short run

The period of time over which it is assumed that plant capacity and certain costs are fixed; often determined to be one year or less (1001).

Step cost

A cost that remains constant in total over a range of output (or sales) but then increases in steps at certain points (1002).

Sunk costs

Past costs about which nothing can be done; they are not relevant in decision making because the costs have already been incurred (1015).

Variable costs

Costs that vary (in total) directly with changes in volume (1002).

Variable cost rate

Variable costs expressed as a percentage of sales; used to find the break-even point (1006).

DEMONSTRATION PROBLEM 26-1

The Boston Company has fixed costs of $250,000 per year and variable costs of $6 per unit. Its product sells for $10 per unit. Full capacity is 100,000 units. Variable costs are 60% of sales ($6/$10).

Required:
  a. Compute the break-even point in (1) sales dollars, (2) units, and (3) percentage of capacity.
  b. Compute the number of units the company must sell if it wishes to have net income of $120,000.

Solution to demonstration problem 26-1

  a. (1) Sales (S) = Fixed costs (FC) + Variable costs (VC)

$$S = \$250,000 + 0.60S$$
$$0.40S = \$250,000$$
$$S = \$250,000 \div 0.40$$
$$S = \$625,000$$

  (2) Break-even point in units = $\$625,000 \div \$10 = \underline{62,500}$ or $\dfrac{\$250,000}{\$10 - \$6} = \underline{62,500}$

  (3) Break-even point as percentage of capacity = $62,500 \div 100,000 = \underline{62.5\%}$

  b. Number of units $= \dfrac{\text{Fixed cost} + \text{Desired net income}}{\text{Contribution margin}}$

$$= \frac{\$250,000 + \$120,000}{\$10 - \$6}$$

$$= \frac{\$370,000}{\$4}$$

$$= \underline{92,500}$$

DEMONSTRATION PROBLEM 26-2

The Detroit Division of the Orvis Company produces a single product that it sells for $10 each. Production costs include $2 per unit variable costs and $330,000 per year of fixed manufacturing overhead costs. Normal activity for fixed manufacturing overhead cost absorption is 110,000 units per year. Thus, fixed manufacturing overhead costs are applied at $3 per unit. Selling and administrative expenses are $25,000 plus $0.50 per unit sold

On December 31, 1987, the division's finished goods inventory consisted of 20,000 units with a total cost of $100,000 ($40,000, variable; $60,000 fixed). Sales and production data for 1988 are:

Sales in units	100,000
Dollars of sales	$1,000,000
Production in units	110,000
Variable production costs . .	$ 220,000

Required:
  a. Prepare an income statement for the division for 1988 under absorption costing.
  b. Prepare an income statement for the division for 1988 under direct costing.

Solution to demonstration problem 26-2

  a. Income statement under absorption costing:

ORVIS COMPANY (Detroit Division)
Income Statement
For the Year Ended December 31, 1988

Sales (100,000 units at $10)		$1,000,000
Cost of goods sold:		
Beginning finished goods inventory (absorption cost $5 per unit)		$ 100,000
Variable production costs ($2 per unit)	$220,000	
Fixed manufacturing overhead costs absorbed ($3 per unit)	330,000	
Cost of goods manufactured		550,000
Ending finished goods inventory (absorption cost $5 per unit)		(150,000)
Cost of goods sold		500,000
Gross margin on sales		$ 500,000
Selling and administrative expenses		75,000
Net income		$ 425,000

b. Income statement under direct costing:

ORVIS COMPANY (Detroit Division)
Income Statement
For the Year Ended December 31, 1988

Sales (100,000 units at $10)		$1,000,000
Cost of goods sold:		
Beginning finished goods inventory (direct cost $2 per unit)	$ 40,000	
Direct cost of goods manufactured ($2 per unit)	220,000	
Ending finished goods inventory (direct cost $2 per unit)	(60,000)	
Cost of goods sold		$ 200,000
Manufacturing margin		$ 800,000
Variable selling and administrative expenses		50,000
Contribution margin		$ 750,000
Period costs:		
Fixed manufacturing overhead	$330,000	
Fixed selling and administrative expenses	25,000	355,000
Net income		$ 395,000

QUESTIONS

1. Name and describe the four cost behavior patterns.

2. What are the various ways in which the cost line for a mixed cost can be determined? Describe each method.

3. What is meant by the term *break-even point?* What factors must be taken into consideration in determining it?

4. What are the different ways in which the break-even point can be expressed?

5. How is the relevant range related to break-even analysis?

6. Why is break-even analysis considered appropriate only for short-run decisions?

7. What is the formula for calculating the break-even point in sales revenue?

8. What formula is used to solve for the break-even point in units? How can this formula be altered to calculate the number of units that must be sold to achieve a desired level of income?

9. Why might a business wish to lower its break-even point? How would it go about lowering the break-even point? What effect would you expect the mechanization and automation of production processes to have upon the break-even point?

10. How is the break-even point calculated for a multiproduct company?

11. What does the label "units" on the horizontal axis of the break-even chart mean?

12. Identify some types of decisions that can be made using differential analysis.

13. What is a committed fixed cost? Give some examples.

14. What is a discretionary fixed cost? Give some examples.

15. Give an example of a fixed cost that might be considered committed for one company and discretionary for another.

16. What assumptions are made in cost-volume-profit (CVP) analysis?

17. What essential feature distinguishes direct costing from absorption costing?

18. Under what specific circumstances would you expect net income to be larger under direct costing than under absorption costing? What is the specific reason for this difference?

EXERCISES

E-1

Analyze mixed cost using high-low method

Use the high-low method to determine the fixed and variable components of a mixed cost, given the following observations:

Volume (units)	Cost
4,000 . . .	$5,000
8,000 . . .	8,000

E-2

Compute break-even point in sales dollars

Compute the break-even point in sales dollars if fixed costs are $55,000 and variable costs are 45% of sales.

E-3

Compute break-even point in units

The Duke Company sells each unit it produces for $15, with fixed costs of $60,000 and variable cost of $9 per unit. Find the break-even point in units.

E-4

Compute break-even point in sales dollars and units under varying assumptions; comment on results

The Sun Company currently sells each unit it produces for $7.50. Variable cost is $2.25 per unit, and fixed costs are $105,000. Compute the break-even point in both dollars and units under each of the following independent assumptions. Comment on why the break-even points are different.

a. The costs and selling price are as given above.
b. Fixed costs are increased to $115,500.
c. Selling price is increased by 2%.
d. Variable cost is increased to $2.70 per unit.

E-5

Decide whether to increase advertising; compute margin of safety

A company sells a product for $20 each, with variable cost of $10 per unit. Fixed costs are $1,000,000. The company currently sells 200,000 units per year. Should this company undertake an advertising campaign that will result in a $100,000 increase in fixed costs, a $2 per unit decrease in variable cost, and a 10% increase in sales? What would the margin of safety be before and after the campaign?

E-6

Compute break-even point in units and sales volume to achieve a specified level of income

If a company has fixed costs of $130,000 and variable cost of $14 per unit, how many units would have to be sold at $21 each to break even? How many units would have to be sold to earn $100,000? If 30,000 units are 100% of capacity, what percentage of capacity do the two levels of output represent?

E-7

Compute multiproduct break-even point and margin of safety

The Shining Company sells three products. Last year's sales were $75,000 for product X, $97,500 for product Y, and $52,500 for product Z. Variable costs were X, $45,000; Y, $60,000; and Z, $33,000. Fixed costs were $36,000. Determine the break-even point and the margin of safety.

E-8

Compute multiproduct break-even point

If the company in Exercise E-7 changes the product mix to 2:2:1, with total dollar sales being the same as last year, what will the new break-even point be? Comment on why it has changed.

E-9

Compute break-even point

The Ringling Company sells each unit it produces for $4. Calculate the break-even point in dollars given the following cost observations:

Volume (units)	Cost
4,000 . . .	$24,000
34,000 . . .	75,000

E-10

Identify relevant and differential revenues and costs

Assume you had invested $120 in a lawn mower to set up a lawn mowing business for the summer. During the first week, you are presented with two opportunities. You can mow the grounds at a housing development for $150, or you can help paint a garage for $125. The additional costs you will incur are $25 and $10, respectively. These costs include $2 under each alternative for a pair of gloves that will last about one week. Prepare a schedule showing:

a. The relevant revenues and expenses (costs).
b. The differential revenue and expense.
c. The net benefit or advantage of selecting one alternative over the other.

E-11

Accept or reject an order

The Step Corporation is operating at 80% of capacity, which means it produces 8,000 units. Variable cost is $90 per unit. Wholesaler A offers to buy 2,000 units at $105 per unit. Wholesaler B proposes to buy 1,500 units at $112.50 per unit. Which offer, if any, should the Lane Corporation accept?

E-12

Compute gross margins for two companies with drop in sales volume

Two companies, Paris, Inc. and Newcomb Company, are competitors. Paris, Inc. has just installed the latest automated equipment so that its fixed costs are $90,000. Newcomb Company operates a run-down plant with only $45,000 of fixed costs. Both companies have $150,000 in sales and gross margins of 20%. Compute gross margins for the two companies assuming a 10% drop in sales volume.

E–13

Decide which company can sell for less

In the situation described in Exercise E–12, which company can bid lower on a special order to regain lost sales? Why?

E–14

Decide whether to retain a product line

Analysis of product C reveals that it is losing $10,000 annually. Ten thousand units of product C are sold at a price of $10 per unit each year. If variable costs are $8 per unit, what would be the increase (decrease) in company net income before taxes if product C were eliminated?

E–15

Decide whether to keep or eliminate a department

Department 3 of the Lee Company has revenues of $200,000, variable expenses of $80,000, direct fixed expenses of $40,000, and allocated, indirect fixed expenses of $100,000. If the department is eliminated, what will be the effect on net income before taxes?

E–16

Decide whether to process joint products further

The Lance Company manufactures two joint products. At the split-off point they have sales values of:

Product 1 . . $14/unit
Product 2 . . $10/unit

After further processing costing $8 and $6, respectively, they can be sold for $30 and $14, respectively. Should further processing be done on these products? Why?

E–17

Decide whether to make or buy a part

The Narlin Corporation currently is manufacturing 40,000 units per year of a part used in its final product. The cost of producing this part is $43 per unit. The variable portion of this cost consists of direct materials of $24, direct labor of $13, and manufacturing overhead of $2. The company could earn $40,000 per year from the space now used to manufacture this part. Assuming equal quality and availability, what is the maximum price Narlin Corporation should pay to buy the part rather than make it?

E–18

Compare net income before taxes and ending inventory under direct and absorption costing

The following data relate to the Garin Company for the year ended December 31, 1987:

Costs of production:
Direct materials	$ 75,000
Direct labor	105,000
Manufacturing overhead:	
Variable	37,500
Fixed	75,000
Sales commissions (variable) . .	22,500
Sales salaries (fixed)	15,000
Administrative expenses (fixed) . .	30,000
Units produced	37,500
Units sold (at $15 each)	30,000

Without making any computations, would you expect net income before taxes to be higher under absorption costing or under direct costing? Compute the amount of net income before taxes and ending inventory under both methods.

E–19

Compute net income before taxes under direct and absorption costing

The following data are for a company for the year 1987:

Sales (20,000 units)	$300,000
Direct materials used (24,000 units at $4.50) . .	108,000
Direct labor cost incurred	36,000
Manufacturing overhead incurred:	
Variable	10,800
Fixed	14,400
Selling and administrative expenses:	
Variable	18,000
Fixed	60,000

Assume that one unit of direct materials goes into each unit of finished goods. There is an ending inventory of finished goods of 4,000 units, and there are no other beginning or ending work in process inventories. The variable and fixed overhead rates (based on normal activity of 24,000 units) are $0.45 and $0.60, respectively. Compute the net income before taxes under *(a)* absorption costing and *(b)* direct costing.

E–20

Discuss how net income before taxes under absorption costing would differ under direct costing

Given below are the costs of the finished goods inventories of the Zee Company:

Cost element	Beginning inventory	Ending inventory
Direct materials	$45,000	$4,500
Direct labor	75,000	7,800
Manufacturing overhead:		
Variable	30,000	3,000
Fixed	22,500	3,000

Assume that the Zee Company uses absorption costing and that there were no work in process inventories at the beginning or end of the year. State by how much Zee Company's net income before taxes for the year would have differed if direct costing had been used.

PROBLEMS, SERIES A

P26–1–A

Analyze mixed cost using high-low method and scatter diagram

The Darken Company assigns you the task of estimating total maintenance cost on its production machinery. This cost is a mixed cost. You are supplied with the following data from past years:

Year	Units	Cost
1979 . .	4,000	$10,000
1980 . .	5,000	10,800
1981 . .	4,500	11,000
1982 . .	5,500	11,600
1983 . .	5,000	11,600
1984 . .	6,500	12,400
1985 . .	7,000	13,400
1986 . .	9,000	14,400
1987 . .	10,000	16,000

Required:

a. Using the high-low method, determine the total amount of fixed costs and the amount of variable cost per unit.

b. Prepare a scatter diagram, plot the actual costs, and visually fit a linear cost line to the points. Estimate the amount of total fixed costs and the amount of variable cost per unit.

P26–2–A

Compute break-even point and sales needed to achieve a specified level of income

If a company has fixed costs of $500,000, variable cost of $6 per unit, and a selling price of $14, how many units must be sold to break even? How many units will it have to sell to earn $80,000 before taxes?

P26–3–A

Determine break-even sales under varying assumptions

Compute the break-even point in sales dollars and units under each of the following independent assumptions. Selling price in each case is $50 per unit unless otherwise stated.

a. Fixed costs are $200,000; variable cost is $34 per unit.

b. Fixed costs are $200,000; variable cost is $30 per unit.

  c. Fixed costs are $160,000; variable cost is $30 per unit.
  d. Fixed costs are $160,000; selling price is $40, and variable cost is $30 per unit.
  e. Use the assumptions in *(d)* above to determine the level of sales required to achieve net income of $100,000.

P26–4–A

Determine break-even point and net income under varying assumptions

  a. Assume that fixed costs of L Corporation are $200,000 per year, variable cost is $4 per unit, and selling price is $10 per unit. Determine the break-even point in sales dollars.
  b. M Company breaks even when sales amount to $2,000,000. In 1987, its sales were $3,000,000, and its variable costs amounted to $900,000. Determine the amount of its fixed costs.
  c. The sales of N Corporation in 1987 amounted to $40,000,000, its variable costs were $10,000,000, and its fixed costs were $20,000,000. At what level of sales would the N Corporation break even?
  d. What would have been the net income of the N Corporation, in part *(c)* above, if sales volume had been 10% higher but selling prices had remained unchanged?
  e. What would have been the net income of the N Corporation, in part *(c)* above, if variable costs had been 10% lower?
  f. What would have been the net income of the N Corporation, in part *(c)* above, if fixed costs had been 10% lower?
  g. Determine the break-even point in sales dollars for the N Corporation on the basis of the data given in *(e)* above and then in *(f)* above.

P26–5–A

Prepare break-even chart; compute break-even point; prepare income statement for two companies

The operating results for two companies are presented below:

	Company A	Company B
Sales (20,000 units) . .	$400,000	$400,000
Variable costs	100,000	220,000
Contribution margin . .	$300,000	$180,000
Fixed costs	200,000	80,000
Net income	$100,000	$100,000

Required:

  a. Prepare a break-even chart for Company A, indicating the break-even point, the contribution margin, and the areas of income and losses.
  b. Compute the break-even point of both companies in sales dollars and units.
  c. Assume that without changes in selling price, the sales of each company decline by 20%. Prepare condensed income statements, similar to the ones above, for both companies.

P26–6–A

Make leasing decision; compute break-even point; compute expected net income

The Sharp Company, a leading manufacturer of stereos, incurred $420,000 of fixed costs while selling 20,000 radios at $100 each. Variable cost was $30 per radio.

  A new machine used in the production of stereos has recently become available and is more efficient than the machine currently being used. The new machine would reduce Sharp's variable costs by 20% and can be leased on an annual basis for $16,000 per year.

Required:

  a. Compute the break-even point in units assuming use of the old machine.
  b. Compute the break-even point in units assuming use of the new machine.
  c. Assuming that total sales remain at $2,000,000 and that the new machine is leased, compute expected net income.
  d. Should the new machine be leased? Why?

P26–7–A

Decide whether to undertake a sales promotion campaign and whether to hire an efficiency expert

  a. Change Company reports sales of $600,000, variable costs of $360,000, and fixed costs of $90,000. If the company spends $60,000 on a sales promotion campaign, it is estimated that sales can be increased by $225,000. Should the company proceed with the campaign? (Show computations.)
  b. The following data pertain to the Dame Corporation:

Sales	$300,000
Variable costs . .	180,000
Fixed costs . .	60,000

The president is considering hiring an efficiency expert at $60,000 this year, who can reduce variable costs by 25%. Assuming that sales will remain at the same level, should the expert be hired?

P26-8-A

Compute multiproduct break- even point assuming change in product mix

The Claxton Corporation sells three products. It has fixed costs of $200,000. The sales and variable costs of these products for 1987 follow:

	Products		
	A	**B**	**C**
Sales	$200,000	$300,000	$500,000
Variable costs . .	140,000	180,000	250,000

Required:

a.   Determine the break-even point in sales dollars for 1988 assuming that the product mix will remain as it was in 1987.

b.   Determine the break-even point in sales dollars for 1988 assuming that the product mix ratio for 1988 is expected to change to 50:30:20 while total sales remain the same.

P26-9-A

Decide whether to keep or eliminate a product line

Following are sales and other operating data for the three products made and sold by the Muntz Company:

	Product			
	A	**B**	**C**	**Total**
Sales	$400,000	$250,000	$150,000	$800,000
Manufacturing costs:				
Fixed	$ 50,000	$ 25,000	$ 45,000	$120,000
Variable	240,000	200,000	60,000	500,000
Total	$290,000	$225,000	$105,000	$620,000
Gross margin	$110,000	$ 25,000	$ 45,000	$180,000
Selling expenses:				
Fixed	$ 5,000	$ 5,000	$ 5,000	$ 15,000
Variable	15,000	10,000	25,000	50,000
Administrative expenses:				
Fixed	5,000	3,000	12,000	20,000
Variable	10,000	3,000	7,000	20,000
Total selling and administra- tive expenses	$ 35,000	$ 21,000	$ 49,000	$105,000
Net income (loss) before taxes . . .	$ 75,000	$ 4,000	$ (4,000)	$ 75,000

In view of the net loss shown above for product C, the company's management is considering dropping that product. All variable costs are direct costs and would be eliminated if product C were dropped; all fixed costs are indirect costs and would not be eliminated. Assume that the space used to produce product C would be left idle.

Required:

Would you recommend the elimination of product C? Give supporting computations.

P26-10-A

Evaluate pricing alternatives; prepare income statement using best alternative

Based on the information given in Problem 26-9-A, assume that the product mix of the company is technologically interchangeable. The company can delete one product and pro- duce a given amount of the existing other products without changes in variable cost per unit, selling prices, or total fixed costs. The company is considering dropping product B because of its low contribution margin.

Assume that dropping product B will allow the company to explore these alternatives:

1.   Produce $412,500 more of product C.
2.   Produce $375,000 more of product A.
3.   Produce $150,000 more of product A and $300,000 more of product C.
4.   Produce $225,000 more of product A and $150,000 more of product C.

   a.   What is the best alternative? Show computations.
   b.   Show what the resulting sales and net income before taxes of the best alternative would be.

P26–11–A

Prepare income statements under direct and absorption costing; discuss reasons for differences

Mann Company employs an absorption cost system in accounting for the single product it manufactures. Following are selected data for the year 1987:

Sales (10,000 units)	$300,000
Direct materials used (12,000 units at $6) . . .	108,000
Direct labor cost incurred	36,000
Variable manufacturing overhead	10,800
Fixed manufacturing overhead	14,400
Variable selling and administrative expenses . .	18,000
Fixed selling and administrative expenses . . .	60,000

   One unit of direct materials goes into each unit of finished goods. Overhead rates are based on a capacity of 12,000 units and are $0.90 and $1.20 per unit for variable and fixed overhead, respectively. The only beginning or ending inventory is the 2,000 units of finished goods on hand at the end of 1987.

Required:
   a.   Prepare an income statement for 1987 under variable costing.
   b.   Prepare an income statement for 1987 under absorption costing.
   c.   Explain the reason for the difference in net income before taxes between *(a)* and *(b)*.

PROBLEMS, SERIES B

P26–1–B

Analyze mixed cost using high-low method and scatter diagram

The Rouche Company has identified certain variable and fixed costs in its operations. A mixed cost exists that needs to be divided into its fixed and variable portions. Actual data pertaining to this cost follow:

Year	Units	Costs
1978 . .	10,400	$19,200
1979 . .	10,000	18,000
1980 . .	11,000	19,500
1981 . .	12,800	19,200
1982 . .	14,200	19,500
1983 . .	15,000	20,700
1984 . .	16,400	21,300
1985 . .	17,800	22,800
1986 . .	18,800	24,000
1987 . .	20,000	25,800

Required:
   a.   Using the high-low method, determine the total amount of fixed costs and the amount of variable cost per unit. Draw the cost line.
   b.   Prepare a scatter diagram, plot the actual costs, and visually fit a linear cost line to the points. Estimate the amount of total fixed costs and the amount of variable cost per unit.

P26–2–B

Determine break-even point under varying assumptions

   a.   Determine the break-even point in sales dollars and units for a company that has fixed costs of $120,000, variable cost of $12 per unit, and a selling price of $22 per unit.
   b.   Y Company breaks even when sales are $200,000. In 1987, sales were $900,000 and variable costs were $540,000. Compute the amount of fixed costs.
   c.   The Ace Company had sales in 1987 of $280,000, variable costs of $154,000, and fixed costs of $70,000. At what level of sales did the company break even?
   d.   What would the break-even point in sales dollars have been in *(c)* above if variable costs had been 10% higher?
   e.   What would the break-even point in sales dollars have been in *(c)* above if fixed costs had been 10% higher?

f. Compute the break-even point in sales dollars for the Ace Company under the assumptions of both (d) and (e) together.

P26-3-B

Prepare break-even chart; compute break-even sales and sales needed to achieve a specified level of income

The Smith Company has a plant capacity of 75,000 units. Variable costs are $600,000 at 100% capacity. Fixed costs are $400,000, but this is true only between 25,000 and 75,000 units.

Required:

a. Prepare a break-even chart for the Smith Company assuming it sells its product for $16 each. Indicate on the chart the relevant range, contribution margin, break-even point, and income and losses.
b. Verify the break-even point on the chart by using the break-even sales formula given in this chapter. Also calculate the break-even point in units.
c. How many units would have to be sold in order to earn $100,000 before taxes?

P26-4-B

Compute break-even point for two companies; analyze effects of decrease in sales volume

Following is a summary of 1987 operations for two companies:

	Company E	Company F
Sales	$1,000,000	$1,000,000
Expenses:		
Fixed	$200,000	$700,000
Variable	600,000	100,000
Total expenses . .	800,000	800,000
Net income	$ 200,000	$ 200,000

Required:

a. Compute the break-even point in sales dollars for each company.
b. Assume that (without changes in selling price) the sales of each company decreased by 25%. Present condensed income statements, similar to the ones above, showing the effect of the decrease in sales on the net income of each company.

P26-5-B

Compute level of sales needed to break even and earn a specified level of income

The Amdohl Company has a plant capacity of 100,000 units, at which level variable costs are $300,000. Fixed costs are expected to be $90,000. Each unit of product sells for $5.

Required:

a. Determine the company's break-even point in sales dollars and units.
b. What level of sales would the company need to attain in order to earn $60,000 before taxes?
c. If the selling price were raised to $6 per unit, what level of sales would the company need to attain in order to earn $60,000 before taxes?

P26-6-B

Compute break-even point under varying assumptions; compute fixed costs

a. The Frey Corporation sells its product for $9 per unit. Variable cost is $6.75 per unit, and fixed costs are $337,500. Compute the break-even point in dollars and units.
b. The Cook Company had sales in 1987 of $900,000, and its variable costs were $360,000. If the company could break even with sales of $262,500, what were the fixed costs?
c. What would the break-even point in sales dollars have been for the Cook Company in part (b) if variable costs had been 15% higher?
d. What would the break-even point in sales dollars have been in part (b) if fixed costs had been 10% lower?
e. What would the break-even point in sales dollars have been under the assumptions of both (c) and (d) together?

P26-7-B

Compute break-even point under varying product mix

The Akins Corporation has fixed costs of $200,000. It sells three products. The cost and revenue data for these products follow:

	Products		
	1	*2*	*3*
Sales	$100,000	$150,000	$200,000
Variable costs . .	60,000	100,000	110,000

Required:

a. Compute the break-even point in sales dollars.
b. Assume the sales mix is expected to be in the ratio of 2:2:1 next year with total sales being the same as this year. What would the break-even point be in sales dollars?

P26-8-B

Prepare condensed income statement showing effects of product pricing decision

A state government has asked for bids on an order for 200,000 units of product X. The Deck Company, which has a production capacity of 1,000,000 units and is currently operating at 80% of capacity, is considering making a bid for the government contract. The Deck Company's fixed costs amount to $2,000,000, and its variable cost is $20 per unit.

Required:

a. What is the minimum price Deck Company should bid?
b. Present two income statements, the first assuming that the bid is unsuccessful and that the price on regular sales is $30 per unit, and the second assuming that the contract is obtained at a bid price of $25 per unit, while regular sales are at $30 per unit.

P26-9-B

Present income statement assuming department elimination; evaluate the decision to eliminate

The new president of Rexford, Inc., Guy Rex, is giving serious consideration to discontinuing Department B. He notes that the income statements of the past few years show the department operating at a loss. He also notes that the other two departments seem quite badly crowded and in need of additional space. He doubts, however, that the closing of Department B will increase the sales of the other two departments. In condensed form, the income statement for the year ending June 30, 1987, is:

	Dept. A	*Dept. B*	*Dept. C*	*Total*
Net sales	$240,000	$60,000	$100,000	$400,000
Cost of goods sold	160,000	37,500	60,000	257,500
Gross margin	$ 80,000	$22,500	$ 40,000	$142,500
Operating expenses:				
Selling	$ 29,000	$15,000	$ 20,000	$ 64,000
Delivery	6,000	1,500	2,500	10,000
Buying	14,500	3,000	5,500	23,000
Occupancy	9,000	3,000	6,000	18,000
Administrative	12,000	3,000	5,000	20,000
Total operating expenses .	$ 70,500	$25,500	$ 39,000	$135,000
Net income from operations . .	$ 9,500	$ (3,000)	$ 1,000	$ 7,500
Interest income	3,000	750	1,250	5,000
Net income before taxes . . .	$ 12,500	$ (2,250)	$ 2,250	$ 12,500
Federal income taxes (credit) . .	2,500	(450)	450	2,500
Net income (loss)	$ 10,000	$ (1,800)	$ 1,800	$ 10,000

The president of the company has asked you to express your opinion on the desirability of the contemplated closing of Department B. He tells you that he believes that all of the selling expenses and half of the delivery, buying, and administrative expenses charged to Department B will be eliminated upon the closing of the department. Also, all of the financial charges earned and allocated to Department B will be eliminated if the department is closed.

Required: State your opinion on the desirability of closing Department B. Support your opinion with a schedule showing what the net income after taxes for the company as a whole would have been if Department B had been closed at the start of the accounting year ending June 30, 1987. The tax rate is 20%.

P26–10–B

Prepare income statements under direct and absorption costing

The following data are for the Winfrey Company for the year 1987:

Sales (10,000 units)	$150,000
Direct materials used (12,000 units at $4.50) . .	54,000
Direct labor cost incurred	18,000
Variable manufacturing overhead incurred . . .	5,400
Fixed manufacturing overhead incurred	7,200
Variable selling and administrative expenses . .	9,000
Fixed selling and administrative expenses . . .	30,000

One unit of direct materials goes into each unit of finished goods. The only beginning or ending inventory is the 2,000 units of finished goods on hand at the end of 1987. Variable and fixed overhead rates (based on 100% of capacity or 12,000 units) are $0.45 and $0.60, respectively.

Required:
a. Prepare an income statement under direct costing.
b. Prepare an income statement under absorption costing.

BUSINESS DECISION PROBLEM 26–1

Compute break-even point and projected net income for two investment alternatives; determine best alternative

The Pitts Company is operating at almost 100% of capacity. The company expects the demand for its product to increase by 25% next year (1988). In order to satisfy the demand for its product, the company is considering two alternatives. The first alternative will increase fixed costs by 15% but will have no effect on variable costs. The second alternative will not affect fixed costs but will cause variable costs to increase to 60% of the selling price of the company's product.

The Pitts Company's condensed income statement for 1987 is shown below:

Sales		$6,000,000
Costs:		
Variable	$2,700,000	
Fixed	1,100,000	3,800,000
Net income before taxes . .		$2,200,000

Required:
a. Determine the break-even point in sales dollars for 1988 under each of the alternatives.
b. Determine projected net income before taxes for 1988 under each of the alternatives.
c. Which alternative would you recommend? Why?

BUSINESS DECISION PROBLEM 26–2

Compute break-even point; determine point at which factory should shut down rather than produce

When the plant of the Foster Company is completely idle, fixed costs amount to $300,000. When the plant operates at levels of 50% of capacity and below, its fixed costs are $350,000; at levels above 50% of capacity its fixed costs are $500,000. The company's variable costs at full capacity (100,000 units) amount to $750,000.

Required: a.   Assuming that the company's product sells for $25.00 per unit, what is the company's break-even point in sales dollars?

b.   Using only the data given, at what level of sales would it be more economical to close the factory than to operate it? In other words, at what level will operating losses approximate the losses incurred if the factory is closed down completely?

c.   Assume that when the Foster Company is operating at half of its capacity, it decides to reduce the selling price from $25 per unit to $15 per unit in order to increase sales. At what percentage of capacity must the company operate in order to break even at the reduced sales price?

BUSINESS DECISION PROBLEM 26–3

Decide whether to make or buy a part; find variable cost and calculate cost to manufacture part

The Cooper's Company has recently been awarded a contract to sell 50,000 units of its product to the federal government. Cooper's manufactures the components of the product rather than purchasing them. When the news of the contract was released to the public, the president of Cooper's, Dan Cooper, received a call from the president of the White Corporation, Joe White. Mr. White offered to sell to Cooper's 50,000 units of one of the needed components, part N, for $12.50. After receiving the offer, Mr. Cooper calls you into his office and assigns you the task of providing him a recommendation (along with any supporting information) on whether to accept or reject Mr. White's offer.

You first go to the company's records and obtain the following information concerning the production of part N:

	Costs at current production level (400,000 units)
Direct labor	$2,080,000
Direct materials	960,000
Manufacturing overhead . .	1,000,000
Total cost	$4,040,000

You calculate the unit cost of part N to be $10.10 ($4,040,000 ÷ 400,000). But you suspect that this unit cost may not hold true at all production levels. To find out, you consult the production manager. She tells you that in order to meet the increased production needs, equipment will have to be rented and the production workers will have to work some overtime. She estimates the machine rental to be $100,000 and the total overtime premiums to be $180,000. She provides you with the following cost information:

	Costs at increased production level (450,000 units)
Direct labor	$2,340,000
Direct materials	1,080,000
Manufacturing overhead (including equipment rental and overtime premiums)	1,380,000
Total cost	$4,800,000

The production manager advises you to reject White's offer, since the unit cost of part N will only rise to $10.67 (4,800,000 ÷ 450,000) even with the additional costs of equipment rental and overtime premiums. This is much less than the $12.50 offered by Mr. White. You are still undecided, so you return to your office to consider the matter further.

Required: a.   Using the high-low method, compute the variable cost portion of manufacturing overhead. (Remember that the costs of equipment rental and overtime premiums are included in manufacturing overhead. Subtract these amounts before performing the calculation.)

b. Compute the total costs to manufacture the additional units of part N. (Note: Include overtime premiums as a part of direct labor.)

c. Compute the unit cost to manufacture the additional units of part N.

d. Should Mr. Cooper accept or reject Mr. White's offer?

BUSINESS DECISION PROBLEM 26–4

Prepare income statement under both absorption costing and direct costing; explain why net income before taxes differs; settle debate between general manager and controller

The general manager of the Chicago Division of the All-Klean Company submitted the company's income statement for the year ended June 30, 1987, (prepared under absorption costing) with the comment that the division was at least profitable. The report showed that sales amounted to 80,000 units at $40 per unit and that the following costs had been incurred:

Direct materials	$ 880,000
Direct labor	380,000
Manufacturing overhead	1,140,000
Selling and administrative expenses . .	1,200,000

A total of 110,000 units was put into process during the year. Regarding the 30,000 units in the June 30, 1987, inventory, all materials costs had been incurred, but the units were only 50% complete as to processing. There were no other finished goods or work in process inventories, either beginning or ending.

The Chicago Division's production process is highly automated, and its costs are largely fixed; $950,000 of the manufacturing overhead costs and $400,000 of the selling and administrative costs are fixed.

Upon receipt of the division's income statement, the company's controller made a few quick calculations and commented that the division actually operated at a loss. The general manager of the division took exception to this statement, causing a long argument.

Required:

a. Prepare the division's income statement under absorption costing. Include a schedule showing the computation of the cost of ending work in process Inventory. Assume that fixed overhead is absorbed under expected activity and that this equaled actual activity for the year.

b. Repeat part *(a)* under direct costing.

c. State exactly what caused the difference in net income between *(a)* and *(b)*.

d. Who is right in this debate? Explain.

BUSINESS SITUATION FOR DISCUSSION

A Tool for Planning and Decision Making*
Frederick J. Turk

☐ Governing boards and administrators in higher education today must cope with their problems under the most difficult circumstances: dynamic change. The dynamics add an extra dimension of complexity to planning and decision making. But an illuminating approach, called breakeven analysis, introduces clarity in ways that this article will explain.

The dynamic elements of change are only too easy to recognize. Costs of faculty and staff salaries and benefits, supplies and equipment, fuel, and other necessities are rising rapidly. The physical facilities at many institutions have deteriorated to a point where deferred maintenance is no longer tolerable. Almost all other costs are jumping mainly at unpredictable rates.

*   *   *   *   *

Competing for Students

Some institutions have suffered a decline in the number of students. Others have recently experienced a slight surge in enrollments. Most are concerned that, whatever the current demand, the acknowledged demographics indicate fewer college-age students in the near future.

* Peat, Marwick Mitchell & Co.: *Management Focus,* March/April 1980, pp. 9–13. Used with permission.

This trend will certainly affect the viability of some of these institutions.

Many colleges and universities have expanded their programs to include adults who are seeking non-degree education. Witnessed by the advertisements in local papers, the competition for non-traditional students is fierce. Some believe that this relatively new market for colleges and universities is already becoming saturated.

This potpourri of troubles facing colleges and universities presents a sober challenge to governing boards and administrators. Yet it is certain that these conditions can significantly affect the future of colleges and universities and, therefore, must be confronted successfully if institutions are to remain healthy and capable of achieving their educational mission.

Complexity of Interlocking Decisions

. . . the difficulties facing higher education in the 1980s are motivating many institutions to devote increasing attention to planning for their future. The problem, however, is to evaluate simultaneously the implications of various actions that might be taken. When considered together, it is impossible to understand the consequences of each action. As a result, many decision makers are following a pattern whereby each individual action is examined separately. With decisions broken down into small elements, each can be examined fully. When the divisible parts of a decision are understood, they can be aggregated to present a complete picture of the entire effect of one or more related decisions. This approach to planning and analysis also promotes rapid examination of variations or alternatives.

The Basics of Breakeven Analysis

Breakeven analysis has been used in commercial enterprises for many years. More recently colleges and universities are beginning to use this technique in planning and decision-making. Sometimes referred to as cost-volume-revenue analysis, it permits planners to examine the potential economic consequences of a proposed course of action.

The primary focus of breakeven analysis is examining how changes in volume will affect cost and revenue. By calculating the relationship of cost and revenue to different levels of volume, the analyst can identify the level of volume at which equilibrium between cost and revenue is achieved. The state of equilibrium is often called "the breakeven point," and the results of the analysis are often presented on a breakeven chart. A diagrammatic representation of such a chart is presented as Exhibit 1. . . . This chart permits decision makers to see at a glance the effect that proposed actions are likely to have on the future finances of an institution.

In order to perform a breakeven analysis, the analyst must be able to identify fixed and variable costs and

Exhibit 1

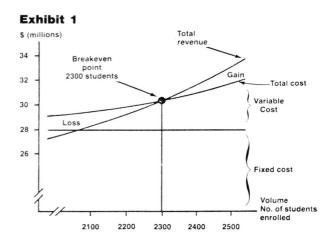

revenues. Costs and revenues are fixed when they remain constant regardless of fluctuations in the level of volume. Costs and revenues are variable when they fluctuate in direct proportion to changes in the level of volume. The separation of costs and revenues into fixed and variable components is difficult. Because high precision is not required for most decisions, estimates of cost behavior based on observation or experience are often applied.

Certain costs behave irregularly, e.g., at a certain level of volume costs are fixed only if volume stays within definite limits. These costs, which act in stairstep fashion, are often referred to as "mixed" or "semivariable" costs. For purposes of simplification in breakeven analysis, mixed costs are usually treated as either fixed or variable.

Another important concept inherent in breakeven analysis relates to the "relevant range of volume." Implied in this concept is the assumption that cost and revenue will behave as expected within the range of volume being examined. Should analysis above or below the relevant range be required, costs and revenues may behave differently.

Applying Breakdown Analysis

Earlier, certain difficult decisions requiring action by many institutions of higher education were mentioned. Breakeven analysis lends itself well to assisting board members and administrators to understand the potential economic consequences of their decisions.

Exhibit I is a breakeven chart that presents a snapshot of the current budget of an institution's costs and revenues. For the most part, the majority of costs are fixed in the short run. For many institutions this is a realistic representation of cost behavior. For example, costs associated with faculty and staff are substantial in colleges and universities. Faculty costs are typically fixed because of tenure or other contractual commitments.

Revenue is composed of both fixed and variable components. For instance, tuition and fees are directly variable with the number of students, while private gifts, grants, and contracts have no relationship to enrollment and thereby act as fixed revenues. What is indicated from the breakeven chart is the expectation that the college will operate on a breakeven basis at 2,300 enrolled students. If more than 2,300 students enroll, there will be an excess of revenue over cost; under 2,300, cost will exceed revenue.

Suppose it were determined to pay greater attention to deferred maintenance. Accordingly, the college may wish to increase expenditures by $2000,000 to refurbish a part of the plant. Exhibit 2 shows the effect such a decision might have on the college, assuming that everything else remains unchanged.[1]

Similarly, if the tuition charge were increased while all other costs and revenues remained unchanged, net revenue would increase. When this is recorded in Exhibit 3, the result is a new breakeven point—i.e., only 2,150 students are required.

Results of Decisions

Through this method many potential decisions can be analyzed to explain the financial impact of each. For instance, other scenarios that might be considered could include:

1. a reduction in potential operating costs, owing to a capital fund-raising campaign that is expected to pay for plant refurbishment costs.
2. a reduction in annual giving revenues because donors may give to the capital campaign instead of to annual giving
3. an increase in student aid costs for certain students should tuition rates be increased.

Each scenario can be analyzed and presented independently.

With an understanding of the effect that each potential decision may have, it may then be useful to summarize the effects of all decisions in one breakeven analysis. Additionally, it is often helpful to see the financial effect that these multiple decisions have on the institution over time, such as a three-to-five year planning horizon. Such analysis over time is frequently essential since all decisions can seldom be implemented in one year. Some decisions, such as refurbishing physical plant or conducting a capital campaign, may have financial effects on the institution for many years.

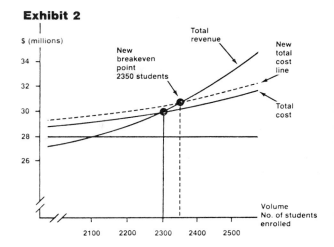

Exhibit 2

This combined analysis over time may require several iterations to arrive at a financial result that presents an acceptable breakeven condition.

Developing a Planning Model

Breakeven analysis is readily applied when one potential decision is examined in the light of all other variables affecting institutional costs and revenues being held constant. In essence the methodology described earlier is a model for analyzing institutional cost and revenue behavior.

The analysis becomes increasingly complex as more variables are examined and the dimension of a planning horizon is introduced. Because the financial consequences of so many variables need to be examined together over time, it becomes necessary to use a computerized planning model to perform the many calculations that are required to complete the analysis. Without such

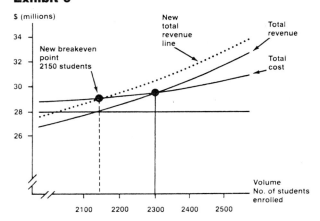

Exhibit 3

---

[1] The reader should be aware that the amounts shown . . . [in the Exhibits] and referred to in the text are for illustrative purposes only and are not subject to verification by precise calculation.

a planning model the ability to examine the financial consequences of various interactive decisions would be difficult. More importantly, planning is a dynamic human activity. Accordingly, it is desirable to calculate rapidly the effects of policy decisions. Planners require prompt feedback so that they can reexamine and modify plans that do not meet institutional financial objectives.

Communicates to Board Members

Breakeven analysis is a useful tool for analyzing the financial consequences of a variety of actions being considered by decision makers. A breakeven chart is a useful device for communicating the financial results of potential decisions to board members and administrators.

Breakeven analysis is used most advantageously when one variable (the independent variable) is changed while other variables (dependent variables) are held constant. Too often, board members and administrators are confused because multiple decisions are combined.

When a variety of possible actions are considered, planners may wish to consider the financial consequences of these actions together and over time. Under these circumstances a computerized planning model is likely to be most useful.

CHAPTER 27

Capital Budgeting: Long-Range Planning

LEARNING OBJECTIVES

After studying this chapter, you should be able to:

1. Determine the net cash inflows, after taxes, for both an asset addition and an asset replacement.

2. Evaluate projects using payback period, unadjusted rate of return, net present value, profitability index, and time-adjusted rate of return.

3. Determine, for project evaluation, the effect of an investment in working capital.

4. Define and use correctly the new terms in the glossary.

In your personal life you make many short-run decisions (such as where to go on vacation this year) and many long-run decisions (such as whether to buy a home). The quality of these decisions determines to a large extent the success of your life. Businesses also face short-run and long-run decisions.

In Chapter 26, you studied how accountants help management make short-run decisions, such as what prices to charge for their products this year. Accountants also play an important role in advising management on long-range decisions, such as investing in new buildings and equipment, that will benefit the company for many years. Long-run decisions have a great impact on the long-run success of a company. Incorrect long-run decisions can threaten the survival of a company.

Whereas short-run decisions involve items such as selling prices, costs, volume, and profits in the current year, long-run decisions involve investments in capital assets, such as buildings and equipment, affecting the current year and many future years. Planning for these investments is referred to as capital budgeting. This chapter discusses the general concepts behind capital budgeting.

■ CAPITAL BUDGETING DEFINED

Capital budgeting is the process of considering alternative capital projects and selecting those alternatives that provide the most profitable return on available funds, within the framework of company goals and objectives. A **capital project** is any long-range endeavor to purchase, build, lease, or renovate buildings, equipment, or other major items of property. Such decisions usually involve very large sums of money and usually bring about a large increase in fixed costs for a number of years in the future. Once a company builds a plant or undertakes some other capital expenditure, it becomes less flexible.

Poor capital-budgeting decisions can be very costly because of the large sums of money and relatively long time periods involved. If a poor capital-budgeting decision is implemented, the company can lose all or part of the funds originally invested in the project and not realize expected benefits. In addition, other actions taken within the company regarding the project, such as finding suppliers of raw materials, are wasted if the capital-budgeting decision must later be revoked. Poor capital-budgeting decisions may also harm the company's competitive position because the company will not have the most efficient productive assets needed to compete in world markets.

Investment of funds in a poor alternative can create other problems as well. Workers who were hired for the project might be laid off if the project fails, creating morale and unemployment problems. Many of the fixed costs will still remain even if a plant is closed or is not producing. Advertising efforts will have been wasted. Stock prices could be affected by the decline in income.

On the other hand, failure to invest enough funds in a good project can also be costly. Ford's Mustang is an excellent example of this. If, at the time of the original capital-budgeting decision, Ford had correctly projected the Mustang's popularity, the company would have expended more funds on the project. Because of an undercommitment of funds, Ford found itself short on production capacity, which caused lost and postponed sales of the automobile.

Finally, the amount of funds available for investment is limited. Thus, once a capital investment decision is made, alternative investment opportunities are lost. The benefits or returns lost by rejecting the best alternative investment are the **opportunity cost** of a given project.

For all these reasons, companies must be very careful in their analyses of capital projects. Capital expenditures do not occur as often as ordinary expenditures (such as payroll or inventory purchases) but involve substantial sums of money that are then committed for a long period of time. Therefore, the means by which companies evaluate capital expenditure decisions need to be much more formal and detailed than would be necessary for ordinary purchase decisions.

■ PROJECT SELECTION: A GENERAL VIEW

Making capital-budgeting decisions involves analyzing cash inflows and outflows. This section identifies benefits and costs that are relevant to capital-budgeting decisions.

Time Value of Money

Money received today is worth more than the same amount of money received at a future date, such as a year from now. This principle is known as the time value of money. Money has a time value because of investment opportunities, not because of inflation. For example, $100 today is worth more than $100 to be received one year from today because the $100 received today may be invested and will grow to some amount greater than $100 in one year. Future value and present value concepts are extremely important in assessing the desirability of long-term investments (capital budgeting). These concepts were covered in the Appendix to Chapter 17. If you need to review these concepts, refer back to the Chapter 17 Appendix before continuing with this chapter.

Net Cash Inflow

The **net cash inflow** (as used in capital budgeting) is the net cash benefit expected from a project in a period. The net cash inflow is the difference between the periodic cash inflows and the periodic cash outflows for a proposed project.

Asset Acquisition.   Assume, for example, that a company is considering the purchase of new equipment for $120,000. The equipment is expected to have a useful life of 15 years and no salvage value. The equipment is expected to produce cash inflows (revenue) of $75,000 per year and cash outflows (costs) of $50,000 per year. Ignoring depreciation and taxes, the annual net cash inflow is computed as follows:

Cash inflows . .	$75,000
Cash outflows . .	50,000
Net cash inflow . .	$25,000

Depreciation and Taxes.   The computation of the net cash inflow usually includes the effects of depreciation and taxes. Although depreciation does not involve a cash outflow, it is deductible in arriving at federal taxable income. Thus, depreciation reduces the amount of cash outflow for income taxes. This reduction is a tax savings made possible by a depreciation tax shield. A **tax shield** is the amount by which taxable income is reduced due to the deductibility of an item. In order to simplify the illustration, we assume the use of straight-line depreciation for tax purposes throughout the chapter. Straight-line depreciation can be elected for tax purposes, even under the new tax law. Thus, if depreciation is $8,000, the tax shield is $8,000.

The tax shield results in a tax savings. The amount of the tax savings can be found by multiplying the tax rate by the amount of the depreciation tax shield. The formula is shown below:

$$\text{Tax rate} \times \text{Depreciation tax shield} = \text{Tax savings}$$

Using the data in the previous example and assuming straight-line depreciation of $8,000 per year and a 40% tax rate, the amount of the tax savings is $3,200 (40% × $8,000 depreciation tax shield). Now, considering taxes and depreciation, the annual net cash inflow from the $120,000 of equipment is computed as follows:

	Change in net income	Change in cash flow
Cash inflows	$75,000	$75,000
Cash outflows	50,000	50,000
Net cash inflow before taxes . .	$25,000	$25,000
Depreciation	8,000	
Net income before taxes . . .	$17,000	
Tax at 40%	6,800	6,800
Net income after taxes	$10,200	
Net cash inflow (after taxes) . .		$18,200

If there was no depreciation tax shield, income tax would have been $10,000 ($25,000 × 40%), and the net after-tax cash inflow from the investment would have been $15,000 ($25,000 − $10,000), or [$25,000 × (1 − 40%)]. The depreciation tax shield, however, reduces income tax by $3,200 ($8,000 × 40%) and increases the investment's after-tax net cash inflow by the same amount. Therefore, the following formula can also be used to determine the after-tax net cash inflow from an investment:

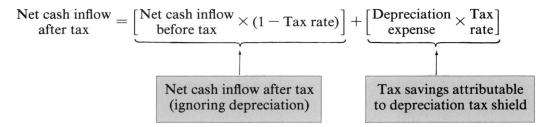

$$\text{Net cash inflow after tax} = \left[\begin{array}{c}\text{Net cash inflow before tax}\end{array} \times (1 - \text{Tax rate})\right] + \left[\begin{array}{c}\text{Depreciation expense}\end{array} \times \begin{array}{c}\text{Tax rate}\end{array}\right]$$

Net cash inflow after tax (ignoring depreciation)

Tax savings attributable to depreciation tax shield

Asset Replacement. Sometimes a company must decide whether or not it should replace existing plant assets. Such replacement decisions often occur when faster and more efficient machinery and equipment appear on the market.

The computation of the net cash inflow is more complex for a replacement decision than for an acquisition decision because cash inflows and outflows for **two** items (the asset being replaced and the new asset) must be considered. To illustrate, assume that a company operates two machines that were purchased four years ago at a cost of $18,000 each. The estimated useful life of each machine is 12 years (with no salvage value). Each machine will produce 30,000 units of product per year. The annual cash operating expenses (labor, repairs, etc.) for the two machines together total $14,000. After the old machines have been used for four years, a new machine becomes available. The new machine can be acquired for $28,000 and has an estimated useful life of eight years (with no salvage value). The new machine will produce 60,000 units annually and will entail annual cash operating expenses of $10,000.

A $28,000 cash outflow is required in the first year to acquire the new machine. In addition to this initial outlay, the annual net cash inflow from replacement is computed as follows:

Annual cash operating expenses:		
Old machines		$14,000
New machine		10,000
Annual net cash inflow (savings) before tax . .		$ 4,000
1 — Tax rate		× 60%
Annual net cash inflow (savings)* after tax		
(ignoring depreciation) (1)		$ 2,400
Annual depreciation expense:		
Old machines	$3,000	
New machine	3,500	
Additional annual depreciation		
expense	$ 500	
Tax rate	× 40%	
Additional depreciation tax savings (2) . . .		200
Net cash inflow after tax (1) + (2)		$ 2,600

* Cash savings are considered to be cash inflows.

Notice that the above figures concentrated only on the differences in costs for each of the two alternatives. Two other items are also relevant to the decision. First, the purchase of the new machine will create a $28,000 cash outflow immediately upon acquisition. Second, the two old machines can probably be sold, and the selling price or salvage value of the old machines will create a cash inflow in the period of disposal. Also, the above example used straight-line depreciation. If the Accelerated Cost Recovery System (ACRS) method had been used, the tax shield would have been larger in the early years and smaller in the later years of the asset's life.

Out-of-Pocket and Sunk Costs.   A distinction between out-of-pocket costs and sunk costs needs to be made for capital-budgeting decisions. An **out-of-pocket cost** is one that requires a future outlay of resources, usually cash; it can be avoided or changed in amount. Future labor and repair costs are examples of out-of-pocket costs.

Sunk costs are costs that have already been incurred. Nothing can be done about sunk costs at the present time; they cannot be avoided or changed in amount. The price paid for a machine becomes a sunk cost the minute the purchase has been made (before that moment it was an out-of-pocket cost). The amount of that past outlay cannot be changed regardless of whether the machine is scrapped or used. Thus, depreciation is a sunk cost because it represents a past cash outlay. Depletion and amortization of assets such as ore deposits and patents are also sunk costs.

A sunk cost is a past cost, while an out-of-pocket cost is a future cost. Only the out-of-pocket costs (the future cash outlays) are relevant to capital-budgeting decisions. Sunk costs are not relevant, except for any effect they have on the cash outflow for taxes.

Initial Cost and Salvage Value.   Any cash outflows necessary to acquire an asset and place it in a position and condition for use are part of the **initial cost of the asset.** If an investment has a salvage value, that value should be treated as a cash inflow in the year of the asset's disposal.

The Cost of Capital.   The cost of capital is important in project selection. Certainly any acceptable proposal should offer a return that exceeds the cost of the funds used to finance it. **Cost of capital,** usually expressed as a rate, is the cost of all sources of capital (debt and equity) employed by a company. For convenience, most current liabilities, such as accounts payable and federal income taxes payable, are treated as being without cost. Every other item on the right (equity) side of the balance sheet has a cost. The subject of determining the cost of capital is a controversial topic in the literature of accounting and finance and will not be discussed here. Assumed rates for the cost of capital will be given in the remainder of the chapter.

■ PROJECT SELECTION: PAYBACK PERIOD

The next few sections of this chapter examine specific techniques used to evaluate capital projects. The first of these is the payback period. The **payback period** is the period of time it takes for the cumulative sum of the annual net cash inflows from a project to equal the initial net cash outlay. In effect, the payback period answers the question: How long will it take the capital project to recover, or pay back, the initial investment? If the net cash inflows each year are a constant amount, the formula for the payback period is:

$$\text{Payback period} = \frac{\text{Initial cash outlay}}{\text{Annual net cash inflows (or benefits)}}$$

The payback period for the two assets discussed previously can be computed as follows. The purchase of the $120,000 equipment discussed on page 1047 will create an annual net cash inflow after taxes of $18,200, so the payback period is 6.6 years, computed as follows:

$$\text{Payback period} = \frac{\$120,000}{\$18,200} = 6.6 \text{ years}$$

The payback period for the replacement machine mentioned above, with a $28,000 cash outflow in the first year and an annual net cash inflow of $2,600, is 10.8 years, computed as follows:

$$\text{Payback period} = \frac{\$28,000}{\$2,600} = 10.8 \text{ years}$$

Remember that the payback period indicates how long it will take the machine to pay for itself. The replacement machine being considered has a payback period of 10.8 years, but a useful life of only 8 years. Therefore, since the investment cannot pay for itself within its useful life, the machine should **not** be purchased to replace the two old machines.

In each of the two examples above, the projected net cash inflow per year was uniform. When the annual returns are uneven, a cumulative calculation must be used to determine payback period, as shown in the following situation.

The Neil Company is considering a capital investment project that costs $40,000 and is expected to last 10 years. The projected annual net cash inflows are as follows:

Year	Investment	Annual net cash inflow	Cumulative net cash inflows
0	$40,000	—	—
1	—	$8,000	$ 8,000
2	—	6,000	14,000
3	—	7,000	21,000
4	—	5,000	26,000
5	—	8,000	34,000
6	—	6,000	40,000
7	—	3,000	43,000
8	—	2,000	45,000
9	—	3,000	48,000
10	—	1,000	49,000

The payback period in this example is six years—the time it takes to recover the $40,000 original investment.

When the payback period analysis is used to evaluate investment proposals, management may use one of the following rules to decide on project selection:

1. Select the investments with the shortest payback periods.
2. Select only those investments that have a payback period of less than a specified number of years.

Both decision rules focus on the rapid return of invested capital. If capital can be recovered rapidly, it can be invested in other projects, thereby generating more cash inflows or profits.

Payback period analysis is used extensively in capital-budgeting decisions due to its simplicity and because cash flow is critical in many businesses. However, this type of analysis has two important limitations:

1. Payback period analysis ignores the time period beyond the payback period. For example, assume the Allen Company is considering two alternative investments that each requires an initial outlay of $30,000. Proposal Y will return $6,000 per year for five years, while proposal Z will return $5,000 per year for eight years. The payback period for Y is five years ($30,000/$6,000) and for Z is six years ($30,000/$5,000). But, if the goal is to maximize income, proposal Z should be selected rather than proposal Y, even though Z has a longer payback period. This is because Z will return a total of $40,000, while Y simply recovers the initial $30,000 outlay.

2. Payback analysis also ignores the time value of money. For example, assume the following net cash inflows are expected in the first three years from two capital projects:

	Net cash inflows	
	Project A	Project B
First year . . .	$15,000	$ 9,000
Second year . .	12,000	12,000
Third year . . .	9,000	15,000
Total . .	$36,000	$36,000

Assume that both projects have the same net cash inflows each year beyond the third year. If the cost of each project is $36,000, then each has a payback period of three years. But common sense indicates that the projects are not equal because money has a time value and can be reinvested to increase income. Since larger amounts of cash are received earlier under project A, it is the preferable project.

■ PROJECT SELECTION: UNADJUSTED RATE OF RETURN

The unadjusted rate of return is another method used in evaluating investment projects. The unadjusted rate of return is an approximation of the rate of return on investment of a capital project. It is computed by dividing the average annual income after taxes by the average amount of investment in the project. The **average investment** is the original cash outlay divided by 2. The formula for the unadjusted rate of return is:

$$\text{Unadjusted rate of return} = \frac{\text{Average annual income after taxes}}{\text{Average amount of investment}}$$

Notice that annual **income** rather than net cash inflow is used in the calculation.[1]

To illustrate the use of the unadjusted rate of return, assume the Thomas Company is considering two capital project proposals that both have useful lives of three years. The company does not have enough funds to undertake both projects. Information relating to the projects is shown below:

Proposal	Initial cost	Average annual before-tax net cash inflow	Average depreciation
1	$72,000	$45,000	$24,000
2	90,000	55,000	30,000

Assuming a 40% tax rate, the unadjusted rate of return for each project is determined as follows:

		Proposal 1	Proposal 2
Average investment:			
Original outlay ÷ 2	(1)	$36,000	$45,000
Annual net cash inflow (before taxes)		$45,000	$55,000
Annual depreciation		24,000	30,000
Annual income (before taxes)		$21,000	$25,000
Income taxes at 40%		8,400	10,000
Average annual net income from investment	(2)	$12,600	$15,000
Rate of return (2) ÷ (1)		35%	33⅓%

---

[1] Some formulas use the initial investment as the denominator instead of the average investment.

From these calculations, if Thomas Company makes an investment decision solely on the basis of unadjusted rate of return, proposal 1 would be selected since it has a higher rate.

The unadjusted rate of return can also be computed with the following formula:

$$\text{Rate of return} = \frac{\left(\begin{array}{c}\text{Average annual before-} \\ \text{tax net cash inflow}\end{array} - \begin{array}{c}\text{Average annual} \\ \text{depreciation}\end{array}\right) \times (1 - \text{Tax rate})}{\text{Average investment}}$$

For proposal 1 above, the computation is as follows:

$$\text{Rate of return} = \frac{(\$45,000 - \$24,000) \times (1 - 0.4)}{(\$72,000/2)} = \frac{(\$21,000) \times (0.6)}{\$36,000}$$

$$= \frac{\$12,600}{\$36,000} = 35\%$$

For proposal 2 above, the computation is as follows:

$$\text{Rate of return} = \frac{(\$55,000 - \$30,000) \times (1 - 0.4)}{(\$90,000/2)} = \frac{(\$25,000) \times (0.6)}{\$45,000}$$

$$= \frac{\$15,000}{\$45,000} = 33\frac{1}{3}\%$$

Sometimes information is provided on the average annual after-tax net cash inflow. Average annual after-tax net cash inflow is equal to annual before-tax cash inflow minus taxes. Given this information, the depreciation can be deducted to arrive at average net income. For instance, for proposal 2 above, average net income would be computed as follows:

After-tax net cash inflow ($55,000 − $10,000) . . $45,000
Less: Depreciation   30,000
Average net income $15,000

The unadjusted rate of return, like payback period analysis, has several limitations:

1. The length of time over which the return will be earned is not considered.
2. The rate allows a sunk cost, depreciation, to enter into the calculation. Since depreciation can be calculated in so many different ways, the rate of return can be manipulated by simply changing the method of depreciation used for the project.
3. The timing of cash flows is not considered. Thus, the time value of money is ignored.

■ PROJECT SELECTION: NET PRESENT VALUE METHOD AND THE PROFITABILITY INDEX

Unlike the two project selection methods just illustrated, the net present value method and the profitability index take into account the time value of money in the analysis. Because of their computational similarities, the net present value method and the profitability index will both be discussed in this section. For purposes of these methods we assume that all net cash inflows occur at the end of the year. This assumption is often used in capital-budgeting analysis and makes the calculation of present values less complicated than if we assume the cash flows occurred at some other time.

A major issue in acknowledging the time value of money in capital-budgeting decisions is determining an appropriate discount rate to use in computing the present value of cash flows. Management requires some minimum rate of return on its investments. This rate should be the company's cost of capital, but that rate is difficult to determine. Therefore, management often selects a target rate that it believes to be at or above the company's cost of capital, and then that rate is used as a basis for present value calculations.

Net Present Value Method

Under the net present value method, all expected after-tax cash inflows and outflows from the proposed investment are discounted to their present values using the company's required minimum rate of return as a discount rate. The **net present value** of the proposed investment is the difference between the present value of the annual net cash inflows and the present value of the required cash outflows. In many projects, the only cash outflow is the initial investment, and since it occurs immediately, the initial investment does not need to be discounted. Therefore, in such projects, the net present value of the proposed project may be computed as the present value of the annual net cash inflows minus the initial investment. Other types of projects require that additional investments, like a major repair, be made at later dates in the life of the project. In those cases, the cash outflows must be discounted to their present value before they are compared to the present value of the net cash inflows.

To illustrate the net present value method, assume the Morris Company is considering a capital investment project that will cost $25,000. Net cash inflows after taxes for the next four years are expected to be $8,000, $7,500, $8,000, and $7,500, respectively. Management requires a minimum rate of return of 14% and wants to know if the project is acceptable. The following analysis is developed, using the tables in Appendix C at the end of the text:

	Annual net cash inflow (after taxes)	Present value of $1 at 14% (from Table 3)	Total present value
First year	$8,000	0.87719	$ 7,018
Second year	7,500	0.76947	5,771
Third year	8,000	0.67497	5,400
Fourth year	7,500	0.59208	4,441
Present value of net cash inflows			$22,630
Cost of investment			25,000
Net present value			$ (2,370)

Since the present value of the net cash inflows, $22,630, is less than the initial outlay of $25,000, the project is not acceptable. The net present value for the project is equal to the present value of its net cash inflows less the present value of its cost (the investment amount), which in this instance is $-2,370 ($22,630 -$25,000).

In general, a proposed capital investment is acceptable if it has a positive net present value. In the previous example, if the expected net cash inflows from the investment had been $10,000 per year for four years, the present value of the benefits would have been (from Appendix Table 4):

$$\$10,000 \times 2.91371 = \$29,137$$

This yields a net present value of $4,137 ($29,137 − $25,000). Since the net present value is positive, the investment proposal is acceptable. But there may be a competing project that has an even higher net present value. When the net present value method is used to screen alternative projects, the higher a project's net present value, the more desirable the project.

Profitability Index

When investment projects costing different amounts are being compared, the net present value method does not provide a valid means by which to rank the projects in order of contribution to income or desirability under limited financial resources. A **profitability index** provides this additional information to management. A profitability index is the ratio of the present value of the expected net cash benefits (after taxes) divided by the initial cash outlay (or present value of cash outlays if future outlays are required). The profitability index formula is:

$$PI = \frac{PV \text{ of net cash inflows}}{\text{Initial outlay (or present value of cash outlays if future outlays are required)}}$$

Only those proposals having a profitability index greater than or equal to 1.00 should be considered by management. Proposals with a profitability index of less than 1.00 will not yield the minimum rate of return because the present value of the projected cash inflows will be less than the initial cost.

To illustrate use of the profitability index, assume that a company is considering two alternative capital outlay proposals that have the following initial costs and expected net cash inflows after taxes:

	Proposal X	*Proposal Y*
Initial cost	$7,000	$9,500
Expected net cash inflow (after taxes):		
Year 1	$5,000	$9,000
Year 2	4,000	6,000
Year 3	6,000	3,000

Management's minimum desired rate of return is 20%.

The net present values and profitability indexes can be computed as follows (using Appendix C, Table 3):

	Present value	
	Proposal X	**Proposal Y**
Year 1 (net cash inflow in year 1 × 0.83333) . .	$ 4,167	$ 7,500
Year 2 (net cash inflow in year 2 × 0.69444) . .	2,778	4,167
Year 3 (net cash inflow in year 3 × 0.57870) . .	3,472	1,736
Present value of net cash inflows	$10,417	$13,403
Initial outlay	7,000	9,500
Net present value	$ 3,417	$ 3,903
	Proposal X	**Proposal Y**
Profitability index:	$\dfrac{\$10,417}{\$7,000} = 1.49$	$\dfrac{\$13,403}{\$9,500} = 1.41$

When net present values are compared, proposal Y appears to be more favorable than X because its net present value is higher. But after computing the profitability indexes, proposal X is found to be a more desirable investment because it has the higher profitability index. The higher the profitability index, the more profitable the project per dollar of investment. Proposal X is earning a higher rate of return on a smaller investment than proposal Y.

■ PROJECT SELECTION: THE TIME-ADJUSTED RATE OF RETURN

Another technique for evaluating capital projects that accounts for the time value of money is the time adjusted rate of return. The **time-adjusted rate of return,** also called the discounted or internal rate of return, equates the present value of expected after-tax net cash inflows from an investment with the cost of the investment by finding the rate at which the net present value of the project is zero. If the time-adjusted rate of return equals or exceeds the cost of capital or target rate of return, then the investment should be considered further. But if the proposal's time-adjusted rate of return is less than the minimum rate, the proposal should be rejected. Ignoring other considerations, the higher the time-adjusted rate of return, the more desirable the project.

Present value tables can be used to approximate the time-adjusted rate of return. To illustrate, assume the Young Company is considering a $90,000 investment that is expected to last 25 years with no salvage value. The investment will yield a $15,000 annual after-tax net cash inflow. This $15,000 is referred to as an **annuity,** which is a series of equal cash inflows.

The first step in computing rate of return is to determine the payback period. In this case, payback period is six years ($90,000 ÷ $15,000). Next, examine Appendix C, Table 4 (present value of an annuity) to find the present value factor that is nearest in amount to the payback period of 6. Since the investment is expected to yield returns for 25 years, look at that row in the table. In that row, the factor nearest to 6 is 5.92745, which appears under the 16.5% interest column. If the annual return of $15,000 is multiplied by the 5.92745 factor, the result is $88,912, which is just below the $90,000 cost of the project. Thus, the actual rate of return is slightly less than 16.5%. It is less than 16.5% but more than 16% because, as interest rates increase, present values decrease since less investment is needed to generate the same income.

The above example involves uniform net cash inflows from year to year. What happens when net cash inflows are not uniform? In such instances, a trial and error procedure is necessary. For example, assume that a company is considering a $200,000 project that will last four years and will yield the following returns:

Year	Net cash inflow (after taxes)
1	$ 20,000
2	40,000
3	80,000
4	150,000
Total	$290,000

The average annual net cash inflow is $72,500 ($290,000 ÷ 4). Based on this average net cash inflow, the payback period is 2.76 years ($200,000 ÷ $72,500). Looking in the four-year row of Appendix C, Table 4, we find that the factor 2.77048 is nearest to the payback period of 2.76. But in this case, cash flows are not uniform. The largest returns will occur in the later years of the asset's life. Since the early returns have the largest present value, it is likely that the rate of return will be less than the 16.5% rate that corresponds to the present value factor of 2.77048. If the returns had been greater during the earlier years of the asset's life, the correct rate of return would have been higher than 16.5%. To find the specific discount rate that yields a present value closest to the initial outlay or $200,000, several interest rates less than 16% are tried out. By trial and error the rate of return is found; the following computation reveals the rate to be slightly higher than 12%:

	Return	Present value factor at 12%	Present value of net cash inflows
Year 1	$ 20,000	0.89286	$ 17,857
Year 2	40,000	0.79719	31,888
Year 3	80,000	0.71178	56,942
Year 4	150,000	0.63553	95,330
			$202,017

Since the cost of capital is not a precise percentage, some financial theorists argue that the time-adjusted rate of return method is better than the net present value method. Under the time-adjusted rate of return method, the cost of capital is used only as a **cutoff point** in deciding which projects are acceptable for more consideration. Under the net present value method, the cost of capital is used **in the calculation** of the present value of the benefits. Thus, if the cost of capital percentage is wrong, the ranking of the projects will be affected. As a result, management may select projects that are really not as profitable as other projects.

No matter which time value of money concept is considered "better," these methods are both theoretically superior to the payback and unadjusted rate of return methods. But the time value of money methods are more difficult to compute. In reality, no single method should be used by itself to make capital-budgeting decisions. All aspects of the investment should be considered, including nonquantitative factors, such as employee morale (layoff of workers due to higher efficiency of a new machine) and company flexibility (versatility of production of one machine over another). The company will be committed to its investment in a capital project for a long period of time and should use the best selection techniques and judgment available.

■ INVESTMENTS IN WORKING CAPITAL

An investment in a capital asset usually must be supported by an investment in working capital, such as accounts receivable and inventory. For example, an investment in a capital project often is expected to increase sales. Increased sales usually bring about an increase in accounts receivable from customers and an increase in inventory to support the higher sales level. The increases in the current assets—accounts receivable and inventory—are investments in working capital that usually are recovered in full at the end of a capital project's life. Such working capital investments should be considered in capital-budgeting decisions.

To illustrate, assume that a company is considering a capital project that will involve a $50,000 investment in machinery and a $40,000 investment in working capital. The machine, which will be used to produce a new product, has a useful life of eight years and has no salvage value. The annual cash inflow (before taxes) is estimated at $25,000, with annual cash outflow (before taxes) of $5,000. The annual net cash inflow from the project is computed below (assuming straight-line depreciation and a 40% tax rate):

Cash inflows	$25,000
Cash outflows	5,000
Net cash inflow before tax	$20,000
1 − Tax rate	× 60%
Net cash inflow after tax (ignoring depreciation) (1)	$12,000
Depreciation tax shield ($50,000 ÷ 8 years)	$ 6,250
Tax rate	× 40%
Depreciation tax savings (2)	$ 2,500
Annual net cash inflow (years 1–8) (1) + (2)	$14,500

The annual net cash inflow from the machine is $14,500 each year for eight years. However, the working capital investment needs to be considered. First, the investment of $40,000 in working capital at the start of the project is an additional outlay that must be made when the project is started. The $40,000 will be tied up every year until the project is finished, or in this case, until the end of the life of the machine. At that point, the working capital will be released, and the $40,000 can be used for other investments. Therefore, the

$40,000 is a cash outlay at the start of the project and a cash inflow at the end of the project.

The net present value of the project is computed as follows (assuming a 14% minimum desired rate of return):

Net cash inflow, years 1–8 ($14,500 × 4.63886)	$67,263
Recovery of investment in working capital ($40,000 × 0.35056) . .	14,022
Present value of net cash inflows	$81,285
Initial cash outlay ($50,000 + $40,000)	90,000
Net present value	$ (8,715)

The discount factor for the cash inflows, 4.63886, comes from Appendix C, Table 4, since the cash inflows in this example are a series of equal payments—an annuity. The recovery of the investment in working capital is assumed to represent a single lump sum that is received at the end of the project's life. As such, it is discounted using a factor (0.35056) that comes from Appendix C, Table 3.

The investment is not acceptable because it has a negative net present value. If the working capital investment had been ignored, the proposal would have had a rather large positive net present value of $17,263 ($67,263 − $50,000). Thus, it should be obvious that investments in working capital must be considered if correct capital budgeting decisions are to be made.

■ THE POSTAUDIT

The last step in the capital-budgeting process is a postaudit review that should be performed by a person not involved in the capital-budgeting decision-making process. Such a person can provide an impartial judgment on the project's worthiness. This step should be performed early in the project's life, but enough time should have passed for any operational "bugs" to have been worked out. Actual operating costs and revenues should be determined and compared with those estimated when the project was originally reviewed and accepted.

The postaudit review performs these functions:

1. Lets management know if the projections were accurate and if the particular project is performing as expected regarding cash inflows and outflows.
2. May identify additional factors for management to consider in upcoming capital-budgeting decisions, such as cash outflows that were forgotten in a particular project.
3. Provides a review of the capital-budgeting process to determine how effectively and efficiently it is working. The postaudit provides information that allows management to compare the actual results of decisions with the expectations it had during the planning and selection phases of the capital-budgeting process.

■ SUMMARY

A capital project is any long-term endeavor to purchase, lease, or renovate buildings, equipment, or other major items of property. Capital budgeting is the process of considering alternative capital projects and selecting those alternatives that provide the most profitable return on available funds, within the framework of company goals and objectives.

Several concepts are important to capital-budgeting decisions. The time value of money concept states that money received today is worth more than money received in the future. The time value of money is considered by discounting future cash flows to their present values. The net cash inflow is the difference between the periodic cash inflows and the periodic cash outflows expected from a project. The net cash inflow is usually computed after considering the tax effect of depreciation. Out-of-pocket costs require future outlays of resources, usually cash, while sunk costs have already been incurred. The initial cost of the project includes any cash outlays necessary to acquire the asset and to place it in a position and condition for use. The expected salvage value represents an expected future cash inflow at the end of the asset's life. The cost of capital, usually expressed as a rate of return, includes the cost of all the company's sources of capital. Management often selects as a discount rate a minimum required rate of return that it believes to be at or above the company's cost of capital.

Various capital project selection techniques are discussed in the chapter. Payback period analysis compares the project's initial investment to its annual net cash inflows and asks how many years it will be before the sum of the net cash inflows equals, or pays back, the initial investment. The unadjusted rate of return compares the project's average annual net income after tax (rather than its net cash inflows) to its average investment and computes an approximate rate of return. Neither of these methods considers the time value of money.

The other techniques examined in the chapter do consider the time value of money. The net present value method involves calculating the difference between the present value of the net cash inflows and the initial investment (or the present value of the cash outlays if future outlays are required). The profitability index, on the other hand, computes the ratio of the present value of the net cash inflows to the initial investment (or the present value of the cash outlays if future outlays are required). Finally, the time-adjusted rate of return method computes the project's rate of return by examining the amount and timing of the net cash inflows and the required cash outlay(s). The resulting rate can then be compared directly to the company's required rate of return to judge the acceptability of the investment.

When preparing a capital-budgeting proposal, management must be careful to include not only the cost of buildings and equipment but also the cost of working capital necessary to operate the project. Such a commitment of resources is part of the overall investment in the project.

The postaudit review is the last step in the capital-budgeting project. The postaudit provides management an opportunity to compare actual results with the projections on which the selection decision was based. This review provides feedback to permit management to revise the current project if necessary and to help management improve future capital-budgeting decisions.

Throughout this text the discussion has centered around businesses—single proprietorships, partnerships, and corporations. In Chapter 28, the final chapter in this text, a personal element is introduced as you study personal income taxes. Two things every person faces are death and taxes. Since corporations are legal "persons," they face the same concerns, although their ultimate death can often be postponed longer than our own. The chapter closes by going back to corporations and discussing corporate federal income taxation.

NEW TERMS INTRODUCED IN CHAPTER 27*

Annuity

A series of equal cash inflows (1056).

Capital budgeting

Process of considering alternative capital projects and selecting those alternatives that provide the most profitable return on available funds, within the framework of company goals and objectives (1046).

Capital project

Any long-range endeavor to purchase, build, lease, or renovate buildings, equipment, or other major items of property (1046).

Cost of capital

The cost of all sources of capital (debt and equity) employed by a company (1050).

Initial cost of an asset

Any cash outflows necessary to acquire an asset and place it in a position and condition for its intended use (1049).

Net cash inflow

The periodic cash inflows from a project less the periodic cash outflows related to the project (1047).

Net present value

A project selection technique that discounts all expected after-tax cash inflows and outflows from the proposed investment to their present values using the company's minimum rate of return as a discount rate. If the amount obtained by this process exceeds or equals the investment amount, the proposal is considered acceptable for further consideration (1054).

—————
* Some terms listed in earlier chapters are repeated here for your convenience.

Opportunity cost

The benefits or returns lost by rejecting the best alternative investment (1046).

Out-of-pocket cost

A cost requiring a future outlay of resources, usually cash (1049).

Payback period

The period of time it takes for the cumulative sum of the annual net cash inflows from a project to equal the initial net cash outlay (1050).

Profitability index

The ratio of the present value of the expected net cash inflows (after taxes) divided by the initial cash outlay (or present value of cash outlays if future outlays are required) (1055).

Sunk costs

Costs that have already been incurred. Nothing can be done about sunk costs at the present time, they cannot be avoided or changed in amount (1049).

Tax shield

The total amount by which taxable income is reduced due to the deductibility of an item (1047).

Time-adjusted rate of return

A project selection technique that finds a rate of return that will equate the present value of future expected net cash inflows (after taxes) from an investment with the cost of the investment (1056).

Unadjusted rate of return

The rate of return computed by dividing average annual income after taxes from a project by the average amount of the investment (1052).

DEMONSTRATION PROBLEM

The Logue Company is considering three different investments. Listed below are some data related to these investments:

Investment	Initial cash outlay	Expected after-tax net cash inflow per year	Expected life of proposals
A . .	$100,000	$20,000	10 years
B . .	120,000	17,600	15
C . .	150,000	21,000	20

Management requires a minimum return on investments of 14%.

Required: Rank these proposals using the following selection techniques. (Ignore income taxes and salvage value.)

a. Payback period.
b. Unadjusted rate of return.
c. Profitability index.
d. Time-adjusted rate of return.

Solution to demonstration problem

a. Payback period:

Proposal	(a) Investment	(b) Annual after-tax cash inflow	(a)/(b) Payback period
A . .	$100,000	$20,000	5.00 years
B . .	120,000	17,600	6.82
C . .	150,000	21,000	7.14

The proposals in order of desirability are A, B, and C.

b. Unadjusted rate of return:

Proposal	(a) Average investment	(b) Average annual after-tax net cash inflow	(c) Average depreciation	(d) = (b) − (c) Average annual income	(d)/(a) Rate of return
A . .	$50,000	$20,000	$10,000	$10,000	20%
B . .	60,000	17,600	8,000	9,600	16
C . .	75,000	21,000	7,500	13,500	18

The proposals in order of desirability are A, C, and B.

c. Profitability index:

Proposal	(a) Annual after-tax net cash inflow	(b) Present value factor at 14%	(c) = (a) × (b) Present value of annual net cash inflow	(d) Initial cash outlay	(c)/(d) Profitability index
A	$20,000	5.21612	$104,322	$100,000	1.04
B	17,600	6.14217	108,102	120,000	0.90
C	21,000	6.62313	139,086	150,000	0.93

The proposals in order of desirability are A, C, and B. (But neither B nor C should be considered acceptable since each has a profitability index of less than one.)

d. Time-adjusted rate of return:

Proposal	Rate	How found
A . . .	15% (slightly above)	($100,000 ÷ $20,000) = Factor of 5 in 10-period row
B . . .	12 (slightly below)	($120,000 ÷ $17,600) = Factor of 6.82 in 15-period row
C . . .	13 (slightly below)	($150,000 ÷ $21,000) = Factor of 7.14 in 20-period row

The proposals in order of desirability are A, C, and B. (But neither B nor C earns the minimum rate of return.)

QUESTIONS

1. How do capital expenditures differ from ordinary expenditures?

2. What effects can capital-budgeting decisions have on a company?

3. What effect does depreciation have on cash flow?

4. Give an example of an out-of-pocket cost and a sunk cost by describing a situation in which both are encountered.

5. A machine is being considered for purchase. The salesperson attempting to sell the machine says that it will pay for itself in five years. What is meant by this statement?

6. Discuss the limitations of the payback period method.

7. What is the profitability index, and of what value is it?

8. What is the time-adjusted rate of return on a capital investment?

9. What role does the cost of capital play in the time-adjusted rate of return method and in the net present value method?

10. What is the purpose of a postaudit? When should a postaudit be performed?

EXERCISES

E-1

Determine estimated income and net cash inflow for an asset addition

The Barclay Athletic Club is considering investing $75,000 in some new sports equipment with an estimated useful life of 10 years and no salvage value. The equipment is expected to produce $30,000 in cash inflows and $20,000 in cash outflows annually. Straight-line depreciation is used by the company, and a 40% tax rate applies. Determine the annual estimated income and net cash inflow.

E–2

Determine additional cash inflow for an asset replacement

The Classic Manufacturing Company is considering replacing a four-year-old machine with a new, advanced model. The old machine was purchased for $30,000, has a useful life of 10 years with no salvage value, and has annual maintenance costs of $7,500. The new machine would cost $22,500 and would produce the same output as the old machine. But annual maintenance costs would be only $3,000. The new machine would have a useful life of 10 years with no salvage value. Using straight-line depreciation and a 40% tax rate, compute the additional annual cash inflow if the old machine is replaced.

E–3

Compute payback period for a new machine

Given the following annual costs, compute the payback period for the new machine if its initial cost is $105,000. (Ignore income taxes.)

	Old machine	New machine
Depreciation	$ 9,000	$21,000
Labor	36,000	31,500
Repairs	10,500	2,250
Other costs	6,000	1,800
	$61,500	56,550

E–4

Compute unadjusted rate of return for a new machine

The Bishop Company is considering investing $25,000 in a new machine. The machine is expected to last five years and to have no salvage value. Annual after-tax net cash inflow from the machine is expected to be $7,000. Calculate the unadjusted rate of return.

E–5

Compute profitability index for two projects and rank projects

Compute the profitability index for each of the following two proposals assuming the desired minimum rate of return is 20%. Based upon the profitability indexes, which proposal is better?

	Proposal F	Proposal G
Initial cash outlay	$16,000	$20,600
Net cash inflow (after taxes):		
First year	10,000	12,000
Second year	9,000	12,000
Third year	6,000	8,000
Fourth year	–0–	5,000

E–6

Rank projects using payback and unadjusted rate of return

The Scooter Company is considering three alternative investment proposals. Using the information presented below, rank the proposals in order of desirability using the (a) payback period method and (b) unadjusted rate of return method.

	M	O	P
Initial outlay	$180,000	$180,000	$180,000
Net cash inflow (after taxes):			
First year	$ –0–	$ 45,000	$ 45,000
Second year	90,000	135,000	90,000
Third year	90,000	45,000	135,000
Fourth year	45,000	90,000	225,000
Total net cash inflows	$225,000	$315,000	$495,000

E–7

Determine acceptability of a project using net present value

The Parker Company is considering the purchase of a new machine costing $45,000. It is expected to save $9,000 cash per year for 10 years. It has an estimated useful life of 10 years and no salvage value. Management will not make any investment unless at least an 18% rate of return can be earned.

Using the net present value method, determine if the proposal is acceptable.

E–8

Compute time-adjusted rate of return

Refer to the data in Exercise E–7. Calculate the time-adjusted rate of return. (Ignore income taxes.)

E–9

Rank projects using payback, net present value, and time-adjusted rate of return

Rank the following investments in order of their desirability using the (a) payback period method, (b) net present value method, and (c) time-adjusted rate of return method. Management requires a minimum rate of return of 14%.

Investment	Initial cash outlay	Expected after-tax net cash inflow per year	Expected life of proposal
A . . .	$30,000	$4,500	8 years
B . . .	37,500	6,500	20
C . . .	60,000	12,000	10

PROBLEMS, SERIES A

P27–1–A

Determine net cash inflow and payback period for an asset addition

Bridges Company is considering the purchase of a new machine that would cost $50,000 and would have a useful life of 10 years with no salvage value. The new machine is expected to have annual cash inflows of $25,000 and annual cash outflows of $10,000. The machine will be depreciated using straight-line depreciation, and the tax rate is 40%.

Required: a. Determine the net after-tax cash inflow for the new machine.
              b. Determine the payback period for the new machine.

P27–2–A

Determine additional cash inflow for an asset replacement

The Gaines Company currently uses four machines to produce 200,000 units annually. The machines were bought three years ago for $50,000 each and have a useful life of 10 years with no salvage value. These machines cost a total of $28,000 per year to repair and maintain.

The company is considering replacing the four machines with one technologically superior machine that is capable of producing the 200,000 units annually by itself. The machine would cost $140,000 and have a useful life of seven years with no salvage value. Annual repair and maintenance costs are estimated at $14,000.

Required: Assuming straight-line depreciation and a 40% tax rate, determine the annual additional after-tax net cash inflow if the new machine is acquired.

P27–3–A

Evaluate asset replacement using payback and net present value

The Paton Manufacturing Company owns five spinning machines that it uses in its manufacturing operations. Each of the machines was purchased four years ago at a cost of $120,000. Each machine has an estimated life of 10 years with no expected salvage value. A new machine has become available. One new machine has the same productive capacity as the five old machines combined; it can produce 400,000 units each year. The new machine will cost $648,000, is estimated to last six years, and will have a salvage value of $72,000. A trade-in allowance of $24,000 is available for each of the old machines.

Operating costs per unit are compared below:

	Five old machines	New machine
Repairs	$0.6795	$0.0855
Depreciation	0.1500	0.2400
Power	0.1890	0.1035
Other operating costs . . .	0.1620	0.0495
Operating costs per unit . .	$1.1805	$0.4785

Required: Ignore income taxes. Use the payback period method for parts *(a)* and *(b)*.

a. Do you recommend replacing the old machines? Support your answer with computations. Disregard all factors except those reflected in the data given above.
b. If the old machines were already fully depreciated, would your answer be different? Why?
c. Using the net present value method with a discount rate of 20%, present a schedule showing whether or not the new machine should be acquired.

P27-4-A

Calculate time-adjusted rate of return for new equipment; determine effect of altering useful life and net cash inflows

The Odiorne Canning Company has used a particular canning machine for several years. The machine has a zero salvage value. The company is considering buying a technologically improved machine at a cost of $232,000. The new machine will save $50,000 per year after taxes in cash operating costs. If the company decides not to buy the new machine, it can use the old machine for an indefinite period of time by incurring heavy repair costs. The new machine will have a useful life of eight years.

Required: a. Compute the time-adjusted rate of return for the new machine.
b. Management thinks the estimated useful life of the new machine may be more or less than eight years. Compute the time-adjusted rate of return for the new machine if its useful life is (1) 5 years and (2) 12 years, instead of 8 years.
c. Suppose the new machine's useful life is eight years, but the annual after-tax cost savings are only $40,000. Compute the time-adjusted rate of return.
d. Assume the annual after-tax cost savings from the new machine will be $44,000 and its useful life will be 10 years. Compute the time-adjusted rate of return.

P27-5-A

Rank investments using payback, unadjusted rate of return, profitability index, and time-adjusted rate of return

The Gover Company is considering three different investments involving depreciable assets with no salvage value. Listed below are some data related to these investments:

Investment	Initial cash outlay	Expected after-tax net cash inflow per year	Expected life of proposal
1	$140,000	$28,000	10 years
2	240,000	48,000	20
3	360,000	68,000	10

Management requires a minimum return on investments of 12%.

Required: Rank these proposals using the following selection techniques. (Ignore income taxes and salvage value.)

a. Payback period.
b. Unadjusted rate of return.

c. Profitability index.
d. Time-adjusted rate of return.

P27–6–A

Make capital-budgeting decision using net present value

The Carter Company has decided to computerize its accounting system. The company has two alternatives—it can lease a computer under a three-year contract, or it can purchase a computer outright.

If the computer is leased, the lease payment will be $18,000 each year. The first lease payment will be due on the day the lease contract is signed. The other two payments will be due at the end of the first and second years. All repairs and maintenance will be provided by the lessor.

If the computer is purchased outright, the following costs will be incurred:

Acquisition cost $42,000

Repairs and maintenance:
  First year   1,200
  Second year   1,000
  Third year   1,400

The computer is expected to have only a three-year useful life because of obsolescence and technological advancements. The computer will have no salvage value and will be depreciated on a double-declining-balance basis. The Carter Company's cost of capital is 16%.

Required: Using the net present value method, show whether the Carter Company should lease or purchase the computer. (Ignore income taxes).

P27–7–A

Make capital-budgeting decision using net present value

The Walker Sports Company is trying to decide whether or not to add tennis equipment to its existing line of football, baseball, and basketball equipment. Market research studies and cost analyses have provided the following information:

1. Additional machinery and equipment will be needed to manufacture the tennis equipment. The machines and equipment will cost $900,000, have a 10-year useful life, and have a $20,000 salvage value.
2. Sales of tennis equipment for the next 10 years have been projected as follows:

Year	Sales in dollars
1	$150,000
2	225,000
3	337,500
4	375,000
5	412,500
6–10 (each year) . .	450,000

3. Variable costs are 60% of selling price, and fixed costs (including straight-line depreciation) will total $177,000 per year.
4. The company will need to advertise its new product line to gain rapid entry into the market. Its advertising campaign costs will be:

Years	Advertising cost
1–3	$150,000 (each year)
4–10	75,000 (each year)

5. The company requires a 14% minimum rate of return on investments.

Required: Using the net present value method, decide whether or not the Walker Sports Company should add the tennis equipment to its line of products. (Ignore income taxes.) Round to the nearest dollar (round down for .5).

P27-8-A

Evaluate investment proposal using net present value

The Wicks Company is considering purchasing new equipment that will cost $450,000. It is estimated that the useful life of the equipment will be five years and that there will be a salvage value of $150,000. The company uses straight-line depreciation. The new equipment is expected to have a net cash inflow (before taxes) of $64,500 annually. Assume that the tax rate is 40% and that management requires a minimum return of 14%.

Required: Using the net present value method, determine whether the equipment is an acceptable investment.

P27-9-A

Make capital-budgeting decision using net present value

The Beech Company has an opportunity to sell some equipment for $40,000. Such a sale will result in a tax-deductible loss of $4,000. If it is not sold, the equipment is expected to produce net cash inflows after taxes of $12,000 for the next 10 years. After 10 years, the equipment can be sold for its book value of $4,000. Assume a 40% tax rate.

Required: Management currently has other opportunities that will yield 18%. Using the net present value method, show whether the company should sell the equipment. Prepare a schedule to support your conclusion.

PROBLEMS, SERIES B

P27-1-B

Determine increase of cash inflow for machine replacement

The Collins Manufacturing Company is currently using three machines that it bought seven years ago to manufacture its product. Each machine produces 20,000 units annually. Each machine originally cost $102,000 and has a life of 17 years with no salvage value.

The new assistant manager of the Ironside Manufacturing Company suggests that the company replace the three old machines with two technically superior machines for $90,000 each. Each new machine would produce 30,000 units annually and would have a life of 10 years with no salvage value.

The new assistant manager points out that the cost of maintaining the new machines would be much lower. Each old machine costs $10,000 per year to maintain; each new machine would cost only $4,000 a year to maintain.

Required: Compute the increase in after-tax annual net cash inflow that would result from replacing the old machines, using straight-line depreciation and a tax rate of 40%.

P27-2-B

Evaluate asset replacement using net present value

Refer to the information given in Problem 27-1-B. The new assistant manager of the Collins Manufacturing Company also points out that the old machines could be sold for $50,000 each. Assume this sale would result in an after-tax cash inflow of $150,000. Ignore the tax effect of the gain or loss on this sale.

Required: Using the net present value method, should the new machines be bought if the company's cost of capital is 14%?

P27-3-B

Determine desirability of asset replacement using payback; develop schedule to aid in project evaluation

The Munson Company is considering replacing 10 of its delivery vans that originally cost $30,000 each; depreciation of $18,300 has already been taken on each van. The vans were originally estimated to have useful lives of eight years and no salvage value. Each van travels an average of 150,000 miles per year. The 10 new vans, if purchased, will cost $36,000 each. Each van will be driven 150,000 miles per year and will have no salvage value at the end of its three-year estimated useful life. A trade-in allowance of $3,000 is available for each of the old vans.

Following is a comparison of costs of operation per mile:

	Old vans	New vans
Fuel, lubricants, etc.	$0.152	$0.119
Tires	0.067	0.067
Repairs	0.110	0.087
Depreciation	0.025	0.080
Other operating costs (variable) . .	0.051	0.043
Operating cost per mile	$0.405	$0.396

Required: Ignore income taxes. Use the payback period method for parts *(a)* and *(b)*.

 a. Do you recommend replacing the old vans? Support your answer with computations, and disregard all factors not related to the cost data given above.
 b. If the old vans were already fully depreciated, would your answer be different? Why?
 c. Assume that all cash flows for operating costs fall at the end of each year and that 18% is an appropriate rate for discounting purposes. Using net present value, present a schedule showing whether or not the new vans should be acquired.

P27–4–B

Compute time-adjusted rate of return for asset replacement and effect of altering useful life and cash flows in calculations

The Bolten Company has been using an old-fashioned forklift for many years. The forklift has no salvage value. The company is considering buying a modern forklift at a cost of $140,000. The new forklift will save $28,000 per year after taxes in cash operating costs. If the company decides not to buy the new forklift, it can use the old one for an indefinite period of time. The new forklift will have a useful life of 10 years.

Required: a. Compute the time-adjusted rate of return for the new forklift.
 b. The company is uncertain about the new forklift's 10-year useful life. Compute the time-adjusted rate of return for the new forklift if its useful life is (1) 6 years and (2) 15 years, instead of 10 years.
 c. Suppose the forklift has a useful life of 10 years, but the annual after-tax cost savings are only $24,000. Compute the time-adjusted rate of return.
 d. Assume the annual after-tax cost savings will be $32,000 and that the useful life will be eight years. Compute the time-adjusted rate of return.

P27–5–B

Rank projects using payback, unadjusted rate of return, probability index, and time-adjusted rate of return

The Hector Company is considering three different investments involving depreciable assets with no salvage value. Listed below are some data related to these investments.

Investment	Initial cash outlay	Expected after-tax net cash inflow per year	Expected life of proposal
1 . . .	$ 45,000	$ 6,600	20 years
2 . . .	120,000	15,000	10
3 . . .	165,000	27,600	10

Management requires a minimum return on investments of 12%.

Required: Rank these proposals using the following selection techniques:

 a. Payback method.
 b. Unadjusted rate of return.
 c. Profitability index.
 d. Time-adjusted rate of return.

P27-6-B

Evaluate asset replacement using net present value

Breck's Moving Company has always purchased its trucks outright and sold them after three years. The company is ready to sell its present fleet of trucks and is trying to decide whether it should continue to purchase trucks or whether it should lease trucks.

If the trucks are purchased, the following costs will be incurred:

	Costs per fleet
Acquisition cost	$156,000
Repairs, first year	1,800
Repairs, second year	3,300
Repairs, third year	4,500
Other annual costs	4,800

At the end of three years, the trucks could be sold for a total of $48,000. Another fleet of trucks would then be purchased. The costs listed above, including the same acquisition cost, would also be incurred with respect to the second fleet of trucks. The second fleet could also be sold for $48,000 at the end of three years.

If the trucks are leased, the lease contract will run for six years. One fleet of trucks will be provided immediately, and a second fleet of trucks will be provided at the end of three years. The company will pay $63,000 per year under the lease contract. The first lease payment will be due on the day the lease contract is signed. The lessor will bear the cost of all repairs.

Required: Using the net present value method, should the company buy or lease the trucks? Assume the company's cost of capital is 18%. (Ignore income taxes.)

P27-7-B

Evaluate project using net present value

Wheeler Manufacturing Company is considering adding a new electronic calculator to its line of products. The following information has been provided by various departments within the company:

1. Additional machinery and equipment will be needed to manufacture the calculator. The machinery and equipment will cost $225,000, have a 15-year useful life, and have a zero salvage value.
2. Sales of Wheeler calculators for the next 15 years have been projected as follows:

Year	Sales in units
1–5	750
6–10	500
11–15	250

3. Selling price per calculator will be $187.50.
4. Variable cost will be $75 per calculator. Fixed costs (including straight-line depreciation) will total $26,250 annually.
5. Advertising campaign costs will be:

Year	Advertising cost per year
1–5	$18,750
6–10	11,250
11–15	3,000

6. The company requires a 12% minimum rate of return on investments.

Required: Using the net present value method, decide whether or not Wheeler Manufacturing Company should add the calculator to its line of products. (Ignore income taxes.) Round to the nearest dollar (round down for .5).

P27–8–B

Evaluate investment using net present value

The Butler Company is considering the purchase of equipment that will cost $600,000. It is estimated that the useful life of the equipment will be 10 years and that it will have a salvage value of $150,000. The company uses straight-line depreciation. The new equipment is expected to have a net cash inflow before taxes of $150,000 annually. Assume that the tax rate is 35% and that management requires a minimum return of 20%.

Required: Using the net present value method, determine whether or not the equipment is an acceptable investment.

P27–9–B

Evaluate decision to sell equipment

The Moore Company has an opportunity to sell a piece of equipment for $120,000. Such a sale will result in a tax-deductible loss of $8,000. If it is not sold, the equipment is expected to produce an annual net cash inflow after taxes of $48,000 for the next 20 years. After 20 years the equipment will have no salvage value. Assume a 30% income tax rate.

Required: The company currently has other investment opportunities that will yield 12%. Should the company sell the equipment? Prepare a schedule to support your conclusion.

BUSINESS DECISION PROBLEM 27–1

Compute net present value of several proposals; rank proposals in order of acceptability

The Duke Company wishes to invest $750,000 in capital projects that have a minimum expected rate of return of 14%. Five proposals are being evaluated. Acceptance of one proposal does *not* preclude acceptance of any of the other proposals. The company's criterion is to select proposals that meet its minimum required rate of return (14%).

The relevant information related to the five proposals is presented below:

Investment	Initial cash outlay	Expected after-tax net cash inflow per year	Expected life of proposal
A . . .	$150,000	$45,000	5 years
B . . .	300,000	60,000	8
C . . .	375,000	82,500	10
D . . .	450,000	78,000	12
E . . .	150,000	31,500	10

Required:
a. Compute the net present value of each of the five proposals.
b. Which projects should be undertaken? Why? Rank them in order of desirability.

BUSINESS DECISION PROBLEM 27–2

Evaluate bookkeeper's computation of a project's net present value; determine acceptability of project

The Vrana Company is considering a capital project that will involve a $225,000 investment in machinery and a $45,000 investment in working capital. The machine has a useful life of 10 years and no salvage value. The annual cash inflows (before taxes) are estimated at $90,000 with annual cash outflows (before taxes) of $30,000. The company uses straight-line depreciation. The income tax rate is 40%.

The company's new bookkeeper computed the net present value of the project using a minimum required rate of return of 16% (the company's cost of capital). The bookkeeper's computations are shown below:

Cash inflows	$ 90,000
Cash outflows	30,000
Net cash inflow	$ 60,000
Present value factor at 16%	×4.833
Present value of net cash inflow	$289,980
Initial cash outlay	225,000
Net present value	$ 64,980

Required: a. Are the bookkeeper's computations correct? If not, compute the correct net present value.

   b. Is this capital project acceptable to the company? Why or why not?

BUSINESS DECISION PROBLEM 27–3

Determine whether to purchase or lease a new machine

The Perry Company is trying to decide whether to purchase or lease a new factory machine. If the machine is purchased, the following costs will be incurred:

Acquisition cost	$400,000
Repairs and maintenance:	
Years 1–5	10,000
Years 6–10	20,000

The machine will be depreciated on a straight-line basis and will have no salvage value. If the machine is leased, the lease payment will be $60,000 each year for 10 years. The first lease payment will be due on the day the lease contract is signed. All repairs and maintenance will be provided by the lessor. The Perry Company's cost of capital is 12%.

Required: Do you recommend that the company purchase or lease the machine? Show computations to support your answer. (Ignore income taxes.)

BUSINESS SITUATION FOR DISCUSSION

Capital Budgeting for Marketing Managers*
Roger Dickinson and Anthony Herbst

☐   Your company must decide whether to market a new product called "Moondust" that has been created by the research and development staff. If you decide to manufacture and market Moondust, you must invest $1,000 now. If Moondust sells, as you expect it will, net cash flows should be $500 for 10 years, *provided your competitors don't begin marketing a similar product.* If they do, then the cash flows would likely fall to $100 a year by the third year. To get the $1,000 required for the investment, you will have to borrow money, and the bank will require you to pledge existing assets as collateral on the loan. This may weaken your firm's credit standing with its bankers, raise its future costs of borrowing, and affect availability of funds. It may also affect the market value of the firm's shares.

If you do not produce Moondust, but your competitors decide to produce a similar product, your existing products will be affected. And the experience gained by your competitor will give it an advantage for future product development. Should you go ahead with this project? Can capital-budgeting techniques help you decide?

Capital budgeting relates to investments that promise cash returns over a span of several years. Typically, such capital investments require sizable amounts of funds, and a single investment often involves a large portion of the firm's total assets. The combination of large cash outlays with long investment horizons make capital-budgeting decisions of great importance to the success of an organization.

Marketing executives have often taken aspects of the capital-budgeting process, such as discount rates, for granted. Recently, however, controversy has grown over the applicability of quantitative capital-budgeting methods to all important decisions, including marketing

---

* *Business,* April–June 1983, pp. 36–40. Used with permission.

decisions. What capital-budgeting methods are popularly used? How valid are capital-budgeting assumptions as they pertain to marketing decisions? And how can marketers avoid obvious pitfalls in evaluating capital investments?

The controversy over the practicality of applying capital-budgeting methods to marketing decisions arises largely because executives use capital-budgeting methods without understanding the implied assumptions. Capital-budgeting methods were developed by finance theorists who assumed either (1) that the cash flows from a prospective investment were known or (2) that the cash flows were distributed according to known probability distributions that could be dealt with by using the tools of statistics. The theorists made other assumptions that developed the theory of capital budgeting, but perhaps did not bear any resemblance to reality, such as the assumptions that: (1) perfect capital markets exist, i.e., that the markets appropriately reflect cash-flow patterns. Numerous marketing decisions are of this kind. The most obvious is the new product decision. But advertising campaigns, sales territories, pricing decisions, and the like also can have implications over time and may be important. Retailers, for example, are often asked to sign 20- or 30-year leases with large-dollar commitments involved.

But marketers have had almost nothing to say about the discount rate. The literature often suggests that future cash flows should be discounted at the "appropriate" rate. However, there are few statements about the assumptions involved in setting a discount rate or the great differences in present values for different discount rates. And indeed, the differences can be substantial. For example, the NPV of a dollar to be received in 20 years is just over a penny at a 25% discount rate. In contrast, for a discount rate of 5% the NPV is 38 cents.

The capital-budgeting process can provide information that may be relevant to marketing decisions that do not involve payouts lasting over many years or that may not be critically important. Executives may wish to discount cash flows over a few years, for example, in comparing the cash flows of proposed new sales territory "A" with the cash flows of proposed new sales territory "B." The capital-budgeting process should provide a set of discount rates that can be used to choose among short-term alternatives.

Another use for a set of discount rates is to establish a rate for anticipation and a rate for imputed interest. Anticipation occurs when a purchasing element in the distribution channel, such as a retailer, pays bills earlier than required, perhaps because the costs of setting up a system for delayed payment to the supplier may be large. The problem is to establish a discount rate that will "equate" payment today with payment later.

Retail organizations will often charge a profit center an imputed interest on inventory even though no debt is incurred and no interest is actually paid. Retailers want to make sure that the person managing the inventory understands that it is a valuable and costly asset. Presumably, imputed interest in most normal financial environments would be at some level above the rate the firm pays for short-term money.

Discount rates may also help in making many other types of short-term decisions. Thus, to some executives it is meaningful to suggest that an increase in the level of inventory should net the firm more than some minimum rate of return, perhaps more than its cost of capital. Put another way, if a firm can make more than its cost of capital on any marketing decision, short term or long term, then the value of the enterprise will be increased by the undertaking. All decisions can be subjected to an evaluation of their return on investment. However, it is necessary to evaluate the return on investment of other marketing decisions the firm may be considering, and to compare the returns. For example, the decision to increase inventory by $4 million for a four-year period might prevent a retailer from opening a new store. Thus, even if a decision to increase inventory meets a minimum investment criterion, it may also have to yield more than a new store. This, of course, assumes that the funds available are limited (i.e., that there is capital rationing). In this last example, short-term alternatives are compared with all other options including long-term options.

It seems clear that marketers (including retailers) have an interest in the capital-budgeting process, including the attendant discount rate determinations.

CHAPTER 28 Personal and Corporate Income Taxes

LEARNING OBJECTIVES

After studying this chapter, you should be able to:

1. Compute gross income, adjusted gross income, and taxable income for personal tax returns.
2. Compute tax liability on personal returns, including the effects of tax credits.
3. Compute the tax liability for corporations.
4. Illustrate the use of tax loss carrybacks and carryforwards.
5. Compute depreciation allowance for tax purposes using the Accelerated Cost Recovery System (ACRS).
6. Identify the nature of permanent and timing differences between taxable income and accounting pretax income.
7. Account for timing differences using interperiod tax allocation.
8. Define and use correctly the new terms in the glossary.

In 1913, the ratification of the 16th Amendment established the constitutionality of the federal income tax in the United States. Without a doubt, you can expect to file income tax forms as long as you have any significant income.

Income taxes play an important role in both personal and business decisions. Whenever a person or a company considers financial opportunities, the tax consequences of those opportunities should be noted and weighed.

The purpose of this chapter is to provide an introductory understanding of federal income taxes, both personal and corporate. This chapter can only provide a general overview of these taxes due to their complexity and the constantly changing nature of tax laws. Coverage in this chapter is based on tax laws in effect as of mid 1985. Provisions of major tax legislation such as the Economic Recovery Act of 1981 and the Tax Equity and Fiscal Responsibility Act of 1982 are included. Recognize that some changes may have been made to the tax law since this chapter was revised. The Business Situation for Discussion at the end of this chapter describes some possible changes that may occur in the tax laws.

■ PERSONAL FEDERAL INCOME TAXES

The first part of this chapter develops the concept of taxable income and illustrates the measurement of the tax liability for individual taxpayers.

Who Must File a Return

In general, all U.S. citizens and resident aliens must file a federal tax return. More specifically, the determination of who must file a return depends on filing status and income level. For 1985, the minimum income levels at which a tax return must be filed are $3,430 for a single person, $4,300 if age 65 or older, $5,620 for a married couple filing a joint return, $6,660 if one spouse is age 65 or older, and $7,700 if both are age 65 or older. All of the minimum income levels at which a tax return must be filed are subject to change because of the indexing of various items in the new IRS code.

Filing Status.   There are four basic filing statuses that can be used in filing an income tax return—single, married filing jointly, married filing separately, and head of household. All of these are self-explanatory except **head of household,** who typically is an unmarried or legally separated person who maintains a residence for someone who qualifies as a dependent of the taxpayer.

Gross Income

Illustration 28.1 contains a general model of the determination of taxable income. The model starts with gross (total) income. **Gross income** includes all of a taxpayer's income from whatever source derived, except for those items specifically excluded, such as social security benefits. Gross income includes wages, interest, dividends, tips, bonuses, gambling winnings, gains from property sales, and prizes (including noncash prizes). Even income generated illegally, such as by theft, must be included in gross income. The general rule is that every income item, unless specifically exempted by law, must be included in gross income.

Exclusions from Gross Income.   Items excluded from gross income are interest on state and municipal bonds, certain social security benefits, workmen's compensation insurance benefits, and several employee "fringe" benefits, such as employer-paid health insurance premiums. Also, gifts, inheritances, certain disability benefits, scholarships, and the proceeds from life insurance policies are excluded. The first $100 of dividend income ($200 on a joint return no matter which spouse earned the dividend) can be excluded.

Illustration 28.1

Determination of Taxable Income for an Individual Taxpayer

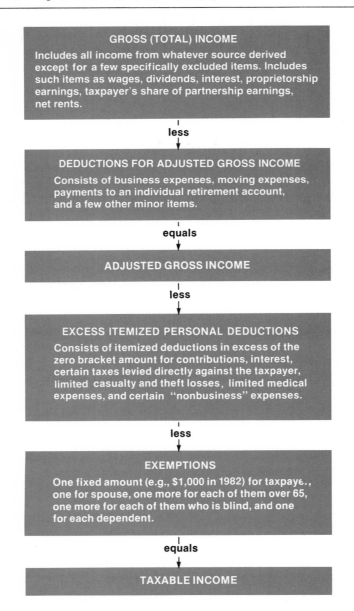

GROSS (TOTAL) INCOME

Includes all income from whatever source derived except for a few specifically excluded items. Includes such items as wages, dividends, interest, proprietorship earnings, taxpayer's share of partnership earnings, net rents.

less

DEDUCTIONS FOR ADJUSTED GROSS INCOME

Consists of business expenses, moving expenses, payments to an individual retirement account, and a few other minor items.

equals

ADJUSTED GROSS INCOME

less

EXCESS ITEMIZED PERSONAL DEDUCTIONS

Consists of itemized deductions in excess of the zero bracket amount for contributions, interest, certain taxes levied directly against the taxpayer, limited casualty and theft losses, limited medical expenses, and certain "nonbusiness" expenses.

less

EXEMPTIONS

One fixed amount (e.g., $1,000 in 1982) for taxpayer, one for spouse, one more for each of them over 65, one more for each of them who is blind, and one for each dependent.

equals

TAXABLE INCOME

Adjusted Gross Income

Taxpayers are allowed to deduct certain items from gross income in arriving at adjusted gross income. The computation of adjusted gross income is necessary in order to compute the allowable amounts of certain personal, itemized deductions.

Deductions for adjusted gross income to arrive at adjusted gross income consist basically of business expenses related to the production of income, moving expenses related to job or business, payments to individual retirement accounts (IRAs) or to Keogh retirement plans, alimony paid to an ex-spouse, and interest penalties assessed on certain investments for early withdrawals of funds. Some of these deductions are discussed below.

Ordinary and necessary business expenses that can be deducted (to the extent that they are unreimbursed) in computing adjusted gross income are any items that fall into the following three categories:

1. Expenses incurred as an employee while away from home on business for travel, food, or accommodations.
2. Transportation expenses incurred as an employee, other than the normal cost of commuting to and from work.
3. Expenses incurred in moving to a new place of employment.

Employees can also deduct from gross income contributions to an individual retirement account (IRA). An IRA is a retirement savings account usually set up in a bank, savings and loan association, insurance company, mutual fund, or brokerage firm. The annual deduction is limited to the lesser of 100% of earnings or $2,000 for an individual, $4,000 for a married couple if both spouses have jobs, and $2,250 for a married couple if only one spouse has earned income. Deductions cannot be based on unearned income, such as interest and dividends.

Since self-employed individuals are not covered by company-established retirement plans as employees are, they are allowed to establish their own retirement plan called a Keogh plan (pronounced Key-oh). The distinction between an IRA and a Keogh plan is that while an IRA is available to anyone, a Keogh plan is available only to self-employed individuals. The annual deduction for a Keogh plan in the early 1980s was limited to 15% of earnings up to a maximum of $15,000. Beginning in 1984 the Keough contribution limits were raised to 20% of earned self-employment income up to a maximum of $30,000.

Taxable Income

Taxpayers are allowed certain additional deductions and exemptions in arriving at taxable income. The deductions from adjusted gross income are called itemized or personal deductions and are specified by law. These itemized deductions are allowable only to the extent that they exceed a specified amount called the zero bracket amount, because the zero bracket amount is built into the tax rate schedules and tables. The zero bracket amount is $2,390 for single persons and for persons filing as a head of household, $3,540 for married couples filing a joint return, and $1,700 for married persons filing separate returns. The amount by which itemized deductions exceed the zero bracket amount is known as excess itemized deductions and can be deducted from adjusted gross income. A taxpayer will itemize deductions only if they exceed the zero bracket amount.

Itemized Deductions.   The more common itemized deductions include:

1. **Taxes.**   Real estate taxes, personal property taxes, state and local income taxes, and sales taxes are deductible. License fees and federal excise taxes are not deductible.

2. **Interest.**   Virtually all interest paid on any type of personal debt is deductible.

3. **Charitable contributions.**   Gifts to educational, religious, scientific, and charitable organizations are deductible if, in total, they do not exceed 50% of adjusted gross income. Donations to individuals, labor unions, and organizations that are established primarily to influence legislation are not deductible.

4. **Medical expenses.**   Within certain limits, unreimbursed health insurance premiums and hospital, medical, and dental expenses incurred by taxpayers and their dependents are deductible. Only that amount of medical costs that exceeds 5% of adjusted gross income is deductible. The entire cost of **prescription** drugs and insulin can be included in medical costs. The cost of other drugs and medicines can not be included.

To clarify the treatment of medical expenses, assume that in 1985, a taxpayer with an adjusted gross income of $20,000 paid $550 of health insurance premiums, incurred other medical expenses of $700, and incurred prescription drug costs of $400. The medical deduction is:

Health insurance premiums	$ 550
Other unreimbursed medical expenses	700
Medicine costs	400
	$1,650
Less: 5% of adjusted gross income (0.05 × $20,000)	1,000
Medical deduction	$ 650

5. **Casualty losses.**   Casualty losses are sudden and unexpected losses resulting from theft, accidents, storms, fire, and similar events. They are deductible to the extent that **each** casualty loss exceeds $100 **and** that the total of all unreimbursed casualty losses for the year exceeds 10% of adjusted gross income. Thus, to compute the deduction, first subtract $100 from the dollar amount of **each** loss (ignore losses of less than $100) to obtain an adjusted casualty loss. Then, from the sum of all of the adjusted casualty losses, subtract 10% of adjusted gross income. The positive difference is the casualty loss deduction. To illustrate, assume a taxpayer had adjusted gross income of $50,000 and suffered two casualty losses during the year—a fire loss of $9,000 and a theft loss of $12,000. The casualty loss deduction is computed as follows:

Adjusted fire loss ($9,000 − $100)	$ 8,900
Adjusted theft loss ($12,000 − $100)	11,900
Total	$20,800
Less 10% of adjusted gross income	5,000
Casualty loss deduction	$15,800

6. **Other deductions.**   In general, this category consists of expenses related to the taxpayer's business or profession that are not deductible from gross income. Included are the costs of professional publications and dues, union dues, safe-deposit box rentals, income tax preparer's fees, business entertainment, and job-related clothing and tools.

Exemptions

The final step in determining taxable income is to deduct the amount of income that is exempt from taxation. This amount was determined by multiplying the number of exemptions allowed the taxpayer by $1,000 in 1984. To adjust the amount of the exemption for inflation, the 1981 Tax Act provided for indexing the amount using the Consumer Price Index beginning in 1985. The exemption allowance increased to $1,040 in 1985 and will increase again in the future because of indexing for inflation. Married persons filing jointly are both considered taxpayers even though only one spouse has income; they are allowed one exemption each, plus one for each dependent. An additional exemption is allowed each taxpayer who is 65 or over or blind. Thus, a married couple with no dependents may be allowed up to six exemptions, three each— one for self, one for age 65 or over, and one for being blind.

A taxpayer is also allowed an exemption for each person who (1) is closely related to the taxpayer or who lived as a member of the taxpayer's family for the entire year; (2) had an income of less than $1,000; (3) received more than half of his or her support from the taxpayer; and (4) who, if married, does not file a joint return with a spouse for the taxable year. The $1,000 income limitation does not apply to the taxpayer's children who are under 19 or who are enrolled as full-time students. Thus, student status may yield two exemptions—one on the parents' return and another on the student's own return.

Computing Tax Liability

As discussed above, the manner of calculating taxable income differs slightly depending upon whether deductions are itemized or not. If deductions are itemized, taxable income is equal to adjusted gross income less excess itemized deductions and exemptions; if deductions are not itemized, taxable income is equal to adjusted gross income less exemptions.

If taxable income is $50,000 or less, tax liability in most cases is determined by using **tax tables** provided by the Internal Revenue Service. Portions of the tax tables used for a recent year are shown in Illustration 28.2. Note there are four tax tables provided; the taxpayer's filing status determines which one will be used.

To illustrate use of the table, assume Mr. and Mrs. Olson file a joint return showing taxable income of $24,610. Their income tax liability is found on the $24,600–$24,650 line in the "Married couple filing jointly" column. The amount is $3,663.

If taxable income is more than $50,000, **tax rate schedules** such as those in Illustration 28.3 must be used to compute the tax. Thus, the tax on $61,000 of taxable income reported by a married couple filing jointly is $16,014 + (0.44 × $1,000), or $16,454.

Marginal and Effective Tax Rates.   A quick look at the tax rate schedules in Illustration 28.3 shows clearly that the rates are progressive. Progressive tax rates increase with successively higher amounts of taxable income. For example, the taxable income of a single taxpayer over $2,300 but not over $3,400 is taxed at an 11% rate. Income over $34,100 but not over $41,500 is taxed at a 40% rate. These percentages are called marginal tax rates. A **marginal tax rate** is the rate applied to the next dollar of taxable income or each incremental amount of income. Such rates are important in decision making because they show the marginal effect of a decision. For example, assume that Joe Hardy, a single taxpayer in the 40% tax bracket, could earn $400 on a plumbing job if he would work on Sunday. But being in the 40% bracket means that Joe would have to pay $160 ($400 × 0.40) more income taxes if he takes the

Illustration 28.2

Partial Tax Table

If line 37 (taxable income) is— At least	But less than	Single	Married filing jointly *	Married filing separately	Head of a house-hold
24,500	24,550	4,677	3,639	5,817	4,294
24,550	24,600	4,693	3,650	5,837	4,309
24,600	24,650	4,709	3,663	5,857	4,323
24,650	24,700	4,725	3,676	5,877	4,338
24,700	24,750	4,741	3,689	5,897	4,352
24,750	24,800	4,757	3,702	5,917	4,367
24,800	24,850	4,773	3,715	5,937	4,381
24,850	24,900	4,789	3,728	5,957	4,396
24,900	24,950	4,805	3,741	5,977	4,410
24,950	25,000	4,821	3,754	5,997	4,425
25,000					
25,000	25,050	4,837	3,767	6,017	4,439
25,050	25,100	4,853	3,780	6,037	4,454
25,100	25,150	4,869	3,793	6,057	4,468
25,150	25,200	4,885	3,806	6,077	4,483
25,200	25,250	4,901	3,819	6,097	4,497
25,250	25,300	4,917	3,832	6,117	4,512
25,300	25,350	4,933	3,845	6,137	4,526
25,350	25,400	4,949	3,858	6,157	4,541
25,400	25,450	4,965	3,871	6,177	4,555
25,450	25,500	4,981	3,884	6,197	4,570
25,500	25,550	4,997	3,897	6,217	4,584
25,550	25,600	5,013	3,910	6,237	4,599
25,600	25,650	5,029	3,923	6,257	4,613
25,650	25,700	5,045	3,936	6,277	4,628
25,700	25,750	5,061	3,949	6,297	4,642
25,750	25,800	5,077	3,962	6,317	4,657
25,800	25,850	5,093	3,975	6,337	4,671
25,850	25,900	5,109	3,988	6,357	4,686
25,900	25,950	5,125	4,001	6,377	4,700
25,950	26,000	5,141	4,014	6,397	4,715
26,000					
26,000	26,050	5,157	4,027	6,417	4,729
26,050	26,100	5,173	4,040	6,437	4,744
26,100	26,150	5,189	4,053	6,457	4,758
26,150	26,200	5,205	4,066	6,477	4,773
26,200	26,250	5,221	4,079	6,497	4,787
26,250	26,300	5,237	4,092	6,517	4,802
26,300	26,350	5,253	4,105	6,537	4,816
26,350	26,400	5,269	4,118	6,557	4,831
26,400	26,450	5,285	4,131	6,577	4,845
26,450	26,500	5,301	4,144	6,597	4,860
26,500	26,550	5,317	4,157	6,617	4,874
26,550	26,600	5,333	4,170	6,637	4,889
26,600	26,650	5,349	4,183	6,657	4,903
26,650	26,700	5,365	4,196	6,677	4,918
26,700	26,750	5,381	4,209	6,697	4,932
26,750	26,800	5,397	4,222	6,717	4,947
26,800	26,850	5,413	4,235	6,737	4,961
26,850	26,900	5,429	4,248	6,757	4,976
26,900	26,950	5,445	4,261	6,777	4,990
26,950	27,000	5,461	4,274	6,797	5,005
27,000					
27,000	27,050	5,477	4,287	6,817	5,019
27,050	27,100	5,493	4,300	6,837	5,034
27,100	27,150	5,509	4,313	6,857	5,048
27,150	27,200	5,525	4,326	6,877	5,063
27,200	27,250	5,541	4,339	6,897	5,077

If line 37 (taxable income) is— At least	But less than	Single	Married filing jointly *	Married filing separately	Head of a house-hold
27,250	27,300	5,557	4,352	6,917	5,092
27,300	27,350	5,573	4,365	6,937	5,106
27,350	27,400	5,589	4,378	6,957	5,121
27,400	27,450	5,605	4,391	6,977	5,135
27,450	27,500	5,621	4,404	6,997	5,150
27,500	27,550	5,637	4,417	7,017	5,164
27,550	27,600	5,653	4,430	7,037	5,179
27,600	27,650	5,669	4,443	7,057	5,193
27,650	27,700	5,685	4,456	7,077	5,208
27,700	27,750	5,701	4,469	7,097	5,222
27,750	27,800	5,717	4,482	7,117	5,237
27,800	27,850	5,733	4,495	7,137	5,251
27,850	27,900	5,749	4,508	7,157	5,266
27,900	27,950	5,765	4,521	7,177	5,280
27,950	28,000	5,781	4,534	7,197	5,295
28,000					
28,000	28,050	5,797	4,547	7,217	5,309
28,050	28,100	5,813	4,560	7,237	5,324
28,100	28,150	5,829	4,573	7,257	5,338
28,150	28,200	5,845	4,586	7,277	5,353
28,200	28,250	5,861	4,599	7,297	5,367
28,250	28,300	5,877	4,612	7,317	5,382
28,300	28,350	5,893	4,625	7,337	5,396
28,350	28,400	5,909	4,638	7,357	5,411
28,400	28,450	5,925	4,651	7,377	5,425
28,450	28,500	5,941	4,664	7,397	5,440
28,500	28,550	5,957	4,677	7,417	5,454
28,550	28,600	5,973	4,690	7,437	5,469
28,600	28,650	5,989	4,703	7,457	5,483
28,650	28,700	6,005	4,716	7,477	5,498
28,700	28,750	6,021	4,729	7,497	5,512
28,750	28,800	6,037	4,742	7,517	5,527
28,800	28,850	6,054	4,755	7,537	5,543
28,850	28,900	6,072	4,768	7,557	5,560
28,900	28,950	6,090	4,781	7,577	5,577
28,950	29,000	6,108	4,794	7,597	5,594
29,000					
29,000	29,050	6,126	4,807	7,617	5,611
29,050	29,100	6,144	4,820	7,637	5,628
29,100	29,150	6,162	4,833	7,657	5,645
29,150	29,200	6,180	4,846	7,677	5,662
29,200	29,250	6,198	4,859	7,697	5,679
29,250	29,300	6,216	4,872	7,717	5,696
29,300	29,350	6,234	4,885	7,737	5,713
29,350	29,400	6,252	4,898	7,757	5,730
29,400	29,450	6,270	4,911	7,777	5,747
29,450	29,500	6,288	4,924	7,797	5,764
29,500	29,550	6,306	4,937	7,817	5,781
29,550	29,600	6,324	4,950	7,837	5,798
29,600	29,650	6,342	4,963	7,857	5,815
29,650	29,700	6,360	4,976	7,877	5,832
29,700	29,750	6,378	4,989	7,897	5,849
29,750	29,800	6,396	5,002	7,917	5,866
29,800	29,850	6,414	5,015	7,937	5,883
29,850	29,900	6,432	5,028	7,957	5,900
29,900	29,950	6,450	5,042	7,977	5,917
29,950	30,000	6,468	5,057	7,997	5,934

If line 37 (taxable income) is— At least	But less than	Single	Married filing jointly *	Married filing separately	Head of a house-hold
30,000					
30,000	30,050	6,486	5,072	8,018	5,951
30,050	30,100	6,504	5,087	8,040	5,968
30,100	30,150	6,522	5,102	8,062	5,985
30,150	30,200	6,540	5,117	8,084	6,002
30,200	30,250	6,558	5,132	8,106	6,019
30,250	30,300	6,576	5,147	8,128	6,036
30,300	30,350	6,594	5,162	8,150	6,053
30,350	30,400	6,612	5,177	8,172	6,070
30,400	30,450	6,630	5,192	8,194	6,087
30,450	30,500	6,648	5,207	8,216	6,104
30,500	30,550	6,666	5,222	8,238	6,121
30,550	30,600	6,684	5,237	8,260	6,138
30,600	30,650	6,702	5,252	8,282	6,155
30,650	30,700	6,720	5,267	8,304	6,172
30,700	30,750	6,738	5,282	8,326	6,189
30,750	30,800	6,756	5,297	8,348	6,206
30,800	30,850	6,774	5,312	8,370	6,223
30,850	30,900	6,792	5,327	8,392	6,240
30,900	30,950	6,810	5,342	8,414	6,257
30,950	31,000	6,828	5,357	8,436	6,274
31,000					
31,000	31,050	6,846	5,372	8,458	6,291
31,050	31,100	6,864	5,387	8,480	6,308
31,100	31,150	6,882	5,402	8,502	6,325
31,150	31,200	6,900	5,417	8,524	6,342
31,200	31,250	6,918	5,432	8,546	6,359
31,250	31,300	6,936	5,447	8,568	6,376
31,300	31,350	6,954	5,462	8,590	6,393
31,350	31,400	6,972	5,477	8,612	6,410
31,400	31,450	6,990	5,492	8,634	6,427
31,450	31,500	7,008	5,507	8,656	6,444
31,500	31,550	7,026	5,522	8,678	6,461
31,550	31,600	7,044	5,537	8,700	6,478
31,600	31,650	7,062	5,552	8,722	6,495
31,650	31,700	7,080	5,567	8,744	6,512
31,700	31,750	7,098	5,582	8,766	6,529
31,750	31,800	7,116	5,597	8,788	6,546
31,800	31,850	7,134	5,612	8,810	6,563
31,850	31,900	7,152	5,627	8,832	6,580
31,900	31,950	7,170	5,642	8,854	6,597
31,950	32,000	7,188	5,657	8,876	6,614
32,000					
32,000	32,050	7,206	5,672	8,898	6,631
32,050	32,100	7,224	5,687	8,920	6,648
32,100	32,150	7,242	5,702	8,942	6,665
32,150	32,200	7,260	5,717	8,964	6,682
32,200	32,250	7,278	5,732	8,986	6,699
32,250	32,300	7,296	5,747	9,008	6,716
32,300	32,350	7,314	5,762	9,030	6,733
32,350	32,400	7,332	5,777	9,052	6,750
32,400	32,450	7,350	5,792	9,074	6,767
32,450	32,500	7,368	5,807	9,096	6,784
32,500	32,550	7,386	5,822	9,118	6,801
32,550	32,600	7,404	5,837	9,140	6,818
32,600	32,650	7,422	5,852	9,162	6,835
32,650	32,700	7,440	5,867	9,184	6,852
32,700	32,750	7,458	5,882	9,206	6,869

*This column must also be used by a qualifying widow(er).

job, which means that he would net only $240 from the job. Joe may decide he would rather watch a football game or go fishing. This type of analysis illustrates the correct use of the marginal tax rate.

The effective tax rate rather than the marginal rate should be used as a measure of total taxes to be paid. The **effective tax rate** is the average rate of taxation for a given amount of taxable income. For example, if Joe Hardy earns $34,600 for the year, he is in the 40% bracket. But he does not pay

Illustration 28.3

Tax Rate Schedules

Tax rate schedule for single individuals

If taxable income is:		Income tax is:	
Over—	**But not over—**	**This amount**	**Of amount over—**
–0–	$ 2,300	–0–	
$ 2,300	3,400	. . . . . + 11%	$ 2,300
3,400	4,400	$ 121 + 13%	3,400
4,400	8,500	251 + 15%	4,400
8,500	10,800	866 + 17%	8,500
10,800	12,900	1,257 + 19%	10,800
12,900	15,000	1,656 + 21%	12,900
15,000	18,200	2,097 + 24%	15,000
18,200	23,500	2,865 + 28%	18,200
23,500	28,800	4,349 + 32%	23,500
28,800	34,100	6,045 + 36%	28,800
34,100	41,500	7,953 + 40%	34,100
41,500	55,300	10,913 + 45%	41,500
55,300	. . . . .	17,123 + 50%	55,300

Tax rate schedule for married individuals filing joint returns and surviving spouses

If taxable income is:		Income tax is:	
Over—	**But not over—**	**This amount**	**Of amount over—**
–0–	$ 3,400	–0–	
$ 3,400	5,500	. . . . . + 11%	$ 3,400
5,500	7,600	$ 231 + 13%	5,500
7,600	11,900	504 + 15%	7,600
11,900	16,000	1,149 + 17%	11,900
16,000	20,200	1,846 + 19%	16,000
20,200	24,600	2,644 + 23%	20,200
24,600	29,900	3,656 + 26%	24,600
29,900	35,200	5,034 + 30%	29,900
35,200	45,800	6,624 + 35%	35,200
45,800	60,000	10,334 + 40%	45,800
60,000	85,600	16,014 + 44%	60,000
85,600	109,400	27,278 + 48%	85,600
109,400	. . . . .	38,702 + 50%	109,400

$13,840 ($34,600 × 0.40) per year in taxes. Joe actually pays taxes at a 23.6% rate computed as follows:

$$\text{Effective (average) tax rate} = \frac{\text{Total taxes paid}}{\text{Total taxable income}}$$

$$\text{Effective tax rate} = \frac{\$7,953 + [0.40 \times (\$34,600 - \$34,100)]*}{\$34,600}$$

$$\text{Effective tax rate} = \frac{\$8,153}{\$34,600} = 23.6\%$$

* These figures were taken from Illustration 28.3 for a single taxpayer.

Capital Gains and Losses

Capital assets are all items of property other than inventories, receivables, copyrights, certain governmental obligations, and real and depreciable property used in a trade or business. Investments in capital stocks and bonds are examples of capital assets. A gain—an excess of selling price over cost—is classified as a **long-term capital gain** if it relates to a capital asset that was held longer than the specified holding period prior to sale. That holding period is six months for assets purchased after June 22, 1984, but before January 1, 1988. For assets purchased before June 23, 1984, or after December 31, 1987, the holding period is one year. Taxpayers seek to report taxable income as long-term capital gains because such gains receive favorable tax treatment.

Even though real and depreciable property used in a trade or business is not a capital asset, gains in excess of losses from the sale of such property are treated as capital gains. Losses on the sale of such property, however, are deductible as ordinary business expenses.

Taxation of Capital Gains.   Some capital gains escape taxation. For example, a taxpayer age 55 or older may exclude from gross income up to $125,000 ($62,500 on a separate return) of any gain on sale of the taxpayer's home.

All other capital gains are short term or long term according to whether the capital asset sold was held for more than the specified holding period. Short-term capital gains are fully taxable; that is, 100% of such gains is included in adjusted gross income. But only 40% of a long-term capital gain is included in adjusted gross income; the remaining 60% escapes taxation.

The tax saving to a taxpayer in the 44% tax rate bracket from qualifying a $1,000 gain from sale of stock investments as long term rather than short term is $264. The tax on the gain, if short term, is $440 ($1,000 × 0.44). The tax on the gain, if long term, is $176 ($1,000 × 0.4 × 0.44). Thus, the total tax saving is $264 ($440 − $176). The effective tax rate on the gain, if long term, is 17.6% ($176/$1,000). With a maximum marginal income tax rate of 50%, the maximum tax on a long-term capital gain is 20% (0.5 × 0.4).

If a taxpayer has both short-term and long-term capital gains and losses, the following procedures are applied:

1. Offset short-term gains and losses into a single net short-term gain or loss.
2. Offset long-term gains and losses into a single net long-term gain or loss.

If net short-term gains exceed net long-term losses, the excess is included in adjusted gross income. If net long-term gains exceed net short-term losses, 40% of the excess is included in adjusted gross income. For example, if a taxpayer has $5,000 of net short-term gains and $2,000 of net long-term losses, the $3,000 difference is included in adjusted gross income. If the taxpayer has net long-term gains of $6,000 and a net short-term loss of $1,000, 40% of the $5,000 difference, or $2,000, is included in adjusted gross income.

If there is both a net short-term gain and a net long-term gain, all of the short-term gain and 40% of the long-term gain is included in adjusted gross income. The tax law relative to net losses is more complex, containing certain limitations. Discussion of losses is left for a more advanced course.

Tax Credits

A **tax credit** is a direct deduction from the amount of taxes to be paid, resulting largely from certain expenditures made by the taxpayer. Because tax credits reduce the amount of taxes to be paid dollar for dollar, they are much more valuable to the taxpayer than deductions. A tax credit of $100 saves $100 of cash; a $100 deduction, on the other hand, is worth only $100 times the taxpayer's marginal tax rate. The maximum value, then, of any deduction is 50% of the amount of the deduction since the highest marginal tax rate is now 50%.

Following are some of the most common tax credits:

A tax credit of 50% of contributions made to candidates for public office is allowed, up to a maximum of $50 ($100 if filing jointly).

If new or used equipment is acquired by a person for use in a trade or business, part of its cost may be taken as an investment tax credit (ITC). For the 1975 tax year the investment credit was increased to 10%. The Tax Equity and Fiscal Responsibility Act (TEFRA) of 1982 changed the standard 10% rate to:

1. Ten percent of the investment if the depreciable base is reduced by one half of the investment credit taken.
2. Eight percent of the investment if there is no reduction in the depreciable base.

Thus, if a person operating an individual proprietorship purchases machinery at a cost of $10,000, $1,000 may be deducted from that person's tax liability and reduce the depreciable base by $500 to $9,500, or $800 may be deducted from the tax liability and leave the depreciable base at $10,000.

A tax credit can be taken for part of the cost of home energy conservation items, such as insulation, storm windows and doors, caulking, and clock thermostats. The credit is 15% of qualified expenditures up to $2,000, or a maximum credit of $300 for all years, not for each year.

A tax credit is available for part of the cost of installing alternative energy equipment such as solar, wind, and geothermal equipment in the taxpayer's home. The credit is 40% of the first $10,000 of such costs, with a maximum credit of $4,000 for all years.

There also are tax credits for persons with low earned income levels, for the elderly, for child and dependent care expenses, for income taxes paid to foreign countries, and for wages paid in work incentive programs.

Filing the Tax Return

Personal tax returns generally must be filed by April 15 of the year following the tax year. Extensions may be filed, but payment of any tax liability is still due on April 15. As discussed in Chapter 12, most taxpayers are also employees and, therefore, taxes are withheld by employers under our pay-as-you-go tax system. Also, taxpayers having income above a prescribed amount that is not subject to withholding must pay an estimated tax. This estimated tax must be paid in four installments. The taxes withheld and the estimated taxes paid are entered as offsets to the total tax liability on the tax return. Any remaining unpaid taxes are paid to the Internal Revenue Service when the return is filed. In some cases, tax withholdings and estimated taxes paid may have exceeded tax liability, and the taxpayer can claim a refund.

■ COMPREHENSIVE ILLUSTRATION—PERSONAL INCOME TAXES

An actual tax return consists of a number of preprinted forms that are filled out by the taxpayer. Most taxpayers will file either Form 1040A, often called the short form, or Form 1040, the long form. A taxpayer who intends to itemize deductions cannot file a short form, 1040A. A taxpayer who uses the long form generally must attach various schedules to it. Two common schedules included in the long form are Schedule A and Schedule B. Schedule A shows the itemized deductions, while Schedule B lists all dividends and interest income when dividend and interest income exceeds $400. As mentioned in Chapter 12, one copy of the taxpayer's Form W-2 is attached to the tax return. The W-2 is issued by the employer and shows wages earned and taxes withheld during the period of these wages.

Illustration 28.4 shows a brief summary schedule of the tax return items for Lee and Dora Bowman for 1985, who are married and file a joint return. Lee is chief engineer for a manufacturing company; Dora is a full-time home-maker. Both taxpayers are under age 65; they have two dependent children, ages 13 and 15. Dora owns a number of bonds and shares of stock, some of which she sold during the year, realizing $10,000 of long-term capital gains and $1,000 of short-term capital losses. Total income taxes withheld during

Illustration 28.4

Joint Tax Return Computations

Salary		$58,000
Interest income		4,000
Dividend income, net of $200 exclusion		6,000
Long-term capital gain ($10,000) less short-term capital loss ($1,000)	$ 9,000	
Less: 60% exclusion	5,400	3,600
Total		$71,600
Contribution to an individual retirement account		2,250
Adjusted gross income		$69,350
Excess itemized deductions:		
Medical expense ($3,618 − $3,468; total medical cost less 5% of adjusted gross income)	$ 150	
Charitable contributions	2,240	
Taxes (real estate on home, state income, sales)	5,670	
Casualty loss ($7,485 − $6,935; total adjusted casualty losses less 10% of adjusted gross income)	550	
Miscellaneous (professional dues, subscriptions, unreimbursed business entertainment expenses, etc.)	440	
	$ 9,050	
Zero bracket amount	3,540	
Excess itemized deductions		5,510
		$63,840
Exemptions (4 × $1,040)		4,160
Taxable income		$59,680
Income tax [$10,334 + (0.40 × $13,880)		$15,886
Credit for political contribution ($250 × 0.5 = $125, limited to $100)		100
Total tax liability		$15,786
Income taxes withheld	$14,700	
Estimated taxes paid	800	15,500
Income taxes payable with return		$ 286

the year amounted to $14,700. In addition, Lee and Dora paid estimated taxes of $800. Other information needed to compute the Bowman's tax liability and tax payment are shown in the illustration. The income tax of $15,786 is computed using the tax rate schedule in Illustration 28.3. These rates are used for illustrative purposes only and may have changed by the time you read this text.

■ CORPORATE FEDERAL INCOME TAXATION

Business managers strive to maximize income in a company, while at the same time attempting to minimize taxes. In a sole proprietorship or partnership, business earnings flow directly to the owner or owners and thus affect personal tax returns. In contrast, the corporation itself is considered a taxpayer by law and, therefore, is the only form of business organization that pays federal income taxes.

Taxable Income

Corporate income taxes are based on the amount of taxable income shown on IRS Form 1120. Corporate taxable income is computed by subtracting all allowable deductions from the corporation's gross income. Corporate gross income is calculated much like the calculation for personal gross income; it basically includes all revenues from sales, services, or investments of the company. Allowable deductions from a corporate standpoint must meet four criteria; such deductions must be business related, reasonable in amount, necessary, and legal.

Once taxable income is determined, a tax rate is applied to find the amount of tax liability. As of this writing, the graduated tax rates applicable to corporations for the years 1983 and beyond are:

Corporate taxable income	Tax rate
First $25,000	15%
Second $25,000	18
Third $25,000	30
Fourth $25,000	40
Over $100,000	46

To illustrate, assume a corporation had taxable income in 1985 of $60,000. The tax due would be $11,250, computed as follows:

Tax on first $25,000 (at 15%)	$ 3,750
Tax on second $25,000 (at 18%)	4,500
Tax on remaining $10,000 (at 30%)	3,000
	$11,250

Earlier we illustrated tax credits for individuals. Tax credits also are available for corporations. One such tax credit that is particularly significant to the corporation is the investment tax credit. The investment tax credit (ITC) when applied to a corporation works the same way as for an individual. When certain qualifying machinery and equipment are purchased, the ITC is (1) a 10% credit to tax liability if the depreciable base is reduced by one half of the investment credit taken; or (2) an 8% credit to tax liability if no reduction in the depreciable base is taken. Therefore, if the corporation in the above example had purchased $47,500 of qualifying plant assets during the year, it could choose a $4,750 tax credit. This ITC would be used to directly reduce the tax liability of $11,250, making the net tax due $6,500 ($11,250 − $4,750).

Tax Loss Carrybacks and Carryforwards

If a corporation suffers a net loss in a given year, it of course owes no income tax in that year. The tax law also provides that the corporation can apply this loss to its taxable income from prior years and recover some or all of the taxes paid during those years. This provision is called a **tax loss carryback.** If the corporation elects to carry the loss back, it may carry the loss back three years. The loss must be applied first to the oldest year, then to the next oldest year, and so on until the loss is used up or until then there is no more prior year income that may be affected. The corporation may then carry the remaining, unused loss forward for up to 15 years to reduce its taxable income in those future years. This is called a **tax loss carryforward.**

To illustrate the application of this provision, assume that a corporation had the amounts of taxable income (or loss) shown below:

Year	Taxable income (or loss)	Taxes paid	Taxes recovered
1984	$ 15,000	$ 2,250	$2,250
1985	20,000	3,000	3,000
1986	5,000	750	750
1987	(100,000)	–0–	–0–
1988	40,000	–0–	–0–
1989	10,000	–0–	–0–
1990	30,000	3,000	–0–
1991	50,000	8,250	–0–
1992	60,000	11,250	–0–

The loss of $100,000 in 1987 would first be offset against the $15,000 of income in 1984, then the $20,000 in 1985, and next the $5,000 in 1986. The company would recover the $6,000 taxes previously paid. At this point it would have a $60,000 loss carryforward. It would apply $40,000 of the loss toward taxable income in 1988, the result is a taxable income of $0 for 1988. This leaves $20,000 of loss carryforward remaining; $10,000 would be used to offset income in the next year (1989), and the other $10,000 would be used to reduce 1990 taxable income. The taxes paid for 1990 are ($30,000 − $10,000) × 0.15 = $3,000. If a corporation decides not to apply the loss to its taxable income from prior years, it can still carry the loss forward to future years. If the loss carryforward is not "used up" by the end of the 15th year, the remaining portion is lost.

Depreciation Methods Used for Tax Purposes

Tax depreciation is substantially different from depreciation used for accounting purposes. In accounting, depreciation methods are designed to match the expense of a capital investment against the revenue the investment produces. The depreciable period or useful life used for tax purposes is based on tax law and has no relationship to the actual useful life of the asset; thus, no attempt is made to match income and expenses.

Prior to 1981, several depreciation methods were available for tax purposes, including the sum-of-years'-digits method and the uniform-rate-on-declining-balance method. The Economic Recovery Tax Act of 1981 introduced a new depreciation system known as the Accelerated Cost Recovery System (ACRS). For the most part, this new system is mandatory for both new and used property placed in service after December 31, 1980.

Under the ACRS, capital assets are rapidly depreciated, thus allowing high tax deductions early in the life of the asset. The cash saved from reduced taxes in the early years of life of the assets can be invested in new productive assets or can be applied to the replacement of the old assets when they become obsolete or worn out. Thus, the main goal of the ACRS is the modernization of productive assets so that companies in the United States can compete more effectively in world markets. Under the ACRS, the concepts of useful life and salvage value are eliminated. Instead, capital assets are grouped into several different classes. Each class has an assigned life over which the assets are depreciated.

The ACRS identifies two major types of capital assets—personal property and real property.

Personal property is any property that is movable (not attached to land). Examples are trucks and machinery. **Real property (real estate)** is land and any property attached to land, such as a building, which cannot be moved. For tangible personal property and real estate, ACRS provides classes of 3, 5, 10, 15, and 18 years. Each class is described below:

Class of investment	Kinds of assets
3 years	Automobiles, light-duty trucks, machinery, and equipment used in research and development
5 years	All other machinery and equipment, such as dies, drills, presses, etc., petroleum storage facilities, furniture, and fixtures
10 years	Some public utility property, coal conversion boilers and equipment, and railroad tank cars
15 years	Low-income residential real estate and public utility property
18 years	All other real property

Once the asset has been classified, the depreciation allowance for each year is determined by referring to the ACRS depreciation table shown in the Appendix to this chapter. Under ACRS, the first year percentage allowance for all assets (except depreciable real property, e.g., a building) is the same regardless of when the property was placed in service during the year.

In using the ACRS table, keep in mind the following three rules:

1. Ignore salvage value. Apply the percentage to the cost of the asset.
2. If an asset is purchased and put into service at any time during the year, it will still receive a full year's depreciation (for tax purposes) for that calendar year.
3. Ignore the estimated useful life of an asset. The number of years that the asset is to be depreciated is determined strictly by its classification, not its useful life.

To illustrate the application of the ACRS, assume that on July 1, 1984, Bigwig Company acquired and placed in service a new machine costing $100,000. The machine falls into the five-year class under ACRS. Using the percentages taken from the five-year column of Table 28.1 in the Appendix, the depreciation allowance for the machine is calculated as follows:

Year	Cost	× Percent allowance	= Depreciation allowance
1984	100,000	0.15	15,000*
1985	100,000	0.22	22,000
1986	100,000	0.21	21,000
1987	100,000	0.21	21,000
1988	100,000	0.21	21,000
1989	100,000	–0–	

* 15% × 100,000 = 15,000.

Depreciation is an expense that does not require the outlay of additional capital or cash by the corporation. Therefore, tax depreciation is very desirable since it decreases taxable income and hence the corporation's tax liability. The great advantage of the ACRS is the early write-off of capital assets for tax purposes. By providing accelerated depreciation for tax purposes, tax savings are provided in the early years of the asset's life. The tax savings in early years can be reinvested and thus increase the earnings per share available for common stockholders for the entire period.

■ INCOME TAX ALLOCATION

Taxable income and net income before income taxes (for simplicity, pre-tax income) for a corporation may differ sharply for a number of reasons. In fact, the tax return may show a loss, while the income statement shows positive pre-tax income. This difference raises a question about the amount of income taxes to be shown on the income statement. The answer lies in the nature of the items causing the difference between taxable income and pre-tax income. Some items create permanent differences, while others create timing differences. Both kinds of differences are discussed below.

Permanent Differences

Certain types of revenue and expense included in the computation of net income for book purposes are excluded from the computation of taxable income. **Permanent differences** between taxable income and financial statement pre-tax income are caused by tax law provisions that exclude an item of expense, revenue, gain, or loss as an element of taxable income. For instance, interest earned on state, county, or municipal bonds is included in book net income but is not subject to tax and therefore is not included in determining taxable income. The same is true for life insurance proceeds received by a corporation. Other items that are expensed for book purposes are not deductible for tax purposes, such as premiums paid for officers' life insurance, costs of attempting to influence legislation, and amortization of goodwill. These are only a few of the numerous items for which the tax treatment is completely different from the accounting treatment. These differences in treatment **never** change or reverse themselves. Therefore, they are called **permanent differences.** Such differences cause no accounting problem—the estimated actual amount of income taxes payable for the year is shown on the income statement even if this results in reporting only $1,000 of income tax expense on $100,000 of pre-tax income.

Timing Differences

Other items of revenue and expense often are recognized at **different times** for tax purposes than for financial reporting purposes. **Timing differences** between taxable income and financial statement pre-tax income are caused by items that affect both taxable income and pre-tax income, but in different periods. For example, interpretations of the tax code generally have held that revenue received in advance is taxable when received and that current expenses based on estimates of future costs (such as costs of performance under service contracts) are not deductible until actually incurred. Timing differences can also result from using accounting methods for tax purposes that are different from the ones used for financial reporting purposes. For example, a corporation may use straight-line depreciation for book purposes and ACRS depreciation for tax purposes. Eventually these revenues and expenses are recognized in computing both accounting income and taxable income; it is the timing of recognition that differs. Therefore, these variations between taxable income and net income are called timing differences.

The reconciliation between income before taxes and taxable income for a given corporation appears below:

Net income before taxes per income statement		$74,000
Add:		
Life insurance premiums paid	$ 700	
Service revenue received in advance	5,000	
Estimated expenses under service contracts	1,000	6,700
		$80,700
Deduct:		
Interest on New York State bonds	$3,000	
Difference in depreciation for tax purposes		
($8,000) and for book purposes ($6,000)	2,000	5,000
Taxable income		$75,700

As discussed above, timing differences include items that will be included in both taxable income and in pre-tax income, but in **different periods.** The items involved thus will have a tax effect. When there are timing differences, generally accepted accounting principles require that **tax allocation** procedures be applied to prevent the presentation of possibly misleading information. **Interperiod tax allocation** is a procedure whereby the tax effects of an element of expense or revenue, or loss or gain, that will affect taxable income are allocated to the period in which the item is recognized for accounting purposes, regardless of the period in which it is recognized for tax purposes.

To illustrate the tax allocation procedure required for timing differences, assume that (1) a company acquires automobiles for $20,000 that have an estimated life of four years with no expected salvage value, (2) it uses the straight-line depreciation method for financial reporting purposes and the ACRS method for tax purposes (the automobiles fall into the three-year class), (3) net income before depreciation and income taxes is $15,000 for each year of the automobiles' lives, (4) there are no other items that cause differences between pretax income and taxable income, and (5) the tax rate is 40% (to simplify the illustration). Under these circumstances, the actual tax liability for each year is shown in Illustration 28.5.

Illustration 28.5

Calculation of Tax Liability

	1983	1984	1985	1986	Total
Income before depreciation and income taxes	$15,000	$15,000	$15,000	$15,000	$60,000
Depreciation (ACRS, three-year class method)	5,000	7,600	7,400	–0–	20,000
Taxable income	$10,000	$ 7,400	$ 7,600	$15,000	$40,000
Income taxes payable (40% of taxable income)	$ 4,000	$ 2,960	$ 3,040	$ 6,000	$16,000

Net income for each year, using the amount of income taxes payable calculated above, is shown in Illustration 28.6. Note that the amount of taxable income to be shown on the corporation's tax return for each year except 1983 (Illustration 28.5) is different from the amount of pre-tax income reported on the corporation's income statement (Illustration 28.6). To report this much year-to-year net income variance under the circumstances described is considered misleading according to generally accepted accounting principles.

Generally accepted accounting principles dictate that the income taxes should be $4,000 per year since the tax rate is 40% and income before taxes is $10,000. This requirement is supported by drawing attention to the fact that the total income taxes paid for the four years in Illustration 28.5 will be

Illustration 28.6

Net Income with No Tax Allocation

	1983	1984	1985	1986	Total
Income before depreciation and income taxes	$15,000	$15,000	$15,000	$15,000	$60,000
Depreciation (straight-line method) . .	5,000	5,000	5,000	5,000	20,000
Net income before taxes	$10,000	$10,000	$10,000	$10,000	$40,000
Income taxes (computed in Illustration 28.5)	4,000	2,960	3,040	6,000	16,000
Net income	$ 6,000	$ 7,040	$ 6,960	$ 4,000	$24,000

$16,000, the same as income tax expense for accounting purposes (4 × $4,000). Any taxes not paid in the early years of the automobiles' lives will be paid later—note the $6,000 of taxes in 1985—when, as the accountant would say, the timing differences reverse. In this case, reversing occurs in 1986 when depreciation is less for tax purposes than for financial reporting purposes.

Consequently, tax allocation procedures should be applied in the above circumstances. Under such procedures, the income statement for each of the four years is shown in Illustration 28.7. Under tax allocation, reported net income is $6,000 per year. Income tax expense is reported on the income statement at $4,000 per year regardless of the taxes actually payable each year.

Illustration 28.7

Net Income with Tax Allocation

	Each year	Total for four years
Income before depreciation and income taxes	$15,000	$60,000
Depreciation expense	5,000	20,000
Net income before taxes	$10,000	$40,000
Income taxes expense	4,000	16,000
Net income	$ 6,000	$24,000

The entries necessary in 1983, 1984, and 1985 to record income taxes on the company's books are given below:

	1983		1984		1985	
Federal Income Tax Expense	4,000		4,000		4,000	
Federal Income Taxes Payable		4,000		2,960		3,040
Deferred Federal Income Taxes Payable		–0–		1,040		960
To record income tax expense.						

The required entry for 1986 is:

Federal Income Tax Expense	4,000	
Deferred Federal Income Taxes Payable	2,000	
Federal Income Taxes Payable		6,000
To record income tax expense.		

The entries are posted to T-accounts below. When payments are actually made to the federal government, the Federal Income Taxes Payable account is debited and Cash is credited for the amount of the payment.

Federal Income Tax Expense		Federal Income Taxes Payable		Deferred Federal Income Taxes Payable	
1983 4,000			1983 4,000	1986 2,000	1983 –0–
1984 4,000			1984 2,960		1984 1,040
1985 4,000			1985 3,040		1985 960
1986 4,000			1986 6,000		
16,000			16,000		–0–

Note again that the amount of tax expense recognized remains constant at $4,000 even though the tax liability increases from $2,960 for 1984 to $6,000 for 1986. The normalizing of the tax expense for each year is accomplished by making entries in the Deferred Federal Income Taxes Payable account. The T-accounts clearly show that the tax expense for the four years is $16,000 and that the tax payments for the four years also sum to $16,000. The only difference is that the tax expense charged to each year is not the same amount as the actual liability for the year.

In this simplified example, the Deferred Federal Income Taxes Payable account has a zero balance at the end of four years. But actual business experience has shown that once a Deferred Federal Income Taxes Payable account is established, it is seldom decreased or reduced to zero. The reason is that most businesses acquire new depreciable assets, usually at higher prices. The result is that depreciation for tax purposes continues to be greater than depreciation for financial reporting purposes, and the balance in the Deferred Federal Income Taxes Payable account also continues to grow. For this reason, many accountants seriously question the validity of tax allocation in circumstances such as those described above. But discussion of this controversial issue must be left to a more advanced text. In the above example, the Deferred Federal Income Taxes Payable account would be reported as a long-term liability on the balance sheet because the item causing its existence (the machine) is classified as a long-term asset.

■ SUMMARY

Income taxes play a significant role in both personal and business decisions. Whenever a company or a person considers financial opportunities, the tax consequences of those opportunities need to be considered.

There are a number of steps in the determination of taxable income for an individual taxpayer. The general rule is that all income from all sources is included in gross income unless the item is specifically excluded. Among items specifically excluded are interest on state and municipal bonds, social security benefits, and workmen's compensation insurance benefits.

Certain deductions are subtracted from gross income to arrive at adjusted gross income. These deductions, called deductions for adjusted gross income, consist primarily of business expenses, contributions to IRA and Keogh retirement plans, and other specified items. A second set of deductions is subtracted from adjusted gross income. These deductions, called itemized deductions, include items such as taxes, interest expense, medical expenses, and charitable contributions. In addition to the itemized deductions, the taxpayer is permitted to subtract from adjusted gross income a certain amount of income that is exempt from taxation. The total amount of the exemptions depends on the taxpayer's marital status, number of dependents, age, and other factors. After the excess itemized deductions and the exemptions are subtracted from adjusted gross income, the result is taxable income.

The amount of tax due is determined by comparing the taxpayer's taxable income with either the tax table or the tax rate schedule that is appropriate for the taxpayer's filing status—single, married filing jointly, married filing separately, or unmarried head of household. The marginal tax rate is the tax rate that is applied to the next dollar of taxable income. The effective tax rate, on the other hand, is the average rate of tax paid on the taxpayer's total income. Long-term capital gains receive more favorable tax treatment than does ordinary income. Only 40% of the total amount of a taxable long-term capital gain is included in adjusted gross income, while the other 60% escapes taxation entirely.

Tax credits directly reduce the taxpayer's tax liability. Among the more common of the tax credits allowed to individual taxpayers are the investment tax credit, home energy conservation tax credit, alternative energy equipment tax credit, child and dependent care tax credit, low earned-income tax credit, and the credit for the elderly.

Personal income tax returns must be filed by April 15 of the year following the tax year. All taxpayers earning more than specified minimum amounts of income must file a tax return. Because of tax withholding requirements, most taxpayers will have paid most, if not all, of their income taxes for the year during the tax year.

Computing gross income for a corporation is much like computing gross income for an individual. Computing gross income for a corporation involves adding revenues from sales, services, and investments of the company. The computation of taxable income for a corporation involves subtracting allowable deductions from gross income; allowable deductions are expenses that are business related, reasonable in amount, necessary, and legal. Once taxable income is determined, a tax rate is applied to find the amount of the tax liability.

As noted with personal tax returns, tax credits are also available for corporations. The investment tax credit is particularly important for corporations. Corporations that suffer net losses for a taxable year may apply the loss to taxable income from prior years and recover some or all of the taxes paid during those years. This provision is known as a tax loss carryback. The corporation may then carry the loss forward and apply it to taxable income in future years, a provision known as a tax loss carryforward.

Tax depreciation is substantially different from depreciation used for accounting purposes. The Accelerated Cost Recovery System (ACRS) is a depreciation system that is mandatory for most property placed in service after December 31, 1980. The ACRS classifies depreciable assets into 3-, 5-, 10-, 15-, and 18-year classes and provides depreciation schedules for each of those classes of assets.

Certain types of revenues and expenses included in the computation of net income for book purposes are excluded from the computation of taxable income. These items give rise to permanent differences between taxable income and financial statement pre-tax income. Certain other revenue and expense items are recognized for tax purposes at different times than they are recognized for financial statement purposes. Those differences are referred to as timing differences. Interperiod tax allocation is a procedure whereby the effects of an element of expense or revenue, or loss or gain, that will affect taxable income are allocated to the period in which the item is recognized for accounting purposes, regardless of the period in which it is recognized for tax purposes.

The subject of personal and corporate income taxes concludes your introduction to the study of accounting. If you have not already done so, you may want to study Appendix A, which shows part of the annual report of the

General Motors Corporation, and Appendix B, which discusses international accounting.

Thank you for studying from our text. The knowledge you have gained will serve you well regardless of the career you choose.

APPENDIX: ACCELERATED COST RECOVERY SYSTEM DEPRECIATION ALLOWANCE TABLES

ACRS depreciation is, for the most part, mandatory for assets (new or used) purchased and put into service **after** December 31, 1980. Table 28.1 gives the depreciation rates for such assets.

Table 28.1

Personal Property Placed in Service after December 31, 1980

	Class of investment			
Ownership year	3 years (%)	5 years (%)	10 years (%)	15-year utility property (%)
1	25	15	8	5
2	38	22	14	10
3	37	21	12	9
4		21	10	8
5		21	10	7
6			10	7
7			9	6
8			9	6
9			9	6
10			9	6
11				6
12				6
13				6
14				6
15				6
	100	100	100	100

In using the ACRS table, keep in mind the following three rules:

1. Ignore salvage value. Apply the percentage to the cost of the asset.
2. If an asset is purchased and put into service at any time during the year, it will still receive a full year's depreciation (for tax purposes) for that calendar year.
3. Ignore the estimated useful life of an asset. The number of years that the asset is to be depreciated is determined strictly by its classification, not its useful life.

NEW TERMS INTRODUCED IN CHAPTER 28

Adjusted gross income

Gross income less deductions for adjusted gross income such as business expenses, employee moving expenses, payments to an individual retirement account (IRA), and certain other deductions (1076).

Capital assets

All items of property other than inventories, trade accounts and notes receivable, copyrights, government obligations due within one year and issued at a discount, and real or depreciable property used in a trade or business. Examples include investments in capital stocks and bonds (1081).

Deductions for adjusted gross income

Expenses of carrying on a trade, business, or practice of a profession, employee moving expenses, payments to an IRA or Keogh plan, forfeited interest penalty, and alimony paid (1076).

Deductions from adjusted gross income

Excess itemized deductions and exemptions (1077).

Effective tax rate

Average rate of taxation for a given amount of taxable income (1080).

Estimated tax

A tax that must be paid in four installments by persons having amounts of income above a certain level that are not subject to withholding (1083).

Excess itemized deductions

The amount by which itemized deductions exceed the zero bracket amount (1077).

Exemptions

A fixed amount, $1,000 in 1984 and $1,040 in 1985 due to indexing, that a taxpayer may deduct from adjusted gross income for the taxpayer, the spouse, and one more for each if blind or over 65, plus one more for each dependent (1078).

Gross income

All items of income from whatever source derived, except for those items specifically excluded by law (1075).

Head of household

Certain unmarried or legally separated persons (and those married to nonresident aliens) who maintain a residence for a relative or dependent (1075).

Interperiod tax allocation

A procedure whereby the tax effects of an element of expense or revenue, or loss or gain, that will affect taxable income are allocated to the period in which the item is recognized for accounting purposes, irrespective of the period in which it is recognized for tax purposes (1090).

Investment tax credit (ITC)

A direct reduction from tax liability equal to (1) 10% of the cost of certain qualifying business machinery and equipment purchased if the depreciable base is reduced by one half of the investment credit taken, or (2) 8% of the cost of certain qualifying business machinery and equipment purchased if there is no reduction in the depreciable base (1085).

Itemized deductions

Deductions from adjusted gross income for items such as contributions, interest paid, taxes, casualty losses, limited medical expenses, and other employment related expenses (1077).

Long-term capital gains

Gains resulting from the sale of capital assets and certain other assets that were held more than one year prior to sale. Preferential tax treatment is accorded such gains (1082).

Marginal tax rate

The tax rate that will be levied against the next dollar of taxable income (1079).

Permanent differences

Differences between taxable income and financial statement pre-tax income caused by tax law provisions that exclude an item of expense, revenue, gain, or loss as an element of taxable income (1089).

Personal property

Any property that is movable (not attached to land). Examples include trucks and machinery (1087).

Real property (real estate)

Land and any property attached to land, such as a building, which cannot be moved (1087).

Tax credit

A direct reduction from the amount of taxes to be paid, resulting largely from certain expenditures made (1082).

Tax loss carryback

Provision in tax law permitting corporations to apply a loss to their taxable income from prior years and recover some or all of the taxes paid during those years (1086).

Tax loss carryforward

Provision in tax law permitting corporations to carry any remaining, unused loss forward for up to 15 years to reduce their taxable income in future years (1086).

Tax rate schedules

Schedules showing the taxes levied on base amounts of income, plus the tax rate to be applied to amounts in excess of the base. Used by taxpayers with taxable incomes in excess of $50,000, and certain others (1079).

Tax tables

Tables provided by the IRS in which taxpayers can look up the amount of income taxes levied upon their taxable incomes (1079).

Taxable income

Adjusted gross income less excess itemized deductions and exemptions (1077).

Timing differences

Differences between taxable income and financial statement pre-tax income caused by items that affect both taxable income and pre-tax income, but in different periods (1089).

Total (gross) income

See Gross income.

Zero bracket amount

An amount that is built into the tax tables as a deduction that all can take. Itemized deductions can be deducted from adjusted gross income only to the extent that they exceed the zero bracket amount (1077).

DEMONSTRATION PROBLEM 28–1

Lee Nash is a CPA employed by a CPA firm at an annual salary of $45,000. He is single and has no dependents. Other information concerning his 1985 finances follows:

Gain on sale of stock acquired in 1982	$ 6,000
Loss on sale of stock purchased in November 1985	600
Interest received	1,500
Dividends received	2,440
Interest paid	690
Taxes paid:	
State income	1,800
Property	750
Sales	900
Professional dues and subscriptions to professional journals	475
Business entertainment expenses	300
Charitable contributions	400
Health insurance premiums	500
Drugs and medicine	700
Other medical and dental expenses	2,470
Income taxes withheld	12,000

Required: a.   Compute the taxable income for Mr. Nash. (Prepare a schedule similar to Illustration 28.4.)

               b.   Using the tax rate schedule in Illustration 28.3, compute the additional taxes due the IRS or the refund due Mr. Nash.

Solution to demonstration problem 28–1

a.		
Salary		$45,000
Interest income		1,500
Dividend income, less $100 exclusion		2,340
Long-term capital gain ($6,000) less short-term		
capital loss ($600)	$5,400	
Less: 60% exclusion	3,240	2,160
Adjusted gross income		$51,000

Excess itemized deductions:			
Interest paid		$ 690	
Taxes paid (state income, property, sales)		3,450	
Miscellaneous business expenses (entertainment,			
professional dues, journal subscriptions)		775	
Charitable contributions		400	
Health care:			
Health insurance premiums	$ 500		
Other medical and dental expenses	2,470		
Drugs and medicine	700		
	$3,670		
Less: 5% of adjusted gross income	2,550		
Medical deduction		1,120	
		$6,435	
Zero bracket amount		2,390	
Excess itemized deductions			4,045
			$46,955
Exemptions (1 × $1,040)			1,040
Taxable income			$45,915

b.		
Income tax [$10,913 + (0.45 × $4,415)]		$12,900
Income taxes withheld		12,000
Additional tax due		$ 900

DEMONSTRATION PROBLEM 28–2

The records of the Vista Corporation show the following for the calendar year 1988:

Sales	$385,000
Interest earned on—	
State of New Jersey bonds	3,000
City of Miami bonds	1,500
Essex County, Ohio, School District No. 2 bonds . .	375
Cost of goods sold and other expenses	315,000
Allowable extra depreciation for tax purposes	4,500
Dividends declared	15,000
Revenue received in advance, considered taxable	
income of this year	3,000
Contribution to influence legislation (included in	
"other expenses")	300

Required: a. Present a schedule showing the computation of taxable income.

b. Compute the amount of the corporation's tax that is payable for the current year. (Use the rates given in the text. Also assume the company acquired $100,000 of new equipment during the year and qualified for the full amount of investment credit [10%] as a reduction in taxes.)

c. Prepare the adjusting entry necessary to recognize federal income tax expense assuming income tax allocation procedures are followed. (The reduction in taxes caused by the investment credit is to be deducted from federal income tax expense and federal income tax currently payable.) The only permanent differences are the contribution to influence legislation and the nontaxable interest.

Solution to demonstration problem 28–2

a.

VISTA CORPORATION
Computation of Taxable Income and Income Taxes
For the Year 1988

Sales	$385,000
Cost of goods sold and other expenses	315,000
Reported income from operations	$ 70,000
Add: Revenue received in advance	3,000
Contribution to influence legislation	300
	$ 73,300
Less: Allowable additional depreciation	4,500
Taxable income	$ 68,800

b. Computation of tax liability:

15% of first $25,000	$ 3,750
18% of the next $25,000	4,500
30% of the remaining $18,800	5,640
Total tax before investment credit	$13,890
Less: Investment credit ($100,000 × 10%)	10,000
Total tax payable	$ 3,890

c.

Federal Income Tax Expense*	4,340	
Federal Income Taxes Payable		3,890
Deferred Federal Income Taxes Payable		450

To record federal income tax expense.

* Federal income tax expense is computed as follows:

Reported income from operations	$70,000
Add back permanent difference—contribution to	
influence legislature	300
Base for computing tax expense	$70,300

Computation of tax expense:

$25,000 at 15%	$ 3,750
$25,000 at 18%	4,500
$20,300 at 30%	6,090
Tax on $70,300	$14,340
Deduct reduction in taxes caused by investment credit†	10,000
Tax expense	$ 4,340

† If Vista chose to take a 10% investment credit the new equipment's depreciable base would have to be reduced by $5,000 (0.5 × $10,000).

DEMONSTRATION PROBLEM 28–3

On January 1, 1988, the Warman Corporation purchased new equipment for $20,000. The equipment falls into the three-year class under ACRS, but will be depreciated for accounting purposes over four years using the straight-line method.

Required: *a.* Using Table 28.1 in the Appendix, compute the depreciation for tax purposes for 1988, 1989, and 1990.

b. Assuming that there are no other timing differences and that net income before depreciation and income taxes is $80,000 for each of the four years, prepare a schedule showing taxable income and income taxes payable. Use a 40% rate.

c. Prepare a schedule showing net income with interperiod tax allocation for each of the four years.

d. Give the required adjusting journal entry at year-end to record income tax expense for each of the four years.

Solution to demonstration problem 28–3

a. 1988: $20,000 × 0.25 = $5,000
1989: $20,000 × 0.38 = $7,600
1990: $20,000 × 0.37 = $7,400

b.

	1988	*1989*	*1990*	*1991*
Income before depreciation and income taxes . . .	$80,000	$80,000	$80,000	$80,000
Depreciation	5,000	7,600	7,400	–0–
Taxable income	$75,000	$72,400	$72,600	$80,000
Income taxes payable (40%)	$30,000	$28,960	$29,040	$32,000

c.

	1988	*1989*	*1990*	*1991*
Income before depreciation and income taxes . . .	$80,000	$80,000	$80,000	$80,000
Depreciation	5,000	5,000	5,000	5,000
Pretax income	$75,000	$75,000	$75,000	$75,000
Income tax expense (40%)	30,000	30,000	30,000	30,000
Net income	$45,000	$45,000	$45,000	$45,000

d. 1988 Federal Income Tax Expense 30,000
          Federal Income Tax Payable   30,000
       To record federal income tax expense.

      1989 Federal Income Tax Expense 30,000
              Deferred Federal Income Taxes Payable   1,040
              Federal Income Tax Payable   28,960
           To record federal income tax expense.

      1990 Federal Income Tax Expense 30,000
              Deferred Federal Income Taxes Payable   960
              Federal Income Taxes Payable   29,040
           To record federal income tax expense.

      1991 Federal Income Tax Expense 30,000
            Deferred Federal Income Taxes Payable 2,000
              Federal Income Taxes Payable   32,000
           To record federal income tax expense.

QUESTIONS

1. What is the general rule for determining whether a particular cash receipt should be included in gross income? Name several items that might be considered income that are excluded from gross income. Why are they excluded?

2. Define the term *adjusted gross income* as it is used for personal income tax purposes.

3. For what kinds of expenditures may personal (itemized) deductions be taken on a personal income tax return? What effect does the zero bracket amount have on the total personal deductions that may be deducted from adjusted gross income?

4. What are exemptions, and by how much does one exemption reduce taxable income?

5. Why does a taxpayer wish a gain to qualify as a long-term capital gain, and how will a gain so qualify?

6. What is a tax credit? Give several examples of tax credits.

7. Which is the most valuable to a taxpayer: *(a)* an investment tax credit of $1,000, *(b)* a $1,000 allowed deduction for a contribution to an IRA, or *(c)* an additional exemption which is currently worth $1,000? In your answer, rank the three items according to their probable value to a taxpayer.

8. What does a person mean when making the statement, "I'm in the 44% bracket"?

9. What is an estimated tax? How is it levied and paid?

10. H Corporation has suffered a loss for the current year. How can the corporation treat this loss for tax purposes?

11. How is depreciation for accounting purposes different from tax depreciation?

12. What is the primary objective of ACRS depreciation? How does it accomplish this objective?

13. Distinguish between permanent differences and timing differences. List two items that might be a cause of each type of difference.

14. When is interperiod tax allocation used?

15. A classmate states: "Why all the fuss about deferring revenue and recognizing expenses sooner for tax purposes? All net taxable income is taxed eventually anyway. It is only a matter of putting off the payment. I don't think these manipulations are worth the effort." Comment.

16. Classified among the long-term liabilities of Corporation A is an account entitled "Deferred Federal Income Taxes Payable." Explain the nature of this account.

EXERCISES

E–1

Determine number of exemptions allowed

C. C. Chapwell is 65 years old; his wife is 65 years old and blind. They have three sons, ages 22, 24, and 30. The son who is 24 is a full-time student in law school and earns $4,000 per year. His parents contribute $6,000 annually toward his living expenses. The other two sons are fully self-supporting. How many exemptions are C. C. Chapwell and his wife entitled to claim on their joint return?

E–2

Compute tax liability

William Martin has gross income of $250,000, deductions for adjusted gross income of $25,000, excess itemized deductions of $60,000, and seven exemptions. He files a joint return with his wife who has no separate income. Using the tax rate schedule in Illustration 28.3 for married taxpayers filing jointly, compute their tax liability.

E–3

Identify items included in gross income

Identify those items listed below that would be included in gross income:

a. Tips received while working as a beautician.
b. Golf clubs won as a door prize while attending a conference.
c. Social security benefits.
d. A check received as reimbursement for medical expenses paid earlier this year.
e. Cash received from an uncle's estate.
f. Cash received from the proceeds of a life insurance policy on an aunt.
g. Employer-paid health insurance premiums amounting to $1,000.
h. Gain on the sale of a personal asset, a sail boat.
i. Interest earned on an IRA.
j. Scholarship received from a state university.

E–4

Calculate adjusted gross income

Using the following data, calculate the adjusted gross income for the joint return of Louise and George Harris:

Interest on State of Virginia bonds	$ 4,700
Salary of George	54,000
Dividend income—George	400
Dividend income—Lou	100
Irish Sweepstakes prize	500
Long-term capital gain on sale of stock	10,000
Cash received as personal award for injury suffered in auto accident	1,000

E–5

Compute amount of tax due or refund claimable

The following data are for Ann Skilman, a single taxpayer:

Salary	$28,000
Contribution to an IRA	2,000
Contribution to candidate running for Senate	60
Itemized personal expenses	2,790
Income taxes withheld from salary	4,500

Using the tax table in Illustration 28.2, compute the amount of tax due or refund claimable.

E–6

Compute taxable income

Lucy Frances has three exemptions even though she is unmarried. Her adjusted gross income is $20,100. Her itemized personal expenses amount to $2,690. Compute her taxable income.

E–7

Indicate effect of capital gains and losses on adjusted gross income

Given below are the capital gains and losses of two taxpayers, Harry and Sue. For each taxpayer, indicate the effect of the capital gains and losses on his or her adjusted gross income for the year.

	Harry	Sue
Long-term capital gains	$4,000	$ 500
Long-term capital losses	1,000	1,500
Short-term capital gains	500	3,000
Short-term capital losses	1,500	1,000

E–8

Compute the tax savings if a gain is long term rather than short term

Joe Murdock has $25,000 of taxable income from various sources. He also has a capital gain of $6,000. Using the tax table in Illustration 28.2, compute the amount of income taxes Joe would save if the gain is a long-term capital gain rather than a short-term capital gain. Assume Joe is single.

E–9

Determine amount of federal income taxes

Wuxtry Corporation had taxable income of $15,000, $30,000, and $45,000 in its first three years of operations. Determine the amount of federal income taxes it will incur each year assuming the first year of operations is 1983.

E–10

Compute tax liability

Sutton Corporation had taxable income of $130,000 in 1987. Compute the tax liability of Sutton Corporation.

E–11

Compute tax liability assuming an investment tax credit

Using the information in Exercise E–10, compute Sutton Corporation's tax liability assuming that during the year, $40,000 of plant assets were purchased which qualify for the investment tax credit and that the company chose to take the full 10% credit.

E–12

Determine amount of taxes recoverable due to a loss carryback

Gordon Company suffered a $60,000 loss in its fifth year of operations. Information from Gordon's previous tax returns is given below:

Year	Taxable income	Taxes paid
1	$30,000	$4,650
2	35,000	5,550
3	15,000	2,250
4	25,000	3,750

Assuming that Gordon elects to carry the loss back, determine the amount of taxes that can be recovered for each of the previous years.

E–13

Compute depreciation using ACRS tables

Sun Company purchased equipment that falls into the three-year class under ACRS. The equipment was purchased for $50,000 on July 1, 1985, and placed into service immediately. Compute the 1987 depreciation for tax purposes (use Appendix Table 28.1).

E–14

Prepare journal entry to record income tax chargeable and tax liability for year

The pre-tax income of the R Corporation for a given year amounts to $200,000, while its taxable income is only $160,000. The difference is attributable entirely to additional depreciation taken for tax purposes. If the current income tax rate is 40%, give the entry to record the income tax expense and income tax liability for the year.

PROBLEMS SERIES A

P28–1–A

Compute amount of tax due or refund claimable

Elizabeth Powers is a professional model and is considered self-employed for tax purposes. She is single and has no dependents. She gathered the following information for your use in preparing her 1985 income tax return:

Business income	$50,000
Royalties received	2,000
Interest received (including $100 on New York City bonds)	1,300
Long-term capital gain	5,000
Contribution to a retirement account (Keogh plan)	7,000
Medical and dental expenses including $400 medical insurance premiums paid and $200 of lotions	3,896
Property taxes on residence	2,690
State sales tax	420
State income tax	4,200
Interest paid	6,500
Contributions to church and charitable organizations	2,800
Theft loss, excess over $100	2,100
Political contributions	200
Estimated taxes paid and income taxes withheld	8,000

Required: Using the tax table in Illustration 28.2, compute the additional income taxes due or the refund claimable.

P28-2-A

Prepare table showing taxes due or refund claimable

Bob and Alice Jensen file a joint tax return. They have three children; the oldest is Dan, who is 20 and a full-time student. Although Dan earned $2,500 in the current year, he still gets most of his support from his parents. Bob earned a salary of $34,000 in 1985. He also received $500 income from interest and $80 from dividends. He sold some bonds held for three years at a gain of $3,000 and also sold some stock held for eight months at a loss of $500. Alice received $330 of interest on City of Detroit bonds and $420 of dividends. Total income taxes withheld were $4,800. Among the personal expenditures of the Jensen family are the following:

Investment in an IRA	$2,000
State income taxes	1,300
Social security taxes withheld	2,212
Property taxes on residence	2,040
State sales tax	400
Charitable contributions	700
Contribution to political candidate	125
Interest paid	1,200
Medical costs, including $400 of health insurance premiums, and cost of drugs and medicine of $500 . . .	2,638
Miscellaneous items consisting of investment advice and subscriptions, and fee paid for income tax return preparation	260

Required: Prepare a schedule similar to Illustration 28.4 showing the taxes due or refund claimable.

P28-3-A

Calculate income tax due

Consider the following data, which pertain to four individuals:

			Expenditures on—			
Individual	Tax status	Taxable income	Assets qualifying for the investment credit of 10%	Energy conservation	Qualified alternative energy equipment	Qualified political contributions
1 . . .	Single	$24,610	$5,000		$3,000	$220
2 . . .	Married filing jointly	54,000		$4,000		250
3 . . .	Head of household	28,000		1,200		
4 . . .	Married filing separately	25,000	4,000		2,500	

Required: None of the individuals has ever before taken a credit for energy conservation or alternative energy equipment. Using the data given above and either the table in Illustration 28.2 or the schedules in Illustration 28.3 (whichever is appropriate), calculate the amount of federal income taxes currently due from each of the individuals.

P28-4-A

Compute taxable income; calculate the tax liability for year

The following information relates to the activities of the Paradise Company for 1984:

Sales	$900,000
Interest income—	
State of Alabama Bonds	8,000
ABC Corporation Bonds	9,000
Cost of goods sold	675,000
Other expenses	125,000
Extra depreciation allowed for tax purposes	15,000
Amortization of goodwill, included in "other expenses"	1,100

In February 1984, Paradise purchased for $50,000 machinery qualifying for an investment tax credit and will take an investment credit of 10%.

Required: a. Compute the taxable income for Paradise Company.

b. Calculate the tax liability for the current year using the tax rates given in the chapter.

P28–5–A

Calculate tax liability making various assumptions about a loss carryback

The Harvest Company had the following amounts of taxable income (loss) in the years indicated:

1983	$40,000
1984	50,000
1985	30,000
1986 . . . . (see parts [a], [b], and [c] below)	
1987	15,000
1988	45,000
1989	20,000
1990	50,000
1991	75,000
1992	90,000

Assume that the rates for 1984 are in effect for the entire period.

Required: a. If the loss in 1986 is $120,000 and is carried back, what amount of back taxes would Harvest be eligible to recover?

b. Assuming that the loss in 1986 is $210,000 and is first carried back, what amount of taxes would Harvest be required to pay for the years 1987–92?

c. If the 1986 loss is $350,000 and is carried back, what amount of taxes would be paid for the years 1987–92?

d. If, after 15 years, there is an unused carryforward remaining, what happens to it?

P28–6–A

Calculate depreciation allowance using the ACRS tables

The Samford Company purchased equipment for $80,000, which has an estimated useful life of six years and falls into the five-year category under ACRS.

Required: For each year that the equipment is expected to be used, calculate the depreciation allowance for tax purposes assuming the equipment was purchased and put into use in 1984. (Use Table 28.1 in the Appendix.)

P28–7–A

Prepare schedule showing tax liability and income tax allocation; prepare year-end entries to recognize income tax expense; summarize the entries in T-accounts

The ABC Telephone Company expects to have income before depreciation and income taxes of $200,000 each year for the period 1984–87. On January 1, 1984, the company acquired light-duty trucks for $160,000, which are expected to last four years and have no salvage value at the end of that period. For financial accounting purposes the company uses the straight-line depreciation method, and for tax purposes it uses the ACRS three-year class (see Appendix, Table 28.1). Assume that the tax rate is 40% and that there are no other items that cause differences between pre-tax income and taxable income.

Required: a. Prepare a schedule showing the actual tax liability for each year.

b. Calculate the income tax expense that should be shown each year assuming that income tax allocation procedures are used.

c. Prepare journal entries to record the tax expense and tax liability for each year.

d. Show how the entries prepared in part *(c)* would be summarized in T-accounts. How would the amounts appearing in these accounts eventually be cleared?

PROBLEMS, SERIES B

P28–1–B

Prepare schedule showing computation of additional taxes due or refund claimable

Alan Grimes is a systems analyst for a computer company at an annual salary of $50,000. He also provides consulting services from which he derived $16,000 of income in 1985 after deducting related expenses. Alan is single and has no dependents. Other data for 1985 include:

Interest received	$ 2,500
Long-term capital gain from sale of securities	2,500
Contribution to a retirement (Keogh) plan	2,400
Interest paid	1,000
Medical and dental expenses, including medical insurance premium paid of $450 and drugs and medicine of $200	2,463
Taxes:	
State income	2,600
Property taxes on residence	2,200
Sales	500
Contributions to charitable organizations	600
Professional dues, subscriptions to professional publications, business entertainment, safe-deposit box rentals, etc.	390
Casualty loss ($550 damage loss to automobile, less $200 deductible amount paid by Alan)	350
Income taxes withheld	10,200
Estimated taxes paid	8,000

Required: Using the tax schedule for a single taxpayer in Illustration 28.3, present a schedule similar to Illustration 28.4 showing the computation of the additional taxes due or the refund claimable.

P28–2–B

Prepare schedule showing computation of additional taxes due or refund claimable

Joy and Rob Bakke, who are married and are the parents of two school-age children, file a joint tax return. They provide almost all of the support for Joy's mother, age 66, who lives with them. In 1985, Rob earned a salary of $43,000. They earned $800 of taxable interest during the year. They received $500 of dividends and realized a long-term capital gain of $5,000. Rob invested $2,000 in an IRA. Other data for the year are:

State income taxes paid	$1,900
State sales taxes paid	350
Property taxes paid on residence	2,080
Contributions (including $200 of clothing donated to neighbors who suffered a loss from fire)	660
Interest paid (on mortgage, $4,500; on auto loan, $1,000)	5,500
Medical expenses paid (including health insurance premium of $500 and drugs and medicine of $300)	2,452
Miscellaneous expenses paid (all deductible)	200
Income tax withheld	8,000

Required: Prepare a schedule similar to Illustration 28.4 showing the additional taxes due or refund claimable.

P28–3–B

Calculate amount of federal income tax due

Consider the following data, which pertain to four individual taxpayers:

Individual	Tax status	Taxable income	Assets qualifying for the investment credit of 10%	Energy conservation	Qualified alternative energy equipment
			Expenditures on—		
A	Married filing jointly	$66,000	$5,000		$3,000
B	Head of household	32,000		$2,500	
C	Married filing separately	32,140			
D	Single	31,720	4,500	1,400	

Required: None of the individuals has ever before taken a credit for energy conservation or alternative energy equipment. Using the data given above and either the table in Illustration 28.2 or the schedules in Illustration 28.3 (whichever is appropriate), calculate the amount of federal income tax due for each individual.

P28–4–B

Prepare schedule showing computation of taxable income; compute the tax liability

The records of the Rawhide Corporation show the following for the year 1984:

Sales	$750,000
Interest earned on—	
State of New York bonds	6,000
City of Detroit bonds	3,000
Howard County, Ohio, School District No. 1 bonds	750
Cost of goods sold and other expenses	630,000
Loss on sale of asset	6,000
Gain on sale of asset	15,000
Allowable extra depreciation deduction for tax purposes	9,000
Dividends declared	30,000
Revenue received in advance, considered taxable income of this year	6,000
Contribution made to influence legislation (included in the $630,000 listed above)	600

Required:
a. Present a schedule showing the computation of taxable income.
b. Compute the corporation's tax for the current year using the tax rates given in this chapter.

P28–5–B

Calculate tax liability making various assumptions about a loss carryback

The Squash Company had the following amounts of taxable income (loss) in the years indicated:

1983	$30,000
1984	20,000
1985	60,000
1986 . . . . (see parts [a], [b], and [c] below)	
1987	40,000
1988	10,000
1989	50,000
1990	70,000
1991	80,000
1992	65,000

Assume that the rates for 1984 are in effect for the entire period.

Required:
a. If the loss in 1986 is $110,000 and is carried back, how much would the company recover in back taxes?
b. If the loss in 1986 is $180,000 and is first carried back, how much would the company have to pay in taxes for the period 1987–92?

c. If the loss in 1986 is $400,000 and is carried back, how much would the company have to pay in taxes for the period 1987–92?

d. If there is an unused carryforward at the end of 15 years, what happens to it?

P28-6-B

Calculate depreciation using the ACRS tables

The We-Haul Company purchased a van for $15,000 to use in making its local deliveries. Under ACRS, the van is classified as a three-year investment.

Required: Compute depreciation for tax purposes for each year assuming that the van was purchased and put into use in 1984. (Use Appendix Table 28.1.)

P28-7-B

Prepare schedules showing taxable income, income taxes due, and income tax allocation; prepare year-end entries to recognize income tax expense

On January 1, 1984, Alexander Corporation acquired light-duty trucks for $100,000 that are expected to have a four-year life and no salvage value. The company uses the ACRS (three-year class) method of depreciation for tax purposes (see the Appendix, Table 28.1) and the straight-line method for book purposes. There are no other timing differences. Net income before depreciation and income taxes is $100,000 for each of the four years.

Required: a. Prepare a schedule showing taxable income and income taxes due for each of the four years using a 40% tax rate.

b. Prepare a schedule showing income tax expense assuming that income tax allocation procedures are used.

c. Prepare the year-end adjusting entry required at the end of each of the four years to recognize federal income tax expense.

BUSINESS DECISION PROBLEM

Determine whether a project is acceptable by using net present value method

J. W. Enterprises is considering whether or not to invest in a fleet of delivery vans, thereby expanding into a new business area for the company. Mike Livingston, president of J. W. Enterprises, estimates that the vans will generate a net cash inflow before income taxes of $150,000 per year for four years. The fleet of vans would cost $400,000 and would have an estimated useful life of four years. The vans will be classified as three-year property under ACRS tax regulations. The vans will qualify for the 10% investment tax credit.

Required: Assume the company is subject to a 40% income tax rate and that all cash flows, except the $400,000 cost, fall at the end of the year. Show whether this project is acceptable, assuming the company requires a minimum return of 15%. (Hint: Use the net present value method of appraising alternative investment projects, as discussed in Chapter 27. Recall that the tax basis of the vans must be reduced 5% when a 10% investment tax credit is claimed.)

BUSINESS SITUATION FOR DISCUSSION

Summary of Major Tax Reform Proposals*

☐   **The Second Time Around.**   President Reagan has launched his version of major tax reform. Referred to as "Treasury II," the new proposals reflect considerable reworking of the first set of proposals released by the Treasury Department last November. Some proposals have been made more economically sound, particularly in light of their practical application, and Treasury II is generally more politically palatable. Similar to its predecessor, Treasury II strives to be revenue-neutral in total although clearly favoring individuals at the expense of the business community.

This issue of the *E&W Washington Tax Reporter* explores the Treasury II proposals in some detail. Most of the proposals are contrasted with current law and the Bradley-Gephardt "Fair Tax" and Kemp-Kasten "Fair and Simple Tax" bills that are also before Congress. Congress will most likely shape any tax reform legislation to restructure the tax code from among these four alternatives. For brevity within this text, we refer to these proposals as "T-II" (Treasury II), "B-G" (Bradley Gephardt), and "K-K" (Kemp-Kasten). [See Table 1 for a summary.]

Now the Trading Begins.   Several congressional committees are currently holding hearings on tax reform. These hearings are expected to last throughout the summer. Of course this is only the beginning, and although the prospects for reform presently appear high, Congress could easily become embroiled in "horse trading" and compromise that substantially alter Treasury II or result in its demise. As the various proposals are scrutinized, one by one, the debate often revolves around whether or not each "fairness" will inevitably override the objective of simplicity.

*   *   *   *   *

Comparison of Major Tax Reform Items

Tax Rates.   Currently, individuals are taxed in 14 brackets (according to taxable income and filing status) at rates varying from 11% to 50%, and corporations are taxed at 46% (except for 15% to 40% on the first $100,000). Treasury II (T-II) compresses the individual brackets to three at 15%, 25% and 35%, with the maximum corporate rate after the first $75,000 being 33%. However, the new rates are not effective until July 1, 1986, so that actual 1986 rates would be halfway between the current and new rates. Bradley-Gephardt

(B-G) proposes individual rates on adjusted gross income (AGI) of 14%, 26%, and 30%, and a flat corporate rate of 30%. An individual's itemized deductions and personal exemptions first reduce taxes at the 14% rate, rather than the highest applicable rate. Kemp-Kasten (K-K) sets forth a 24 percent rate for individuals, although the effective rates on earned income may be as low as 19.2% due to a progressive exclusion, and the rate on investment income may be as high as 28.8% because of a technical adjustment for gross income in excess of the FICA maximum wage base (at least $41,700 in 1986). The K-K maximum corporate rate is 35% (15% to 25% on the first $100,000).

The top corporate tax rate would be reduced to 33%. The first $75,000 of taxable income would be subject to rates of 15%, 18%, and 25% in $25,000 brackets. The graduated ratio would be phased out for corporations with income in excess of $140,000 and would be totally eliminated for those with $360,000 of taxable income.

Personal/Dependent Exemptions.   Under current law, for 1986 the personal exemption for an individual and each dependent will be approximately $1,080 because of indexing for inflation. T-II increases exemptions to $2,000 beginning in 1986 but removes the exemptions for blindness and persons 65 or over. T-II also provides that the $2,000 would be indexed for inflation. B-G calls for a $1,600 personal exemption for each taxpayer ($1,800 for head of household) with a $1,000 exemption for each dependent. K-K has $2,000 personal and dependent exemptions.

Zero Bracket Amount.   As currently projected, the standard deduction (zero bracket amount) for single, head of household, and joint returns is expected to be about $2,480, $2,480 and $3,670 in 1986 when adjusted for inflation. This compares to $2,900, $3,600 and $4,000 under T-II; $3,000, $3,000 and $6,000 under B-G; and $2,600, $3,200 and $3,300 under K-K. Both T-II and K-K provide for indexing of the standard deduction. The deduction for the married filing separately status is one-half the amount for a joint return in all instances.

*   *   *   *   *

Bad Debt Deductions.   If a taxpayer uses the direct write-off method under current law, deductions are allowed for debts that are determined worthless during the taxable year. Alternatively, a taxpayer may use the reserve method, which allows a current deduction based on estimated future uncollectible debts. T-II limits all taxpayers to the direct write-off method and eliminates the reserve method. Both B-G and K-K retain current law

Table 1 Comparison of Major Tax Reform Proposals on Selected Items

Item for 1986	Current law	Treasury II	Bradley-Gephardt	Kemp-Kasten
Regular Tax Rates Personal	14 brackets from 11% to 50%	15%, 25%, 35% beginning 7-1-86	14%, 26%, 30% (exemptions and itemized deductions first reduce taxes at the 14% rate)	24% although effective rates vary between 19.2% and 28.8%
Corporate	46%, except 15% to 40% on first $100,000	33%, except 15% to 25% on first $75,000, begins 7-1-86	Flat rate of 30%	35%, except 15% to 25% on first $100,000
Personal and dependent exemptions	$1,080 (1986 estimate), indexed for inflation	$2,000 for 1986, indexed for inflation, no elderly or blind exemption	$1,600 ($1,800 for household) personal exemption, $1,000 exemption for dependents	$2,000 per exemption
Zero bracket amount (standard deduction)	$2,480 single and head of household returns $3,670 joint return (1986 indexed estimates)	$2,900 single return $3,600 head of household $4,000 joint return (all indexed for inflation)	$3,000 single return $3,000 head of household $6,000 joint return (not indexed)	$2,600 single return $3,200 head of household $3,300 joint return (all indexed for inflation)
Life insurance and annuity inside build-up	Increases in cash surrender value not included in gross income	Coverage added after action by a tax-writing committee will create interest income equal to the increase in cash surrender value over investment in contract	Add to gross income the annual excess of change in cash surrender value, withdrawals, insurance cost and policy dividends over premiums paid	Add to gross income the annual excess of change in cash surrender value, withdrawals, insurance cost and policy dividends over premiums paid
Employer-paid health insurance	Exclusion of employer-paid insurance premiums	Taxed up to $10 per month for single individuals and $25 per month for families	Exclusion limited to payments made during periods when an employee is absent from work due to illness or disability	Retain current law
Long-term capital gains (individuals)	Net long-term capital gain (LTCG) deduction of 60%, top rate of 20%, no indexed basis	50% LTCG deduction, top rate of 17.5% for stocks and other non-depreciable investment property, optional indexation after 1990; depreciable property and business property generally taxed on 100% of gain after inflation adjustment	All capital gains are ordinary income, top rate of 30%	Yearly election to (1) have all capital gains indexed for inflation and taxed at ordinary rates, or (2) take a 40% of net LTCG deduction without the benefit of indexation
State and local taxes (as itemized deductions)	Fully deductible	Repeal the deduction by individual taxpayers for state and local taxes	Repeal the deduction for personal property and general sales taxes for individuals, but retain the income and real estate tax deductions	Repeal the deduction for income, personal property, and general sales taxes for individuals, but retain real estate tax deduction
Interest expense	Fully deductible, except investment interest in excess of net investment income plus $10,000	Interest deduction for individuals limited to principal residence mortgage, $5,000 ($10,000 until 1988) and net investment income	Interest deduction for qualified residences plus nonbusiness interest to the extent of net investment income	No personal interest deduction in excess of certain housing interest and certain educational loan

Table 1 *(concluded)*

Item for 1986	Current law	Treasury II	Bradley-Gephardt	Kemp-Kasten
Retirement plans (IRAs)	$2,000 maximum contribution ($2,250 total with a non-working spouse)	$2,000 maximum contribution ($4,000 total with a non-working spouse)	Retain current law	Retain current
40(k) (cash deferred)	Maximum contribution limit of the lesser of $30,000 or 25% of compensation	Maximum contribution limit of $8,000; IRA contributions reduce limit	Retain current law, except the $30,000 limit is reduced to $20,000	Retain current law
Business meals and entertainment	Deduction allowed for all ordinary and necessary expenses	Deny most entertainment expenses, business meals in a clear business setting, limited to $25 per person plus 50% of the excess over $25	Retain current law	Retain current law
Investment tax credit	10% (4%–25% on selected property)	Repeal credit	Repeal credit	Repeal credit
Depreciation	ACRS—3, 5, 10, 15 and 18 year property classes with liberal writeoffs	CCRS—6 classes with 4 to 28 year lives, ranges from approximately 200% declining balance to straight-line depreciation indexed for inflation	SCRS—6 classes with 4 to 40 year lives, approximately 250% declining balance depreciation, not indexed	NCRS—5 classes with 4 to 25 year lives, modifies current ACRS, economic equivalent of expensing, indexed for inflation
Percentage depletion and intangible drilling costs	Percentage depletion allowed, intangible drilling costs deducted in year incurred	Percentage depletion generally phased out for all minerals over five-year period except for stripper wells, expense option for intangible drilling costs retained	Repeal percentage depletion and replace with SCRS, repeal expensing intangible drilling costs for oil, gas and geothermal wells, repeal depletion allowance for timber	Retain current law, except that depletion allowance for timber is repealed
Bad debt deductions	Deduction allowed for worthless debt within the taxable year or, if under the reserve method, expected worthless debts are provided for	All taxpayers limited to actual bad debt write-offs during the year	Increase in the reserve for bad debts for any financial institution is limited to the experience method, otherwise current law retained	Increase in the reserve for bad debts for any financial institution is limited to the experience method, otherwise current law retained
Restrict use of cash-basis accounting	Compute taxable income under the method used in keeping the books and records of the business	Accrual method mandatory for businesses with more than $5 million in receipts or accrual basis reporting to outsiders	Require taxable income from farming (including timber) to be computed on the accrual basis, except for certain taxpayers with gross receipts not exceeding $1 million	Require taxable income from farming (including timber) to be computed on the accrual basis, except for certain taxpayers with gross receipts not exceeding $1 million
Dividends-paid deduction	No provision	Deduction for 10% of dividends paid	No provision	No provision
Corporate minimum tax	Tax equal to 15% of the amount by which the sum of tax preference items exceeds the greater of $10,000 or the regular tax	Replace add-on minimum tax with 20% alternative minimum tax containing an expanded list of preference items	Repeal corporate minimum tax	Retain current law

except for limiting the reserve for bad debts of any financial institution to the experience method.

Use of Cash-Basis Accounting Restricted. Personal service proprietorships, partnerships and corporations may currently compute taxable income on either the cash method or the accrual method. T-II makes the accrual method mandatory for those businesses with more than $5 million in receipts *or* those businesses that report on the accrual basis to outsiders (e.g., shareholders, partners, or for credit purposes). Both B-G and K-K require taxable income from farming (including tim-

ber) to be computed on the accrual basis except for certain taxpayers whose gross receipts do not exceed $1 million.

Dividends-Paid Deduction. There is no provision in either current law, B-G or K-K for a dividends-paid deduction. T-II would permit a deduction equal to 10% of "qualified" dividends paid to stockholders of most domestic corporations. To the extent applicable, a dividends-paid deduction avoids the double taxation of corporate earnings.

*   *   *   *   *

APPENDIX

A

A Set of Consolidated Financial Statements and Other Financial Data for General Motors Corporation

GENERAL MOTORS ANNUAL REPORT 1984

HIGHLIGHTS

(Dollars in Millions Except Per Share and Hourly Amounts)

	1984	1983	1982
Sales and Revenues			
United States operations			
Automotive products	$73,053.1	$63,665.0	$47,391.2
Nonautomotive products	2,107.6	1,670.3	2,138.9
Defense and space	1,322.7	826.8	793.8
Computer systems services (since October 18, 1984)	148.7	—	—
Total United States operations	76,632.1	66,162.1	50,323.9
Canadian operations	12,581.6	11,232.4	7,972.6
Overseas operations	11,345.5	11,955.5	12,212.8
Elimination of interarea sales and revenues	(16,669.3)	(14,768.4)	(10,483.7)
Total	$83,889.9	$74,581.6	$60,025.6
Worldwide automotive products	$80,499.3	$71,904.7	$56,676.8
Worldwide nonautomotive products	$ 3,390.6	$ 2,676.9	$ 3,348.8
Worldwide Factory Sales of Cars and Trucks (units in thousands)	8,256	7,769	6,244
Net Income			
Amount	$ 4,516.5	$ 3,730.2	$ 962.7
As a percent of sales and revenues	5.4%	5.0%	1.6%
As a percent of stockholders' equity	18.7%	18.0%	5.3%
Attributable to:			
$1-2/3 par value common stock	$ 4,485.3	$ 3,717.3	$ 949.8
Class E common stock (issued in 1984)	$ 18.7	—	—
Earnings per share of common stocks:			
$1-2/3 par value common	$14.22	$11.84	$3.09
Class E common (issued in 1984)	$1.03	—	—
Cash dividends per share of common stocks:			
$1-2/3 par value common	$4.75*	$2.80	$2.40
Class E common (issued in 1984)	$0.09	—	—
Taxes			
United States, foreign and other income taxes (credit)	$ 1,805.1	$ 2,223.8	($ 252.2)
Other taxes (principally payroll and property taxes)	3,572.4	2,675.8	2,470.3
Total	$ 5,377.5	$ 4,899.6	$ 2,218.1
Taxes per share of $1-2/3 par value common stock	$16.98	$15.61	$7.22
Investment as of December 31			
Cash and marketable securities	$ 8,567.4	$ 6,216.9	$ 3,126.2
Working capital	$ 6,276.7	$ 5,890.8	$ 1,658.1
Stockholders' equity	$24,214.3	$20,766.6	$18,287.1
Book value per share of common stocks:			
$1-2/3 par value common	$72.16	$64.88	$57.64
Class E common (issued in 1984)	$36.08	—	—
Number of Stockholders as of December 31 (in thousands)			
$1-2/3 par value common and preferred	957	998	1,050
Class E common	623	—	—
Worldwide Employment (including financing and insurance subsidiaries)			
Average number of employes (in thousands)	748	691	657
Total payrolls (including profit sharing)	$22,505.4	$19,605.3	$17,043.8
Total cost of an hour worked—U.S. hourly employes	$22.60	$21.80	$21.50
Property			
Real estate, plants and equipment—Expenditures	$ 3,595.1	$ 1,923.0	$ 3,611.1
—Depreciation	$ 2,663.2	$ 2,569.7	$ 2,403.0
Special tools—Expenditures	$ 2,452.1	$ 2,083.7	$ 2,601.0
—Amortization	$ 2,236.7	$ 2,549.9	$ 2,147.5
Total expenditures	$ 6,047.2	$ 4,006.7	$ 6,212.1

What Happened to the Revenue GM Received During 1984

100%

Suppliers 49.5%

Employes 32.8%

Taxes 6.4%

Depreciation and Amortization 5.9%

Use in the Business 3.6%

Stockholders 1.8%

*In addition, in December 1984 holders of $1-2/3 par value common stock received one share of Class E common stock for every 20 shares of $1-2/3 par value common stock held.

LETTER TO STOCKHOLDERS

February 4, 1985

*I*n all the 76-year history of General Motors, there has been no other year like 1984—a year of profound and unprecedented change affecting GM people, products, plants, and processes. At the same time, it was a second successive year of record performance as General Motors earned net income of $4.5 billion, or $14.22 per share of $1-2/3 par value common stock, on worldwide sales and revenues of $83.9 billion.

The first of many milestone events in 1984 was a major reorganization announced in January to consolidate GM's North

---

"...1984—a year of profound and unprecedented change affecting GM people, products, plants, and processes."

American passenger car operations into two integrated car groups which function as self-contained business units. Each of the restructured groups is totally responsible for the engineering, manufacturing, assembly, and marketing of its own cars; each is accountable for its own quality, performance, and profitability. Primary objectives of this organizational change are to provide more effective use of people and to accelerate the response to the changing marketplace. Within each group, GM passenger cars will continue to be marketed in North America under the Chevrolet and Pontiac and the Buick, Oldsmobile, and Cadillac nameplates through our well-established and aggressive wholesale selling and dealer organizations to continue to serve the customer most effectively.

April marked the introduction of all-new Buick Electra, Oldsmobile Ninety-Eight, and Cadillac DeVille and Fleetwood luxury cars built in GM's newest plants in Wentzville, Missouri and Orion Township, Michigan.

*Y*our Corporation was honored in July when President Reagan came to Michigan to dedicate the Orion Township plant and view GM's high-technology Project Saturn at the GM Technical Center. Saturn, a new approach to building a line of subcompact cars competitive with small cars made anywhere in the world, became an operating unit six months later with the announcement of Saturn Corporation, a separate subsidiary formed to add a sixth nameplate to GM's domestic passenger car marques.

October saw the introductions of more all-new models. These included sporty Buick Somerset Regal, Oldsmobile Calais, and Pontiac Grand Am coupes and Chevrolet Astro and GMC Safari compact vans built in completely modernized plants in Lansing, Michigan and Baltimore, Maryland, respectively. Chevrolet Sprint and Spectrum small cars imported from GM's Japanese affiliates, Suzuki and Isuzu, debuted regionally.

The year was also a milestone in labor relations as General Motors and the United Auto Workers reached accord on a historic new national agreement. The three-year contract ratified in October provides unprecedented job security as well as solid economic gains for our U.S. employes, and also affords GM the opportunity to achieve increased competitiveness. New agreements also were negotiated with the UAW in Canada and with other unions representing our employes. These pacts enabled us to resume building upon the spirit of cooperation already taking hold between management and labor.

Roger B. Smith

Compensation changes to address the unique needs of GM's salaried work force were subsequently approved. Progress in equal employment opportunity was encouraging as employment of minorities and women in GM's work force reflected further improvement in 1984.

In October, the alliance between General Motors and Electronic Data Systems Corporation was formally approved. EDS is a world leader in the design of large-scale data processing systems, the operation of cost-effective data processing centers and networks, and the integration of large data processing and communications systems. Operating as an independent consolidated subsidiary, EDS will benefit GM by more effective control of health insurance costs, increased data processing capabilities within General Motors Acceptance Corporation, and improved delivery of computer services throughout GM. In addition, GM will work with EDS to develop advanced computer systems for manufacturing process control and order entry—for GM's own use, for use by our dealers and suppliers, and for sale to other customers. EDS' expertise will play a major role in Saturn and the Factory of the Future, a "learning laboratory" being built at Saginaw Steering Gear Division. The 1984 acquisition of an interest in an artificial intelligence firm and a number of high-technology companies specializing in machine vision also is helping us move toward the Factory of the Future.

"The year was also a milestone in labor relations as General Motors and the United Auto Workers reached accord on a historic new national agreement."

In our continuing commitment to product quality, GM acquired an interest in Philip Crosby Associates, Inc., a quality consulting firm that operates Quality College in Winter Park, Florida. GM people have trained there, and the association was the impetus for GM's own Quality Institute.

As the year ended, the Opel Kadett/Vauxhall Astra won the prestigious European "Car of the Year" award, the first time for a General Motors product. New United Motor Manufacturing, Inc., the joint venture with Japan's Toyota Motor Corporation, bore fruit in December when the new Chevrolet Nova made its first appearance at Fremont, California. This sparkling new star goes on sale in the late spring of 1985.

*T*he year sparkled in the financial statements as well. Net income of $4.5 billion on sales and revenues of $83.9 billion surpassed previous highs of $3.7 billion earned on sales of $74.6 billion in 1983. Earnings per share of $14.22 on $1-2/3 par value common stock compared with $11.84 per share in 1983 and the previous record of $12.24 per share on fewer shares outstanding in 1978. Net income was $963 million, or $3.09 per share, on sales of $60.0 billion in 1982.

F. James McDonald

Worldwide factory sales (sales of vehicles to GM dealers) in 1984 totaled 8.3 million cars and trucks, up from 7.8 million units in 1983 and 6.2 million units in 1982.

Late June brought a metalworkers' strike in the Federal Republic of Germany, resulting in production losses that kept General Motors from record overseas factory sales volume. This disruption and local strikes in the United States and Canada reduced net income in 1984 by about $450 million.

Reflecting GM's strong performance and prospects, the Board of Directors increased the cash dividend on the $1-2/3 par value common stock from $1.00 to $1.25 per share in the second quarter of 1984 and continued this rate through the fourth quarter. This resulted in cash dividends of $4.75 per share for the year, compared with $2.80 per share paid in 1983 and $2.40 per share in 1982.

In addition, the Board declared a fourth quarter dividend of one share of the new Class E common stock—first issued in connection with the acquisition of EDS—for every 20 shares of the $1-2/3 par value common stock. The Class E common stock issued as a dividend provided GM stockholders an immediate identification with EDS. This dividend, valued at $1.90 per share of $1-2/3 par value common stock, resulted in a total 1984 dividend payout on the $1-2/3 par value common stock equivalent to $6.65 per share. The 1984 dividend actions also recognized the continuing need for substantial investments in the business to achieve international cost competitiveness.

Earnings per share of Class E common stock for the period October 18 to December 31, 1984 amounted to $1.03. A fourth quarter cash dividend of $0.09 per share was paid on Class E common stock prior to its distribution to $1-2/3 par value common stockholders.

*I*n all, stockholders participated in the success of 1984 through dividends in cash and stock totaling more than $2 billion, more than double the amount received the year before. U.S. hourly and salaried employes participated fully in GM's 1984 success with payrolls and benefit costs increasing to a new high

"...capital spending represents a further major commitment to product quality, new products, new facilities, and factory efficiencies."

of $24.6 billion, up 18% over a year earlier. Earnings from U.S. operations were strong enough to provide profit sharing funds totaling nearly $282 million to be distributed among some 547,000 U.S. hourly and salaried GM employes, or an average of $515 per employe. In addition, those who wish to will be able to increase the value of their profit share by 25% if they apply their payment toward the purchase of a new GM vehicle during 1985. The reduction in profit sharing from last year was more

than accounted for by the production lost in North America before labor agreements could be reached. Since March of 1984, GM has paid out more than $600 million in profits to its U.S. employes. No other company has ever distributed such a large amount of profit sharing to employes in so short a span of time.

Based on the stockholder-approved formula, the Incentive Program generated a record fund of over $304 million on record worldwide profits of $4.5 billion. On the recommendation of GM management, however, the Bonus and Salary Committee determined that the amount awarded for 1984 would be $80 million less than the maximum amount available under the incentive compensation formula. Of this amount, $35 million has been returned to income and $45 million will be carried over to future years. The $224 million awarded to GM's managers will be paid in instalments over a three-year period, generally in equal portions of GM stock and cash.

*F*or the 1985 calendar year, we anticipate that GM's capital expenditures, including the annual requirements of EDS, will be approximately $9 billion worldwide, up significantly from the 1984 spending level of $6.0 billion. Largely driven by our forward product programs, this would be the second highest spending in GM's history.

This level of capital spending represents a further major commitment to product quality, new products, new facilities, and factory efficiencies. Saturn Corporation, for example, encompasses all of these. Moreover, there will be additional changes, and there will be more diversification.

There are those who would compare the changing General Motors of these times to the Corporation in the era of Alfred P. Sloan, Jr., who shaped and led GM two generations ago. We

"...one thing does not change: the efforts of everyone ...to build on past achievement while attaining or maintaining GM leadership throughout the world."

leave such comparisons to the historians. Still, it is worth noting what was perhaps Mr. Sloan's most basic perception of the Corporation: "No company ever stops changing...Each new generation must meet changes—in the automotive market, in the general administration of the enterprise, and in the involvement of the corporation in a changing world...The work is only beginning...The work of creating goes on." But one thing does not change: the efforts of everyone in the organization on behalf of the owners of General Motors to build on past achievement while attaining or maintaining GM leadership throughout the world.

Chairman

President

FINANCIAL REVIEW: MANAGEMENT'S DISCUSSION AND ANALYSIS*

Results of Operations

General Motors' net income in 1984 of $4,516.5 million was $786.3 million higher than in 1983.

As detailed in the table below, worldwide factory sales (sales of General Motors cars and trucks to its dealers) in 1984 totaled 8,256,000 units, 6% above 1983 unit sales. Worldwide dollar sales and revenues in 1984 were $83.9 billion, 13% above 1983. Dollar sales and revenues include price adjustments of $2.9 billion in 1984, compared with $3.2 billion in 1983 and $2.9 billion in 1982.

The table shows the percentage contribution to GM's total worldwide dollar sales and revenues, before elimination of interarea sales and revenues, by U.S., Canadian, and overseas operations. Automotive products accounted for more than 94% of GM's sales and revenues in each of the last three years.

In analyzing the earnings for the three years, it should be noted, as shown on page 1, that the two largest cost elements are payments to suppliers (for raw materials and expenses) and the cost of labor. Efforts to control supplier costs, particularly for raw materials and energy, have continued. The cost of labor reflects the U.S. labor agreement, ratified in April 1982, that

*The comments covering power products and defense sales (page 8), people of General Motors (pages 10 through 13), and the effects of inflation on financial data (pages 32 and 33) also should be read as an integral part of this discussion and analysis.

expired in September 1984 and the new three-year contract ratified in October 1984.

Taxes represent the third largest cost element of the Corporation. The significance of GM's tax burden is illustrated by comparing it with the level of cash dividends paid. For example, holders of $1-2/3 par value common stock received cash dividends of $4.75, $2.80, and $2.40 per share on their investment in 1984, 1983, and 1982, respectively. During the same period, taxes incurred were equivalent to $16.98, $15.61, and $7.22 per $1-2/3 par value common share, respectively.

The Corporation's net income as a percent of sales and revenues was 5.4% in 1984, compared with 5.0% in 1983 and 1.6% in 1982.

1984 Compared With 1983

The 1984 net income of $4,516.5 million compares with 1983 net income of $3,730.2 million. As shown in the table below, that income was earned principally in the United States and Canada. Earnings reflect the inclusion, for the period from October 18 to December 31, 1984, of the net income of Electronic Data Systems (EDS).

Earnings per share of $1-2/3 par value common stock amounted to $14.22 in 1984 versus $11.84 per share in 1983. The $2.38 per share improvement in earnings in 1984 is primarily attributable to higher volume, improved operating performance and the reversal of deferred income taxes related to the domestic international sales corporation (DISC), partially offset by increased

costs not fully recovered through prices.

Earnings per share of Class E common stock amounted to $1.03 in 1984. These earnings are based on the Separate Consolidated Net Income of EDS as defined in Note 8 to the Financial Statements.

Interest expense decreased from 1983 due in part to the lower interest costs associated with reduced levels of long-term borrowings.

Total taxes of General Motors, including payroll and property taxes but excluding the taxes of GM's financing and insurance operations, General Motors Acceptance Corporation (GMAC) and its subsidiaries as discussed below, totaled $5,377.5 million in 1984 compared with $4,899.6 million in 1983. The provision for U.S., foreign and other income taxes in 1984 reflects $1,317.1 million U.S. taxes, which includes the favorable impact of U.S. investment tax credits. These taxes are net of a deferred income tax reversal of $421.3 million, or $1.34 per share of $1-2/3 par value common stock, reflecting a change in the provisions covering DISCs in accordance with the Deficit Reduction Act of 1984.

GMAC and its subsidiaries earned $784.8 million in 1984, compared with a record $1,002.0 million in 1983. The decline in earnings was principally a result of higher short-term borrowing costs in the U.S., combined with the impact of earnings on retail receivables acquired in previous years at lower yields. GMAC's income taxes, which are provided for separately from GM, decreased $202.2 million to a total of $591.9 million for 1984 as a result of decreased pretax earnings.

Worldwide Factory Sales
(Units in Thousands)

	CARS			TRUCKS & BUSES			TOTAL		
	1984	1983	1982	1984	1983	1982	1984	1983	1982
United States	4,338	3,996	3,147	1,338	1,123	895	5,676	5,119	4,042
Canada	549	539	335	277	263	230	826	802	565
Overseas†	1,485	1,606	1,388	269	242	249	1,754	1,848	1,637
Total	6,372	6,141	4,870	1,884	1,628	1,374	8,256	7,769	6,244

†Includes units which are manufactured overseas by other companies and which are imported and sold by General Motors and affiliates.

Percentage of Net Income (Loss) Attributable to:

	1984	1983	1982
United States	86%	93%	111%
Canada	17	16	(3)
Overseas	(3)	(9)	(8)
Total	100%	100%	100%
Automotive	100%	102%	101%
Nonautomotive	—	(2)	(1)
Total	100%	100%	100%

Percentage of Worldwide Dollar Sales and Revenues Attributable to:

	1984	1983	1982
United States	76%	74%	72%
Canada	13	13	11
Overseas	11	13	17
Total	100%	100%	100%
Automotive	96%	96%	94%
Nonautomotive	4	4	6
Total	100%	100%	100%

1983 Compared With 1982

The 1983 net income of $3,730.2 million or $11.84 per share of common stock compared with 1982 net income of $962.7 million or $3.09 per share of common stock.

The $8.75 per share improvement in earnings in 1983 was primarily attributable to increased volume, an improved product mix, efficiencies due to cost reduction efforts, and increased earnings of GMAC and its subsidiaries. As explained in Note 1 to the Financial Statements, the Corporation implemented Statement of Financial Accounting Standards No. 52, Foreign Currency Translation, effective January 1, 1983 and the effect was to reduce net income for 1983 by about $422.5 million ($1.35 per share).

Interest expense decreased from 1982 due to the lower interest costs associated with reduced levels of long-term borrowings.

The provision for U.S., foreign and other income taxes in 1983 reflected $1,811.4 million U.S. taxes, which included the favorable impact of U.S. investment tax credits.

GMAC and its subsidiaries earned a record $1,002.0 million in 1983, compared with the previous record of $688.0 million in 1982, reflecting lower short-term borrowing costs and a higher level of earning assets.

Liquidity and Capital Resources

In 1984, cash and marketable securities increased by $2,350.5 million, or 38%, principally reflecting funds provided by current operations and the net decrease in other working capital items, only partially offset by expenditures for property and for the intangible assets acquired in the acquisition of EDS. The net decrease in other working

OLDSMOBILE DELTA 88 ROYALE BROUGHAM Sedan

capital items consisted primarily of an increase in loans payable due principally to the fluctuating rate GM notes issued in connection with the acquisition of EDS.

In 1983, cash and marketable securities increased by $3,090.7 million, or 99%, principally reflecting funds provided by current operations, only partially offset by expenditures for property, the net reduction in long-term debt and the net increase in other working capital items (principally accounts and notes receivable). The increase in accounts and notes receivable of $4,099.7 million in 1983 reflected the sales increase as well as an increase in the receivable from GMAC, which provides the majority of the wholesale financing of General Motors' products. That increase included $2,562.4 million related to dealer vehicle stocks for which payment from GMAC was due at a later date than previously had been the practice.

Long-term debt was reduced by $719.8 million in 1984 as a result of decreases in long-term debt of $1,793.9 million exceeding increases of $1,074.1 million. Accordingly, the ratio of long-term debt to the total of long-term debt and stockholders' equity declined to 9.1% at December 31, 1984.

During 1983, long-term debt had decreased $1,314.8 million because decreases of $4,491.9 million exceeded increases of $3,177.1 million. As a result, the long-term debt ratio had declined to 13.1% at year-end 1983.

The ratio of long-term debt and short-term loans payable to the total of this debt and stockholders' equity amounted to 18.5% at December 31, 1984, an increase of one point from the 17.5% ratio at December 31, 1983 reflecting the notes issued in the EDS acquisition.

Sales and Revenues

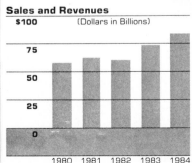

Net Income

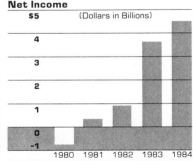

Earnings Per Share of $1-2/3 Par Value Common Stock

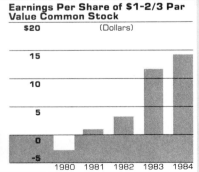

The senior long-term debt ratings of GM and GMAC carry the second highest possible rating, while the short-term commercial paper of GMAC continues to carry the highest possible rating. In line with the past practice of maintaining lines of credit, at year-end 1984 the Corporation and its subsidiaries (excluding GMAC) had unused short-term credit lines of approximately $2.4 billion and unused long-term credit agreements of approximately $1.4 billion.

Of the 1984 worldwide expenditures for real estate, plants and equipment, approximately 82% were made in the United States (78% in 1983 and 73% in 1982), 4% in Canada (7% in 1983 and 5% in 1982), and 14% overseas (15% in 1983 and 22% in 1982).

Product programs necessary to respond to the demands of the marketplace for quality and fuel economy, to improve General Motors' competitive position worldwide, to improve plant efficiency, and to meet government standards require continued high capital expenditures. In each of the last nine years, GM has introduced substantially redesigned or new models in the United States and Canada. Significant product redesign programs also have been undertaken by overseas subsidiaries. Commitments for capital spending at December 31, 1984 totaled $4.2 billion, and it is anticipated that total capital expenditures, including the annual requirements of EDS, will be approximately $9 billion in 1985.

The decrease in preferred stocks reflects the Corporation's previously announced long-term program to repurchase such stock when it is considered economically attractive to GM. The difference between repurchase prices and the stated value of $100 per share has been credited to capital surplus.

The issuance of Class E common stock reflects primarily the acquisition of EDS, as described more fully in Note 1 to the Financial Statements, and the dividend of one share of Class E common stock for every 20 shares of $1-2/3 par value common stock on December 10, 1984.

Increases in $1-2/3 par value common stock and other capital surplus in 1984 reflect use of newly issued stock for purposes of bonus deliveries, the Stock Option Plans (SOP) and the General Motors Dividend Reinvestment Plan (DRP). In 1983 and 1982, newly issued stock was used for the SOP, the DRP, the Savings-Stock Purchase Programs, and the Employe Stock Ownership Plans. In addition, the Corporation exchanged common stock for long-term debt in the earlier two years.

It is the Corporation's policy with respect to $1-2/3 par value common stock to distribute from current earnings such amounts as the outlook and the indicated capital needs of the business permit. In this regard, a strong capital position must be maintained in order to meet capital expenditures in the years ahead. The Class E com-

mon stock dividend policy is discussed on page 19 and in Note 8 to the Financial Statements.

Accumulated foreign currency translation adjustments of ($789.5) million at December 31, 1984 and ($661.8) million at December 31, 1983 are included in a separate section of stockholders' equity.

Book value per share of $1-2/3 par value common stock increased in 1984 to $72.16 from $64.88 at the end of 1983. Book value was $57.64 at the end of 1982. Book value per share of Class E common stock was $36.08 at the end of 1984. Net income as a percent of stockholders' equity was 18.7% in 1984, compared with 18.0% in 1983 and 5.3% in 1982.

GM's liquidity can be measured by its current ratio (ratio of current assets to current liabilities). For the years ended December 31, 1984, 1983, and 1982, the current ratio, based on last-in, first-out (LIFO) inventories, was 1.36, 1.40, and 1.13, respectively. The LIFO method, while improving Corporate cash flow, adversely affects the current ratio. The first-in, first-out (FIFO) value of inventories, which more nearly reflects replacement cost, exceeded LIFO amounts at December 31, 1984, 1983, and 1982 by approximately $2.2 billion, $2.0 billion, and $1.9 billion, respectively. If inventories were valued at FIFO cost, the current ratio would be 1.40, 1.47, and 1.21, respectively.

Quality control checks occur throughout the assembly line process. Shown here is a Cadillac Sedan DeVille receiving final front- and rear-wheel alignment in a "toe-in" machine. This machine feeds information back to camber equipment — which made the suspension alignment further up the assembly line — and double checks that original setting. The new Cadillac's four-wheel independent suspension makes front- and rear-wheel alignment necessary.

EARNINGS ON CLASS E COMMON STOCK

On October 18, 1984, General Motors acquired Electronic Data Systems (EDS), a leader in the computer services industry. The operations of EDS since October 18 are included in the consolidated results of General Motors shown on pages 20-33 for the period ended December 31, 1984.

The earnings of EDS and its subsidiaries since acquisition by GM, including income earned from services provided to GM and its other subsidiaries but excluding purchase accounting adjustments, form the base out of which any dividends paid on the Class E common stock will be declared. These earnings are designated as the "Separate Consolidated Net Income of EDS" and are described as "Earnings on Class E Common Stock" in the Financial Statements. The rights of Class E common stockholders to participate in dividends are described more fully in Note 8 to the Financial Statements.

In the 22 years since it began operations, EDS has helped to shape many of the technologies and business practices now prominent in the data processing field.

☐ In the early 1960s, EDS created an entirely new service—Facilities Management, whereby EDS, in effect, assumes data processing responsibility for its client companies, providing all hardware, software, personnel, and computer services. The company was the first computer services firm to sign extended, multi-year contracts with its customers. EDS helped pioneer interactive systems, distributed processing, satellite communications and computer telecommunications, and in the early 1970s began work on EDS•NET, the company's nationwide data communications network. Currently, EDS•NET handles more than 5 million data transactions each day from more than 25,000 on-line customer terminals.

☐ In 1974, EDS began to serve credit unions by developing systems for CUNADATA Corporation, a subsidiary of the Credit Union National Association; within 10 years, EDS has become the industry leader in service to credit unions.

☐ In 1978, EDS began an effort to serve another specifically targeted customer—the Federal government. In 1984, Federal government contracts brought EDS over $250 million in revenues. Multi-year arrangements with the Departments of Defense, Interior, Energy, Justice and Agriculture, the U.S. Postal Service, the Social Security Administration, and the Environmental Protection Agency, as well as the Army, Navy, and Marines, make this one of the largest, fastest-growing parts of EDS' business.

☐ In 1982, the company demonstrated its ability to transfer its service technologies from one area to another related one. EDS•NET, for example, helped prepare EDS for the procurement and implementation of the 10-year, $656 million project VIABLE (Vertical Installation Automation Base Line) for the U.S. Army—one of the largest computer services contracts ever awarded by the Federal government. VIABLE, in turn, proved EDS' readiness in 1984 to take on a systems integration contract with the U.S. Navy. These projects are helping position the company for similar major contracts not only with the government but with the commercial sector as well.

If a single reason could be credited for EDS' steady sustained growth, it is the ability to find, develop and retain the right people for the job. The company's recruiting, training and employe recognition practices help keep EDS personnel ready to anticipate and meet the needs of current customers, and prepare for the business opportunities ahead. The company's training programs, such as the Systems, Engineering and Development (SED) Program, were ahead of their time when first developed, and remain so today. Extensive initial and ongoing education is available for EDS personnel, and the highest priority is given to providing individuals with the tools and work environment necessary for maximum productivity. This people-oriented approach has sustained

EDS Headquarters, Dallas, Texas

EARNINGS ON CLASS E COMMON STOCK (continued)

EDS' leadership in the data processing industry.

This expertise in data processing and communications will be applied across a broad spectrum of General Motors operations worldwide. It will assist in the development of the advanced computer systems needed to enhance GM's leadership position and enable GM to achieve greater efficiencies in operations.

While the merger with GM was the most significant event of 1984 in EDS' operations, its outside business continued to grow also. EDS signed more commercial business than ever before and several long-term government contracts. Revenues from commercial business are now at their highest point ever.

EDS is not limited to a reliance on any one business category or industry; therefore, the company's well-being is less vulnerable to the downturns of a single industry. Among computer services companies, EDS leads in its ability to serve large companies in a diverse range of industries, both nationally and internationally—including health care, financial services, commercial insurance, industrial, and Federal, state and local government organizations. EDS pioneered the concept of industry specialization and servicing many different industries. While a number of firms compete with EDS in a given industry, most specialize in service to only that one industry.

One traditional EDS stronghold has been the health care market. The year 1984 was no exception. Blue Cross and Blue Shield of Colorado extended its facilities management contract with EDS for an additional three years—until 1992. Blue Shield of Western New York also extended its contract for 10 more years. In addition, EDS recently signed a 10-year contract with Blue Cross/Blue Shield United of Wisconsin, one of the nation's largest plans, bringing the current total of Blue Cross and Blue Shield customers to 13.

EDS continued its steady and progressive growth in the credit union market during 1984. Today, EDS serves 3,100 credit unions with 10 million members. That is an increase of 2 million members in the past year.

EDS' success in the industrials market has been growing. This year, EDS signed a seven-year contract to provide complete data processing services to the six companies that comprise the Specialty Retailing Group of General Mills, Inc.

EDS also signed a new seven-year facilities management contract with Vista Chemicals of Houston, Texas. During the first six months of the agreement, EDS will transfer Vista's data processing activities to EDS' Dallas Information Processing Centers.

AT&T and EDS announced a major expansion of their business arrangement with the signing of a multi-year agreement designed to strengthen the ability of both companies to integrate tailor-made communications and data processing systems. The agreement combines AT&T's technological expertise in communications and data products and services with EDS' knowledge and skills with software and systems integration.

AT&T and EDS project teams will identify and qualify potential sales opportunities that require custom-designed system solutions. If a customer accepts a recommended solution, critical elements will be evaluated and tested before installation.

In 1984, an eight-year, $350 million agreement with the U.S. Navy to update data processing facilities at the Navy's two major inventory control points was also signed. In addition, EDS will build a nationwide telecommunications network, provide both hardware and software, and train more than 5,500 Navy personnel. The contract contains two eight-year extension options, making it a potential 24-year agreement.

Another major government contract is a seven-year, potential $200 million contract with the U.S. Postal Service to automate tracking and handling of airmail. The new system uses laser scanning equipment to sort mail at 351 locations in the continental United States.

In international activities, EDS won a 10-year contract with Unilever PLC of London, England to manage and operate Unilever's United Kingdom telecommunications network. EDS also signed a major contract with British United Provident Association that is believed to be one of the largest contracts for data processing services ever awarded in the United Kingdom.

The Control Room of an EDS Information Processing Center

EARNINGS ON CLASS E COMMON STOCK (concluded)

The following are selected summary financial data relating to the EDS operations which form the Class E common stock Dividend Base for the period from October 18 to December 31, 1984. For purposes of analysis, pro forma calendar year data for 1984 and 1983 are also presented.

Selected Summary Financial Data

(Dollars in Millions Except Per Share Amounts)	Oct. 18 to Dec. 31, 1984	Pro Forma Year Ended December 31, 1984	Pro Forma Year Ended December 31, 1983
Revenues:			
Systems and other contracts:			
Outside customers	$184.5	$866.6	$701.7
GM and affiliates	36.4	59.3	–
Interest and other income	4.8	21.5	30.1
Total Revenues	225.7	947.4	731.8
Costs and Expenses	191.1	808.1	614.9
Income Taxes	15.9	58.6	51.7
Earnings on Class E Common Stock	$ 18.7	$ 80.7	$ 65.2
Average number of shares of Class E common stock outstanding (in millions)	18.2	–	–
Earnings per share of Class E common stock	$1.03	–	–
Dividend Base Per Share of Class E common stock*	$0.31	–	–
Cash dividends per share of Class E common stock	$0.09	–	–
Payout Ratio**	29.0%	–	–

*The Dividend Base Per Share represents earnings on Class E common stock divided by 60.0 million shares.
**The Payout Ratio represents dividends per share divided by the Dividend Base Per Share.

(Dollars in Millions)	December 31, 1984	December 31, 1983
Current Assets:		
Cash and marketable securities	$162.5	$ 95.4
Accounts receivable	191.4	113.6
Other current assets	37.3	26.0
Total Current Assets	391.2	235.0
Current Liabilities:		
Accounts payable	35.4	40.1
Notes payable—current portion	5.7	3.5
Deferred revenue	24.0	27.1
Other accrued liabilities	140.8	75.8
Total Current Liabilities	205.9	146.5
Working Capital	$185.3	$ 88.5
Data Processing Facilities, Property and Equipment	$106.7	$ 94.9
Other Assets:		
Investment in nonconsolidated subsidiaries	$ .6	$ 7.8
Land held for investment and development	72.5	60.5
Other operating assets	36.3	73.0
Total Other Assets	$109.4	$141.3
Long-Term Debt and Deferred Credits:		
Notes payable—long-term portion	$ 27.2	$ 28.4
Deferred income taxes payable	15.3	9.4
Deferred revenue	13.4	6.1
Total Long-Term Debt and Deferred Credits	$ 55.9	$ 43.9

EDS experienced continued growth during the calendar year ended December 31, 1984. During the past year:
☐ Revenues rose 29.5% to $947.4 million, including $59.3 million derived from GM and affiliates.
☐ On a pro forma basis, earnings on Class E common stock increased 23.8% to $80.7 million.
☐ Working capital totaled $185.3 million, an increase of over 100% in 1984.
☐ Total assets were $607.3 million.
☐ The number of EDS employes surpassed 22,000, including 7,000 transferred from GM and affiliates, effective January 1, 1985.

The current policy of the GM Board of Directors is to pay dividends on the Class E common stock approximately equal to 25% of the quotient of (a) the Separate Consolidated Net Income of EDS, as defined, divided by (b) the greater of 60 million or the number of shares of Class E common stock outstanding. The Board has also adopted the policy that dividends per share of Class E common stock for the first four quarters following the acquisition of EDS will equal at least $0.09 per share per quarter.

The data do not include the cost of $2,006.3 million to GM of the EDS customer contracts, computer software programs and intangible assets arising from the acquisition of EDS by GM. The cost of these assets is being amortized by GM over their estimated useful lives. Amortization for the period from the date of acquisition to December 31, 1984 was $68.4 million. The unamortized balance at December 31, 1984 was $1,937.9 million. For the purpose of determining earnings per share and amounts available for dividends on common stocks, the amortization of these assets is charged against earnings attributable to $1-2/3 par value common stock. The effect on the 1984 consolidated net income of General Motors is a net charge of $26.1 million, consisting of earnings on Class E common stock less the amortization of the applicable assets and the elimination of intercompany transactions.

People and Technology—The Key to EDS' Success

CONSOLIDATED FINANCIAL STATEMENTS

General Motors Corporation
and Consolidated Subsidiaries

RESPONSIBILITIES FOR FINANCIAL STATEMENTS

The following financial statements of General Motors Corporation and consolidated subsidiaries were prepared by the management which is responsible for their integrity and objectivity. The statements have been prepared in conformity with generally accepted accounting principles and, as such, include amounts based on judgments of management. Financial information elsewhere in this Annual Report is consistent with that in the financial statements.

Management is further responsible for maintaining a system of internal accounting controls, designed to provide reasonable assurance that the books and records reflect the transactions of the companies and that its established policies and procedures are carefully followed. From a stockholder's point of view, perhaps the most important feature in the system of control is that it is continually reviewed for its effectiveness and is augmented by written policies and guidelines, the careful selection and training of qualified personnel, and a strong program of internal audit.

Deloitte Haskins & Sells, independent certified public accountants, are engaged to examine the consolidated financial statements of General Motors Corporation and its subsidiaries and issue reports thereon. Their examination is conducted in accordance with generally accepted auditing standards which comprehend a review of internal accounting controls and a test of transactions. The Accountants' Report appears on page 30.

The Board of Directors, through the Audit Committee (composed entirely of non-employe Directors), is responsible for assuring that management fulfills its responsibilities in the preparation of the financial statements. The Committee selects the independent public accountants annually in advance of the Annual Meeting of Stockholders and submits the selection for ratification at the Meeting. In addition, the Committee reviews the scope of the audits and the accounting principles being applied in financial reporting. The independent public accountants, representatives of management, and the internal auditors meet regularly (separately and jointly) with the Committee to review the activities of each and to ensure that each is properly discharging its responsibilities. To ensure complete independence, Deloitte Haskins & Sells have full and free access to meet with the Committee, without management representatives present, to discuss the results of their examination, the adequacy of internal accounting controls, and the quality of the financial reporting.

Chairman

Chief Financial Officer

STATEMENT OF CONSOLIDATED INCOME

For the Years Ended December 31, 1984, 1983 and 1982
(Dollars in Millions Except Per Share Amounts)

	1984	1983	1982
Net Sales and Revenues (Note 2)			
Manufactured products	$83,699.7	$74,581.6	$60,025.6
Computer systems services	190.2	—	—
Total Net Sales and Revenues	83,889.9	74,581.6	60,025.6
Costs and Expenses			
Cost of sales and other operating charges, exclusive of items listed below	70,217.9	60,718.8	51,548.3
Selling, general and administrative expenses	4,006.3	3,234.8	2,964.9
Depreciation of real estate, plants and equipment	2,663.2	2,569.7	2,403.0
Amortization of special tools	2,236.7	2,549.9	2,147.5
Amortization of intangible assets (Note 1)	65.8	—	—
Total Costs and Expenses	79,189.9	69,073.2	59,063.7
Operating Income	4,700.0	5,508.4	961.9
Other income less income deductions—net (Note 5)	1,713.5	815.8	476.3
Interest expense (Note 1)	(909.2)	(1,352.7)	(1,415.4)
Income before Income Taxes	5,504.3	4,971.5	22.8
United States, foreign and other income taxes (credit) (Note 7)	1,805.1	2,223.8	(252.2)
Income after Income Taxes	3,699.2	2,747.7	275.0
Equity in earnings of nonconsolidated subsidiaries and associates (dividends received amounted to $706.1 in 1984, $757.3 in 1983 and $412.7 in 1982)	817.3	982.5	687.7
Net Income	4,516.5	3,730.2	962.7
Dividends on preferred stocks	12.5	12.9	12.9
Earnings on Common Stocks	$ 4,504.0	$ 3,717.3	$ 949.8
Attributable to:			
$1-2/3 par value common stock	$ 4,485.3	$ 3,717.3	$ 949.8
Class E common stock (issued in 1984)	$ 18.7	—	—
Average number of shares of common stocks outstanding (in millions):			
$1-2/3 par value common	315.3	313.9	307.4
Class E common (issued in 1984)	18.2	—	—
Earnings Per Share of Common Stocks (Note 8):			
$1-2/3 par value common	$14.22	$11.84	$3.09
Class E common (issued in 1984)	$1.03	—	—

Reference should be made to notes on pages 23 through 30.

CONSOLIDATED BALANCE SHEET

December 31, 1984 and 1983
(Dollars in Millions Except Per Share Amounts)

ASSETS	1984	1983
Current Assets		
Cash	$ 467.5	$ 369.5
United States Government and other marketable securities and time deposits—at cost, which approximates market of $8,108.7 and $5,834.6	8,099.9	5,847.4
Total cash and marketable securities	8,567.4	6,216.9
Accounts and notes receivable (including GMAC and its subsidiaries—$3,868.5 and $3,560.7)—less allowances (Note 9)	7,357.9	6,964.2
Inventories (less allowances) (Note 1)	7,359.7	6,621.5
Prepaid expenses and deferred income taxes	428.3	997.2
Total Current Assets	23,713.3	20,799.8
Equity in Net Assets of Nonconsolidated Subsidiaries and Associates (principally GMAC and its subsidiaries—Note 9)	4,603.0	4,450.8
Other Investments and Miscellaneous Assets—at cost (less allowances)	2,344.4	1,221.2
Common Stocks Held for the Incentive Program (Note 3)	144.2	56.3
Property		
Real estate, plants and equipment—at cost (Note 10)	39,354.1	37,777.8
Less accumulated depreciation (Note 10)	21,649.8	20,116.8
Net real estate, plants and equipment	17,704.3	17,661.0
Special tools—at cost (less amortization)	1,697.2	1,504.1
Total Property	19,401.5	19,165.1
Intangible Assets—at cost (less amortization) (Note 1)	1,938.5	1.3
Total Assets	$52,144.9	$45,694.5

LIABILITIES AND STOCKHOLDERS' EQUITY		
Current Liabilities		
Accounts payable (principally trade)	$ 4,743.5	$ 4,642.3
Loans payable (Note 12)	3,086.0	1,255.2
United States, foreign and other income taxes payable	618.9	202.3
Accrued liabilities (Note 11)	8,988.2	8,809.2
Total Current Liabilities	17,436.6	14,909.0
Long-Term Debt (Note 12)	2,417.4	3,137.2
Capitalized Leases	355.5	384.6
Other Liabilities (including GMAC and its subsidiaries—$300.0 in 1984 and 1983)	5,971.9	4,698.2
Deferred Credits (including investment tax credits—$1,259.9 and $1,281.1)	1,749.2	1,798.9
Stockholders' Equity (Notes 3, 4 and 13)		
Preferred stocks ($5.00 series, $169.8 and $183.6; $3.75 series, $85.8 and $100.0)	255.6	283.6
Common stocks:		
$1-2/3 par value (issued, 317,504,133 and 315,711,299 shares)	529.2	526.2
Class E (issued, 29,082,382 shares in 1984)	2.9	—
Capital surplus (principally additional paid-in capital)	3,347.8	2,136.8
Net income retained for use in the business	20,796.6	18,390.5
Subtotal	24,932.1	21,337.1
Accumulated foreign currency translation and other adjustments (Note 1)	(717.8)	(570.5)
Total Stockholders' Equity	24,214.3	20,766.6
Total Liabilities and Stockholders' Equity	$52,144.9	$45,694.5

Reference should be made to notes on pages 23 through 30.
Certain amounts for 1983 have been reclassified to conform with 1984 classifications.

STATEMENT OF CHANGES
IN CONSOLIDATED FINANCIAL POSITION

For the Years Ended December 31, 1984, 1983 and 1982
(Dollars in Millions)

	1984	1983	1982
Source of Funds			
Net income	$ 4,516.5	$ 3,730.2	$ 962.7
Depreciation of real estate, plants and equipment	2,663.2	2,569.7	2,403.0
Amortization of special tools	2,236.7	2,549.9	2,147.5
Amortization of intangible assets (Note 1)	65.8	—	—
Deferred income taxes, undistributed earnings of nonconsolidated subsidiaries and associates, etc.—net	(1,316.1)	645.5	75.8
Total funds provided by current operations	8,166.1	9,495.3	5,589.0
Decrease (Increase) in other working capital items	1,964.6	(1,142.0)	1,306.2
Increase in long-term debt	1,074.1	3,177.1	2,497.4
Issuances of common stocks, less repurchases of preferred stocks	602.2	212.0	353.5
Other—net	2,013.9	772.8	1,459.2
Total	13,820.9	12,515.2	11,205.3
Use of Funds			
Cash dividends paid to stockholders (Note 13)	1,523.7	892.2	750.2
Expenditures for real estate, plants and equipment	3,595.1	1,923.0	3,611.1
Expenditures for special tools	2,452.1	2,083.7	2,601.0
Intangible assets acquired in acquisition of EDS (Note 1)	2,006.3	—	—
Decrease in long-term debt	1,793.9	4,491.9	1,846.5
Investments in nonconsolidated subsidiaries and associates	99.3	33.7	591.0
Total	11,470.4	9,424.5	9,399.8
Increase in cash and marketable securities	2,350.5	3,090.7	1,805.5
Cash and marketable securities at beginning of the year	6,216.9	3,126.2	1,320.7
Cash and marketable securities at end of the year	$ 8,567.4	$ 6,216.9	$ 3,126.2
Decrease (Increase) in Other Working Capital Items by Element			
Accounts and notes receivable	($ 393.7)	($ 4,099.7)	$ 778.8
Inventories	(738.2)	(437.3)	1,038.5
Prepaid expenses and deferred income taxes	568.9	871.0	(341.1)
Accounts payable	101.2	1,041.6	(99.0)
Loans payable	1,830.8	72.7	(545.3)
United States, foreign and other income taxes payable	416.6	131.5	(461.4)
Accrued liabilities	179.0	1,278.2	935.7
Decrease (Increase) in other working capital items	$ 1,964.6	($ 1,142.0)	$ 1,306.2

Reference should be made to notes on pages 23 through 30.
Certain amounts for 1983 and 1982 have been reclassified to conform with 1984 classifications.

NOTES TO FINANCIAL STATEMENTS

NOTE 1. Significant Accounting Policies

Principles of Consolidation
The consolidated financial statements include the accounts of the Corporation and all domestic and foreign subsidiaries which are more than 50% owned and engaged principally in manufacturing or wholesale marketing of General Motors products and in computer services. General Motors' share of earnings or losses of nonconsolidated subsidiaries and of associates in which at least 20% of the voting securities is owned is included in consolidated income under the equity method of accounting.

Income Taxes
Investment tax credits are deferred and amortized over the lives of the related assets. The tax effects of timing differences between pretax accounting income and taxable income (principally related to depreciation, sales and product allowances, vehicle instalment sales, and benefit plans expense) are deferred. Provisions are made for estimated United States and foreign taxes, less available tax credits and deductions, which may be incurred on remittance of the Corporation's share of subsidiaries' undistributed earnings less those deemed to be permanently reinvested. Possible taxes beyond those provided would not be material.

Inventories
Inventories are stated generally at cost, which is not in excess of market. The cost of substantially all domestic inventories was determined by the last-in, first-out (LIFO) method. If the first-in, first-out (FIFO) method of inventory valuation had been used by the Corporation for such inventories, it is estimated they would be $2,183.0 million higher at December 31, 1984, compared with $2,038.6 million higher at December 31, 1983. As a result of decreases in unit sales and actions taken to reduce inventories, certain LIFO inventory quantities carried at lower costs prevailing in prior years, as compared with the costs of current purchases, were liquidated in 1982. These inventory adjustments favorably affected income before income taxes by approximately $305.0 million in 1982. The cost of inventories outside the United States was determined generally by the FIFO or the average cost method.

Major Classes of Inventories

(Dollars in Millions)	1984	1983
Productive material, work in process and supplies	$5,264.2	$4,202.2
Finished product, service parts, etc.	2,095.5	2,419.3
Total	$7,359.7	$6,621.5

Depreciation and Amortization
Depreciation is provided on groups of property using, with minor exceptions, an accelerated method which accumulates depreciation of approximately two-thirds of the depreciable cost during the first half of the estimated lives of the property.

Expenditures for special tools are amortized, with the amortization applied directly to the asset account, over short periods of time because the utility value of the tools is radically affected by frequent changes in the design of the functional components and appearance of the product. Replacement of special tools for reasons other than changes in products is charged directly to cost of sales.

Pension Program
The Corporation and its subsidiaries have several pension plans covering substantially all of their employes. Benefits under the plans are generally related to an employe's length of service, wages and salaries, and, where applicable, contributions. The costs of these plans are determined on the basis of actuarial cost methods and include amortization of prior service cost over periods not in excess of 30 years from the later of October 1, 1979 or the date such costs are established. With the exception of certain Canadian and overseas subsidiaries, pension costs accrued are funded within the limitations set by the Employee Retirement Income Security Act.

Product Related Expenses
Expenditures for advertising and sales promotion and for other product related expenses are charged to costs and expenses as incurred; provisions for estimated costs related to product warranty are made at the time the products are sold. Expenditures for research and develop-

ment are charged to expenses as incurred and amounted to $3,075.8 million in 1984, $2,602.2 million in 1983 and $2,175.1 million in 1982.

Interest Cost
Total interest cost incurred in 1984, 1983 and 1982 amounted to $932.5 million, $1,401.8 million and $1,544.6 million, respectively, of which $23.3 million, $49.1 million and $129.2 million related to certain real estate, plants and equipment acquired in those years was capitalized.

Foreign Currency Translation
As required by the Financial Accounting Standards Board, effective January 1, 1983, the Corporation implemented Statement of Financial Accounting Standards (SFAS) No. 52, Foreign Currency Translation. Under SFAS No. 52, all assets and liabilities of operations outside the United States, except for operations in highly inflationary economies (principally in Latin America) or those that are highly integrated with operations of the Corporation (principally in Canada), are translated into U.S. dollars using current exchange rates, and the effects of foreign currency translation adjustments are deferred and included as a component of stockholders' equity. For operations in highly inflationary economies or that are highly integrated, foreign currency translation adjustments are included in income. The effect of adopting SFAS No. 52 was to reduce net income for 1983 by about $422.5 million ($1.35 per share of $1-2/3 par value common stock). The financial statements for 1982 have not been restated for this change. Exchange and translation gains (losses) included in net income in 1984, 1983 and 1982 amounted to ($114.8) million, ($52.3) million and $348.4 million, respectively.

Acquisition
On October 18, 1984, the Corporation acquired Electronic Data Systems Corporation (EDS) and its subsidiaries, whose activities include the design of large-scale data processing systems and the operation of data centers and communications networks, for $2,501.9 million. The acquisition was consummated through an offer to exchange EDS common stock for either (a) $44 in cash or (b) $35.20 in cash plus two-tenths of a share of Class E common stock plus a nontransferable contingent promissory note issued by GM. Certain EDS stockholders elected to receive fluctuating rate GM notes due in 1985 in lieu of cash. The nontransferable contingent promissory note is payable seven years after closing in an amount equal to .2 times the excess of $125 over the market price of the Class E common stock at the maturity date of the note. Holders may tender their notes for prepayment at discounted amounts beginning five years after closing. If the market price of Class E common stock at the maturity date of the notes were to equal the market price at December 31, 1984, $42.00 a share, the aggregate contingent consideration would be $940 million.

The acquisition has been accounted for as a purchase. The purchase price exceeded the net book value of EDS by $2,179.5 million. This amount relates primarily to existing customer contracts, $1,069.9 million, computer software programs developed by EDS, $646.2 million, and other intangible assets, $164.0 million. The cost assigned to these assets, $1,880.1 million, is being amortized on a straight-line basis over five years for computer software programs, about seven years for customer contracts and varying years for the remainder, with the amortization applied directly to the asset account. The cost assigned to goodwill, $126.2 million, is being amortized on a straight-line basis over ten years, with the amortization applied directly to the asset account. Amortization of goodwill amounted to $2.6 million in 1984.

The Statement of Consolidated Income includes the operations of EDS since October 18, 1984. The effect of the acquisition on the 1984 consolidated net income of GM is a net charge of $26.1 million, consisting of the Separate Consolidated Net Income of EDS (see Note 8) less the amortization of the intangible and other assets arising from the acquisition and the elimination of intercompany transactions. For the purpose of determining earnings per share and amounts available for dividends on common stocks, the amortization of these assets is charged against earnings attributable to $1-2/3 par value common stock. Earnings per share of $1-2/3 par value common stock would have been reduced by $0.66 in 1984 and $0.83 in 1983 if the acquisition had been consummated at the beginning of those years.

NOTES TO FINANCIAL STATEMENTS (continued)

NOTE 2. Net Sales and Revenues

Net sales and revenues includes sales to:

(Dollars in Millions)	1984	1983	1982
Nonconsolidated subsidiaries and associates	$ 121.6	$ 111.2	$ 96.3
Dealerships operating under dealership assistance plans	$1,917.4	$1,634.3	$1,253.7

Unrealized intercompany profits on sales to nonconsolidated subsidiaries and to associates are deferred.

NOTE 3. General Motors Incentive Program

The Incentive Program consists of the General Motors Bonus Plan, the General Motors Stock Option Plans and the General Motors Performance Achievement Plan. The By-Laws provide that the Plans in which directors or officers of the Corporation may participate shall be presented for action at a stockholders' meeting at least once in every five years. The Program was last approved by stockholders at the 1982 Annual Meeting, while amendments to the Stock Option Plans were approved at the 1984 Annual Meeting.

The Corporation maintains a reserve for purposes of the Bonus Plan. Under the current Plan provisions, for any year a maximum credit may be made to the reserve equal to the amount which the independent public accountants of the Corporation determine to be 8% of the net earnings which exceed $1 billion, but not in excess of the amount paid out as dividends on the $1-2/3 par value common stock during the year. The Bonus and Salary Committee may, at its discretion, direct that for any year an amount less than the maximum amount available under the formula be credited. Further, the Committee may, but is not obligated to, award as bonus in any year the full amount available in the reserve for such awards, or it may award less than the amount available. Bonus awards under the Bonus Plan and such other amounts arising out of the operation of the Bonus Plan as the Committee may determine are charged to the reserve.

The Bonus and Salary Committee has determined to limit the credit for 1984 to the reserve to $269.2 million. The credit so determined was $35.0 million less than the maximum which could have been credited to the reserve under the Bonus Plan approved by stockholders in 1982 and, as required by the Bonus Plan, less than the amount distributed as dividends to holders of GM $1-2/3 par value common stock in 1984. On February 4, 1985, the Committee granted awards to 5,804 employes of $224.1 million. These awards consisted of 1,564,870 shares of GM $1-2/3 par value common stock valued at an average of $70.69 per share for award purposes in accordance with the Bonus Plan, and $113.5 million in cash. A balance of $45.1 million is available in the reserve for future awards. A credit of $180.0 million was made to the Bonus Plan reserve in 1983, substantially all of which was awarded to participants for that year. No credit or awards were made for 1982, 1981, and 1980.

In 1982, the Committee established performance achievement levels for the initial three-year phase-in period ending in 1984 and for the first five-year period ending in 1986 under the Performance Achievement Plan approved by stockholders in 1982. In 1984, the Committee established performance achievement levels for a new five-year period ending in 1988. Under the Plan, the annual average of the aggregate final awards relating to the aggregate target awards granted in the years 1982 through 1986 shall not exceed $60 million. Payment of these awards is contingent upon achievement of earnings in relation to average worldwide industry sales volume targets over the term of the performance period related to each grant. In the future, it is anticipated that new grants will be made every two years. Employes selected to participate in the Plan are granted target awards payable in cash and/or $1-2/3 par value common stock which are, in general, expressed as a percentage of the participant's salary at the beginning of the performance period. Accruals of $12.3 million and $20.9 million were made in 1984 to recognize progress toward achieving the three-year and five-year earnings targets, respectively, through 1984. Awards for the 1982-1984 grant will be paid in cash in early 1985. The awards for the 1982-1986 and 1984-1988 periods will not be paid until 1987 and 1989,

respectively, with the ultimate amounts dependent on actual performance. Accruals of $15.5 million and $11.0 million were made for the 1982-1984 and 1982-1986 performance periods in 1983. There was no accrual in 1982 for the Plan.

Under the provisions of the Bonus Plan, participants receive their awards in instalments in as many as three years. Performance Achievement Plan awards are to be paid as soon as is practicable following completion of the performance period. If participants in the Plans fail to meet conditions precedent to receiving undelivered instalments of bonus and performance achievement awards (and contingent credits related to the Stock Option Plan prior to 1977), the amount of any such instalments is credited to income.

On April 2, 1984, the Committee granted Stock Appreciation Rights (SARs) on outstanding nonqualified stock options under the 1977 and 1982 Plans to certain officers of the Corporation, subject to stockholder approval of the proposed SAR amendments to the 1977 and 1982 Plans. Such approval was received at the May 25, 1984 Annual Meeting of Stockholders. On October 1, 1984, the Committee granted SARs to certain officers of the Corporation in conjunction with the incentive and nonqualified stock options granted on that day. SARs provide officers with the right to receive payment equal in value to the appreciation in the Corporation's $1-2/3 par value common stock over the option exercise price of the shares so granted. Such payment would be made in lieu of the related option's exercise, with the corresponding option shares cancelled and not available for regrant under the Plan. SARs are exercisable at such time as determined by the Committee, but only upon surrender of the related option and only to the extent that the related option is exercisable. SARs expire no later than the date of the underlying option, are not transferable under any circumstances and may be exercised only when the market value of the stock subject to the related option exceeds the applicable option price.

The utilization of SARs requires an expense accrual each year for the appreciation on the rights expected to be exercised. The amount of such accrual is dependent upon the extent to which such rights are granted and the amount, if any, by which the fair market value of General Motors $1-2/3 par value common stock exceeds the option price provided for in the related options. An accrual of $13.9 million was made for SARs in 1984.

Changes during 1982, 1983 and 1984 in the status of options granted under the Stock Option Plans are shown in the table below. The option prices are 100% of the average of the highest and lowest sales prices of GM $1-2/3 par value common stock on the dates the options were granted as reported (1) on the New York Stock Exchange for options granted prior to 1976, and (2) on the Composite Tape of transactions on all major exchanges and nonexchange markets in the U.S. for options granted in 1976 and subsequent years. Incentive stock options expire ten years from date of grant. Nonqualified stock options granted prior to 1982 expire ten years from date of grant and nonqualified stock options granted in 1982 and thereafter expire ten years and two days from date of grant. Options are subject to earlier termination under certain conditions.

	Years Granted	Option Prices	Shares Under Option
Outstanding at Jan. 1, 1982	1973-1981	$50.00-$73.38	1,807,673
Granted:	March 1982	38.25	897,150
	Oct. 1982	46.50	740,420
Exercised	1980-1981	50.00-53.25	(1,635)
Terminated	1973-1982		(191,469)
Outstanding at Dec. 31, 1982			3,252,139
Granted	1983	72.88	586,820
Exercised	1974-1982	38.25-66.57	(627,318)
Terminated	1973-1983		(111,347)
Outstanding at Dec. 31, 1983			3,100,294
Granted	1984	77.19	615,355
Exercised: Options	1974-1983	38.25-72.88	(794,828)
SARs	1984	38.25-72.88	(231,539)
Terminated	1974-1983		(48,039)
Outstanding at Dec. 31, 1984			2,641,243

(continued)

NOTES TO FINANCIAL STATEMENTS (continued)

NOTE 3. (concluded)

The Corporation intends to deliver newly issued $1-2/3 par value common stock upon the exercise of any of the stock options. The maximum number of shares for which additional options might be granted under the Plans was 931,405 at January 1, 1982, 6,760,945 at December 31, 1982, 6,195,185 at December 31, 1983, and 5,595,283 at December 31, 1984. Options outstanding at December 31, 1984 consisted of:

	Years Granted	Option Prices	Shares Under Option
1972 Plan	1976	$65.19	37,722
1977 Plan	1977	66.57	138,185
	1978	63.75	158,346
	1979	59.50	175,245
	1980	53.25	195,001
	1981	50.00	186,728
	1982	38.25	202,647
1982 Plan	1982	46.50	376,812
	1983	72.88	555,202
	1984	77.19	615,355
Total $1-2/3 Par Value Shares Under Option			2,641,243

On December 3, 1984, the Committee approved, subject to a favorable Internal Revenue Service ruling, adjustment of the number and the exercise prices of shares under option to reflect the $1.90 value per share of the December 1984 dividend of Class E common stock. The adjustment will have the effect of increasing the number of $1-2/3 par value common shares under option on the record date for receipt of the dividend by about 70,000 shares and reducing the related option prices.

Common stocks held for the Incentive Program are stated substantially at cost and used exclusively for payment of Program liabilities.

(Dollars in Millions)	1984		1983	
	Shares	Amount	Shares	Amount
Bal. at Jan. 1	828,273	$ 56.3	592,207	$35.2
Acquired: $1-2/3	1,869,391	133.1	594,680	42.6
Class E	19,134	.7	—	—
Delivered	(663,238)	(45.9)	(358,614)	(21.5)
Bal. at Dec. 31: $1-2/3	2,034,426	143.5	828,273	56.3
Class E	19,134	.7	—	—
Total	**2,053,560**	**$144.2**	**828,273**	**$56.3**

NOTE 4. EDS Incentive Plan

At its meeting on December 3, 1984, the Board of Directors approved and adopted the 1984 Electronic Data Systems Corporation Stock Incentive Plan in accordance with stockholder approval obtained as part of the consent of stockholders to the Amendment Proposal concerning GM's acquisition of EDS. The Stock Incentive Plan is designed to provide officers and key employes of EDS with incentive for individual creativity and contribution to ensure the future growth of EDS. Under this Plan, which covers up to 20 million shares of Class E common stock during the ten-year life of the Plan, shares, rights or options to acquire shares, which may be subject to restrictions, may be granted or sold. The Class E common stock shares granted and sold under the 1984 Plan vest over a ten-year period from the date of grant.

With regard to the unvested shares under the EDS 1977 Stock Incentive Plan, as a part of the acquisition agreement the 2,270,160 unvested shares of EDS common stock issued under the 1977 Plan were converted at the date of the acquisition into an equal number of unvested shares of Class E common stock.

The EDS employe who holds unvested shares under the 1977 Plan received a guarantee from GM to make a deferred compensation payment under certain conditions. This payment is intended to provide the employe with the same after Federal income tax proceeds that would have been realized after seven years if he had received an amount equal to the product of (a) the excess of $125.00 over the then average market price per share of Class E common stock and (b) one-half of the number of unvested shares of Class E common stock received by the employe, and had been eligible for long-term capital gain treatment.

NOTE 5. Other Income Less Income Deductions

(Dollars in Millions)	1984	1983	1982
Other income: Interest	$1,466.8	$719.5	$483.6
Other*	302.4	161.7	174.5
Income deductions	(55.7)	(65.4)	(181.8)
Net	$1,713.5	$815.8	$476.3

*Includes gains of $13.9 million in 1983 and $48.7 million in 1982 from early retirements of long-term debt.

NOTE 6. Pension Program and Postemployment Benefits

Total pension expense of the Corporation and its consolidated subsidiaries amounted to $1,618.4 million in 1984, $1,714.2 million in 1983 and $1,565.9 million in 1982. For purposes of determining pension expense, the Corporation uses a variety of assumed rates of return on pension funds in accordance with local practice and regulations, which rates approximate 7%. The following table compares accumulated plan benefits and plan net assets for the Corporation's defined benefit plans in the United States as of October 1 (the plans' anniversary date) of both 1984 and 1983:

(Dollars in Millions)	1984	1983
Actuarial present value of accumulated plan benefits:		
Vested	$20,216.2	$18,239.5
Nonvested	1,814.2	3,159.9
Total	$22,030.4	$21,399.4
Net assets available for benefits:		
Trustees	$16,245.5	$14,817.8
Insurance companies	3,211.8	3,310.2
Total	$19,457.3	$18,128.0

The assumed rates of return used in determining the actuarial present value of accumulated plan benefits shown in the table above were based upon those published by the Pension Benefit Guaranty Corporation, a public corporation established under the Employee Retirement Income Security Act (ERISA), adjusted in 1984 to reflect a fixed income management technique under which an immunized rate is being earned on certain pension fund assets. Such rates averaged approximately 10¼% for 1984 and approximately 9% for 1983. The effect of the 1984 immunized rate adjustment was to reduce the unfunded liability by $663.5 million in 1984.

The pension plans of subsidiaries outside the United States are not required to report to governmental agencies pursuant to ERISA and the actuarial value of accumulated benefits for these plans has not been determined in the manner calculated and shown above. The total of these plans' pension funds and balance sheet accruals, less pension prepayments and deferred charges, exceeded the actuarially computed value of vested benefits by approximately $340 million at December 31, 1984 and $497 million at December 31, 1983.

In addition to providing pension benefits, the Corporation and its subsidiaries provide certain health care and life insurance benefits for retired employes. Substantially all of the Corporation's employes, including employes in some foreign countries, may become eligible for those benefits if they reach normal retirement age while working for the Corporation. The Corporation recognizes the cost of providing those benefits by expensing annual insurance premiums, which amounted to $798 million in 1984 for United States retirees.

NOTES TO FINANCIAL STATEMENTS (continued)

NOTE 7. United States, Foreign and Other Income Taxes (Credit)

(Dollars in Millions)	1984	1983	1982
Taxes estimated to be payable (refundable) currently:			
United States Federal	$1,151.7	$ 254.4	($168.6)
Foreign	662.5	146.0	98.6
State and local	140.1	126.0	(8.1)
Total	1,954.3	526.4	(78.1)
Taxes deferred—net:			
United States Federal	8.3	1,241.3	(146.3)
Foreign	(170.6)	192.7	(35.0)
State and local	32.1	142.0	(40.4)
Total	(130.2)	1,576.0	(221.7)
Investment tax credits deferred—net:			
United States Federal	(15.1)	47.7	85.3
Foreign	(3.9)	73.7	(37.7)
Total	(19.0)	121.4	47.6
Total taxes (credit)	$1,805.1	$2,223.8	($252.2)

Investment tax credits entering into the determination of taxes estimated to be payable (refundable) currently amounted to $311.6 million in 1984, $406.2 million in 1983 and $403.0 million in 1982.

The deferred taxes (credit) for timing differences consisted principally of the following: 1984—$762.6 million for benefit plans expense, ($305.5) million for sales and product allowances, $387.6 million for vehicle instalment sales; ($240.3) million for interest; ($125.1) million for pollution control bonds; and ($435.7) million for the domestic international sales corporation (DISC); 1983—$519.2 million for benefit plans expense, ($438.0) million for sales and product allowances, $379.5 million for vehicle instalment sales and $707.5 million for depreciation; and 1982—($164.0) million for benefit plans expense, ($172.0) million for sales and product allowances and $275.0 million for depreciation.

Income before income taxes included the following components:

(Dollars in Millions)	1984	1983	1982
Domestic income	$4,513.6	$4,387.6	$170.4
Foreign income (loss)	990.7	583.9	(147.6)
Total	$5,504.3	$4,971.5	$ 22.8

The consolidated income tax (credit) was different than the amount computed at the United States statutory income tax rate for the reasons set forth in the table at the top of the next column.

(Dollars in Millions)	1984	1983	1982
Expected tax at U.S. statutory income tax rate	$2,532.0	$2,286.9	$ 10.5
Investment tax credits amortized	(330.6)	(284.8)	(355.4)
Foreign tax rate differential	135.9	43.9	131.3
State and local income taxes	93.0	144.7	(26.2)
Deferred income tax reversal on the DISC	(421.3)	—	—
Taxes on undistributed earnings of subsidiaries	(112.2)	54.4	(4.7)
Other adjustments	(91.7)	(21.3)	(7.7)
Consolidated income tax (credit)	$1,805.1	$2,223.8	($252.2)

NOTE 8. Earnings and Cash Dividends Per Share of Common Stocks

Earnings per share of common stocks have been determined using the "two-class" method. Under that method, earnings per share have been determined based on the relative rights of $1-2/3 par value common and Class E common stocks to participate in dividends. Cash dividends on the Class E common stock are to be paid out of the earnings of EDS and its subsidiaries since acquisition by GM, excluding the effects of purchase accounting adjustments arising from the acquisition (Separate Consolidated Net Income of EDS). Cash dividends on the $1-2/3 par value common stock are to be paid out of the earnings of GM and its subsidiaries, excluding the earnings of EDS and its subsidiaries since acquisition by GM as defined above. At December 31, 1984, consolidated net income retained for use in the business attributable to Class E common stock and $1-2/3 par value common stock was $17.5 million and $20,779.1 million, respectively.

The current policy of the Board of Directors is to pay cash dividends on the Class E common stock approximately equal to 25% of the quotient of (a) the Separate Consolidated Net Income of EDS, divided by (b) the greater of 60,000,000 or the number of shares of Class E common stock outstanding. The Board has also adopted the policy that cash dividends per share of Class E common stock for the first four quarters following the acquisition of EDS will equal at least $0.09 per share per quarter. The cash dividend for the period from acquisition of EDS through December 31, 1984 amounted to $0.09 per share.

Earnings per share of common stocks are based on the average number of shares outstanding during each year. The effect on earnings per share of $1-2/3 par value common stock resulting from the assumed exercise of outstanding options and delivery of bonus awards and contingent credits under the General Motors Incentive Program is not material.

NOTE 9. General Motors Acceptance Corporation and Subsidiaries

Condensed Consolidated Balance Sheet (Dollars in Millions)	1984	1983
Cash and investments in securities	$ 2,100.1	$ 2,002.6
Finance receivables—net (including GM and affiliates—$300.0 in 1984 and 1983)	50,051.5	48,124.4
Other assets	2,273.8	1,271.0
Total Assets	$54,425.4	$51,398.0
Short-term debt	$27,629.5	$26,257.9
Accounts payable and other liabilities (including GM and affiliates—$3,868.5 and $3,560.7)	6,913.7	6,216.6
Long-term debt	15,715.5	14,798.1
Stockholder's equity	4,166.7	4,125.4
Total Liabilities and Stockholder's Equity	$54,425.4	$51,398.0

Condensed Statement of Consolidated Income (Dollars in Millions)	1984	1983	1982
Gross Revenue	$8,098.6	$7,391.1	$7,255.4
Interest and discount	4,772.4	4,099.1	4,482.1
Other expenses	2,541.4	2,290.0	2,085.3
Total Expenses	7,313.8	6,389.1	6,567.4
Net Income	$ 784.8	$1,002.0	$ 688.0

NOTES TO FINANCIAL STATEMENTS (continued)

NOTE 10. Real Estate, Plants and Equipment and Accumulated Depreciation

(Dollars in Millions)	1984	1983
Real estate, plants and equipment (Note 12):		
Land	$ 414.9	$ 347.2
Land improvements	1,170.0	1,145.1
Leasehold improvements—less amortization	59.7	47.1
Buildings	8,162.6	8,010.2
Machinery and equipment	26,269.9	25,669.1
Furniture and office equipment	752.5	469.0
Capitalized leases	814.6	754.7
Construction in progress	1,709.9	1,335.4
Total	$39,354.1	$37,777.8
Accumulated depreciation:		
Land improvements	$ 665.5	$ 628.3
Buildings	4,120.3	3,937.0
Machinery and equipment	16,207.9	15,057.8
Furniture and office equipment	289.8	196.4
Capitalized leases	366.3	297.3
Total	$21,649.8	$20,116.8

NOTE 11. Accrued Liabilities

(Dollars in Millions)	1984	1983
Taxes, other than income taxes	$ 990.0	$1,016.5
Payrolls	1,764.3	1,633.5
Employe benefits	630.4	1,297.2
Dealer and customer allowances, claims, discounts, etc.	3,896.7	3,589.8
Other	1,706.8	1,272.2
Total	$8,988.2	$8,809.2

NOTE 12. Long-Term Debt

(Dollars in Millions)	Interest Rate	Maturity	1984	1983
GM:				
U.S. dollars:				
Notes	8.05 %		$ —	$ 300.0
Notes	10.00	1986	50.0	125.0
Notes	12.20	1986-88	200.0	200.0
Notes	10.00	1991	250.0	250.0
Debentures	8.625	2005	102.4	102.4
Other	5.23	1986-2001	69.1	80.1
Other currencies	7.44	1986-87	17.7	19.9
Consolidated subsidiaries:				
U.S. dollars	11.24	1986-2006	960.6	1,005.7
Spanish pesetas	12.74	1986-90	527.8	597.9
German marks	6.01	1986-96	143.5	106.0
Australian dollars	13.70	1986-89	27.3	177.1
Austrian schillings	7.10	1986-88	17.6	132.9
Other currencies	Various	1986-2004	155.3	149.2
Total			2,521.3	3,246.2
Less unamortized discount (principally on 10% notes due 1991)			103.9	109.0
Total			$2,417.4	$3,137.2

At year-end 1984, the Corporation and its consolidated subsidiaries had unused short-term credit lines of approximately $2.4 billion and unused long-term credit agreements of approximately $1.4 billion. Long-term debt at December 31, 1984 and 1983 included approximately $624 million and $883 million, respectively, of short-term obligations which are intended to be renewed or refinanced under long-term credit agreements. Long-term debt (including current portion) bore interest at a weighted average rate of approximately 12.3% at December 31, 1984 and 11.8% at December 31, 1983.

In 1981, the Corporation and a subsidiary arranged a private financing of $500 million in 10% notes due 1991. The difference between the 10% stated interest rate and the 14.7% effective rate reflects the discount which is being amortized over the lives of the notes. An option to acquire certain real estate in 1991 was also granted. The option holder may deliver the notes in payment for the real estate.

Under the sinking fund provisions of the trust indenture for the Corporation's 8⅝% Debentures due 2005, the Corporation is to make annual sinking fund payments of $3.0 million in 2002 and $11.8 million in each of the years 2003 and 2004.

Maturities of long-term debt in the years 1985 through 1989 are (in millions) $735.5 (included in loans payable at December 31, 1984), $674.2, $474.2, $218.5 and $97.8. Loans payable at December 31, 1983 included $423.4 million current portion of long-term debt.

NOTE 13. Stockholders' Equity

The preferred stock is subject to redemption at the option of the Board of Directors on any dividend date on not less than thirty days' notice at the redemption prices stated on the next page plus accrued dividends.

The Class E common stock has one-half vote per share and votes with the $1-2/3 par value common stock on all general Corporate matters. Liquidation rights are based on voting rights with each share of Class E common stock being treated as one-half of a share of $1-2/3 par value common stock.

After December 31, 1994, the Board of Directors may exchange $1-2/3 par value common for Class E common stock if the Board has declared and paid certain minimum cash dividends on the Class E common stock during each of the five years preceding the exchange. If GM should sell, liquidate, or otherwise dispose of EDS, the Corporation will be required to exchange $1-2/3 par value common for Class E common stock. In the event of any exchange, the Class E common stockholders will receive $1-2/3 par value common stock having a market value at the time of the exchange equal to 120% of the market value of the Class E common stock exchanged.

The Certificate of Incorporation provides that no cash dividends may be paid on the $1-2/3 par value common stock, Class E common stock or any series of preference stock so long as current assets (excluding prepaid expenses) in excess of current liabilities of the Corporation are less than $75 per share of outstanding preferred stock. Such current assets (with inventories calculated on the FIFO basis) in excess of current liabilities were greater than $75 in respect of each share of outstanding preferred stock at December 31, 1984.

The equity of the Corporation and its consolidated subsidiaries in the accumulated net income or loss, since acquisition, of associates has been included in net income retained for use in the business.

(continued)

NOTES TO FINANCIAL STATEMENTS (continued)

NOTE 13. (concluded)

(Dollars in Millions Except Per Share Amounts)	1984	1983	1982
Capital Stock:			
Preferred Stock, without par value, cumulative dividends (authorized, 6,000,000 shares):			
$5.00 series, stated value $100 per share, redeemable at Corporation option at $120 per share:			
Issued at beginning of the year (1,875,366 shares); in treasury (39,722 shares)	$ 183.6	$ 183.6	$ 183.6
Reacquired on the open market (137,350 shares)	13.8	–	–
Outstanding at end of the year (1,698,294 shares in 1984)	169.8	183.6	183.6
$3.75 series, stated value $100 per share, redeemable at Corporation option at $100 per share:			
Issued at beginning of the year (1,000,000 shares)	100.0	100.0	100.0
Reacquired on the open market (142,000 shares)	14.2	–	–
Outstanding at end of the year (858,000 shares in 1984)	85.8	100.0	100.0
Preference Stock, $0.10 par value (authorized, 100,000,000 shares in 1984), no shares issued	–	–	–
Class E Common Stock, $0.10 par value (authorized, 190,000,000 shares in 1984):			
Issued in the acquisition of EDS (11,371,268 shares)	1.1	–	–
Issued in conjunction with the EDS 1977 Stock Incentive Plan (2,270,160 shares) (Note 4)	.2	–	–
Issued to $1-2/3 par value common stockholders as a dividend (15,440,954 shares)	1.6	–	–
Issued at end of the year (29,082,382 shares in 1984)	2.9	–	–
Common Stock, $1-2/3 par value (authorized, 1,000,000,000 shares):			
Issued at beginning of the year (315,711,299 shares in 1984, 312,363,657 in 1983 and 304,804,228 in 1982)	526.2	520.6	508.0
Newly issued stock used for bonus deliveries, sold under provisions of the Stock Option Plans, Employe Stock Ownership Plans, Savings-Stock Purchase Programs and the Dividend Reinvestment Plan (1,792,834 shares in 1984, 3,029,593 in 1983 and 6,459,429 in 1982) and exchanged for long-term debt (318,049 shares in 1983 and 1,100,000 in 1982)	3.0	5.6	12.6
Issued at end of the year (317,504,133 shares in 1984, 315,711,299 in 1983 and 312,363,657 in 1982)	529.2	526.2	520.6
Total capital stock at end of the year	787.7	809.8	804.2
Capital Surplus (principally additional paid-in capital):			
Balance at beginning of the year	2,136.8	1,930.4	1,589.5
Stated value in excess of repurchase price of preferred stock reacquired in open market transactions	16.2	–	–
Amounts in excess of par value of Class E common stock issued in the acquisition of EDS	499.2	–	–
Amounts in excess of par value of Class E common stock issued as a dividend	585.1	–	–
Proceeds in excess of par value of newly issued $1-2/3 par value common stock used for bonus deliveries, sold under provisions of the Stock Option Plans, Employe Stock Ownership Plans, Savings-Stock Purchase Programs and the Dividend Reinvestment Plan and, in 1983 and 1982, exchanged for long-term debt	110.5	206.4	340.9
Balance at end of the year	3,347.8	2,136.8	1,930.4
Net Income Retained for Use in the Business:			
Balance at beginning of the year	18,390.5	15,552.5	15,340.0
Net income	4,516.5	3,730.2	962.7
Total	22,907.0	19,282.7	16,302.7
Dividend of one Class E common share for each 20 shares of $1-2/3 par value common	586.7	–	–
Cash dividends:			
Preferred stock, $5.00 series, $5.00 per share	8.9	9.2	9.2
Preferred stock, $3.75 series, $3.75 per share	3.6	3.7	3.7
Class E common stock, $0.09 per share in 1984	1.2	–	–
$1-2/3 par value common stock, $4.75 per share in 1984, $2.80 in 1983 and $2.40 in 1982	1,497.5	879.3	737.3
Cash payments in lieu of fractional shares of Class E common stock issued as a dividend	12.5	–	–
Total cash dividends	1,523.7	892.2	750.2
Balance at end of the year	20,796.6	18,390.5	15,552.5
Accumulated Foreign Currency Translation and Other Adjustments:			
Balance at beginning of the year:			
Accumulated foreign currency translation adjustments	(661.8)	(668.0)	–
Net unrealized gains on marketable equity securities	91.3	68.1	–
Changes during the year:			
Accumulated foreign currency translation adjustments	(127.7)	6.2	–
Net unrealized gains (losses) on marketable equity securities	(19.6)	23.2	–
Balance at end of the year	(717.8)	(570.5)	–
Total Stockholders' Equity	$24,214.3	$20,766.6	$18,287.1

NOTES TO FINANCIAL STATEMENTS (continued)

NOTE 14. Segment Reporting

General Motors is a highly vertically-integrated business operating primarily in a single industry consisting of the manufacture, assembly and sale of automobiles, trucks and related parts and accessories classified as automotive products. Because of the high degree of integration, substantial interdivisional and intercompany transfers of materials and services are made. Consequently, any determination of income by area of operations or class of products is necessarily arbitrary because of the allocation and reallocation of costs, including Corporate costs, benefiting more than one division or product.

Substantially all of General Motors' products are marketed through retail dealers and through distributors and jobbers in the United States and Canada and through distributors and dealers overseas. To assist in the merchandising of General Motors' products, GMAC and its subsidiaries offer financial services and certain types of automobile insurance to dealers and customers.

Net sales and revenues, net income (loss), total and net assets and average number of employes in the U.S. and in locations outside the U.S. for 1984, 1983 and 1982 are summarized below. Net income (loss) is after provisions for deferred income taxes applicable to that portion of the undistributed earnings deemed to be not permanently invested, less available tax credits and deductions, and appropriate consolidating adjustments for the geographic areas set forth below. Interarea sales and revenues are made at negotiated selling prices.

1984	United States	Canada	Europe	Latin America	All Other	Total*
Net Sales and Revenues:			(Dollars in Millions)			
Outside	$69,355.6	$ 4,411.6	$6,735.7	$1,642.0	$1,745.0	$83,889.9
Interarea	7,276.5	8,170.0	242.2	823.6	401.7	–
Total net sales and revenues	$76,632.1	$12,581.6	$6,977.9	$2,465.6	$2,146.7	$83,889.9
Net Income (Loss)	$ 3,872.0	$ 762.2	($ 291.1)	$ 94.4	$ 61.5	$ 4,516.5
Total Assets	$41,692.7	$ 2,833.5	$4,425.7	$2,874.0	$ 932.0	$52,144.9
Net Assets	$22,149.7	$ 1,628.9	($ 439.2)	$1,016.7	$ 41.7	$24,214.3
Average Number of Employes (in thousands)	511	41	122	49	25	748

1983						
Net Sales:						
Outside	$59,668.7	$ 3,866.4	$7,761.7	$1,742.7	$1,542.1	$74,581.6
Interarea	6,493.4	7,366.0	208.6	653.1	295.4	–
Total net sales	$66,162.1	$11,232.4	$7,970.3	$2,395.8	$1,837.5	$74,581.6
Net Income (Loss)	$ 3,469.0	$ 592.3	($ 228.3)	($ 15.0)	($ 91.1)	$ 3,730.2
Total Assets	$34,670.4	$ 2,385.5	$5,379.1	$2,834.3	$ 813.9	$45,694.5
Net Assets	$18,749.3	$ 1,332.9	($ 120.5)	$ 919.6	$ 8.9	$20,766.6
Average Number of Employes (in thousands)	463	39	123	41	25	691

1982						
Net Sales:						
Outside	$45,650.1	$ 2,621.9	$7,150.5	$2,699.5	$1,903.6	$60,025.6
Interarea	4,673.8	5,350.7	234.3	310.2	192.9	–
Total net sales	$50,323.9	$ 7,972.6	$7,384.8	$3,009.7	$2,096.5	$60,025.6
Net Income (Loss)	$ 1,079.3	($ 33.5)	$ 6.2	($ 16.5)	($ 63.2)	$ 962.7
Total Assets	$29,227.4	$ 2,299.0	$5,952.3	$2,973.3	$1,063.5	$41,397.8
Net Assets	$15,756.0	$ 774.7	$ 803.3	$ 894.3	$ 170.7	$18,287.1
Average Number of Employes (in thousands)	441	34	114	38	30	657

*After elimination of interarea transactions.

NOTE 15. Profit Sharing Plans

Profit Sharing Plans were established, effective January 1, 1983, under which eligible United States hourly and salaried employes will share in the success of the Corporation's U.S. operations. Under the Plans' provisions, 10% of profits, as defined, will be shared when the Corporation's U.S. income before income taxes plus equity in U.S. earnings of nonconsolidated subsidiaries (principally GMAC) exceeds 10% of the net worth of U.S. operations plus 5% of the difference between total assets of U.S. operations and net worth of U.S. operations. Amounts applicable to subsidiaries incorporated in the U.S. that are operating outside of the U.S., as well as amounts applicable to associates, are excluded from the calculation. Ten percent of the profits in excess of the minimum annual return, less a diversion for the Guaranteed Income Stream Benefit Program and Income Protection Plan, will be distributed to eligible U.S. employes by March 31 following the year earned. $322.2 million was accrued for profit sharing in 1983. The calculation of the profit sharing accrual for 1984 is shown on the next page.

(continued)

NOTES TO FINANCIAL STATEMENTS (concluded)

NOTE 15. (concluded)

(Dollars in Millions)   1984

Minimum Annual Return	January 1, 1984	December 31, 1984	Average		
Total Assets in the U.S.	$34,670.4	$41,692.7			
Deduct assets of excluded subsidiaries and associates	1,329.8	2,018.5			
Total Assets of U.S. operations as defined in the Plans	$33,340.6	$39,674.2	$36,507.4		
Net Assets in the U.S.	$18,749.3	$22,149.7			
Deduct net assets of excluded subsidiaries and associates	1,143.6	1,609.3			
Net Worth of U.S. operations as defined in the Plans	$17,605.7	$20,540.4	19,073.0	X 10% =	$1,907.3
Other assets of U.S. operations			$17,434.4	X 5% =	871.7
Minimum Annual Return as defined in the Plans					$2,779.0

Profits as Defined in the Plans

Net Income in the U.S.	$3,872.0
Add: Net loss of excluded subsidiaries and associates	24.7
Income taxes of U.S. operations	1,322.9
Provision for the General Motors Incentive Program applicable to U.S. operations	271.0
Profit sharing accrual	281.9
Profits as defined in the Plans	$5,772.5

Profit Sharing Accrual

Profits as defined in the Plans	$5,772.5		
Deduct Minimum Annual Return as defined in the Plans	2,779.0		
Profits in excess of Minimum Annual Return	$2,993.5	X 10% =	$299.3
Deduct diversion for Guaranteed Income Stream Benefit Program and Income Protection Plan			17.4
Profit Sharing Accrual			$281.9

NOTE 16. Contingent Liabilities

There are various claims and pending actions against the Corporation and its subsidiaries with respect to commercial matters, including warranties and product liability, governmental regulations including environmental and safety matters, civil rights, antitrust, patent matters, taxes and other matters arising out of the conduct of the business. Certain of these actions purport to be class actions, seeking damages in very large amounts. The amounts of liability on these claims and actions at December 31, 1984 were not determinable but, in the opinion of the management, the ultimate liability resulting will not materially affect the consolidated financial position of the Corporation and its consolidated subsidiaries.

— **ACCOUNTANTS' REPORT** —

Deloitte Haskins + Sells
CERTIFIED PUBLIC ACCOUNTANTS

1114 Avenue of the Americas
New York, New York 10036

General Motors Corporation, its Directors and Stockholders: February 4, 1985

We have examined the Consolidated Balance Sheet of General Motors Corporation and consolidated subsidiaries as of December 31, 1984 and 1983 and the related Statements of Consolidated Income and Changes in Consolidated Financial Position for each of the three years in the period ended December 31, 1984. Our examinations were made in accordance with generally accepted auditing standards and, accordingly, included such tests of the accounting records and such other auditing procedures as we considered necessary in the circumstances.

In our opinion, these financial statements present fairly the financial position of the companies at December 31, 1984 and 1983 and the results of their operations and the changes in their financial position for each of the three years in the period ended December 31, 1984, in conformity with generally accepted accounting principles consistently applied during the period except for the change in 1983, with which we concur, in the method of accounting for foreign currency translation as described in Note 1 to the Financial Statements.

Deloitte Haskins + Sells

SUPPLEMENTARY INFORMATION

Selected Quarterly Data
(Dollars in Millions Except Per Share Amounts)

	1984 Quarters				1983 Quarters			
	1st	2nd	3rd	4th	1st	2nd	3rd	4th
Net sales and revenues	$22,886.4	$21,583.3	$18,542.6	$20,877.6	$16,743.8	$19,400.2	$17,619.3	$20,818.3
Operating income	2,424.7	1,546.8	306.9	421.6	692.9	1,775.2	866.0	2,174.3
Income before income taxes	2,487.4	1,786.5	526.0	704.4	518.5	1,655.7	738.7	2,058.6
United States, foreign and other income taxes	1,097.5	384.7	277.8	45.1	112.3	860.8	236.1	1,014.6
Income after income taxes	1,389.9	1,401.8	248.2	659.3	406.2	794.9	502.6	1,044.0
Equity in earnings of nonconsolidated subsidiaries and associates	224.1	207.0	168.6	217.6	246.9	248.5	234.3	252.8
Net income	1,614.0	1,608.8	416.8	876.9	653.1	1,043.4	736.9	1,296.8
Dividends on preferred stocks	3.2	3.2	3.1	3.0	3.2	3.3	3.2	3.2
Earnings on common stocks	$ 1,610.8	$ 1,605.6	$ 413.7	$ 873.9	$ 649.9	$ 1,040.1	$ 733.7	$ 1,293.6
Attributable to:								
$1-2/3 par value common stock	$ 1,610.8	$ 1,605.6	$ 413.7	$ 855.2	$ 649.9	$ 1,040.1	$ 733.7	$ 1,293.6
Class E common stock (issued in 1984)	—	—	—	$ 18.7	—	—	—	—
Average number of shares of common stocks outstanding (in millions):								
$1-2/3 par value common	315.2	315.5	315.3	315.3	312.4	313.5	314.7	314.8
Class E common (issued in 1984)	—	—	—	18.2	—	—	—	—
Earnings Per Share of Common Stocks:								
$1-2/3 par value common*	$5.11	$5.09	$1.31	$2.71	$2.08	$3.32	$2.33	$4.11
Class E common (issued in 1984)	—	—	—	$1.03	—	—	—	—
Cash dividends per share of common stocks:								
$1-2/3 par value common	$1.00	$1.25	$1.25	$1.25	$0.60	$0.60	$0.60	$1.00
Class E common (issued in 1984)	—	—	—	$0.09	—	—	—	—
Stock price range:								
$1-2/3 par value common**								
High	$80.50	$68.25	$80.25	$82.75	$65.75	$75.25	$77.50	$80.00
Low	$62.63	$61.00	$64.25	$73.38	$57.38	$56.00	$65.50	$72.00
Class E common (issued in 1984)***								
High	—	—	—	$42.50	—	—	—	—
Low	—	—	—	$33.00	—	—	—	—

*Includes favorable (unfavorable) effects on earnings per share of: an adjustment of income taxes of $1.34 in the 1984 second quarter reflecting a change in the provisions covering domestic international sales corporations (DISC) in accordance with the Deficit Reduction Act of 1984; and foreign exchange/translation activity [1984: first quarter—$0.24, second quarter—($0.23), third quarter—($0.45), fourth quarter—$0.24; 1983: first quarter—$0.51, second quarter—($0.45), third quarter—($0.12), fourth quarter—($0.11)].

**The principal market is the New York Stock Exchange and prices are based on the Composite Tape. $1-2/3 par value common stock is also listed on the Midwest, Pacific and Philadelphia stock exchanges. As of December 31, 1984, there were 943,831 holders of record of $1-2/3 par value common stock.

***The principal market is the New York Stock Exchange and prices are based on the Composite Tape. As of December 31, 1984, these were 623,210 holders of record of Class E common stock.

The effective income tax rate for the 1984 second quarter reflects the $421.3 million reversal of deferred income taxes related to DISC legislation; the rate for the third quarter reflects losses at overseas subsidiaries where no applicable tax credits were available; and the rate for the fourth quarter reflects higher investment tax credits due to increased capital expenditures and the effect of foreign tax credits on dividends declared by subsidiaries, applied to lower pretax earnings. The effective income tax rates for the 1983 quarters reflect the continuing high level of U.S. investment tax credits.

(continued)

SUPPLEMENTARY INFORMATION (concluded)

Selected Financial Data

(Dollars in Millions Except Per Share Amounts)	1984	1983	1982	1981	1980
Net sales and revenues	$83,889.9	$74,581.6	$60,025.6	$62,698.5	$57,728.5
Earnings (loss) on $1-2/3 par value common stock	$ 4,485.3	$ 3,717.3	$ 949.8	$ 320.5	($ 775.4)
Cash dividends on $1-2/3 par value common stock	1,510.0	879.3	737.3	717.6	861.2
Dividend of Class E common shares	586.7	–	–	–	–
Net income (loss) retained in the year	$ 2,388.6	$ 2,838.0	$ 212.5	($ 397.1)	($ 1,636.6)
Earnings (loss) on $1-2/3 par value common stock—per share	$14.22	$11.84	$3.09	$1.07	($2.65)
Cash dividends on $1-2/3 par value common stock—per share	4.75	2.80	2.40	2.40	2.95
Dividend of Class E common shares—per share	1.90	–	–	–	–
Net income (loss) retained in the year—per share	$ 7.57	$ 9.04	$0.69	($1.33)	($5.60)
Earnings on Class E common stock (issued in 1984)	$ 18.7	–	–	–	–
Cash dividends on Class E common stock (issued in 1984)	1.2	–	–	–	–
Net income retained in the year	$ 17.5	–	–	–	–
Earnings on Class E common stock—per share	$1.03	–	–	–	–
Cash dividends on Class E common stock—per share	0.09	–	–	–	–
Net income retained in the year—per share	$0.94	–	–	–	–
Average number of shares of common stocks outstanding (in millions):					
$1-2/3 par value common	315.3	313.9	307.4	299.1	292.4
Class E common (issued in 1984)	18.2	–	–	–	–
Cash dividends on capital stocks as a percent of net income	33.7%	23.9%	77.9%	219.1%	N.A.
Expenditures for real estate, plants and equipment	$ 3,595.1	$ 1,923.0	$ 3,611.1	$ 6,563.3	$ 5,160.5
Expenditures for special tools	$ 2,452.1	$ 2,083.7	$ 2,601.0	$ 3,178.1	$ 2,600.0
Cash and marketable securities	$ 8,567.4	$ 6,216.9	$ 3,126.2	$ 1,320.7	$ 3,715.2
Working capital	$ 6,276.7	$ 5,890.8	$ 1,658.1	$ 1,158.8	$ 3,212.1
Total assets	$52,144.9	$45,694.5	$41,397.8	$38,979.0	$34,581.0
Long-term debt and capitalized leases	$ 2,772.9	$ 3,521.8	$ 4,745.1	$ 4,044.0	$ 2,058.3

Financial data for years prior to 1983 have not been restated for the adoption of Statement of Financial Accounting Standards No. 52, Foreign Currency Translation.

EFFECTS OF INFLATION ON FINANCIAL DATA

The accompanying Schedules display the basic historical cost financial data adjusted for changes in specific prices (current cost) for use in the evaluation of comparative financial results.

One method by which to analyze the effects of inflation on financial data (and thus the business) is by adjusting the historical cost data to the current costs for the major balance sheet items which have been accumulated through the accounting system over a period of years and which thus reflect different prices for the same commodities and services.

The current cost of inventories was estimated based on costs in effect at December 31, 1984. Cost of sales for inventories maintained on a first-in, first-out basis was restated to a current cost basis using the specific level of prices at the time the goods were sold.

The current cost of property owned and the related depreciation and amortization expense for U.S. operations were calculated by applying (1) selected producer price indices to historical book values of machinery and equipment and (2) the Marshall Valuation Service index to buildings, and the use of assessed values for land. For locations outside the United States, such amounts were calculated generally by applying indices closely related to the assets being measured and translating the resulting amounts using year-end foreign currency exchange rates.

The purpose of this type of restatement is to furnish estimates of the effects of price increases for replacement of inventories and property on the potential future net income of the business and thus assess the probability of future cash flows. Although these data may be useful for this purpose, they do not reflect specific plans for the replacement of property. A more meaningful estimate of the effects of such costs on future earnings is the estimated level of future capital expenditures which is set forth on page 16 in the Financial Review: Management's Discussion and Analysis.

Under the current cost method, the net income of General Motors is lower (or the net loss is higher) than that determined under the historical cost method. This means that businesses, as well as individuals, are affected by inflation and that the purchasing power of business dollars also has declined. In addition, the costs of maintaining the productive capacity, as reflected in the current cost data (and estimate of future capital expenditures), have increased, and thus management must seek ways to cope with the effects of inflation through accounting methods such as the LIFO method of inventory valuation, which matches current costs with current revenues, and through accelerated methods of depreciation and amortization.

It must be emphasized that there is a continuing need for national monetary and fiscal policies designed to control inflation and to provide adequate capital for future business growth which, in turn, will mean increased productivity and employment.

EFFECTS OF INFLATION ON FINANCIAL DATA (concluded)

Comparison of Selected Data Adjusted for Effects of Changing Prices
(Dollars in Millions Except Per Share Amounts)
Historical cost data adjusted for changes in specific prices (current cost):*

	1984	1983	1982	1981	1980
Net Income (Loss)—as reported	$ 4,516.5	$ 3,730.2	$ 962.7	$ 333.4	($ 762.5)
—in current cost 1967 dollars	1,403.1	1,144.0	71.7	(252.8)	(829.5)
Earnings (Loss) per share of $1-2/3 par value common stock					
—as reported	$14.22	$11.84	$3.09	$1.07	($2.65)
—in current cost 1967 dollars	4.42	3.63	0.22	(0.86)	(2.86)
Earnings per share of Class E common stock (issued in 1984)					
—as reported	$1.03	—	—	—	—
—in current cost 1967 dollars	0.33	—	—	—	—
Cash dividends per share of $1-2/3 par value common stock					
—as reported	$4.75	$2.80	$2.40	$2.40	$2.95
—in constant 1967 dollars	1.53	0.94	0.83	0.88	1.20
Cash dividends per share of Class E common stock (issued in 1984)					
—as reported	$0.09	—	—	—	—
—in constant 1967 dollars	0.03	—	—	—	—
Net assets at year-end—as reported	$24,214.3	$20,766.6	$18,287.1	$17,721.1	$17,814.6
—in current cost 1967 dollars	10,938.7	10,635.1	9,818.3	10,450.9	11,377.2
Accumulated foreign currency translation adjustments					
—as reported	($ 127.7)	($ 661.8)	—	—	—
—in current cost 1967 dollars	(51.8)	(129.8)	—	—	—
Unrealized gain from decline in purchasing power of dollars of net amounts owed	$ 50.5	$ 86.5	$ 130.5	$ 241.3	$ 182.3
Excess of increase in general price level over increase in specific prices of inventories and property	$ 320.8	$ 78.4	$ 861.2	$ 619.0	$ 689.2
Market price per $1-2/3 par value common share at year-end					
—unadjusted	$78.38	$74.38	$62.38	$38.50	$45.00
—in constant 1967 dollars	25.19	24.93	21.58	14.13	18.23
Market price per Class E common share at year-end (issued in 1984)					
—unadjusted	$42.38	—	—	—	—
—in constant 1967 dollars	13.62	—	—	—	—
Average Consumer Price Index	311.1	298.4	289.1	272.4	246.8

*Current cost data have been adjusted to 1967 dollars by applying the Consumer Price Index—Urban to the data with 1967 (CPI-100) as the base year. Depreciation has been determined on a straight-line basis for this calculation.

Schedule of Income Adjusted for Changing Prices
For the Year Ended December 31, 1984
(Dollars in Millions Except Per Share Amounts)

	As Reported in the Financial Statements (Historical Cost)	Adjusted for Changes in Specific Prices (1984 Current Cost)
Net Sales and Revenues	$83,889.9	$83,889.9
Cost of sales	70,217.9	70,270.1
Depreciation and amortization of property	4,899.9	4,999.5
Other operating and nonoperating items—net	2,450.5	2,450.5
United States and other income taxes	1,805.1	1,805.1
Total costs and expenses	79,373.4	79,525.2
Net Income	$ 4,516.5	$ 4,364.7
Earnings per share of $1-2/3 par value common stock	$14.22	$13.74
Earnings per share of Class E common stock	$1.03	$1.03
Accumulated foreign currency translation adjustments	($ 127.7)	($ 161.0)
Unrealized gain from decline in purchasing power of dollars of net amounts owed		$ 157.2
Excess of increase in general price level over increase in specific prices of inventories and property		$ 998.1**

**At December 31, 1984, current cost of inventories was $9,535.2 million and current cost of property (including special tools), net of accumulated depreciation and amortization, was $27,042.0 million.

APPENDIX
B

International Accounting

■ WHY ACCOUNTING PRINCIPLES AND PRACTICES DIFFER AMONG NATIONS

In today's world we do not find it surprising to discover a British bank in Atlanta, Coca-Cola in Paris, and French airplanes in Zaire. German auto parts are assembled in Spain and sold in the United States. Japan buys oil from Saudi Arabia and sells cameras in Italy. Soviet livestock eat American grain, and the British sip tea from Sri Lanka and China. Business has become truly international, but accounting, often described as the language of business, does not cross borders so easily. Accounting principles and reporting practices differ from country to country, and international decision making is made more difficult by the lack of a common communication system. But, since business is practiced at an international level, accounting must find a way to provide its services at that level.

The problem is that accounting must first reflect the national economic and social environment in which it is practiced, and this environment is not the same in Bangkok as in Boston. Some economies, for example, are mainly agricultural. Others are based on manufacturing, trade, or service industries. Still others export natural resources, such as oil or gold, while a few derive most of their income from tourism. Accounting for inventories and natrual resources, cost accounting techniques, and methods of foreign currency translation naturally have a different orientation, emphasis, and degree of refinement in these different economies.

Other accounting differences stem from the various legal or political systems of nations. In centrally controlled economies, for instance, the state owns all or most of the property. It makes little sense to prescribe full disclosure of accounting procedures to protect investors when there is little or no private ownership of property. Some of these countries standardize their accounting methods and incorporate them into law. But in market-oriented economies, the development of accounting principles and reporting practices is left mainly to the private sector. Where uniformity exists, it occurs more by general agreement or consensus of interested parties than by governmental decree. In market-oriented economies, accounting principles and practices must be more flexible to serve the needs of business firms which differ widely in ownership, size, and complexity. In countries where business firms are predominately family owned, disclosure practices can be less complete than in countries where large, publicly held corporations dominate.

The degree of development of the accounting profession and the general level of education of a country also influence accounting practices and procedures. Nations that lack a well-organized accounting profession may adopt almost wholesale the accounting methods of other countries. Commonwealth countries, for example, tend to follow British accounting standards; the former French colonies of Africa use French systems; Bermuda follows Canadian pronouncements; and the influence of the United States is widespread. At the same time, levels of expertise vary. There is no point in advocating statistical accounting and auditing techniques in countries where there is little knowledge or understanding of statistics. Accounting systems designed for electronic data processing are not helpful in countries where few or no businesses use computers.

Even in advanced countries, genuine differences of opinion exist regarding accounting theory and appropriate accounting methods. American standards, for example, require the periodic amortization of goodwill to expense, but British, German, and Dutch standards do not. Accounting methods also differ within nations. Most countries, including the United States, permit several depreciation methods and two or more inventory costing methods. Such flexibility is essential if accounting is to serve a useful purpose in economic, political, and social environments that are not uniform.

■ ATTEMPTED HARMONIZATION OF ACCOUNTING PRACTICES

The question arises as to whether financial statements that reflect the economic and social environment of, say, France can also be useful to a potential American investor. Can some of the differences between French and American accounting be eliminated or at least explained so that French and American investors will understand each other's reports and find them useful when they make decisions?

Several organizations are working to achieve greater understanding and harmonization of different accounting practices. These include the United Nations Commission on Transnational Corporations, the Organization for Economic Cooperation and Development (OECD), the European Economic Community (EEC), the International Federation of Accountants (IFAC), and the International Accounting Standards Committee (IASC). These organizations study the information needs and accounting and reporting practices of different nations and issue pronouncements recommending specific practices and procedures for adoption by all members.

The IASC is making a significant contribution to the development of international accounting standards. It was founded in London in 1973 by the professional accountancy bodies of 10 countries: Australia, Canada, France, Germany, Ireland, Japan, Mexico, the Netherlands, the United Kingdom, and the United States. Since 1973, the professional bodies of more than 30 countries have joined the IASC as associate members. The IASC selects a topic for study from lists of problems submitted by the profession all over the world. After research and discussion by special committees, the IASC issues an exposure draft of a proposed standard for consideration by the profession and the business and financial communities. After about six months' further study of the topic in light of the comments received, the IASC issues the final international accounting standard. To date, 19 standards have been issued on topics as varied as *Disclosure of Accounting Policies* (IAS 1), *Depreciation Accounting* (IAS 4), *Statement of Changes in Financial Position* (IAS 7), and *Revenue Recognition* (IAS 18, effective January 1, 1984). Setting international standards is not easy. If the standards are too detailed or rigid, then the flexibility needed to reflect different national environments will be lost. On the other hand, if pronouncements are vague and allow too many alternative methods, then there is little point in setting international standards.

One major problem is the enforcement of these standards. There is no organization, nor is there likely to be, to ensure compliance with international standards. Enforcement is left to national standard-setting bodies or legislatures, which may or may not adopt a recommended international standard. Generally, members commit themselves to support the objectives of the international body. The members promise to use their best endeavors to see that international standards are formally adopted by local professional accountancy bodies, by government departments or other authorities that control the securities markets, and by the industrial, business, and financial communities of their respective countries.

The American Institute of Certified Public Accountants (AICPA), for example, issued a revised statement in 1975 reaffirming its support for the implementation of international standards adopted by the IASC. The AICPA's position is that international accounting standards must be specifically adopted by the Financial Accounting Standards Board (FASB), which is not a member of the IASC, is order to achieve acceptance in the United States. But if there is no significant difference between an international standard and U.S. practice, compliance with U.S. generally accepted accounting principles (GAAP) constitutes compliance with the international standard. Where a significant difference exists, the AICPA publishes the IASC standard together with comments on how it differs from U.S. GAAP and undertakes to urge the FASB to give early consideration to harmonizing the differences.[1] Significant support for IASC standards has also resulted from a resolution adopted by the World Federation of Stock Exchanges in 1975. The resolution binds members to require conformance with IASC standards in securities listing agreements.[2]

Although these developments are important for international harmonization of accounting, ultimately the success of international pronouncements depends on the willingness of the members to support them. In some cases, national legislation is required and may be slow or difficult to pass. The EEC, for example, issues "Directives" which must be accepted as compulsory objectives

---

[1] American Institute of Certified Public Accountants, *CPA Letter,* August 1975.

[2] *CA Magazine,* January 1975, p. 52.

by the 10 member states (Belgium, Denmark, France, Germany, Greece, Ireland, Italy, Luxembourg, the Netherlands, and the United Kingdom) but which are translated into national legislation at the discretion of each member state. The EEC's important *Fourth Directive* was adopted in 1978 to regulate the preparation, content, presentation, audit, and publication of the accounts and reports of companies. It applies to all limited-liability companies (corporations) registered in the EEC, except for banks and insurance companies. Under the directive, member states were to introduce legislation by July 1980 so that accounts in all EEC countries would conform to the directive as of the fiscal year beginning January 1, 1982. Yet by that date, only Belgium, Denmark, and the United Kingdom had passed the necessary legislation, although most of the other member countries were close to doing so.

The general movement toward international harmonization of accounting standards is increasing in other areas of society. The accounting profession, national standard-setting bodies, universities, academic societies, and multinational corporations have all shown an increased interest in international accounting problems in recent years. The AICPA has an International Practice Division as a formal part of its line organization. The American Accounting Association officially established an International Accounting Section in 1976. The University of Lancaster (England) and the University of Illinois have international accounting research centers that support research studies and conduct international conferences and seminars. Georgia State University received a Touche Ross & Co. grant to internationalize its accounting curriculum. Many universities currently offer courses in international business and accounting.

All this activity helps to increase the flow of information and our understanding of the accounting and reporting practices in other parts of the world. Greater understanding improves the likelihood that unnecessary differences will be eliminated and enhances the general acceptance of international standards.

The rest of this appendix gives examples of the accounting methods used in different countries and of the concepts that underlie them to illustrate the difficulty of achieving international harmonization.

▋ FOREIGN CURRENCY TRANSLATION

Foreign currency translation is probably the most common problem in an international business environment. Foreign currency translation has two main components: accounting for transactions in a foreign currency and translating the financial statements of foreign enterprises into a different, common currency.

Accounting for Transactions in a Foreign Currency

Suppose an American automobile dealership imports vehicles from Japan and promises to pay for them in yen 90 days after receiving them. If there is no change in the dollar-yen exchange rate between the date the goods are received and the date the invoice is paid, there is no problem. Both the purchase and the payment will be recorded at the same dollar value. But if the yen appreciates against the dollar during the 90-day period, the importer must pay more dollars for the yen needed on the settlement date.[3] Which exchange rate should the importer use to record payment of the invoice—the rate in effect on the purchase date or on the payment date?

One approach to the problem is to regard the purchase of the automobiles and settlement of the invoice as two separate transactions and record them at two different exchange rates. The difference between the amount recorded in Accounts Payable on the purchase date and the decrease in Cash on the settlement date is considered an exchange gain or loss (a loss in this case). This approach, known as the "time-of-transaction" method, was the prescribed or predominant practice in 61 of 64 countries surveyed in 1979,[4] including the United States.[5] The time-of-transaction method is also the method recommended in the IASC's exposure draft, *Accounting for the Effects of Changes in Foreign Exchange Rates,* issued in March 1982.

Another approach, known as the "time-of-settlement" method, regards the transaction and its settlement as a single event. If this method is used, the amount recorded on the purchase date is regarded as an estimate of the settlement amount. Any fluctuations in the exchange rate between the purchase date and the settlement date are accounted for as part of the transaction and are not treated as a separate gain or loss. Consequently there is no effect on earnings.

Although the time-of-transaction method is widely used, the treatment of resulting exchange gains and losses is not uniform. If the gains or losses are realized, that is, if settlement is made within the same accounting period as the purchase, then most countries recognize such gains and losses in the income statement for that period. If the exchange gains or losses are unrealized, that is, if they result from translating Accounts Payable (or Accounts Receivable for the vendor) at the balance sheet date, the treatment varies. Recording losses unrealized was the prescribed or predominant practice in 54 countries in 1979. But only 40 countries similarly recognized exchange gains in income, the remaining nations preferring to defer them until settlement. In the United States, under the provisions of FASB *Statement No. 52,* both realized and unrealized transaction gains and losses are recognized in earnings of the period in which the exchange rate changes.

Translating Financial Statements

Financial statements of foreign subsidiaries are translated into a single common unit of measurement, such as the dollar, for purposes of consolidation. Considerable argument has arisen in recent years as to the correct way to do this; that is, which exchange rate should be used to translate items in the balance sheet and income statement, and what treatment is appropriate for any resulting exchange gains and losses? Items that translated at the historical rate cannot

---

[3] This example ignores the possibility that the importer might obtain a forward exchange contract, a discussion of which is beyond the scope of this text.

[4] Price Waterhouse International *International Survey.* Data on the different methods used and on the number of countries using each method described in these examples are derived substantially from this publication.

[5] FASB *Statement of Financial Accounting Standards No. 8,* "Accounting for the Translation of Foreign Currency Transactions and Foreign Currency Financial Statements" (Stamford, Conn., 1975). The "time-of-transaction" method is also prescribed by FASB *Statement No. 52,* "Foreign Currency Translation" (Stamford, Conn., 1981) which supersedes FASB *Statement No. 8.*

result in exchange gains or losses. But items that are translated at the exchange rate in effect on the balance sheet data (the current rate) can result in exchange gains and losses if the current rate differs from the rate in effect when those items were recorded (the historical rate). If the current rate is used, a related question arises: Should the resulting exchange gains or losses be recognized immediately in income or deferred in some way?

The methods used to translate financial statements fall basically into two groups: translation of all items at the current rate and translation of some items at the current rate and others at the historical rates. The two groups are based on different concepts of both consolidation and international business.

The Current-Rate Approach.   The current- or closing-rate method translates all assets and liabilities at the exchange rate in effect on the balance sheet date. The main advantage of this method is its simplicity; it treats all items uniformly. The approach is based on the view that a foreign subsidiary is a separate unit from the domestic parent company. The subsidiary's assets are viewed as being acquired largely out of local borrowing. Multinational groups, therefore, consist of entities that operate independently but which contribute to a central fund of resources. Consequently, in consolidation it is believed that stockholders of the parent company are interested primarily in the parent company's net investment in the foreign subsidiary.

The Current/Historical-Rates Approach.   This approach regards the parent company and its foreign subsidiaries as a single business undertaking. Assets owned by a foreign subsidiary are viewed as indistinguishable from assets owned by the parent company. Foreign assets should, therefore, be reflected in consolidated statements in the same way that similar assets of the parent company are reported, that is, at historical cost in the parent company's currency.

Three translation methods are commonly used under this approach. The **current-noncurrent method** translates current assets and current liabilities at the current rate—the rate in effect on the balance sheet date—while noncurrent items are translated at their respective historical rates. Under the **monetary-nonmonetary method,** the current rate is used for monetary assets and liabilities—that is, for those that have a fixed, nominal value in terms of the foreign currency—while historical rates are applied to nonmonetary items. The **temporal method** is a variation of the monetary-nonmonetary method. Cash, receivables and payables, and other assets and liabilities carried at current prices (for example, marketable securities carried at current market value) are translated at the current rate of exchange. All other assets and liabilities are translated at historical rates.

Disagreement over the appropriate translation method seems likely to continue because of the different concepts of parent-subsidiary relations on which they are founded. In 1979, only six countries prescribed a single method. The temporal method was required in Austria, Canada, Bermuda, Jamaica, and the United States (under FASB *Statement No. 8*), while Uruguay required the current-rate method. Since that time the United States has changed to the current-rate method (FASB *Statement No. 52*), and Canada is reconsidering its position, a decision which will also affect Bermuda. Apart from these six nations, 24 countries, including most of Europe, Japan, and Australia, followed predominantly the current-rate approach, while in 25 countries, including Germany, South Africa, and most of Central and South America, some variation of the current/historical-rates approach was common practice.

The treatment of exchange gains and losses produced by translating items at the current rate varies and is not strictly related to the translation method used. In 1979, the predominant practice in 42 nations, including much of Europe, Latin America, Japan, and the United States, was to recognize all gains and losses immediately in income. Eighteen of these countries used the current-rate translation method and 23 followed one of the current/historical-rates methods. Alternative treatments of translation gains and losses included recording them directly in stockholders' equity (Australia), recognizing some of them immediately in income and deferring others (United Kingdom), and recognizing some in income and deferring and amortizing others over the remaining life of the items concerned (Canada and Bermuda).

Since the issuance of FASB *Statement No. 52,* the immediate recognition of translation gains and losses in income is not permitted in the United States. Instead, they are reported separately and accumulated in a separate component of stockholders' equity until the parent company's investment in the foreign subsidiary is sold or liquidated, at which time they are reported as part of the gain or loss on sale or liquidation of the investment.

■ INVENTORIES

Variations in accounting for inventories relate principally to the basis for determining cost, whether cost once determined should be increased or decreased to reflect the market value of the inventories, and whether the variable (direct) costing or the absorption (full) costing approach should be used to allocate overhead.

Determination of Cost

Although other methods are occasionally used in some countries, this text will only discuss the three principal bases for determining inventory cost: first-in, first-out (Fifo); last-in, first-out (Lifo); and average cost.

The most frequently used methods in 1979 were Fifo and average cost. Each of these methods was predominant in 31 countries, although no country required the use of one method to the exclusion of the other. Fifo was more common in Europe, although Austria, France, Greece, and Portugal used an average method. Fifo also predominated in Australia, Canada, South Africa, and the United States. The average method was generally followed in Latin America, Japan, and much of Africa. Lifo was the principal method in only one country—Italy—although it was a common minority method in Japan, the United States, most of Latin America, and several European countries. Lifo was considered an unacceptable method in Australia, Brazil, France, Ireland, Malawi, Norway, Peru, and the United Kingdom. IASC's Statement No. 2, *Valuation and Presentation of Inventories in the Context of the Historical Cost System,* supports the preference of the majority of countries and recommends the use of Fifo or average cost.

Market Value of Inventories

Only seven countries in 1979 did not require or predominantly follow the principle that inventories should be carried at the lower of cost or market value. Five of these countries, including Japan, used cost, even when cost exceeded market value. In the other two countries—Portugal and Switzerland—most enterprises wrote down inventories to amounts below both cost and market value, a practice permitted by law.

The main difference in the countries that did use the lower of cost or market approach was in the interpretation of "market value." Forty-eight countries equated it with net realizable value, meaning estimated selling price in the ordinary course of business less costs of completion and necessary selling expenses. This view was essentially required in 22 countries, including Australia, France, Ireland, South Africa, and the United Kingdom. IASC Statement No. 2 also requires this interpretation. Austria, Greece, Italy, and Venezuela interpreted market value as replacement cost—the current cost of replacing the inventories in their present condition and location.

The United States defines market value as replacement cost, with the stipulation that it cannot exceed net realizable value or fall below net realizable value reduced by the normal profit margin. In 1979, Chile, the Dominican Republic, Mexico, Panama, and the Philippines also used this interpretation of market value.

Allocation of Overhead

Recall from Chapter 22 that under direct (variable) costing, all variable manufacturing costs are charged to the product and all fixed costs (including fixed manufacturing costs) are charged to expense. Manufacturing overhead costs must, therefore, be separated into variable and fixed portions. The variable portion is assigned to production and included in inventory costs until the goods are sold, whereas the fixed portion is expensed immediately. In contrast, under absorption (full) costing all manufacturing costs, including fixed overhead costs, are applied to production and included in inventories.

Fifty-one countries in 1979 required or predominantly used absorption costing based on a level of normal capacity. IASC Statement No. 2 requires this approach. Ecuador, Ivory Coast, Malaysia, Morocco, and Senegal used direct costing, while in Botswana, the Netherlands, South Africa, and Switzerland there was no predominant practice. Chile, Denmark, India, and Malawi normally excluded all overhead—fixed and variable—from inventories.

In view of the importance of inventories and the wide variation in accounting for them, it is fortunate for the users of financial statements that most countries require disclosure of information relating to the valuation of inventories. Only 8 of the countries surveyed in 1979 did not generally disclose whether the basis of valuation was cost, market, or the lower of cost or market, while all but 13 countries usually disclosed the basis for determining cost. IASC Statement No. 2 also recommends adequate disclosure of the inventory valuation methods that were used in preparing the financial statements.

■ ACCOUNTING FOR THE EFFECTS OF CHANGING PRICES

The final example of international differences illustrates an opportunity for international harmonization that is almost unique. Accounting for the effects of inflation is still in its infancy, so it may be possible to achieve a general international approach to the problem before national practices become too varied and too entrenched.

In Chapter 13, two approaches to accounting for the effects of inflation on business enterprises were discussed: general price-level accounting and current-cost accounting. The FASB, in *Statement No. 33,* requires both methods.[6] The first approach attempts to reflect the effects of changes in general purchasing power on historical-cost financial statements, while the second is concerned with the impact of specific price changes.

A number of countries are concerned about the loss of relevance of historical-cost financial reporting in inflationary environments, and several have adopted one of the two approaches. So far only the United States and Mexico require both. Some countries, usually those with the longest history of severe inflation, have issued standards that are mandatory for all enterprises, or at least for large or publicly held entities. In other countries, the accounting profession recommends, but does not prescribe, a form of inflation-adjusted statements, usually as supplementary information. The accountancy bodies of several nations have issued exposure drafts but have not yet adopted formal standards. But few countries are prepared to abandon the historical-cost basis for their primary financial statements, at least until decision makers have had sufficient experience with inflation accounting to give an opinion on its utility. Exceptions to this view are Argentina, Brazil, and Chile, which now require incorporation of general price-level accounting in the primary financial statements of all enterprises.

The United Kingdom's standard prescribes the provision of current-cost information either in the primary financial statements or as supplementary statements or additional information. New Zealand requires a supplementary income statement and balance sheet on a current-cost basis. Australia and South Africa recommended, but do not yet require, similar supplementary current-cost statements. Germany recommends the incorporation of current-cost information in notes to the historical-cost financial statements, while in the Netherlands, some companies prepare the primary statements on a current-cost basis, and some provide only supplementary information.

The fact that the accountancy bodies of various nations are adopting neither a uniform approach nor a uniform application of any approach, even with something as relatively new as inflation accounting, highlights the difficulty of achieving international harmonization of accounting standards. Adoption of different approaches to inflation accounting by different countries will make the preparation of consolidated financial statements by multinational corporations especially difficult, while at the same time comparability of the financial reports of companies in different nations will be further reduced. But even if all countries adopted a similar approach, a major barrier to comparability would still remain: the price indices used in each country to compute adjustments for price changes are not comparable in composition, accuracy, frequency of publication, or timeliness.

Many accountants are reluctant to see inflation-adjusted statements replace historical-cost financial statements because they believe historical cost is the most objective basis of valuation. But business entities may be more likely to favor inflation accounting, once they become accustomed to it, because of its tax implications. Since inflation accounting generally leads to lower profit figures than those computed on the historical-cost basis, there is a strong incentive for companies to adopt inflation accounting in those countries where computation of the tax liability is based on reported net income. Governments, on

---

[6] FASB *Statement of Financial Accounting Standards No. 33,* "Financial Reporting and Changing Prices" (Stamford, Conn., FASB, 1979).

the other hand, may decide to prohibit the use of inflation accounting for tax purposes when a decline in tax revenues becomes apparent.

The current trend in the use of inflation-accounting approaches appears to be toward current-cost accounting and away from general price-level accounting. It has been suggested that, of the two approaches, governments prefer current-cost accounting, and this preference may influence the decisions of the accounting profession in some countries. As one British writer has pointed out,

> No government wants to have the effects of its currency debasement measured by anyone—certainly not by every business enterprise in the country. Much better to point the finger at all those individual prices moving around because of the machinations of big business, big labour and big aliens.[7]

Whether current-cost accounting will become common practice or whether some combination of current-cost and general price-level accounting will gain favor, perhaps along the lines of FASB *Statement No. 33,* should depend on the usefulness to decision makers of the information provided by each approach. One thing is clear: Unless inflation abates, more countries will adopt some form of inflation accounting. The opportunity to achieve a higher level of international harmonization while national standards are still at the development stage should not be missed.

We have attempted in these few pages to provide a broad and general picture of the variety of accounting principles and reporting practices that exist across the world. This variety is inevitable and necessary if accounting is to be useful within widely differing national business environments. At the same time, the information needs of international business must also be satisfied. It is a challenging problem and one that will receive increasing attention in the years to come.

■ SELECTED BIBLIOGRAPHY

Arthur Anderson & Co. (London). *European Review* nos. 1–5 (January 1981–May 1982).

Choi, Frederick D. S. and Gerhard G. Mueller. *An Introduction to Multinational Accounting.* Englewood Cliffs, N.J.: Prentice-Hall, Inc., 1978.

Hauworth, William P., II. "A Comparison of Various International Proposals on Inflation Accounting: A Practitioner's View." Monograph, 1980.

International Centre for Research in Accounting. *International Financial Reporting Standards: Problems and Prospects. ICRA Occasional Paper No. 13.* Lancaster, England: ICRA, University of Lancaster, 1977.

Price Waterhouse International. *International Survey of Accounting Principles and Reporting Practices,* 1979.

Stamp, Edward. *The Future of Accounting and Auditing Standards. ICRA Occasional Paper No. 18.* Lancaster, England: International Centre for Research in Accounting, University of Lancaster, 1979.

Stamp, Edward, and Maurice Moonitz. "International Auditing Standards—Parts I and II." *The CPA Journal* LII, nos. 6 and 7 (June–July 1982).

---

[7] P. H. Lyons, "Farewell to Historical Costs?" *CA Magazine,* February 1976, p. 23.

APPENDIX

C

Compound Interest and Annuity Tables

Table 1 *Future Value of $1 at Compound Interest: 0.5%–10%* $\qquad F_{i,n} = (1 + i)^n$

Period	.5%	1%	1.5%	2%	2.5%	3%	3.5%	4%	4.5%	5%
1	1.00500	1.01000	1.01500	1.02000	1.02500	1.03000	1.03500	1.04000	1.04500	1.05000
2	1.01003	1.02010	1.03023	1.04040	1.05063	1.06090	1.07123	1.08160	1.09203	1.10250
3	1.01508	1.03030	1.04568	1.06121	1.07689	1.09273	1.10872	1.12486	1.14117	1.15762
4	1.02015	1.04060	1.06136	1.08243	1.10381	1.12551	1.14752	1.16986	1.19252	1.21551
5	1.02525	1.05101	1.07728	1.10408	1.13141	1.15927	1.18769	1.21665	1.24618	1.27628
6	1.03038	1.06152	1.09344	1.12616	1.15969	1.19405	1.22926	1.26532	1.30226	1.34010
7	1.03553	1.07214	1.10984	1.14869	1.18869	1.22987	1.27228	1.31593	1.36086	1.40710
8	1.04071	1.08286	1.12649	1.17166	1.21840	1.26677	1.31681	1.36857	1.42210	1.47746
9	1.04591	1.09369	1.14339	1.19509	1.24886	1.30477	1.36290	1.42331	1.48610	1.55133
10	1.05114	1.10462	1.16054	1.21899	1.28008	1.34392	1.41060	1.48024	1.55297	1.62889
11	1.05640	1.11567	1.17795	1.24337	1.31209	1.38423	1.45997	1.53945	1.62285	1.71034
12	1.06168	1.12683	1.19562	1.26824	1.34489	1.42576	1.51107	1.60103	1.69588	1.79586
13	1.06699	1.13809	1.21355	1.29361	1.37851	1.46853	1.56396	1.66507	1.77220	1.88565
14	1.07232	1.14947	1.23176	1.31948	1.41297	1.51259	1.61869	1.73168	1.85194	1.97993
15	1.07768	1.16097	1.25023	1.34587	1.44830	1.55797	1.67535	1.80094	1.93528	2.07893
16	1.08307	1.17258	1.26899	1.37279	1.48451	1.60471	1.73399	1.87298	2.02237	2.18287
17	1.08849	1.18430	1.28802	1.40024	1.52162	1.65285	1.79468	1.94790	2.11338	2.29202
18	1.09393	1.19615	1.30734	1.42825	1.55966	1.70243	1.85749	2.02582	2.20848	2.40662
19	1.09940	1.20811	1.32695	1.45681	1.59865	1.75351	1.92250	2.10685	2.30786	2.52695
20	1.10490	1.22019	1.34686	1.48595	1.63862	1.80611	1.98979	2.19112	2.41171	2.65330
21	1.11042	1.23239	1.36706	1.51567	1.67958	1.86029	2.05943	2.27877	2.52024	2.78596
22	1.11597	1.24472	1.38756	1.54598	1.72157	1.91610	2.13151	2.36992	2.63365	2.92526
23	1.12155	1.25716	1.40838	1.57690	1.76461	1.97359	2.20611	2.46472	2.75217	3.07152
24	1.12716	1.26973	1.42950	1.60844	1.80873	2.03279	2.28333	2.56330	2.87601	3.22510
25	1.13280	1.28243	1.45095	1.64061	1.85394	2.09378	2.36324	2.66584	3.00543	3.38635
26	1.13846	1.29526	1.47271	1.67342	1.90029	2.15659	2.44596	2.77247	3.14068	3.55567
27	1.14415	1.30821	1.49480	1.70689	1.94780	2.22129	2.53157	2.88337	3.28201	3.73346
28	1.14987	1.32129	1.51722	1.74102	1.99650	2.28793	2.62017	2.99870	3.42970	3.92013
29	1.15562	1.33450	1.53998	1.77584	2.04641	2.35657	2.71188	3.11865	3.58404	4.11614
30	1.16140	1.34785	1.56308	1.81136	2.09757	2.42726	2.80679	3.24340	3.74532	4.32194

5.5%	6%	6.5%	7%	7.5%	8%	8.5%	9%	9.5%	10%
1.05500	1.06000	1.06500	1.07000	1.07500	1.08000	1.08500	1.09000	1.09500	1.10000
1.11303	1.12360	1.13423	1.14490	1.15563	1.16640	1.17723	1.18810	1.19903	1.21000
1.17424	1.19102	1.20795	1.22504	1.24230	1.25971	1.27729	1.29503	1.31293	1.33100
1.23882	1.26248	1.28647	1.31080	1.33547	1.36049	1.38586	1.41158	1.43766	1.46410
1.30696	1.33823	1.37009	1.40255	1.43563	1.46933	1.50366	1.53862	1.57424	1.61051
1.37884	1.41852	1.45914	1.50073	1.54330	1.58687	1.63147	1.67710	1.72379	1.77156
1.45468	1.50363	1.55399	1.60578	1.65905	1.71382	1.77014	1.82804	1.88755	1.94872
1.53469	1.59385	1.65500	1.71819	1.78348	1.85093	1.92060	1.99256	2.06687	2.14359
1.61909	1.68948	1.76257	1.83846	1.91724	1.99900	2.08386	2.17189	2.26322	2.35795
1.70814	1.79085	1.87714	1.96715	2.06103	2.15892	2.26098	2.36736	2.47823	2.59374
1.80209	1.89830	1.99915	2.10485	2.21561	2.33164	2.45317	2.58043	2.71366	2.85312
1.90121	2.01220	2.12910	2.25219	2.38178	2.51817	2.66169	2.81266	2.97146	3.13843
2.00577	2.13293	2.26749	2.40985	2.56041	2.71962	2.88793	3.06580	3.25375	3.45227
2.11609	2.26090	2.41487	2.57853	2.75244	2.93719	3.13340	3.34173	3.56285	3.79750
2.23248	2.39656	2.57184	2.75903	2.95888	3.17217	3.39974	3.64248	3.90132	4.17725
2.35526	2.54035	2.73901	2.95216	3.18079	3.42594	3.68872	3.97031	4.27195	4.59497
2.48480	2.69277	2.91705	3.15882	3.41935	3.70002	4.00226	4.32763	4.67778	5.05447
2.62147	2.85434	3.10665	3.37993	3.67580	3.99602	4.34245	4.71712	5.12217	5.55992
2.76565	3.02560	3.30859	3.61653	3.95149	4.31570	4.71156	5.14166	5.60878	6.11591
2.91776	3.20714	3.52365	3.86968	4.24785	4.66096	5.11205	5.60441	6.14161	6.72750
3.07823	3.39956	3.75268	4.14056	4.56644	5.03383	5.54657	6.10881	6.72507	7.40025
3.24754	3.60354	3.99661	4.43040	4.90892	5.43654	6.01803	6.65860	7.36395	8.14027
3.42615	3.81975	4.25639	4.74053	5.27709	5.87146	6.52956	7.25787	8.06352	8.95430
3.61459	4.04893	4.53305	5.07237	5.67287	6.34118	7.08457	7.91108	8.82956	9.84973
3.81339	4.29187	4.82770	5.42743	6.09834	6.84848	7.68676	8.62308	9.66836	10.83471
4.02313	4.54938	5.14150	5.80735	6.55572	7.39635	8.34014	9.39916	10.58686	11.91818
4.24440	4.82235	5.47570	6.21387	7.04739	7.98806	9.04905	10.24508	11.59261	13.10999
4.47784	5.11169	5.83162	6.64884	7.57595	8.62711	9.81822	11.16714	12.69391	14.42099
4.72412	5.41839	6.21067	7.11426	8.14414	9.31727	10.65277	12.17218	13.89983	15.86309
4.98395	5.74349	6.61437	7.61226	8.75496	10.06266	11.55825	13.26768	15.22031	17.44940

Table 1 *(concluded)* *Future Value of $1 at Compound Interest: 10.5%–20%*

Period	10.5%	11%	11.5%	12%	12.5%	13%	13.5%	14%	14.5%	15%
1	1.10500	1.11000	1.11500	1.12000	1.12500	1.13000	1.13500	1.14000	1.14500	1.15000
2	1.22103	1.23210	1.24323	1.25440	1.26563	1.27690	1.28822	1.29960	1.31102	1.32250
3	1.34923	1.36763	1.38620	1.40493	1.42383	1.44290	1.46214	1.48154	1.50112	1.52088
4	1.49090	1.51807	1.54561	1.57352	1.60181	1.63047	1.65952	1.68896	1.71879	1.74901
5	1.64745	1.68506	1.72335	1.76234	1.80203	1.84244	1.88356	1.92541	1.96801	2.01136
6	1.82043	1.87041	1.92154	1.97382	2.02729	2.08195	2.13784	2.19497	2.25337	2.31306
7	2.01157	2.07616	2.14252	2.21068	2.28070	2.35261	2.42645	2.50227	2.58011	2.66002
8	2.22279	2.30454	2.38891	2.47596	2.56578	2.65844	2.75402	2.85259	2.95423	3.05902
9	2.45618	2.55804	2.66363	2.77308	2.88651	3.00404	3.12581	3.25195	3.38259	3.51788
10	2.71408	2.83942	2.96995	3.10585	3.24732	3.39457	3.54780	3.70722	3.87307	4.04556
11	2.99906	3.15176	3.31149	3.47855	3.65324	3.83586	4.02675	4.22623	4.43466	4.65239
12	3.31396	3.49845	3.69231	3.89598	4.10989	4.33452	4.57036	4.81790	5.07769	5.35025
13	3.66193	3.88328	4.11693	4.36349	4.62363	4.89801	5.18736	5.49241	5.81395	6.15279
14	4.04643	4.31044	4.59037	4.88711	5.20158	5.53475	5.88765	6.26135	6.65697	7.07571
15	4.47130	4.78459	5.11827	5.47357	5.85178	6.25427	6.68248	7.13794	7.62223	8.13706
16	4.94079	5.31089	5.70687	6.13039	6.58325	7.06733	7.58462	8.13725	8.72746	9.35762
17	5.45957	5.89509	6.36316	6.86604	7.40616	7.98608	8.60854	9.27646	9.99294	10.76126
18	6.03283	6.54355	7.09492	7.68997	8.33193	9.02427	9.77070	10.57517	11.44192	12.37545
19	6.66628	7.26334	7.91084	8.61276	9.37342	10.19742	11.08974	12.05569	13.10039	14.23177
20	7.36623	8.06231	8.82058	9.64629	10.54509	11.52309	12.58686	13.74349	15.00064	16.36654
21	8.13969	8.94917	9.83495	10.80385	11.86323	13.02109	14.28608	15.66758	17.17573	18.82152
22	8.99436	9.93357	10.96597	12.10031	13.34613	14.71383	16.21470	17.86104	19.66621	21.64475
23	9.93876	11.02627	12.22706	13.55235	15.01440	16.62663	18.40369	20.36158	22.51781	24.89146
24	10.98233	12.23916	13.63317	15.17863	16.89120	18.78809	20.88818	23.21221	25.78290	28.62518
25	12.13548	13.58546	15.20098	17.00006	19.00260	21.23054	23.70809	26.46192	29.52141	32.91895
26	13.40971	15.07986	16.94910	19.04007	21.37793	23.99051	26.90868	30.16658	33.80202	37.85680
27	14.81772	16.73865	18.89824	21.32488	24.05017	27.10928	30.54135	34.38991	38.70331	43.53531
28	16.37359	18.57990	21.07154	23.88387	27.05644	30.63349	34.66443	39.20449	44.31529	50.06561
29	18.09281	20.62369	23.49477	26.74993	30.43849	34.61584	39.34413	44.69312	50.74101	57.57545
30	19.99256	22.89230	26.19667	29.95992	34.24330	39.11590	44.65559	50.95016	58.09846	66.21177

15.5%	16%	16.5%	17%	17.5%	18%	18.5%	19%	19.5%	20%
1.15500	1.16000	1.16500	1.17000	1.17500	1.18000	1.18500	1.19000	1.19500	1.20000
1.33402	1.34560	1.35722	1.36890	1.38063	1.39240	1.40422	1.41610	1.42802	1.44000
1.54080	1.56090	1.58117	1.60161	1.62223	1.64303	1.66401	1.68516	1.70649	1.72800
1.77962	1.81064	1.84206	1.87389	1.90613	1.93878	1.97185	2.00534	2.03926	2.07360
2.05546	2.10034	2.14600	2.19245	2.23970	2.28776	2.33664	2.38635	2.43691	2.48832
2.37406	2.43640	2.50009	2.56516	2.63164	2.69955	2.76892	2.83976	2.91211	2.98598
2.74204	2.82622	2.91260	3.00124	3.09218	3.18547	3.28117	3.37932	3.47997	3.58318
3.16706	3.27841	3.39318	3.51145	3.63331	3.75886	3.88818	4.02139	4.15856	4.29982
3.65795	3.80296	3.95306	4.10840	4.26914	4.43545	4.60750	4.78545	4.96948	5.15978
4.22493	4.41144	4.60531	4.80683	5.01624	5.23384	5.45989	5.69468	5.93853	6.19174
4.87980	5.11726	5.36519	5.62399	5.89409	6.17593	6.46996	6.77667	7.09654	7.43008
5.63617	5.93603	6.25045	6.58007	6.92555	7.28759	7.66691	8.06424	8.48037	8.91610
6.50977	6.88579	7.28177	7.69868	8.13752	8.59936	9.08528	9.59645	10.13404	10.69932
7.51879	7.98752	8.48326	9.00745	9.56159	10.14724	10.76606	11.41977	12.11018	12.83918
8.68420	9.26552	9.88300	10.53872	11.23487	11.97375	12.75778	13.58953	14.47167	15.40702
10.03025	10.74800	11.51370	12.33030	13.20097	14.12902	15.11797	16.17154	17.29364	18.48843
11.58494	12.46768	13.41346	14.42646	15.51114	16.67225	17.91480	19.24413	20.66590	22.18611
13.38060	14.46251	15.62668	16.87895	18.22559	19.67325	21.22904	22.90052	24.69575	26.62333
15.45460	16.77652	18.20508	19.74838	21.41507	23.21444	25.15641	27.25162	29.51143	31.94800
17.85006	19.46076	21.20892	23.10560	25.16271	27.39303	29.81035	32.42942	35.26615	38.33760
20.61682	22.57448	24.70839	27.03355	29.56618	32.32378	35.32526	38.59101	42.14305	46.00512
23.81243	26.18640	28.78527	31.62925	34.74026	38.14206	41.86043	45.92331	50.36095	55.20614
27.50335	30.37622	33.53484	37.00623	40.81981	45.00763	49.60461	54.64873	60.18134	66.24737
31.76637	35.23642	39.06809	43.29729	47.96327	53.10901	58.78147	65.03199	71.91670	79.49685
36.69016	40.87424	45.51433	50.65783	56.35684	62.66863	69.65604	77.38807	85.94045	95.39622
42.37713	47.41412	53.02419	59.26966	66.21929	73.94898	82.54240	92.09181	102.69884	114.47546
48.94559	55.00038	61.77318	69.34550	77.80767	87.25980	97.81275	109.58925	122.72511	137.37055
56.53216	63.80044	71.96576	81.13423	91.42401	102.96656	115.90811	130.41121	146.65651	164.84466
65.29464	74.00851	83.84011	94.92705	107.42321	121.50054	137.35111	155.18934	175.25453	197.81359
75.41531	85.84988	97.67373	111.06465	126.22227	143.37064	162.76106	184.67531	209.42916	237.37631

Table 2 *Future Value of an Ordinary Annuity of $1 per Period: 0.5%–10%* $F_{A_{i,n}} = \dfrac{(1+i)^n - 1}{i}$

Period	.5%	1%	1.5%	2%	2.5%	3%	3.5%	4%	4.5%	5%
1	1.00000	1.00000	1.00000	1.00000	1.00000	1.00000	1.00000	1.00000	1.00000	1.00000
2	2.00500	2.01000	2.01500	2.02000	2.02500	2.03000	2.03500	2.04000	2.04500	2.05000
3	3.01502	3.03010	3.04522	3.06040	3.07562	3.09090	3.10622	3.12160	3.13702	3.15250
4	4.03010	4.06040	4.09090	4.12161	4.15252	4.18363	4.21494	4.24646	4.27819	4.31012
5	5.05025	5.10101	5.15227	5.20404	5.25633	5.30914	5.36247	5.41632	5.47071	5.52563
6	6.07550	6.15202	6.22955	6.30812	6.38774	6.46841	6.55015	6.63298	6.71689	6.80191
7	7.10588	7.21354	7.32299	7.43428	7.54743	7.66246	7.77941	7.89829	8.01915	8.14201
8	8.14141	8.28567	8.43284	8.58297	8.73612	8.89234	9.05169	9.21423	9.38001	9.54911
9	9.18212	9.36853	9.55933	9.75463	9.95452	10.15911	10.36850	10.58280	10.80211	11.02656
10	10.22803	10.46221	10.70272	10.94972	11.20338	11.46388	11.73139	12.00611	12.28821	12.57789
11	11.27917	11.56683	11.86326	12.16872	12.48347	12.80780	13.14199	13.48635	13.84118	14.20679
12	12.33556	12.68250	13.04121	13.41209	13.79555	14.19203	14.60196	15.02581	15.46403	15.91713
13	13.39724	13.80933	14.23683	14.68033	15.14044	15.61779	16.11303	16.62684	17.15991	17.71298
14	14.46423	14.94742	15.45038	15.97394	16.51895	17.08632	17.67699	18.29191	18.93211	19.59863
15	15.53655	16.09690	16.68214	17.29342	17.93193	18.59891	19.29568	20.02359	20.78405	21.57856
16	16.61423	17.25786	17.93237	18.63929	19.38022	20.15688	20.97103	21.82453	22.71934	23.65749
17	17.69730	18.43044	19.20136	20.01207	20.86473	21.76159	22.70502	23.69751	24.74171	25.84037
18	18.78579	19.61475	20.48938	21.41231	22.38635	23.41444	24.49969	25.64541	26.85508	28.13238
19	19.87972	20.81090	21.79672	22.84056	23.94601	25.11687	26.35718	27.67123	29.06356	30.53900
20	20.97912	22.01900	23.12367	24.29737	25.54466	26.87037	28.27968	29.77808	31.37142	33.06595
21	22.08401	23.23919	24.47052	25.78332	27.18327	28.67649	30.26947	31.96920	33.78314	35.71925
22	23.19443	24.47159	25.83758	27.29898	28.86286	30.53678	32.32890	34.24797	36.30338	38.50521
23	24.31040	25.71630	27.22514	28.84496	30.58443	32.45288	34.46041	36.61789	38.93703	41.43048
24	25.43196	26.97346	28.63352	30.42186	32.34904	34.42647	36.66653	39.08260	41.68920	44.50200
25	26.55912	28.24320	30.06302	32.03030	34.15776	36.45926	38.94986	41.64591	44.56521	47.72710
26	27.69191	29.52563	31.51397	33.67091	36.01171	38.55304	41.31310	44.31174	47.57064	51.11345
27	28.83037	30.82089	32.98668	35.34432	37.91200	40.70963	43.75906	47.08421	50.71132	54.66913
28	29.97452	32.12910	34.48148	37.05121	39.85980	42.93092	46.29063	49.96758	53.99333	58.40258
29	31.12439	33.45039	35.99870	38.79223	41.85630	45.21885	48.91080	52.96629	57.42303	62.32271
30	32.28002	34.78489	37.53868	40.56808	43.90270	47.57542	51.62268	56.08494	61.00707	66.43885

5.5%	6%	6.5%	7%	7.5%	8%	8.5%	9%	9.5%	10%
1.00000	1.00000	1.00000	1.00000	1.00000	1.00000	1.00000	1.00000	1.00000	1.00000
2.05500	2.06000	2.06500	2.07000	2.07500	2.08000	2.08500	2.09000	2.09500	2.10000
3.16802	3.18360	3.19922	3.21490	3.23062	3.24640	3.26222	3.27810	3.29402	3.31000
4.34227	4.37462	4.40717	4.43994	4.47292	4.50611	4.53951	4.57313	4.60696	4.64100
5.58109	5.63709	5.69364	5.75074	5.80839	5.86660	5.92537	5.98471	6.04462	6.10510
6.88805	6.97532	7.06373	7.15329	7.24402	7.33593	7.42903	7.52333	7.61886	7.71561
8.26689	8.39384	8.52287	8.65402	8.78732	8.92280	9.06050	9.20043	9.34265	9.48717
9.72157	9.89747	10.07686	10.25980	10.44637	10.63663	10.83064	11.02847	11.23020	11.43589
11.25626	11.49132	11.73185	11.97799	12.22985	12.48756	12.75124	13.02104	13.29707	13.57948
12.87535	13.18079	13.49442	13.81645	14.14709	14.48656	14.83510	15.19293	15.56029	15.93742
14.58350	14.97164	15.37156	15.78360	16.20812	16.64549	17.09608	17.56029	18.03852	18.53117
16.38559	16.86994	17.37071	17.88845	18.42373	18.97713	19.54925	20.14072	20.75218	21.38428
18.28680	18.88214	19.49981	20.14064	20.80551	21.49530	22.21094	22.95338	23.72363	24.52271
20.29257	21.01507	21.76730	22.55049	23.36592	24.21492	25.09887	26.01919	26.97738	27.97498
22.40866	23.27597	24.18217	25.12902	26.11836	27.15211	28.23227	29.36092	30.54023	31.77248
24.64114	25.67253	26.75401	27.88805	29.07724	30.32428	31.63201	33.00340	34.44155	35.94973
26.99640	28.21288	29.49302	30.84022	32.25804	33.75023	35.32073	36.97370	38.71350	40.54470
29.48120	30.90565	32.41007	33.99903	35.67739	37.45024	39.32300	41.30134	43.39128	45.59917
32.10267	33.75999	35.51672	37.37896	39.35319	41.44626	43.66545	46.01846	48.51345	51.15909
34.86832	36.78559	38.82531	40.99549	43.30468	45.76196	48.37701	51.16012	54.12223	57.27500
37.78608	39.99273	42.34895	44.86518	47.55253	50.42292	53.48906	56.76453	60.26384	64.00250
40.86431	43.39229	46.10164	49.00574	52.11897	55.45676	59.03563	62.87334	66.98891	71.40275
44.11185	46.99583	50.09824	53.43614	57.02790	60.89330	65.05366	69.53194	74.35286	79.54302
47.53800	50.81558	54.35463	58.17667	62.30499	66.76476	71.58322	76.78981	82.41638	88.49733
51.15259	54.86451	58.88768	63.24904	67.97786	73.10594	78.66779	84.70090	91.24593	98.34706
54.96598	59.15638	63.71538	68.67647	74.07620	79.95442	86.35455	93.32398	100.91430	109.18177
58.98911	63.70577	68.85688	74.48382	80.63192	87.35077	94.69469	102.72313	111.50116	121.09994
63.23351	68.52811	74.33257	80.69769	87.67931	95.33883	103.74374	112.96822	123.09377	134.20994
67.71135	73.63980	80.16419	87.34653	95.25526	103.96594	113.56196	124.13536	135.78767	148.63093
72.43548	79.05819	86.37486	94.46079	103.39940	113.28321	124.21473	136.30754	149.68750	164.49402

Table 2 (concluded) *Future Value of an Ordinary Annuity of $1 per Period: 10.5%–20%*

Period	10.5%	11%	11.5%	12%	12.5%	13%	13.5%	14%	14.5%	15%
1 ...	1.00000	1.00000	1.00000	1.00000	1.00000	1.00000	1.00000	1.00000	1.00000	1.00000
2 ...	2.10500	2.11000	2.11500	2.12000	2.12500	2.13000	2.13500	2.14000	2.14500	2.15000
3 ...	3.32602	3.34210	3.35822	3.37440	3.39062	3.40690	3.42322	3.43960	3.45602	3.47250
4 ...	4.67526	4.70973	4.74442	4.77933	4.81445	4.84980	4.88536	4.92114	4.95715	4.99337
5 ...	6.16616	6.22780	6.29003	6.35285	6.41626	6.48027	6.54488	6.61010	6.67594	6.74238
6 ...	7.81361	7.91286	8.01338	8.11519	8.21829	8.32271	8.42844	8.53552	8.64395	8.75374
7 ...	9.63404	9.78327	9.93492	10.08901	10.24558	10.40466	10.56628	10.73049	10.89732	11.06680
8 ...	11.64561	11.85943	12.07744	12.29969	12.52628	12.75726	12.99273	13.23276	13.47743	13.72682
9 ...	13.86840	14.16397	14.46634	14.77566	15.09206	15.41571	15.74675	16.08535	16.43166	16.78584
10 ...	16.32458	16.72201	17.12997	17.54874	17.97857	18.41975	18.87256	19.33730	19.81425	20.30372
11 ...	19.03866	19.56143	20.09992	20.65458	21.22589	21.81432	22.42036	23.04452	23.68731	24.34928
12 ...	22.03772	22.71319	23.41141	24.13313	24.87913	25.65018	26.44711	27.27075	28.12197	29.00167
13 ...	25.35168	26.21164	27.10372	28.02911	28.98902	29.98470	31.01746	32.08865	33.19966	34.35192
14 .:.	29.01361	30.09492	31.22065	32.39260	33.61264	34.88271	36.20482	37.58107	39.01361	40.50471
15 ...	33.06004	34.40536	35.81102	37.27971	38.81422	40.41746	42.09247	43.84241	45.67058	47.58041
16 ...	37.53134	39.18995	40.92929	42.75328	44.66600	46.67173	48.77496	50.98035	53.29282	55.71747
17 ...	42.47213	44.50084	46.63616	48.88367	51.24925	53.73906	56.35958	59.11760	62.02027	65.07509
18 ...	47.93170	50.39594	52.99932	55.74971	58.65541	61.72514	64.96812	68.39407	72.01321	75.83636
19 ...	53.96453	56.93949	60.09424	63.43968	66.98733	70.74941	74.73882	78.96923	83.45513	88.21181
20 ...	60.63081	64.20283	68.00508	72.05244	76.36075	80.94683	85.82856	91.02493	96.55612	102.44358
21 ...	67.99704	72.26514	76.82566	81.69874	86.90584	92.46992	98.41541	104.76842	111.55676	118.81012
22 ...	76.13673	81.21431	86.66062	92.50258	98.76908	105.49101	112.70149	120.43600	128.73249	137.63164
23 ...	85.13109	91.14788	97.62659	104.60289	112.11521	120.20484	128.91619	138.29704	148.39871	159.27638
24 ...	95.06985	102.17415	109.85364	118.15524	127.12961	136.83147	147.31988	158.65862	170.91652	184.16784
25 ...	106.05219	114.41331	123.48681	133.33387	144.02081	155.61956	168.20806	181.87083	196.69941	212.79302
26 ...	118.18767	127.99877	138.68780	150.33393	163.02341	176.85010	191.91615	208.33274	226.22083	245.71197
27 ...	131.59737	143.07864	155.63689	169.37401	184.40134	200.84061	218.82483	238.49933	260.02285	283.56877
28 ...	146.41510	159.81729	174.53513	190.69889	208.45151	227.94989	249.36618	272.88923	298.72616	327.10408
29 ...	162.78868	178.39719	195.60668	214.58275	235.50795	258.58338	284.03062	312.09373	343.04145	377.16969
30 ...	180.88149	199.02088	219.10144	241.33268	265.94644	293.19922	323.37475	356.78685	393.78246	434.74515

15.5%	16%	16.5%	17%	17.5%	18%	18.5%	19%	19.5%	20%
1.00000	1.00000	1.00000	1.00000	1.00000	1.00000	1.00000	1.00000	1.00000	1.00000
2.15500	2.16000	2.16500	2.17000	2.17500	2.18000	2.18500	2.19000	2.19500	2.20000
3.48902	3.50560	3.52222	3.53890	3.55562	3.57240	3.58922	3.60610	3.62302	3.64000
5.02982	5.06650	5.10339	5.14051	5.17786	5.21543	5.25323	5.29126	5.32951	5.36800
6.80945	6.87714	6.94545	7.01440	7.08398	7.15421	7.22508	7.29660	7.36877	7.44160
8.86491	8.97748	9.09145	9.20685	9.32368	9.44197	9.56172	9.68295	9.80568	9.92992
11.23897	11.41387	11.59154	11.77201	11.95533	12.14152	12.33064	12.52271	12.71779	12.91590
13.98101	14.24009	14.50415	14.77325	15.04751	15.32700	15.61181	15.90203	16.19776	16.49908
17.14807	17.51851	17.89733	18.28471	18.68082	19.08585	19.49999	19.92341	20.35632	20.79890
20.80602	21.32147	21.85039	22.39311	22.94997	23.52131	24.10749	24.70886	25.32580	25.95868
25.03095	25.73290	26.45570	27.19994	27.96621	28.75514	29.56737	30.40355	31.26433	32.15042
29.91075	30.85017	31.82089	32.82393	33.86030	34.93107	36.03734	37.18022	38.36088	39.58050
35.54692	36.78620	38.07134	39.40399	40.78585	42.21866	43.70424	45.24446	46.84125	48.49660
42.05669	43.67199	45.35311	47.10267	48.92337	50.81802	52.78953	54.84091	56.97529	59.19592
49.57548	51.65951	53.83638	56.11013	58.48496	60.96527	63.55559	66.26068	69.08547	72.03511
58.25968	60.92503	63.71938	66.64885	69.71983	72.93901	76.31338	79.85021	83.55714	87.44213
68.28993	71.67303	75.23307	78.97915	82.92080	87.06804	91.43135	96.02175	100.85079	105.93056
79.87486	84.14072	88.64653	93.40561	98.43194	103.74028	109.34615	115.26588	121.51669	128.11667
93.25547	98.60323	104.27321	110.28456	116.65753	123.41353	130.57519	138.16640	146.21244	154.74000
108.71007	115.37975	122.47829	130.03294	138.07260	146.62797	155.73160	165.41802	175.72387	186.68800
126.56013	134.84051	143.68721	153.13854	163.23531	174.02100	185.54194	197.84744	210.99002	225.02560
147.17695	157.41499	168.39560	180.17209	192.80149	206.34479	220.86720	236.43846	253.13308	271.03072
170.98937	183.60138	197.18087	211.80134	227.54175	244.48685	262.72763	282.36176	303.49403	326.23686
198.49272	213.97761	230.71571	248.80757	268.36155	289.49448	312.33225	337.01050	363.67536	392.48424
230.25910	249.21402	269.78381	292.10486	316.32482	342.60349	371.11371	402.04249	435.59206	471.98108
266.94926	290.08827	315.29813	342.76268	372.68167	405.27211	440.76975	479.43056	521.53251	567.37730
309.32639	337.50239	368.32233	402.03234	438.90096	479.22109	523.31215	571.52237	624.23135	681.85276
358.27198	392.50277	430.09551	471.37783	516.70863	566.48089	621.12490	681.11162	746.95647	819.22331
414.80414	456.30322	502.06127	552.51207	608.13264	669.44745	737.03300	811.52283	893.61298	984.06797
480.09878	530.31173	585.90138	647.43912	715.55585	790.94799	874.38411	966.71217	1068.86751	1181.88157

Table 3 *Present Value of $1 at Compound Interest: 0.5%–7%*

$$P_{i,n} = \frac{1}{(1+i)^n}$$

Period	.5%	1%	1.5%	2%	2.5%	3%	3.5%	4%	4.5%	5%	5.5%	6%	6.5%	7%
1 ...	0.99502	0.99010	0.98522	0.98039	0.97561	0.97087	0.96618	0.96154	0.95694	0.95238	0.94787	0.94340	0.93897	0.93458
2 ...	0.99007	0.98030	0.97066	0.96117	0.95181	0.94260	0.93351	0.92456	0.91573	0.90703	0.89845	0.89000	0.88166	0.87344
3 ...	0.98515	0.97059	0.95632	0.94232	0.92860	0.91514	0.90194	0.88900	0.87630	0.86384	0.85161	0.83962	0.82785	0.81630
4 ...	0.98025	0.96098	0.94218	0.92385	0.90595	0.88849	0.87144	0.85480	0.83856	0.82270	0.80722	0.79209	0.77732	0.76290
5 ...	0.97537	0.95147	0.92826	0.90573	0.88385	0.86261	0.84197	0.82193	0.80245	0.78353	0.76513	0.74726	0.72988	0.71299
6 ...	0.97052	0.94205	0.91454	0.88797	0.86230	0.83748	0.81350	0.79031	0.76790	0.74622	0.72525	0.70496	0.68533	0.66634
7 ...	0.96569	0.93272	0.90103	0.87056	0.84127	0.81309	0.78599	0.75992	0.73483	0.71068	0.68744	0.66506	0.64351	0.62275
8 ...	0.96089	0.92348	0.88771	0.85349	0.82075	0.78941	0.75941	0.73069	0.70319	0.67684	0.65160	0.62741	0.60423	0.58201
9 ...	0.95610	0.91434	0.87459	0.83676	0.80073	0.76642	0.73373	0.70259	0.67290	0.64461	0.61763	0.59190	0.56735	0.54393
10 ...	0.95135	0.90529	0.86167	0.82035	0.78120	0.74409	0.70892	0.67556	0.64393	0.61391	0.58543	0.55839	0.53273	0.50835
11 ...	0.94661	0.89632	0.84893	0.80426	0.76214	0.72242	0.68495	0.64958	0.61620	0.58468	0.55491	0.52679	0.50021	0.47509
12 ...	0.94191	0.88745	0.83639	0.78849	0.74356	0.70138	0.66178	0.62460	0.58966	0.55684	0.52598	0.49697	0.46968	0.44401
13 ...	0.93722	0.87866	0.82403	0.77303	0.72542	0.68095	0.63940	0.60057	0.56427	0.53032	0.49856	0.46884	0.44102	0.41496
14 ...	0.93256	0.86996	0.81185	0.75788	0.70773	0.66112	0.61778	0.57748	0.53997	0.50507	0.47257	0.44230	0.41410	0.38782
15 ...	0.92792	0.86135	0.79985	0.74301	0.69047	0.64186	0.59689	0.55526	0.51672	0.48102	0.44793	0.41727	0.38883	0.36245
16 ...	0.92330	0.85282	0.78803	0.72845	0.67362	0.62317	0.57671	0.53391	0.49447	0.45811	0.42458	0.39365	0.36510	0.33873
17 ...	0.91871	0.84438	0.77639	0.71416	0.65720	0.60502	0.55720	0.51337	0.47318	0.43630	0.40245	0.37136	0.34281	0.31657
18 ...	0.91414	0.83602	0.76491	0.70016	0.64117	0.58739	0.53836	0.49363	0.45280	0.41552	0.38147	0.35034	0.32189	0.29586
19 ...	0.90959	0.82774	0.75361	0.68643	0.62553	0.57029	0.52016	0.47464	0.43330	0.39573	0.36158	0.33051	0.30224	0.27651
20 ...	0.90506	0.81954	0.74247	0.67297	0.61027	0.55368	0.50257	0.45639	0.41464	0.37689	0.34273	0.31180	0.28380	0.25842
21 ...	0.90056	0.81143	0.73150	0.65978	0.59539	0.53755	0.48557	0.43883	0.39679	0.35894	0.32486	0.29416	0.26648	0.24151
22 ...	0.89608	0.80340	0.72069	0.64684	0.58086	0.52189	0.46915	0.42196	0.37970	0.34185	0.30793	0.27751	0.25021	0.22571
23 ...	0.89162	0.79544	0.71004	0.63416	0.56670	0.50669	0.45329	0.40573	0.36335	0.32557	0.29187	0.26180	0.23494	0.21095
24 ...	0.88719	0.78757	0.69954	0.62172	0.55288	0.49193	0.43796	0.39012	0.34770	0.31007	0.27666	0.24698	0.22060	0.19715
25 ...	0.88277	0.77977	0.68921	0.60953	0.53939	0.47761	0.42315	0.37512	0.33273	0.29530	0.26223	0.23300	0.20714	0.18425
26 ...	0.87838	0.77205	0.67902	0.59758	0.52623	0.46369	0.40884	0.36069	0.31840	0.28124	0.24856	0.21981	0.19450	0.17220
27 ...	0.87401	0.76440	0.66899	0.58586	0.51340	0.45019	0.39501	0.34682	0.30469	0.26785	0.23560	0.20737	0.18263	0.16093
28 ...	0.86966	0.75684	0.65910	0.57437	0.50088	0.43708	0.38165	0.33348	0.29157	0.25509	0.22332	0.19563	0.17148	0.15040
29 ...	0.86533	0.74934	0.64936	0.56311	0.48866	0.42435	0.36875	0.32065	0.27902	0.24295	0.21168	0.18456	0.16101	0.14056
30 ...	0.86103	0.74192	0.63976	0.55207	0.47674	0.41199	0.35628	0.30832	0.26700	0.23138	0.20064	0.17411	0.15119	0.13137
31 ...	0.85675	0.73458	0.63031	0.54125	0.46511	0.39999	0.34423	0.29646	0.25550	0.22036	0.19018	0.16425	0.14196	0.12277
32 ...	0.85248	0.72730	0.62099	0.53063	0.45377	0.38834	0.33259	0.28506	0.24450	0.20987	0.18027	0.15496	0.13329	0.11474
33 ...	0.84824	0.72010	0.61182	0.52023	0.44270	0.37703	0.32134	0.27409	0.23397	0.19987	0.17087	0.14619	0.12516	0.10723
34 ...	0.84402	0.71297	0.60277	0.51003	0.43191	0.36604	0.31048	0.26355	0.22390	0.19035	0.16196	0.13791	0.11752	0.10022
35 ...	0.83982	0.70591	0.59387	0.50003	0.42137	0.35538	0.29998	0.25342	0.21425	0.18129	0.15352	0.13011	0.11035	0.09366
36 ...	0.83564	0.69892	0.58509	0.49022	0.41109	0.34503	0.28983	0.24367	0.20503	0.17266	0.14552	0.12274	0.10361	0.08754
37 ...	0.83149	0.69200	0.57644	0.48061	0.40107	0.33498	0.28003	0.23430	0.19620	0.16444	0.13793	0.11579	0.09729	0.08181
38 ...	0.82735	0.68515	0.56792	0.47119	0.39128	0.32523	0.27056	0.22529	0.18775	0.15661	0.13074	0.10924	0.09135	0.07646
39 ...	0.82323	0.67837	0.55953	0.46195	0.38174	0.31575	0.26141	0.21662	0.17967	0.14915	0.12392	0.10306	0.08578	0.07146
40 ...	0.81914	0.67165	0.55126	0.45289	0.37243	0.30656	0.25257	0.20829	0.17193	0.14205	0.11746	0.09722	0.08054	0.06678
41 ...	0.81506	0.66500	0.54312	0.44401	0.36335	0.29763	0.24403	0.20028	0.16453	0.13528	0.11134	0.09172	0.07563	0.06241
42 ...	0.81101	0.65842	0.53509	0.43530	0.35448	0.28896	0.23578	0.19257	0.15744	0.12884	0.10554	0.08653	0.07101	0.05833
43 ...	0.80697	0.65190	0.52718	0.42677	0.34584	0.28054	0.22781	0.18517	0.15006	0.12270	0.10003	0.08163	0.06668	0.05451
44 ...	0.80296	0.64545	0.51939	0.41840	0.33740	0.27237	0.22010	0.17805	0.14417	0.11686	0.09482	0.07701	0.06261	0.05095
45 ...	0.79896	0.63905	0.51171	0.41020	0.32917	0.26444	0.21266	0.17120	0.13796	0.11130	0.08988	0.07265	0.05879	0.04761
46 ...	0.79499	0.63273	0.50415	0.40215	0.32115	0.25674	0.20547	0.16461	0.13202	0.10600	0.08519	0.06854	0.05520	0.04450
47 ...	0.79103	0.62646	0.49670	0.39427	0.31331	0.24926	0.19852	0.15828	0.12634	0.10095	0.08075	0.06466	0.05183	0.04159
48 ...	0.78710	0.62026	0.48936	0.38654	0.30567	0.24200	0.19181	0.15219	0.12090	0.09614	0.07654	0.06100	0.04867	0.03887
49 ...	0.78318	0.61412	0.48213	0.37896	0.29822	0.23495	0.18532	0.14634	0.11569	0.09156	0.07255	0.05755	0.04570	0.03632
50 ...	0.77929	0.60804	0.47500	0.37153	0.29094	0.22811	0.17905	0.14071	0.11071	0.08720	0.06877	0.05429	0.04291	0.03395
51 ...	0.77541	0.60202	0.46798	0.36424	0.28385	0.22146	0.17300	0.13530	0.10594	0.08305	0.06518	0.05122	0.04029	0.03173
52 ...	0.77155	0.59606	0.46107	0.35710	0.27692	0.21501	0.16715	0.13010	0.10138	0.07910	0.06178	0.04832	0.03783	0.02965
53 ...	0.76771	0.59016	0.45426	0.35010	0.27017	0.20875	0.16150	0.12509	0.09701	0.07533	0.05856	0.04558	0.03552	0.02771
54 ...	0.76389	0.58431	0.44754	0.34323	0.26358	0.20267	0.15603	0.12028	0.09284	0.07174	0.05551	0.04300	0.03335	0.02590
55 ...	0.76009	0.57853	0.44093	0.33650	0.25715	0.19677	0.15076	0.11566	0.08884	0.06833	0.05262	0.04057	0.03132	0.02420
56 ...	0.75631	0.57280	0.43441	0.32991	0.25088	0.19104	0.14566	0.11121	0.08501	0.06507	0.04987	0.03827	0.02941	0.02262
57 ...	0.75255	0.56713	0.42799	0.32344	0.24476	0.18547	0.14073	0.10693	0.08135	0.06197	0.04727	0.03610	0.02761	0.02114
58 ...	0.74880	0.56151	0.42167	0.31710	0.23879	0.18007	0.13598	0.10282	0.07785	0.05902	0.04481	0.03406	0.02593	0.01976
59 ...	0.74508	0.55595	0.41544	0.31088	0.23297	0.17483	0.13138	0.09886	0.07450	0.05621	0.04247	0.03213	0.02434	0.01847
60 ...	0.74137	0.55045	0.40930	0.30478	0.22728	0.16973	0.12693	0.09506	0.07129	0.05354	0.04026	0.03031	0.02286	0.01726

Period	.5%	1%	1.5%	2%	2.5%	3%	3.5%	4%	4.5%	5%	5.5%	6%	6.5%	7%
61 ..	0.73768	0.54500	0.40325	0.29881	0.22174	0.16479	0.12264	0.09140	0.06822	0.05099	0.03816	0.02860	0.02146	0.01613
62 ..	0.73401	0.53960	0.39729	0.29295	0.21633	0.15999	0.11849	0.08789	0.06528	0.04856	0.03617	0.02698	0.02015	0.01507
63 ..	0.73036	0.53426	0.39142	0.28720	0.21106	0.15533	0.11449	0.08451	0.06247	0.04625	0.03428	0.02545	0.01892	0.01409
64 ..	0.72673	0.52897	0.38563	0.28157	0.20591	0.15081	0.11062	0.08126	0.05978	0.04404	0.03250	0.02401	0.01777	0.01317
65 ..	0.72311	0.52373	0.37993	0.27605	0.20089	0.14641	0.10688	0.07813	0.05721	0.04195	0.03080	0.02265	0.01668	0.01230
66 ..	0.71952	0.51855	0.37432	0.27064	0.19599	0.14215	0.10326	0.07513	0.05474	0.03995	0.02920	0.02137	0.01566	0.01150
67 ..	0.71594	0.51341	0.36879	0.26533	0.19121	0.13801	0.09977	0.07224	0.05239	0.03805	0.02767	0.02016	0.01471	0.01075
68 ..	0.71237	0.50833	0.36334	0.26013	0.18654	0.13399	0.09640	0.06946	0.05013	0.03623	0.02623	0.01902	0.01381	0.01004
69 ..	0.70883	0.50330	0.35797	0.25503	0.18199	0.13009	0.09314	0.06679	0.04797	0.03451	0.02486	0.01794	0.01297	0.00939
70 ..	0.70530	0.49831	0.35268	0.25003	0.17755	0.12630	0.08999	0.06422	0.04590	0.03287	0.02357	0.01693	0.01218	0.00877
71 ..	0.70179	0.49338	0.34746	0.24513	0.17322	0.12262	0.08694	0.06175	0.04393	0.03130	0.02234	0.01597	0.01143	0.00820
72 ..	0.69830	0.48850	0.34233	0.24032	0.16900	0.11905	0.08400	0.05937	0.04204	0.02981	0.02117	0.01507	0.01074	0.00766
73 ..	0.69483	0.48366	0.33727	0.23561	0.16488	0.11558	0.08116	0.05709	0.04023	0.02839	0.02007	0.01421	0.01008	0.00716
74 ..	0.69137	0.47887	0.33229	0.23099	0.16085	0.11221	0.07842	0.05490	0.03849	0.02704	0.01902	0.01341	0.00947	0.00669
75 ..	0.68793	0.47413	0.32738	0.22646	0.15693	0.10895	0.07577	0.05278	0.03684	0.02575	0.01803	0.01265	0.00889	0.00625
76 ..	0.68451	0.46944	0.32254	0.22202	0.15310	0.10577	0.07320	0.05075	0.03525	0.02453	0.01709	0.01193	0.00835	0.00585
77 ..	0.68110	0.46479	0.31777	0.21766	0.14937	0.10269	0.07073	0.04880	0.03373	0.02336	0.01620	0.01126	0.00784	0.00546
78 ..	0.67772	0.46019	0.31308	0.21340	0.14573	0.09970	0.06834	0.04692	0.03228	0.02225	0.01536	0.01062	0.00736	0.00511
79 ..	0.67434	0.45563	0.30845	0.20921	0.14217	0.09680	0.06603	0.04512	0.03089	0.02119	0.01456	0.01002	0.00691	0.00477
80 ..	0.67099	0.45112	0.30389	0.20511	0.13870	0.09398	0.06379	0.04338	0.02956	0.02018	0.01380	0.00945	0.00649	0.00446
81 ..	0.66765	0.44665	0.29940	0.20109	0.13532	0.09124	0.06164	0.04172	0.02829	0.01922	0.01308	0.00892	0.00609	0.00417
82 ..	0.66433	0.44223	0.29497	0.19715	0.13202	0.08858	0.05955	0.04011	0.02707	0.01830	0.01240	0.00841	0.00572	0.00390
83 ..	0.66102	0.43785	0.29062	0.19328	0.12880	0.08600	0.05754	0.03857	0.02590	0.01743	0.01175	0.00794	0.00537	0.00364
84 ..	0.65773	0.43352	0.28632	0.18949	0.12566	0.08350	0.05559	0.03709	0.02479	0.01660	0.01114	0.00749	0.00504	0.00340
85 ..	0.65446	0.42922	0.28209	0.18577	0.12259	0.08107	0.05371	0.03566	0.02372	0.01581	0.01056	0.00706	0.00473	0.00318
86 ..	0.65121	0.42497	0.27792	0.18213	0.11960	0.07870	0.05190	0.03429	0.02270	0.01506	0.01001	0.00666	0.00445	0.00297
87 ..	0.64797	0.42077	0.27381	0.17856	0.11669	0.07641	0.05014	0.03297	0.02172	0.01434	0.00948	0.00629	0.00417	0.00278
88 ..	0.64474	0.41660	0.26977	0.17506	0.11384	0.07419	0.04845	0.03170	0.02079	0.01366	0.00899	0.00593	0.00392	0.00260
89 ..	0.64154	0.41248	0.26578	0.17163	0.11106	0.07203	0.04681	0.03048	0.01989	0.01301	0.00852	0.00559	0.00368	0.00243
90 ..	0.63834	0.40839	0.26185	0.16826	0.10836	0.06993	0.04522	0.02931	0.01903	0.01239	0.00808	0.00528	0.00346	0.00227
91 ..	0.63517	0.40435	0.25798	0.16496	0.10571	0.06789	0.04369	0.02818	0.01821	0.01180	0.00766	0.00498	0.00324	0.00212
92 ..	0.63201	0.40034	0.25417	0.16173	0.10313	0.06591	0.04222	0.02710	0.01743	0.01124	0.00726	0.00470	0.00305	0.00198
93 ..	0.62886	0.39638	0.25041	0.15856	0.10062	0.06399	0.04079	0.02606	0.01668	0.01070	0.00688	0.00443	0.00286	0.00185
94 ..	0.62573	0.39246	0.24671	0.15545	0.09816	0.06213	0.03941	0.02505	0.01596	0.01019	0.00652	0.00418	0.00269	0.00173
95 ..	0.62262	0.38857	0.24307	0.15240	0.09577	0.06032	0.03808	0.02409	0.01527	0.00971	0.00618	0.00394	0.00252	0.00162
96 ..	0.61952	0.38472	0.23947	0.14941	0.09343	0.05856	0.03679	0.02316	0.01462	0.00924	0.00586	0.00372	0.00237	0.00151
97 ..	0.61644	0.38091	0.23594	0.14648	0.09116	0.05686	0.03555	0.02227	0.01399	0.00880	0.00555	0.00351	0.00222	0.00141
98 ..	0.61337	0.37714	0.23245	0.14361	0.08893	0.05520	0.03434	0.02142	0.01338	0.00838	0.00526	0.00331	0.00209	0.00132
99 ..	0.61032	0.37341	0.22901	0.14079	0.08676	0.05359	0.03318	0.02059	0.01281	0.00798	0.00499	0.00312	0.00196	0.00123
100 ..	0.60729	0.36971	0.22563	0.13803	0.08465	0.05203	0.03026	0.01980	0.01226	0.00760	0.00473	0.00295	0.00184	0.00115
101 ..	0.60427	0.36605	0.22230	0.13533	0.08258	0.05052	0.03098	0.01904	0.01173	0.00724	0.00448	0.00278	0.00173	0.00108
102 ..	0.60126	0.36243	0.21901	0.13267	0.08057	0.04905	0.02993	0.01831	0.01122	0.00690	0.00425	0.00262	0.00162	0.00101
103 ..	0.59827	0.35884	0.21577	0.13007	0.07860	0.04762	0.02892	0.01760	0.01074	0.00657	0.00403	0.00247	0.00152	0.00094
104 ..	0.59529	0.35529	0.21258	0.12752	0.07669	0.04623	0.02794	0.01693	0.01028	0.00626	0.00382	0.00233	0.00143	0.00088
105 ..	0.59233	0.35177	0.20944	0.12502	0.07482	0.04488	0.02699	0.01627	0.00984	0.00596	0.00362	0.00220	0.00134	0.00082
106 ..	0.58938	0.34828	0.20635	0.12257	0.07299	0.04358	0.02608	0.01565	0.00941	0.00567	0.00343	0.00208	0.00126	0.00077
107 ..	0.58645	0.34484	0.20330	0.12017	0.07121	0.04231	0.02520	0.01505	0.00901	0.00540	0.00325	0.00196	0.00118	0.00072
108 ..	0.58353	0.34142	0.20029	0.11781	0.06947	0.04108	0.02435	0.01447	0.00862	0.00515	0.00308	0.00185	0.00111	0.00067
109 ..	0.58063	0.33804	0.19733	0.11550	0.06778	0.03988	0.02352	0.01391	0.00825	0.00490	0.00292	0.00174	0.00104	0.00063
110 ..	0.57774	0.33469	0.19442	0.11324	0.06613	0.03872	0.02273	0.01338	0.00789	0.00467	0.00277	0.00165	0.00098	0.00059
111 ..	0.57487	0.33138	0.19154	0.11101	0.06451	0.03759	0.02196	0.01286	0.00755	0.00445	0.00262	0.00155	0.00092	0.00055
112 ..	0.57201	0.32810	0.18871	0.10884	0.06294	0.03649	0.02122	0.01237	0.00723	0.00423	0.00249	0.00146	0.00086	0.00051
113 ..	0.56916	0.32485	0.18592	0.10670	0.06140	0.03543	0.02050	0.01189	0.00692	0.00403	0.00236	0.00138	0.00081	0.00048
114 ..	0.56633	0.32164	0.18318	0.10461	0.05991	0.03440	0.01981	0.01143	0.00662	0.00384	0.00223	0.00130	0.00076	0.00045
115 ..	0.56351	0.31845	0.18047	0.10256	0.05845	0.03340	0.01914	0.01099	0.00633	0.00366	0.00212	0.00123	0.00072	0.00042
116 ..	0.56071	0.31530	0.17780	0.10055	0.05702	0.03243	0.01849	0.01057	0.00606	0.00348	0.00201	0.00116	0.00067	0.00039
117 ..	0.55792	0.31218	0.17518	0.09858	0.05563	0.03148	0.01786	0.01016	0.00580	0.00332	0.00190	0.00109	0.00063	0.00036
118 ..	0.55514	0.30908	0.17259	0.09665	0.05427	0.03056	0.01726	0.00977	0.00555	0.00316	0.00180	0.00103	0.00059	0.00034
119 ..	0.55238	0.30602	0.17004	0.09475	0.05295	0.02967	0.01668	0.00940	0.00531	0.00301	0.00171	0.00097	0.00056	0.00032
120 ..	0.54963	0.30299	0.16752	0.09289	0.05166	0.02881	0.01611	0.00904	0.00508	0.00287	0.00162	0.00092	0.00052	0.00030

Table 3 (continued)   Present Value of $1 at Compound Interest: 7.5%–14%

Period	7.5%	8%	8.5%	9%	9.5%	10%	10.5%	11%	11.5%	12%	12.5%	13%	13.5%	14%
1 ...	0.93023	0.92593	0.92166	0.91743	0.91324	0.90909	0.90498	0.90090	0.89686	0.89286	0.88889	0.88496	0.88106	0.87719
2 ...	0.86533	0.85734	0.84946	0.84168	0.83401	0.82645	0.81898	0.81162	0.80436	0.79719	0.79012	0.78315	0.77626	0.76947
3 ...	0.80496	0.79383	0.78291	0.77218	0.76165	0.75131	0.74116	0.73119	0.72140	0.71178	0.70233	0.69305	0.68393	0.67497
4 ...	0.74880	0.73503	0.72157	0.70843	0.69557	0.68301	0.67073	0.65873	0.64699	0.63553	0.62430	0.61332	0.60258	0.59208
5 ...	0.69656	0.68058	0.66505	0.64993	0.63523	0.62092	0.60700	0.59345	0.58026	0.56743	0.55493	0.54276	0.53091	0.51937
6 ...	0.64796	0.63017	0.61295	0.59627	0.58012	0.56447	0.54932	0.53464	0.52042	0.50663	0.49327	0.48032	0.46776	0.45559
7 ...	0.60275	0.58349	0.56493	0.54703	0.52979	0.51316	0.49712	0.48166	0.46674	0.45235	0.43846	0.42506	0.41213	0.39964
8 ...	0.56070	0.54027	0.52067	0.50187	0.48382	0.46651	0.44989	0.43393	0.41860	0.40388	0.38974	0.37616	0.36311	0.35056
9 ...	0.52158	0.50025	0.47988	0.46043	0.44185	0.42410	0.40714	0.39092	0.37543	0.36061	0.34644	0.33288	0.31992	0.30751
10 ...	0.48519	0.46319	0.44229	0.42241	0.40351	0.38554	0.36845	0.35218	0.33671	0.32197	0.30795	0.29459	0.28187	0.26974
11 ...	0.45134	0.42888	0.40764	0.38753	0.36851	0.35049	0.33344	0.31728	0.30198	0.28748	0.27373	0.26070	0.24834	0.23662
12 ...	0.41985	0.39711	0.37570	0.35553	0.33654	0.31863	0.30175	0.28584	0.27083	0.25668	0.24332	0.23071	0.21880	0.20756
13 ...	0.39056	0.36770	0.34627	0.32618	0.30734	0.28966	0.27308	0.25751	0.24290	0.22917	0.21628	0.20416	0.19278	0.18207
14 ...	0.36331	0.34046	0.31914	0.29925	0.28067	0.26333	0.24713	0.23199	0.21785	0.20462	0.19225	0.18068	0.16985	0.15971
15 ...	0.33797	0.31524	0.29414	0.27454	0.25632	0.23939	0.22365	0.20900	0.19538	0.18270	0.17089	0.15989	0.14964	0.14010
16 ...	0.31439	0.29189	0.27110	0.25187	0.23409	0.21763	0.20240	0.18829	0.17523	0.16312	0.15190	0.14150	0.13185	0.12289
17 ...	0.29245	0.27027	0.24986	0.23107	0.21378	0.19784	0.18316	0.16963	0.15715	0.14564	0.13502	0.12522	0.11616	0.10780
18 ...	0.27205	0.25025	0.23028	0.21199	0.19523	0.17986	0.16576	0.15282	0.14095	0.13004	0.12002	0.11081	0.10235	0.09456
19 ...	0.25307	0.23171	0.21224	0.19449	0.17829	0.16351	0.15001	0.13768	0.12641	0.11611	0.10668	0.09806	0.09017	0.08295
20 ...	0.23541	0.21455	0.19562	0.17843	0.16282	0.14864	0.13575	0.12403	0.11337	0.10367	0.09483	0.08678	0.07945	0.07276
21 ...	0.21899	0.19866	0.18029	0.16370	0.14870	0.13513	0.12285	0.11174	0.10168	0.09256	0.08429	0.07680	0.07000	0.06383
22 ...	0.20371	0.18394	0.16617	0.15018	0.13580	0.12285	0.11118	0.10067	0.09119	0.08264	0.07493	0.06796	0.06167	0.05599
23 ...	0.18950	0.17032	0.15315	0.13778	0.12402	0.11168	0.10062	0.09069	0.08179	0.07379	0.06660	0.06014	0.05434	0.04911
24 ...	0.17628	0.15770	0.14115	0.12640	0.11326	0.10153	0.09106	0.08170	0.07335	0.06588	0.05920	0.05323	0.04787	0.04308
25 ...	0.16398	0.14602	0.13009	0.11597	0.10343	0.09230	0.08240	0.07361	0.06579	0.05882	0.05262	0.04710	0.04218	0.03779
26 ...	0.15254	0.13520	0.11990	0.10639	0.09446	0.08391	0.07457	0.06631	0.05900	0.05252	0.04678	0.04168	0.03716	0.03315
27 ...	0.14190	0.12519	0.11051	0.09761	0.08626	0.07628	0.06749	0.05974	0.05291	0.04689	0.04158	0.03689	0.03274	0.02908
28 ...	0.13200	0.11591	0.10185	0.08955	0.07878	0.06934	0.06107	0.05382	0.04746	0.04187	0.03696	0.03264	0.02885	0.02551
29 ...	0.12279	0.10733	0.09387	0.08215	0.07194	0.06304	0.05527	0.04849	0.04256	0.03738	0.03285	0.02889	0.02542	0.02237
30 ...	0.11422	0.09938	0.08652	0.07537	0.06570	0.05731	0.05002	0.04368	0.03817	0.03338	0.02920	0.02557	0.02239	0.01963
31 ...	0.10625	0.09202	0.07974	0.06915	0.06000	0.05210	0.04527	0.03935	0.03424	0.02980	0.02596	0.02262	0.01973	0.01722
32 ...	0.09884	0.08520	0.07349	0.06344	0.05480	0.04736	0.04096	0.03545	0.03070	0.02661	0.02307	0.02002	0.01738	0.01510
33 ...	0.09194	0.07889	0.06774	0.05820	0.05004	0.04306	0.03707	0.03194	0.02754	0.02376	0.02051	0.01772	0.01532	0.01325
34 ...	0.08553	0.07305	0.06243	0.05339	0.04570	0.03914	0.03355	0.02878	0.02470	0.02121	0.01823	0.01568	0.01349	0.01162
35 ...	0.07956	0.06763	0.05754	0.04899	0.04174	0.03558	0.03036	0.02592	0.02215	0.01894	0.01621	0.01388	0.01189	0.01019
36 ...	0.07401	0.06262	0.05303	0.04494	0.03811	0.03235	0.02748	0.02335	0.01987	0.01691	0.01440	0.01228	0.01047	0.00894
37 ...	0.06885	0.05799	0.04888	0.04123	0.03481	0.02941	0.02487	0.02104	0.01782	0.01510	0.01280	0.01087	0.00923	0.00784
38 ...	0.06404	0.05369	0.04505	0.03783	0.03179	0.02673	0.02250	0.01896	0.01598	0.01348	0.01138	0.00962	0.00813	0.00688
39 ...	0.05958	0.04971	0.04152	0.03470	0.02903	0.02430	0.02036	0.01708	0.01433	0.01204	0.01012	0.00851	0.00716	0.00604
40 ...	0.05542	0.04603	0.03827	0.03184	0.02651	0.02209	0.01843	0.01538	0.01285	0.01075	0.00899	0.00753	0.00631	0.00529
41 ...	0.05155	0.04262	0.03527	0.02921	0.02421	0.02009	0.01668	0.01386	0.01153	0.00960	0.00799	0.00666	0.00556	0.00464
42 ...	0.04796	0.03946	0.03251	0.02680	0.02211	0.01826	0.01509	0.01249	0.01034	0.00857	0.00711	0.00590	0.00490	0.00407
43 ...	0.04461	0.03654	0.02996	0.02458	0.02019	0.01660	0.01366	0.01125	0.00927	0.00765	0.00632	0.00522	0.00432	0.00357
44 ...	0.04150	0.03383	0.02761	0.02255	0.01844	0.01509	0.01236	0.01013	0.00832	0.00683	0.00561	0.00462	0.00380	0.00313
45 ...	0.03860	0.03133	0.02545	0.02069	0.01684	0.01372	0.01119	0.00913	0.00746	0.00610	0.00499	0.00409	0.00335	0.00275
46 ...	0.03591	0.02901	0.02345	0.01898	0.01538	0.01247	0.01012	0.00823	0.00669	0.00544	0.00444	0.00362	0.00295	0.00241
47 ...	0.03340	0.02686	0.02162	0.01742	0.01405	0.01134	0.00916	0.00741	0.00600	0.00486	0.00394	0.00320	0.00260	0.00212
48 ...	0.03107	0.02487	0.01992	0.01598	0.01283	0.01031	0.00829	0.00668	0.00538	0.00434	0.00350	0.00283	0.00229	0.00186
49 ...	0.02891	0.02303	0.01836	0.01466	0.01171	0.00937	0.00750	0.00601	0.00483	0.00388	0.00312	0.00251	0.00202	0.00163
50 ...	0.02689	0.02132	0.01692	0.01345	0.01070	0.00852	0.00679	0.00542	0.00433	0.00346	0.00277	0.00222	0.00178	0.00143
51 ...	0.02501	0.01974	0.01560	0.01234	0.00977	0.00774	0.00615	0.00488	0.00388	0.00309	0.00246	0.00196	0.00157	0.00125
52 ...	0.02327	0.01828	0.01438	0.01132	0.00892	0.00704	0.00556	0.00440	0.00348	0.00276	0.00219	0.00174	0.00138	0.00110
53 ...	0.02164	0.01693	0.01325	0.01038	0.00815	0.00640	0.00503	0.00396	0.00312	0.00246	0.00194	0.00154	0.00122	0.00096
54 ...	0.02013	0.01567	0.01221	0.00953	0.00744	0.00582	0.00455	0.00357	0.00280	0.00220	0.00173	0.00136	0.00107	0.00085
55 ...	0.01873	0.01451	0.01126	0.00874	0.00680	0.00529	0.00412	0.00322	0.00251	0.00196	0.00154	0.00120	0.00094	0.00074
56 ...	0.01742	0.01344	0.01037	0.00802	0.00621	0.00481	0.00373	0.00290	0.00225	0.00175	0.00137	0.00107	0.00083	0.00065
57 ...	0.01621	0.01244	0.00956	0.00736	0.00567	0.00437	0.00338	0.00261	0.00202	0.00157	0.00121	0.00094	0.00073	0.00057
58 ...	0.01508	0.01152	0.00881	0.00675	0.00518	0.00397	0.00305	0.00235	0.00181	0.00140	0.00108	0.00083	0.00065	0.00050
59 ...	0.01402	0.01067	0.00812	0.00619	0.00473	0.00361	0.00276	0.00212	0.00162	0.00125	0.00096	0.00074	0.00057	0.00044
60 ...	0.01305	0.00988	0.00749	0.00568	0.00432	0.00328	0.00250	0.00191	0.00146	0.00111	0.00085	0.00065	0.00050	0.00039

Period	7.5%	8%	8.5%	9%	9.5%	10%	10.5%	11%	11.5%	12%	12.5%	13%	13.5%	14%
61 ..	0.01214	0.00914	0.00690	0.00521	0.00394	0.00299	0.00226	0.00172	0.00131	0.00099	0.00076	0.00058	0.00044	0.00034
62 ..	0.01129	0.00847	0.00636	0.00478	0.00360	0.00271	0.00205	0.00155	0.00117	0.00089	0.00067	0.00051	0.00039	0.00030
63 ..	0.01050	0.00784	0.00586	0.00439	0.00329	0.00247	0.00185	0.00140	0.00105	0.00079	0.00060	0.00045	0.00034	0.00026
64 ..	0.00977	0.00726	0.00540	0.00402	0.00300	0.00224	0.00168	0.00126	0.00094	0.00071	0.00053	0.00040	0.00030	0.00023
65 ..	0.00909	0.00672	0.00498	0.00369	0.00274	0.00204	0.00152	0.00113	0.00085	0.00063	0.00047	0.00035	0.00027	0.00020
66 ..	0.00845	0.00622	0.00459	0.00339	0.00250	0.00185	0.00137	0.00102	0.00076	0.00056	0.00042	0.00031	0.00023	0.00018
67 ..	0.00786	0.00576	0.00423	0.00311	0.00229	0.00169	0.00124	0.00092	0.00068	0.00050	0.00037	0.00028	0.00021	0.00015
68 ..	0.00732	0.00534	0.00390	0.00285	0.00209	0.00153	0.00113	0.00083	0.00061	0.00045	0.00033	0.00025	0.00018	0.00014
69 ..	0.00680	0.00494	0.00359	0.00262	0.00191	0.00139	0.00102	0.00075	0.00055	0.00040	0.00030	0.00022	0.00016	0.00012
70 ..	0.00633	0.00457	0.00331	0.00240	0.00174	0.00127	0.00092	0.00067	0.00049	0.00036	0.00026	0.00019	0.00014	0.00010
71 ..	0.00589	0.00424	0.00305	0.00220	0.00159	0.00115	0.00083	0.00061	0.00044	0.00032	0.00023	0.00017	0.00012	0.00009
72 ..	0.00548	0.00392	0.00281	0.00202	0.00145	0.00105	0.00075	0.00055	0.00039	0.00029	0.00021	0.00015	0.00011	0.00008
73 ..	0.00510	0.00363	0.00259	0.00185	0.00133	0.00095	0.00068	0.00049	0.00035	0.00026	0.00018	0.00013	0.00010	0.00007
74 ..	0.00474	0.00336	0.00239	0.00170	0.00121	0.00086	0.00062	0.00044	0.00032	0.00023	0.00016	0.00012	0.00009	0.00006
75 ..	0.00441	0.00311	0.00220	0.00156	0.00111	0.00079	0.00056	0.00040	0.00028	0.00020	0.00015	0.00010	0.00008	0.00005
76 ..	0.00410	0.00288	0.00203	0.00143	0.00101	0.00071	0.00051	0.00036	0.00026	0.00018	0.00013	0.00009	0.00007	0.00005
77 ..	0.00382	0.00267	0.00187	0.00131	0.00092	0.00065	0.00046	0.00032	0.00023	0.00016	0.00012	0.00008	0.00006	0.00004
78 ..	0.00355	0.00247	0.00172	0.00120	0.00084	0.00059	0.00041	0.00029	0.00021	0.00014	0.00010	0.00007	0.00005	0.00004
79 ..	0.00330	0.00229	0.00159	0.00110	0.00077	0.00054	0.00038	0.00026	0.00018	0.00013	0.00009	0.00006	0.00005	0.00003
80 ..	0.00307	0.00212	0.00146	0.00101	0.00070	0.00049	0.00034	0.00024	0.00017	0.00012	0.00008	0.00006	0.00004	0.00003
81 ..	0.00286	0.00196	0.00135	0.00093	0.00064	0.00044	0.00031	0.00021	0.00015	0.00010	0.00007	0.00005	0.00004	0.00002
82 ..	0.00266	0.00182	0.00124	0.00085	0.00059	0.00040	0.00028	0.00019	0.00013	0.00009	0.00006	0.00004	0.00003	0.00002
83 ..	0.00247	0.00168	0.00115	0.00078	0.00054	0.00037	0.00025	0.00017	0.00012	0.00008	0.00006	0.00004	0.00003	0.00002
84 ..	0.00230	0.00156	0.00106	0.00072	0.00049	0.00033	0.00023	0.00016	0.00011	0.00007	0.00005	0.00003	0.00002	0.00002
85 ..	0.00214	0.00144	0.00097	0.00066	0.00045	0.00030	0.00021	0.00014	0.00010	0.00007	0.00004	0.00003	0.00002	0.00001
86 ..	0.00199	0.00134	0.00090	0.00060	0.00041	0.00028	0.00019	0.00013	0.00009	0.00006	0.00004	0.00003	0.00002	0.00001
87 ..	0.00185	0.00124	0.00083	0.00055	0.00037	0.00025	0.00017	0.00011	0.00008	0.00005	0.00004	0.00002	0.00002	0.00001
88 ..	0.00172	0.00114	0.00076	0.00051	0.00034	0.00023	0.00015	0.00010	0.00007	0.00005	0.00003	0.00002	0.00001	0.00001
89 ..	0.00160	0.00106	0.00070	0.00047	0.00031	0.00021	0.00014	0.00009	0.00006	0.00004	0.00003	0.00002	0.00001	0.00001
90 ..	0.00149	0.00098	0.00065	0.00043	0.00028	0.00019	0.00013	0.00008	0.00006	0.00004	0.00002	0.00002	0.00001	0.00001
91 ..	0.00139	0.00091	0.00060	0.00039	0.00026	0.00017	0.00011	0.00008	0.00005	0.00003	0.00002	0.00001	0.00001	0.00001
92 ..	0.00129	0.00084	0.00055	0.00036	0.00024	0.00016	0.00010	0.00007	0.00004	0.00003	0.00002	0.00001	0.00001	0.00001
93 ..	0.00120	0.00078	0.00051	0.00033	0.00022	0.00014	0.00009	0.00006	0.00004	0.00003	0.00002	0.00001	0.00001	0.00001
94 ..	0.00112	0.00072	0.00047	0.00030	0.00020	0.00013	0.00008	0.00005	0.00004	0.00002	0.00002	0.00001	0.00001	0.00000
95 ..	0.00104	0.00067	0.00043	0.00028	0.00018	0.00012	0.00008	0.00005	0.00003	0.00002	0.00001	0.00001	0.00001	0.00000
96 ..	0.00097	0.00062	0.00040	0.00026	0.00016	0.00011	0.00007	0.00004	0.00003	0.00002	0.00001	0.00001	0.00001	0.00000
97 ..	0.00090	0.00057	0.00037	0.00023	0.00015	0.00010	0.00006	0.00004	0.00003	0.00002	0.00001	0.00001	0.00000	0.00000
98 ..	0.00084	0.00053	0.00034	0.00021	0.00014	0.00009	0.00006	0.00004	0.00002	0.00002	0.00001	0.00001	0.00000	0.00000
99 ..	0.00078	0.00049	0.00031	0.00020	0.00013	0.00008	0.00005	0.00003	0.00002	0.00001	0.00001	0.00001	0.00000	0.00000
100 ..	0.00072	0.00045	0.00029	0.00018	0.00011	0.00007	0.00005	0.00003	0.00002	0.00001	0.00001	0.00000	0.00000	0.00000
101 ..	0.00067	0.00042	0.00026	0.00017	0.00010	0.00007	0.00004	0.00003	0.00002	0.00001	0.00001	0.00000	0.00000	0.00000
102 ..	0.00063	0.00039	0.00024	0.00015	0.00010	0.00006	0.00004	0.00002	0.00002	0.00001	0.00001	0.00000	0.00000	0.00000
103 ..	0.00058	0.00036	0.00022	0.00014	0.00009	0.00005	0.00003	0.00002	0.00001	0.00001	0.00001	0.00000	0.00000	0.00000
104 ..	0.00054	0.00033	0.00021	0.00013	0.00008	0.00005	0.00003	0.00002	0.00001	0.00001	0.00000	0.00000	0.00000	0.00000
105 ..	0.00050	0.00031	0.00019	0.00012	0.00007	0.00005	0.00003	0.00002	0.00001	0.00001	0.00000	0.00000	0.00000	0.00000
106 ..	0.00047	0.00029	0.00018	0.00011	0.00007	0.00004	0.00003	0.00002	0.00001	0.00001	0.00000	0.00000	0.00000	0.00000
107 ..	0.00044	0.00027	0.00016	0.00010	0.00006	0.00004	0.00002	0.00001	0.00001	0.00001	0.00000	0.00000	0.00000	0.00000
108 ..	0.00041	0.00025	0.00015	0.00009	0.00006	0.00003	0.00002	0.00001	0.00001	0.00000	0.00000	0.00000	0.00000	0.00000
109 ..	0.00038	0.00023	0.00014	0.00008	0.00005	0.00003	0.00002	0.00001	0.00001	0.00000	0.00000	0.00000	0.00000	0.00000
110 ..	0.00035	0.00021	0.00013	0.00008	0.00005	0.00003	0.00002	0.00001	0.00001	0.00000	0.00000	0.00000	0.00000	0.00000
111 ..	0.00033	0.00019	0.00012	0.00007	0.00004	0.00003	0.00002	0.00001	0.00001	0.00000	0.00000	0.00000	0.00000	0.00000
112 ..	0.00030	0.00018	0.00011	0.00006	0.00004	0.00002	0.00001	0.00001	0.00001	0.00000	0.00000	0.00000	0.00000	0.00000
113 ..	0.00028	0.00017	0.00010	0.00006	0.00004	0.00002	0.00001	0.00001	0.00000	0.00000	0.00000	0.00000	0.00000	0.00000
114 ..	0.00026	0.00015	0.00009	0.00005	0.00003	0.00002	0.00001	0.00001	0.00000	0.00000	0.00000	0.00000	0.00000	0.00000
115 ..	0.00024	0.00014	0.00008	0.00005	0.00003	0.00002	0.00001	0.00001	0.00000	0.00000	0.00000	0.00000	0.00000	0.00000
116 ..	0.00023	0.00013	0.00008	0.00005	0.00003	0.00002	0.00001	0.00001	0.00000	0.00000	0.00000	0.00000	0.00000	0.00000
117 ..	0.00021	0.00012	0.00007	0.00004	0.00002	0.00001	0.00001	0.00000	0.00000	0.00000	0.00000	0.00000	0.00000	0.00000
118 ..	0.00020	0.00011	0.00007	0.00004	0.00002	0.00001	0.00001	0.00000	0.00000	0.00000	0.00000	0.00000	0.00000	0.00000
119 ..	0.00018	0.00011	0.00006	0.00004	0.00002	0.00001	0.00001	0.00000	0.00000	0.00000	0.00000	0.00000	0.00000	0.00000
120 ..	0.00017	0.00010	0.00006	0.00003	0.00002	0.00001	0.00001	0.00000	0.00000	0.00000	0.00000	0.00000	0.00000	0.00000

Table 3 *(concluded)* *Present Value of $1: 14.5%–20%*

Period	14.5%	15%	15.5%	16%	16.5%	17%	17.5%	18%	18.5%	19%	19.5%	20%
1	0.87336	0.86957	0.86580	0.86207	0.85837	0.85470	0.85106	0.84746	0.84388	0.84034	0.83682	0.83333
2	0.76276	0.75614	0.74961	0.74316	0.73680	0.73051	0.72431	0.71818	0.71214	0.70616	0.70027	0.69444
3	0.66617	0.65752	0.64901	0.64066	0.63244	0.62437	0.61643	0.60863	0.60096	0.59342	0.58600	0.57870
4	0.58181	0.57175	0.56192	0.55229	0.54287	0.53365	0.52462	0.51579	0.50714	0.49867	0.49038	0.48225
5	0.50813	0.49718	0.48651	0.47611	0.46598	0.45611	0.44649	0.43711	0.42796	0.41905	0.41036	0.40188
6	0.44378	0.43233	0.42122	0.41044	0.39999	0.38984	0.37999	0.37043	0.36115	0.35214	0.34339	0.33490
7	0.38758	0.37594	0.36469	0.35383	0.34334	0.33320	0.32340	0.31393	0.30477	0.29592	0.28736	0.27908
8	0.33850	0.32690	0.31575	0.30503	0.29471	0.28478	0.27523	0.26604	0.25719	0.24867	0.24047	0.23257
9	0.29563	0.28426	0.27338	0.26295	0.25297	0.24340	0.23424	0.22546	0.21704	0.20897	0.20123	0.19381
10	0.25819	0.24718	0.23669	0.22668	0.21714	0.20804	0.19935	0.19106	0.18315	0.17560	0.16839	0.16151
11	0.22550	0.21494	0.20493	0.19542	0.18639	0.17781	0.16966	0.16192	0.15456	0.14757	0.14091	0.13459
12	0.19694	0.18691	0.17743	0.16846	0.15999	0.15197	0.14439	0.13722	0.13043	0.12400	0.11792	0.11216
13	0.17200	0.16253	0.15362	0.14523	0.13733	0.12989	0.12289	0.11629	0.11007	0.10421	0.09868	0.09346
14	0.15022	0.14133	0.13300	0.12520	0.11788	0.11102	0.10459	0.09855	0.09288	0.08757	0.08258	0.07789
15	0.13120	0.12289	0.11515	0.10793	0.10118	0.09489	0.08901	0.08352	0.07838	0.07359	0.06910	0.06491
16	0.11458	0.10686	0.09970	0.09304	0.08685	0.08110	0.07575	0.07078	0.06615	0.06184	0.05782	0.05409
17	0.10007	0.09293	0.08632	0.08021	0.07455	0.06932	0.06447	0.05998	0.05582	0.05196	0.04839	0.04507
18	0.08740	0.04081	0.07474	0.06914	0.06399	0.05925	0.05487	0.05083	0.04711	0.04367	0.04049	0.03756
19	0.07633	0.07027	0.06471	0.05961	0.05493	0.05064	0.04670	0.04308	0.03975	0.03670	0.03389	0.03130
20	0.06666	0.06110	0.05602	0.05139	0.04715	0.04328	0.03974	0.03651	0.03355	0.03084	0.02836	0.02608
21	0.05822	0.05313	0.04850	0.04430	0.04047	0.03699	0.03382	0.03094	0.02831	0.02591	0.02373	0.02174
22	0.05085	0.04620	0.04199	0.03819	0.03474	0.03162	0.02879	0.02622	0.02389	0.02178	0.01986	0.01811
23	0.04441	0.04017	0.03636	0.03292	0.02982	0.02702	0.02450	0.02222	0.02016	0.01830	0.01662	0.01509
24	0.03879	0.03493	0.03148	0.02838	0.02560	0.02310	0.02085	0.01883	0.01701	0.01538	0.01390	0.01258
25	0.03387	0.03038	0.02726	0.02447	0.02197	0.01974	0.01774	0.01596	0.01436	0.01292	0.01164	0.01048
26	0.02958	0.02642	0.02360	0.02109	0.01886	0.01687	0.01510	0.01352	0.01211	0.01086	0.00974	0.00874
27	0.02584	0.02297	0.02043	0.01818	0.01619	0.01442	0.01285	0.01146	0.01022	0.00912	0.00815	0.00728
28	0.02257	0.01997	0.01769	0.01567	0.01390	0.01233	0.01094	0.00971	0.00863	0.00767	0.00682	0.00607
29	0.01971	0.01737	0.01532	0.01351	0.01193	0.01053	0.00931	0.00823	0.00728	0.00644	0.00571	0.00506
30	0.01721	0.01510	0.01326	0.01165	0.01024	0.00900	0.00792	0.00697	0.00614	0.00541	0.00477	0.00421
31	0.01503	0.01313	0.01148	0.01004	0.00879	0.00770	0.00674	0.00591	0.00518	0.00455	0.00400	0.00351
32	0.01313	0.01142	0.00994	0.00866	0.00754	0.00658	0.00574	0.00501	0.00438	0.00382	0.00334	0.00293
33	0.01147	0.00993	0.00861	0.00746	0.00648	0.00562	0.00488	0.00425	0.00369	0.00321	0.00280	0.00244
34	0.01001	0.00864	0.00745	0.00643	0.00556	0.00480	0.00416	0.00360	0.00312	0.00270	0.00234	0.00203
35	0.00875	0.00751	0.00645	0.00555	0.00477	0.00411	0.00354	0.00305	0.00263	0.00227	0.00196	0.00169
36	0.00764	0.00653	0.00559	0.00478	0.00410	0.00351	0.00301	0.00258	0.00222	0.00191	0.00164	0.00141
37	0.00667	0.00568	0.00484	0.00412	0.00352	0.00300	0.00256	0.00219	0.00187	0.00160	0.00137	0.00118
38	0.00583	0.00494	0.00419	0.00355	0.00302	0.00256	0.00218	0.00186	0.00158	0.00135	0.00115	0.00098
39	0.00509	0.00429	0.00362	0.00306	0.00259	0.00219	0.00186	0.00157	0.00133	0.00113	0.00096	0.00082
40	0.00444	0.00373	0.00314	0.00264	0.00222	0.00187	0.00158	0.00133	0.00113	0.00095	0.00080	0.00068
41	0.00388	0.00325	0.00272	0.00228	0.00191	0.00160	0.00134	0.00113	0.00095	0.00080	0.00067	0.00057
42	0.00339	0.00282	0.00235	0.00196	0.00164	0.00137	0.00114	0.00096	0.00080	0.00067	0.00056	0.00047
43	0.00296	0.00245	0.00204	0.00169	0.00141	0.00117	0.00097	0.00081	0.00068	0.00056	0.00047	0.00039
44	0.00259	0.00213	0.00176	0.00146	0.00121	0.00100	0.00083	0.00069	0.00057	0.00047	0.00039	0.00033
45	0.00226	0.00186	0.00153	0.00126	0.00104	0.00085	0.00071	0.00058	0.00048	0.00040	0.00033	0.00027
46	0.00197	0.00161	0.00132	0.00108	0.00089	0.00073	0.00060	0.00049	0.00041	0.00033	0.00028	0.00023
47	0.00172	0.00140	0.00114	0.00093	0.00076	0.00062	0.00051	0.00042	0.00034	0.00028	0.00023	0.00019
48	0.00150	0.00122	0.00099	0.00081	0.00066	0.00053	0.00043	0.00035	0.00029	0.00024	0.00019	0.00016
49	0.00131	0.00106	0.00086	0.00069	0.00056	0.00046	0.00037	0.00030	0.00024	0.00020	0.00016	0.00013
50	0.00115	0.00092	0.00074	0.00060	0.00048	0.00039	0.00031	0.00025	0.00021	0.00017	0.00014	0.00011
51	0.00100	0.00080	0.00064	0.00052	0.00041	0.00033	0.00027	0.00022	0.00017	0.00014	0.00011	0.00009
52	0.00088	0.00070	0.00056	0.00044	0.00036	0.00028	0.00023	0.00018	0.00015	0.00012	0.00009	0.00008
53	0.00076	0.00061	0.00048	0.00038	0.00031	0.00024	0.00019	0.00015	0.00012	0.00010	0.00008	0.00006
54	0.00067	0.00053	0.00042	0.00033	0.00026	0.00021	0.00017	0.00013	0.00010	0.00008	0.00007	0.00005
55	0.00058	0.00046	0.00036	0.00028	0.00022	0.00018	0.00014	0.00011	0.00009	0.00007	0.00006	0.00004
56	0.00051	0.00040	0.00031	0.00025	0.00019	0.00015	0.00012	0.00009	0.00007	0.00006	0.00005	0.00004
57	0.00044	0.00035	0.00027	0.00021	0.00017	0.00013	0.00010	0.00008	0.00006	0.00005	0.00004	0.00003
58	0.00039	0.00030	0.00023	0.00018	0.00014	0.00011	0.00009	0.00007	0.00005	0.00004	0.00003	0.00003
59	0.00034	0.00026	0.00020	0.00016	0.00012	0.00009	0.00007	0.00006	0.00004	0.00003	0.00003	0.00002
60	0.00030	0.00023	0.00018	0.00014	0.00010	0.00008	0.00006	0.00005	0.00004	0.00003	0.00002	0.00002

Period	14.5%	15%	15.5%	16%	16.5%	17%	17.5%	18%	18.5%	19%	19.5%	20%
61	0.00026	0.00020	0.00015	0.00012	0.00009	0.00007	0.00005	0.00004	0.00003	0.00002	0.00002	0.00001
62	0.00023	0.00017	0.00013	0.00010	0.00008	0.00006	0.00005	0.00003	0.00003	0.00002	0.00002	0.00001
63	0.00020	0.00015	0.00011	0.00009	0.00007	0.00005	0.00004	0.00003	0.00002	0.00002	0.00001	0.00001
64	0.00017	0.00013	0.00010	0.00007	0.00006	0.00004	0.00003	0.00003	0.00002	0.00001	0.00001	0.00001
65	0.00015	0.00011	0.00009	0.00006	0.00005	0.00004	0.00003	0.00002	0.00002	0.00001	0.00001	0.00001
66	0.00013	0.00010	0.00007	0.00006	0.00004	0.00003	0.00002	0.00002	0.00001	0.00001	0.00001	0.00001
67	0.00011	0.00009	0.00006	0.00005	0.00004	0.00003	0.00002	0.00002	0.00001	0.00001	0.00001	0.00000
68	0.00010	0.00007	0.00006	0.00004	0.00003	0.00002	0.00002	0.00001	0.00001	0.00001	0.00001	0.00000
69	0.00009	0.00006	0.00005	0.00004	0.00003	0.00002	0.00001	0.00001	0.00001	0.00001	0.00000	0.00000
70	0.00008	0.00006	0.00004	0.00003	0.00002	0.00002	0.00001	0.00001	0.00001	0.00001	0.00000	0.00000
71	0.00007	0.00005	0.00004	0.00003	0.00002	0.00001	0.00001	0.00001	0.00001	0.00000	0.00000	0.00000
72	0.00006	0.00004	0.00003	0.00002	0.00002	0.00001	0.00001	0.00001	0.00000	0.00000	0.00000	0.00000
73	0.00005	0.00004	0.00003	0.00002	0.00001	0.00001	0.00001	0.00001	0.00000	0.00000	0.00000	0.00000
74	0.00004	0.00003	0.00002	0.00002	0.00001	0.00001	0.00001	0.00000	0.00000	0.00000	0.00000	0.00000
75	0.00004	0.00003	0.00002	0.00001	0.00001	0.00001	0.00001	0.00000	0.00000	0.00000	0.00000	0.00000
76	0.00003	0.00002	0.00002	0.00001	0.00001	0.00001	0.00000	0.00000	0.00000	0.00000	0.00000	0.00000
77	0.00003	0.00002	0.00002	0.00001	0.00001	0.00001	0.00000	0.00000	0.00000	0.00000	0.00000	0.00000
78	0.00003	0.00002	0.00001	0.00001	0.00001	0.00000	0.00000	0.00000	0.00000	0.00000	0.00000	0.00000
79	0.00002	0.00002	0.00001	0.00001	0.00001	0.00000	0.00000	0.00000	0.00000	0.00000	0.00000	0.00000
80	0.00002	0.00001	0.00001	0.00001	0.00000	0.00000	0.00000	0.00000	0.00000	0.00000	0.00000	0.00000
81	0.00002	0.00001	0.00001	0.00001	0.00000	0.00000	0.00000	0.00000	0.00000	0.00000	0.00000	0.00000
82	0.00002	0.00001	0.00001	0.00001	0.00000	0.00000	0.00000	0.00000	0.00000	0.00000	0.00000	0.00000
83	0.00001	0.00001	0.00001	0.00000	0.00000	0.00000	0.00000	0.00000	0.00000	0.00000	0.00000	0.00000
84	0.00001	0.00001	0.00001	0.00000	0.00000	0.00000	0.00000	0.00000	0.00000	0.00000	0.00000	0.00000
85	0.00001	0.00001	0.00000	0.00000	0.00000	0.00000	0.00000	0.00000	0.00000	0.00000	0.00000	0.00000
86	0.00001	0.00001	0.00000	0.00000	0.00000	0.00000	0.00000	0.00000	0.00000	0.00000	0.00000	0.00000
87	0.00001	0.00001	0.00000	0.00000	0.00000	0.00000	0.00000	0.00000	0.00000	0.00000	0.00000	0.00000
88	0.00001	0.00000	0.00000	0.00000	0.00000	0.00000	0.00000	0.00000	0.00000	0.00000	0.00000	0.00000
89	0.00001	0.00000	0.00000	0.00000	0.00000	0.00000	0.00000	0.00000	0.00000	0.00000	0.00000	0.00000
90	0.00001	0.00000	0.00000	0.00000	0.00000	0.00000	0.00000	0.00000	0.00000	0.00000	0.00000	0.00000
91	0.00000	0.00000	0.00000	0.00000	0.00000	0.00000	0.00000	0.00000	0.00000	0.00000	0.00000	0.00000
92	0.00000	0.00000	0.00000	0.00000	0.00000	0.00000	0.00000	0.00000	0.00000	0.00000	0.00000	0.00000
93	0.00000	0.00000	0.00000	0.00000	0.00000	0.00000	0.00000	0.00000	0.00000	0.00000	0.00000	0.00000
94	0.00000	0.00000	0.00000	0.00000	0.00000	0.00000	0.00000	0.00000	0.00000	0.00000	0.00000	0.00000
95	0.00000	0.00000	0.00000	0.00000	0.00000	0.00000	0.00000	0.00000	0.00000	0.00000	0.00000	0.00000
96	0.00000	0.00000	0.00000	0.00000	0.00000	0.00000	0.00000	0.00000	0.00000	0.00000	0.00000	0.00000
97	0.00000	0.00000	0.00000	0.00000	0.00000	0.00000	0.00000	0.00000	0.00000	0.00000	0.00000	0.00000
98	0.00000	0.00000	0.00000	0.00000	0.00000	0.00000	0.00000	0.00000	0.00000	0.00000	0.00000	0.00000
99	0.00000	0.00000	0.00000	0.00000	0.00000	0.00000	0.00000	0.00000	0.00000	0.00000	0.00000	0.00000
100	0.00000	0.00000	0.00000	0.00000	0.00000	0.00000	0.00000	0.00000	0.00000	0.00000	0.00000	0.00000
101	0.00000	0.00000	0.00000	0.00000	0.00000	0.00000	0.00000	0.00000	0.00000	0.00000	0.00000	0.00000
102	0.00000	0.00000	0.00000	0.00000	0.00000	0.00000	0.00000	0.00000	0.00000	0.00000	0.00000	0.00000
103	0.00000	0.00000	0.00000	0.00000	0.00000	0.00000	0.00000	0.00000	0.00000	0.00000	0.00000	0.00000
104	0.00000	0.00000	0.00000	0.00000	0.00000	0.00000	0.00000	0.00000	0.00000	0.00000	0.00000	0.00000
105	0.00000	0.00000	0.00000	0.00000	0.00000	0.00000	0.00000	0.00000	0.00000	0.00000	0.00000	0.00000
106	0.00000	0.00000	0.00000	0.00000	0.00000	0.00000	0.00000	0.00000	0.00000	0.00000	0.00000	0.00000
107	0.00000	0.00000	0.00000	0.00000	0.00000	0.00000	0.00000	0.00000	0.00000	0.00000	0.00000	0.00000
108	0.00000	0.00000	0.00000	0.00000	0.00000	0.00000	0.00000	0.00000	0.00000	0.00000	0.00000	0.00000
109	0.00000	0.00000	0.00000	0.00000	0.00000	0.00000	0.00000	0.00000	0.00000	0.00000	0.00000	0.00000
110	0.00000	0.00000	0.00000	0.00000	0.00000	0.00000	0.00000	0.00000	0.00000	0.00000	0.00000	0.00000
111	0.00000	0.00000	0.00000	0.00000	0.00000	0.00000	0.00000	0.00000	0.00000	0.00000	0.00000	0.00000
112	0.00000	0.00000	0.00000	0.00000	0.00000	0.00000	0.00000	0.00000	0.00000	0.00000	0.00000	0.00000
113	0.00000	0.00000	0.00000	0.00000	0.00000	0.00000	0.00000	0.00000	0.00000	0.00000	0.00000	0.00000
114	0.00000	0.00000	0.00000	0.00000	0.00000	0.00000	0.00000	0.00000	0.00000	0.00000	0.00000	0.00000
115	0.00000	0.00000	0.00000	0.00000	0.00000	0.00000	0.00000	0.00000	0.00000	0.00000	0.00000	0.00000
116	0.00000	0.00000	0.00000	0.00000	0.00000	0.00000	0.00000	0.00000	0.00000	0.00000	0.00000	0.00000
117	0.00000	0.00000	0.00000	0.00000	0.00000	0.00000	0.00000	0.00000	0.00000	0.00000	0.00000	0.00000
118	0.00000	0.00000	0.00000	0.00000	0.00000	0.00000	0.00000	0.00000	0.00000	0.00000	0.00000	0.00000
119	0.00000	0.00000	0.00000	0.00000	0.00000	0.00000	0.00000	0.00000	0.00000	0.00000	0.00000	0.00000
120	0.00000	0.00000	0.00000	0.00000	0.00000	0.00000	0.00000	0.00000	0.00000	0.00000	0.00000	0.00000

Table 4   Present Value of an Ordinary Annuity of $1 per Period: 0.5%–7%

$$P_{A_{i,n}} = \frac{1 - \dfrac{1}{(1+i)^n}}{i}$$

Period	.5%	1%	1.5%	2%	2.5%	3%	3.5%	4%	4.5%	5%	5.5%	6%	6.5%	7%
1	0.99502	0.99010	0.98522	0.98039	0.97561	0.97087	0.96618	0.96154	0.95694	0.95238	0.94787	0.94340	0.93897	0.93458
2	1.98510	1.97040	1.95588	1.94156	1.92742	1.91347	1.89969	1.88609	1.87267	1.85941	1.84632	1.83339	1.82063	1.80802
3	2.97025	2.94099	2.91220	2.88388	2.85602	2.82861	2.80164	2.77509	2.74896	2.72325	2.69793	2.67301	2.64848	2.62432
4	3.95050	3.90197	3.85438	3.80773	3.76197	3.71710	3.67308	3.62990	3.58753	3.54595	3.50515	3.46511	3.42580	3.38721
5	4.92587	4.85343	4.78264	4.71346	4.64583	4.57971	4.51505	4.45182	4.38998	4.32948	4.27028	4.21236	4.15568	4.10020
6	5.89638	5.79548	5.69719	5.60143	5.50813	5.41719	5.32855	5.24214	5.15787	5.07569	4.99553	4.91732	4.84101	4.76654
7	6.86207	6.72819	6.59821	6.47199	6.34939	6.23028	6.11454	6.00205	5.89270	5.78637	5.68297	5.58238	5.48452	5.38929
8	7.82296	7.65168	7.48593	7.32548	7.17014	7.01969	6.87396	6.73274	6.59589	6.46321	6.33457	6.20979	6.08875	5.97130
9	8.77906	8.56602	8.36052	8.16224	7.97087	7.78611	7.60769	7.43533	7.26879	7.10782	6.95220	6.80169	6.65610	6.51523
10	9.73041	9.47130	9.22218	8.98259	8.75206	8.53020	8.31661	8.11090	7.91272	7.72173	7.53763	7.36009	7.18883	7.02358
11	10.67703	10.36763	10.07112	9.78685	9.51421	9.25262	9.00155	8.76048	8.52892	8.30641	8.09254	7.88687	7.68904	7.49867
12	11.61893	11.25508	10.90751	10.57534	10.25776	9.95400	9.66333	9.38507	9.11858	8.86325	8.61852	8.38384	8.15873	7.94269
13	12.55615	12.13374	11.73153	11.34837	10.98318	10.63496	10.30274	9.98565	9.68285	9.39357	9.11708	8.85268	8.59974	8.35765
14	13.48871	13.00370	12.54338	12.10625	11.69091	11.29607	10.92052	10.56312	10.22283	9.89864	9.58965	9.29498	9.01384	8.74547
15	14.41662	13.86505	13.34323	12.84926	12.38138	11.93794	11.51741	11.11839	10.73955	10.37966	10.03758	9.71225	9.40267	9.10791
16	15.33993	14.71787	14.13126	13.57771	13.05500	12.56110	12.09412	11.65230	11.23402	10.83777	10.46216	10.10590	9.76776	9.44665
17	16.25863	15.56225	14.90765	14.29187	13.71220	13.16612	12.65132	12.16567	11.70719	11.27407	10.86461	10.47726	10.11058	9.76322
18	17.17277	16.39827	15.67256	14.99203	14.35336	13.75351	13.18968	12.65930	12.15999	11.68959	11.24607	10.82760	10.43247	10.05909
19	18.08236	17.22601	16.42617	15.67846	14.97889	14.32380	13.70984	13.13394	12.59329	12.08532	11.60765	11.15812	10.73471	10.33560
20	18.98742	18.04555	17.16864	16.35143	15.58916	14.87747	14.21240	13.59033	13.00794	12.46221	11.95038	11.46992	11.01851	10.59401
21	19.88798	18.85698	17.90014	17.01121	16.18455	15.41502	14.69797	14.02916	13.40472	12.82115	12.27524	11.76408	11.28498	10.83553
22	20.78406	19.66038	18.62082	17.65805	16.76541	15.93692	15.16712	14.45112	13.78442	13.16300	12.58317	12.04158	11.53520	11.06124
23	21.67568	20.45582	19.33086	18.29220	17.33211	16.44361	15.62041	14.85684	14.14777	13.48857	12.87504	12.30338	11.77014	11.27219
24	22.56287	21.24339	20.03041	18.91393	17.88499	16.93554	16.05837	15.24696	14.49548	13.79864	13.15170	12.55036	11.99074	11.46933
25	23.44554	22.02316	20.71961	19.52346	18.42438	17.41315	16.48151	15.62208	14.82821	14.09394	13.41393	12.78336	12.19788	11.65358
26	24.32402	22.79520	21.39863	20.12104	18.95061	17.87684	16.89035	15.98277	15.14661	14.37519	13.66250	13.00317	12.39237	11.82578
27	25.19803	23.55961	22.06762	20.70690	19.46401	18.32703	17.28536	16.32959	15.45130	14.64303	13.89810	13.21053	12.57500	11.98671
28	26.06769	24.31644	22.72672	21.28127	19.96489	18.76411	17.66702	16.66306	15.74287	14.89813	14.12142	13.40616	12.74648	12.13711
29	26.93302	25.06579	23.37608	21.84438	20.45355	19.18845	18.03577	16.98371	16.02189	15.14107	14.33310	13.59072	12.90749	12.27767
30	27.79405	25.80771	24.01584	22.39646	20.93029	19.60044	18.39205	17.29203	16.28889	15.37245	14.53375	13.76483	13.05868	12.40904
31	28.65080	26.54229	24.64615	22.93770	21.39541	20.00043	18.73628	17.58849	16.54439	15.59281	14.72393	13.92909	13.20063	12.53181
32	29.50328	27.26959	25.26714	23.46833	21.84918	20.38877	19.06887	17.87355	16.78889	15.80268	14.90420	14.08404	13.33393	12.64656
33	30.35153	27.98969	25.87895	23.98856	22.29188	20.76579	19.39021	18.14765	17.02286	16.00255	15.07507	14.23023	13.45909	12.75379
34	31.19555	28.70267	26.48173	24.49859	22.72379	21.13184	19.70068	18.41120	17.24676	16.19290	15.23703	14.36814	13.57661	12.85401
35	32.03537	29.40858	27.07559	24.99862	23.14516	21.48722	20.00066	18.66461	17.46101	16.37419	15.39055	14.49825	13.68696	12.94767
36	32.87102	30.10751	27.66068	25.48884	23.55625	21.83225	20.29049	18.90828	17.66604	16.54685	15.53607	14.62099	13.79057	13.03521
37	33.70250	30.79951	28.23713	25.96945	23.95732	22.16724	20.57053	19.14258	17.86224	16.71129	15.67400	14.73678	13.88786	13.11702
38	34.52985	31.48466	28.80505	26.44064	24.34860	22.49246	20.84109	19.36786	18.04999	16.86789	15.80474	14.84602	13.97921	13.19347
39	35.35309	32.16303	29.36458	26.90259	24.73034	22.80822	21.10250	19.58448	18.22966	17.01704	15.92866	14.94907	14.06499	13.26493
40	36.17223	32.83469	29.91585	27.35548	25.10278	23.11477	21.35507	19.79277	18.40158	17.15909	16.04612	15.04630	14.14553	13.33171
41	36.98729	33.49969	30.45896	27.79949	25.46612	23.41240	21.59910	19.99305	18.56611	17.29437	16.15746	15.13802	14.22115	13.39412
42	37.79830	34.15811	30.99405	28.23479	25.82061	23.70136	21.83488	20.18563	18.72355	17.42321	16.26300	15.22454	14.29216	13.45245
43	38.60527	34.81001	31.52123	28.66156	26.16645	23.98190	22.06269	20.37079	18.87421	17.54591	16.36303	15.30617	14.35884	13.50696
44	39.40823	35.45545	32.04062	29.07996	26.50385	24.25427	22.28279	20.54884	19.01838	17.66277	16.45785	15.38318	14.42144	13.55791
45	40.20720	36.09451	32.55234	29.49016	26.83302	24.51871	22.49545	20.72004	19.15635	17.77407	16.54773	15.45583	14.48023	13.60552
46	41.00219	36.72724	33.05649	29.89231	27.15417	24.77545	22.70092	20.88465	19.28837	17.88007	16.63292	15.52447	14.53543	13.65002
47	41.79322	37.35370	33.55319	30.28658	27.46748	25.02471	22.89944	21.04294	19.41471	17.98102	16.71366	15.58903	14.58725	13.69161
48	42.58032	37.97396	34.04255	30.67312	27.77315	25.26671	23.09124	21.19513	19.53561	18.07716	16.79020	15.65003	14.63592	13.73047
49	43.36350	38.58808	34.52468	31.05208	28.07137	25.50166	23.27656	21.34147	19.65130	18.16872	16.86275	15.70757	14.68161	13.76680
50	44.14279	39.19612	34.99969	31.42361	28.36231	25.72976	23.45562	21.48218	19.76201	18.25593	16.93152	15.76186	14.72452	13.80075
51	44.91820	39.79814	35.46767	31.78785	28.64616	25.95123	23.62862	21.61749	19.86795	18.33898	16.99670	15.81308	14.76481	13.83247
52	45.68975	40.39419	35.92874	32.14495	28.92308	26.16624	23.79576	21.74758	19.96933	18.41807	17.05848	15.86139	14.80264	13.86212
53	46.45746	40.98435	36.38300	32.49505	29.19325	26.37499	23.95726	21.87267	20.06634	18.49340	17.11705	15.90697	14.83816	13.88984
54	47.22135	41.56866	36.83054	32.83828	29.45683	26.57766	24.11330	21.99296	20.15918	18.56515	17.17255	15.94998	14.87151	13.91573
55	47.98145	42.14719	37.27147	33.17479	29.71398	26.77443	24.26405	22.10861	20.24802	18.63347	17.22517	15.99054	14.90282	13.93994
56	48.73776	42.71999	37.70588	33.50469	29.96486	26.96546	24.40971	22.21982	20.33303	18.69854	17.27504	16.02881	14.93223	13.96256
57	49.49031	43.28712	38.13387	33.82813	30.20962	27.15094	24.55045	22.32675	20.41439	18.76052	17.32232	16.06492	14.95984	13.98370
58	50.23911	43.84863	38.55554	34.14523	30.44841	27.33101	24.68642	22.42957	20.49224	18.81954	17.36712	16.09898	14.98577	14.00346
59	50.98419	44.40459	38.97097	34.45610	30.68137	27.50583	24.81780	22.52843	20.56673	18.87575	17.40960	16.13111	15.01011	14.02192
60	51.72556	44.95504	39.38027	34.76089	30.90866	27.67556	24.94473	22.62349	20.63802	18.92929	17.44985	16.16143	15.03297	14.03918

Period	.5%	1%	1.5%	2%	2.5%	3%	3.5%	4%	4.5%	5%	5.5%	6%	6.5%	7%
61 ...	52.46324	45.50004	39.78352	35.05969	31.13040	27.84035	25.06738	22.71489	20.70624	18.98028	17.48801	16.19003	15.05443	14.05531
62 ...	53.19726	46.03964	40.18080	35.35264	31.34673	28.00034	25.18587	22.80278	20.77152	19.02883	17.52418	16.21701	15.07458	14.07038
63 ...	53.92762	46.57390	40.57222	35.63984	31.55778	28.15567	25.30036	22.88729	20.83399	19.07508	17.55847	16.24246	15.09350	14.08447
64 ...	54.65435	47.10287	40.95785	35.92141	31.76369	28.30648	25.41097	22.96855	20.89377	19.11912	17.59096	16.26647	15.11127	14.09764
65 ...	55.37746	47.62661	41.33779	36.19747	31.96458	28.45289	25.51785	23.04668	20.95098	19.16107	17.62177	16.28912	15.12795	14.10994
66 ...	56.09698	48.14516	41.71210	36.46810	32.16056	28.59504	25.62111	23.12181	21.00572	19.20102	17.65096	16.31049	15.14362	14.12144
67 ...	56.81291	48.65857	42.08089	36.73343	32.35177	28.73305	25.72088	23.19405	21.05811	19.23907	17.67864	16.33065	15.15833	14.13219
68 ...	57.52529	49.16690	42.44423	36.99356	32.53831	28.86704	25.81727	23.26351	21.10824	19.27530	17.70487	16.34967	15.17214	14.14223
69 ...	58.23411	49.67020	42.80219	37.24859	32.72030	28.99712	25.91041	23.33030	21.15621	19.30981	17.72974	16.36762	15.18511	14.15162
70 ...	58.93942	50.16851	43.15487	37.49862	32.89786	29.12342	26.00040	23.39451	21.20211	19.34268	17.75330	16.38454	15.19728	14.16039
71 ...	59.64121	50.66190	43.50234	37.74374	33.07108	29.24604	26.08734	23.45626	21.24604	19.37398	17.77564	16.40051	15.20872	14.16859
72 ...	60.33951	51.15039	43.84467	37.98406	33.24008	29.36509	26.17134	23.51564	21.28808	19.40379	17.79682	16.41558	15.21945	14.17625
73 ...	61.03434	51.63405	44.18194	38.21967	33.40495	29.48067	26.25251	23.57273	21.32830	19.43218	17.81689	16.42979	15.22953	14.18341
74 ...	61.72571	52.11292	44.51422	38.45066	33.56581	29.59288	26.33092	23.62762	21.36680	19.45922	17.83591	16.44320	15.23900	14.19010
75 ...	62.41365	52.58705	44.84160	38.67711	33.72274	29.70183	26.40669	23.68041	21.40363	19.48497	17.85395	16.45585	15.24788	14.19636
76 ...	63.09815	53.05649	45.16414	38.89913	33.87584	29.80760	26.47989	23.73116	21.43888	19.50950	17.87104	16.46778	15.25623	14.20220
77 ...	63.77926	53.52127	45.48191	39.11680	34.02521	29.91029	26.55062	23.77996	21.47262	19.53285	17.88724	16.47904	15.26407	14.20767
78 ...	64.45697	53.98146	45.79498	39.33019	34.17094	30.00999	26.61896	23.82689	21.50490	19.55510	17.90260	16.48966	15.27142	14.21277
79 ...	65.13132	54.43709	46.10343	39.53940	34.31311	30.10679	26.68498	23.87201	21.53579	19.57628	17.91716	16.49968	15.27833	14.21755
80 ...	65.80231	54.88821	46.40732	39.74451	34.45182	30.20076	26.74878	23.91539	21.56534	19.59646	17.93095	16.50913	15.28482	14.22201
81 ...	66.46996	55.33486	46.70672	39.94560	34.58714	30.29200	26.81041	23.95711	21.59363	19.61568	17.94403	16.51805	15.29091	14.22617
82 ...	67.13428	55.77709	47.00170	40.14275	34.71916	30.38059	26.86996	23.99722	21.62070	19.63398	17.95643	16.52646	15.29663	14.23007
83 ...	67.79531	56.21494	47.29231	40.33603	34.84796	30.46659	26.92750	24.03579	21.64660	19.65141	17.96818	16.53440	15.30200	14.23371
84 ...	68.45304	56.64845	47.57863	40.52552	34.97362	30.55009	26.98309	24.07287	21.67139	19.66801	17.97932	16.54188	15.30704	14.23711
85 ...	69.10750	57.07768	47.86072	40.71129	35.09621	30.63115	27.03680	24.10853	21.69511	19.68382	17.98987	16.54895	15.31178	14.24029
86 ...	69.75871	57.50265	48.13864	40.89342	35.21582	30.70986	27.08870	24.14282	21.71781	19.69887	17.99988	16.55561	15.31622	14.24326
87 ...	70.40668	57.92342	48.41246	41.07198	35.33251	30.78627	27.13884	24.17579	21.73953	19.71321	18.00936	16.56190	15.32040	14.24604
88 ...	71.05142	58.34002	48.68222	41.24704	35.44635	30.86045	27.18728	24.20749	21.76032	19.72687	18.01835	16.56783	15.32431	14.24864
89 ...	71.69296	58.75249	48.94800	41.41867	35.55741	30.93248	27.23409	24.23797	21.78021	19.73987	18.02688	16.57342	15.32800	14.25106
90 ...	72.33130	59.16088	49.20985	41.58693	35.66577	31.00241	27.27932	24.26728	21.79924	19.75226	18.03495	16.57870	15.33145	14.25333
91 ...	72.96647	59.56523	49.46784	41.75189	35.77148	31.07030	27.32301	24.29546	21.81746	19.76406	18.04261	16.58368	15.33470	14.25545
92 ...	73.59847	59.96557	49.72201	41.91362	35.87462	31.13621	27.36523	24.32256	21.83489	19.77529	18.04987	16.58838	15.33774	14.25743
93 ...	74.22734	60.36195	49.97242	42.07218	35.97524	31.20021	27.40602	24.34861	21.85156	19.78599	18.05675	16.59281	15.34060	14.25928
94 ...	74.85307	60.75441	50.21913	42.22762	36.07340	31.26234	27.44543	24.37367	21.86753	19.79619	18.06327	16.59699	15.34329	14.26101
95 ...	75.47569	61.14298	50.46220	42.38002	36.16917	31.32266	27.48350	24.39776	21.88280	19.80589	18.06945	16.60093	15.34581	14.26262
96 ...	76.09522	61.52770	50.70168	42.52943	36.26261	31.38122	27.52029	24.42092	21.89742	19.81513	18.07531	16.60465	15.34818	14.26413
97 ...	76.71166	61.90862	50.93761	42.67592	36.35376	31.43808	27.55584	24.44319	21.91140	19.82394	18.08086	16.60816	15.35040	14.26555
98 ...	77.32503	62.28576	51.17006	42.81953	36.44269	31.49328	27.59018	24.46461	21.92479	19.83232	18.08612	16.61147	15.35249	14.26687
99 ...	77.93536	62.65917	51.39907	42.96032	36.52946	31.54687	27.62337	24.48520	21.93760	19.84031	18.09111	16.61460	15.35445	14.26810
100 ...	78.54264	63.02888	51.62470	43.09835	36.61411	31.59891	27.65543	24.50500	21.94985	19.84791	18.09584	16.61755	15.35629	14.26925
101 ...	79.14691	63.39493	51.84700	43.23368	36.69669	31.64942	27.68640	24.52404	21.96158	19.85515	18.10032	16.62033	15.35802	14.27033
102 ...	79.74817	63.75736	52.06601	43.36635	36.77726	31.69847	27.71633	24.54234	21.97281	19.86205	18.10457	16.62295	15.35964	14.27133
103 ...	80.34644	64.11619	52.28178	43.49642	36.85586	31.74609	27.74525	24.55995	21.98355	19.86862	18.10860	16.62542	15.36117	14.27228
104 ...	80.94173	64.47148	52.49437	43.62394	36.93255	31.79232	27.77318	24.57687	21.99382	19.87488	18.11241	16.62776	15.36260	14.27315
105 ...	81.53406	64.82325	52.70381	43.74896	37.00736	31.83720	27.80018	24.59315	22.00366	19.88083	18.11603	16.62996	15.36394	14.27398
106 ...	82.12344	65.17153	52.91016	43.87153	37.08035	31.88078	27.82626	24.60879	22.01307	19.88651	18.11946	16.63204	15.36521	14.27474
107 ...	82.70989	65.51637	53.11346	43.99170	37.15156	31.92308	27.85146	24.62384	22.02208	19.89191	18.12271	16.63400	15.36639	14.27546
108 ...	83.29342	65.85779	53.31375	44.10951	37.22104	31.96416	27.87581	24.63831	22.03070	19.89706	18.12579	16.63585	15.36750	14.27613
109 ...	83.87405	66.19583	53.51108	44.22501	37.28882	32.00404	27.89933	24.65222	22.03894	19.90196	18.12872	16.63759	15.36855	14.27676
110 ...	84.45180	66.53053	53.70550	44.33824	37.35494	32.04276	27.92206	24.66560	22.04684	19.90663	18.13148	16.63924	15.36953	14.27735
111 ...	85.02666	66.86191	53.89704	44.44926	37.41946	32.08035	27.94402	24.67846	22.05439	19.91108	18.13411	16.64079	15.37045	14.27789
112 ...	85.59867	67.19001	54.08576	44.55810	37.48240	32.11684	27.96523	24.69082	22.06162	19.91531	18.13659	16.64226	15.37131	14.27840
113 ...	86.16783	67.51486	54.27168	44.66480	37.54380	32.15227	27.98573	24.70272	22.06853	19.91934	18.13895	16.64364	15.37212	14.27888
114 ...	86.73416	67.83649	54.45486	44.76941	37.60371	32.18667	28.00554	24.71415	22.07515	19.92318	18.14119	16.64494	15.37289	14.27933
115 ...	87.29767	68.15494	54.63533	44.87197	37.66216	32.22007	28.02467	24.72514	22.08148	19.92684	18.14331	16.64617	15.37360	14.27975
116 ...	87.85838	68.47024	54.81313	44.97252	37.71918	32.25250	28.04316	24.73571	22.08754	19.93033	18.14531	16.64733	15.37428	14.28014
117 ...	88.41630	68.78242	54.98831	45.07110	37.77481	32.28398	28.06103	24.74588	22.09334	19.93364	18.14722	16.64843	15.37491	14.28050
118 ...	88.97144	69.09150	55.16089	45.16775	37.82908	32.31454	28.07829	24.75565	22.09889	19.93680	18.14902	16.64946	15.37550	14.28084
119 ...	89.52382	69.39753	55.33093	45.26250	37.88203	32.34421	28.09496	24.76505	22.10420	19.93981	18.15073	16.65043	15.37606	14.28116
120 ...	90.07345	69.70052	55.49845	45.35539	37.93369	32.37302	28.11108	24.77409	22.10929	19.94268	18.15235	16.65135	15.37658	14.28146

Table 4 (continued)   Present Value of an Ordinary Annuity of $1 per Period: 7.5%–14%

Period	7.5%	8%	8.5%	9%	9.5%	10%	10.5%	11%	11.5%	12%	12.5%	13%	13.5%	14%
1	0.93023	0.92593	0.92166	0.91743	0.91324	0.90909	0.90498	0.90090	0.89686	0.89286	0.88889	0.88496	0.88106	0.87719
2	1.79557	1.78326	1.77111	1.75911	1.74725	1.73554	1.72396	1.71252	1.70122	1.69005	1.67901	1.66810	1.65732	1.64666
3	2.60053	2.57710	2.55402	2.53129	2.50891	2.48685	2.46512	2.44371	2.42262	2.40183	2.38134	2.36115	2.34125	2.32163
4	3.34933	3.31213	3.27560	3.23972	3.20448	3.16987	3.13586	3.10245	3.06961	3.03735	3.00564	2.97447	2.94383	2.91371
5	4.04588	3.99271	3.94064	3.88965	3.83971	3.79079	3.74286	3.69590	3.64988	3.60478	3.56057	3.51723	3.47474	3.43308
6	4.69385	4.62288	4.55359	4.48592	4.41983	4.35526	4.29218	4.23054	4.17029	4.11141	4.05384	3.99755	3.94250	3.88867
7	5.29660	5.20637	5.11851	5.03295	4.94961	4.86842	4.78930	4.71220	4.63704	4.56376	4.49230	4.42261	4.35463	4.28830
8	5.85730	5.74664	5.63918	5.53482	5.43344	5.33493	5.23919	5.14612	5.05564	4.96764	4.88205	4.79877	4.71774	4.63886
9	6.37889	6.24689	6.11906	5.99525	5.87528	5.75902	5.64632	5.53705	5.43106	5.32825	5.22848	5.13166	5.03765	4.94637
10	6.86408	6.71008	6.56135	6.41766	6.27880	6.14457	6.01477	5.88923	5.76777	5.65022	5.53643	5.42624	5.31952	5.21612
11	7.31542	7.13896	6.96898	6.80519	6.64730	6.49506	6.34821	6.20652	6.06975	5.93770	5.81016	5.68694	5.56786	5.45273
12	7.73528	7.53608	7.34469	7.16073	6.98384	6.81369	6.64996	6.49236	6.34058	6.19437	6.05348	5.91765	5.78666	5.66029
13	8.12584	7.90378	7.69095	7.48690	7.29118	7.10336	6.92304	6.74987	6.58348	6.42355	6.26976	6.12181	5.97943	5.84236
14	8.48915	8.24424	8.01010	7.78615	7.57185	7.36669	7.17018	6.98187	6.80133	6.62817	6.46201	6.30249	6.14928	6.00207
15	8.82712	8.55948	8.30424	8.06069	7.82818	7.60608	7.39382	7.19087	6.99671	6.81086	6.63289	6.46238	6.29893	6.14217
16	9.14151	8.85137	8.57533	8.31256	8.06226	7.82371	7.59622	7.37916	7.17194	6.97399	6.78479	6.60388	6.43077	6.26506
17	9.43396	9.12164	8.82519	8.54363	8.27604	8.02155	7.77939	7.54879	7.32909	7.11963	6.91982	6.72909	6.54694	6.37286
18	9.70601	9.37189	9.05548	8.75563	8.47127	8.20141	7.94515	7.70162	7.47004	7.24967	7.03984	6.83991	6.64928	6.46742
19	9.95908	9.60360	9.26772	8.95011	8.64956	8.36492	8.09515	7.83929	7.59644	7.36578	7.14652	6.93797	6.73946	6.55037
20	10.19449	9.81815	9.46334	9.12855	8.81238	8.51356	8.23091	7.96333	7.70982	7.46944	7.24135	7.02475	6.81890	6.62313
21	10.41348	10.01680	9.64363	9.29224	8.96108	8.64869	8.35376	8.07507	7.81149	7.56200	7.32565	7.10155	6.88890	6.68696
22	10.61719	10.20074	9.80980	9.44243	9.09688	8.77154	8.46494	8.17574	7.90269	7.64465	7.40058	7.16951	6.95057	6.74294
23	10.80669	10.37106	9.96295	9.58021	9.22089	8.88322	8.56556	8.26643	7.98447	7.71843	7.46718	7.22966	7.00491	6.79206
24	10.98297	10.52876	10.10410	9.70661	9.33415	8.98474	8.65662	8.34814	8.05782	7.78432	7.52638	7.28288	7.05279	6.83514
25	11.14695	10.67478	10.23419	9.82258	9.43758	9.07704	8.73902	8.42174	8.12361	7.84314	7.57901	7.32998	7.09497	6.87293
26	11.29948	10.80998	10.35409	9.92897	9.53203	9.16095	8.81359	8.48806	8.18261	7.89566	7.62578	7.37167	7.13213	6.90608
27	11.44138	10.93516	10.46460	10.02658	9.61830	9.23722	8.88108	8.54780	8.23552	7.94255	7.66736	7.40856	7.16487	6.93515
28	11.57338	11.05108	10.56645	10.11613	9.69707	9.30657	8.94215	8.60162	8.28298	7.98442	7.70432	7.44120	7.19372	6.96066
29	11.69617	11.15841	10.66033	10.19828	9.76902	9.36961	8.99742	8.65011	8.32554	8.02181	7.73717	7.47009	7.21914	6.98304
30	11.81039	11.25778	10.74684	10.27365	9.83472	9.42691	9.04744	8.69379	8.36371	8.05518	7.76638	7.49565	7.24153	7.00266
31	11.91664	11.34980	10.82658	10.34280	9.89472	9.47901	9.09271	8.73315	8.39795	8.08499	7.79234	7.51828	7.26126	7.01988
32	12.01548	11.43500	10.90008	10.40624	9.94952	9.52638	9.13367	8.76860	8.42866	8.11159	7.81541	7.53830	7.27864	7.03498
33	12.10742	11.51389	10.96781	10.46444	9.99956	9.56943	9.17074	8.80054	8.45619	8.13535	7.83592	7.55602	7.29396	7.04823
34	12.19295	11.58693	11.03024	10.51784	10.04526	9.60857	9.20429	8.82932	8.48089	8.15656	7.85415	7.57170	7.30745	7.05985
35	12.27251	11.65457	11.08778	10.56682	10.08699	9.64416	9.23465	8.85524	8.50304	8.17550	7.87036	7.58557	7.31934	7.07005
36	12.34652	11.71719	11.14081	10.61176	10.12511	9.67651	9.26213	8.87859	8.52291	8.19241	7.88476	7.59785	7.32982	7.07899
37	12.41537	11.77518	11.18969	10.65299	10.15992	9.70592	9.28700	8.89963	8.54072	8.20751	7.89757	7.60872	7.33904	7.08683
38	12.47941	11.82887	11.23474	10.69082	10.19171	9.73265	9.30950	8.91859	8.55670	8.22099	7.90895	7.61833	7.34718	7.09371
39	12.53899	11.87858	11.27625	10.72552	10.22074	9.75696	9.32986	8.93567	8.57103	8.23303	7.91906	7.62684	7.35434	7.09975
40	12.59441	11.92461	11.31452	10.75736	10.24725	9.77905	9.34829	8.95105	8.58389	8.24378	7.92806	7.63438	7.36065	7.10504
41	12.64596	11.96723	11.34979	10.78657	10.27146	9.79914	9.36497	8.96491	8.59541	8.25337	7.93605	7.64104	7.36621	7.10969
42	12.69392	12.00670	11.38229	10.81337	10.29357	9.81740	9.38006	8.97740	8.60575	8.26194	7.94316	7.64694	7.37111	7.11376
43	12.73853	12.04324	11.41225	10.83795	10.31376	9.83400	9.39372	8.98865	8.61502	8.26959	7.94947	7.65216	7.37543	7.11733
44	12.78003	12.07707	11.43986	10.86051	10.33220	9.84909	9.40608	8.99878	8.62334	8.27642	7.95509	7.65678	7.37923	7.12047
45	12.81863	12.10840	11.46531	10.88120	10.34904	9.86281	9.41727	9.00791	8.63080	8.28252	7.96008	7.66086	7.38258	7.12322
46	12.85454	12.13741	11.48877	10.90018	10.36442	9.87528	9.42739	9.01614	8.63749	8.28796	7.96451	7.66448	7.38554	7.12563
47	12.88794	12.16427	11.51038	10.91760	10.37847	9.88662	9.43656	9.02355	8.64349	8.29282	7.96846	7.66768	7.38814	7.12774
48	12.91902	12.18914	11.53031	10.93358	10.39130	9.89693	9.44485	9.03022	8.64887	8.29716	7.97196	7.67052	7.39043	7.12960
49	12.94792	12.21216	11.54867	10.94823	10.40301	9.90630	9.45235	9.03624	8.65369	8.30104	7.97508	7.67302	7.39245	7.13123
50	12.97481	12.23348	11.56560	10.96168	10.41371	9.91481	9.45914	9.04165	8.65802	8.30450	7.97785	7.67524	7.39423	7.13266
51	12.99982	12.25323	11.58119	10.97402	10.42348	9.92256	9.46529	9.04653	8.66190	8.30759	7.98031	7.67720	7.39580	7.13391
52	13.02309	12.27151	11.59557	10.98534	10.43240	9.92960	9.47085	9.05093	8.66538	8.31035	7.98250	7.67894	7.39718	7.13501
53	13.04474	12.28843	11.60882	10.99573	10.44055	9.93600	9.47588	9.05489	8.66850	8.31281	7.98444	7.68048	7.39839	7.13597
54	13.06487	12.30410	11.62103	11.00525	10.44799	9.94182	9.48043	9.05846	8.67130	8.31501	7.98617	7.68184	7.39947	7.13682
55	13.08360	12.31861	11.63229	11.01399	10.45478	9.94711	9.48456	9.06168	8.67382	8.31697	7.98771	7.68304	7.40041	7.13756
56	13.10103	12.33205	11.64266	11.02201	10.46099	9.95191	9.48829	9.06457	8.67607	8.31872	7.98907	7.68411	7.40124	7.13821
57	13.11723	12.34449	11.65222	11.02937	10.46666	9.95629	9.49166	9.06718	8.67809	8.32029	7.99029	7.68505	7.40198	7.13878
58	13.13231	12.35601	11.66104	11.03612	10.47183	9.96026	9.49472	9.06954	8.67990	8.32169	7.99137	7.68589	7.40262	7.13928
59	13.14633	12.36668	11.66916	11.04231	10.47656	9.96387	9.49748	9.07165	8.68152	8.32294	7.99232	7.68663	7.40319	7.13972
60	13.15938	12.37655	11.67664	11.04799	10.48088	9.96716	9.49998	9.07356	8.68298	8.32405	7.99318	7.68728	7.40369	7.14011

Period	7.5%	8%	8.5%	9%	9.5%	10%	10.5%	11%	11.5%	12%	12.5%	13%	13.5%	14%
61....	13.17152	12.38570	11.68354	11.05320	10.48482	9.97014	9.50225	9.07528	8.68429	8.32504	7.99394	7.68786	7.40413	7.14044
62....	13.18281	12.39416	11.68990	11.05798	10.48842	9.97286	9.50430	9.07683	8.68546	8.32593	7.99461	7.68837	7.40452	7.14074
63....	13.19331	12.40200	11.69576	11.06237	10.49171	9.97532	9.50615	9.07822	8.68651	8.32673	7.99521	7.68882	7.40487	7.14100
64....	13.20308	12.40926	11.70116	11.06640	10.49471	9.97757	9.50783	9.07948	8.68745	8.32743	7.99574	7.68922	7.40517	7.14123
65....	13.21217	12.41598	11.70614	11.07009	10.49745	9.97961	9.50935	9.08061	8.68830	8.32807	7.99621	7.68958	7.40544	7.14143
66....	13.22062	12.42221	11.71073	11.07347	10.49996	9.98146	9.51072	9.08163	8.68906	8.32863	7.99663	7.68989	7.40567	7.14160
67....	13.22848	12.42797	11.71496	11.07658	10.50224	9.98315	9.51196	9.08255	8.68974	8.32913	7.99701	7.69017	7.40588	7.14176
68....	13.23580	12.43330	11.71885	11.07943	10.50433	9.98468	9.51309	9.08338	8.69035	8.32958	7.99734	7.69042	7.40606	7.14189
69....	13.24260	12.43825	11.72245	11.08205	10.50624	9.98607	9.51411	9.08413	8.69090	8.32999	7.99764	7.69063	7.40622	7.14201
70....	13.24893	12.44282	11.72576	11.08445	10.50798	9.98734	9.51503	9.08480	8.69139	8.33034	7.99790	7.69083	7.40636	7.14211
71....	13.25482	12.44706	11.72881	11.08665	10.50957	9.98849	9.51586	9.08541	8.69183	8.33066	7.99813	7.69100	7.40648	7.14221
72....	13.26030	12.45098	11.73162	11.08867	10.51102	9.98954	9.51662	9.08595	8.69222	8.33095	7.99834	7.69115	7.40659	7.14229
73....	13.26539	12.45461	11.73421	11.09052	10.51235	9.99049	9.51730	9.08644	8.69257	8.33121	7.99852	7.69128	7.40669	7.14236
74....	13.27013	12.45797	11.73660	11.09222	10.51356	9.99135	9.51792	9.08688	8.69289	8.33143	7.99869	7.69140	7.40678	7.14242
75....	13.27454	12.46108	11.73880	11.09378	10.51467	9.99214	9.51848	9.08728	8.69318	8.33164	7.99883	7.69150	7.40685	7.14247
76....	13.27864	12.46397	11.74083	11.09521	10.51568	9.99285	9.51899	9.08764	8.69343	8.33182	7.99896	7.69160	7.40692	7.14252
77....	13.28246	12.46664	11.74270	11.09653	10.51660	9.99350	9.51945	9.08797	8.69366	8.33198	7.99908	7.69168	7.40698	7.14256
78....	13.28601	12.46911	11.74443	11.09773	10.51744	9.99409	9.51986	9.08826	8.69387	8.33213	7.99918	7.69175	7.40703	7.14260
79....	13.28931	12.47140	11.74601	11.09883	10.51821	9.99463	9.52024	9.08852	8.69405	8.33226	7.99927	7.69181	7.40707	7.14263
80....	13.29238	12.47351	11.74748	11.09985	10.51892	9.99512	9.52057	9.08876	8.69422	8.33237	7.99935	7.69187	7.40711	7.14266
81....	13.29524	12.47548	11.74883	11.10078	10.51956	9.99556	9.52088	9.08897	8.69436	8.33247	7.99942	7.69192	7.40715	7.14268
82....	13.29790	12.47729	11.75007	11.10163	10.52015	9.99597	9.52116	9.08916	8.69450	8.33257	7.99949	7.69197	7.40718	7.14270
83....	13.30037	12.47897	11.75122	11.10241	10.52068	9.99633	9.52141	9.08934	8.69462	8.33265	7.99955	7.69201	7.40721	7.14272
84....	13.30267	12.48053	11.75228	11.10313	10.52117	9.99667	9.52164	9.08949	8.69472	8.33272	7.99960	7.69204	7.40723	7.14274
85....	13.30481	12.48197	11.75325	11.10379	10.52162	9.99697	9.52185	9.08963	8.69482	8.33279	7.99964	7.69207	7.40725	7.14275
86....	13.30680	12.48331	11.75415	11.10440	10.52202	9.99724	9.52203	9.08976	8.69490	8.33285	7.99968	7.69210	7.40727	7.14277
87....	13.30865	12.48455	11.75497	11.10495	10.52240	9.99749	9.52220	9.08987	8.69498	8.33290	7.99972	7.69212	7.40729	7.14278
88....	13.31037	12.48569	11.75574	11.10546	10.52274	9.99772	9.52235	9.08998	8.69505	8.33294	7.99975	7.69214	7.40730	7.14279
89....	13.31197	12.48675	11.75644	11.10593	10.52305	9.99793	9.52249	9.09007	8.69511	8.33299	7.99978	7.69216	7.40731	7.14280
90....	13.31346	12.48773	11.75709	11.10635	10.52333	9.99812	9.52262	9.09015	8.69517	8.33302	7.99980	7.69218	7.40732	7.14280
91....	13.31485	12.48864	11.75768	11.10675	10.52359	9.99829	9.52273	9.09023	8.69522	8.33306	7.99982	7.69219	7.40733	7.14281
92....	13.31614	12.48948	11.75823	11.10711	10.52383	9.99844	9.52283	9.09029	8.69526	8.33309	7.99984	7.69221	7.40734	7.14282
93....	13.31734	12.49026	11.75874	11.10744	10.52404	9.99859	9.52293	9.09036	8.69530	8.33311	7.99986	7.69222	7.40735	7.14282
94....	13.31846	12.49098	11.75921	11.10774	10.52424	9.99871	9.52301	9.09041	8.69534	8.33314	7.99988	7.69224	7.40736	7.14283
95....	13.31949	12.49165	11.75964	11.10802	10.52442	9.99883	9.52309	9.09046	8.69537	8.33316	7.99989	7.69224	7.40736	7.14283
96....	13.32046	12.49227	11.76004	11.10827	10.52458	9.99894	9.52315	9.09050	8.69540	8.33318	7.99990	7.69225	7.40737	7.14284
97....	13.32136	12.49284	11.76040	11.10851	10.52473	9.99903	9.52322	9.09054	8.69543	8.33319	7.99991	7.69225	7.40737	7.14284
98....	13.32219	12.49337	11.76074	11.10872	10.52487	9.99912	9.52327	9.09058	8.69545	8.33321	7.99992	7.69226	7.40738	7.14284
99....	13.32297	12.49386	11.76105	11.10892	10.52500	9.99920	9.52332	9.09061	8.69547	8.33322	7.99993	7.69226	7.40738	7.14284
100....	13.32369	12.49432	11.76134	11.10910	10.52511	9.99927	9.52337	9.09064	8.69549	8.33323	7.99994	7.69227	7.40738	7.14284
101....	13.32437	12.49474	11.76160	11.10927	10.52522	9.99934	9.52341	9.09067	8.69551	8.33324	7.99995	7.69227	7.40739	7.14284
102....	13.32499	12.49513	11.76184	11.10942	10.52531	9.99940	9.52345	9.09069	8.69552	8.33325	7.99995	7.69228	7.40739	7.14285
103....	13.32557	12.49549	11.76207	11.10956	10.52540	9.99945	9.52348	9.09071	8.69553	8.33326	7.99996	7.69228	7.40739	7.14285
104....	13.32611	12.49582	11.76227	11.10969	10.52548	9.99950	9.52351	9.09073	8.69555	8.33327	7.99996	7.69228	7.40739	7.14285
105....	13.32662	12.49613	11.76246	11.10981	10.52555	9.99955	9.52354	9.09075	8.69556	8.33328	7.99997	7.69229	7.40739	7.14285
106....	13.32709	12.49642	11.76264	11.10991	10.52562	9.99959	9.52357	9.09077	8.69557	8.33328	7.99997	7.69229	7.40740	7.14285
107....	13.32752	12.49668	11.76280	11.11001	10.52568	9.99963	9.52359	9.09078	8.69558	8.33329	7.99997	7.69229	7.40740	7.14285
108....	13.32793	12.49693	11.76295	11.11010	10.52573	9.99966	9.52361	9.09079	8.69558	8.33329	7.99998	7.69229	7.40740	7.14285
109....	13.32831	12.49716	11.76309	11.11019	10.52578	9.99969	9.52363	9.09080	8.69559	8.33330	7.99998	7.69230	7.40740	7.14285
110....	13.32866	12.49737	11.76322	11.11026	10.52583	9.99972	9.52365	9.09082	8.69560	8.33330	7.99998	7.69230	7.40740	7.14285
111....	13.32898	12.49756	11.76333	11.11033	10.52587	9.99975	9.52366	9.09082	8.69560	8.33330	7.99998	7.69230	7.40740	7.14285
112....	13.32929	12.49774	11.76344	11.11040	10.52591	9.99977	9.52368	9.09083	8.69561	8.33331	7.99999	7.69230	7.40740	7.14285
113....	13.32957	12.49791	11.76354	11.11046	10.52595	9.99979	9.52369	9.09084	8.69561	8.33331	7.99999	7.69230	7.40740	7.14285
114....	13.32983	12.49807	11.76363	11.11051	10.52598	9.99981	9.52370	9.09085	8.69562	8.33331	7.99999	7.69230	7.40740	7.14286
115....	13.33008	12.49821	11.76371	11.11056	10.52601	9.99983	9.52371	9.09085	8.69562	8.33332	7.99999	7.69230	7.40740	7.14286
116....	13.33030	12.49834	11.76379	11.11060	10.52603	9.99984	9.52372	9.09086	8.69562	8.33332	7.99999	7.69230	7.40740	7.14286
117....	13.33051	12.49846	11.76386	11.11065	10.52606	9.99986	9.52373	9.09086	8.69563	8.33332	7.99999	7.69230	7.40741	7.14286
118....	13.33071	12.49858	11.76393	11.11069	10.52608	9.99987	9.52374	9.09087	8.69563	8.33332	7.99999	7.69230	7.40741	7.14286
119....	13.33089	12.49868	11.76399	11.11072	10.52610	9.99988	9.52374	9.09087	8.69563	8.33332	7.99999	7.69230	7.40741	7.14286
120....	13.33106	12.49878	11.76405	11.11075	10.52612	9.99989	9.52375	9.09088	8.69563	8.33332	7.99999	7.69230	7.40741	7.14286

Table 4 (concluded)   Present Value of an Ordinary Annuity of $1 per Period: 14.5%–20%

Period	14.5%	15%	15.5%	16%	16.5%	17%	17.5%	18%	18.5%	19%	19.5%	20%
1	0.87336	0.86957	0.86580	0.86207	0.85837	0.85470	0.85106	0.84746	0.84388	0.84034	0.83682	0.83333
2	1.63612	1.62571	1.61541	1.60523	1.59517	1.58521	1.57537	1.56564	1.55602	1.54650	1.53709	1.52778
3	2.30229	2.28323	2.26443	2.24589	2.22761	2.20958	2.19181	2.17427	2.15698	2.13992	2.12309	2.10648
4	2.88410	2.85498	2.82634	2.79818	2.77048	2.74324	2.71643	2.69006	2.66412	2.63859	2.61346	2.58873
5	3.39223	3.35216	3.31285	3.27429	3.23646	3.19935	3.16292	3.12717	3.09208	3.05763	3.02382	2.99061
6	3.83600	3.78448	3.73407	3.68474	3.63645	3.58918	3.54291	3.49760	3.45323	3.40978	3.36721	3.32551
7	4.22358	4.16042	4.09876	4.03857	3.97979	3.92238	3.86631	3.81153	3.75800	3.70570	3.65457	3.60459
8	4.56208	4.48732	4.41451	4.34359	4.27449	4.20716	4.14154	4.07757	4.01519	3.95437	3.89504	3.83716
9	4.85771	4.77158	4.68789	4.60654	4.52746	4.45057	4.37578	3.30302	4.23223	4.16333	4.09627	4.03097
10	5.11591	5.01877	4.92458	4.83323	4.74460	4.65860	4.57513	4.49409	4.41538	4.33893	4.26466	4.19247
11	5.34140	5.23371	5.12951	5.02864	4.93099	4.83641	4.74479	4.65601	4.56994	4.48650	4.40557	4.32706
12	5.53834	5.42062	5.30693	5.19711	5.09098	4.98839	4.88918	4.79322	4.70037	4.61050	4.52349	4.43922
13	5.71034	5.58315	5.46055	5.34233	5.22831	5.11828	5.01207	4.90951	4.81044	4.71471	4.62217	4.53268
14	5.86056	5.72448	5.59355	5.46753	5.34619	5.22930	5.11666	5.00806	4.90333	4.80228	4.70474	4.61057
15	5.99176	5.84737	5.70870	5.57546	5.44747	5.32419	5.20567	5.09158	4.98171	4.87586	4.77384	4.67547
16	6.10634	5.95423	5.80840	5.66850	5.53422	5.40529	5.28142	5.16235	5.04786	4.93770	4.83167	4.72956
17	6.20641	6.04716	5.89472	5.74870	5.60878	5.47461	5.34589	5.22233	5.10368	4.98966	4.88006	4.77463
18	6.29381	6.12797	5.96945	5.81785	5.67277	5.53385	5.40075	5.27316	5.15078	5.03333	4.92055	4.81219
19	6.37014	6.19823	6.03416	5.87746	5.72770	5.58449	5.44745	5.31624	5.19053	5.07003	4.95443	4.84350
20	6.43680	6.25933	6.09018	5.92884	5.77485	5.62777	5.48719	5.35275	5.22408	5.10086	4.98279	4.86958
21	6.49502	6.31246	6.13868	5.97314	5.81532	5.66476	5.52101	5.38368	5.25239	5.12677	5.00652	4.89132
22	6.54587	6.35866	6.18068	6.01133	5.85006	5.69637	5.54980	5.40990	5.27628	5.14855	5.02638	4.90943
23	6.59028	6.39884	6.21704	6.04425	5.87988	5.72340	5.57430	5.43212	5.29644	5.16685	5.04299	4.92453
24	6.62907	6.43377	6.24852	6.07263	5.90548	5.74649	5.59515	5.45095	5.31345	5.18223	5.05690	4.93710
25	6.66294	6.46415	6.27577	6.09709	5.92745	5.76623	5.61289	5.46691	5.32780	5.19515	5.06853	4.94759
26	6.69252	6.49056	6.29937	6.11818	5.94631	5.78311	5.62799	5.48043	5.33992	5.20601	5.07827	4.95632
27	6.71836	6.51353	6.31980	6.13636	5.96250	5.79753	5.64084	5.49189	5.35014	5.21513	5.08642	4.96360
28	6.74093	6.53351	6.33749	6.15204	5.97639	5.80985	5.65178	5.50160	5.35877	5.22280	5.09324	4.96967
29	6.76064	6.55088	6.35281	6.16555	5.98832	5.82039	5.66109	5.50983	5.36605	5.22924	5.09894	4.97472
30	6.77785	6.56598	6.36607	6.17720	5.99856	5.82939	5.66901	5.51681	5.37219	5.23466	5.10372	4.97894
31	6.79288	6.57911	6.37755	6.18724	6.00734	5.83709	5.67576	5.52272	5.37738	5.23921	5.10771	4.98245
32	6.80601	6.59053	6.38749	6.19590	6.01489	5.84366	5.68150	5.52773	5.38175	5.24303	5.11106	4.98537
33	6.81747	6.60046	6.39609	6.20336	6.02136	5.84928	5.68638	5.53197	5.38545	5.24625	5.11386	4.98781
34	6.82749	6.60910	6.40354	6.20979	6.02692	5.85409	5.69054	5.53557	5.38856	5.24895	5.11620	4.98984
35	6.83623	6.61661	6.40999	6.21534	6.03169	5.85820	5.69407	5.53862	5.39119	5.25122	5.11816	4.99154
36	6.84387	6.62314	6.41558	6.22012	6.03579	5.86171	5.69708	5.54120	5.39341	5.25312	5.11980	4.99295
37	6.85054	6.62881	6.42041	6.22424	6.03930	5.86471	5.69965	5.54339	5.39528	5.25472	5.12117	4.99412
38	6.85637	6.63375	6.42460	6.22779	6.04232	5.86727	5.70183	5.54525	5.39686	5.25607	5.12232	4.99510
39	6.86146	6.63805	6.42823	6.23086	6.04491	5.86946	5.70368	5.54682	5.39820	5.25720	5.12328	4.99592
40	6.86590	6.64178	6.43136	6.23350	6.04713	5.87133	5.70526	5.54815	5.39932	5.25815	5.12408	4.99660
41	6.86978	6.64502	6.43408	6.23577	6.04904	5.87294	5.70660	5.54928	5.40027	5.25895	5.12475	4.99717
42	6.87317	6.64785	6.43643	6.23774	6.05068	5.87430	5.70775	5.55024	5.40107	5.25962	5.12532	4.99764
43	6.87613	6.65030	6.43847	6.23943	6.05208	5.87547	5.70872	5.55105	5.40175	5.26019	5.12579	4.99803
44	6.87872	6.65244	6.44024	6.24089	6.05329	5.87647	5.70955	5.55174	5.40232	5.26066	5.12618	4.99836
45	6.88098	6.65429	6.44176	6.24214	6.05433	5.87733	5.71026	5.55232	5.40280	5.26106	5.12651	4.99863
46	6.88295	6.65591	6.44308	6.24323	6.05522	5.87806	5.71086	5.55281	5.40321	5.26140	5.12679	4.99886
47	6.88467	6.65731	6.44423	6.24416	6.05598	5.87868	5.71137	5.55323	5.40355	5.26168	5.12702	4.99905
48	6.88618	6.65853	6.44522	6.24497	6.05664	5.87922	5.71180	5.55359	5.40384	5.26191	5.12721	4.99921
49	6.88749	6.65959	6.44608	6.24566	6.05720	5.87967	5.71217	5.55389	5.40409	5.26211	5.12738	4.99934
50	6.88864	6.66051	6.44682	6.24626	6.05768	5.88006	5.71249	5.55414	5.40429	5.26228	5.12751	4.99945
51	6.88964	6.66132	6.44746	6.24678	6.05809	5.88039	5.71275	5.55436	5.40447	5.26242	5.12762	4.99954
52	6.89052	6.66201	6.44802	6.24722	6.05845	5.88068	5.71298	5.55454	5.40461	5.26254	5.12772	4.99962
53	6.89128	6.66262	6.44850	6.24760	6.05876	5.88092	5.71318	5.55469	5.40474	5.26264	5.12780	4.99968
54	6.89195	6.66315	6.44892	6.24793	6.05902	5.88113	5.71334	5.55483	5.40484	5.26272	5.12786	4.99974
55	6.89253	6.66361	6.44928	6.24822	6.05924	5.88131	5.71348	5.55494	5.40493	5.26279	5.12792	4.99978
56	6.89304	6.66401	6.44959	6.24846	6.05944	5.88146	5.71360	5.55503	5.40500	5.26285	5.12797	4.99982
57	6.89348	6.66435	6.44987	6.24868	6.05960	5.88159	5.71370	5.55511	5.40507	5.26290	5.12801	4.99985
58	6.89387	6.66466	6.45010	6.24886	6.05974	5.88170	5.71379	5.55518	5.40512	5.26294	5.12804	4.99987
59	6.89421	6.66492	6.45030	6.24902	6.05987	5.88180	5.71386	5.55524	5.40516	5.26297	5.12807	4.99989
60	6.89451	6.66515	6.45048	6.24915	6.05997	5.88188	5.71393	5.55529	5.40520	5.26300	5.12809	4.99991

Period	14.5%	15%	15.5%	16%	16.5%	17%	17.5%	18%	18.5%	19%	19.5%	20%
61	6.89477	6.66534	6.45063	6.24927	6.06006	5.88195	5.71398	5.55533	5.40523	5.26303	5.12811	4.99993
62	6.89499	6.66552	6.45076	6.24937	6.06014	5.88200	5.71403	5.55536	5.40526	5.26305	5.12812	4.99994
63	6.89519	6.66567	6.45088	6.24946	6.06020	5.88206	5.71406	5.55539	5.40528	5.26307	5.12814	4.99995
64	6.89536	6.66580	6.45098	6.24953	6.06026	5.88210	5.71410	5.55542	5.40530	5.26308	5.12815	4.99996
65	6.89551	6.66591	6.45106	6.24960	6.06031	5.88214	5.71413	5.55544	5.40532	5.26309	5.12816	4.99996
66	6.89565	6.66601	6.45114	6.24965	6.06035	5.88217	5.71415	5.55546	5.40533	5.26310	5.12816	4.99997
67	6.89576	6.66609	6.45120	6.24970	6.06039	5.88219	5.71417	5.55547	5.40534	5.26311	5.12817	4.99998
68	6.89586	6.66617	6.45125	6.24974	6.06042	5.88222	5.71419	5.55548	5.40535	5.26312	5.12818	4.99998
69	6.89595	6.66623	6.45130	6.24978	6.06045	5.88224	5.71420	5.55549	5.40536	5.26313	5.12818	4.99998
70	6.89602	6.66629	6.45134	6.24981	6.06047	5.88225	5.71421	5.55550	5.40537	5.26313	5.12819	4.99999
71	6.89609	6.66634	6.45138	6.24983	6.06049	5.88227	5.71422	5.55551	5.40537	5.26314	5.12819	4.99999
72	6.89615	6.66638	6.45141	6.24986	6.06050	5.88228	5.71423	5.55552	5.40538	5.26314	5.12819	4.99999
73	6.89620	6.66642	6.45144	6.24988	6.06052	5.88229	5.71424	5.55552	5.40538	5.26314	5.12819	4.99999
74	6.89624	6.66645	6.45146	6.24989	6.06053	5.88230	5.71425	5.55553	5.40539	5.26314	5.12820	4.99999
75	6.89628	6.66648	6.45148	6.24991	6.06054	5.88231	5.71425	5.55553	5.40539	5.26315	5.12820	4.99999
76	6.89632	6.66650	6.45150	6.24992	6.06055	5.88231	5.71426	5.55554	5.40539	5.26315	5.12820	5.00000
77	6.89635	6.66653	6.45151	6.24993	6.06056	5.88232	5.71426	5.55554	5.40540	5.26315	5.12820	5.00000
78	6.89637	6.66654	6.45153	6.24994	6.06057	5.88232	5.71427	5.55554	5.40540	5.26315	5.12820	5.00000
79	6.89640	6.66656	6.45154	6.24995	6.06057	5.88233	5.71427	5.55554	5.40540	5.26315	5.12820	5.00000
80	6.89642	6.66657	6.45155	6.24996	6.06058	5.88233	5.71427	5.55555	5.40540	5.26315	5.12820	5.00000
81	6.89643	6.66659	6.45156	6.24996	6.06058	5.88234	5.71427	5.55555	5.40540	5.26315	5.12820	5.00000
82	6.89645	6.66660	6.45157	6.24997	6.06058	5.88234	5.71428	5.55555	5.40540	5.26315	5.12820	5.00000
83	6.89646	6.66661	6.45157	6.24997	6.06059	5.88234	5.71428	5.55555	5.40540	5.26316	5.12820	5.00000
84	6.89647	6.66661	6.45158	6.24998	6.06059	5.88234	5.71428	5.55555	5.40540	5.26316	5.12820	5.00000
85	6.89648	6.66662	6.45158	6.24998	6.06059	5.88234	5.71428	5.55555	5.40540	5.26316	5.12820	5.00000
86	6.89649	6.66663	6.45159	6.24998	6.06059	5.88234	5.71428	5.55555	5.40540	5.26316	5.12820	5.00000
87	6.89650	6.66663	6.45159	6.24998	6.06060	5.88235	5.71428	5.55555	5.40540	5.26316	5.12820	5.00000
88	6.89651	6.66664	6.45159	6.24999	6.06060	5.88235	5.71428	5.55555	5.40540	5.26316	5.12820	5.00000
89	6.89651	6.66664	6.45160	6.24999	6.06060	5.88235	5.71428	5.55555	5.40540	5.26316	5.12820	5.00000
90	6.89652	6.66664	6.45160	6.24999	6.06060	5.88235	5.71428	5.55555	5.40540	5.26316	5.12820	5.00000
91	6.89652	6.66665	6.45160	6.24999	6.06060	5.88235	5.71428	5.55555	5.40540	5.26316	5.12820	5.00000
92	6.89652	6.66665	6.45160	6.24999	6.06060	5.88235	5.71428	5.55555	5.40540	5.26316	5.12820	5.00000
93	6.89653	6.66665	6.45160	6.24999	6.06060	5.88235	5.71428	5.55555	5.40540	5.26316	5.12820	5.00000
94	6.89653	6.66665	6.45160	6.24999	6.06060	5.88235	5.71428	5.55555	5.40540	5.26316	5.12820	5.00000
95	6.89653	6.66666	6.45161	6.25000	6.06060	5.88235	5.71428	5.55555	5.40540	5.26316	5.12820	5.00000
96	6.89654	6.66666	6.45161	6.25000	6.06060	5.88235	5.71428	5.55555	5.40540	5.26316	5.12820	5.00000
97	6.89654	6.66666	6.45161	6.25000	6.06060	5.88235	5.71428	5.55555	5.40541	5.26316	5.12820	5.00000
98	6.89654	6.66666	6.45161	6.25000	6.06060	5.88235	5.71428	5.55556	5.40541	5.26316	5.12820	5.00000
99	6.89654	6.66666	6.45161	6.25000	6.06060	5.88235	5.71429	5.55556	5.40541	5.26316	5.12821	5.00000
100	6.89654	6.66666	6.45161	6.25000	6.06060	5.88235	5.71429	5.55556	5.40541	5.26316	5.12821	5.00000
101	6.89654	6.66666	6.45161	6.25000	6.06060	5.88235	5.71429	5.55556	5.40541	5.26316	5.12821	5.00000
102	6.89654	6.66666	6.45161	6.25000	6.06061	5.88235	5.71429	5.55556	5.40541	5.26316	5.12821	5.00000
103	6.89655	6.66666	6.45161	6.25000	6.06061	5.88235	5.71429	5.55556	5.40541	5.26316	5.12821	5.00000
104	6.89655	6.66666	6.45161	6.25000	6.06061	5.88235	5.71429	5.55556	5.40541	5.26316	5.12821	5.00000
105	6.89655	6.66666	6.45161	6.25000	6.06061	5.88235	5.71429	5.55556	5.40541	5.26316	5.12821	5.00000
106	6.89655	6.66666	6.45161	6.25000	6.06061	5.88235	5.71429	5.55556	5.40541	5.26316	5.12821	5.00000
107	6.89655	6.66666	6.45161	6.25000	6.06061	5.88235	5.71429	5.55556	5.40541	5.26316	5.12821	5.00000
108	6.89655	6.66666	6.45161	6.25000	6.06061	5.88235	5.71429	5.55556	5.40541	5.26316	5.12821	5.00000
109	6.89655	6.66667	6.45161	6.25000	6.06061	5.88235	5.71429	5.55556	5.40541	5.26316	5.12821	5.00000
110	6.89655	6.66667	6.45161	6.25000	6.06061	5.88235	5.71429	5.55556	5.40541	5.26316	5.12821	5.00000
111	6.89655	6.66667	6.45161	6.25000	6.06061	5.88235	5.71429	5.55556	5.40541	5.26316	5.12821	5.00000
112	6.89655	6.66667	6.45161	6.25000	6.06061	5.88235	5.71429	5.55556	5.40541	5.26316	5.12821	5.00000
113	6.89655	6.66667	6.45161	6.25000	6.06061	5.88235	5.71429	5.55556	5.40541	5.26316	5.12821	5.00000
114	6.89655	6.66667	6.45161	6.25000	6.06061	5.88235	5.71429	5.55556	5.40541	5.26316	5.12821	5.00000
115	6.89655	6.66667	6.45161	6.25000	6.06061	5.88235	5.71429	5.55556	5.40541	5.26316	5.12821	5.00000
116	6.89655	6.66667	6.45161	6.25000	6.06061	5.88235	5.71429	5.55556	5.40541	5.26316	5.12821	5.00000
117	6.89655	6.66667	6.45161	6.25000	6.06061	5.88235	5.71429	5.55556	5.40541	5.26316	5.12821	5.00000
118	6.89655	6.66667	6.45161	6.25000	6.06061	5.88235	5.71429	5.55556	5.40541	5.26316	5.12821	5.00000
119	6.89655	6.66667	6.45161	6.25000	6.06061	5.88235	5.71429	5.55556	5.40541	5.26316	5.12821	5.00000
120	6.89655	6.66667	6.45161	6.25000	6.06061	5.88235	5.71429	5.55556	5.40541	5.26316	5.12821	5.00000

Index

*This book has been set VideoComp in 11 and 9 point
Times Roman, leaded 1 point. Part numbers are 30 point
Spectra Bold and part titles are 36 point Spectra Black;
chapter numbers are 18 point Spectra Black and chapter
titles are 14 point Spectra Bold. The size of the type page
is 39 by 53½ picas.*

ACCOUNTING PRINCIPLES-VOLUME II

Date: _____

This questionnaire is designed to get reader opinions on the adequacy and relevance of the text. Your comments, both positive and negative, will influence the design and content of future AIB textbooks. Thank you for your assistance.

I. Background Information

A. In this course I was a(n): ☐ Instructor   ☐ Student

B. Highest educational attainment:
☐ High School   ☐ Some College   ☐ BA/BS Degree   ☐ Advanced Degree

C. I am a(n): ☐ Officer   ☐ Non-Officer   ☐ Non-Bank Employee

D. Asset Size of Bank:
☐ $0-100m   ☐ $101-500m   ☐ $501m-1b   ☐ Over $1b

E. My major job responsibility is _____

F. I am pursuing an AIB diploma: ☐ Yes   ☐ No

II. The Materials

Please rate the text according to the criteria below. Check the box that most closely corresponds with your opinion.

Thoroughness:	☐ Covers too little of subject	☐ Covers sufficient content	☐ Covers too much unrelated content
Difficulty Level:	☐ Too basic	☐ Appropriate for level of course	☐ Too difficult
Interest Level:	☐ Dull and uninteresting	☐ Acceptable	☐ Very interesting
Organization:	☐ Sequenced logically	☐ Not in logical sequence	
Timeliness:	☐ Most content was current	☐ Most content was outdated	
Practicality:	☐ Too theoretical	☐ Has sufficient practical application	

Please rate the *overall effectiveness* of the text by circling the number which represents your opinion.

Very effective as a learning aid   Ineffective as a learning aid

5   4   3   2   1

III. Comments

A. Can you make any suggestions for improving the book?

_____

_____

_____

B. Would you recommend this book to someone who needs to know this information?
☐ Yes   ☐ No

STAPLE HERE

FOLD IN HALF AND STAPLE

FOLD HERE

BUSINESS REPLY MAIL

First Class   Permit No. 10579   Washington, D.C.

Postage Will Be Paid by

Education & Field Relations
Education Policy & Development Group
American Bankers Association
1120 Connecticut Avenue
Washington, D.C. 20036